A Companion to

Blackwell Companions to Literature and Culture

This series offers comprehensive, newly written surveys of key periods and movements and certain major authors, in English literary culture and history. Extensive volumes provide new perspectives and positions on contexts and on canonical and post-canonical texts, orientating the beginning student in new fields of study and providing the experienced undergraduate and new graduate with current and new directions, as pioneered and developed by leading scholars in the field.

Forthcoming

A COMPANION TO
MILTON

EDITED BY THOMAS N. CORNS

Blackwell
Publishing

© 2001, 2003 by Blackwell Publishing Ltd
except for editorial material and organization © 2001, 2003 by Thomas N. Corns

350 Main Street, Malden, MA 02148-5020, USA
108 Cowley Road, Oxford OX4 1JF, UK
550 Swanston Street, Carlton, Victoria 3053, Australia

The right of Thomas N. Corns to be identified as the Author of the Editorial Material in this Work
has been asserted in accordance with the UK Copyright, Designs, and Patents Act 1988.

First published 2001
First published in paperback 2003 by Blackwell Publishing Ltd

Library of Congress Cataloging-in-Publication Data

A companion to Milton / edited by Thomas N. Corns.
p.   cm. — (Blackwell companions to literature and culture; 10)
Includes bibliographical references (p.) and index.
ISBN 0–631–21408–9 (hb : alk. paper) — ISBN 1–4051–1370–7 (pb. : alk. paper)
1. Milton, John, 1608–1674—Criticism and interpretation.   2. Milton, John,
1608–1674—Handbooks, manuals, etc.   I. Corns, Thomas N.   II. Series.

PR3588 .C58 2001
821'.4—dc21

00-051915

A catalogue record for this title is available from the British Library.

Set in 11 on 13 pt Garamond 3
by Kolam Information Services Pvt. Ltd, Pondicherry, India
Printed and bound in the United Kingdom
by T. J. International Ltd, Padstow, Cornwall

For further information on
Blackwell Publishing, visit our website:
http://www.blackwellpublishing.com

Contents

Preface

Early in the eighteenth century, Joseph Addison, probably the most influential journalist and cultural commentator of his age, dedicated eighteen issues of *The Spectator*, the journal he co-authored, to guiding a wide readership towards a more informed and enthusiastic appreciation of *Paradise Lost*. He did so knowing that there existed already a substantial readership for Milton and believing that it needed encouragement, education and a kind of aesthetic reassurance. Milton was already the subject of academic enquiry and sustained popularization in the form of annotated editions of his poetry and critical narratives about his life. Addison's project reflected his own political and cultural agenda. A Whig eager to pass over his party's remoter connections with mid-seventeenth-century republicanism, Addison offered to his readers a depoliticized Milton to be appreciated, according to the canons of Augustan neoclassicism, as a vernacular writer who aspired to match classical masters, pre-eminently Virgil and Homer, and who sometimes succeeded in that high ambition.

In sharp contrast, this collection appears at a time when Milton's standing with a wide readership appears altogether more insecure. From colleagues in the United States, I hear frequently rehearsed anxieties about the future of early modern literary studies in universities responsive to students' preferences for a literature that speaks directly to their own experience in the language of today. In the British context, changes in school curricula and increased levels of optionality in first degree pro-grammes make it possible to graduate from many institutions with little familiarity with earlier literature apart from Shakespeare. Yet the academic study of Milton has never been healthier. Historically informed interpretation is refreshed by significant developments in early modern historiography that are recharting the history of the early Stuart church, the origins of the English Civil War, and the informing phil-osophies of English republicanism. Milton's own theology and its place in radical Protestantism are under investigation with a new precision. Major critical movements of the final quarter of the twentieth century, such as feminist criticism, cultural materialism and genre theory, remain vital and productive components in an array of methodologies that also reflects ecological awareness, postcolonialism and Habermasian neo-Marxism. There have been four new and important editions of Milton's works since 1997. Academic associations for Milton studies flourish in Japan and Korea, and support programmes of conferences and seminars. The Milton Society of America has well over 500 members. There are thriving and prestigious research seminars in North America and the United Kingdom. The International Milton Symposium will hold its seventh meeting in 2002. The vital signs for Milton studies, at research level, are very encouraging.

The primary objective of this volume is to bring an awareness of that academic vigour to a wider readership and, in so doing, to promote and stimulate the study and enjoyment of a rich, profound, diverse and fascinating œuvre. But the collection neither simplifies nor ignores the controversial nature of contemporary Milton criticism. Readers will discern that different contributors take rather different views on a number of key issues. For a decade now there has been some dispute about the place of *De Doctrina Christiana*, a Latin exegetical treatise, within the canon of Milton's works. Within this collection, there are those who regard it fairly straightforwardly as Miltonic, and accordingly available as a kind of explicit account of views more obliquely expressed, for example, in *Paradise Lost*. Others treat it more sceptically, regarding its status as genuinely uncertain. Again, the nature of seventeenth-century republicanism, particularly in its intellectual origins and its earliest history in the constitutional crises of the 1620s, emerges as a keenly disputed issue with profound implications for the understanding of Milton's political prose; and sharp disagreements surround the aetiology of his radical Protestantism. Where appropriate, this volume aims to define problems rather than to offer premature syntheses and the facile resolution of issues that in reality remain unresolved.

I have endeavoured to give a platform to some of the most distinctive and influential voices in contemporary Milton studies. Scholars have been asked, not to offer a bland overview of a critical tradition, but to develop readings that express the freshness and originality of their own approaches. The 'companionship' this collection is designed to offer is not one of condescending reassurance but rather an invitation to join in challenging forays to the edge of what is known about early modern literary culture and Milton's place in it. Addison's project sought to equip readers aspiring towards cultural respectability with a unified and confident account of Milton as England's national poet and laureate of Anglican Protestantism. This collection, in its critical pluralism, expresses the controversial, questioning, and vital characteristics of Milton studies in our own age.

I should like to thank Andrew McNeillie, who commissioned this collection and supported and encouraged it throughout, Alison Dunnett, who saw it through to publication with tact and energy, and Gillian Bromley, for her meticulous and constructive work as copy-editor. I am grateful to my contributors for responding promptly and constructively to suggestions and queries. Not for the first time on a major project, my greatest debt is to Linda Jones, research administrator of the

Department of English, University of Wales, Bangor, who has done so much to bring the work to completion.

Thomas N. Corns
University of Wales, Bangor
August 2000

Acknowledgements, Abbreviations and a Note on Editions Used

Unless otherwise stated, all biblical references are to the Authorized Version (AV); all references to Milton's vernacular prose are to the *Complete Prose Works of John Milton*, edited by Don M. Wolfe et al. (New Haven: Yale University Press, 1953–82) (*CPW*); all references to his poetry are either to the second edition of *Complete Shorter Poems*, edited by John Carey (London and New York: Longman, 1997) (*CSP*), or to the second edition of *Paradise Lost*, edited by Alastair Fowler (London and New York: Longman, 1998) (*PL*). Milton's Latin prose is sometimes cited from *The Works of John Milton*, edited by Frank Allen Patterson et al. (New York: Columbia University Press, 1931–8) (*WJM*). The author and publisher are grateful for permission to reproduce copyright material from these editions.

The principal texts considered within each chapter are listed under 'Writings', followed by a list of suggested 'References for Further Reading'.

The Contributors

Sharon Achinstein teaches at the University of Maryland. She has edited *Gender, Literature and the English Revolution* (*Women's Studies* 24 [1994]), and authored *Milton and the Revolutionary Reader* (1994). Her *Zion's Ashes: Poetics of Dissent in Restoration England* is forthcoming.

Amy Boesky is Associate Professor of English at Boston College. She is the author of *Founding Fictions: Utopias in Early Modern England* (1996) and of various articles on Milton in journals, among them *Modern Philology* and *Milton Studies*. She is currently writing a book on time and representation in early modern England.

Cedric C. Brown is Professor of English at the University of Reading, Co-Director of the Renaissance Texts Research Centre at Reading, and Dean of the Faculty. His major research interests at the moment concern the social transmission and various appropriations of poetry texts in the seventeenth century. Recent publications include *John Milton: A Literary Life* (1995) and the co-edited volume *Texts and Cultural Change in Early Modern England* (1997, with Arthur F. Marotti).

Gordon Campbell is Professor of Renaissance Literature at the University of Leicester. In recent years his work on Milton has concentrated on issues arising from manuscripts associated with Milton. He is the editor of the Everyman edition of Milton's poems and co-editor and translator of the poems of Edward King, Milton's Lycidas. He has published *A Milton Chronology* (1997) and a revised edition of W. R. Parker's biography of Milton (2 vols, 1996) and, within the group (led by Thomas Corns) investigating the provenance of *De Doctrina Christiana*, has been responsible for the archival research. He is General Editor of *Review of English Studies* and is at present writing *The Oxford Companion to the Renaissance*.

Thomas N. Corns is Professor of English and Head of the School of Arts and Humanities at the University of Wales, Bangor. His principal publications include *The Development of Milton's Prose Style* (1982), *Milton's Language* (1990), *Uncloistered Virtue: English Political Literature 1640–1660* (1992), *Regaining 'Paradise Lost'* (1994), and the Twayne guide to Milton's prose (1998). He edited *The Cambridge Companion to English Poetry, Donne to Marvell* (1993) and *The Royal Image: Representations of Charles I* (1999). With Ann Hughes and David Loewenstein he is editing the complete works of Gerrard Winstanley, and he is the lead researcher of a group considering the provenance of *De Doctrina Christiana*.

Martin Dzelzainis is Reader in Renaissance Literature and Thought at Royal Holloway, University of London. He has edited *John Milton: Political Writings* (1991) for Cambridge Texts in the History of Political Thought, and, with Warren Chernaik, *Marvell and Liberty* (1999). He is currently editing both parts of *The Rehearsal Transpros'd* for the forthcoming Yale *Prose Works of Andrew Marvell*, under the general editorship of Annabel Patterson, and is also working on a study of Restoration censorship.

Stephen M. Fallon teaches at Notre Dame University. He is author of *Milton among the Philosophers* (1991) and winner of the Milton Society of America's Hanford Award, and has published articles on Milton and on the Renaissance in the *Journal of the History of Ideas*, *English Literary Renaissance*, *PMLA* and multi-contributor volumes. Twice the recipient of NEH Fellowships, he is writing a book on self-representation, intention and authority in Milton. He co-founded a course in literary and philosophical classics at the Center for the Homeless in South Bend, Indiana.

Achsah Guibbory is Professor of English, and affiliated with the Religious Studies Program, at the University of Illinois, Urbana-Champaign. She is the author of *The Map of Time: Seventeenth-Century English Literature and Ideas of Pattern in History* (1986), *Ceremony and Community from Herbert to Milton: Literature, Religion and Cultural Conflict in Seventeenth-Century England* (1998), and numerous articles on seventeenth-century literature and culture. Her essay on Donne's *Elegies* published in *ELH* (1990) was winner of the award from the John Donne Society for Distinguished Publication.

Andrew Hadfield is Professor of English at the University of Wales, Aberystwyth. He is the author of a number of books on Renaissance literature and culture, most recently *Literature, Travel and Colonial Writing in the English Renaissance, 1545–1625* (1998) and *The English Renaissance, 1500–1620* (2000). He is currently working on a book provisionally entitled *Shakespeare and Political Culture*. For 2001–4 he has been awarded a Leverhulme Major Research Fellowship to work on Shakespeare and republicanism.

John K. Hale is Associate Professor in the Department of English at the University of Otago. His publications include *Milton's Languages: The Impact of Multilingualism on Style* (1997), *John Milton: Latin Writings, A Selection* (1998, editor and translator), *The Shakespeare of the Comedies: A Multiple Approach* (1996) and *Sonnets of Four Centuries, 1500–1900* (1992, editor). He has written numerous essays on Milton, with some further concentration on Aristotle, Dante and Shakespeare.

Margaret Kean is Fellow and Tutor in English at St Hilda's College, Oxford. She is currently completing a study of creativity and image production in John Milton's *Paradise Lost*.

N. H. Keeble is a Professor and currently Head of the Department of English Studies at the University of Stirling. He has published studies of *Richard Baxter: Puritan Man of Letters* (1982) and *The Literary Culture of Nonconformity in Later Seventeenth-Century England* (1987); a two-volume *Calendar of the Correspondence of Richard Baxter* (1991, with Geoffrey F. Nuttall); an edited collection of tercentenary essays, *John Bunyan: Conventicle and Parnassus* (1988); an anthology illustrating *The Cultural Identity of Seventeenth-Century Woman* (1994); and editions of texts by Richard Baxter, John Bunyan and Lucy Hutchinson. He is currently editing a tract for the Yale edition of the *Prose Works of Andrew Marvell* and completing a study of the 1660s.

Peter J. Kitson is Professor of English at the University of Dundee. He is the editor of *Romantic Criticism 1800–1825* (1989), *Coleridge and the Armoury of the Human Mind: Essays on His Prose Writings* (1991, with Thomas N. Corns), *Coleridge, Keats and Shelley* (1996), *Slavery, Abolition and Emancipation* (1999, with Debbie Lee), *Romanticism and Colonialism* (1998, with Tim Fulford) and *Travels, Explorations and Empires* (2001, with Tim Fulford). He was Editor of *The Year's Work in English Studies* from 1995 to 2001.

Laura Lunger Knoppers is Associate Professor of English at Pennsylvania State University. She is author of *Historicizing Milton: Spectacle, Power, and Poetry in Restoration England* (1994) and of *Constructing Cromwell: Ceremony, Portrait, and Print, 1645–1661* (2000). Her essays on Milton's poetry and prose, on Shakespeare, on representations of Oliver Cromwell and on Charles I have appeared in various scholarly journals and book collections. She is currently working on a book-length study of Charles I and Henrietta Maria.

John Leonard teaches at the University of Western Ontario. He has published *Naming in Paradise* (1990, co-winner of the Milton Society of America's James Holly Hanford Award), the Penguin edition of *Milton's Complete Poems* (1998) and related edition of *Paradise Lost* (2000), and many articles on Milton.

Barbara Kiefer Lewalski is William R. Kenan Professor of History and Literature and of English Literature at Harvard University. She has just published *The Life of*

John Milton: A Critical Biography (2000). Other books include *Writing Women in Jacobean England, 1603–1625* (1993), *Paradise Lost and the Rhetoric of Literary Forms* (1985), *Protestant Poetics and the Seventeenth-Century Religious Lyric* (1979), *Donne's Anniversaries and the Poetry of Praise* (1973) and *Milton's Brief Epic: The Genre, Meaning, and Art of* Paradise Regained (1966).

David Loewenstein is Professor of English at the University of Wisconsin-Madison. His publications include *Milton and the Drama of History: Historical Vision, Iconoclasm, and the Literary Imagination* (1990), *Politics, Poetics, and Hermeneutics in Milton's Prose* (1990), *Milton*: Paradise Lost (1993) and *Representing Revolution in Milton and His Contemporaries: Religion, Politics, and Polemics in Radical Puritanism* (2001). With Ann Hughes and Thomas Corns, he is co-editing the complete works of Gerrard Winstanley.

Diane Kelsey McColley teaches British Literature and the Literature of Nature at Rutgers, the State University of New Jersey, Camden College of Arts and Sciences. She is the author of *Milton's Eve* (1983), *A Gust for Paradise: Milton's Eden and the Visual Arts* (1993), and *Poetry and Music in Seventeenth-Century England* (1997). She became an Honored Scholar of the Milton Society of America in 1999. Research for her essay was aided by a Mellon Fellowship at the Huntington Library.

Leah S. Marcus is Edwin Mims Professor of English at Vanderbilt University. She is the author of *Childhood and Cultural Despair* (1978), *The Politics of Mirth* (1986), *Puzzling Shakespeare* (1988) and *Unediting the Renaissance* (1996), and, along with Janel Mueller and Mary Beth Rose, edited *Elizabeth I: Collected Works* (2000).

Graham Parry is Professor of English at the University of York. His most recent book is *The Trophies of Time: English Antiquarians of the Seventeenth Century* (1995). He is currently writing a book on the arts of the Church in the time of Archbishop Laud. He was the organizer of the Sixth International Milton Symposium at York in 1999.

Annabel Patterson is the Karl Young Professor of English at Yale University. Among her books are *Early Modern Liberalism* (1997), which has much to say about Milton, and *John Milton*, a Longman Critical Reader (1992). She is currently Editor-in-Chief of the Yale edition of the *Prose Works of Andrew Marvell*, and has just finished a short book subtitled *A New Whig Interpretation of History*.

Joad Raymond is a Lecturer in English Literature at the University of East Anglia. He is the editor of *Making the News: An Anthology of the Newsbooks of Revolutionary England, 1641–1660* (1993) and of *News, Newspapers, and Society in Early Modern Britain* (1999), and the author of *The Invention of the Newspaper: English Newsbooks, 1641–1649* (1996) and of articles on literature and politics in the mid-seventeenth century. He is presently completing a study of pamphlets and pamphleteering between 1588 and 1688.

Stella P. Revard is Professor Emerita from Southern Illinois University, Edwardsville. She is currently President of the International Association for Neo-Latin Studies. She is an Honored Scholar of the Milton Society of America and has published numerous articles and two books on Milton – *The War in Heaven* (1980) and *Milton and the Tangles of Neaera's Hair* (1997) – both of which were awarded the Hanford Prize from the Milton Society of America. A forthcoming book is entitled *Pindar and the Renaissance Hymn-Ode: 1450–1700*.

John Rumrich is Professor of English at the University of Texas, Austin. He is the author of *Matter of Glory: A New Preface to Paradise Lost* (1987) and *Milton Unbound* (1996), and editor of *Texas Studies in Literature and Language*.

Michael Schoenfeldt is Professor of English and Director of the Program in Medieval and Early Modern Studies at the University of Michigan, Ann Arbor. He is the author of *Prayer and Power: George Herbert and Renaissance Courtship* (1991), *Bodies and Selves in Early Modern England: Physiology and Inwardness in Spenser, Shakespeare, Herbert, and Milton* (1999), and articles on Herbert, Donne, Spenser, Amelia Lanyer, Herrick, Shakespeare, Jonson and Milton.

Regina Schwartz is Professor of English and Religion at Northwestern University. She is the author of *Remembering and Repeating: On Milton's Theology and Poetics* (winner of the James Holly Hanford Book Award in 1989) and *The Curse of Cain: The Violent Legacy of Monotheism* (1997). She is editor of *The Book and the Text: The Bible and Literary Theory* (1990), and co-editor of *Desire in the Renaissance: Psychoanalysis and Literature* (1994, with Valeria Finucci). Her essays on Milton appear in *Representations*, *Milton Studies*, *English Literary History*, *PMLA* and *Religion and Literature*. She was President of the Milton Society of America in 1999 and is co-chair of the Newberry Milton Seminar. She is currently writing on English Reformation poetics.

Kay Gilliland Stevenson is Senior Lecturer in Literature at the University of Essex. She is co-author, with Clive Hart, of *Heaven and the Flesh: Imagery of Desire from the Renaissance to the Rococo* (1995) and, with Margaret Seares, of *Paradise Lost in Short: Smith, Stillingfleet and the Transformation of Epic* (1998). Her most recent book is a period volume in Palgrave's 'transitions' series, *Milton to Pope: 1650–1720* (2001).

Elizabeth Skerpan Wheeler is Professor of English at Southwest Texas State University, where she teaches seventeenth-century and modern literature and rhetoric. The author of *The Rhetoric of Politics in the English Revolution, 1642–1660* (1992), she is completing a book on Milton's poetics and seventeenth-century language theory, and working on a CD-ROM edition of *Eikon Basilike*.

PART I
The Cultural Context

1

Genre

Barbara K. Lewalski

Milton shows a constant concern with form, with genre, to a degree remarkable even in his genre-conscious era. Among the first questions to ask about any of his poems are what conventions he embraced and what freight of shared cultural significances he took on by casting a poem in a particular genre. In poem after poem he achieves high art from the tension between his immense imaginative energy and the discipline of form. Yet he is never a mere follower of convention and neoclassical rules: his poems gain much of their power from his daring mixtures of generic elements and from radical transformations that disrupt and challenge reader expectation.

In 1642, in the preface to the Second Book of *The Reason of Church-Government*, Milton provided his most extended comment on poetry and poetics. Among other topics, he points to some of the literary genres he hopes to attempt, offering an important insight into his ideas about and ways with genre:

> Time servs not now, and perhaps I might seem too profuse to give any certain account of what the mind at home in the spacious circuits of her musing hath liberty to propose to her self, though of highest hope, and hardest attempting, whether that Epick form whereof the two poems of *Homer*, and those other two of *Virgil* and *Tasso* are a diffuse, and the book of *Job* a brief model: or whether the rules of *Aristotle* herein are strictly to be kept, or nature to be follow'd . . . Or whether those Dramatick constitutions, wherein *Sophocles* and *Euripides* raigne shall be found more doctrinal and exemplary to a Nation, the Scripture also affords us a divine pastoral Drama in the Song of *Salomon* consisting of two persons and a double *Chorus*, as *Origen* rightly judges. And the Apocalyps of Saint *John* is the majestick image of a high and stately Tragedy, shutting up and interminging her solemn Scenes and Acts with a sevenfold *Chorus* of halleluja's and harping symphonies: . . . Or if occasion shall lead to imitat those magnifick Odes and Hymns wherein *Pindarus* and *Callimachus* are in most things worthy, some others in their frame judicious, in their matter most an end faulty: But those frequent songs throughout the law and prophets beyond all these, not in their divine argument alone, but in the very

critical art of composition may be easily made appear over all the kinds of Lyrick poesy, to be incomparable. (*CPW* I: 812–16)

Much as the Renaissance Italian critic Minturno did (Minturno 1559: 3), Milton thought in terms of three general categories or 'parts' of poetry – epic, dramatic, lyric – and within each of these categories he identified certain historical genres or 'kinds' (the Renaissance term). Here he mentions 'diffuse' and 'brief' epic, pastoral dramas and tragedies, odes and hymns. Renaissance theorists and poets also recognized many other kinds, identified by a mix of formal and thematic elements, conventions and topics: metre, structure, size, scale, subject, values, occasion, style and more (Fowler 1982: 1–74). Milton's reference to 'pastoral' drama in the passage quoted calls attention to the category of literary modes – what Sidney in *The Defence of Poesie* called 'species' and defined chiefly by tone, topics and affect: e.g. pastoral, satiric, comedic, heroic, elegiac (Sidney 1595, sigs C2^r, E3^v–F1^r). These modes may govern works or parts of works in several kinds: we might have a pastoral comedy, or pastoral eclogue, or pastoral song; or a satiric verse epistle, or epigram, or novel. Also, Milton links biblical with classical models – Homer and Job for epic, Sophocles and the Apocalypse for tragedy, Pindar and the Psalms for the high lyric – indicating his sense of the Bible as a compendium of literary genres and poetic art. His final comment privileging biblical lyric over all other lyric poetry not only for truth but also for art assumes a Platonic union of truth and beauty.

Renaissance poets and critics often repeated the Horatian formula for the purpose of poetry, to teach and delight, and Sidney added to these aims the function of rhetoric, to move. Milton was thinking in these terms as he debated with himself whether epic or tragedy might be more 'doctrinal and exemplary' to the nation. But Milton's poetic teaching is not a matter of urging a message or doctrine: it involves representing human life and human values in all their complexity, in a richly imagined poetic universe. Genre is a major element in that representation, for genres afford, in Rosalie Colie's terms, a series of frames or fixes upon the world (Colie 1973: vii), transmitting the culture's shared imaginative experience. By his virtuoso use of the literary genre system, and especially by his characteristic mixture of generic elements in most of his poems, Milton can invite his readers to weigh and consider the values the several kinds have come to embody, and to make discriminating choices (Lewalski 1985: 17–24).

During Milton's earlier career, genres associated with and promoted by the Caroline court took on special political and cultural import. Court masques and pastoral dramas mystified the virtue, power and benevolence of Charles I and Henrietta Maria. Cavalier poets associated with the court wrote witty, sophisticated, playful love lyrics imbued with the fashionable neoplatonism and pastoralism or treated *carpe diem* themes with a light-hearted licentiousness. Other common royalist kinds were panegyrics on members of the royal family and their celebratory occasions, and religious poems treating the 'high church' rituals, feasts, ceremonies and arts promoted by Archbishop Laud. During the period of the Commonwealth and Protectorate (1649–60), royalists in retreat from London and without a court often wrote works in pastoral and romance modes, celebrating retirement and friendship, or courtly chivalry (Potter 1989; Smith 1994: 233–41). By contrast, some writers associated with the revolution reached towards the sublime or prophetic register to celebrate heroic action, as in Marvell's *Horatian Ode* (Norbrook 1999: 251–71). Restoration court culture, with Dryden at its centre, promoted heroic drama, satire and Virgilian panegyric, written in smooth and graceful pentameter couplets.

Milton wrote many kinds of poems: sonnets in Italian and English, elegies and verse epistles in Latin elegiac verse, funeral elegies in English and Latin, songs, literary hymns, odes, epitaphs, encomiums, a masque, an entertainment, a tragedy, an epic and a brief epic. He also wrote several kinds of prose treatises and polemics, both in English and in Latin – college orations, controversial tracts promoting particular causes or answering attacks, defences of the regicide and the Commonwealth, histories and theological exposition. As poet, he identified his career path with that defined by Virgil and imitated by Spenser: beginning with the lesser kinds, pastoral and lyric, and proceeding to the highest – assumed by Renaissance theorists to be epic, though Aristotle gave pride of place to tragedy. Milton wrote both.

In several early poems Milton invokes the genre system to weigh alternative lifestyles, in both personal and cultural terms. 'Elegy VI', a Latin verse epistle addressed to his close friend Charles Diodati, is a counterstatement to his own 'Elegy V', an ecstatic celebration of love and springtime in Ovidian terms, written a few months earlier. 'Elegy VI' contrasts two kinds of poetry and the lifestyles appropriate to each. He identifies Diodati with the 'gay elegy', which is consonant with a festive life of 'grand banquets' and 'frequent potions of old wine', and locates himself with epic and hymnic poets – Homer, Tiresias, Linus and Orpheus – whose high subjects require an ascetic and chaste life: 'For the poet is sacred to the gods: he is their priest' (line 77). Also, the graceful, urbane companion poems, 'L'Allegro' and 'Il Penseroso', explore and contrast in generic terms the ideal pleasures appropriate to contrasting lifestyles – 'heart-easing Mirth' (line 13), 'divinest Melancholy' (line 12) – that a poet might choose, or might choose at different times, or in sequence. As celebrations of their respective deities, the Grace Euphrosone (Youthful Mirth) and the allegorical figure imagined as a deity, Melancholy, both poems are modelled on the classical hymn. But they also incorporate elements of several other kinds, among them the academic debate, the Theocritan pastoral idyll of the ideal day and its festivals, the Theophrastian prose 'character' with such titles as 'The Happy Man' or 'The Melancholy Man', the encomium, and the demonstrative or eulogistic oration with its traditional categories of praise: the goods of nature (ancestry and birth), the goods of fortune (friends and circumstances of life), and the goods of character (actions and virtues). The final couplet of each poem echoes and answers the question posed in Marlowe's 'Come live with me and be my love' and its Elizabethan analogues. But despite the familiarity of these elements, Milton's paired poems have no close antecedents.

The title personages of both poems are drawn with some playfulness, as ideal but exaggerated types, their pleasures and values adumbrated through literary kinds. The essence of 'L'Allegro', youthful mirth, is displayed in the activities and values of the pastoral mode and the literary genres harmonious with it: rural folk and fairy tales of Queen Mab and Goblin; court masques and pageants; Jonson's 'learned' comedy; romantic comedies in which 'sweetest Shakespeare fancy's child / Warble[s] his native wood-notes wild' (lines 133–4); and love songs in the Greek Lydian mode. In 'Il Penseroso' the romance mode presents the activities, pleasures and values of a solitary scholar-errant. He wanders through a mysterious gothic landscape with a melancholy nightingale, a 'high lonely tower' (line 86), a drowsy bellman, a cathedral cloister with 'high embowed roof' (line 157), stained glass windows, 'dim religious light' (line 160), a 'pealing organ' and a 'full-voiced choir' engaged in 'service high' (lines 161–3) and a hermitage with mossy cells. These images are appropriate to the medievalism and romance decorum of the poem. Melancholy's devoté enjoys the esoteric philosophy of Plato and Hermes Trismegistus, romances like Chaucer's unfinished *Squire's Tale* for their marvels and their allegory, Greek tragedies about Thebes and Troy by Aeschylus and Euripides, and bardic hymns like those of Orpheus. Finally, Il Penseroso turns to Christian hymns that produce ecstasy and vision.

L'Allegro might seem to show some affinity with the Cavalier poets in his pastoralism, his apparent elitist denial of rural labour, and his attendance at masques and stage plays. And Il Penseroso's fondness for the architecture, art and organ music of cathedrals, and his final retreat to a monastic hermitage, seem to register a surprising affinity with Roman Catholic or Laudian ritual (Patterson 1988: 9–22). But Milton uses these images to another purpose: to define and evaluate lifestyles in terms of literary modes, and to reclaim debased genres and art forms to good uses. Milton does not, here or elsewhere, repudiate pastoral, stage plays or masques because he thinks Cavaliers have debased them, or church music and art because he thinks Laudians use them in the service of idolatry. Rather, these poems reclaim such art for innocent delight by excising any hint of licentiousness, or courtly neoplatonism, or idolatry. Through them, Milton contrasts kinds of art and life and sets them in some hierarchical relation. A progression is implied from the genres L'Allegro enjoys to the higher kinds Il Penseroso delights in: from folk tales to allegorical romance, from comedy to tragedy, from Lydian airs to bardic and Christian hymns. More important, the eight-line coda of 'Il Penseroso' disrupts the poems' parallelism by opening to the future:

> And may at last my weary age
> Find out the peaceful hermitage,
> The hairy gown and mossy cell,
> Where I may sit and rightly spell
> Of every star that heaven doth shew,
> And every herb that sips the dew;

> Till old experience do attain
> To something like prophetic strain.
> (lines 167–74)

The coda makes Milton's poetic strategy clear. He does not, obviously, plan a monastic retreat for himself or hold it forth as an ideal; but he makes those images, which are appropriate to the medievalizing, romance mode of the poem, figure his aspiration to prophetic poetry. In 'Il Penseroso', age has its place, bringing true knowledge of nature and the ripening of 'old experience' into 'something like prophetic strain'. A natural progression from 'L'Allegro' to the higher life and art of 'Il Penseroso' offers to lead, at last, beyond ecstatic vision to prophetic poetry that can convey that vision to others.

When Milton was invited to contribute a poetic entertainment as part of the festivities in honour of Alice Spencer, Dowager Countess of Derby, he had to decide how to situate himself *vis-à-vis* genres traditionally associated with the court. The court masques of the 1630s promoted a fashionable cult of Platonic Love as a benign representation and vindication of royal absolutism and the personal rule of 1629–40, when Charles ruled without Parliament (Parry 1981). The royal pair displayed themselves under various mythological and pastoral guises as enacting the union of Heroic Virtue (Charles) and Divine Beauty or Love (Henrietta Maria). Caroline masques were exotic and prodigiously expensive. Sets and machinery were elaborate, and the ideality of Charles's reign was often imaged in pastoral terms: the Queen is Chloris/Flora in *Chloridia* (1631); the court is imaged as the Valley of Tempe in *Tempe Restored* (1632); and in *Coelum Britannicum* (1634) the reformed heaven (modelled on the court of Charles) is represented as a garden with parterres, fountains and grottoes (Lewalski 1998: 298–301). The King and Queen danced in many masques, symbolizing their personal and active control of all the discordant elements represented in the antimasques – unruly passions, discontented and mutinous elements in the populace, and threats from abroad. At the end the royal and noble masquers unmasked and participated with other members of the court in elaborate dances (the Revels), figuring the continual intermixing of the ideal world and the Stuart court.

Milton's *Arcades* was performed in the great hall of the Countess of Derby's Harefield estate by some of the Countess's resident and visiting grandchildren and some others. It proposed to reclaim pastoral from the court, intimating the superiority of these festivities and the virtues of this noble Protestant lady and her household over the Queen and her suspect pastoral entertainments. Milton's designation, 'Part of an Entertainment', relates *Arcades* to the genre usually employed to welcome visiting royalty or their surrogates to a noble house; most often its topics praise the visitor, who brings the benefits and virtues of the court to the hosts. But in Milton's reformed entertainment it is the visitors, coming in pastoral guise from the 'Arcadian' court, who pay homage to a far superior rural queen of a better Arcadia, directed by Genius, its guardian spirit. The Countess replaces the King in the chair of State, and displays royal and divine accoutrements. A 'sudden blaze of majesty' (line 2) flames from her 'radiant state' and 'shining throne' (lines 14–15), which is also a 'princely shrine' (line 36) for an 'unparalleled' maternal deity (line 25): 'Such a rural queen / All Arcadia hath not seen' (lines 94–5). The critique of the court is sharpened in a pair of lines in the last song of Genius: 'Though Syrinx your Pan's mistress were, / Yet Syrinx well might wait on her' (lines 106–7). The Arcadia/Pan myth had been taken over by the Stuarts, so these lines exalt the Countess above Henrietta Maria and the Caroline court. Milton begins to explore here what his *Masque* develops fully – a stance towards art and recreation that repudiates both the court aesthetics and wholesale puritan prohibitions. The virtues of Harefield are said to be nurtured by good art as well as by the ruling Lady. Genius, the gardener/guardian of the place, embodies and displays the curative and harmony-producing powers of music and poetry, associating his better aesthetics with the virtues of a sound Protestant aristocracy.

Milton's *Masque*, commonly known as *Comus*, challenges the cultural politics of that court genre. In form, theme and spirit this is a reformed masque, projecting reformist religious and political values. Performed in 1634 on Michaelmas night (29 September) in the great hall at Ludlow Castle to honour the Earl of Bridgewater, the newly appointed Lord Lieutenant of Wales and the border counties, Milton's masque builds brilliantly upon the specific occasion, presenting the Earl's three unmarried children on a journey to their Father's house for a celebration, aided by a Guardian Spirit who is their own music master, Henry Lawes. But their journey takes on overtones of the journey of life and of contemporary life, with the children lost in the dark woods and Lady Alice confronting the temptations of Comus, who in Milton's version is not the traditional belly god of drunkenness and gluttony but has the power and attractiveness of a natural force and a contemporary cultural ideal. As Cedric Brown argues, he is the right tempter for the occasion, presenting these young aristocrats with the refined, dissolute, licentious Cavalier lifestyle they must learn to resist (Brown 1985: 57–77). He embodies as well the seductive power of false rhetoric and the threat of rape. With his bestial rout Comus is made to figure not only Cavalier licentiousness, but also Laudian ritual, the depravities of court masques and feasts, and the unruly holiday pastimes – maypoles, Morris dances, Whitsunales – promoted by the court and decried by puritans. Milton's masque requires no expensive and elaborate machinery: no cloud machines for the Attendant Spirit, no elaborate sets. The ideal masque world is Ludlow Castle, not the Stuart court, and it does not, as is usual in masques, simply appear and dispel all dangers: it is attained through pilgrimage. Nor are the monarchs the agents of cure and renewal: that role belongs to Sabrina as an instrument of divine grace from the region, the Welsh countryside, and as an embodiment of the transformative power of song and poetry. Also, the Platonism in this masque is a far cry from that of the Caroline court: external form does not reflect internal worth, and evil is conceived in Protestant, not Platonic terms. At the end of this masque evil remains: the dark wood is still dangerous to pass through and Comus is neither conquered, nor transformed, nor reconciled.

Comus himself is a species of court masquer, enacting 'dazzling spells' and marvellous spectacles, but they only 'cheat the eye with blear illusion' (lines 154–5;

McGuire 1983: 39–40). He deceptively claims the world of pastoral by his shepherd disguise and his offer to guide the Lady to a 'low / But loyal cottage' (lines 318–19), alluding to the pastoralism so prevalent in court masques. But instead he leads her to a decadent court with an elaborate banquet and a beast-headed entourage – a none-too-subtle allusion to the licentious Cavaliers. In formal terms, this is a surprise: a masque audience would expect the court scene to be the main masque after the antimasque in the dark wood with the antic dances of Comus's rout. Instead, the court is another antimasque – not the locus of virtue and grace but Comus's own residence. Poised against the Comus-ideal is the Lady's chastity as the principle that orders sensuality, pleasure and love, holding nature, human nature and art to their right uses. And poised against the 'dazzling fence' of Comus's 'dear wit, and gay rhetoric' (lines 789–90) is the better art embodied in the songs of the Lady, the Attendant Spirit and Sabrina, and especially the masque dances at Ludlow Castle that figure and display the children's 'triumph in victorious dance / O'er sensual folly, and intemperance' (lines 973–4). The scene images the virtuous pleasure, beauty and art that accord with the life of chastity, intimating that they can be best nurtured in the households of the country aristocracy. If we compare *Coelum Britannicum*, Thomas Carew's sumptuous court masque of 1634 in which the Caroline court is a model for the reformation of Olympus itself, it will be evident how completely Milton has reversed the usual politics of masquing.

Milton's pastoral funeral elegy, 'Lycidas', is the *chef d'œuvre* of his early poetry and one of the greatest lyrics in the language. In it he confronts and works through his most profound personal concerns: about vocation, early death, belatedness and unful-filment, fame, and the value of poetry. He also sounds some leitmotifs of reformist politics: the dangers posed by a corrupt clergy and church, the menace of Rome, adumbrations of apocalypse and the call to prophecy. The opening phrase, 'Yet once more', places this poem in the long series of pastoral funeral elegies stretching back to Theocritus, and in a series of biblical warnings and apocalyptic prophecies beginning with those words, especially Hebrews 12: 26–8 (Wittreich 1979: 137–53). The headnote identifies this poem as a monody, a funeral song by a single singer (Putten-ham 1589: 39), though in fact other speakers are quoted in the poem and the coda introduces another poetic voice. The generic topics of funeral elegy – praise, lament, consolation – are present, though not as distinct parts of the poem. Virtually every line echoes other pastoral elegies by classical, neo-Latin and vernacular Renaissance poets: Theocritus, Moschus, Bion, Virgil, Petrarch, Castiglione, Mantuan, Joannes Secundus, Sannazaro, Spenser and many more (Woodhouse and Bush 1972b: 544–65). Yet no previous, or I think subsequent, funeral poem has the scope, dimension, poignancy and power of 'Lycidas'; it is, paradoxically, at once the most derivative and the most original of elegies. Milton's choice of the pastoral mode was by then out of fashion for funeral elegies, but that choice enabled him to call upon the rich symbolic resonances Renaissance pastoral had come to embody. Imaging the harmony of nature and humankind in the Golden Age, pastoral traditionally portrays the rhythms of human life and death in harmony with the rhythms of the seasons. In classical tradition the shepherd is the poet, and pastoral is a way of exploring the relation of art and nature. In biblical tradition the shepherd is pastor of his flock, like Christ the Good Shepherd. He may also be a prophet like Moses, Isaiah or David, all of whom were called to that role from tending sheep. Pastoral also allows for political comment, as in Spenser's *Shepheards Calender* and several other poems (Revard 1997a: 190–3).

As Milton develops the usual topics of pastoral elegy, he evokes the pastoral vision again and again, then dramatizes its collapse. The dead poet and the living mourner are presented as companion shepherds singing and tending sheep in a *locus amoenus* – an idealized Cambridge University characterized by pastoral *otium*. The first collapse of pastoral obliterates this poignantly nostalgic pastoral scene in which nature, humankind and poetic ambitions seem to be in harmony, unthreatened by the fact or even the thought of mortality. Lycidas's death shatters this idyll, revealing in nature not the ordered seasonal processes of mellowing and fruition that pastoral assumes, but rather the wanton destruction of youth and beauty: the blighted rosebud, the taintworm destroying the weanling sheep, and the frostbitten flowers in early spring. The swain then questions the nymphs, the muses and the classical gods as to why they did not prevent the death of a poet, and they cannot answer. Twice Milton signals the collapse of pastoral by genre shifts, as the pastoral oaten flute is interrupted by notes in a 'higher mood' (line 87): the epic speech of divine Apollo assuring the living swain and the dead Lycidas of enduring fame in heaven, and the 'dread voice' of St Peter promising that some formidable if ambiguous 'two-handed engine' stands ready 'at the door' to smite the guilty and cleanse the church (lines 130–2). These consolations, however incomplete, allow the swain to recall pastoral, first with a procession of mourners and later with an imagined funereal tribute of pastoral flowers. But it collapses again, based as it is on a 'false surmise' (line 153) of nature's empathy with and care for humans: Lycidas's body is not here to be honoured by the floral tribute of nature's beauty, but is subject to all the horrors of the monstrous deep. At length, various adumbrations of resurrection throughout the poem are caught up in the swain's ecstatic vision of a heavenly pastoral scene in which Lycidas enjoys true *otium* beside heavenly streams, with his twin roles of poet and pastor preserved. Painfully inadequate to the fallen human condition, pastoral is seen to have its true locus in heaven. That vision enables the swain, in the coda, to take up his several pastoral roles in the world: to warble his 'Doric lay' (pastoral poetry) and, twitching his symbolic blue mantle, to assume poetry's prophetic/ teaching role (Wittreich 1979: 142–3). He can now move on to the next stage of life and poetry and national reformation: 'fresh woods, and pastures new' (lines 189, 193).

Milton's sonnets, written over a period of some twenty-five years, offer a prime example of his experiments with, and transformations of, genre. He wrote twenty-three sonnets, almost all in Petrarchan form, and he did so after the great age of sonnet writing in England (the 1590s) had passed. But all over Europe for more than two centuries the sonnet had been used by Petrarch and his many followers as the major vernacular lyric genre to treat of love and lovers' emotional states, and sometimes also to represent the power relations of patrons and clients. Milton vastly expanded the sonnet's range, using it for all sorts of subjects and incorporating other generic elements as well as a new complexity of rhetoric and tone. In several sonnets, especially those on his blindness and on the massacre of the Waldensians, syntax and rhetoric play off against the formal metrical pattern of octave and sestet, intensifying tensions and providing a formal mimesis of theme.

He began with traditional love sonnets. His first sonnet has in its generic background medieval lovers' complaints which set the nightingale, the bird of true love, against the cuckoo, the bird of hate whose song doomed the lover to disappointment. His Petrarchan mini-sequence of five sonnets and a canzone in Italian displays debts to Petrarch, Tasso, Bembo and especially Giovanni della Casa (Prince 1954): having mastered the Ovidian love elegy in Latin, Milton evidently decided to try out the other major mode of love poetry in the European tradition in *its* original language. Milton's sequence employs familiar Petrarchan topics: his lady's beauty and virtue are 'the bows and arrows of love' (Sonnet II, line 7); potent fire flashes from her eyes which are like suns; and the humble, devoted lover sighs painful sighs and suffers from love's incurable dart. But this speaker resists and redefines conventional Petrarchan roles. His sonnet lady is not coy or reserved or forbidding, but gentle and gracious; she is no silent object of adoration, but charms her lover with bilingual speech and enthralling songs. Also, this lover-poet carefully avoids Petrarchan subjection to the bonds of Cupid and the lady's power, retaining his autonomy and insisting on his own virtue and worth. The sonnet lady is not his Muse, like Petrarch's Laura: indeed, the Italian love poetry she inspires diverts him from greater poetic achievements in English which promise, his friends remind him, an 'immortal reward' of fame ('Canzone', line 11). And the last sonnet in the sequence is a curious self-blazon, praising the speaker's own moral virtues and poetic aspirations rather than the physical beauties of the lady.

Several of Milton's political sonnets take on some characteristics of the comic or satiric epigram – those short, witty, acerbic poems that look back to Martial and often end with a surprising turn at the end, called a 'sting in the tail'. One engages with contemporary history, a threatened assault on the city; others respond to attacks on Milton's Divorce Tracts and threats to religious toleration. They transport into the lyric mode the satiric persona Milton developed in his prose tracts of the early 1640s. Other sonnets to male and female friends – Henry Lawes and Margaret Ley, and the epitaph-sonnet to Catherine Thomason – find some generic antecedents in epigrams of praise as practised by Ben Jonson, with Milton's speaker adopting the Jonsonian stance of an honest man giving well-considered and well-deserved praise. Two other epigram-like sonnets invite young friends to enjoy the pleasant recreation of good conversation and a light repast: they adopt a Horatian tone and recall Jonson's Epigram 101, 'On Inviting a Friend to Dinner'. Three 'heroic' sonnets – to Sir Thomas Fairfax, Oliver Cromwell and Sir Henry Vane – import into the small form of the sonnet the elevated diction, lofty epithets and style of address appropriate to

odes for great heroes and statesmen. But Milton mixes his high praises with admonitions to these statesmen to meet the still greater challenges that remain in settling
civil government and religious toleration.

Several of Milton's finest sonnets dramatize moments of personal moral crisis, and
in this owe something to the traditions of Protestant occasional meditation on the self
and on personal experience. Topics include an anxious analysis of belatedness in the
choice of vocation and the catastrophe of blindness striking in mid-career. 'When I
consider how my light is spent' (Sonnet XVI, line 1) voices a bitter complaint against
a taskmaster God who seems to demand service even from a blind poet, then moves
towards resolving that problem by projecting a regal God who needs no service but
whose kingdom has place for all. A later sonnet on blindness insists, perhaps too
urgently, on Milton's calm resignation and pride in having lost his sight in the service
of liberty. A moving sonnet to his dead wife, couched as a dream vision, plays off the
classical myth of Alcestis restored to her husband Admetus. Here the sestet offers no
resolution but ends with a poignant sense of loss – of sight and of love: 'But O as to
embrace me she inclined / I waked, she fled, and day brought back my night' (Sonnet
XIX, lines 13–14). Most remarkable, perhaps, is 'On the late Massacre in Piedmont',
which transforms the sonnet into a prophetic Jeremiad, calling down God's vengeance
for the Waldensians slaughtered by the forces of the Roman Catholic Duke of Savoy. It
incorporates many details of the atrocities from contemporary news accounts, and
creates for the sonnet a high, epic-like style. When Wordsworth revived the sonnet for
the Romantics, Milton was his acknowledged model.

In his Proem to Book IX of *Paradise Lost*, the Miltonic Bard alludes to a long period
of gestation for his epic poem: 'this subject for heroic song / Pleased me long
choosing, and beginning late' (*PL* IX. 25–6). He had been thinking about writing
epic for decades – as far back as his collegiate *Vacation Exercise* in 1628. When he wrote
The Reason of Church-Government in 1642, he was thinking about an epic on the model
of Virgil and Tasso, with a great national hero like King Arthur. But at some point
the Virgilian model, celebrating the founding of the Roman empire and the concomitant ruin of the Roman republic, came to be problematic for this republican
poet. And Tasso's model, celebrating within the story of the first crusade the restoration of Counter-Reformation hegemony over all kinds of rebellion and dissent, was
not very useful to this staunch Protestant independent (Quint 1993: 213–47). We
cannot be sure just when Milton decided that the great epic subject for his own times
had to be the Fall and its consequences – 'all our woe' (*PL* I. 3): not the founding of a
great empire or nation, but the loss of an earthly paradise and the need for a new epic
heroism conceived in moral and spiritual terms.

By complex generic strategies and specific allusions, Milton set his poem in
relation to other great epics and works in a variety of genres, involving readers in a
critique of the values associated with those other heroes and genres, as well as with
issues of contemporary politics and theology. He included the full range of topics and
conventions common to the Homeric and Virgilian epic tradition (Blessington 1979):
invocations to the Muse; a beginning *in medias res*; an Achilles-like hero in Satan; a

Homeric catalogue of Satan's generals; councils in hell and in heaven; epic pageants and games; supernatural powers – God, the Son, and good and evil angels. The poem also has a fierce battle in heaven between two armies, replete with chariot clashes, taunts and vaunts, and hill-hurlings; single combats of heroes; reprises of past actions in Raphael's narratives of the War in Heaven and the Creation; and prophecies of the hero's descendants in Michael's summary of biblical history. Yet at a more funda-mental level, Milton's epic is defined against the traditional epic subject – wars and empire – and the traditional epic hero as the epitome of courage and battle prowess. His protagonists are a domestic pair; the scene of their action is a pastoral garden; and their primary challenge is, 'under long obedience tried' (*PL* VII. 159), to make themselves, their marital relationship and their garden – the nucleus of the human world – ever more perfect. Into this radically new kind of epic, Milton incorporates many particular genres in many modes: romance, pastoral, georgic, comedic, tragic, rhetorical, lyric (Ide and Wittreich 1983; Lewalski 1985). And into his sublime epic high style he incorporated a wide range of other styles: colloquial, dialogic, lyric, hymnic, elegiac, mock-heroic, denunciatory, ironic, oratorical, ornate, plain.

In the Proems to Books I, III, VII and IX, Milton explores the problematics of authorship (Grossman 1987). In no other formal epic does the poet insert himself so directly and extensively into his work, making his own experience in writing the poem a part of and an analogue to his story as he struggles to understand the roles played by prophetic inspiration, literary tradition and authorial originality in the writing of his poem. By his choice of subject and use of blank verse, he distances himself from Dryden, Davenant, Cowley and other contemporary aspirants to epic; but his allusions continually acknowlege debts to the great ancients – Homer, Virgil, Ovid, Lucan and Lucretius – and to such moderns as Ariosto, Tasso, Du Bartas, Camoens and Spenser. Yet he hopes and expects to surpass them, since his subject is both truer and more heroic than theirs, and since he looks for illumination and collaboration to the divine source of both truth and creativity.

With the striking portrait of Satan in Books I and II, Milton prompts his readers to begin a poem-long exploration and redefinition of heroes and heroism, the funda-mental concern of epic. Often he highlights discrepancies between Satan's noble rhetoric and his motives and actions; also, by associating Satan with the heroic genres and the great heroes of literary tradition, he invites the reader to discover how he in some ways exemplifies but in essence perverts those models (Lewalski 1985: 55–78). Satan at the outset is a heroic warrior indomitable in the face of defeat and staggering obstacles, manifesting fortitude, determination, endurance and leadership. He prides himself on an Achilles-like obduracy, a 'fixed mind / And high disdain, from sense of injured merit' (I. 97–8), and he commits himself, like Virgil's Turnus, to revenge, hate and 'eternal war / Irreconcilable' (I. 121–2) – though he has not been wronged as those heroes were. He makes martial prowess the test of worth: 'our own right hand / Shall teach us highest deeds, by proof to try / Who is our equal' (V. 864–6). But instead of winning Achilles-like victories on the battlefield, he is defeated by the Son who wields God's omnipotence yet displays it first and chiefly in acts of restoration and new creation (*PL* VI. 780–90). Like Aeneas, Satan departs from a burning city to conquer and lead his followers to a new kingdom; but he finds that hell is his proper kingdom, and that he carries it with him wherever he goes. Like Odysseus, he makes a perilous journey requiring the use of wit and craft, but not to return home to wife and son; rather, before he ventures into Chaos he meets but does not recognize his daughter-wife Sin and the offspring of their incestuous union, Death.

Satan casts himself in the mould of the tragic hero Prometheus, enduring with constancy, indomitable will and 'courage never to submit or yield' the punishment meted out by an implacable divine tyrant (I. 108) – though Prometheus angered Zeus by bringing humans the gift of fire, whereas Satan brings them misery and death. Satan claims that his mind will remain unchanged and will transform his surroundings: 'The mind is its own place, and in itself / Can make a heaven of hell, a hell of heaven' (I. 254–5). But he finds the reverse: 'Which way I fly is hell; myself am hell' (IV. 75). Like many romance heroes, Satan enters a Garden of Love and courts its lady with exaggerated Petrarchan compliments (Giamatti 1966: 295–351), but he cannot win love, or find sensual delight, or enjoy sensuous refreshment or ease there; on the contrary, he feels more intensely than before the agony of his own loneliness, lovelessness and unsatisfied desire. Against the model of Camoens's *Lusiads*, Satan is represented as an explorer bent on conquest and colonization, a 'great adventurer' undertaking to search 'foreign worlds' (X. 440–1). He sets out courageously to sail through an uncharted sea (Chaos) enduring as yet unknown dangers and difficulties; he discovers the site of a future colony, the Paradise of Fools, to be peopled chiefly by Roman Catholics; and he discovers the paradise of Eden where, after conquering Adam and Eve, he means to settle the fallen angels. At his first sight of Adam and Eve, he makes clear in soliloquy that he means to use Eden and its inhabitants for his own purposes, that his excursion is about empire-building as well as revenge. He justifies his enterprise by 'public reason just, / Honour and empire with revenge enlarged' – characterized by the narrator as 'necessity, / The tyrant's plea' (IV. 389–94). He then practises fraud on Eve, causing her to lose her rightful domain. Such associations do not mean that Milton thought exploration and colonization necessarily Satanic, but they do suggest how susceptible the imperial enterprise is to evil purposes. All these Satanic perversions of the heroic find their climax in Book X, when Satan returns to hell intending a Roman triumph like that attending the formal coronation of Charles II (Knoppers 1994: 96–114) – to be greeted instead with a universal hiss from his followers turned into snakes, as all of them are forced to enact a grotesque black comedy of God's devising. Milton does not use these comparisons to condemn the various literary genres, nor yet to exalt Satan as hero, but to let readers discover how Satan has perverted the noblest qualities of literature's greatest heroes, and so realize how susceptible those models of heroism are to perversion. He invites readers to measure all other versions of the heroic against the poem's standard: the self-sacrificing love of the Son, the moral courage of Abdiel, and the 'better fortitude' (IX. 31) of Christ in life and death, with which Adam and Eve at last identify.

Milton's representations of hell, heaven and Eden employ a variety of generic resources to challenge readers' stereotypes, and their bases in literature and theology. In his poem, all these places are in process: their physical conditions are fitted to the beings that inhabit them, but the inhabitants interact with and shape their environments, creating societies in their own images. Hell is first presented in traditional terms with Satan and his crew chained on a lake of fire, but they soon rise up and begin to mine gold and gems, build a government centre (Pandæmonium), hold a parliament, send Satan on a mission of exploration and conquest, investigate their spacious and varied though sterile landscape, engage in martial games and parades, perform music, compose epic poems and argue hard philosophical questions. Milton portrays hell as a damned society in the making, with royalist politics, perverted language, perverse rhetoric, political manipulation and demagoguery. By contrast, he portrays heaven as a unique place, a celestial city combining courtly magnificence and the pleasures of pastoral nature. The mixture of heroic, georgic and pastoral activities and modes – elegant hymns suited to various occasions, martial parades, warfare, pageantry, masque dancing, feasting, lovemaking, political debate, the protection of Eden – provides an ideal of wholeness. But, surprisingly, Milton's heaven is also a place of process, not stasis, of complexity, not simplicity, and the continuous and active choice of good rather than the absence of evil. Eden is a lush and lovely enclosed garden with a superabundance of natural delights and a wide range of pastoral and georgic activities, and it is pre-eminently a place of growth and change. Adam and Eve are expected to cultivate and control their burgeoning garden and their own sometimes wayward impulses and passions; to work out their relationship to God and to each other; and to deal with a constant succession of challenges relating to work, education, love and sex, intellectual curiosity, the duties pertaining to their places in a hierarchical universe, and temptations from Satan. Milton presents these challenges as components of an ideal human life in innocence and as preparation for a more exalted state.

Paradise Lost also uses the resources of genre to engage with contemporary political and cultural issues. At some point while he was writing and revising his epic for its first publication in 1667 Milton decided on a ten-book format, thereby distinguishing his poem from the twelve-book Virgilian model consciously followed by Tasso and others. He may have rejected the Virgilian format to emphasize that his is not an epic of conquest and empire, but another reason was surely that royalists had appropriated the Virgilian heroic mode before and especially after the Restoration. In what Laura Knoppers terms the 'politics of joy' following the Restoration, poets hailed the new era in Virgilian terms as a Golden Age restored, and celebrated Charles II as a new Augustus (Knoppers 1994: 67–122). His coronation procession was designed as a magnificent Roman triumph through elaborate Roman arches that identified him with Augustus, Aeneas and Neptune. Dryden's *Astraea Redux* (1660) rings explicit changes on those motifs: 'Oh Happy Age! Oh times like those alone / By Fate reserv'd for Great *Augustus* Throne' (lines 320–1). By contrast, Milton's opening lines indicate that the true restoration will not be effected by an English

Augustus but must await a divine hero: 'till one greater man / Restore us, and regain the blissful seat' (*PL* I. 4–5). And his portrayal of Satan contains a powerful critique of monarchy as civil idolatry, with allusion to Charles I and Charles II. By adopting a ten-book format, Milton associates his poem explicitly with the republican Lucan's unfinished epic, *Pharsalia*, or *The Civil War*, which was the font of a countertradition to Virgil's celebration of an Augustan empire predestined by the Gods. Lucan celebrated the resistance of the Roman republic and its heroes, Pompey and Cato, and by Milton's time the *Pharsalia* was firmly associated with antimonarchical or republican politics through several editions and translations, especially the 1627 English translation by the Long Parliament's historian-to-be, Thomas May (Norbrook 1999: 23–63). Milton alludes to and echoes Lucan especially in the treatment of contingency in Satan's flight through Chaos, in the portrayal of the War in Heaven as a civil war, and in Satan's echo of Caesar's opportunistic republican rhetoric (Norbrook 1999: 438–67; Quint 1993: 255–6, 305–7). In 1674 Milton produced an edition of *Paradise Lost* in twelve books by dividing Books VII and X but adding very little new material. By then, Virgil was no longer so obvious a signifier of royalism, and Milton seems to have decided to reclaim that central epic tradition from Dryden and the court for his own sublime poem and its values.

In the last two books of *Paradise Lost* Milton reworks another common epic topic, the prophecy of future history. The series of visions and narratives Michael presents to Adam show over and over again the few righteous overwhelmed by the many wicked, and the collapse of all attempts to found a permanent version of the Kingdom of God on earth. Adam and Milton's readers must learn to read that history, with its tragic vision of an external paradise irretrievably lost – 'so shall the world go on, / To good malignant, to bad men benign, / Under her own weight groaning' (XII. 537–9) – offset only by the projected millennial restoration of all things at Christ's second coming and the possibility, now, of inhabiting a pastoral of the spirit, 'A paradise within thee, happier far' (XII. 587). This might seem a recipe for retreat from political engagement, but the thrust of Michael's prophecy is against any kind of quietism or passivity, spiritual, moral or political. His history shows that in every age the just rise to oppose, when God calls them to do so, the Nimrods, or the Pharaohs, or the royalist persecutors of puritans, even though – like the loyal angels in the Battle in Heaven – they can win no decisive victories and can effect no lasting reforms until the Son appears. Eve learns something of the history to come through dreams, which lead her to recognize her divinely appointed agency in bringing the messianic promise into history. Remarkably, Milton's poem ends with Eve's recognition of herself as the primary human agent in God's redemptive plan and the primary protagonist of *Paradise Lost*: 'though all by me is lost, / Such favour I unworthy am vouchsafed, / By me the promised seed shall all restore' (XII. 621–3). The poem ends in the elegiac register: the poignant, quiet, wonderfully evocative final lines conjoin loss and consolation. Prophecy and Providence provide part of that consolation, but so does the human love of Adam and Eve, as those new domestic heroes wander forth 'hand in hand' to meet the harsh challenges of life in the fallen world.

In a note added in 1668 explaining his use of blank verse, Milton openly contested the new norm for heroic poetry and drama, the heroic couplet. By remarkable coincidence, his blank verse epic greeted the reading public at about the same time as Dryden's essay *Of Dramatick Poesie* (1668) with its claim that rhyme is now the norm for modern poetry of all sorts, and especially for tragedy and heroic drama. Dryden's persona, Neander, affirms categorically that 'Blank Verse is acknowledg'd to be too low for a Poem, nay more, for a paper of verses; but if too low for an ordinary Sonnet, how much more for Tragedy' (lines 66–7) – or for epic, he implies, since drama and epic are of the same genus. In the preface, Dryden states that rhyme enjoys the favour of the court, 'the last and surest judge of writing' (sig. A3^r). Though Milton's note on the verse form was requested by his publisher, who recognized that in this cultural milieu readers expected rhyme, Milton did rather more than was expected, challenging not only the new poetic norms but also the court culture and royalist politics that fostered them: 'This neglect then of rhyme so little is to be taken for a defect, though it may seem so perhaps to vulgar readers, that it rather is to be esteemed an example set, the first in English, of ancient liberty recovered to heroic poem from the troublesome and modern bondage of rhyming' (*PL*: 54–5). That language of liberty and bondage associates Milton's blank verse with (it is implied) the restoration of English liberty from the bondage of Stuart tyranny (Zwicker 1987: 249), making Milton's epic an aesthetic complement to republican politics and culture.

In 1671 Milton published in a single volume a brief epic, *Paradise Regained*, and a tragedy, *Samson Agonistes*, which offer two models of political response in conditions of severe trial and oppression after the Restoration. The brief epic presents in its hero Jesus an example of unflinching resistance to and forthright denunciation of all versions of the sinful or disordered life, and all faulty and false models of church and state. The tragedy presents a warrior hero through whose deeds and final catastrophic act God offered the Israelites opportunities to free themselves from ignominious defeat and slavery, though only if he and they can rise to the moral and political challenges involved. These poems continue Milton's redefinition of the heroic. Even more directly than *Paradise Lost*, they challenge the aesthetics and cultural politics of the contemporary heroic drama: its pentameter couplets and what Steven Zwicker terms 'its bombast and cant, its aristocratic code of virtue and honor, its spectacle and rhetoric...its warring heroes and virgin queens, its exaltation of passion and elevation of empire' (1995: 139–40, 151). Milton's largely dialogic brief epic celebrates in blank verse the heroism of intellectual and moral struggle and entirely redefines the nature of empire and glory. And his severe classical tragedy, written in a species of free verse with varying line lengths and some irregular rhyme, eschews every vestige of exotic spectacle, links erotic passion with idolatry, and presents a tragic hero whose intense psychic suffering leads to spiritual growth.

Paradise Regained offers a daring challenge to and revision of epic norms. Its epic proposition makes the quite startling claim that this poem treats a vastly more noble and heroic subject than *Paradise Lost*, with a hero who conquers his enemy, regains the regions lost to Satan and establishes his own realm. These lines allude to the verses, then widely accepted as genuine, that introduce the *Aeneid* in most Renaissance editions (Virgil 1960: 240–1) and supposedly announce Virgil's turn from pastoral and georgic to an epic subject:

> I who ere while the happy garden sung,
> By one man's disobedience lost, now sing
> Recovered Paradise to all mankind,
> By one man's firm obedience fully tri'd
> Through all temptation, and the Tempter foil'd
> In all his wiles, defeated and repulsed,
> And Eden raised in the waste wilderness
>
> (I. 1–7)

That echo, and the reference to *Paradise Lost* as a poem about a happy garden, suggest with witty audacity that Milton has now, like Virgil, graduated from pastoral apprentice-work to the true epic subject: in his case, the spiritual warfare and victory of Jesus. Also, several allusions to the Book of Job suggest that Milton is now carrying out the poetic project he imagined a quarter of a century earlier in *The Reason of Church-Government*, when he proposed the Book of Job as a 'brief model' for epic (*CPW* I: 813). This poem is in part shaped by the exegetical tradition that interpreted Job as epic, and also by the long tradition of biblical 'brief epics' in three or four books, in Latin and in the vernacular literatures (Lewalski 1966: 3–129).

Contemporary readers were no doubt surprised, as many modern critics have been, by Milton's choosing as his subject the Temptation in the Wilderness instead of the Passion–Crucifixion narrative, and by his portrait of an austere, nay-saying Jesus who discounts and refuses all worldly pleasures and goods. But this choice of subject follows naturally from Milton's belief that self-knowledge and self-rule are preconditions for any worthy public action in the world. The temptation episode allows Milton to present Jesus's moral and intellectual trials as a higher epic heroism, as a model for right knowing and choosing, and as a creative and liberating force in history. As a political gesture, it allowed him to develop a model of nonviolent yet active and forceful resistance to the Restoration church and state (Loewenstein 1994: 63–89). The debates between Jesus and Satan can lead readers to think rightly about kingship, prophecy, idolatry, millenarian zeal, the proper uses of civil power, the place of secular learning, and the abuses of pleasure, glory and power. The poem's structure gives primary attention to the Messiah's kingdom and its relation to secular monarchies and their values, with Books II and III, and much of Book IV, given over to that issue.

Milton reworked and adapted epic conventions and topics to this unusual subject. He transformed the central epic episode, the single combat of hero and antagonist, into a three-day verbal battle, a poem-long intellectual and moral struggle. The poem begins *in medias res* with Jesus's baptism. There are two Infernal Councils in which

Satan plots his temptation, and a Council in Heaven in which God prophesies his Son's immediate and ultimate victory over Satan. Also, there are two transformed epic recitals – Christ's meditation about his youthful experiences and aspirations, and Mary's reminiscences about the prophecies and promises attending the hero's early life – as well as a transformed prophetic vision in which the hero, instead of viewing his own destined kingdom (as Aeneas does), sees and rejects all the kingdoms that are not his. There is an epic catalogue of the Kingdoms of the World displayed to Jesus, a martial pageant of the Parthian warriors and a few striking epic similes. Like *Paradise Lost*, this poem incorporates other genres into the epic frame: continuous dialogue in which Satan's inflated epic rhetoric is met by Jesus's spare answers; a pastoral grove where Satan presents a sensuous banquet, and the still more enchanting 'Olive Groves of Academe'; a romance situation in which Jesus reprises the trials of a young knight in the wilderness before he is recognized as champion or king; and angelic hymns at the beginning and end of the temptations. But this poem forgoes the soaring, eloquent style of *Paradise Lost* for one appropriate to this subject: more restrained, dialogic, and tense with the parry and thrust of intellectual exchange.

The title page of *Samson Agonistes* terms it a 'Dramatic Poem', not a drama: Milton did not suppose that it might be presented on the Restoration stage alongside Dryden's exotic tragedies. But as a written text it might still prove 'doctrinal and exemplary to a Nation', the effect he had projected for tragedy in *The Reason of Church-Government* (*CPW* I: 815). Milton made large alterations in the biblical story from Judges 13–16: conflating the biblical strong man with Job and the Psalmist (Radzinowicz 1978: 188–260), he creates a hero capable of self-analysis, intellectual struggle, tragic suffering and bitter self-castigation as he seeks to understand God's ways to him. In the preface, Milton's only extended commentary on a poem of his own, he explicitly sets his practice against that of his contemporaries, describing his tragedy as 'coming forth after the ancient manner, much different from what among us passes for best' (*CSP*: 356). Milton begins by paraphrasing Aristotle's famous definition of tragedy (*Poetics* 6.1, 1973: 24–5) in terms tailored to his own poem:

> TRAGEDY, as it was anciently composed, hath been ever held the gravest, moralest, and most profitable of all other poems: therefore said by Aristotle to be of power by raising pity and fear, or terror, to purge the mind of those and such-like passions, that is to temper and reduce them to just measure with a kind of delight, stirred up by reading or seeing those passions well imitated. (*CSP*: 355)

Unlike Aristotle, Milton emphasizes the moral profit of tragedy. He glosses catharsis as a purging or tempering of the passions by aesthetic delight – a concept encapsulated in the drama's final line: 'calm of mind all passion spent'. He also changes the object of imitation: for Aristotle, it is an action, the plot or mythos; for Milton, it is the tragic passions, pity or fear and terror, that are to be 'well imitated' –

a definition that locates the essence of tragedy in the scene of suffering, the agonies and passions of Samson. In Aristotle's paradigmatic tragedy, Sophocles's *Oedipus Rex*, the hero falls from prosperity into abject misery through an error or fault (*hamartia*) that enmeshes him in the toils of Fate. Milton's tragedy begins with Samson already fallen into misery, like the heroes of Aeschylus's *Prometheus Bound* or Sophocles's *Oedipus at Colonnus*. Again, as he did in *The Reason of Church-Government*, Milton finds a biblical model for tragedy in the Book of Revelation and the commentary of David Pareus, who described that book's tragic subject as the 'sufferings and agons' of the saints throughout history (Lewalski 1970: 1050–62). Whatever intimations of providential design or apocalyptic destruction of the wicked are conveyed by Milton's drama, they do not dispel the tragedy of Samson's agony and his people's loss.

Pointing to Aeschylus, Sophocles and Euripides as 'the best rule to all who endeavour to write tragedy' in regard to the disposition of the plot, Milton follows the structure of Greek tragedy closely (*CSP*: 357). There is a prologue spoken by Samson, a parados or entry song of the Chorus, five agons or dialogic struggles with visitors separated by choral odes, an exode containing the report of and responses to Samson's death, and a kommos containing a funeral dirge and consolations (Parker 1970). Like Oedipus in *Oedipus Rex*, Samson gains self-knowledge through the dialogic agons, in this case partly by encountering and overcoming versions of his former self: as a Danite circumscribed by his tribe and family, as a sensualist enslaved by passion, and as a swaggering strong man. Milton states that his Chorus of Danites is designed 'after the Greek manner', but it is much more than the voice of community mores. Especially in the long segment after Samson leaves the scene, it falls to them to try to understand what Samson's life and death mean for Israel, and what they themselves are called to do. The preface also indicates the drama's adherence to the neoclassical unities of time and place: the action takes only a few hours with no intervals of time, and the single locale is a shady bank in front of Samson's prison, with all the action in the Philistine Temple reported by a messenger.

The tragic effect of *Samson Agonistes* is intensified by its portrayal of the great obstacles to political liberation, whether in Israel or England. All human heroes are flawed, and peoples generally are more disposed to choose 'Bondage with ease than strenuous liberty' (line 271). Yet in the drama's historical moment a future in bondage is not yet fixed and choices are still possible. If the Israelites, or the English, could truly value liberty, could reform themselves, could read the signs and events with penetration, could benefit from the 'new acquist / Of true experience' (lines 1755–6), moral and political, that Samson's experience offers to the Danites and that Milton's dramatization of it offers to his compatriots, liberation might be possible. But that can only happen when a virtuous citizenry understands the political stakes and places a true value on liberty. Milton's exemplary tragedy makes a fitting poetic climax to his lifelong effort to use the resources of genre to help create such citizens.

BIBLIOGRAPHY

Writings

Aristotle (1973); Dryden (1668); Lucan (1928); Minturno (1559); Puttenham (1589); Sidney (1595); Virgil (1960).

References for Further Reading

Blessington (1979); Brown (1985); Colie (1973); Fowler (1982); Giamatti (1966); Grossman (1987); Ide and Wittreich (1983); Knoppers (1994); Lewalski (1966, 1970, 1985, 1998); Loewenstein (1994); McGuire (1983); Norbrook (1999); Parker, William R. (1968, 1970, 1996); Parry (1981); Patterson (1988); Potter (1989); Prince (1954); Quint (1993); Radzinowicz (1978); Revard (1997a); Smith (1994); Wittreich (1979); Woodhouse and Bush (1972b); Zwicker (1987, 1995).

2
The Classical Literary Tradition

John K. Hale

What have Milton's modern-day readers to gain from awareness of the classical literary tradition in which he repeatedly and explicitly placed himself? Should we press that question, indeed, and ask what is lost by unawareness or neglect of the tradition? Or should we put it aside, taking the view that nothing is lost, since there is always some other way of reading him which will yield the same understanding, and hence pleasure? Although these questions are too large and personal to receive balanced answers here, some suggestive ones will emerge from the following case studies.

Being case studies, they cannot help privileging texture above structure (close reading above detached meditation); but truly it *is* moment-to-moment, textural reading which makes Milton's voice distinctive, and gains him his readership. I shall be glancing at a few larger structures too, since these certainly draw benefit from his classical attainments; the emphasis, none the less, should remain on the texturing. Similarly, Milton's power to speak to us is not at all limited to *Paradise Lost*. But since readers who do not enjoy *Paradise Lost* seldom enjoy his other poetry, still less his prose, where better to begin on case studies than with that poem's own beginning?

The Opening Sentence of *Paradise Lost*

> Of man's first disobedience, and the fruit
> Of that forbidden tree, whose mortal taste
> Brought death into the world, and all our woe,
> With loss of Eden, till one greater man
> Restore us, and regain the blissful seat,   5
> Sing heavenly Muse, that on the secret top
> Of Oreb or of Sinai, didst inspire
> That shepherd, who first taught the chosen seed,

In the beginning how the heavens and earth
Rose out of chaos: or if Sion hill   10
Delight thee more, and Siloa's brook that flowed
Fast by the oracle of God[,] I thence
Invoke thy aid to my advent'rous song,
That with no middle flight intends to soar
Above the Aonian mount, while it pursues   15
Things unattempted yet in prose or rhyme.

(I. 1–16)

Any reader meeting this for the first time and willing to confront its texture in detail will check the allusions, and perhaps observe that most are biblical, in accordance with the chosen subject (Jesus in line 4, Moses in lines 6–11, three sacred mountains and Siloa's brook). Thus 'Aonian' sticks out, as the kind of classical allusion which must receive a gloss, but which may also irritate the reader who is eager to get up steam. 'Aonian' means 'belonging to Mount Helicon, sacred home of the classical Muses'; and so it links back to the 'heavenly Muse' of line 6, differentiating that from the Homerical / pagan one ... yes, but so what? The eager reader might object – and how readers enjoy objecting to this poet! – that the sense boils down to a routine claim that the biblical subject is loftier than those of Greek and Roman epics. The same reader might object that the distinction between the regular classical sisterhood of Muses and the '*heavenly* Muse' of line 6 is a footling or confusing one.

A fit reply to the first misgiving would be that precisely because the ploy is routine the point lies in listening to *how* this poet appropriates it, how he makes the detail arresting in his opening bid for our attention. The second point is the more important one: Milton has a new Muse, a 'heavenly' one (perhaps the divine Logos of John's Gospel), and yet to call it a *Muse* is his way of upholding both originality and continuity, indeed, originality because of continuity. The two Greek names together have brought into view, this early in the poem, a persistent dialectic within Milton's texture. He will persist in two related mental acts: to affirm that his subject holds greater spiritual worth than the pagan predecessors' do; but yet to avail himself of their resources, while still carrying on a dialectic with himself about the truth status and moral worth of his classical inheritance.

He avails himself of the classical resources as if by second nature. In the passage, for example, he claims to 'sing' (line 6) and 'soar' (line 14): both are classical images of the poet's activity. And by 'Aonian' (line 15) or (in the same verse paragraph) 'what in me is dark' (line 22) Milton may begin moving his opening utterance closer to Homer as the archetypal, originary blind poet (with pun on 'seer'). The alignment will become wholly explicit in his next invocation, the 'blind Maeonides' of Book III, line 35. Here at the poem's opening Milton undertakes an emulation with Homer, and yet not one where the competitor is slighted, for the self-image is the same.

The Dialectic, as Seen in Further Allusions

The dialectic appears in innumerable forms, each unique. Let us take three further instances of classical allusion. One is an abrupt dismissal of a particular detail of classical myth, as false. The second is a generalizing address to the issue we have just adumbrated, explicitly problematizing it. In the third, however, conflict is absent: the back-reference to Virgil becomes (to use a favourite Renaissance metaphor) a grateful making of fresh honey from the ancient flowers.

First he tells the famous myth of Hephaestus (Mulciber, Vulcan) thrown from Olympus by angry Zeus; then he says it is lies!

> Nor was his name unheard or unadored
> In ancient Greece; and in Ausonian land
> Men called him Mulciber; and how he fell   740
> From heaven, they fabled, thrown by angry Jove
> Sheer o'er the crystal battlements: from morn
> To noon he fell, from noon to dewy eve,
> A summer's day; and with the setting sun
> Dropped from the zenith like a falling star,   745
> On Lemnos the Ægæan isle: thus they relate,
> Erring; for he with this rebellious rout
> Fell long before;
>
>   (I. 738–48)

The thought-content here is insisting on the primacy, the aboriginality and superior truth, of the biblical over the classical. But the main impact within the reading experience is less of solemn triumphalism than of a witty surprise. The allusion is a '*dis*simile', a 'narrative intrusion like a simile but declared by the intrusive author to be unlike' (*PL*: 106; my italics). It disconcerts the attentive reader, who is led up the path of a lengthy retelling of Homer, only to be informed that close attention was a waste of time. Yet not a total waste, surely, because the rhetorical lurch is diverting and alerting. And the jape itself may come from a classical author, Lucretius (*De Rerum Natura* I. 393, *PL*: 105–6).

Rather different is the invocation by which Milton girds the bardic loins to narrate the Fall itself:

>   sad task, yet argument
> Not less but more heroic than the wrath
> Of stern Achilles on his foe pursued   15
> Thrice fugitive about Troy wall; or rage
> Of Turnus for Lavinia disespoused,
> Or Neptune's ire or Juno's, that so long
> Perplexed the Greek and Cytherea's son;

If answerable style I can obtain   20
Of my celestial patroness, who deigns
Her nightly visitation unimplored,
And díctates to me slumbering, or inspires
Easy my unpremeditated verse:
Since first this subject for heroic song   25
Pleased me long choosing, and beginning late;
Not sedulous by nature to indite
Wars, hitherto the only argument
Heroic deemed, chief mastery to dissect
With long and tedious havoc fabled knights   30
In battles feigned; the better fortitude
Of patience and heroic martyrdom
Unsung; or to describe races and games,
Or tilting furniture, emblazoned shields,
Impreses quaint, caparisons and steeds;   35
Bases and tinsel trappings, gorgeous knights
At joust and tournament; then marshalled feast
Served up in hall with sewers, and seneschals;
The skill of artifice or office mean,
Not that which justly gives heroic name   40
To person or to poem. Me of these
Nor skilled nor studious, higher argument
Remains,

(PL IX. 27–43)

The main thrust is certainly to propose that a Christian fortitude is 'better' than the ancient, martial varieties. But the proposal comes in the course of an epic invocation, one among a host of features of classical epic on which the poet relies; I almost said, has to rely. And as the comparison proceeds, from classical epics (lines 14–19) to medieval and romance ones (lines 30–9) we find him *more* scathing towards the latter, whose trappings of feasts and colourful detail sound lesser – and are excoriated for longer – than the fortitude of Homeric heroes and those of secondary epics like those of Virgil or Lucan. Indeed, it has recently been argued with force that Milton owed much to Roman stoic writers, whose creed (whether in action or when undergoing exile or political repression) was precisely an inner fortitude (Shifflett 1998: 129–54). The ranking of biblical above classical in the poem does not seem to have been decided once and for all. Milton keeps coming back to it, thinking it out afresh, viewing it from another angle. What is more, he always uses classical weapons to address it, so begetting a further dialectic within the main one. There seems to be a tension, even a threat, or at any rate a perpetually altering issue for him.

In a third instance, however, no tension is felt. When Satan first finds voice in the poem, speaking to his chief ally Beelzebub as they lie weltering upon the livid flood of hell, his words are

> If thou beest he; but oh how fallen! how changed
> From him, who in the happy realms of light   85
> Clothed with transcendent brightness didst outshine
> Myriads though bright:
>
>   (*PL* I. 84–7)

Many readers have found here an allusion to the shock with which Virgil's Aeneas meets the ghost of his kinsman Hector: 'quantum mutatus ab illo / Hectore qui redit exuvias indutus Achilli', 'How greatly changed from that / Hector who returned wearing the armour of Achilles' (*Aeneid* II. 274–5). Why does this matter? Even if it does allude, what is the reader to do with this ostensibly indigestible hunk of information? Gilbert Highet rightly declares that while the poignancy of the phrase is owed to the translating from Virgil and acquires the charm of reminiscence, 'the meaning also is enriched': without any more description Milton is making us feel the 'anguish, and foreboding, and defeat', of fallen but still heroic persons, with strong recognizable human passions (Highet 1949: 156–7). In short, the allusion enables Milton to implant several pertinent things at once in the responsive reader; to start up a turmoil of sympathies, and to do it economically and mimetically.

The variety by now observed within the dialectic suggests, then, a provisional answer to our opening questions. Where the dialectic is overt, awareness of the classical side of the tussle is the most direct way of joining in Milton's acts of thought. Where the dialectic is quiescent it can be ignored or savoured at will. Where it becomes a special effect, however, awareness must stretch and keep up with the moment-to-moment energy of this poet's mind. And lastly, the dialectic is so frequent that awareness of the classical literary tradition seems the quickest way to chart it.

The Variety of the Debts, and their Treatment Here

So far I have been examining Milton's use of classical literary resources in terms of allusions. The resources in question go much wider. They include such further textural features as syntax and diction, as well as more structural ones such as invocation and prosopopoeia, motifs or themes, bardic stance and metaphor. They include large structures such as the division of *Paradise Lost* into ten and then twelve books. One could go on listing. Instead, it is best to perceive the resources energizing the poem locally, and so savour the diversity of the usage and of its benefits. I continue first with examples from Book I, as being the portion in which the problems with classical influence arise first, and perhaps most often; for here Milton is using his epic and other classical reading to establish his very credentials. Then I look outside *Paradise Lost* in a mainly chronological order, so as to work back to it. However, chronology sometimes yields to generic coverage: Milton's genres, not his highest poetic ones alone but one and all, draw their vitality from the classical literary tradition. They never cease to help make Milton Milton. And this I finally demonstrate by examples from Book IX of his epic, that obvious climax of his life's whole work.

Further Examples from *Paradise Lost*, Book I

Plunging like Homer and the rest *in medias res* ('into the midst of things'), Milton invokes, then narrates, then hands over to speeches, before going on into a series of full-length and profoundly felt similes, which then usher in a catalogue. All of these bear the hallmark of the ancient epics. If anything, Milton (as a latecomer to the tradition of epic) is assailing the reader with a *concentration* of the recognized distinctive elements of ancient epic. Thus an unusual number of epic's extended similes populate Book I; the poem's epic catalogue comes far earlier than in Homer or Virgil; and so on. It behoves modern readers, as best we may, to receive the impact as thus designed if we want the expressive pleasures that result.

Consider, for example, the simile of the fallen leaves:

> Natheless he [Satan] so endured, till on the beach
> Of that inflamèd sea, he stood and called   300
> His legions, angel forms, who lay entranced
> Thick as autumnal leaves that strew the brooks
> In Vallombrosa, where the Etrurian shades
> High overarched embower;
>
> > (*PL* I. 299–304)

The numberless dead of Homer and Virgil and many another poet become the lost fallen angels. But the repetition gives much more than the pleasure of recognition. These fallen leaves are *not* dead: so much the worse for them, since they will know their own loss for ever, will suffer from that knowledge for ever. The effect of the simile as read within its classical subtradition is of a simple, but ironic and most incremental repetition.

Or consider two apparently minor matters: the spelling of the biblical place names in the catalogue of the fallen angels; and Milton's 1674 revision of a ten-book poem into the twelve-book one which we read. The spellings are often neither the usual English ones nor the Hebrew transliterated, but Latinate or Greekish. 'Azotus', not 'Ashdod' (I. 464); 'Oreb' not 'Horeb' (I. 484). Was this an acoustic preference, or a philological/etymological one? I have found that although the latter aspect might enter into the matter where a secondary meaning was to be gained, Milton also does it where that is not the case: there was something about Greek or Latin *sounds* which he on occasion preferred to those of Hebrew or English. Whether the preference was conscious aural taste or some unexamined predilection, either way we are catching an instinctive reliance on the classical, which has governed how he hears.

As for the revision of the ten books of 1667 into the twelve of 1674, not only is the idea of a 'book' itself classical, but the change moves their number and the poem's whole large shaping towards the classical. Though Homer's two epics were articulated by others into twenty-four books apiece, the number of the letters of the Greek alphabet, Virgil deliberately kept the number-base, as a sort of arithmetical if not numerological allusion to Homer, while making it his own by the choice of twelve. As Virgil, so – finally, and upon reflection – Milton (Hale 1995: 131–49).

In short, Milton's borrowings from antiquity are appropriations, made for his own new, original creation. They empower him to say many things at once, to say them densely and strongly, to acquire and maintain a voice which has *authority*. He seeks that authority by seeking, like his ancient models, to be heard as a *doctus poeta*, a 'learned poet', in the same way that the ancient world esteemed its greatest poets. As readers, we ignore this role and its ancestry at considerable cost (Hale 1997: 114–15).

Development and Range

The diminutive scale in the spelling of those names and the opposite scale of that late redivision of the books emphasize that Milton heeded antiquity in multiple ways. Next, beginning a sketch of Milton's classicizing imagination outside *Paradise Lost*, I offer further passages which show Milton's debate with himself upon our theme. As Yeats put it, 'Out of the quarrel with others we make rhetoric; out of the quarrel with ourselves we make poetry.'

Just as most readers feel that 'Lycidas' marks a growth-point in the development of Milton's poetic voice, so the growth stems from the degree and kind of its engagement with Virgil's *Eclogues*. Individual debts can readily be documented – by names, including 'Lycidas' itself, or by allusions, or by portions of speeches. The number of them makes a stronger point, as does the weightiness of individual *cris de coeur* ('Alas! What boots it . . .', line 64; 'Were it not better . . .', line 67). While these are listed in editions, they become far more instructive when used to drive a whole new interpretation of a still problematic poem. Such an interpretation is that of J. Martin Evans, done in terms of the whole argument of the poem, as it absorbs or inverts or extends several eclogues, and (in one word, again) appropriates them. 'If the muse is not only thankless but powerless to boot, then what is the point of serving her so strictly?' (Evans 1998a: 80). Evans shows that Virgil's Tenth Eclogue provides impetus and theme as well as forms and texture, and that from all this together can be gained a *secure* basis of interpretation, a measure of Milton's appropriation, a sharp sense of the ultimate difference and uniqueness of his poem. For the poem requires an answer to the underlying question: why is it termed a 'monody', yet ends with a narrative eight lines said by another voice? Who, in fact, says the last words of all, 'Tomorrow to fresh woods, and pastures new'? To overstate for emphasis, Milton's Virgil finds him this sudden new voice.

Now, Evans's approach is not the only one, nor indeed does he rely exclusively on insights deriving from Virgil. Yet Virgil begins, grounds and controls his reading. Virgil's were not the only ancient or Latin eclogues, but they have always taken pride of place in the genre: Evans starts where Milton in all probability started. And that security leads into a very fresh reading.

That the oldest approach may here be the freshest suggests a wider need for awareness of Milton's classical inheritance. Not just 'Lycidas' but many of his works have Latin or Greek titles. We can see this with special clarity in cases where we have only the titles, from his list of titles of projected tragedies in the Trinity Manuscript (Milton 1970: 34–9). It teems with hellenizing epithets, and I shall dwell on them here as a rare chance to watch his imagination at the initial, sketching stage. His classical languages and his sense of Greek tragedy combine to express his ruminations, as he sought for a tragic theme.

At page 34 we read a run of the hellenizing epithets: 'Elias *in the mount*. 2 Reg. 1 *oreibates*. or better Elias *Polemistes*. Elisaeus *Hydrochoos*. 2 Reg. 3. *Hudrophantes Aquator* Elisaeus *Adorodocetos*. Elisaeus *Menutes* sive in Dothaimis 2 Reg....' (emphases added). A title like those of the great Greek tragedies ('Prometheus *Vinctus*', 'Oedipus *Tyrannus*', 'Hercules *Furens*' and so on) is being built into each such project. He is *thinking* in Greek or Latin about these English projects, trying to capture the essence of each projected dramatic action by the classicizing epithet. Indeed, we catch him in the very process of the thinking, his thinking in Greek about a Hebrew subject which he might make into an English tragedy, as he dawdles through the pages of his Old Testament. For when he says 'or better Elias Polemistes' (Elijah as warrior) he is pushing his conception closer to the essential, its conflicted-ness. We can watch him 'pushing'. Elijah is at first baldly 'in the mount', but swells into the more grandiloquent Greek *oreibates*, 'mountain-ranging' – a word found in Sophocles and Euripides. And yet *polemistes* is 'better' still, either because it is a Homeric word or because the sense comes nearer to catching what Elijah is *doing* on those mountains – not hiking or gazing up there, but warfaring, for the Lord against Beelzebub (2 Kings 1: 2–3).

Milton is less vivid, and more headscratching, when he moves onward in his contemplation of possible subjects for biblical tragedy to Elijah's successor as prophet, Elisha. Is Elisha best epithetized as 'water-pourer' (Hydrochoos)? Or as 'water-revealer' (Hudrophantes)? After the two Greek attempts, the Latin 'Aquator' (water-carrier) still does not clinch the matter. It may again be worth going into more detail, to show how Milton's thoughts were shifting, and shifting among classical thought-forms, as he brainstormed the subjects of his proposed tragedy. In 2 Kings 3, Elisha is summoned by the three kings because he 'poured water on the hands of Elijah' (verse 11); in other words, had been his servant or acolyte. Thus 'water-pourer' was a sensible, if prosaic, *first* attempted epithet. But in the sequel Elisha creates a landscape of ditches which are filled with water in such a way that the watching Moabites see it as blood. They are lured by the sight to think the three kings' armies have destroyed one another: Hastening forward 'to the spoil' (verse 23), they are slaughtered by the Israelites – who then, to complete this 'water' motif in the chapter as a whole, stop up all the wells of Moab. So Milton altered 'Hydrochoos', to 'Hudro*phantes*', 'water-revealer' (with a side-glance at 'hierophant'?), to shift the title's attention on to the decisive stratagem: how Elisha made the water – prophetically and ironically – look like blood. But the suffix '-phantes' is a little obscure, a little indecisive. 'Aquator' is weaker still. It may be significant that the ancient users of all the three epithets are minor, compared with the earlier heavyweights, *oreibates* versus *polemistes*. At all events, Milton's page-turning and pen-pushing went on, to Elisha 'incorruptible' (*adorodoketos*, 'accepting no bribe') – presumably the story of Naaman and his simoniac servant Gehazi (2 Kings 5), on which he would come next. Though one and all of these tragedy projects from Kings proved abortive, the Trinity Manuscript lists the moving of his thoughts, and their instinctively classical thought-forms. There is a continual grecizing preoccupation in Milton's searches for a theme, and to keep it in mind is constantly enlightening, since after all the search is for the fittest subject for the work (be it tragedy or epic) by which Milton hoped his name should live 'to aftertimes' (*CPW* I: 810).

Areopagitica is another Greek title, and this one is no abortive gesture but decisive and central to the whole speech-act, the 'oratio' of which 'Areopagitica' is the adjective. If in 'Lycidas' a close attention to classical sources helps readers ask the right questions, in *Areopagitica* Milton's readings in ancient history provide him with his best exemplars, the substantiation of his theme (the liberty of printing). It is not simply that the 'speech' is named after the Athenian Areopagus, which had been addressed by Orestes and Paul as well as Demosthenes and Isocrates, though that is quite a roll-call of predecessors. Nor is it simply that the historical examples of right and wrong responses to the dilemmas of government control versus liberties come densely from the histories of Greece and Rome. Even the *non*-classical examples had come to Milton through massive readings in world history, readings to which his Greek and Latin had given him the access (Hale 1997: 67). And precisely because his views on history were so coloured by naïve acceptance of the sympathies and emphases of his sources – in favour of Athens, in favour of republican institutions at Rome – the modern reader must reckon these enthusiasms *into* the interpretation of *Areopagitica*. It is a work of rhetoric, of would-be persuasion; a speech, albeit not spoken but printed. We need to feel the enthusiasms on our own pulses, and the English prose fervour impels this; but the reader's mind needs to be engaged as the writer's was, and with the same evidence.

To expand the point, although Milton's classical languages gave him best access to the classical evidence, they gave him equivalent access to evidence from many more ages and cultures. Among these we must include the Bible and biblical history, because he read exegesis in Latin and church history in Greek as well. Milton was resolute upon the matter, because for him Paul who spoke on the Areopagus did more than use Greek to do it: he 'thought it no defilement to insert into holy Scripture the sentences [*sententiae*, maxims] of three Greek poets, and one of them a Tragedian' (*CPW* II: 508).

A sonnet from the same decade, and a polemical prose extract from the next, both attest this gravitational pull within Milton's mind to classical or at least classically mediated proofs.

In the sonnet he imagines himself, a poet, speaking with an army leader from the opposing side in the Civil War, whatever officer of the invading royalists comes seeking billets (or worse):

> Captain or colonel, or knight in arms,
> Whose chance on these defenceless doors may seize,
> If deed of honour did thee ever please,
> Guard them, and him within protect from harms,
> He can requite thee, for he knows the charms   5
> That call fame on such gentle acts as these,
> And he can spread thy name o'er lands and seas,
> Whatever clime the sun's bright circle warms.
> Lift not thy spear against the muses' bower,
> The great Emathian conqueror bid spare   10
> The house of Pindarus, when temple and tower
> Went to the ground: and the repeated air
> Of sad Electra's poet had the power
> To save the Athenian walls from ruin bare.
>
> (*CSP*: 288–9)

Although one could call the two closing anecdotes 'allusions', really they are more than that. They are the climax and the whole point.

Ignoring as side-issues the moral dubieties of Alexander in line 10 and of the repellent Athenian imperialism which had brought the city's own walls under threat, Milton keeps his focus on what was once felt due to poets as such. First, Pindar's 'house' was spared during the general act of reprisal. The defeated city of Athens, Milton's beloved Periclean Athens, was saved from razing by the thought that it had produced a Euripides. His power to arouse pity towards a fiction aroused pity in return towards his fellow citizens. Milton in turn is moving the putative officer, and thus his actual readers, through personal fear to a thrilling moral, by simple appropriations from the classical literary tradition.

To put that another way, the poem depends throughout on the figure by which the poet's 'doors' (where the poem is imagined to be affixed) stand for the whole house, which in turn stands for the household or indwelling people. They are quite as 'defenceless' as the doors. Thus the comparison proceeds from the London house 'when the City expected an assault', as a note in Milton's hand in the Trinity Manuscript observes (*CSP*: 288) in late 1642, to the 'house of Pindarus'. Plutarch had recorded that Pindar's descendants were spared, but Arrian makes it explicit that house and descendants alike were spared; the *oikia*, embracing both these senses, comes within Milton's view, because delicately though he mentions buildings throughout, he intends the extension to their inhabitants.

Similarly for the closing anecdote, Milton entreats that some human rights should obtain even in wartime. Humans need protection in their social living from other humans as well as from the elements. Let not war become mere vengeance and pillage. The point has been questioned on the grounds that after the Peloponnesian War the Spartans and their allies did not just debate whether to pull down the walls of Athens but did pull them down. Milton, however, knew that the walls pulled down were not those which protected the citizens' houses but the 'Long Walls', which ran from city to port and (by ensuring that supplies went in and out) had enabled the Athens of Pericles to use sea power to maintain a far-flung empire. By dismantling the Long Walls Lysander ensured the end of that empire. Enough was enough, for Lysander, what with the contribution of Euripides. The closing moral exemplum of the sonnet makes many points at once for Milton in his own time, his own situation of internecine conflict, and danger to non-combatants.

In his important *Defences* of the Commonwealth and Protectorate, composed in Latin for European consumption, Milton wields classical knowledge and Latin style in tandem against his opponents, as a way of gaining credibility with the uncommitted reading public on the continent. He not only keeps sounding a patriotic Ciceronian note, of the republic saved by resolute citizens against a domestic tyrant; he also mimics the Roman style and voice alongside the Roman content, while incorporating as a clincher that he does it 'with this over and above of being a Christian'. For instance,

> Meminisses quid te non solùm libri sacri, sed etiam Lyricus doceat:
> —*Valet ima summis*
> *Mutare, et insignem attenuat Deus*
> *Obscura promens.*—
>
> (WJM 7: 32)

('You [the opponent, Salmasius] should have recalled what not only the scriptures but the lyric poet Horace teach us: "God has power to make high and low change places; God enfeebles the mighty and raises up the lowly." ')

Milton drives home the paradox he has already made from the Magnificat – 'Deposuit potentes de sede, et exaltavit humiles' (Luke 1: 52, 'He hath put down the mighty from their seats, and exalted them of low degree') – by a secular corroboration from the esteemed Horace. Nor should we think it weak to follow up sacred with secular; for Milton makes the argument *a fortiori*: this must be true for Christians, since even the pagans knew it. He is using the dialectic he has felt on his own pulse to win an argument with an opponent.

Moving past *Paradise Lost* before returning to it, we can discern within Milton's last two poems a similar intimate and critical but admiring reliance on classical literature. *Paradise Regained* and *Samson Agonistes* were published together in 1671: the one seems to contest this assertion of reliance, the other to presuppose it, but the two brought together as in a diptych demonstrate its importance and ubiquity.

In the strange (because generically unclassifiable) sequel to *Paradise Lost*, when Satan tempts the Son with the delights and depths of classical literature itself, our present topic (*Paradise Regained*, IV. 221–84), the Son rejects them in favour of biblical Hebrew, both its genres and their insight (IV. 286–364). In the heat of the argument he prefers 'Sion's songs, to all true tastes excelling' (IV. 347). In the wider context of the whole debate he is rejecting the assumption that classical literature holds sufficient truth. After all, the Messiah is given the reflections of the Roman historian Tacitus to criticize the Rome of Tiberius. It is a nice irony that the question: What is world power worth if built on sleaze? is itself a Roman thought. Tacitus implies it in *Annals*, Book VI, when describing the degradation of Rome's emperor, Tiberius, his 'daily perishing' and innermost anguish (see *CSP*: 487, 489). Milton's Satan and his Messiah are arguing as Romans also did, about how to deal with the crisis of an ailing tyrant. Thus it is the classical literary tradition which hands Milton the terms of his critique. *Samson Agonistes* has a considered preface which seeks to grasp and advance on Aristotle in the understanding of his highest genre, tragedy; a preface which answers to the poem's own reflection on tragic effect, as 'calm of mind all passion spent' (line 1758, the poem's closing words). Milton to his very last writings used antiquity to think with; to critique everything, including antiquity. Two of his last acts as a writer were to publish his Latin letters, and to modify the architecture of *Paradise Lost* towards the Virgilian.

Classical Tradition in the Fall of Eve and Adam

Since for most readers Book IX of *Paradise Lost* is the climax of all Milton's work, we might wonder whether the classical tradition of literature contributes to it less, or more, than elsewhere; and whether, in particular, Milton's reliance on the tradition here surpasses that of Book I, eager as that was to establish epic credentials. It would be agreeable but merely partisan of me to argue (as I draw to a close) for a surpassing reliance. Book IX does *not* so thrust its epic appurtenances upon the reader. They contribute, none the less, distinctively at apposite points throughout, and to widely varying effect.

The book opens with an epic invocation which surveys the epic tradition itself. It hinges on extended similes, and on extended or crowded allusions to the culture of antiquity. Just as in ancient epic, speeches are important: many of the key transactions are persuasions, by means of speeches; what Wittgenstein called 'speech-acts'. The action might be read as five acts, formed as in Greek tragedy by the punctuations of the poet as Chorus. For sure, the poet declares that he must change his 'notes' to 'tragic' ones (IX. 6) – a reminder that Milton had hesitated between presenting Adam's fall as tragedy and as epic, the two highest genres of mimesis according to Aristotle in the *Poetics*. For detail here, however, two case studies of epic simile must suffice.

To feel their force, we need again to see that Milton does not work as rigidly as a classifying pedagogy does. The first simile is also an allusion, or indeed a bunch of such, and is so discriminating that it might be called instead a figure of intensifying qualification (*PL*: 491). The second simile could equally be read as allusion or as irony. The inherited motif of extended or epic simile is nevertheless the natural place to begin, since Milton inherited not only the thing but also the discussions and scholarship of antiquity concerning it. He heralds both similes with the formulaic syntax or recognition-devices of simile: 'like' and 'As when'.

Eve has had her way, and sets off on her separate gardening:

> Thus saying, from her husband's hand her hand   385
> Soft she withdrew, and like a wood nymph light
> Oread or dryad, or of Delia's train,
> Betook her to the groves, but Delia's self
> In gait surpassed and goddess-like deport,
> Though not as she with bow and quiver armed,   390
> But with such gardening tools as art yet rude,
> Guiltless of fire had formed, or angels brought.
> To Pales, or Pomona, thus adorned,
> Likest she seemed, Pomona when she fled
> Vertumnus, or to Ceres in her prime,   395
> Yet virgin of Proserpina from Jove.
>
> (IX. 385–96)

The outstanding features of the comparisons are, first, that they are manifold (seven-fold!); and second, that each is qualified. Milton is far from demonstrating a torrential fluency of mythological allusion, a fault which bedevilled his early Latin verse but which by this date he had long outgrown. He is *ransacking* his lore, as if eager in his own or epic voice to express the moment exactly before it is gone for ever. It is expressed all the more exactly because whereas no single avatar is enough, perhaps all of them together may approach exactness. The sequence reaches its climax upon Ceres 'Yet virgin of Proserpina' (Ceres before her losses began). The mythological lore conveys the poet's mental act here, a piercing precision of praise.

It instantly becomes Adam's mental act also: 'Her long with ardent look his eye pursued' (IX. 397). Ancient similes regularly included an observer-figure in the extended comparison of the primary scene with a scene from some other life, real or mythical: Milton is using the 'other life' that pagan culture comprises in order to increase Adam the loser's sense of loss, felt before it happens. The logical impossibility of unfallen innocence knowing what loss could be is obliterated here because the extended crowding allusions from the epic voice bring in the reader's own ironic awareness. That irony is not at all the irony of detachment or superior awareness. Rather, the wrenching slowness of the pacing, the persevering lingering upon the watching Adam's ache, are producing the emotions of tragedy, namely pity and fear – to which, in fact, the epic voice has begun by referring: 'I now must change / Those notes to tragic' (IX. 5–6). Without heavily glossing that some nymphs are mortal (die when their trees die) or that the birth of Proserpina led to the infliction of winter on mankind, the allusions which gather at speed to become the whole simile – in their brevity and cumulative impact – avail the reader of such further meanings for Eve's slow departure. Milton's classical appropriations are not only apt, they free the reader to make his or her own appropriations.

This same holds good but differently in my second instance, the speech by which Satan finally ensnares Eve, beside the tree of the knowledge of good and evil:

> As when of old some orator renowned   670
> In Athens or free Rome, where eloquence
> Flourished, since mute, to some great cause addressed,
> Stood in himself collected, while each part,
> Motion, each act won audience ere the tongue,
> Sometimes in height began, as no delay   675
> Of preface brooking through his zeal of right.
>
> (IX. 670–6)

Two things at once distinguish this simile. First, there is no particular, named orator: the simile is general ('*some* orator'). Second, there is no observer within this simile. Both of these distinguishing features challenge the reader to think and feel what Milton is communicating by this secondary world, the world of the politics of antiquity.

The first feature keeps our attention on the public world as a whole (undeflected into thoughts about Cicero or Demosthenes or whoever), thereby avoiding contentious value judgements of policy, and keeping focus on the oratorical arts as arts; which in turn keeps us detached, cool, and discerning – just the opposite of the impact of the female-victim simile preceding. The names which do enter into the allusion, 'Athens or free Rome', show Milton himself at his most discerning. These are the societies which were the heroes of *Areopagitica*: the Athens which (for Milton anyway) represented 'free speech'; and the Rome of the republic, the Rome of self-discipline and patriotic sacrifice and free speech which was ended (for Milton as for Lucan and Tacitus) by the Caesars. Milton seeks his kind of desired authority from the reader by the gratuitous yet judicious mental exercising which the sidelong phrasing here encourages.

The second feature, the absence for once of a witness figure inside the simile, is another deft touch of obliquity. 'Audience' (IX. 674) can mean not only 'attention, hearing' but also the people who comprise the entailed auditory. But the precision lies in the generality and focus: we are made to think about the oratorical powers which compel listening, not about who is listening or to what. That is forgotten. Indeed, that is the whole trouble with political eloquence: Hitler was a terrific orator. In other words, Eve is the audience but we forget her, just as she forgets conscience while she listens – an especially powerful instance of Milton's constant onomatopoeia. Compatible with this is the further reflection, however, that God is listening (IX. 826, 'what if God have seen?') Are we, then, we the readers, in another sense the missing 'audience'? The extreme generality, going as it does with the absence of usual specificity and of audience within the secondary discourse ('vehicle'), encourages the thought that we are the helpless witnesses; and hence like the audiences of tragedy, watching Oedipus or Othello make his hideous misjudgement.

The many meanings co-present typify Milton's engrossment in his subject, such that we sense the whole in every part. Such readings of a wider whole in the given part will not all convince everyone, of course, and other readings may seem more important. For example, Alastair Fowler finds the simile to have no fewer than 'three vehicles: oratorical, theatrical, and theological' (*PL*: 509). Though I can find only the first two, the essential thing is the emphasis, the sense that Milton in this simile is (rather like Satan) pulling out all the stops. And this sense of an extra-special, purpose-built, unique synergy of allusion and tradition with simile is what the awareness of classical literature produces. Knowing what had been done by Homer and Virgil, and by the continuing line of epics before Milton gives one the most natural and relevant standpoint from which to watch him doing the same differently, doing their thing in his own way, and because of them. It is seeing with his eyes.

Conclusion

I conclude, accordingly, that at the supreme moments of the poem (rather than just at its quieter places or its flat ones) the classical literary tradition provides us with reliable instruments and starting places for a most active researching as our own response. I hope to have illustrated some of the typical as well as best evidence. I hope to have shown that awareness of the classical within the texture encourages a richer reading than could exist without that awareness; and offers a flexible, many-sided method of seeking pleasure from the moment-to-moment experience of the reading. To my own sense of things, so far from being a worm-eaten crutch, the awareness of the tradition – from Addison to Highet, from Curtius to Martindale and beyond – has given readers of *Paradise Lost* a strong lens through which to see for themselves. Without claiming that similar insights could not be gained by other, perhaps newer lenses (such as intertextuality or reader-response theory), I see huge advantages in principle as well as practice when we try to stand first where Milton himself, composing, had placed himself.

BIBLIOGRAPHY

Writings

Milton (1970) [Trinity Manuscript].

References for Further Reading

Curtius (1953); Daiches (1971); Evans (1998a); Hale (1995, 1997); Highet (1949); Martindale (1986); Porter (1993); Shifflett (1998).

3
Milton on the Bible

Regina M. Schwartz

John Milton was not only a poet, thinker, theologian and political figure; he was also one of the most astute 'literary critics' of the Bible. That is not to say, of course, that the Bible was only a work of literature to him. Scripture was the revealed Word of God. But it does mean that when Milton interpreted the Bible, he did so not only with the thought of a theologian and with the faith of a believer, but also with the sensibility of a poet. For him, biblical theology was inseparable from biblical poetics – *what* the Bible means is bound to *how* it means – and it is no accident that despite writing a lengthy theological treatise, Milton wrote his own theology most forcefully in his poetry. He lived during a period when biblical interpretation was part of everyday life. The legacies of the Renaissance, with its humanist emphasis on the text, and the Reformation, with its emphasis on interpretation of the Bible, were to infuse common vocabulary with scripture. During the English Civil War, soldiers carried a Bible into battle; before entering the fray, they sang its psalms; before bedtime, parents recounted its narratives; during parliamentary conflicts, proponents cited its verses. The Bible was used in Parliament, in pamphlet wars, in education, in courtship and in conversation to an extent that is hardly imaginable today. As Christopher Hill warns, 'the Bible was central to the whole of the life of the society: we ignore it at our peril':

> [The Bible] was everywhere in the lives of men, women and children. Not only in the church services they had to attend, but in the ballads they bought and sang, and in their daily surroundings . . . almost all houses had hangings to keep out draughts and to cover the rough walls. These often took the form of 'painted cloths', 'the real poor man's pictures', among which Biblical scenes seem to have preponderated. In accordance with Deuteronomy XI. 20, Biblical texts were very often painted on walls or posts in houses, 'probably representing the most common form in which an "illiterate" would encounter the written word'. In addition, walls were covered with printed matter – almanacs, illustrated ballads and broadsides, again often on Biblical subjects. More elusive, 'godly

tables [tablets]' specially printed for decorating walls and 'most fit to be set up in every house', often contained texts from the Bible . . . (Hill 1993: 38)

The 'use' of the sacred text was not always savoury, for the Bible was not only invoked to inspire ethical conduct and goodwill, but also asked to lend authority to less charitable positions: for bolstering self-interest, for justifying lawlessness, for slaughtering innocents and for defeating enemies. Because God's will was conveyed to fallen humanity and employed by fallen humanity, fallen interpretations of God's word were not always synonymous with divine will. Between human understanding and divine will was a murky realm of interpretation. 'It is no hard thing', wrote John Hales in his *Golden Remains* (1659: 4), 'for a man that hath wit, and is strongly possessed of an opinion, and resolute to maintain it, to find some place of Scripture which by good handling will be wooed to cast a favourable countenance upon it' (cited in Hill 1993: 43). The hermeneutical feats performed to turn the word of God into justification for any and every agenda had begun to make biblical interpretation overtly suspect; the hazards of interpreting the word of God were notable even to its interpreters. Shakespeare, among others, took this un-holy instrumentality for granted.

> *Gloucester*: But then I might; and, with a piece of Scripture,
> Tell them that God bids us do good for evil:
> And thus I clothe my naked villainy
> With odd old ends, stol'n forth of Holy Writ.
> (Shakespeare, *The Tragedy of King Richard III*, I. iii)

John Milton was no exception: he accused Justin Martyr, Clement, Origen and Tertullian, among other church fathers, of 'the ridiculous wresting of Scripture' (*Of Reformation*, CPW I: 551) and the church of being 'so rash to raise up such lofty Bishops and Bishopricks out of places in Scripture meerly misunderstood' (*Of Pre-latical Episcopacy*, CPW I: 631).

With his three great epics, *Paradise Lost*, *Paradise Regained* and *Samson Agonistes*, all based upon episodes in biblical narratives, Milton is surely the most biblical of English poets. His prose is also saturated with biblical citation: whether he writes on divorce, on censorship, on church government, on the sins of Charles I's monarchy or the virtue of Cromwell's republic, whether he defends the English revolution or the justice of God, his method is to invoke biblical verses and with them, biblical authority. As an adept practitioner of biblical hermeneutics himself – even going so far as to craft consistency between two completely contradictory biblical mandates about marriage in order to justify his doctrine of divorce – Milton was well aware of the uses and abuses of scripture. His enemies cite the Bible as frequently as he does, so he must counter them by rejecting their use of scripture; for 'a wise man will make better use of an idle pamphlet, then a fool will do of sacred Scripture' (*Areopagitica*, II: 521). Those who misinterpret the Bible are guilty of 'resting in the meere element of the Text', and of committing the grave error of 'not consulting with charitie, *the interpreter* and guide of our faith' (*The Doctrine and Discipline of Divorce, CPW* II: 236; my italics).

In the tracts that Milton devotes to 'personal liberty', his four tracts on divorce, he is so preoccupied with biblical hermeneutics – interpreting the Bible according to the right principles completely justifies divorce – that *The Doctrine and Discipline of Divorce* could have been justifiably titled *The Doctrine and Discipline of Biblical Exegesis*. It almost is: the full title of the first version, 1643, reads *The Doctrine and Discipline of Divorce: Restor'd to the Good of Both Sexes, From the bondage of Canon Law, and other mistakes, to Christian freedom, guided by the Rule of Charity*. While the Old Testament Mosaic law (Deuteronomy 24: 1–2) maintains that a husband can divorce his wife if 'she find no favour in his eyes, because he hath found some uncleanness in her', in the New Testament Christ seems to forbid divorce, except on grounds of 'fornication', which the church interpreted as adultery. Determined to reconcile these differences, Milton claims that the church has interpreted the words of Christ erroneously. The main passage of contention within the New Testament is Matthew 19: 3–9:

> The Pharisees also came unto him, tempting him, and saying unto him, Is it lawful for a man to put away his wife for every cause? And he answered and said unto them, Have ye not read, that he which made them at the beginning made them male and female, And said, For this cause shall a man leave father and mother, and shall cleave to his wife: and they twain shall be one flesh? Wherefore they are no more twain, but one flesh. What therefore God hath joined together, let not man put asunder. They say unto him, Why did Moses then command to give a writing of divorcement, and to put her away? He saith unto them, Moses because of the hardness of your hearts suffered you to put away your wives: but from the beginning it was not so. And I say unto you, Whosoever shall put away his wife, except it be for fornication, and shall marry another, committeth adultery: and whoso marrieth her which is put away doth commit adultery.

Milton asserts that those who interpret the scripture as forbidding divorce except for adultery are imagining that Christ is willing to abrogate the law of Moses despite his explicit refusal to ignore '*one jot or tittle*' (*CPW* II: 283) of that law. Not only do they fail to take into account the 'precedent law of *Moses*' which they should do because 'God hath not two wills, but one will, much lesse two contrary'; they also misinterpret the 'attestation of Christ himself' (*CPW* II: 325). According to Milton, Christ left the Mosaic permission for divorce intact. To interpret the words of Christ correctly, they must be interpreted according to the principles he himself embraced. That is, ultimately, Christ must be interpreted so as 'to preserve those his fundamental and superior laws of nature and charitie, *to which all other ordinances give up their seals*' (*CPW* II: 325, my italics). Milton argues here and elsewhere that all biblical laws are submitted to the higher divine laws of nature and charity – it is by these principles that we should judge the validity of biblical injunctions and by these principles that he will labour to interpret them. Milton tells us directly what he means by 'nature': the 'two prime statutes' of nature are 'to joyn it self to that which is good and acceptable and friendly; and to turn aside and depart from what is disagreeable, displeasing and unlike' (*CPW* II: 297, 345–6).

What, then, does Milton mean by the other principle, of 'charitie'? This principle of charity is so crucial to Milton as not only to be included in the title of his first divorce tract but also to figure as the very last word of the tract, which concludes by enjoining readers, yet again, to submit the biblical text to the rule of charity. While he began his treatise with the considerable claim that charity is 'the interpreter and guide of our faith' (*CPW* II: 236), when he signs off he strengthens his rhetoric further with the warning that if his readers cannot learn (1) that the Law and the Prophets depend upon mercy and not sacrifice, and (2) that the purpose of the Gospel is mercy and peace, then (3) 'how will they hear this, which yet I shall not doubt to leave with them as a conclusion: That God the Son hath put all other things under his own feet; but his Commandments he hath left all under the feet of charity' (*CPW* II: 356; see also 1 Corinthians 15: 27 and 1 Timothy 1: 5). When we try to discern both how to interpret God's will and how to act, we must remember that God never intends ill for us (like bondage to a tyrannical government in the state or the church, or the bondage of a miserable failed union in marriage), nor does he intend for us to do ill (commit adultery to satisfy the longing for a helpmeet that a failed marriage does not address). Charity dictates not only Milton's biblical hermeneutics, but also his revolutionary politics, his personal life and his critique of church government. To drive home the centrality of charity, he challenges a rebellious Parliament pointedly, 'if charity be...excluded and expulst, how yee will defend the untainted honour of your own actions and proceedings'. And he maintains, 'If [a whole people] against any authority, Covnant, or Statute, may by the soveraign edict of charity, save not only their lives, but honest liberties from unworthy bondage, as well may he against any private Covnant...redeem himself from unsupportable disturbances' (*CPW* II: 229).

Furthermore, in his charity, God has made available to human reason the justness and goodness – indeed, the charity – of his laws. While many of God's way are mysterious, this is not: 'hee hath taught us to love and to extoll his Lawes, not only as they are his, but as they are just and good to every wise and sober understanding' (*CPW* II: 297–8). This may not sound radical to our ears; it may even ring of some vaguely familiar early modern piety; but it is an astonishing claim. Except for Nicolas Malebranche in a provocative essay, 'The Treatise on Nature and Grace', none of the philosophers of this burgeoning age of reason – not even Descartes – was willing to make the claim that divine justice could be apprehended by human reason. Such a correspondence between divinity and humanity – between divine justice and the law of nature imprinted in us – was unthinkable. None the less, Milton asserts that while 'God indeed in some wayes of his providence, is high and secret past finding out: but in the delivery and execution of his Law...hath plain anough reveal'd himself, and requires the observance therof not otherwise then to the law of nature and of equity imprinted in us seems correspondent' (*CPW* II: 297). The Bible lay open to reason; and, interpreted according to the principle of charity, God's justness and goodness also lay open to reason. This explains why Abraham had the temerity to question God's actions, for Abraham well understood the principle of charity and understood that God is the giver of charity: 'Therefore *Abraham* ev'n to the face of God himselfe, seem'd to doubt of divine justice, if it should swerve from that irradiation wherewith it had enlight'ned the mind of man, and bound it selfe to observe its own rule. *Wilt thou destroy the righteous with the wicked? That be far from thee; shall not the Judge of the earth doe right?*' (*CPW* II: 298). Here justice or charity or the right has irradiated the mind of man, and Abraham is at pains to correct the Lord according to the Lord's own principle which is now internal to Abraham.

But how does one interpret according to charity? Perhaps the most succinct example is Milton's explication of 1 Corinthians 7 – an exegesis that adopts the technique of the divorce tracts in miniature. His discussion begins, in the method followed throughout the tract, with a comparison to another biblical text, here Genesis 2: 18:

> For God does not heer precisely say, I make a female to this male, as he did briefly before, but expounding himselfe heer on purpos, he saith, because it is not good for man to be alone, I make him therefore a meet help. God supplies the privation of not good, with the perfect gift of a reall and positive good; *it is mans pervers cooking who hath turn'd this bounty of God into a Scorpion, either by weak and shallow constructions, or by proud arrogance and cruelty to them who neither in their purposes nor in their actions have offended against the due honour of wedlock.* (*Tetrachordon*, *CPW* II: 595–6, my italics)

Milton, interpreting according to the principle of charity, sees God's charity, his bounty, in correcting something which is not good (aloneness) by turning it into something good (having a companion). Only an interpretation that is weak or perverse could turn this correction, by God, of what is not good into a new problem. He then turns to a troubling text, 1 Corinthians 7:

> Now whereas the Apostle speaking in the Spirit, I *Cor.* 7. pronounces quite contrary to this word of God, *It is good for a man not to touch a woman*, and God cannot contradict himself, it instructs us that his commands and words, especially such as bear the manifest title of som good to man, are not to be so strictly wrung, as to command without regard to the most naturall and miserable necessities of mankind. (*Tetrachordon*, *CPW* II: 596)

When Milton interprets the command according to the principle of charity, it becomes clear that God could not mean that man cannot touch a woman at all times – after all, he made woman as a companion for man, and he cannot contradict himself. And he made his commands to respond charitably to the 'natural' and even 'miserable' (i.e. lowly) needs of man. Surely, the Apostle cannot mean that a man is never to touch a woman. How then does Milton resolve the apparent contradiction? By explaining that the Apostle only means his pronouncement to apply in this circumstance or 'present necessity': 'Therefore the Apostle adds a limitation in the 26 v. of that chap. for the present necessity it is good; *which he gives us doubtlesse as a pattern how to reconcile other places by the generall rule of charity*' (*CPW* II: 596, my italics). This example suggests that the rule of charity reconciles biblical passages that seem harsh and unpleasant to those that seem kind and generous. Such a hermeneutical exercise is no small task.

Milton will understand Genesis 2: 24 according to the same interpretive rule of charity: 'Thus a man leaves his father and his mother and cleaves unto his wife and they become one flesh.' He asserts that the biblical injunction for a man and a woman to become one flesh cannot refer only to legitimating the carnal act, but must signal a union of souls 'that can never be where no correspondence is of the minde'. And he proceeds to assert that to understand 'one flesh' in any other way, to understand it as a physical joining, would not be one flesh, but would 'be rather two carkasses chain'd unnaturally together; or as it may happ'n, a living soule bound to a dead corpse' (*The Doctrine and Discipline of Divorce, CPW* II: 326). Milton goes on to explain that God intended a wife as a remedy for loneliness, and since 'joyning ... another body' will not 'remove loneliness', 'it is no blessing but a torment, nay a base and brutish condition to be one flesh, unless where nature can in some measure fix a unity of disposition' (*CPW* II: 327). Now, according to Milton, yoking together such dead corpses, torments, etc., cannot be the right interpretation of the biblical injunction to become 'one flesh', for to create such a condition for mankind is not charitable. Hence, Christ must (according to the principle of charity) endorse the law of the 'inspired Law-giver *Moses*'. '[T]he Gospel enjoyns no new morality, save only the infinit enlargement of charity, which in this respect is call'd the *new Commandement* by St. *John*; as being the accomplishment of every command' (*CPW* II: 330–1). The 'accomplishment' or fulfilment of *every* command, according to Milton's understanding, is quite simply to love one another. His precedent is biblical: 'A new commandment I give unto you, That ye love one another; as I have loved you, that ye also love one another. By this shall all men know that ye are my disciples, if ye have love one to another' (John 13: 34–5).

The words of Christ simply 'can not command us to self-cruelty, cannot hinder and set us back, as they are vulgarly tak'n', argues Milton (*CPW* II: 331), for 'if we mark diligently the nature of our Saviours commands, wee shall finde that both their beginning and their end consists in charity: whose will is that wee should so be good to others, as that wee be not cruel to our selves' (*CPW* II: 330). In Milton's exquisite version of Christ's version of the golden rule, he has embedded two meanings: not only that we should be good to others as we are good to ourselves, but also we should be good to others because anything less would be cruelty to ourselves. He unequivocally asserts that charity is the cause informing Christ's commands, and that their purpose is charity. 'It is no command of perfection further then it partakes of charity, which is *the bond of perfection*' (*CPW* II: 331). Those who think differently from Milton about the biblical injunctions are in error, and sorely lacking in clear thinking: 'this recited law of *Moses* contains a cause of divorce greater beyond compare then that for adultery; and whoso cannot so conceive it errs and wrongs exceedingly a law of deep wisdom for want of well fadoming' (*CPW* II: 332). What follows is a strong gloss on so many Reformers' assertion that the Bible is perspicuous, on the commitment of many to what Milton perceives as a 'pretious literalism' (*CPW* II: 334): *'we cannot safely assent to any precept writt'n in the Bible, but as charity commends it to us'* (*CPW* II: 340, my italics). This is Milton's radical reinterpretation of 'charity beleeveth all things' (1 Corinthians 13); that is, charity guides us in what to believe: we should 'hold that for truth, which accords most with charity' (*CPW* II: 340).

If charity is the principle that will govern Milton's biblical interpretation, it must be the principle that governs that procedure not only in his prose, but also in his most remarkable and enduring biblical interpretation, *Paradise Lost*. Charity, the ability of man to apprehend the justice and goodness of divine law, must govern his understanding of the narratives of the Fall and expulsion of humankind from Paradise. If not, then charity would not be the 'sovereign' that governs all belief, but an expedient principle for his argument on divorce alone, easily exchanged for other guiding principles when the occasion serves. Contrary to any accusation of such opportunism, Milton turns to charity repeatedly. In the wide wilderness of interpretation it is John Milton's guide, assuring him that each step in his interpretation is a safe one so long as charity charts the course.

How, then, does Milton choose to interpret the episode from Genesis relating the loss of Paradise? Does he interpret this narrative according to the principle of charity? Milton seems to have chosen the most difficult test case from the spectrum of biblical narratives. It is a brutal story – the story of the temptation of innocent humanity by a vengeful Satan, the succumbing of humankind answered with the most terrible consequence, for man's first disobedience 'Brought death into the world, and all our woe' (*PL* I. 3). How could *this* story, of the introduction of evil and of death into the world, be interpreted according to the principle of charity? It is plausible, I would argue, to read *Paradise Lost* as just that: an interpretation of the narrative of the Fall according to the principle of charity, that is, according to the principle that the goodness and justice of God prevail, and that they are even available to human reason. Adam and Eve do not live in Paradise without ample explanation of the goodness of God, and Adam and Eve do not leave Paradise without knowledge of God's forgiveness, knowledge that their punishment will be mitigated and their disaster redeemed. In *Paradise Lost* humankind is offered motivation for obeying God: they are taught that God created the world and its creatures, given certain knowledge, not just intuitive awareness, of their contingency so that they cannot deny their creator. They are given an explanation of the purpose of the divine law: to grant to humans freedom of the will; and they are shown the consequences of making the wrong choice, with vivid descriptions of the punishment for Satan's disobedience. Through these narrations and explanations, Milton's God gives not only checks but also goads. Furthermore, the account of the Fall of humankind could hardly have been made more sympathetic: at the hour of noon, hungry and alone, Eve is duped, and she falls, not out of narcissism (although any such tendency is also depicted sympathetically, as part of her created nature), but out of hunger for more knowledge. When Adam follows in sin, he is not deceived; rather, he falls for love of Eve. At the very moment when our sympathies should be furthest from the criminals who brought death into our world and all our woe, Milton makes their Fall seem so understandable. Who would condemn anyone for craving more knowledge? Who would condemn anyone so devoted to his partner that he willingly shares her misery? And yet, throughout all this charitable interpreting, Milton unflinchingly depicts the first error as terrible: 'Earth felt the wound, and nature through her seat / . . . gave signs of woe, / That all was lost' (*PL* IX. 782–4), even while those who commit it inspire our love and our compassion, not our stern judgement. After the horrible event, humankind is again offered explanations, not only of the consequences of their disobedience, with visions and auditions, but also, charitably, a disclosure of the final redemption, a disclosure that the terrible consequences of their disobedience will eventually end. Death will be that charitable end. In short, Milton endeavours to make divine justice, mercy and goodness available to human reason. Whether or not he succeeds depends on the reader, who can freely accept or reject these charitable explanations. Regardless, Milton certainly offered them. It is no accident that grace functions in this way in the Arminianism Milton embraced: grace is offered freely, and one can either reject or accept it. Milton, as creator of his poem, is doubtless modelling himself on his Creator. He sets out to exonerate a God who might seem punitive, to depict human freedom as no burden but a gift, and to understand the psychology of evil, even admiring the courage of one foolish enough to rebel against the Almighty. Charitable indeed.

In his dogged commitment to the processes of reason, Milton asks questions of the biblical narrative that the Bible does not ask: Where does the serpent come from? Why does God command Adam and Eve not to eat the fruit? He presses contradictions in the biblical narrative that the Bible story gracefully elides: how can God know the outcome and not determine it? How can man be condemned to death, but Adam and Eve go on living? He demands that the story offer explanations for more than the biblical narrative purports to explain: the nature of evil and of divine justice; the aspirations and limits of human knowledge; the relations between the sexes, between man and nature, between man and God; and the origin of just about everything. So powerful is his reading of the brief biblical story, so compelling his interpretation in his own epic, that generations of readers have proceeded to confuse Milton's narrative with the Bible's. They think that Satan, rather than a serpent, tempted Eve, that Satan fell from heaven before tempting humankind, that Eve was alone during her temptation, that Adam fell for love – none of which is biblical. In the Bible, the story of a paradise that is lost takes up only forty-five verses. The narrative is cryptic, and, as Erich Auerbach described in his important distinction between biblical and Homeric prose, it brings certain parts into high relief while others are left obscure (1953: 23). While Auerbach describes the story of the 'sacrifice' of Isaac (Genesis 22), his insights are equally applicable to the Fall in the first chapters of Genesis:

> In the story of Isaac, it is not only God's intervention at the beginning and the end, but even the factual and psychological elements which come between, that are mysterious,

merely touched upon, fraught with background; and therefore they require subtle investigation and interpretation, they demand them. Since so much in the story is dark and incomplete, and since the reader knows that God is a hidden God, his effort to interpret it constant finds something new to feed upon. (1953: 15)

About two millennia after the terse biblical story of the Fall was written, Milton presumes to fill in its background, turning full light upon it. When he does so, he not only lights up the background of the story, but also illuminates his understanding of it: 'what in me is dark / Illumine' (*PL* I. 22–3). He invokes the Celestial Light to brighten his reason:

> So much the rather thou celestial light
> Shine inward, and the mind through all her powers
> Irradiate, there plant eyes, all mist from thence
> Purge and disperse, that I may see and tell
> Of things invisible to mortal sight.
>
> (III. 51–5)

Painting descriptions, seeking causes, offering explanations, exploring motives and delineating consequences to make a fairly unintelligible story intelligible: for Milton, these are the methods for interpreting according to the principle of charity.

When Milton applies his brush to filling in the dark background of Paradise, he fills it copiously. Charity abounds. Paradise is a place where our first ancestors know no deprivation, feel no dearth. Paradise has more fruits than Adam and Eve can possibly eat, more varieties of trees than they can possibly know, more growth than they can tame. Remarkably enough, Eve describes Paradise that way to her tempter; in the face of his wily allusion to a prohibited fruit, Eve recalls the bounty of Paradise's gifts.

> many are the trees of God that grow
> In Paradise, and various, yet unknown
> To us, in such abundance lies our choice,
> As leaves a greater store of fruit untouched,
> Still hanging incorruptible, till men
> Grow up to their provision, and more hands
> Help to disburden nature of her birth.
>
> (IX. 618–24)

Paradise is so fecund that there are not enough midwives to attend her constant births. And according to Raphael, the God who so provided humankind did so out of generosity:

> He brought thee into this delicious grove,
> This garden, planted with the trees of God,

> Delectable both to behold and taste;
> And freely all their pleasant fruit for food
> Gave thee, all sorts are here that all the earth yields,
> Variety without end;
>
> (VII. 537–42)

Gratitude for the bounty of Paradise comprises the heart of the liturgy in Adam and Eve's evening prayer:

> Thou also mad'st the night
> Maker omnipotent, and thou the day,
> . . .
>
> and this delicious place
> For us too large, where thy abundance wants
> Partakers, and uncroped falls to the ground.
> But thou hast promised from us two a race
> To fill the earth, who shall with us extol
> Thy goodness infinite,
>
> (IV. 724–34)

All of these passages are Milton's elaborations of one verse in Genesis: 'And out of the ground made the Lord God to grow every tree that is pleasant to the sight, and good for food; the tree of life also in the midst of the garden, and the tree of knowledge of good and evil' (Genesis 2: 9). Here, as elsewhere, Milton interprets the Bible according to a biblical principle to come up with a new Bible. Presupposing that the canon is not closed, that revelation is ongoing, Milton is its most recent recipient. The Muse who inspired Moses to write the Bible is the Muse Milton invokes to inspire his epic, *Paradise Lost*.

> Sing heavenly Muse, that on the secret top
> Of Oreb, or of Sinai, didst inspire
> That Shepherd, who first taught the chosen seed,
> In the beginning how the heavens and earth
> Rose out of chaos:
>
> (I. 6–10)

This Muse 'prefer[s] / Before all temples the upright heart and pure' (I. 17–18). Surely this is not a Muse of institutions (all temples). Is this the Muse of charity?

While the many descriptions of a bountiful garden may tend to convey the impression that Adam and Eve have no experience of deprivation, the divine command prohibiting them to enjoy the fruit of one tree poses a serious challenge. For here, even in Paradise, God issues a strange command: 'Of every tree of the garden thou mayest freely eat: But of the tree of the knowledge of good and evil, thou shalt not eat of it: for in the day that thou eatest thereof thou shalt surely die' (Genesis 2: 16–17). Why? asks Milton. The biblical narratives offer little help: no explanation at all is given in the Genesis story; elsewhere, the scriptures describe God's ways as unfathomable, beyond human reason – and, as the 'friends' of Job demonstrate, man is foolish or even sinful to presume to understand divine justice. Milton nods towards the mystery of divine ways – 'God to remove his ways from human sense, / Placed heaven from earth so far, that earthly sight, / If it presume, might err in things too high' (*PL* VIII. 119–21) – but he is none the less compelled to find answers to his questions. He is determined to render divine creation and redemption accessible to human knowledge; moreover, he even submits divine justice to human reason, intending to 'justify the ways of God to men' (I. 26). This requires that the mysterious first command be scrutinized. Is it a fair command? A just command? Is humankind capable of obeying it?

Milton offers two distinctly different explanations for the prohibition: one from God and his messengers, another from Satan. Whether or not the explanation that Milton's God offers for his command is indeed charitable has been hotly debated for centuries. On the one side, his God has been depicted by Shelley as 'one who in the cold security of undoubted triumph inflicts the most horrible revenge upon his enemy, not from any mistaken notion of inducing him to repent of a perseverance in enmity, but with the alleged design of exasperating him to deserve new torments' ('A Defence of Poetry', 1821; Shelley 1948/1973: 38). But on the other, Tillyard cautions:

> It must not be thought that Milton blamed God for an unsatisfactory world. What he did was to blame mankind for having hopelessly thrown away their chances: they could have made the world a second paradise, and it was utterly their own fault that they failed to do so. Never for a moment does Milton disbelieve in this significance of the Fall. And in the sense that Milton believed God to be just he does not lose his faith in him. (1930/1956: 287–8)

I will refrain from taking sides, because what is far more interesting is *the very fact of the explanation* of the divine command. That Milton tries to explain what is left unexplained in the biblical account is itself to interpret according to charity. Explanations, causes, descriptions, motives, revelations of the past and of the future: these are the methods of Milton's hermeneutic of charity. For Milton, the first command is not an arbitrary law given by a voluntarist deity, nor is it a mysterious law whose motive is inaccessible. The divine purpose, stated clearly and repeatedly in *Paradise Lost*, was to give human beings choice, the exercise of reason: 'reason also is choice' (III. 108; and cf. *Areopagitica*, where 'reason is but choosing', *CPW* II: 527). Far from intending to lower humankind through this command, God claims in the poem that his intention was to ennoble man by offering him freedom. True liberty always dwells twinned with right reason; man suffers outward tyranny when his own reason is enthralled to lower powers (XII. 83–101). Furthermore, if humankind is not free, 'what proof could they have given sincere / Of true allegiance ...? / ... what praise could they receive?' (III. 103–6).

Milton has asked that all commands be subject to the greater command of charity, *'wee cannot safely assent to any precept writt'n in the Bible, but as charity commends it to us'* (*CPW* II: 340, my italics). That principle of biblical interpretation enables us better to understand Milton's answer to the crucial question of why God gave that command: to give the gift of human freedom. And only by understanding the first command through the principle of charity can Adam and Eve assent to it with confidence. They must see that command as a gift, not as an exercise of tyranny, and see that Milton's God is so far from tyranny that *in his very command* he is offering the opposite: freedom. In Milton's theological treatise *De Doctrina Christiana*, where he sets out to describe the nature of God, under the category of 'divine will' Milton asserts not that God exercises his will in any way he chooses, but that God is 'supremely kind', quoting a host of biblical allusions to support this contention: Exodus 34: 6; Psalms 86: 15, 103: 8, 25: 6, et al.; culminating in 1 John 4: 8: 'God is charity' (*CPW* VI: 150–1). Not only our understanding, but also the divine will, is defined in terms of charity.

To interpret the first command according to charity suggests, too, that man is happiest under divine law. When Milton tackles the problem of divine justice head-on and at its theologically most sensitive place – the exile from Paradise into suffering and death – he does not hesitate to assert that reason can indeed demonstrate both the justice and the goodness of divine law. In his tract on divorce, he reiterates the reasonableness of divine goodness: 'And hee hath taught us to love and to extoll his Lawes, not onely as they are his, but as they are just and good to every wise and sober understanding' (*Doctrine and Discipline of Divorce*, *CPW* II: 297–8). None the less, this understanding requires interpretation. And right interpretation requires not only the operations of reason, but also faith, hope and charity as guiding principles.

> The right method of interpreting the scriptures has been laid down by theologians . . . The requisites are linguistic ability, knowledge of the original sources, consideration of the overall intent, distinction between literal and figurative language, examination of the causes and circumstances, and of what comes before and after the passage in question, and comparison of one text with another. *It must always be asked, too, how far the interpretation is in agreement with faith.* (*De Doctrina Christiana*, *CPW* VI: 582; my italics)

As it turns out, the intellect is not self-sufficient; ultimately it is aided by the help of the Spirit: 'the truth / . . . Left only in those written records pure, / Though not but by the Spirit understood' (*PL* XII. 511–13). In his prose, Milton offers a fine paraphrase of his poetry: 'The prophecy, then, must not be interpreted by the intellect of a particular individual, that is to say, not by his merely human intellect, but with the help of the Holy Spirit, promised to each individual believer' (*De Doctrina Christiana*, *CPW* VI: 579–80). Everything we need to know, Milton writes in his theological treatise, is 'supplied either from other passages of scripture' or by the 'Spirit operating in us through faith and charity' (*CPW* VI: 586). The Bible, he tells us (quoting 2 Corinthians 3: 3) '*is written not with ink, but with the Spirit of the living God; not on tablets of stone, but on the fleshly tablets of the heart*'. This means we have 'a double scripture', an external one and an internal one, and because the written one does not address many concerns and because it must be interpreted, 'all things are eventually to be referred to the Spirit and the unwritten word' (*De Doctrina Christiana*, *CPW* VI: 587–90; see Schwartz 1990). Beliefs deduced from scripture which are not informed by this Spirit are as misguided as Adam's interpretive errors. Milton quotes Colossians 2: 8: '*look out, lest anyone rob you by means of philosophy and delusive vanities, based on human traditions and worldly principles, and not on Christ*' (*CPW* VI: 591). Even the prelates are guilty of this error, turning to tradition rather than to the (double) Scripture: 'But let them chaunt while they will of prerogatives, we shall tell them of Scripture; of custom, we of Scripture; of Acts and Statutes, stil of Scripture, til the quick and pearcing word enter to the dividing of their soules, & the mighty weaknes of the Gospel throw down the weak mightines of mans reasoning' (*Reason of Church-Government*, *CPW* I: 827).

So much for the charitable *intentions* of the first command itself. But how can a God who metes out such a punishment – 'Die he or justice must' (*PL* III. 210) – be charitable? Amazingly enough, that harsh, stern, uncompromising verdict is explained, by the deity, as an act of charity.

> I at first with two fair gifts
> Created him endowed, with happiness
> And immortality: that fondly lost,
> This other served but to eternize woe;
> Till I provided death; so death becomes
> His final remedy,
>
> (*PL* XI. 57–62)

God the Father also offers another gift: an explanation for how he wants his sentence to be understood – not as a disaster, 'all terror hide', but as the fulfilment of justice. He directs that it be delivered compassionately by asking Michael to 'intermix' the sentence with the revelation of 'My cov'nant in the woman's seed renewed'. The objective is to achieve an exquisitely defined effect, to 'send them forth, though sorrowing, yet in peace' (XI. 111–17). This divine charity has its counterpart in the narrator's acts of charity, his gifts of interpretation.

The explanation for Adam's sin is not that he disregards God, flaunting his command, but that he is unable to separate from the woman who was made of his flesh. When he falls, he is 'submitting to what seemed remediless' (IX. 919). As the argument to Book IX explains, 'Adam at first amazed, but perceiving her lost, resolves through vehemence of love to perish with her' (*PL*: 466). Interpreting Adam's fall according to the principle of charity, Milton has him fall for love. In a bold exegetical move, Milton takes the lines from the Bible that constitute the original marriage vow and has Adam utter them at his fall:

> if Death
> Consort with thee, death is to me as life;
> So forcible within my heart I feel
> The bond of nature draw me to my own,
> My own in thee, for what thou art is mine;
> Our state cannot be severed, we are one,
> One flesh; to lose thee were to lose myself.
>   (IX. 953–9)

Adam would need to renounce his marriage, that is, to separate his flesh from his flesh, his bone from his bone, in order to obey God. Such obedience is hard. Over-much love of a woman, dying for a woman: this may show a lack of good judgement, according to the narrator, but it is far from the opprobrious explanation given for Satan's fall. He falls for envy, revenge and pride – although, as a whole century of critics argued, even Satan's fall is depicted with much sympathy for the defeated one.

How would the first command be interpreted according to the opposite principle, the principle not of charity but of scarcity? We need not imagine such an interpretation, for Milton offers one. Not only Milton's God and the narrator, but Satan too is an interpreter. He interprets Paradise, the command of obedience from God, the Fall of man – and he interprets them all, not from the principle of charity, but from that of scarcity. God is the great forbidder, who has denied the fruit to man. Satan's motives for acting – revenge (against God), envy (of humanity) and hate – are the precise opposite of giving, of *caritas*, of love.

> What hither brought us, hate, not love, nor hope
> Of Paradise for hell, hope here to taste
> Of pleasure, but all pleasure to destroy,
> Save what is in destroying, other joy
> To me is lost.
>   (IX. 475–9)

And yet Satan is clever enough to know the power of love. He explains that his method of temptation will be to feign Love: 'Hate stronger, under show of love well feigned, / The way which to her ruin now I tend' (IX. 492–3). In his version, an envious God who is determined to keep man inferior denies him the knowledge of good and evil that would elevate him. Rather than regarding the first injunction as a gift to strengthen humankind, enabling them to exercise their judgement and freedom, Satan interprets the command as designed to lessen and injure humanity.

> One fatal tree there stands of knowledge called,
> Forbidden them to taste: knowledge forbidden?
> Suspicious, reasonless. Why should their Lord

Envy them that? Can it be sin to know,
Can it be death? And do they only stand
By ignorance, is that their happy state,
The proof of their obedience and their faith?

(IV. 514–20)

Satan does not understand the command as a sign of freedom (to reason), but as
a deprivation (of knowledge) and a condemnation (to inferiority). Anticipating
Nietzsche, he even equates this inferiority with faith. Satan's thinking is based
upon the presupposition that there is only room for one at the top, that only
one can prosper and only at the others' expense. Satan is hardly alone in this.
The Bible is often interpreted according to the scarcity principle (see Schwartz
1998). Everything about Satan belies his presupposition of scarcity. He interprets
the elevation of the Son of God as the diminution of his own glory: 'by decree /
Another now hath to himself ingrossed / All power, and us eclipsed' (V. 774–6).
He suffers from humiliation: 'Ay me, they little know / How dearly I abide that
boast so vain, / Under what torments inwardly I groan; /...The lower still I fall,
only supreme / In misery;' (IV. 86–92). And he suffers from envy, believing that
others unfairly have what he cannot have: 'aside the devil turned / For envy, yet
with jealous leer malign / Eyed them askance, and to himself thus plained. /
Sight hateful, sight tormenting! Thus these two / Imparadised in one another's
arms /...while I to hell am thrust' (IV. 502–8) Other symptoms follow suit:
his sense of injured merit: 'that fixed mind / And high disdain, from sense of
injured merit, / That with the mightiest raised me to contend' (I. 97–9), his belief
in winners and losers, and the compulsion to compete to avoid feeling like the
loser: 'To wage by force or guile eternal war / Irreconcilable to our grand foe, /
Who now triúmphs, and in the excess of joy / Sole reigning holds the tyranny of
heaven' (I. 121–4).

Accordingly, Satan imagines that everyone cannot attain godhead, even though
that fulfilment is explicitly enunciated by God the Father: 'Then thou thy regal
sceptre shalt lay by, / For regal sceptre then no more shall need, / God shall be all in
all' (III. 339–41) and Raphael teaches Adam of this possibility early in their conversation:

time may come when men
With angels may participate, and find
No inconvenient diet, nor too light fare:
And from these corporal nutriments perhaps
Your bodies may at last turn all to spirit,
Improved by tract of time, and winged ascend
Ethereal, as we, or may at choice
Here or in heavenly paradises dwell;
If ye be found obedient,

(V. 493–501)

Does this deferred, conditional achievement mean that, as the colloquial expression goes, the glass is half-empty or half-full? With that *promise* of 'all in all', a hermeneutic of charity is beginning to look very much like faith. Raphael, who interprets that promise according to the principle of charity, sees it as achievable. As Milton asserts in *De Doctrina Christiana*, 'saving faith' is 'the firm persuasion implanted in us by the gift of God, by virtue of which we believe, on the authority of God's promise, that all those things which God has promised us in Christ are ours, and especially the grace of eternal life' (*CPW* VI: 471). Milton proceeds to offer his interpretation of Hebrews 11. 1, 'faith is the substance of things hoped for...' He writes: 'Here *substance* means that we are persuaded that the *things hoped for* will be ours, just as firmly as if they not only already existed but were actually in our possession' (VI: 472). For Satan, who interprets according to the principle of scarcity, the glass is half-empty, that is, the promise is empty: 'as far / From granting he, as I from begging peace' (*PL* IV. 103–4).

Milton is perhaps most overt about the problem of interpretation in his poetry in the last two books of *Paradise Lost*. There, he confronts Adam with the task of interpreting all of biblical history; and we should not be surprised that his stress is repeatedly on the hermeneutics of charity. Since the eighteenth century, critics have been complaining about the last two books of *Paradise Lost*. The real drama of the epic has ended in Books IX and X with the Fall of our first parents (except for the inevitable swift expulsion, achieved in four lines, XII. 637–40). In Books XI and XII, the epic not only illustrates the consequences of that disobedience for Adam and Eve's progeny in horrid visions and narrations, it also recounts the rest of biblical history, with Milton broadening his debt to biblical plot far beyond the story in Genesis. These Bible stories are not dramatized as Adam and Eve's story is; they are *taught*, and the lesson is in biblical hermeneutics. In short, in the final books of *Paradise Lost*, Milton portrays the angel Michael teaching Adam how to interpret the Bible.

As Michael opens the Bible, first to Adam's sight and then to his hearing, Adam responds to each biblical episode. 'Cain and Abel' provokes his first of many misreadings. After their respective sacrifices, when Cain murders Abel, Adam responds indignantly, 'Is piety thus and pure devotion paid?' (XI. 452), and the sight of death provokes despair: 'Better end here unborn. Why is life giv'n / To be thus wrested from us?' (XI. 502–3). Indeed, Adam is prompted, when he sees the horrors of death, to ask the same question about divine justice that haunts Milton throughout his work: why man, made in his Maker's image, could suffer such deformity.

> Can thus
> The image of God in man created once
> So goodly and erect, though faulty since,
> To such unsightly sufferings be debased
> Under inhuman pains?
>   (XI. 507–11)

The answer, that man gave away that divine image when he rejected divine guidance and disfigured himself, sobers his indignation, and the promise – that man will be restored – tempers his despair.

Adam misinterprets the Bible just as radically when he responds to it with elation. His vision of the 'sons of God' cavorting with the daughters of Cain inspires a misguided delight.

> True opener of mine eyes, prime angel blest,
> Much better seems this Vision, and more hope
> Of peaceful days portends, than those two past;
> Those were of hate and death, or pain much worse,
> Here nature seems fulfilled in all her ends.
> (XI. 598–602)

Now he must learn that such pleasure seekers, if 'Unmindful of their maker' (XI. 611), fail to achieve goodness.

Adam is evidently an unstable biblical interpreter, whose skill needs to be honed. His teacher explains,

> good with bad
> Expect to hear, supernal grace contending
> With sinfulness of men; thereby to learn
> True patience, and to temper joy with fear
> And pious sorrow, equally inured
> By moderation either state to bear,
> Prosperous or adverse:
> (XI. 358–64)

To interpret according to the principle of charity is to understand that each tragedy of human history will be not corrected, but redeemed; hence, the intermixing of loss and gain should not generate swings from despair to elation, but the more stable sorrow that knows peace. Milton's oft-noted emphasis on the Flood at the end of Book XI, separating, as it does, the biblical visions from the narrations, pausing between a world destroyed and another created, underscores the theology of re-creation that informs his work (Schwartz 1993). When we assign that metaphor of a half-empty or half-full glass to the world itself, we confront the risk of interpreting the Flood according to the principle of scarcity: if there is only one world and it is inundated, only complete destruction and despair can follow. But when Adam learns to read the Flood story with charity, he understands it as enabling a second chance, a newly cleansed world. This time Adam is closer to getting it right:

> Far less I now lament for one whole world
> Of wicked sons destroyed, than I rejoice
> For one man found so perfet and so just,

> That God vouchsafes to raise another world
> From him, and all his anger to forget.
>   (XI. 874–8)

And yet, throughout the final book of *Paradise Lost*, the Angel must temper Adam's premature enthusiasm for the restoration wrought by Christ (Schwartz 1988). Before then, his progeny must endure the tragedies of history; and before then, he must be exiled from Paradise. The heavenly instructor's final lesson is that Adam and Eve live in faith 'though sad' for the evils past, 'yet much more cheered / With meditation on the happy end' (XII. 603–5), and this balance of sorrow and hope, deeply considered by Milton theologically, informs the many yoked contraries in the final lines of the poem, where Adam and Eve leave Paradise weeping but wiping their tears. For Milton, to interpret the Bible – that is, our past, our present and our future – according to the principle of charity is not to succumb to despair or elation, but to achieve inner peace, and to interpret biblical/human history with charity is to maintain faith that the achievement of outer peace is possible.

BIBLIOGRAPHY

Writings

Auerbach (1953); Shelley, Percy Bysshe (1948/ 1973); Tillyard (1930/1956).

References for Further Reading

Conklin (1949); Evans (1968); Gallagher (1990); Haskin (1994); Hill (1993); Kerrigan (1974); Lewalski (1985); Lieb (1981); Radzinowicz (1978); Rosenblatt (1994); Ryken and Sims (1984); Schwartz (1988, 1990, 1993, 1998); Sims (1962); Wittreich (1986).

4

Literary Baroque and Literary Neoclassicism

Graham Parry

Milton's poetic art appears to have numerous affinities with the baroque style prevalent in European painting and architecture in the mid-seventeenth century. Although the baroque had developed as a style closely associated with the Catholic faith, its power and appeal were recognized by Protestant artists too as a way of heightening and dramatizing religious experience. From an early stage Milton ventured to appropriate some of the features of baroque art for his own purposes. In this chapter we shall look at his achievements in this mode; and, since baroque was a development from a neoclassical base, we shall also survey the substantial neoclassical background of Milton's verse.

The baroque style was effectively evolved by artists in the service of the Catholic Church as part of the programme to revitalize the Catholic faith after the setbacks of the Reformation. The Council at Trento, in Italy ('the Council of Trent'), in the course of its long deliberations, lasting from 1545 to 1563, over how to combat the formidable appeal of the doctrines of the Reformed churches of northern Europe, began to encourage a more intensive manner of devotion among the followers of Rome. The faculty of wonder was invoked, greater emphasis was given to the element of the miraculous in religion, the sacraments were shown greater veneration, and the cults of saints and martyrs were favoured. The Jesuit order was also founded in the Reformation years to strengthen the Catholic Church intellectually and devotionally, and it was the Jesuits who particularly promoted the use of more dramatic and expressive art forms in their churches, in line with the Counter-Reformation doctrines of the Council of Trent. The characteristic features of the new baroque style began to appear in the later years of the sixteenth century, reaching their height in the middle of the seventeenth. Under the ingenious control of men such as Pietro da Cortona, Maderno, Borromini and Bernini, the firm lines of classical architecture began to develop a novel exuberance, and the decorative motifs became more animated and surprising. The dynamics of this architecture lifted the viewer's eyes upwards to the illusionistic spaces of the ceilings, which increasingly gave the impression that the heavens opened directly out of the fabric of the building, as one gazed up into a seemingly limitless sky crowded with saints and angelic figures, who were often moving towards a source of intense light. Painting responded to the need for an intensely energized devotional art, so the altarpieces commissioned for these new churches shared the vitality of the architecture, with a marked fondness for scenes of martyrdom and extreme suffering, or for moments of vision or miracle. The heroes and heroines of the spiritual life underwent their exemplary experiences in paintings where divine energy had become a visible force surging through the faithful. In Caravaggio's dramatic scenes of shadow and light, in the eventful works of Guido Reni or the strenuous canvasses of the Carracci, the vitalism of the baroque is at its height. In northern Europe, Rubens and Jordaens transmitted the new style among the Catholic communities of Flanders.

When Milton made his journey to Italy in 1638–9, baroque was the predominant art form in the design and decoration of buildings both religious and secular. In Rome especially he would have been exposed to the baroque at its most uninhibited. St Peter's was nearing its completion; many of its recent tombs were in the full-blown baroque manner, and Bernini's spectacular baldacchino or altar canopy had been installed only a few years before Milton's arrival. The Roman churches of the Counter-Reformation period were alive with baroque decoration, though whether the Protestant Milton ventured into the Jesuit churches of Rome is an open question. He must have visited St Peter's, however, for it was one of the wonders of the world, and as much a public monument as the headquarters of the Catholic Church. More to the point, the Palazzo Barberini, to which Milton was invited as a guest of Cardinal Barberini, the nephew of the Pope, had just had its ceilings newly painted with frescoes of exceptional splendour: Andrea Sacchi's refined and dignified 'Divine Wisdom' in 1633–4, and Pietro da Cortona's tumultuous 'Divine Providence and Barberini Power', completed in 1638. This last is an extraordinary confection in the high baroque manner: myriads of allegorical figures swarm upwards into the luminous vault, drawn by the influence of Divine Providence, an illuminated figure gesturing in the void. Gods and humans, pagan and Christian heroes, all mingle promiscuously. There is an overwhelming sense of crowded space and restless motion.

Was Milton's imagination fired by what he saw in Rome and in the Barberini Palace? We should remember that he was present in February 1639 at the perform-ance of an opera in the Palace, an opera that had illusionistic sets designed by Bernini. Although Milton returned to an England sliding into civil war, an episode during which he would become a political activist, when he eventually returned to poetry and the composition of his epic, did the memory of the great baroque scenarios, mostly devoted to the operations of divine power with heavenly vistas and occasionally with infernal depths, return to shape his conceptions of how divine history might be presented?

A number of commentators believe this to be the case. The most persuasive study is that by Murray Roston, whose book *Milton and the Baroque* (1980) draws attention to many aspects of *Paradise Lost* that seem to share the imaginative ethos of the Italian practitioners of the baroque. The very project of an epic of cosmic dimensions, involving the depiction of God, Satan, Christ, heaven, hell and earth, together with the rebellion of the angels, the creation of the world and the panorama of providential history, was one eminently suited to baroque treatment. Its exponents handled celestial transactions with confidence, and the interplay of the divine with the human on an immense scale was a characteristic scenario. It is easy to see the vast, thronged angelic gatherings in Book III, and their elaborate choric celebrations of divine wisdom, as baroque visions, just as Milton's God, hidden in light, has affinities with the deity whose light radiates through those painted heavens of *seicento* Roman churches.

> Thee Father first they sung omnipotent,
> Immutable, immortal, infinite,
> Eternal king; thee author of all being,
> Fountain of light, thyself invisible
> Amidst the glorious brightness where thou sitst
> Throned inaccessible, but when thou shad'st
> The full blaze of thy beams, and through a cloud
> Drawn round about thee like a radiant shrine,
> Dark with excessive bright thy skirts appear,
> Yet dazzle heaven, that brightest seraphim
> Approach not, but with both wings veil their eyes.
>   (III. 372–82)

A passage such as this, with the unimaginable imagined, with a tremendous vitality of technique, strikes an authentic baroque note. So, for example, does the scene of the angels assembling in Book V to hear the will of God pronounced:

>   the empyreal host
> Of angels by imperial summons called,
> Innumerable before the almighty's throne
> Forthwith from all the ends of heaven appeared
> Under their heirarchs in orders bright
> Ten thousand thousand ensigns high advanced,
> Standards, and gonfalons twixt van and rear
> Stream in the air, and for distinction serve
> Of hierarchies, of orders, and degrees;
> Or in thir glittering tissues bear imblazed
> Holy memorials, acts of zeal and love
> Recorded eminent. Thus when in orbs
> Of circuit inexpressible they stood,
> Orb within orb, the Father infinite,
> By whom in bliss embosomed sat the Son,
> Amidst as from a flaming mount, whose top
> Brightness had made invisible, thus spake.
>   (V. 583–99)

In the darker regions of the poem, the bridge that Sin and Death throw over chaos from hell to earth in Book X can be seen as an achievement of baroque engineering, spanning the metaphysical gulfs with a structure of delusive solidity. The teeming scenes of fallen angels at the opening of *Paradise Lost*, the dramatic landscapes of Paradise and the dense succession of historical events in the last books can all be imagined in pictorial form in contemporary art.

Numerous commentators have remarked how the new awareness of infinite space transmitted by the astronomers with their 'optic tubes' and advanced mathematics – Copernicus, Tycho Brahe and Galileo – contributed significantly to the baroque vision of the universe. In Roman painting as in Milton's poetry there is a sense of illimitable depth of space, of a cosmic vastness unknown to earlier generations. The heaven of *Paradise Lost* belongs to this new consciousness of infinity, as do the aerial journeys of Satan across the void. The account of the wheeling universe with all its planetary motions that Raphael offers to Adam in Book VIII gives an insight into Milton's responsiveness to the infinity of worlds and the unending creativity revealed by the new astronomy.

There can be no doubt, then, that many features of *Paradise Lost* reveal what might be termed a baroque way of conceiving and dramatizing the physical and metaphysical worlds. These features have much in common with the Italian *seicento* artists whose work Milton must have encountered in 1638–9. Not all painterly or artistic details of the epic need to be regarded as expressions of the baroque, however. For example, the only major architectural description in *Paradise Lost*, that of the construction of Pandæmonium in Book I, seems to combine recollections of St Peter's, Rome and the Pantheon, buildings of magnificent but restrained classicism; Milton's account emphasizes the magnificence, but does not introduce any details that could be deemed distinctively baroque. In reflecting on Milton's indebtedness to Italian artistic forms, one should bear in mind the general indifference to painting throughout his work. Among the seventeenth-century poets, Milton is unusual in never referring explicitly to paintings, neither in his verse nor in his prose. The letters and poems associated with his Italian visit give no indication of an interest in the visual arts. One should therefore be wary of making claims of any immediate relationship between his poetry and the contemporary arts of Italy. For all this blankness, however, Milton can hardly have been unaware of the dominant artistic movement of the age, especially in Rome where so much of its recent achievement was on display.

Yet long before Milton began to compose *Paradise Lost*, and some years before he visited Italy, he had been incorporating recognizably baroque touches into his early poems. These passages occur most prominently in some of his early Latin poems, the elegies for the Bishops of Ely and of Winchester providing notable examples. In the poem on the death of Nicholas Felton, Bishop of Ely ('*In Obitum Praesulis Eliensis*'), written in 1626 when Milton was a student at Cambridge, aged seventeen, the bishop experiences that particularly baroque phenomenon, apotheosis, an ascension to glory. Apotheosis combined the conventions of the Assumption of the Virgin and the deification of a Roman emperor, and it was a device much used by the baroque painters of the Counter-Reformation. The body of the illustrious deceased was whirled up to heaven accompanied by welcoming and acclamatory figures. Such a scene offered opportunities for unusual vertical perspectives and for the depiction of illusory heights of space. Rubens was especially effective in painting apotheoses, and depicted the celestial ascent of King Henri IV of France, James I of Great Britain and the Duke of Buckingham, among others. Here is the Bishop of Ely's account of his experience, in a prose translation of Milton's Latin:

> I was carried in blessedness high up to the stars amidst winged warriors, just as that aged prophet was swept up into the heavens in a chariot of fire. I was not frightened by the Wain of gleaming Bootes, crawling along because of the cold, nor by the claws of the fearsome Scorpion, nor even, Orion, by your sword. I flew past the glowing globe of the sun, and saw, far away beneath my feet, the triform goddess steering her dragon team with golden reins. I was carried past the courses of the wandering planets, and through the expanses of the Milky Way, often marvelling at my new-found speed, until I reached the shining gates of Olympus, the palace of crystal and the halls paved with emerald . . . (my translation)

The bishop's spectacular ascent to heaven is a fine conflation of Old Testament and pagan motifs. Elijah and Diana are seen manoeuvring their chariots in the crowded skies, though poetic decorum causes Milton not to pronounce their names. Elijah is the *'senex / Auriga currus ignei'* – the old man with the chariot of fire – and Diana the *'deam triformem'* – the threefold goddess – who is driving her team of dragons (here she personifies the moon). We notice, too, that the Bishop's destination is a composite of classical Olympus and Christian heaven. Milton from his earliest years as a poet was ever the Christian humanist, willing to draw his imagery from both the classical and the Judeo-Christian traditions, in the confidence that the two traditions were parallel and compatible, the principal difference being that the Judeo-Christian history communicated revealed truth, while the pagan fables only shadowed truth.

This apotheosis was something of a novelty in verse by Englishmen at this time. The Bishop of Ely hurtling through the planets and along the Milky Way *'Velocitatem saepe miratus novam'* – 'marvelling at my new-found speed' – was probably the first Anglican to make this starry journey, though Catholic saints had frequently sped towards heaven in Counter-Reformation painting. But the young Milton seems very familiar with the conventions of apotheosis; and he writes with assurance, and with a knowledge of the incidents required to enliven a celestial journey. His poem on the death of Lancelot Andrewes, Bishop of Winchester (*'Elegia tertia. In Obitum Praesulis Wintoniensis'*), also written in 1626, shares the same baroque richness of florid detail as its counterpart poem. It takes the form of a vision in which the poet sees the elderly bishop entering the Garden of the Hesperides, transfigured by death into a radiant saint:

> While I marvel at the close-set shadows cast by the clustering vines, and at the shining
> spaces all around me, suddenly near me appeared the Bishop of Winchester. A radiance
> as of the stars shone in his face. His white robe flowed down to his golden ankles, and a
> white crown wreathed his god-like head. While the aged figure moved on, so gloriously
> dressed, the flowery earth vibrated with a joyful sound. The heavenly hosts clap their
> jewelled wings, and the pure upper air rings with the notes of a triumphal trumpet.
> Each angel greets his new companion with embraces and songs, and one of them, with
> peaceful lips, uttered these words: 'Come, my son, and receive in happiness the joys of
> your Father's kingdom; henceforth be free from cruel toil, my son, for ever'. This said,
> the winged squadrons touched their harps ... (my translation)

This scenario is strongly pictorial, employing an unusually high level of artifice. The
resplendent figure of Lancelot Andrewes, with his golden ankles – an odd touch –
amid squadrons of angels, the earth and air vibrating with music, has obvious
affinities with painting; but there are similarities here too with the action of a
masque.

If we ask how Milton's imagination was fired to conceive of these dynamic scenes,
at once so visual and so remote from experience, we might find that the English
court masque was a more likely source of inspiration than contemporary European
painting. In the later 1620s, when Milton was writing in this exuberant manner,
there was virtually no baroque painting in England that Milton could have seen. It
is true that in these years Rubens was painting canvasses for the Duke of Buckingham, one of which showed a full baroque apotheosis as the Duke was swept upwards
to a celestial temple of Virtue, but it is most improbable that the young Milton
would have gained entry into York House, Buckingham's London residence. Rubens
had not yet been commissioned to paint the panels for the Banqueting House
ceiling at Whitehall, which would eventually put mature baroque inventions before
a fairly large audience. But the masques that were performed in the Banqueting
House were another kind of baroque art form that was much more relevant to Milton's
practice. In these lavish shows, men and women were transformed into divinities
with magical ease. Magnificently and fantastically dressed in bejewelled and multi-
coloured costumes, the noble masquers were revealed to the audience in settings of
intense light; they moved and danced to music, and seemed like creatures of another
element. Clouds and chariots bore them heavenwards, as the ingenious technical
devices of Inigo Jones operated behind the scenes to produce effects of wonder for
the spectators. Transformation scenes produced rapid changes of landscape, and everywhere images of perfection were realized by art. The vocabulary of the masque was
largely classical, for the action of a masque was usually worked around a fable
involving the gods, with Greek or Roman allusions in abundance. In addition, the
architectural structures that were part of the scenery were generally designed in the
classical manner.

The court masque can legitimately be regarded as a baroque art form, for its
hybrid or multimedia character, composed of drama, music, dancing, light and

spectacle, places it, like opera, its close relative, in that area where the arts combine and interact to enrich each other in ways typical of seventeenth-century inventiveness. Illusions of space, exuberant and at times almost hallucinatory overloading of the senses with colour, music, poetry and decorative splendour, technical and intellectual virtuosity: all these make masque a distinctive production of the baroque era.

Had Milton ever seen a masque? The answer is probably no, for these spectacles were presented on rare occasions to a highly privileged audience in a court setting. Milton was too young, and seems unlikely to have had the right kind of connections at court to gain entry to its most prestigious form of entertainment. Even when he wrote *Comus* in 1634 it is not certain that he had ever seen a masque, for his own creation is quite unlike the kind that had become conventional at court. But he could certainly have read the published accounts of masques that were issued by Ben Jonson, Thomas Campion, Samuel Daniel and other inventors of these fictions. In some ways, the written descriptions may have been more compelling than the actual performance, for they present the ideal realization of the masque, as it existed in the writer's mind. Consider, for example, one of Jonson's descriptions of a scene in his masque *Hymenaei*:

> Here the upper part of the scene, which was all of clouds and made artificially to swell and ride like the rack, began to open, and, the air clearing, in the top thereof was discovered Juno sitting in a throne supported by two beautiful peacocks; her attire rich and like a queen, a white diadem on her head from whence descended a veil, and that bound a fascia of several-coloured silks, set with all sorts of jewels and raised in the top with lilies and roses; in her right hand she held a sceptre, in the other a timbrel; at her golden feet the hide of a lion was placed; round about her sat the spirits of the air, in several colours, making music. Above her the region of fire with a continual motion was seen to whirl circularly, and Jupiter standing in the top, figuring the heaven, brandishing his thunder; beneath her the rainbow, Iris ... (Orgel and Strong 1973, 1: 108, lines 198–213)

One can well imagine the inspirational effect of such scenes on a receptive young poet.

The poem 'On the Morning of Christ's Nativity' (the Nativity Ode) clearly shows its indebtedness to the masque. It is a poem of high artifice, in which Milton appropriates a form that had been frequently used to reveal the divine qualities of Stuart kingship and applies it to a purer and more exalted end, the revelation of the true divinity of Christ, 'the Prince of Light'. The light and music that are such prominent features of the Nativity Ode were habitually used in masques to express the presence of divinity and the harmony between heaven and earth. By transferring the conventions of masque from a secular to a religious setting, Milton is allying his poetry to truth rather than fiction, and finds an appropriate structure for the shaping of his poem. Several of the Jonsonian masques had dramatized the reign of the Stuarts as the return of the golden age, a time when innocence and justice prevailed among humankind, and heaven and earth were in harmony. In the Ode, with Christ's birth revealing that the link between heaven and earth has been renewed, Milton briefly imagines the restoration of the age of gold:

> For if such holy song
> Enwrap our fancy long,
>   Time will run back, and fetch the age of gold,
> And speckled vanity
> Will sicken soon and die,
>   And lep'rous sin will melt from earthly mould,
>   (lines 133–8)

The imagery of the masque is again mobilized to effect the transformation:

> Yea Truth, and Justice then
> Will down return to men,
>   Orbed in a rainbow; and like glories wearing
> Mercy will sit between,
> Throned in celestial sheen,
>   With radiant feet the tissued clouds down steering,
> And heaven as at some festival,
> Will open wide the gates of her high palace hall.
>   (lines 141–8)

This vision is cut short by the cold realization that Providence has arranged otherwise, that Christ must suffer and die, that time must run its course until the Last Judgement thunders through the deep. The poet has to be content to express his understanding of the significance of Christ's birth in the process of universal history. Milton then describes the procession of pagan gods as they depart from their temples and shrines; but he casts them as figures from an antimasque, the section of a masque that features forces hostile to the benevolent operation of the figures in the main masque proper, and which have to be expelled by the power of the positive characters. Antimasque figures were frequently grotesque or unnatural. In keeping with this conception, Milton gives the pagan gods the music and dances appropriate to their debased condition in the antimasque of spiritual history. They leave with 'hideous hum', with 'hollow shriek', 'with midnight plaint', 'with timbrelled anthems dark', and they move 'In dismal dance about the furnace blue'. In contrast, against them rises the music of the main masque of Christ's birth, the 'full consort' of 'the angelic symphony'. The Ode ends with a tableau, a final revelation of the masquers, as it were, with the Virgin and Child surrounded by the 'bright-harnessed angels' 'in order serviceable'; the setting, although a stable, is none the less 'courtly'. The Nativity Ode is truly Milton's Masque of Christmas.

What other literary influences might have been at work on Milton in the composition of the Nativity Ode, or indeed of those other early poems on high moments of the Christian year, 'Upon the Circumcision' and 'The Passion'? Along with 'At a Solemn Music', these are all written in an elevated, ornate and magniloquent style, and deal with the mysterious relationships between heaven and humankind. This gorgeous manner was extremely uncommon in English verse at the time. Some critics have pointed in the direction of Giles and Phineas Fletcher, brothers who had been poetically prominent at Cambridge in the decade before Milton arrived, and whose poems were being published in the 1620s and 1630s. Their grand designs, on subjects such as *Christ's Victorie, and Triumph* (Giles Fletcher, 1610), or on the Gunpowder Plot (presented by Phineas Fletcher as a conspiracy of the Jesuits under the influence of Satan and Sin) – (*The Locusts or Apollyonists*, 1627), undoubtedly were known to Milton and had some effect on passages in *Paradise Lost* and *Paradise Regained*, and on his early Latin poems on the Gunpowder Plot. But stylistically the poetic diction of the Fletchers was heavily Spenserian, archaic, stilted and slow-moving, quite unlike Milton's splendid, robust and vigorous diction, which has a wonderful reverberative power. The poet who developed a thoroughgoing baroque manner was Richard Crashaw, another Cambridge product; but his works were being written just too late to affect Milton. His Latin Sacred Epigrams (*Epigrammatum sacrorum liber*) were published in 1634, but his religious poems in English, in which he exhibited an extravagant diction suited to his exotic religious sensibility, did not appear until 1646. His florid and emotional style of devotion was expressed in a language of sensuous richness that has no equal in English.

The poet who comes nearest to Milton's youthful grand style, from whom he might have learnt how to create the baroque effects we have been discussing here, was not English, but Scottish. William Drummond of Hawthornden was the leading northern poet, and enjoyed a high reputation in England. It was with Drummond that Ben Jonson had stayed for some three weeks in the winter of 1618–19 at the end of his walk to Scotland, and it is from Drummond's record of their conversations together that we know so much about Jonson's literary opinions. As a religious poet, Drummond moved into new territory with his volume *Flowers of Sion*, published in 1623. Here he wrote an intellectually elevated poetry that explored the great structure of the Christian system in an objective, philosophical way that has clear affinities with Milton's own approach to a similar range of subject matter. He is able to achieve an eloquent and sustained celebration of the noblest themes: 'An Hymn of the Passion', 'To the Angels for the Passion', 'An Hymn of the Resurrection', 'The Miserable Estate of the World before the Incarnation of God', 'On the Great and General Judgment of the World' and 'A Prayer for Mankind'. His most ambitious poem is 'An Hymn of the Fairest Fair: of the Nature, Attributes and Works of God', in wondering praise of the infinite creativity and goodness of the Almighty. Some sample lines convey the tone; here is Drummond imagining the source of all being:

As far beyond the starry walls of heaven,
As is the loftiest of the planets seven
Sequester'd from this earth, in purest light,
Outshining ours, as ours doth sable night,
Thou, all-sufficient, omnipotent,
Thou ever glorious, most excellent,
God various in names, in essence one,
High art installed on a golden throne,
Outreaching heaven's wide vasts, the bounds of nought,
Transcending all the circles of our thought:
With diamantine sceptre in thy hand,
There thou giv'st laws, and dost this world command,
This world of concords rais'd unlikely sweet,
Which like a ball lies prostrate to thy feet.

Drummond's Christian thought is broadly infused with Platonism, another point of appeal to Milton. Numerous verbal echoes of Drummond's 'Hymn of the Ascension' have been identified in Milton's Nativity Ode (see the article by H. Neville Davies [1985]), but it seems likely that there was a more pervasive influence coming from Drummond, who was one of the few contemporary poets to have a comparable grandeur of imagination. It is suggestive, too, to learn that Drummond was an appreciative reader of modern Italian poetry, and had a particular responsiveness to the work of Giovanni Battista Marino, the quintessentially baroque poet, whose manner of expression was, in the opinion of Drummond's editor, William Ward, 'nearly akin to Drummond's own way of thinking'. There is certainly a sense of an Italian Counter-Reformation aesthetic of ornate and high-aspiring splendour in the work of both poets.

One particular motif that recurs in Milton's poetry and is part of a complex of baroque images is that of cosmic flight. We have already noted the early account of an apotheosis, one form of this motif, in which the soaring spirit passes by symbolic groupings of gods in mid-air, en route to its heavenly destination. Another form of this occurs at the end of *Comus*, where the Attendant Spirit describes his path back to the region of divine light that is his home. This is the path that the enlightened soul aspiring to follow Platonic Virtue will take. He flies by the Gardens of the Hesperides, where the Graces dance, past Venus and Adonis engaged in a perpetual cycle of death and revival, up towards Cupid and Psyche who are expressive of a mortal's ultimate ability to know God, before he reaches his home, 'Higher than the sphery chime' (line 1020) in the serene region of complete enlightenment and knowledge of God. This is a mystery both Platonic and Christian that is being shadowed here, and one very dear to Milton. He had already hinted at his own desire to make such a journey in the lines in 'Il Penseroso' when he imagined the figure of the aspiring philosopher, not unlike the young Milton, whose mind can arise from the reading of hermetic mysteries to

> unsphere
> The spirit of Plato to unfold
> What worlds, or what vast regions hold
> The immortal mind that hath forsook
> Her mansion in this fleshly nook:
>
> (lines 88–92)

making an intellectual ascent not unlike that of the Attendant Spirit in *Comus*. But this fantasy goes back right to the beginning of Milton's career as a poet. In some of his earliest lines of English verse, the 'Vacation Exercise' performed at Christ's College in 1628 when he was nineteen, he disclosed to his fellow students his poetic ambitions for the future, which included the composition of a philosophical epic. He spoke of how

> the deep transported mind may soar
> Above the wheeling poles, and at heaven's door
> Look in, and see each blissful deity
> How he before the thunderous throne doth lie,
> Listening to what unshorn Apollo sings
> To the touch of golden wires, while Hebe brings
> Immortal nectar to her kingly sire:
> Then passing through the spheres of watchful fire,
> And misty regions of wide air next under,
> And hills of snow and lofts of piled thunder,
> May tell at length how green-eyed Neptune raves,
> In heaven's defiance mustering all his waves;
> Then sing of secret things that came to pass
> When beldam Nature in her cradle was;
>
> (lines 33–46)

(Drummond's 'Hymn of the Fairest Fair' has a 'Rose-cheeked Youth' who 'pours / Immortal nectar in a cup of gold' – is this mere coincidence, or did Milton, with a poet's retentive memory, assimilate the phrase?)

This adventurous sky-journey seems to have struck a personal chord with Milton: he associated it with philosophical and spiritual exploration; it was an imaginative escape from the limitations of the body and of local space that as a philosophical poet and spiritual prophet he found so restrictive. It is a recurring feature of his poetry, and it finally takes a parodic form in Satan's cosmic journey in Book III of *Paradise Lost*.

> Round he surveys, and well might, where he stood
> So high above the circling canopy
> Of night's extended shade; from eastern point
> Of Libra to the fleecy star that bears
> Andromeda far off Atlantic seas
> Beyond the horizon; then from pole to pole

> He views in breadth, and without longer pause
> Down right into the world's first region throws
> His flight precipitant, and winds with ease
> Through the pure marble air his oblique way
> Among innumerable stars, that shone
> Stars distant, but nigh hand seemed other worlds,
> Or other worlds they seemed, or happy isles,
> Like those Hesperian gardens famed of old,
> Fortunate fields, and groves and flowery vales,
> Thrice happy isles, but who dwelt happy there
> He stayed not to enquire: above them all
> The golden sun in splendour likest heaven
> Allured his eye: thither his course he bends
> Through the calm firmament; but up or down
> By centre, or eccentric, hard to tell,
>
> (III. 555–75)

Milton here sets up the familiar features of the sky-journey: the evocation of vast space, the constellations, clear air and shining light of the firmament, allusions to the Gardens of the Hesperides – these look back to the elegies for the bishops, and to the flight at the end of *Comus*. But here the tone is different, for the heroic splendour of the description is undercut by the narrative voice in the last quoted line, as also by the later image of Satan as a spot upon the sun; and we know too that this is no spiritual or philosophical quest, but a journey whose sole purpose is destruction.

There were various literary antecedents for these aerial voyages, going back as far as the late Greek writer Lucian, who wrote a satirical dialogue, 'Icaromenippus', that described a flight by the cynic philosopher Menippus through the starry heavens to the realm of the gods. More recently, there was the flight to the moon by Astolfo in Ariosto's *Orlando Furioso*, and in English writings there were imaginary voyages by Joseph Hall and Francis Goodwin; and even Ben Jonson's masque *News from the New World Discovered in the Moon* could contribute to stellar fantasies. John Donne had invented an apotheosis for Elizabeth Drury in *The Second Anniversary*, although the account of her progress through the heavens is so encumbered with witty conceits that the reader can scarcely detect any movement. But in truth one does not need to accumulate precedents for Milton's flights of imagination, for star-gazing was in vogue in the intellectual world as a result of the astonishing discoveries of the astronomers, and Milton's thoughts were heaven-directed from his early years. Like many a major poet, his creative faculties assimilated influences promiscuously and comprehensively.

When one tries to relate the extravagant passages we have been concerned with here, the emanations of a baroque sensibility, to the larger body of Milton's work, then one has to recognize that they have evolved from structures that are basically classical. Although he had a variety of stylistic registers at his command, his enduring sense of himself was as a poet in the mainstream classical tradition as it flowed though Europe in the sixteenth and seventeenth centuries. Milton's instinct for poetry was essentially an instinct for Latin poetry. In his early years he expressed himself more readily and more fluently in Latin verse than in English, and he wrote a Latin of exceptional richness and eloquence. It was for him the most intimate form of expression, and if we want to know the young Milton's feelings about love or friendship, it is to his Latin elegies that we must turn, for it was through this medium that he spoke most freely of his private self. It was as a Latin poet that Milton was known to the literary communities on the continent, and it was for the quality and power of his writing that he was celebrated by the members of the academies in Italy in 1638–9. When he published his collected poems in 1645, the volume was fairly evenly divided between his English *Poems* and his Latin *Poemata*. This continuation of the ancient traditions and genres of Roman poetry in the Renaissance we may call neoclassical, on the analogy with neoclassical architecture, as practised, for instance, by Alberti, Palladio or Inigo Jones, consciously following the example of antique models in structure and detail, while retaining the liberty to produce new combinations of the old components and ultimately innovate new structures in the spirit of the classical tradition they were working in.

The admiration for Roman ways of imagining the world and the desire to restore the classical forms were major driving forces for the arts throughout the Renaissance in all countries. In the early seventeenth century, the belief that Stuart England should recognize an affinity with ancient Rome was a dominant conviction of Ben Jonson, who devoted a good deal of his literary career to demonstrating how Roman values could be applied to English life, and how Roman literary forms could be used to classicize his own society. Through a poetry of civilized discourse based on Horace and Martial, through satire that derived from Martial and Juvenal, and comedy that looked back to Plautus and Terence, to pastoral from Virgil, Jonson strove to establish a consonance between societies of different ages and reveal the secret affinities between them. After the faltering attempts by Sidney and Spenser to apply Roman forms to English circumstances in Elizabethan times, Jonson was able to introduce a thorough-going classicism into English letters, which ultimately led on to the mature Augustanism of Dryden and Pope. Jonson's desire was to make educated Englishmen feel that they were naturalized citizens of Rome, sharing the same liberal civilized values as educated Romans of the first century. Jonson was a social poet in a way that Milton was not: he was above all interested in social behaviour, feelings about the nation, and piety. But he showed how important it was to master the forms and styles of Roman poetry in order to reclothe contemporary life in classical dress. Jonson's endeavour was complemented by the work of his collaborator in the masques, Inigo Jones, who first in his designs for masques and then in his building designs began to provide for his aristocratic patrons authentically Roman architectural settings.

Milton grew up in a world in which these neoclassical tendencies were strengthening. His intensively classical education at St Paul's School helped him to participate in these literary trends, but his bent was more mythological, philosophical and religious than Jonson's. Saturated in Roman poetry, and familiar with much Greek, Milton was eager to recreate the eloquent richness of expression that he found especially in Ovid's Epistles and in Virgil's Eclogues. Not so interested in the contemporary scene as Jonson was, he was more consciously 'literary' and artificial.

So, for example, 'Lycidas' is a beautifully crafted pastoral elegy that owes a great deal to Virgil's Eclogues, and also to the heavily embroidered tradition of Virgilian pastoral elegy that had been developed by Renaissance poets in Italy and England; Milton still manages, however, to strike a distinctive note. The classical vocabulary always allows the personal accent to be heard: it is a case of tradition and the individual talent, where the conventions dominate, but stylistic nuance and selective emphasis convey the poet's private concerns. Given the displacement of language, 'Lycidas' is both authentically Virgilian and recognizably Miltonic. The names of the figures within the poem are Roman and also Greek, looking back to the originators of the pastoral tradition in poetry, Theocritus and Bion, whom Virgil himself was following, with a change in language. The rituals of mourning, with the procession of mourners and the scattering of flowers, are those of the Greco-Roman world; the gods and the mythologies invoked are all scrupulously classical. Yet the hope of resurrection expressed in the poem is Christian, and the mourning has a personal note. There is an admirable correctness, or decorum, about the poem, until the expostula-tion by St Peter (who, of course, cannot be named as such in this pastoral setting, but is introduced in a periphrasis as 'The pilot of the Galilean lake' [line 109]). This outburst breaks the decorum of the poem, using the language and tone of satire in place of smooth pastoral, as it introduces a vehement protest about the state of the church (though still maintaining the imagery of the shepherd's world). The neoclas-sical formality gives way to a pressing personal concern of the poet's, and the denunciation disrupts the shapeliness and stately movement of the elegy. The clash of genres here, of pastoral against satire, elegy against philippic, is startling and memorable; but the neoclassical architecture of the poem can accommodate this extrusion because the passage maintains the diction of pastoralism, even if the tone has changed radically from the evenness of elegy. None the less, it is a disconcerting and inappropriate passage; to continue the architectural analogy, it is like pushing out a one-storey Doric projection from a two-storey Corinthian facade. It breaks the ordered stateliness of the structure, and is disproportionate. Here is Milton trying to innovate within the tradition, but not really succeeding.

The pastoral manner was deeply appealing to Milton, and he was able to indulge his love of it extensively in *Comus*. The masque was a modern form, with no classical antecedent, but the classical mode of pastoral verse could be applied to the new form, for the ancient conventions were wonderfully adaptable. The secret of the durability of classical forms is that they can be so freely adapted to new requirements. So the children of the Earl of Bridgewater are introduced into a fable that is a Greco-Roman pastoral populated with Greco-Roman figures, and a theme that combines the pursuit of philosophical virtue with the temptations facing those who undertake this quest. The contemporary world is nowhere visible, for the whole adventure has been classicized. Only at the very end do we see the town of Ludlow in the background of the shepherds' dances. The lengthy descriptions of the natural world are rendered in the leisurely, elaborate, self-indulgent diction that derived from Greek pastoral. So, when Comus tells that Lady that he saw her brothers in the evening near a row of vines, he puts it thus:

> Two such I saw, what time the laboured ox
> In his loose traces from the furrow came,
> And the swinked hedger at his supper sat;
> I saw them under a green mantling vine
> That crawls along the side of yon small hill,
> Plucking ripe clusters from the tender shoots,
>
> (lines 290–5)

The conventions of pastoral shape the presentation of the characters. The Attendant Spirit, the neoplatonic guide to Virtue, changes into shepherd's 'weeds' at the beginning of the masque and takes the pastoral name of Thyrsis; the tempter Comus is placed in a rustic setting; the action takes place in and around a dark wood; and release from the spell is provided by a river spirit, Sabrina.

Pastoral was the mode that Milton chose when he came to mourn the death of his closest friend, Charles Diodati, in 1638. Under the title '*Epitaphium Damonis*', Milton in a long, heartfelt poem remembers his friend, who is figured as the shepherd Damon; their times together and their ambitions are rendered in the elemental language of the countryside, and the poet's intense grief is absorbed by the dense descriptions of the natural world. Pastoral had an undoubted power to soothe disturbed emotions, by turning them towards the consoling beauty of nature. Even today, flowers are the fullest expression of sorrow at funerals. Part of the appeal of pastoral elegy was its timeless character, the sense that particular feelings are common to the race, and that death is part of an ever-renewing cycle of nature.

The early phase of Milton's poetic career came to an end with the elegy for Diodati, for on his return to England he became increasingly involved in bitter debates about reformation in church and state. Prose was the medium for contemporary matters. On his return to sustained poetic composition, however, after a lapse of many years, Milton found the re-use of classical forms not only the weightiest but also the most natural way of communicating his thought. *Paradise Lost* is the most successful epic in English, and it is a major achievement of Milton's neoclassical art. Antique structures are imitated and applied to new uses. Just as ancient Roman architecture was revived and applied to churches in the Renaissance, so the ancient form of epic is Christianized and becomes the vehicle for a sublime account of divine history and God's providence towards humankind.

With its many echoes of Virgil's *Aeneid*, far outnumbering Homeric allusions, *Paradise Lost* is more indebted to Roman than to Greek precedents, and the latinate syntax of Milton's English reinforces the impression that the spirit of Roman poetry lives on in Milton's verse. The pagan Muse who inspires epic has been Christianized as

Urania, and she in turn is indistinguishable from the divine spirit that pervaded the creation. The mythology of Greece and Rome is everywhere present in the epic, yet always seen as a parallel to, analogous with, or an imperfect recollection of, some incident in biblical history, which is true history. The beauty of classical fables has never been so fully realized as in *Paradise Lost* (though Keats and Shelley come close); but even as Milton imagines the perfection of mythological figures in their ideal settings, he has to admit that they are exquisite and compelling fictions, not images of truth. '[T]hus they relate, / Erring' is how he ends the famous description of Mulciber falling from the ramparts of heaven, cast out by Jove (I. 746–7). 'Hesperian fables true, / If true, here only' is how he qualifies the accounts of classical paradises in his account of Eden in Book IV (lines 250–1). Elsewhere in that book he begins a long passage about the supreme beauty of mythological landscapes with a controlling negative: 'Not that fair field / ... might with this Paradise / Of Eden strive' (IV. 268–75). In writing a Christian epic within a classical frame, Milton had to be circumspect, and not give overmuch acclaim to the pagan stories and learning that had formed so large a part of his education and subsequent reading, and occupied so large a part of his imagination. Working with classical materials was a challenge for any writer in the tradition of Christian humanism; one had to be careful to get the balance right in favour of the Christian scheme, and not let the passion for the antique prevail over one's commitment to the faith.

The most satisfying design of Milton's was *Samson Agonistes*. Here is a work with the form of a Greek tragedy, the subject of a Hebrew legend, and a relevance that is Christian. Familiarity with Greek literature was rare among seventeenth-century writers, and knowledge of the Greek language rarer still. So here was neoclassicism with a difference, as Milton produced an accurate replica of a Greek play, found a viable language that is austere, lofty and religiously intense, and raised the ancient question of the justness of God's – or the gods' – dealings with man. Technically, *Samson Agonistes* obeys the Aristotelian precepts for tragedy. It has a protagonist and antagonists, and the chorus is correctly handled. Samson has committed *hubris* in disregarding the law of his God; he possesses the tragic flaw, *harmartia*, in his susceptibility to women; he experiences *anagnorisis* or discovery of self, when he realizes that God is still with him; he undergoes *peripateia* or reversal of fortune when he revives and overthrows the theatre of the Philistines; and that moment is coincidental with the *catastrophe* of the play that brings about his death. Throughout there has been an emphasis on *proairesis* or moral purpose, and the play ends with the famous expression of *catharsis*, the purgative experience of tragedy: 'And calm of mind all passion spent'.

Samson Agonistes is an immensely impressive work, but the society into which it was published paid it no attention. It remained, a beautifully constructed monument of neoclassicism, largely unvisited. Those who entered might find it a temple of Christian mysteries, but most regarded it as a cold, forbidding mausoleum of dead ideas, quite out of place in the modern landscape. It is, however, highly appropriate that the last poem that Milton published should have been so perfect a piece of neoclassicism, for he had always had the most intense feelings of admiration and pleasure for the literatures of Greece and Rome, and his whole career was in some ways an act of homage to their excellence.

BIBLIOGRAPHY

Writings

Drummond (n.d.); Orgel and Strong (1973).

References for Further Reading

Daniells (1963); Davies, H. Neville (1985); Di Cesare (1991); Eriksen (1997); Highet (1957); Revard (1997a); Roston (1980); Sowerby (1994).

5

Milton and English Poetry

Achsah Guibbory

Milton's reworkings and transformations of classical texts and conventions are well known. But Milton's ties were also to the English past, though he became disillusioned with the English people after the failure of the Revolution. While he felt part of a cosmopolitan literary community that reached on to the European continent and into the ancient past, he wrote with a strong sense of his immediate English literary past. Like classical literature, English literature constituted a field to be negotiated; to be valued, but also evaluated. The recent English literary tradition – the literature of post-Reformation England – stretched from Sir Philip Sidney and Edmund Spenser through Ben Jonson and John Donne to the Cavalier poets like Thomas Carew and Robert Herrick. In his treatment of classical texts and conventions, Milton felt compelled to judge them from his position as a Christian even as he was attracted to and incorporated their glorious achievements. In a similar way, Milton engaged in critical dialogue with English literature, not all of which conformed to his Protestant values.

Milton was influenced by a broad range of English texts. Despite his puritan suspicion of theatrical performance, we see the legacy of Renaissance drama (particularly Marlowe's *Dr Faustus* and revenge tragedy) in the portrait of Satan in *Paradise Lost*, and sense the presence of Shakespeare in the language and imagination of *Comus* and *Paradise Lost* (Gardner 1965: 99–120; Guillory 1983: 68–75; Stevens 1985). As a poet, Milton wrote within (and sometimes against) the tradition of English poetry. I will first locate Milton's notion of poetry within its English context, and then focus on his connection with Spenser's *The Faerie Queene*, whose influence he acknowledged and has been widely recognized (Quilligan 1983; Guillory 1983; Helgerson 1983; Norbrook 1984a; Gregerson 1995), and Renaissance lyric love poetry, which has a less obvious and more complicated presence in his major poetry.

The Moral Function of Poetry

Milton inherited from his English predecessors a sense of the poet's exalted role and the moral function of poetry. Milton is one of the most serious of poets, and his seriousness, though in part a matter of personal disposition, was grounded in the view of the poet's responsibilities expressed by Sir Philip Sidney. Sidney's *Defence of Poesie* defined an exalted, heroic view of poetry shared by Spenser, Jonson and Milton, all of whom claimed a moral as well as a poetic authority in their society. Sidney spoke of the poet's power and obligation to move human beings to virtue through 'feigning notable images of virtues, [and] vices'; the true poet aims to perfect people, 'furnishing the mind with knowledge' and 'moving' them to 'well-doing' (Sidney 1989: 219, 226). Spenser claimed that the 'end' or purpose of his epic was 'to fashion a gentleman or noble person in vertuous and gentle discipline' ('Letter... to Raleigh'; Spenser 1965). Jonson went further, insisting in *Timber: or, Discoveries* that the good poet must be a good man (Jonson 1965, 8: 595), and he presented his own poetry as an expression of his active virtue and reason. In his epigrammatic poetry as well as his plays and masques, Jonson discriminated between virtue and vice, as if the moral arbiter of his society.

Milton embraced this activist, moral notion of poetry. Like Sidney, Spenser and Jonson, he believed in the ethical function of literature. He embraced the high responsibility of the writer, whether he was seeking to effect religious, social and political reforms in his polemical tracts, or writing poetry. All of Milton's writing was driven by an educative, redemptive purpose. Echoing Jonson, Milton insisted that the true poet 'ought him selfe to bee a true Poem, that is, a composition, and patterne of the best and honourablest things'. His hopes to produce great literature that later ages would 'not willingly let... die' put him firmly in the line of Spenser and Jonson (*An Apology Against a Pamphlet*, *CPW* I: 890; *Reason of Church-Government*, *CPW* I: 810). But Milton took a more oppositional stance towards the established political and religious structures of authority in England – and the literature associated with them – than either Spenser or Jonson, who, for all their criticism, discomfort or disillusion, were part of the system of patronage in England and whose writings praised the monarch or others in positions of power. Jonson wrote poems for noble patrons and masques for the court, eventually gaining a stipend from the crown. Spenser's epic was dedicated to Queen Elizabeth in an effort to position himself as England's laureate and to gain patronage. It is telling of Milton's difference that his major poetry was not dedicated to royal or noble persons, and indeed was often sharply critical of monarchy. Milton's religious zeal, combined with his sense that the Reformation was threatened in England by the country's political and religious institutions, produced a different, more oppositional sense of his role as a poet – and of his relation to his society and its cultural productions.

If Milton embraced the moral function of literature voiced by Sidney, Spenser and Jonson, he gave it a more sharply religious emphasis. Where Spenser praised the

Queen as his Muse and Jonson traced his inspiration to the Muse of the classical poets, Milton suggested he was inspired by God. His invocations in *Paradise Lost* and *Paradise Regained* recall the claims of divine inspiration by the devotional poets George Herbert (*The Temple*, 1633) and Aemelia Lanyer (*Salve Deus Rex Judaeorum*, 1611) as well as the prophetic claims of religious radicals during the 1640s and 1650s. Jonson's ethical poet, upholding virtue and castigating vice, becomes a decidedly religious and prophetic figure in Milton, who in all of his writing, whether poetry or prose, is concerned with furthering the cause of true religion and attacking the forces and examples of ungodliness and idolatry in his society. Sixteenth-century Christian humanism, which sought to assimilate to Christianity the literary and ethical legacy of the classical world, had focused its attention on ethical rather than religious issues, which were becoming increasingly divisive with the Reformation. But for Milton, 'reformed' religion was at the centre of life. For him, all human experience – politics, love, the writing of literature – existed in relation to God. Thus, not only does religion assume an important place in his sense of the role of the poet and literature, but his religious beliefs colour his view of his literary predecessors and contemporaries and mark his revaluations of English literary tradition.

Comus, Spenser and Cavalier Poetry

As early as *Comus* (1634), written almost a decade before the Revolution when political and religious troubles were brewing, Milton adopts this critical stance as he positions himself in relation to recent English literature. In writing his masque, Milton announced his affiliation to Spenser's *Faerie Queene*, with its Protestant, reformed perspective, as he revalued literary forms and conventions that were linked with a religious politics and court with which he was increasingly at odds.

The court masque had been the pre-eminent literary genre supporting royalist culture and the values of absolutist monarchy (Orgel 1975; Goldberg 1983: 55–112). The masques of Jonson and his poetic sons exalted the god-like power of the king to order the world and subdue his subjects, though Jonson tried to insist that such power was godlike only so far as it was characterized by reason and virtue. Jonson had tried to turn the masque into a more serious form; he insisted that poetry (not spectacle) was its soul, hoping to make his masques an instrument of instruction (not mere flattery) for the royalty and nobility. Nevertheless, Jonson's masques, for all his assertions of ethical independence, embodied the absolutist ideology of the early Stuart kings, James I and Charles I.

Milton learned much from Jonson about the ethical possibilities of the masque and borrowed the figure of Comus from Jonson's *Pleasure Reconciled to Virtue*. By the 1630s, however, the masque was for Milton a tainted form. It expressed the ethos of a court that embraced the notion of the 'divine right' of kings and a religious ceremonialism that Milton thought suspiciously Catholic.

In writing *Comus* Milton reformed the masque, making it politically independent of the court and emphatically Protestant. Performed in Ludlow in the [Welsh] Marches, his 'puritan' masque turned the genre away from the court of Charles, criticizing the court's luxury and its ethos of sensuality and corrupt ritual, which Milton represented in the seductive but villainous Comus and his speeches (McGuire 1983; Norbrook 1984a: 245–65; Marcus 1986: 169–212; Wilding 1987: 28–88; Guibbory 1998: 157–72). Milton's 'reformed' masque directed his praise, not to the king or the representatives of monarchy, but to virtue, chastity and religious purity as embodied in the person of the Lady. Her resistance to the forces of evil represented by Comus demonstrated the qualities Milton identified with true religion and suggested that England in the 1630s was threatened by dangerous forces of irreligion. *Comus*'s strongly Protestant vision of the godly beset by threats to their purity but triumphing is finally more indebted to Spenser than to Jonson (Norbrook 1984a: 251–3; Guillory 1983: 89–90; Quilligan 1983: 209–18; Guibbory 1998: 158–9, 163).

Part of Spenser's appeal lay not just in the beauty and skill of his poetry but in his commitment to the Reformation. In Spenser, Milton found a shared Protestant ethos and sense of what constituted the virtuous life. In *Areopagitica*, defending the need to allow even bad books to be published, Milton invoked Spenser as his exemplary teacher: 'That vertue therefore which is but a youngling in the contemplation of evil, and knows not the utmost that vice promises to her followers, and rejects it, is but a blank vertue, not a pure; . . . Which was the reason why our sage and serious Poet *Spenser*, whom I dare be known to think a better teacher then *Scotus* or *Aquinas*, describing true temperance under the person of *Guion*, brings him in with his palmer through the cave of Mammon, and the bowr of earthly blisse that he might see and know, and yet abstain' (*CPW* II: 515–16). For Milton, Spenser properly understood life, representing it in *The Faerie Queene* as a series of temptations or trials in which humans must make choices, rejecting evil and choosing the good. The hero's life and the reader's experience enact the arduous process of discerning the good in a complex, deceptive world (Quilligan 1983: 46). Spenser's chivalric, Protestant heroes are engaged in combat, resisting and destroying incarnations of evil. This Spenserian model of virtuous action informs all of Milton's mature writing: Milton assumes a combative, oppositional stance in his polemical prose, attacking the evil of prelacy, censorship and tyrannical monarchy; the heroes in *Comus*, *Paradise Lost* and *Paradise Regained*, and *Samson Agonistes*, all face temptation; and Milton challenges his readers to discriminate between good and evil and make virtuous choices in their own lives beyond the literary text.

Virtue for Milton is inseparable from religion. Where Spenser wished 'to fashion a gentleman' (who was a Protestant Christian), Milton wanted to fashion a godly person, who would incorporate the whole spectrum of Spenserian and humanist virtues, but whose primary, all-encompassing quality would be absolute devotion to God. Spenser devoted the first three books of *The Faerie Queene* to the distinct though related virtues of Holiness, Temperance and Chastity. Milton makes them inseparable in *Comus*.

In Book I of *The Faerie Queene*, in the allegory of the Redcrosse Knight and Una, Spenser presented England as on guard against the seductions of Roman Catholicism and defined the virtue of Holiness in a distinctly Protestant, anti-Catholic way. Under Elizabeth I, who enacted anti-Catholic legislation in response to a perceived Catholic threat to her reign, England positioned itself religiously and nationally against Rome. When Milton was writing *Comus*, the Church of England, under the influence of Archbishop William Laud and Charles I, seemed to be softening its stance towards Rome and placing a greater emphasis on ceremonial worship. Milton looked back in his masque to Spenser's strongly Protestant poetic as he undertook to defend true religion and combat the resurgence of idolatry.

Milton's *Comus*, with its journey through the dark woods and its trial of the Lady, who must resist temptation, draws on *The Faerie Queene* in important, some-times subtle ways. As the masque celebrates Chastity, embodied in the Lady and extolled by her brothers, it reveals its genealogical link with the third book of *The Faerie Queene*, the Book of Chastity. Milton's Lady has the 'secret powre unseen' of Britomart, who fells knights (III. i. 6–7), though the Lady also exhibits the vulnerability of Spenser's Florimell, who is pursued by a forester threatening rape (III. i. 17) and excites the brutish lust of the witch's son (canto vii). The influence of Spenser is not limited to Book III. Milton identifies the Lady's Chastity with Temperance, the subject of Book II of *The Faerie Queene*. But the Lady is stronger than Guyon, who is aroused by the sight of the naked wrestling nymphs he encounters in Acrasia's Bower of Bliss and must be pulled away by the Palmer (II. xii. 63–9). Milton's heroine never for a moment wavers in resisting Comus's seductive speeches.

Comus himself recalls not just Jonson's figure of vice but Spenser's evil characters. Though Milton calls him Circe's son, Comus is also, in a sense, the offspring of Acrasia – the evil figure Guyon must subdue, the 'witch' who, like Comus, makes her companions 'drunken mad', who has a charmed 'cup', and binds them to 'her will' in 'chaines of lust and lewd desires' (II. i. 52, 55, 54). Guyon rejects Excesse's offer of Acrasia's charmed cup, much as the Lady refuses Comus's offer of wine. Acrasia's victims, who have been transformed into beasts, re-appear in Milton's masque as Comus's 'rout of monsters' (stage direction after line 92) who have lost their 'human countenance' (line 68).

If Comus recalls Acrasia in Book II, he also is related to Archimago, the evil enchanter of Book I. Comus appears to the Lady disguised as a humble shepherd, much as Archimago first appears to Redcrosse Knight and Una; and, like them, the Lady is taken in by his appearance of holiness and humility. Spenser's association of Archimago (maker of false images, the evil force behind Duessa) with the Roman Catholic Church allows Milton through his Spenserian echo to link Comus with Catholicism – an association reinforced as Milton describes Comus's Italian origins and his infiltration into England, where he, like Duessa (I. viii. 14) and Acrasia (II. xii. 49, 56), offers his followers a false Communion with his enchanting 'cup' (line 524) (Guibbory 1998: 157–72).

Spenser's Redcrosse Knight is not only deceived by Archimago but seduced by Duessa (the embodiment of false religion) once he is separated from Una. Milton's Lady is more like Una than the seriously flawed Redcrosse Knight. Chaste and temperate, she embodies true faith and is steadfast and unmoved by Comus's temptations. That the Satanic figure of Comus is ready to resort to violence suggests Milton's sense that in the 1630s faith was at special risk from the forces of antireligion. Heavenly providence (the Attendant Spirit) and grace (Sabrina) must rescue the Lady, much as Arthur comes to Redcrosse's aid (I. viii). But where Spenser was celebrating England's successful resistance of the Roman Catholic threat, Milton's adaptation of Spenser represents the danger he believed England currently faced from the infiltration of Catholicism in its culture, politics and worship.

Milton rewrites and critiques the Stuart masque through his creative adaptation of Spenser's Protestant epic. But Milton also draws on another body of English poetry in presenting the seductive power of evil. Comus speaks in the voice of the libertine and *carpe diem* poetry that had become associated with the court of Charles I when, with 'glozing courtesy' (line 161), he seeks to seduce the Lady and convince her to drink his wine. Comus urges the Lady to enjoy and use Nature's abundance –

> Wherefore did Nature pour her bounties forth,
> With such a full and unwithdrawing hand,
> Covering the earth with odours, fruits, and flocks,
> Thronging the seas with spawn innumerable,
> But all to please, and sate the curious taste?
>
> (lines 709–13)

He urges her to make use of her beauty and youth –

> List Lady be not coy, and be not cozened
> With that same vaunted name virginity,
> Beauty is Nature's coin, must not be hoarded,
> . . .
> If you let slip time, like a neglected rose
> It withers on the stalk with languished head.
>
> (lines 736–8, 742–3)

Comus recalls Spenser's temptress Acrasia, who sings a *carpe diem* song, hovering over her youthful victim who has been 'molten into lust' (II. xii. 73–5). In its focus on the body and sensual pleasure, in its lack of reference to the soul or an afterlife, *carpe diem* poetry (derived from classical culture) seemed to some English Christians to conflict with Christian values. Spenser had labelled it as dangerous and idolatrous by making it the poetry of Acrasia, much as Jonson did in *Volpone*, when his villain sang a *carpe diem* song to the virtuous Celia (III. vii. 165–82).

By the 1630s, the libertine stance of *carpe diem* poetry was the currency of the Cavalier poets associated with Charles I. Comus's invitation to love shares generic affiliation with such poems as Carew's 'Song: Persuasions to Enjoy', 'To A. L., Persuasions to Love' or 'A Rapture' ('We only sin when Love's rites are not done', line 114), and Herrick's more chaste 'Corinna's Going a-Maying' and 'To the Virgins, To Make Much of Time' (Maclean 1974). Comus's invitation to the Lady to drink 'this cordial julep here / That flames and dances in his crystal bounds / With spirits of balm' (lines 671–3) evokes both the offers of false Communion in *The Faerie Queene* and the royalist culture of ceremonial drinking attacked by William Prynne's pamphlet *Healthes: Sicknesse* (1628) and celebrated by Herrick in such poems as the 'His Farewell to Sack', 'The Welcome to Sack' and 'To Live Merrily, and To Trust to Good Verses'. Milton presents Comus's courtly revels as a false religion, luring Christians from their proper devotion to God and reason. By making Comus a Cavalier poet and spokesman for a life of pleasure and consumption (Marcus 1986: 187–8), Milton judges this poetry as the expression of a corrupt sensuality and luxury identified with the court of Charles I. Though Charles had set a tone of refinement and morality, Milton here continues to identify the court with corruption, and he distances himself from the king and his image-makers of the early 1630s, who presented the Caroline court as the locus of sexual morality, piety and decorum (Corns 1999: 16–21).

If luxury and sensuality are marked as unholy, chastity and temperance are given religious value. '[T]he sun-clad power of chastity' (line 781) manifests the Lady's temperance and devotion to God. Milton's view of chastity is indebted not just to Plato's ideal of chastity as loyalty to reason, but to Spenser, who depicted chastity as an attribute and symbol of holiness when he celebrated Una's virginal purity. Drawing on the metaphorical language of the Hebrew prophets (e.g. Jeremiah 3: 6 '[Israel] is gone up upon every high mountain and under every green tree, and there hath played the harlot') and Revelation (Revelation 18: 3: 'the kings of the earth have committed fornication with [the Whore of Babylon]'), Spenser's allegory of Holiness described spiritual transgression as yielding to seduction and fornication (*Faerie Queene*, I. ii. 14, I. vii. 2–7). Milton learned from Spenser (and the Bible) that chastity could be a powerful symbol for holiness, and that pure, uncontaminated faith could be represented by the closed, contained female body. Spenser's allegorical fictions and narrative tropes showed Milton how erotic relations between men and women – and personal virtues like chastity – could embody and represent moral and religious states.

Paradise Lost: Reforming Love

In early modern English culture, sexual and domestic relations between men and women were understood to be politically significant. In the reign of Elizabeth I, courtly or Petrarchan love became a coded discourse for political relations. Elizabeth enjoyed being addressed as a divine mistress. Sir Thomas Wyatt's and Sidney's love poetry used Petrarchan conventions to describe the frustrations of private, erotic relationships, but also to suggest their authors' struggles, anxieties and disappointments in seeking political favour (Marotti 1982). With this sense of the analogy between love and politics (the recognition that love poetry could simultaneously describe private erotic relations and public, political ones), Donne signified his disaffected distance from the court by rejecting Petrarchan conventions in the frankly sexual love poetry of his *Elegies* and *Songs and Sonets*. Yet a different connection between politics and love appears in the libertine strain of Cavalier poetry, which expressed the anti-puritan ethos of Charles's court culture while representing the absolutist power of the king in the powerful male speakers who claim all pleasures for themselves. Where libertinism in Donne had signified his opposition to political authority, in the Cavalier poets it could serve the established monarchy.

Not only were poetic discourses of love politically inflected, marriage itself was imagined in relation to the sociopolitical order. Marriage was the glue of the monarchical order – which is why Milton's pamphlets arguing for divorce seemed so radical. The patriarchal family (in which the husband was master and the wife chaste, silent and obedient) reflected and supported the monarchical system, in which subjects owed obedience to their king. Paul's view of marriage (as expressed in, for example, Ephesians 5. 22–33 and 1 Corinthians 11: 3), with the wife's subjection to the husband mirroring the church's obedience to Christ, was appropriated to give religious sanction to the connection between the patriarchal family and the Stuart state.

Understanding how conceptions of love, sexuality and domestic relations had political and religious significance in early modern England provides a necessary context for Milton's late major poems, especially *Paradise Lost*, in which the domestic relation of Adam and Eve assumes central importance.

From his early years, Milton shared the Renaissance ambition to produce great literature rivalling or surpassing the classics. At some point he thought of writing an Arthurian poem, perhaps in the manner of Spenser. *The Faerie Queene* had celebrated England, in the tradition of classical epics about the founding of countries and empires. In his patriotic epic romance, Spenser praised Elizabeth as Gloriana and offered genealogies suggesting a mythical, magical, chivalric past and a glorious future destiny for England. He connected Elizabeth/Gloriana (beloved of Arthur in the poem) to the idealized Arthurian past and identified England with true reformed religion through Una, who is betrothed to England's Redcrosse Knight at the end of Book I. But Milton published his epic, not at the end of the sixteenth century when the Spanish Armada had just been defeated (1588), but in the 1660s, when it seemed to him that false religion was flourishing. The Revolution, which had promised to establish a godly nation, had failed. In 1660 the English seemed to have demonstrated their preference for the bondage of idolatry by restoring the monarchy and the Church of England, both of which Milton saw as institutionalized idolatry. Rather than celebrating England, *Paradise Lost* presents the origins of idolatry and in the figure of Satan exposes the restored monarchy as Satanic in its origins and ambitions.

Instead of writing a patriotic epic, Milton focuses on the domestic sphere, perhaps reflecting the nonconformist values of religious dissenters in the Restoration, for whom the home was the site of their worship. In *Paradise Lost* erotic relations are primary, religiously significant and politically resonant, at their best constituting a sphere of value against the contemporary public world.

In *Paradise Lost* Milton shifts his hopes for the godly reconstruction of society from the public to the private sphere. Adam and Eve's harmonious relation before the Fall is an image of the proper relation between humans and God. Milton wrests the marriage of the first married couple away from those Elizabethan and Stuart writers who, invoking Adam's rule over Eve in Genesis, made the originary, hierarchical domestic relation a necessary image of and support for monarchy. In Milton's hands, Eve's submission to Adam is not the grounding of the patriarchal, monarchical politics of the Stuarts, but a sign of 'man's' obedience to God. Though it may offend our contemporary sensibilities, Eve's obedience to Adam, taught to her by God soon after her creation (IV. 449–91) and reinforced in the judgement after the Fall (X. 195–6), is used by Milton to represent human beings' necessary dependence on and loyalty to God, not to earthly rulers.

In *The Faerie Queene*, Spenser had presented both good and bad examples of love: as he writes, good 'may more notably be rad [i.e. discerned]' by a 'paragone / Of euill' (III. ix. 2). Milton similarly distinguishes between good and evil, holy and idolatrous erotic love, in the process drawing upon and speaking to earlier constructions of human love and sexuality in English poetry.

One of Milton's most radical departures from tradition in *Paradise Lost* is his insistence that the first couple enjoyed fully sexual relations in Paradise. Whereas Christian tradition generally held that Adam and Eve did not have intercourse before the Fall, Milton has them enjoy nuptial 'Rites' (IV. 742) in a 'bower' (IV. 738) which is the 'holiest' (IV. 759) part of Eden. They pray to God and then retire:

> Straight side by side were laid, nor turn'd I ween
> Adam from his fair spouse, nor Eve the rites
> Mysterious of connubial love refused:
> Whatever hypocrites austerely talk
> Of purity and place and innocence,
> Defaming as impure what God declares
> Pure, and commands to some, leaves free to all.
>   (IV. 741–7)

Behind the nuptial 'bower', created by God, stands Spenser's 'Garden of Adonis' (*Faerie Queene*, III. vi), where Venus raises Amoret, the twin sister of Belphoebe, the perpetual virgin. Amoret is destined for marriage and reproduction, a path which Spenser insists is good and divinely sanctioned. Like Milton, Spenser is concerned to redeem sexuality, and his Protestant emphasis on marriage rejects the Catholic privileging of celibacy. Spenser's celebration of married, sexual love in Book III, canto vi, anticipates Milton's defence of this 'Perpetual fountain of domestic sweets' (*PL* IV. 760). Nevertheless, if Spenser endorses a chaste (female) reproductive sexuality contained within marriage, he also glorifies the virginity of Britomart and Belphoebe in a way Milton never does in his epic.

Moreover, if the Garden of Adonis embodies a positive, reproductive sexuality, Spenser's *Faerie Queene* also associates sexuality with sin – not only by representing idolatry as seduction in Book I, but in its depiction of Acrasia's Bower of Bliss in Book II. In Acrasia's Bower, where sex is solely for pleasure, sexuality is dangerous and marked as unholy. At the end of Book II, Guyon destroys the Bower of Bliss – his greatest temptation – with the zeal of a reformer destroying a site of idolatry (King 1990: 100–2; Greenblatt 1980: 157–92).

Spenser's identification of sexual desire with idolatry and sin bears the weighty sanction of Christian tradition. In the New Testament, Paul had reinterpreted the Fall in light of his dualistic, eroticized contrast between the 'flesh' and the 'spirit' (see Romans 8; 1 Corinthians 6, 7, 9: 27). Paul's suspicions about sexuality were intensified by Augustine, whose negative representations of sexuality in *Confessions* and *The City of God* powerfully influenced Christianity. By the seventeenth century, the link between sexual love and idolatry, and between sexual desire and sin, had become a fixture of Western culture. It found expression in love poetry even as that poetry privileged erotic desire as constitutive of human identity. Petrarch, whose sonnet sequence influenced English lyric poetry long after Petrarchanism ceased to be fashionable (Dubrow 1995), idealized his beloved Laura but nevertheless associated his passion for her with idolatry. Sonnet 3 describes how he fell in love with Laura on Good Friday, when he should have been thinking about Christ's passion. After Laura's death, having suffered his own passion, Petrarch turns to God, converting (like Augustine in his *Confessions*) from his former idolatry.

Such an association of sexual love with sin and idolatry haunts sixteenth- and early seventeenth-century English poetry. We might think of the 'farewell to love' poems by Wyatt (Sonnet 31) and Donne ('Farewell to love'), which identify sexual love with self-destructiveness and disease. Donne's and Shakespeare's frequent punning on the word 'die' identifies orgasm with death, the universal punishment for original sin. Donne asked in 'Loves Alchymie', why we should 'Our ease, our thift, our honor, and our day . . . for this vaine Bubles shadow pay?' (lines 13–14). Sidney too renounced sexual love in the poem that begins: 'Leave me, O love which leadeth but to dust'.

Given this weight of negative associations, Milton's *Paradise Lost* seems revolutionary in its ecstatic portrayal of Edenic sexuality (Turner 1987: 12). In representing Adam and Eve's lovemaking as holy and describing the sanctity of the nuptial bower, Milton departs from the recent lyric tradition that had imaged active sexual desire as 'expense of spirit in a waste of shame' (as Shakespeare put it in Sonnet 129), and male desire for woman as excessive and idolatrous – though, as we shall see, these suspicions about love resurface in Milton's depiction of Adam's fall. The extent of Milton's departure from Christian orthodoxy and English poetic tradition might be seen in the fact that his Edenic nuptial bower recalls not just Spenser's good Garden of Adonis but Acrasia's evil Bower of Bliss, which Milton echoes but radically transforms.

Spenser tells us that Acrasia's 'Bowre of *Blisse*', the final and greatest temptation Guyon encounters, was situated in

> A place pickt out by choice of best aliue,
> That nature worke by art can imitate:
> In which what euer in this worldly state
> Is sweet, and pleasing vnto liuing sense,
> Or that may dayntiest fantasie aggrate,
> Was poured forth with plentifull dispence.
> (II. xii. 42)

This place is 'enclosed round about' (II. xii. 43). Its arbor is 'Framed' of 'wanton Yuie', 'fragrant Eglantine', roses; it is 'garnished' with 'flowres' of 'bounteous smels, and painted colors' (II. v. 29).

Milton's nuptial bower redeems Spenser's Bower of Bliss from sin, artifice and Excesse (who stood at the entrance: II. xii. 55–7). The bower in paradise

> was a place
> Chosen by the sovereign planter, when he framed
> All things to man's delightful use; the roof
> Of thickest covert was inwoven shade
> Laurel and myrtle, and what higher grew
> Of firm and fragrant leaf; on either side
> Acanthus, and each odorous bushy shrub
> Fenced up the verdant wall; each beauteous flower,
> Iris all hues, roses, and jessamin
> Reared high their flourished heads between, and wrought
> Mosaic; underfoot the violet,
> Crocus, and hyacinth with rich inlay
> Broidered the ground, more coloured than with stone
> Of costliest emblem: other creature here
> Beast, bird, insect, or worm durst enter none;
> (*PL* IV. 690–704)

Milton draws on the biblical description of the 'holy of holies' (Exodus 26: 31–3) as he rewrites Spenser's text (Guibbory 1996). Perhaps the connection between the nuptial bower, decorated by Eve, and Acrasia's ominously associates Eve with Spenser's beautiful, charming witch who lures men to their destruction – an association later confirmed when the narrator remarks that Adam in his fall was 'fondly overcome with Female charm' (IX. 999). Nevertheless, Milton's transformation of Spenser's site of sinful sexuality into the holiest place shows how far Milton has gone to redeem sex.

Milton was not the first English poet to write positively about sex. As noted above, Spenser celebrated married reproductive sexuality. So did some of the Caroline masques celebrating and idealizing the marriage of Charles I and Henrietta Maria (Corns 1999: 20–2) – though Milton's dislike of Charles's politics and religion, and his sense that Charles effeminately allowed himself to be ruled by his Catholic wife, made the marriage of the royal couple hardly exemplary for him. Other English poets glorified eros by separating human sexuality from religious and social prohibitions. Donne's *Elegies* and *Songs and Sonets*, like 'Confined Love' or 'The Indifferent', presented libertine arguments for unrestrained (usually male) sexual pleasure, attacking the legislation of monogamy as repressive and unnatural. In the 1630s and 1640s libertinism took a new turn with the *carpe diem* urgings of Carew's 'A Rapture' and Richard Lovelace's 'Love Made in the First Age: To Chloris', the explicit, pornographic eroticism of Herrick's 'The Vine' and Lovelace's 'To Amarantha, That She Would Dishevel Her Hair', and the cynical pragmatism of John Suckling's 'Sonnets'. But while Milton drew on the libertine tradition in describing the role of Eve's 'coy submission' before the Fall (Kerrigan and Braden 1986), he could not find in this poetry adequate resources for representing Adam and Eve's prelapsarian married sexuality.

Indeed, Milton's lyric epithalamion, embedded in Book IV of *Paradise Lost*, sharply condemns the ethos of Cavalier libertine poetry, identifying it with the court culture of Charles I and the recently restored Charles II, who was notorious for favouring libertines like John Wilmot, Earl of Rochester, and for his own sexual promiscuity, playfully alluded to by John Dryden in the opening of 'Absalom and Achitophel' (1681). Milton distinguishes the chaste but sexual conjugal relations of Adam and Eve from both fallen shamefulness and libertine licentiousness (Turner 1987: 166, 172).

> Hail wedded love...
>
> . . .
>
> Far be it, that I should write thee sin or blame,
> Or think thee unbefitting holiest place,
> Perpetual fountain of domestic sweets,
> Whose bed is undefiled and chaste pronounced,
> Present, or past, as saints and patriarchs used.
> Here Love his golden shafts employs, here lights
> His constant lamp, and waves his purple wings,
> Reigns here and revels; not in the bought smile
> Of harlots, loveless, joyless, unendeared,
> Casual fruition, nor in court amours
> Mixed dance, or wanton masque, or midnight ball,
>
> (IV. 750, 758–68)

Perhaps Adam and Eve's erotically charged married chastity might recall the royalist celebrations in the 1630s of Charles I's and Henrietta Maria's chaste marital sexuality (Corns 1999: 20–1). But for Milton, with his intense dislike of Charles, the royal couple could have only seemed a perverse parody of the Edenic couple, whose love Milton here distinctly separates from the realm of the court – a court he, as in *Comus*, identifies with libertine sensuality.

It was, I would argue, not the literary celebrations of Charles I and Henrietta Maria, nor the tradition of libertine poetry, but Donne's poetry of mutual love that offered an English poetic precedent for Milton's description of the sacredness of sexual love in Eden (Guibbory 1996). Donne might seem an unlikely literary ancestor for Milton, given their religious and political differences (Donne became a priest in the Church of England and a supporter of monarchy). But there was more to Donne than Ovidian, libertine poetry. Some of his *Songs and Sonets* had celebrated sexual love as sacramental, as possessing an integrating, transformative power. Donne too had broken from Christian orthodoxy, suggesting that sexuality and spirituality are intertwined and that the body is the 'booke' of spiritual love ('The Extasie', line 72). In 'The Good-morrow' and 'The Sunne Rising', the experience of consummated sexual love is redemptive, recapturing for the lovers an originary wholeness and giving them access to the divine. 'The Canonization' suggests that sexual love has conferred a special grace on the lovers and is spiritually exemplary for others.

Donne's celebration of the holiness of sexual love anticipates Milton's. But what may have also made Donne attractive to Milton is that these poems locate supreme value in the love relationship, which is defined *against* the corrupt public world of politics. The speaker in 'The Canonization' sets love against a world marked by competition, materialistic ambition, conflict and war; the speakers in 'The Sunne Rising' and 'The Good-morrow' contrast the wealth possessed by the lovers with the power and wealth of princes. The lovers in 'A Valediction Forbidding Mourning' are priests. Like Donne, Milton depicts his priests of love as enjoying a fully holy sexuality, and a purity and devotion in their 'rites' (which are both religious and sexual) that contrasts with the public realm of institutions, including the church, and with the mundane or decadent practices of other lovers lacking a transcendent connection with the divine. And, like Donne, Milton uses his celebration of love to criticize and mark his distance from his own contemporary political world, the world of 'court amours' (IV. 767).

Appropriating and transforming Spenser's bowers and echoing Donne's celebration of the sacredness of sexual, monogamous love, *Paradise Lost* challenges the traditional Christian suspicion of sexuality. Yet Milton's poem does not escape the influence of the Christian identification of sexual love with sin. Immediately after eating the forbidden fruit, Adam and Eve engage in sex that is the 'solace of thir sin' (IX. 1044). Moreover, Milton makes the cause of Adam's fall uxoriousness. His desire for Eve is stronger than his love of God – 'How can I live without thee, how forgo / Thy sweet converse and love so dearly joined' (IX. 908–9).

Even before Adam has fallen we hear in Raphael's ominous warnings the grim echo of Paul and those Renaissance poets who describe man's erotic desire for woman as self-destructive idolatry, a surrender to the weight of flesh, the body's pull of the spirit away from God. When Adam confesses to Raphael his 'passion' for Eve, his feeling that she is 'absolute . . . And in herself complete' (VIII. 530, 547–8), Milton's Raphael (like Spenser and Sidney) distinguishes between 'heavenly love', grounded in 'reason' (VIII. 591–2), and the earthly love that is 'carnal pleasure' (VIII. 593). Warning

Adam not to overvalue Eve or her 'fair' 'outside' (VIII. 568), Raphael invokes both the traditional suspicions of sexuality and the gendered linking of sexuality with sin that goes back at least to Paul and Augustine, who both identify sexual desire and the body with woman, who supposedly lures man from the spirit and God. Spenser had vividly represented this association of sexuality, sin and women in *The Faerie Queene*, when he described the evil Error and Duessa as women with monstrous, deformed 'nether' parts (I. i. 14–15, I. viii. 46–8). Acrasia, leaning over her sleeping lover, 'through his humid eyes did sucke his spright' (II. xii. 73). Despite Milton's eloquent defence of prelapsarian sexuality and of Eve's natural goodness, *Paradise Lost* similarly links sin with sexuality and woman. Sin (conceived by Satan at the moment of his rebellion), possesses the monstrous, repulsive sexual organs of Error and Duessa, the perverted progeny and ugliness of Error (Quilligan 1983: 80–98) and the superficially pleasing beauty of Duessa.

We see even in prelapsarian Eden that human love, from the first, contains the seeds of idolatry. From the moment that Eve is created, Adam feels that she is most valuable ('what seem'd fair in all the world, seemed now / Mean, or in her summed up', VIII. 472–3), that he cannot live without her. Milton makes human love both the most important, valuable part of human experience and the most dangerous. Adam's innocent account to Raphael of his feelings when Eve was created is suggestive of the idolatry that will be his downfall. He tells Raphael that, as he lay in a trance, Eve 'disappeared, and left me dark, I waked / To find her, or for ever to deplore / Her loss, and other pleasures all abjure' (VIII. 478–80). Adam's words strangely echo Donne's 'A Nocturnall upon S. Lucies Day', which voices a lover's grief at the death of his beloved – a woman who had been his soul, his life, his sun. Donne's speaker, like Adam, feels abandoned in a dark world, condemned to a living death, and all his thoughts are directed towards the woman. Donne's difficult poem represents erotic desire for the female beloved (which is sexual but not 'only' sexual) as both sacred and potentially idolatrous (she has become his God, his 'Sunne' (line 37), the source of his life and happiness), and the complexity of Donne's poem anticipates the tension in Milton's, where Adam's love for Eve is described as holy and desired by God but is also marked as (almost) inevitably idolatrous.

Milton's representation of Adam's feeling for Eve before the Fall recalls Donne's celebration of love as integrative and supremely valuable. In Adam's repeated insistence that he and Eve are one ('Bone of my bone, flesh of my flesh', VIII. 495, IX. 914–15), we hear not only the spare, cool statement of Genesis 2: 23 ('And Adam said, This is now bone of my bones, and flesh of my flesh: she shall be called Woman') but also the voice of Donne's impassioned lover in 'A Nocturnall' – or the lover in 'The Good-morrow' who announces with surprise and awe his sense of new-found completeness in love. Yet in Adam's powerful expressions of love we see the human condition that will make him choose, instinctively and instantly, to eat the fruit with Eve and share her fate.

Milton's account of the Fall multiplies the connections between sin and erotic desire. 'Sin', immediately after her birth in heaven, becomes the object of Satan's lust

– he takes 'joy' with her 'in secret' and she conceives Death (II. 765–6). After his Fall, Satan comes to earth to seduce the new creatures. He feels the 'fierce' (IV. 509), unsatisfied 'longing' of the Petrarchan lover (Kerrigan and Braden 1986: 43–7) – the desire Sidney and Mary Wroth had portrayed in their sonnets as agonizing, destructive, tormenting. Satan 'groan[s]' under 'torments inwardly' (IV. 88). Watching Adam and Eve embrace, he feels envy and jealousy (IV. 505–11). Satan's soliloquys or 'plaints', into which he pours 'His bursting passion' (IX. 98), recall not only the soliloquys of villains in Renaissance drama but the frustrations of Petrarchan lovers suffering in their unrequited desire.

Satan's language also echoes Cavalier poetry, which continued to have contemporary relevance in the late 1660s. The Cavalier poets were particularly congenial to Restoration court culture, with its Hobbesian view of human beings motivated by appetite and aversion, seeking to fulfil their desires. The libertine hero, Willmore, in Aphra Behn's play *The Rover* repeatedly echoes Suckling and Lovelace (III. 5. 25–32, 45–8; V. 430–6); and Congreve's heroine Millamant in *The Way of the World* praises 'Natural, easy Suckling' (Act IV, line 92). Satan's frustrated desire, intertwined with hate, is predatory as well as Petrarchan. As Milton compares Satan, bent on seduction, leaping over the wall of Paradise, to a 'prowling wolf, / Whom hunger drives to seek new haunt for prey' (IV. 183–4), we should recall not only the description in *Lycidas* of the corrupt clergy but also Suckling's cynical poems like 'Loves Feast' about the predatory sport of love, in which the interest of the male is in proportion to the difficulty of bagging the prey.

Satan's seduction of Eve is distinctly sexual and eroticized (Turner 1987: 260–3). While she sleeps in the bower, he, 'Squat like a toad, close at the ear of Eve', tries 'by his devilish art to reach / The organs of her fancy', attempting in a kind of rape to make her conceive 'phantasms and dreams' (IV. 800–3). Satan's words arousing Eve – 'Why sleepst thou Eve? Now is the pleasant time' (V. 38) – echo not only the Song of Songs (Song of Solomon 2: 10–13) but Herrick's 'Corinna's Going a-Maying', which (alluding to Charles's controversial 'Proclamation' endorsing the traditional festivals) urges Corinna to 'get up' from bed and 'come forth' and enjoy the rites of spring (lines 40, 1, 5, 16). Though Satan's first attempt on Eve is a kind of coitus interruptus, thwarted when Ithuriel touches Satan with his spear (IV. 810–11), in Book IX he succeeds. Here the seduction is couched in still more explicit sexual terms, even as Satan's address to Eve recalls the delicate seductive rhetoric of courtly or Petrarchan lovers, whose language of flattery and devotion masks their desire for control.

When Satan finds Eve alone in the Garden, his appearance is curiously phallic and his approach to her sexually charged (IX. 499–503). He addresses her boldly, 'as in gaze admiring' (IX. 524). 'Fawning' like a submissive but insistent courtly lover, he 'licked the ground whereon she trod' (IX. 526). Milton's Satan addresses Eve in the hyperbolic language of courtly love – 'Wonder not, sovereign mistress . . . who art sole wonder' (IX. 532–3) – summing up and critiquing courtly and Petrarchan love poetry as well as the libertine seduction lyric, which turns out to be its fraternal twin.

Satan tells her she is the creature 'all things living gaze on' (IX. 539), as Milton exposes the idolatrous nature of such worship as well as the desire for power behind seduction.

In encouraging Eve to taste the fruit, Satan, like Comus, echoes the Cavalier poets. His insistence that Eve deserves universal admiration – that 'here / In this enclosure wild, these beasts among, /... one man except, / Who sees thee? (And what is one?) Who shouldst be seen / A goddess among gods, adored and served / By angels numberless' (IX. 542–3, 545–8) – sounds very much like Edmund Waller's famous 'Song' (Maclean 1974) –

> Tell her that's young,
> And shuns to have her graces spied,
>   That hadst thou sprung
> In deserts where no men abide,
>   Thou must have uncommended died.
>
>   Small is the worth
> Of beauty from the light retired;
>   Bid her come forth,
> Suffer herself to be desired,
>   And not blush so to be admired.
>   (lines 6–15)

As Satan offers Eve knowledge, his invitation carries the sexual associations of the word 'to know', which make the seductive language of Cavalier *carpe diem* poetry peculiarly appropriate. 'Goddess humane, reach then, and freely taste' (IX. 732), he says, awakening the 'longing' (IX. 743) that will lead her to eat the fruit and for the first but not last time to experience 'Carnal desire' (IX. 1013), where sex is divorced from the worship of God.

Samson Agonistes: Renouncing Love

Despite the suspicions about love and sexuality, *Paradise Lost* glows with a sense of potential in love that is emphasized by the reconstruction of Adam and Eve's relation after the Fall and by their departure hand in hand at the end of the poem. The case is very different in the last poems Milton published. In *Paradise Regained* (1671), Satan does not even bother to tempt the Son with sex, knowing that the Son is not attracted to women. In *Samson Agonistes* (1671), women, sexuality and male erotic desire for women are firmly associated with idolatry, as sexual love is stripped of sacred possibilities.

In *Samson*, idolatry is identified with sexual desire, and holiness is defined as distinctly 'masculine' – an important change both from *Paradise Lost*, with its glorification of Edenic sexuality, and from *Comus*, where the Lady represented the godly person. Samson characterizes the attraction to Dalila that led him to betray God by revealing the secret of his strength as a 'foul effeminacy' which 'held me yoked / Her bond-slave' (lines 410–11). Samson's sense of being unmanned not just by Dalila but by his own sexual desire recalls Spenser's description of Redcrosse Knight, who in his 'solace' with Duessa took off his 'armour' and 'shield' (I. vii. 4–8): 'his manly forces gan to faile, / And mightie strong was turnd to feeble fraile' (I. vii. 6). We might also see in the emasculated Samson the effeminized young victim of Acrasia, who lies 'sleeping by her', 'His warlike armes . . . hong vpon a tree' (II. xii. 79–80). In *Samson Agonistes* as in the first two books of *The Faerie Queene*, sexuality is identified with effeminacy and idolatry, with betrayal of God. Distinctly absent from *Samson* is any effort to counterbalance negative images of sexuality with positive ones of marriage and generation.

As in *Comus*, echoes of Spenser invest *Samson Agonistes* with a reformed religious perspective that has contemporary point. When Dalila approaches Samson, the Chorus describes her as 'bedecked, ornate, and gay' (line 712) – metaphors that represent her as a 'ship' (line 714), traditionally an image of prostitution. But Milton's language also recalls Spenser's Duessa, 'robd of royall robes, and purple pall, / And ornaments that richly were displaid' (I. viii. 46). As Spenser's description of Duessa is modelled on the Whore of Babylon in Revelation (17: 3–5), identified by ardent Protestants with the Church of Rome, so Milton's echo of Spenser identifies Dalila as a figure of false religion. Milton transforms the biblical Dalila into the literary daughter of Duessa, suggesting the dangerous power of the idolatry that Samson must resist – and making that idolatry carry anti-Catholic associations relevant in the 1660s, when the restoration of the Church of England seemed to Milton to have revived the idolatrous ceremonial worship of the 1630s. Evoking the contemporary relevance of Samson's story through the echoes of the anti-Catholic Spenser, Milton implies that his contemporaries also must reject the lure of Dalila, of a false ornamental religion.

Once again we find love and religion, seduction and idolatry, linked. But in *Samson Agonistes*, in a striking departure from *Paradise Lost*, Samson's regaining his status as God's chosen depends on his conquest of his own sexuality and his desire for women. In Samson's divorce from his wife Dalila, Milton represents Samson's successful rejection of idolatry, his renunciation of his idolatrous past. Divorce, not marriage, becomes the symbolic act that figures 'man's' proper relation to God, as now marriage is identified with the destructive idolatry that Spenser had reserved for non-marital sexual desire.

I would suggest that we might also, finally, see in Milton's solitary hero – rejecting the lures of sexuality and marriage to be only God's spouse – Milton's own turning away from the seductive lure of English love poetry. In *Comus* and particularly *Paradise Lost*, Milton had echoed and preserved the beautiful erotic lyric poetry of seventeenth-century England even as he judged it and found it morally, religiously wanting – much as the pagan gods in his early Nativity Ode were lovingly described even as they were cast out at the birth of Christ. In Milton's last poems, however, English love poetry, with its privileging of human erotic experience, seems finally set aside in the masculine service of God.

BIBLIOGRAPHY

Writings

Donne (1967); Herbert (1974); Jonson (1965); Lanyer (1993); Maclean (1974); Shakespeare (1997); Sidney (1989); Spenser (1965).

References for Further Reading

Corns (1999); Dubrow (1995); Gardner (1965); Goldberg (1983); Greenblatt (1980); Gregerson (1995); Guibbory (1996, 1998); Guillory (1983); Helgerson (1983); Kerrigan and Braden (1986); King (1990); Marcus (1986); Marotti (1982); McGuire (1983); Norbrook (1984a); Orgel (1975); Quilligan (1983); Stevens (1985); Turner (1987); Wilding (1987).

6

Milton's English

Thomas N. Corns

Alastair Fowler, in the introduction to his first edition of *Paradise Lost*, put the issue declaratively: 'What was left of the attack [on Milton's style] has been routed – surely with finality' (Milton 1968: 430). He alluded to the conclusion of what Christopher Ricks, its eventual victor, had termed 'The Milton Controversy' (Ricks 1967: 1–21). The sometimes fierce and always animated critical exchange – Ricks with hindsight called it 'bitter and important' (Ricks 1968: xi) – originated in F. R. Leavis's revaluative (or more precisely devaluative) account of Milton's style, first published in 1933 in *Scrutiny*, the periodical he had founded, and reissued in his sweeping and influential *Revaluation: Tradition and Development in English Poetry* (Leavis 1936: 42–67). I say 'originated', though at the core of Leavis's objection to Milton is a reservation about his Englishness which can be traced with facility to some of his eighteenth-century editors and critics, and most decisively to Dr Johnson, whose asseveration that 'He was desirous to use English words with a foreign idiom' (Johnson 1963: 142) confirmed earlier prejudices. Jonathan Richardson, an early editor, had observed, 'Milton's language is English, but 'tis Milton's English; 'tis Latin, 'tis Greek English; not only the words, the phraseology, the transpositions, but the ancient idiom is seen in all he writes' (quoted by Fowler, *PL*: 15). I shall return shortly to consider the malign legacy of eighteenth-century scholarship.

In fairness to Leavis I should concede that some of his comments, on Milton's prosody, have received a less than complete response. Though there have been technical accounts of the metre, by Robert Bridges (rev. edn 1921) and by S. Ernest Sprott (1953), our understanding of prosody at theoretical and methodological levels has in recent years been carried further, most influentially in the work of Derek Attridge (see especially Attridge 1982). A thorough engagement from an Attridgean perspective, perhaps augmented by the evidence of experimental phonology, is overdue. Meanwhile, Leavis's challenge remains unanswered. It is based on a responsiveness to the *sound* of the poetry: 'Here, if this were a lecture, would come illustrative reading-out . . . ' (Leavis 1936: 44). The passage he discusses, 'one of the exceptionally good passages', is *Paradise Lost* I: 730–47. In lieu of a no doubt purposeful reading, Leavis, with stresses and italics, demonstrates 'the usual heavy rhythmic pattern, the hieratic stylization, the swaying ritual movement back and forth, the steep cadences' (45). And certainly one could read the passage in that way – just as one could read it in ways that sensitively explore the subtle accommodations between its demanding syntax, its rhetorical figuring and the residual pulls of an underlying prosodic pattern. Reading it intelligently and sensitively has some obvious advantages over the alternative. The opening illustrates well some demonstrable characteristics of Milton's mature verse:

> The hasty multitude   730
> Admiring entered, and the work some praise
> And some the architect: his hand was known
> In heaven by many a towered structure high,
> Where sceptred angels held their residence,
> And sat as princes, whom the súpreme king   735
> Exalted to such power, and gave to rule,
> Each in his hierarchy, the orders bright.
>
>   (*PL* I. 730–7)

Lineation and syntax are in a highly distinctive and unusual relationship in Milton's verse. Compared with contemporary narrative poets, who eschew blank verse, he is far less likely to have sentences end or begin at line endings, though the coincidence of sentence-ending and line-ending is far higher than were the positioning within the decasyllabic lines wholly random. Again, Milton's lines frequently have major syntactic divisions within them. Major caesuras often occur towards the middle of lines. Sentence breaks are commonest between the fourth and fifth syllables and the sixth and seventh syllables (Corns 1990a: 37–40). Such connections between the prosodic and syntactic levels provide the recurrent patterning of his verse form, allowing complex grammatical structures to be reconciled to the exigencies of metre and lineation. We see it well here, in combination with rhetorical patterning. The first sentence begins in syllable five and wraps over the line ending. Of line 731, three of the first four syllables carry some kind of stress. Then, after a major syntactic break between main clauses, occurring between syllables five and six, two half lines subtly balance each other:

> the work [noun phrase – object] some praise [verb phrase]
> and some ['praise' deleted] [verb phrase] the architect [noun phrase – object].

Leavis notes a stress on 'some' in line 732, but a nimble reader, recognizing the rhetorical pattern, would probably put some stress, too, on the corresponding word in line 731. Thereafter, one sentence fills lines 732–7, with major clausal or phrasal breaks within all lines except 734, though the caesura falls differently in each case – in 733 between syllables 2 and 3; in 735 between syllables 5 and 6; in 736 between syllables 6 and 7; in 737 (probably, depending quite how you read 'the orders' and 'hierarchy') between syllables 7 and 8. The double end-stopping of line 734 and the end-stopping of line 737 reassert the underlying metrical structure. So too, in a context of considerable variation in stress, does the regularity of the last four syllables of the concluding lines:

the	sú	preme	king [on the stress on 'sú', see Fowler, *PL*: 105]
and	gave	to	rule,
the	or	ders	bright.

In each line, the stress pattern in syllables 1–6 is not regular. This example seems to me much removed from a 'swaying ritual movement'. Rather, Milton observes the subtlest of variations in stress pattern and caesura placement, while producing a sentence of considerable syntactical complexity – a main clause followed by two dependent clauses ('Where . . . residence' and 'And sat as princes'), the last of which supports two further dependent clauses, which conclude the sentence. Yet the prosodic framework is carefully and precisely restated, the 'usual . . . pattern' still recognizable in a context that still allows neatly turned rhetoric and extended syntactic development.

One example can scarcely support a convincing larger argument, though the fact that it is an example that Leavis had selected for censure has some polemical value. Till the work is done, the best guidance the reader can have about Milton's verse is the evidence of his or her own ears. Hearing the poem read by competent readers – and reading it aloud oneself – are exercises of enormous value.

I turn from prosody, a neglected area of Milton studies, to the core of Leavis's case and the responses it has elicited. As he has it,

> The extreme and consistent remoteness of Milton's medium from any English that was ever spoken is an immediately relevant consideration. It became, of course, habitual to him; but habituation could not sensitize a medium so cut off from speech – speech that belongs to the emotional and sensory texture of actual living and is in resonance with the nervous system; it could only confirm an impoverishment of sensibility. In any case, the Grand Style barred Milton from essential expressive resources of English that he had once commanded. [Leavis has just discussed a passage from *Comus* which he quite liked.] (Leavis 1936: 51)

We are back with Richardson and Johnson, though remoteness from spoken English is now unequivocally damning. Battle-lines of some complexity were soon drawn. T. S. Eliot, in an essay of 1936, bemoaned the abiding influence of Milton's 'damage to the English language' (Eliot 1936: 40), and even in his later, more sympathetic reconsideration he observes, 'Every distortion of construction, the foreign idiom, the use of a word in a foreign way or with the meaning of the foreign word from which it is derived rather than the accepted meaning in English, every idiosyncrasy is a particular act of violence which Milton has been the first to commit' (Eliot 1947: 69). In response, some – foremost among them, C. S. Lewis – argued that Milton's language was indeed remote from ordinary speech, but appropriately so, in decorum with its genre: 'To blame it for being ritualistic or incantatory, for lacking intimacy or the speaking voice, is to blame it for being just what it intends to be and ought to be. It is like damning an opera or an oratorio because the personages sing instead of speaking' (Lewis 1967: 40). Others, led initially by William Empson, developed a different approach, seeking to demonstrate the inadequacy of Leavis's and Eliot's account of Milton's style by showing it to possess the kinds of precision and subtlety that its opponents so value in Shakespeare or in Donne. In a remarkable essay from 1935 Empson plays off the strictures of Milton's eighteenth-century commentators to identify examples of detailed, nuanced stylistic achievement, to show a Milton who puns, who quibbles, who writes with a concreteness and clarity, who develops a 'fluid grammar' that demands his reader's creative attention as surely as Donne at his trickiest (Empson 1967: 123–55).

Ricks's victory is secured by taking the Empson approach and making from it a larger argument, showing *Paradise Lost* to possess – sometimes in the very places that its detractors had cited – expressive qualities of the kind that mid-twentieth-century criticism valued. Fowler, therefore, felt evident confidence in drawing a line under 'The Milton Controversy'.

Ricks remained convinced that his debate with Leavis and others really mattered, that the business of criticism rested – at its most fulfilling – in 'the verbal criticism which now seems one of the most important and useful ways of approaching literature' (Ricks 1967: 1). Yet even as he celebrated Milton's genius (and his own demonstration of it), that critical mode was rapidly approaching its eclipse. In subsequent decades, questions of content and ideology, relating to Milton's politics, his views on gender, his theories of salvation, his views on the Trinity, and the like, have predominated in Milton studies, often producing genuinely illuminating answers. They predominate in this collection; apart from this chapter, 'verbal criticism' figures significantly only in the contributions of John Hale and John Leonard. The new emphases, if such they are ('The Milton Controversy' was pretty much a British game; North American attention was largely directed elsewhere), may well reflect the failure of a larger project of the later 1960s and the 1970s, the development of a critical methodology that rested on appropriation of the categories, assumptions and methodologies of linguistics. The failure of this approach to break through as a major perspective in English studies in part reflected the popularity in influential circles of linguistic systems premised on the semiotics of Saussure, rather than then current models, which owed much to the followers of J. R. Firth and to Noam Chomsky. In part, the failure owed something to Stanley Fish's withering critique, most devastatingly expressed in his essay 'What is stylistics and why are they saying such terrible things about it?' (Fish 1980: 68–96). Thus, he avers, 'they [stylisticians] produce interpretations which are either circular, mechanical reshufflings of the data – or arbitrary – readings of the data that are unconstrained by anything in their machinery' (90). Addressing the questions central to verbal criticism within a linguistics-influenced framework has certainly proved unattractive to most Miltonists.

But that is not to say that there has been no development of the controversy surrounding Milton's English. As the position stood in 1968, the accomplishment of some passages of *Paradise Lost* was convincingly demonstrated. But our real knowledge and appreciation of the minor poems and Milton's prose was very undeveloped, nor had the typicality of the phenomena Ricks identified been established – his account rests on close reading of about 500 lines in total. The issues were addressed by Archie Burnett, who demonstrated effectively how a linguistic-stylistic account could illuminate most of the minor poems (Burnett 1981), while I published a study of the prose (Corns 1982) and a wider-ranging account of all the vernacular poetry (Corns 1990a).

Milton's Englishness emerges strongly both in Burnett's work and my own. Burnett is deeply sceptical about too readily advancing the larger arguments: 'Generalizations about an author's style all too often amount to little more than hastily indulged prejudices or crude abstractions, but some provide useful beginnings for investigation of the more specific functions of style in varying contexts' (Burnett 1981: 99). His book follows the latter course, as, with great deftness, he distinguishes Milton's stylistic preferences in 'L'Allegro' from those in 'Il Penseroso' or ponders the high incidence of adjectives in 'Lycidas'. His study demonstrates that Milton's style is subtly inflected in different contexts, and those variations usually take the form of the atypically high or low incidence of linguistic variables that are present in all texts: what is distinctive is not the appearance of unique features but their relative frequency.

My own accounts have attempted more generalization; what emerges is that Milton, in his syntax and his lexis, escapes the strictures of un-Englishness that his eighteenth-century critics, and Leavis and Eliot, directed against him.

In many respects, his prose syntax typically resembles that of those contemporaries who engaged in the controversies in which he immersed himself. Broadly, it conforms to the norms of the prose written by serious, educated, mid-seventeenth-century Englishmen, adapting the discourses of oratory and academic exposition to the exigencies of polemic in a variety of subgenres which emerged rapidly as the conflicts of the 1640s and 1650s unfolded.

Certainly, among situationally analogous contemporaries, there are some prose styles that are syntactically very different from Milton's own. Indeed, there are some remarkable prose stylists among his contemporaries, and the interest often inheres in their syntactical predilections. Most await patient investigation – only Thomas Browne, among Milton's contemporaries, has in recent years received appropriate attention (Haverstein 1999). But I can confidently say that Milton produces nothing like this passage from the Ranter writer, Abiezer Coppe:

Deare hearts! Where are you, can you tell? Ho! where be you, ho? are you *within*? what,
no body at *home*? Where are you? What are you? Are you asleepe? for shame, rise, its
break aday, the *day* breaks, the *Shaddows* flie away, the *dawning* of the *day* woes [i.e.
woos] you to arise, and let him *into* your *hearts*. (Smith 1983: 51)

An incipient pastiche of the Song of Solomon is nudged into a syntactical framework
imitative of a colloquial and oral discourse, with discourse markers like 'Ho!' and
'ho?'.

Again, Milton's prose, while it frequently quotes scripture and incorporates biblical
imagery into its figurative language, avoids the kinds of mock-liturgical syntax we
find in the prayers in *Eikon Basilike*, the posthumously published apologia apparently
written by Charles I:

Arise O Lord, lift up thy selfe, because of the rage of mine Enemies, which increaseth more and
more. Behold them that have conceived mischiefe, travelled with iniquity, and brought forth
falshood. (Charles I 1649: 65)

Again, models outside the usual discourse of prose controversy are shaping the syntax;
here, of course, English translations of the Psalms (specifically, Psalm 7) and the Book
of Common Prayer. Hence the short and relatively simple sentences, often in the
imperative or optative moods. Not a feature of Milton's English prose.

Among Milton's earlier adversaries was Bishop Joseph Hall, highly regarded in his
own day as a mannered prose stylist, appreciated for his pithy, epigrammatical style,
and contemporaneously called 'the English Seneca'. Here's an example of that Senecan
style:

But stay; Where are we, or what is this we speak of, or to whom? ... Which Church we
mean? My simplicity never thought of any more Churches of *England* but one; Now this
very dayes wiser discovery tels us of more.... (Hall 1640[/1]: 39)

Of course, there is nothing especially latinate about these sentences. Hall, writing
straightforwardly English syntax and using straightforwardly English words, observes
the aesthetic imperatives of a brief, non-periodic style of Latin prose, qualities like
precision and ellipsis, which characterize the prose of Seneca. As such, his style
diverges widely from most polemicists of the 1640s. His sentences are much shorter,
much simpler, and Milton remarks on his eccentricity as something affected; they are
'curtall gibes, by one who makes sentences by the Statute, as if all above three inches
long were confiscat' (*CPW* I: 873; see Corns 1982: 31–4).

Milton's own sentence structure in prose largely resembles that of many of his
contemporaries engaged in the debates that animated him. In terms of length and
clausal structure there are broad affinities with writers like William Prynne or
Marchamont Nedham or the Smectymnuans. Nor is there anything un-English
about the way he orders clauses within sentences. There is no evidence that he

postpones main clauses in ways which may be adduced as latinate. Certainly he writes a lot of very long sentences, but they would have struck his original readers as less remarkable than they do his modern readers unfamiliar with the broad range of early modern prose polemic. In a marginal way, Milton's sentences are perhaps a little more complicated than most. In his case main clauses often support lots of subordinate clauses, and subordinate clauses often themselves support a number of clauses dependent upon them (though others also generate sentences like these). Consider a typical example, from *Of Prelatical Episcopacy*:

> Now come the Epistles of *Ignatius* to shew us first, that *Onesimus* was Bishop of *Ephesus*; next to assert the difference of *Bishop* and *Presbyter*, wherin I wonder that men teachers of the Protestant Religion, make no difficulty of imposing upon our belief a supposititious ofspring of some dozen Epistles, whereof five are rejected as spurious, containing in them Heresies and trifles, which cannot agree in Chronologie with *Ignatius*, entitling him Arch-Bishop of *Antioch Theopolis*, which name of *Theopolis* that City had not till *Iustinians* time long after, as *Cedrenus* mentions, which argues both the barbarous time, and the unskilfull fraud of him that foisted this Epistle upon *Ignatius*. (*CPW* I: 635–6)

Here is a sentence of over a hundred words, no great rarity in the prose of Milton or many of his contemporaries, though this one (like so many in Milton) is beautifully organized and controlled. Milton's sentence structure is sometimes erroneously termed 'circular'. This sentence is circular only in the sense that it begins and ends with the contemplation of the church father Ignatius; in between a driving polemical force, carried from dependent clause to dependent clause, compellingly convinces his readers of the folly of the argument he is destroying. Main clause: here are the epistles of Ignatius; dependent clause: this is what they purport to do; dependent clause: in this, advocates of basing church government on patristic evidence foist in phoney epistles; dependent clause: among these epistles five are certainly spurious; dependent participial construction: they contain heresies; dependent clause: they violate chronology; dependent participial construction: they call him archbishop of Antioch Theopolis; dependent clause: 'Theopolis' wasn't part of its name till Justinian's time; dependent clause: citation of Cedrenus; dependent clause: it goes to prove that the epistles are not only fakes, they're fakes originating in a time of barbarous ignorance. So the epistles, which entered the sentence in its first clause as champions of prelatical church government, are dismissed at the end as feeble imposters; and a great deal has happened in between (Corns 1982: 41).

The example is, I think, typical of the experience of reading Milton's prose. It often incorporates the reader into quite complex arguments expressed in sentences of matching complexity; lots of components of the argument, which in modern prose may be distinguished into shorter sentences, hang together, persuasively and inextricably interconnected, in large structures. But seventeenth-century prose was often like this. Indeed, Francis Bacon saw in the persuasive power of such large syntactical structures a positive impediment to the emergence of a scientific – rather than polemical or forensic – discourse in English. Such structures – he termed them 'methods' (*OED* 6. b) – make for convincing exposition, though, on his account, they preclude or discourage a critical reading, constituting 'a kind of contract of error between the deliverer and the receiver, for he that delivereth knowledge, desireth to deliver it in such a form as may be best believed, and not as may be best examined; and he that receiveth knowledge, desireth present satisfaction, than expectant enquiry' (Bacon 1965: 141; see also 32–3).

Milton, of course, aims in his prose to persuade (though, no doubt, he often believed in the truth of what he was saying). His chosen syntactical preferences perhaps tell us something about his intended readership. Certainly, no educated reader of Milton's own age would have found his prose hard to understand; he attracts a great deal of hostile response, but the charge of unintelligibility is never laid against him. The closest anyone comes is Samuel Parker, in an acerbic comment in *A Reproof to the Rehearsal Transprosed* on a passage from *Areopagitica*, that 'Such fustian bombast as this past for stately wit and sence in that Age of politeness and reformation' (Parker 1673: 191). But he writes from a Restoration perspective, when a new aesthetic of elegant plainness informed standards in prose style. However, if the educated reader could cope, the uneducated probably could not. Milton's prose is never populist. He addresses those who shared his own class culture in ways that excluded a wide readership. For Milton, theological speculation and political debate belong among a fairly narrowly defined community of scholars and among a narrowly defined political nation. Leveller manifestos were on occasion worn in the hatbands of the rank and file of the New Model Army as emblems of ideological affiliation. Milton's prose has also been iconized, though only in later ages, and then as inscriptions to adorn public institutions of learning (Corns 1992a: 55). Milton never attempts the common touch.

Milton's poetic syntax often approaches the complexities of his prose, in ways that do indeed distinguish his style from that of contemporary poets (though the proposition is not supportable in his non-narrative or non-dramatic verse). Stylistically, what really sets him apart from other poets is the high incidence of long sentences of considerable clausal complexity (Corns 1990a: 13–16). He transposes to poetic genres a syntax that is probably commonplace in educated prose, while still meeting the exigencies of the prosodic systems he has adopted.

Milton's longer sentences typically consist of a high incidence of subordinate clauses that are themselves dependent on subordinate clauses. The structural variants are very numerous, ranging from sentences in which the main clause supports a subordinate clause on which several clauses directly depend (relatively rare), through to sentences in which the main clause supports a dependent clause which supports a dependent clause which in turn supports a dependent clause and so on, perhaps through five or more levels of dependency. Of course, these two principal structures may be variously combined. I have illustrated the effects of such syntax elsewhere (Corns 1990a: 24–30; Corns 1994: 116–18). But let me here give just one example, in which I have marked the clausal and principal phrasal division. Satan is answering Gabriel's charge of pusillanimity:

A

[I therefore, I alone first undertook]

B

[To wing the desolate abyss,] [and spy

C   D

This new-created world,] [whereof in hell

E

Fame is not silent,] [here in hope to find

F

Better abode,] [and my afflicted powers

To settle here on earth, or in mid-air;]

G   H

[Though for possession put] [to try once more]

I

[What thou and thy gay legions dare against;]

J   K

[Whose easier business were] [to serve their Lord

L

High up in heaven,] [with songs to hymn his throne,]

M   N

[And practised distances to cringe,] [not fight.]

(*PL* IV. 935–45)

Figure 1 represents a plausible way of interpreting the relationship between the phrases and clauses, though, as so often, the syntax of Milton's sentence – like that of many complex sentences – is tractable to alternative constructions. What we have is a sentence that organizes a series of propositions in an intricate way. The main clause begins the sentence, its redundancy ('I . . . I') establishing a declarative mood. Satan lists the tasks he has undertaken in B, C and E, anticipating in D a practical objection – how could he have known about the earth? Then a complex of dependent clauses,

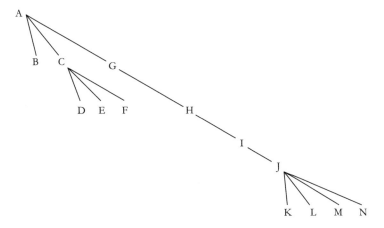

Figure 1　Paradise Lost IV. 935–45

tied to clause G, juxtaposes Satan's high-risk commitment with the lifestyle of the gay legions who still serve. A large rhetorical organization shapes the conflict between the issue developed in the C and G clusters, and the adversive asyndeton between M and N mirrors that implied antithesis. The sentence is both wholly typical of the processes by which Milton generates his longer sentences and in itself a beautifully fashioned syntactical structure. Note the way that, as in *Paradise Lost* I. 730–7, considered above, the concluding three lines are marked by perfect metrical regularity in their final four syllables:

to	serve	their	Lord
to	hymn	his	throne,
to	cringe,	not	fight.

The complex sentence, though its clauses may run over line endings and though its metrical pattern may exhibit a range of variation, concludes in a re-affirmation of the underlying prosodic discipline of the poem.

But besides the long and complex sentences Milton's verse is also characterized by distinctively high incidences of very short sentences, which are in turn characterized by their incidence of monosyllables (Corns 1990a: 16–21). Sometimes a ten-syllabled sentence, end-stopped, links passages of rhetorical elevation and syntactical complexity, as in the long exchange of which the last sentence was part:

> To whom with stern regard thus Gabriel spake.
>
> . . .
>
> To whom thus Satan, with contemptuous brow.
>
> . . .
>
> To which the fiend thus answered frowning stern.

> . . .
> To whom the warrior angel soon replied.
>   (*PL* IV. 877, 885, 924, 946)

The short sentences function in effect as scene directions, though again they contribute towards the assertion of the prosodic structure of the poem. But the effects can
sometimes be much more dramatic, especially when the words used are also short.
Thus, Manoa breaks off a long and rather ponderous account of his lobbying on behalf
of Samson with 'What noise or shout was that? It tore the sky' (*Samson Agonistes*, line
1472). Again, adversarial exchanges are often marked by such sentences. In the War in
Heaven Abdiel confronts Satan with 'Proud, art thou met?' (*PL* VI. 131). The Son
frequently speaks thus to Satan in *Paradise Regained*, as for example in:

>   do as thou find'st
> Permission from above; thou canst not more.
> They all had need, I as thou seest have none.
> Get thee behind me . . .
> Think not but that I know these things, or think
> I know them not . . .
> Me worse than wet thou find'st not . . .
>   Also it is written,
> Tempt not the Lord thy God, he said and stood.
>   (*PR* I. 495–6; II. 318; IV. 193, 286–7, 486, 560–1)

Of course, the kinds of variety in syntactical effect we have been considering reflect
Milton's alertness to the importance of variations, within a straightforwardly English
syntax, in the production of changes in rhetorical or emotional affect. As Ricks
perceptively observed,

> The Leavisite position assumes that Milton's style is continuously grand, and therefore
> continuously deviating from the usual spoken or written-word order. This is an odd idea
> to have about a poet who begins the most important book of his epic with the laconic
> audacity of
>   No more of talk where God and Angel Guest . . .
>   (Ricks 1967: 36)

Of course, in many of the examples we have been considering, 'normal' word
order, that gives us subject–verb–object or adjective–noun sequences among many
others, is not always followed. But English is a language that, throughout its written
history, has allowed considerable variation. In contemporary spoken English numerous variations in word order abound (famously in 'Do I not like that,' for example).
Fowler sharply observes that some of the allegedly un-English 'deviations' are common in seventeenth-century English and indeed in Old English too (Milton 1968:
434). Moreover, poetic genres admit such variations far more frequently than prose

ones, in part because of the need to meet exigencies of rhyme and metre. Thus, in 'Bermudas', Andrew Marvell uses a subject–object–verb sequence in the couplet 'Where he the huge Sea-Monsters wracks, / That lift the Deep upon their Backs'. Again, he inverts the adjective–noun sequence in 'He hangs in shades the Orange bright, / Like golden lamps in a green Night', to secure the iambic rhythm at the line end and effect the rhyme (Marvell 1984: 10–11). Such effects are so commonplace as to be unremarkable in early modern English verse, especially when it is rhymed. Milton, for the most part eschewing rhyme in his longer poems, is probably less constrained than Marvell in these examples, though inversions offer opportunities for rhetorical expressive and dramative effect ('Me worse than wet . . .'), and surely no experienced reader can be surprised or perplexed by inversion like 'orders bright' (*PL* I. 737, considered above), recognizing its contribution to the metrical organization of the line.

Ricks, following Empson, frequently invokes the commentary of eighteenth-century critics and editors of Milton to illuminate nuances of expression unremarked in the criticism of the first half of the twentieth century. Yet that critical and editorial tradition really has its origins in the cultural and linguistic changes that divide Milton's age – and Milton's English – from a subsequent readership. About his poetry and his prose, among close contemporaries there is no suggestion that his English cannot be straightforwardly understood. In Marvell's phrase, 'Thou singest with so much gravity and ease' (*PL*: 54); he would scarcely have attributed 'ease', presumably facility in composition, to a text if it were at the expense of his readers' understanding.

But Milton, we must recall, wrote without compromise to an educated readership, a readership expected to understand both complex sentences and a large vocabulary containing many 'hard words', to use a term contemporaneously current. The word stock of English had expanded very rapidly in the latter part of the sixteenth century and into the opening decades of the seventeenth, mainly through the adoption of loan-words from Greek and more particularly from Latin. Milton, like educated contemporaries writing in both verse and prose, freely uses the expanded words stock, probably no more aware of the words as 'foreign' than we are when we use them ourselves. Of course, the new vocabulary may indeed occasion some kinds of cultural exclusion. An obvious anxiety lies behind the production of the English-language dictionaries which appeared for the first time in the mid-seventeenth century, an anxiety that relatively uneducated readers, unfamiliar with the Latin words from which the new vocabulary derives, are excluded from properly understanding demanding texts. Tellingly, Robert Cawdrey in 1604 addresses his dictionary of hard words to 'Ladies, gentlewomen, and any other unskilful persons' (Green 1996: 149). The gambit shrewdly illuminates the patterns of literacy in early modern England (Cressy 1980): 'Ladies' and 'gentlewomen' because on the whole only such women could read at all; 'unskilful persons' because more educated men would have known Latin and so have understood the new words.

That last point is crucial. As new words entered the language, for the most part they did so in significations that were very close to what they meant in Latin (or

Greek). If you knew Latin (and Greek) you didn't need a dictionary to understand them, because they had senses close to the senses of the corresponding words in the source language. Over the seventeenth century the dynamics of semantic change very often carried them rapidly into new significations, and the original, point-of-entry meanings fell into desuetude. Thus it is that eighteenth-century commentators found it necessary to gloss words which Milton is using in senses no longer current. In so doing, those commentators characteristically ascribed to Milton latinate senses, when really he was simply using them in the senses which they were current when he wrote. These constitute the 'innumerable ghost Latinisms, which were raised by early editors and superstitiously believed in by their successors', as Fowler terms them (Milton 1968: 432). Their exorcism is a major accomplishment of his first edition, as 'not a Latinism' recurs persistently in his footnotes, and I have attempted to dispel a few shades that cling still to the text (Corns 1990a: 95–100).

The Englishness of Milton's English is established beyond dispute, but major questions remain about the relationships between the neoclassical cultural ideology inscribed in much of his work and the complex, multilingual intertext within which he writes and his chosen readers read.

The issues may usefully be related both to the continuing accumulation of evidence in linguistics relating to bilingualism and multilingualism (very usefully reviewed in Hamers and Blanc 1989) and to the linguistic agenda of Renaissance humanism. Milton probably knew ten languages – English, Latin, Greek, Hebrew, Aramaic, Syriac, Italian, French, Spanish and Dutch (Hale 1997: 8), though no doubt his competence varied widely, from first-language competence in English, to absolute competence in reading and considerable fluency in writing and speaking in Latin, to a much more limited reading competence in some of the other languages.

One of the principal indicators of language competence is the capacity to use a second language without 'interference', to use the current technical term, from a first language. Thus, a first-language German-speaker, speaking English, sometimes may extend the appropriate usage of 'make', under the influence of 'machen', to idioms where it is inappropriate (just as a correspondingly inept English-speaker will misuse 'tun', etymologically cognate with 'do', in German). These are errors eliminated by greater competence. They are of the kind that may occur in any bilingual context, and language teaching has recognized and for long sought to eliminate them.

Indeed, Latin itself had been substantially reformed in the fifteenth and sixteenth centuries to exclude from it vocabulary items introduced in the medieval period and to fix its word stock at what was current in the classical period. Many of those expunged neologisms no doubt were word formations from Latin, but interference too may have had a part, in the semantic extension of Latin words. Latin loan-words changed their meaning, through semantic extension, in the vernaculars into which they were borrowed, and quite probably these new significations adjusted how the words were used in neo-Latin writing (Jensen 1996). By Milton's age, impure Latinity carried a potent stigma among the educated. When Milton takes on Salmasius, the defender of Charles I against the English Republic, his own Latinity would have been subject to closest scrutiny, as his enemies' Latin is scrutinized by him. Hale has brilliantly demonstrated the deftness of Milton's Latin, especially his prose, illuminating its 'chief constant . . . its inventive variety' (Hale 1997: 83), but that is a variety premised upon the purest, the most classical of Latin idioms.

Milton's sense of pure Latin corresponds to his defence of pure English. In his prose, he seizes opportunities to pillory gratuitous neologizing through borrowing. William Prynne, by the early 1640s among Milton's enemies, had for long affected the word 'subitane', from the Latin 'subitaneus', as a redundant synonym for the long-native 'sudden'; Milton mocks him as 'him who in his *Subitanes* hath thus censur'd' his divorce tracts (*Colasterion, CPW* II: 723). 'Smelling of the inkhorn', to which I return shortly, seems implicit in the charge. Indeed, when Charles I or his ghost writer coin the word 'demagogue', in the phrase *'the chief Demagoges to send for those Tumults'* (Charles I 1649: 17), Milton bridles as he would at a barbarism in Latin, and he sees, too, an infringement of the English language (and, thus, the rights and freedoms of the English people), lashing 'the affrightment of this Goblin word; for the King by his leave cannot coine English as he could Money, to be current' (*Eikonoklastes, CPW* III: 392–3). In a sense, Milton picks the wrong case to fight. 'Demagogue' proved a useful addition to the word stock, achieving rapid currency, and was picked up and adopted by Hobbes. A contemporary apologist for Charles I defended the term, pointing to the long history of 'pedagogue' in English, and the first element in the word was already current in 'democracy', first borrowed through French in the early sixteenth century (Corns 1982: 69–70). What is nevertheless remarkable is the touchy defence of English purity. But after all, when Milton does coin a word directly from Greek, the effect of alienness, of un-Englishness, is usually sought; 'Pandæmonium' (*PL* I. 756) is both the appropriate home of devils and the appropriate name for it.

In his gibes at Charles, and probably more especially at Prynne, Milton is also displaying the uncomfortable relationship between scholarship and pedantry. Gratuitous affectation of elements of a perceived high-status language within a vernacular extends to what is known in studies of bilingualism as 'code-switching', 'the alternate use of two of more languages in the same utterance or conversation' (Hamers and Blanc 1989: 148). It may be perceived by the speakers to reflect cultural achievement or to mark a social decorum, though it may also prove tractable to hostile interpretation. Thus, Tolstoy in his novels frequently has his aristocrats break into French, at once depicting a social habit and suggesting the speakers' distance from the experiences and sufferings of fellow Russians. In the context of the English Renaissance, the language that breaks through vernacular discourse is Latin, and its societal associations are rather different. When Shakespeare in *Love's Labour's Lost* has Sir Nathaniel, a curate, and Holofernes, a schoolmaster, break into Latin or adopt redundant Latin words into English discourse, he depicts a code-mixing which the characters use to distinguish themselves socially from the likes of Dull, the constable, but which just as surely marks them down from the aristocratic culture of the play. 'Smelling of the inkhorn' – being pedantic – was a familiar charge, and 'inkhorn', as a pejorative term, is first recorded by the *OED* in 1543.

Again, besides voicing a negative response to the apparent malpractices of others, Milton writes positively in praise of his native tongue, most memorably in the ringing declaration, 'Hail native language', with which he marks a transition from the Latin of a vacation exercise to the vernacular in which he will best clothe his 'naked thoughts' ('At a Vacation Exercise in the College', lines 1, 23, *CSP*: 79).

Yet, while certainly eschewing inkhornism, Milton rightly figures within English literary history as the single most important neoclassicist and fitting heir to the cultural agenda set by George Chapman and Ben Jonson. But just as eighteenth-century commentators sometimes failed to recognize changes between Milton's English and theirs, so too they sometimes rather misunderstood what Milton intended in his apparent imitation of classical models. For Joseph Addison, the most influential early critic, Milton's epic achievements may be substantiated because they approach or match those of Homer and Virgil. Milton, however, sets a higher target, to transcend the work of his models and masters. As such, he follows the ambition of Jonson, who had asserted the superiority of his epigrams over Martial's in terms of their subject matter – Martial had flattered an unworthy emperor, but he gives due praise to a worthy king ('Thou flatter'd'st thine, mine cannot flatter'd be', *Epigrammes* xxxvi; Jonson 1947: 38). In similar fashion, Milton's epic transcends those of Virgil and Homer since they celebrate pagan heroes and his describes the central events of Christian history: his is a genius 'Not sedulous by nature to indite / Wars, hitherto the only argument / Heroic deemed (*PL* IX. 27–9). Milton's cultural respect and profound sense of tradition no more concede the bays to the classical world than his mastery of classical languages acknowledges their superiority to native English.

Yet the issues are indeed complex, and latterly they have been illuminated by excellent scholarship (Blessington 1979; Porter 1993; Reid 1993; Hale 1997). As Hale in particular has demonstrated, Milton is a persistently playful writer, in a manner consonant with the achievements and aspirations of Renaissance humanism, drawing his intended readership into an interpretative experience characterized by 'serious play': 'Throughout, he is heeding that humanist topos, *serio ludere*' (Hale 1997: 25). To take an egregious example: in his reductive description of military display in *Paradise Regained*, Milton writes of 'Chariots or elephants endorsed with towers / Of archers' (III. 329–30), which, as Carey notes (*CSP*: 478), puns on the sense 'carrying on their backs' and the sense 'confirmed, strengthened': a piece of wordplay that undermines the seriousness of the account (see also Corns 1990a: 68). There is no reason to suppose the former sense had any real currency in seventeenth-century English, though the wordplay, as Carey notes, occurs also in Jonson. Indeed, the word from which it is borrowed, *indorsare*, as Milton would almost certainly have known, does not occur in classical Latin. It is formed in medieval Latin and occurs in law books for the legal transaction of writing on the back of documents, especially bills or cheques, to confirm their validity for payment. Milton's joke only works because a reader with some Latin can recognize the ultimate etymology of the word in '*in* upon + *dorsum* back' (*OED*, s.v. 'Endorse, indorse'). The catachrestic phrase obliges the reader to see the Latin words inside a neo-Latin formation long adopted into English.

Again, words of Latin origin sometimes sit on the surface of the text as cultural markers, reminders that Milton's major poetry positions itself aggressively in the cultural ideology of early modern neoclassicism. The word 'error', used in its etymological sense of 'wandering' (e.g. *PL* IV. 239; VII. 302), offers the reader an interpretative *frisson* of recognizing its literal signification – and discounting, provisionally, its moral meaning; and the effect has for long received perceptive critical comment (see Ricks 1967: 109–10, discussing Stein 1953: 66–7). But it is also pertinent that the usage occurs in Jonson, too. Other examples of words of Latin origin used in etymological senses that may contemporaneously have felt un-English to Milton's readers can sometimes be found in Jonson, and in Chapman (Corns 1990a: 96–7). Such markers are part of a much larger literary idiom that simultaneously works as a literature of allusion and as an assertion of a vernacular literary culture that actively seeks comparison with classical models. Hale's chapter in this volume illustrates both effects in detailed analyses. Milton's relations to classical precursors are indeed complex. In his Latin prose, his debts to Cicero are obvious, and sometimes technical: periods may end in rhythmic patterns of Ciceronean perfection (Hale 1997: 94). Sentences in his vernacular prose do not, so far as I can detect, exhibit in their conclusions the rhythmic *clausulae* of his Latin prose. But their copiousness, while generated by a wholly English syntax, matches the aesthetic of Ciceronean oratory, as do their clausal density and complexity. While culturally the alignment asserts the values of neoclassicism, endorsement of the Roman republic's most eloquent spokesman may well carry political resonances (Norbrook 1999: 53, 207).

More obviously, perhaps, the major poems, and pre-eminently *Paradise Lost*, seek out comparison with classical analogues, pre-eminently Homer and Virgil. The connections are multifaceted, relating to verbal echoes and to structural similarities in a poetry of dense allusion. Porter's fine account discloses the richness of the connections and suggests how they may shape the reading strategies of the classically informed. As he demonstrates (and as I have, here and elsewhere, asserted) Milton's intersection with classical tradition is neither passive nor supine. Rather, he invites the recognition of allusion in order to demonstrate his own distinction from precursors and constitute a kind of commentary on them. As Porter summarizes, 'The attitude toward the classics that one elaborates from *Paradise Lost* as a whole is at once profoundly ambivalent, ironic, serious, and playful ... a thoughtful reading of Milton's allusions ... should reinvigorate our understanding of the ancient poems and their meaningfulness for us' (1993: 81–2).

The allusions are often flagged through verbal echoes which connect Milton's discourse with Latin (or Greek) analogues through some shared vocabulary: the English words he uses may connect, in their origins, with the words of the classical intertext. Thus, when Milton calls Adam's locks 'hyacinthine', he stimulates, as commentators have for long recognized, recollection of Homer's description of Odysseus (*Odyssey* 6: 231), for reasons that are open to interpretation. Hale (1997) identifies numerous neatly turned allusions driven by verbal proximities, and indeed Dzelzainis, in this volume, demonstrates how such connections may be crucial in the interpretation of key sections of his political prose.

We may attempt to locate what perhaps is happening in the psychology of both linguistic production and interpretation. Certainly there is no reason to suppose that Milton – or his ideal reader – is functioning simultaneously in two or more languages with the effect that interference in encoding and decoding occurs in a manner indicative of linguistic incompetence. Rather, Milton's occasional Latinisms – and Grecisms – occur in ways that are formally governed. Sometimes, he adopts an alien idiom used by other neoclassical writers. Sometimes, a catachresis – rarely as blatant as in the case of 'endorsed' – signals that a multilingual playfulness has entered his discourse and requires interpretation in those terms. Of course, since words of Latin origin are usually closer to their Latin significations in seventeenth-century than later English, verbal echoes, as well as other allusional mechanisms, tie Milton's vernacular to its classical intertext. None of this makes Milton, in the old Leavisite (and Johnsonian) charge un-English, though this aspect of his style renders the reading experience more challenging, more playful, and culturally more complex. In some senses Milton may indeed be the English Cicero and the English Virgil; but his Englishness emerges uncompromised.

BIBLIOGRAPHY

Writings

Attridge (1982); Bacon (1965); Bridges (1921); Charles I (1649); Corns (1992a, 1994); Cressy (1980); Empson (1967); Fish (1980); Green, Jonathon (1996); Hall (1640[/1]); Hamers and Blanc (1989); Haverstein (1999); Jensen (1996); Johnson (1963); Jonson (1947); Lewis (1967); Marvell (1984); Milton (1968); Norbrook (1999); Parker, Samuel (1673); Ricks (1968); Smith (1983); Sprott (1953); Stein (1953).

References for Further Reading

Blessington (1979); Burnett (1981); Corns (1982, 1990a); Eliot (1936, 1947); Hale (1997); Leavis (1936); Porter (1993); Reid (1993); Ricks (1967).

PART II
Politics and Religion

7

The Legacy of the Late Jacobean Period

Cedric C. Brown

There has been a tendency in much writing about the sixteenth and seventeenth centuries, especially in the broadly empirical British tradition, to subordinate the categories of religion to those of politics. British historians, for example, have often treated the Reformation less as an ideological development and more as a series of 'legislative enactments' (Tyacke 1998: 1). The old Whig interpretation of history had put revolutionary Protestantism at the centre of social and political change in early modern England, so had placed ideology in a central position. However, after its collapse as the dominant paradigm, revisionist historians for a while at least found religion displaced in their explanations. (For the older ideological argument see the work of Christopher Hill, especially Hill [1958] and in this context Hill [1977], and Michael Walzer [1965].) Later, some revisionist historians, for example Nicholas Tyacke (1987) and John Morrill (1993), sought to place religion on the agenda again. Literary scholars, too, have used various materialist categories or wished, as recently with the influential book of David Norbrook (1999), to trace revolutionary thought in the seventeenth century by following secular ideas of republicanism. This largely historical chapter sketches some Jacobean cultural contexts for the young John Milton, touching on aspects of his boyhood experience in London and young manhood at Cambridge. In it, I shall put the emphasis the other way round. I shall take as my organizing principle some religious ideas authorized by biblical sources: of the exemplary Protestant pastor, and of the modelling of kings according to the historical books of the Old Testament. Both are identified by the Homeric phrase 'the shepherds of the people'. The influence of these ideas is so strong that they deserve to be followed into some of their textual manifestations, and the concepts were so pervasive that they could function as what Fredric Jameson (1981) calls ideologemes. Or, to put it another way, they reflect material conditions through the way they were perceived. In many ways, the perception is all. Their dissemination often relied, too, upon the most important medium of the pastor, the sermon. At the same time, these religious paradigms are so deeply politicized, connected with the historical ideas and structures of English Protestantism, royal policy and the institutions of education, that religious and political categories are finally impossible to separate.

It seems all the more appropriate to begin with models of the ministry, because Milton himself reported that the vocation of pastor had been the leading idea behind his education. The statement is put most plainly in 1642 in *The Reason of Church-Government*: 'the difficult labours of the Church, to whose service by the intentions of my parents and friends I was destin'd of a child, and in mine own resolutions' (*CPW* I: 822). The context there is one of apologetic self-representation, but the fact of his being designed for the ministry is supported in many other places in his writings. In any case, Milton's eagerness to attribute ideas of the priestly vocation to his own career, often displacing it on to other activities, is further indication of the cultural importance and wide recognition of the values involved. It may be significant that Milton's father, leaving a recusant family in Oxfordshire when he moved to London to make his fortune, was a first-generation convert and seems to have many connections among ministers in London (Parker 1996, esp. 4–23, 684–722).

To follow this line of enquiry means identifying models of leadership; and that in turn is also to remember a climate of great anxiety in late Jacobean England about those in authority in church and state. The role models I shall use are not just of princes but also of bishops, shepherds of the people whom Milton was so comprehensively to attack in the early 1640s. The vigour of that attack may well be in proportion to the persuasiveness and, despite long-running arguments in Protestant cultures about forms of church government, wide acceptance of the model which had been familiar to him as a boy. I wish to take seriously for a moment Milton's two Cambridge elegies for bishops, 'Elegy III' and '*In Obitum Praesulis Eliensis*', not as expressions of a mature technique or viewpoint – he was only seventeen at the time he wrote them, in his second year at the university – but of an ideology in which he had been bred. These two Latin poems are complementary in their definitions, and it is worth putting the two models side by side.

'Elegy III' mourns the death on 25 September 1626, aged seventy-one, of Lancelot Andrewes, Bishop of Winchester. It is also about the leadership of Protestant England and Protestant Europe, marking the death of Andrewes in a time of significant loss, when large numbers of people, including many notables, had succumbed to the plague in England, and various leaders of Protestant forces in Europe had also died. Not inappropriately – Andrewes had been connected to the court as preacher, administrator and privy councillor – the poem treats bishops alongside princes as inhabitants of glorious, marble-filled palaces (line 5), and with no sense of criticism. The alliance between secular and ecclesiastical powers is in the defence of Protestantism, whether at home or in the Thirty Years War on the continent. The poem presents a long historical perspective, ideologically defined: the Belgia in this text (line 12) is the site of religious struggle against Catholic tyranny mythologized by Spenser and Sidney. As the white-haired bishop is pictured being welcomed to the other court, of heaven, and applauded by the assembled hosts, he is celebrated as one who deserves rest after long striving in that heroic cause.

The second poem, marking the death on 5 October, 1626, aged seventy, of Nicholas Felton, Bishop of Ely, presents a bishop in quite another guise, as a *teacher*. Here the young poet begins his poem with expressions of overwhelming grief, being unreconciled to Providence and noting as in the other poem the worrying numbers of deaths after the end of James's reign. But he is corrected by the voice of the bishop himself, who explains God's purposes with death (line 27ff). There is an anticipation here of the 'dramatic' method of 'Lycidas', and the role of the bishop as instructor could be put against the voice of the mitred Peter in the later poem. As the men ultimately responsible for appointing young scholars from the two universities to the ministry, bishops were supposed to monitor their care of the flock, and to lead by example in their own instruction to congregations in their areas, sometimes by going on preaching tours.

These two poems are conventional memorials of the kind expected from apt scholars in colleges, which produced showpiece collections of elegies in Latin and Greek to mark notable deaths. Both Andrewes and Felton had been Bishop of Ely, the Cambridge diocese; both had strong Cambridge connections, having graduated there and been Master of Pembroke Hall. The occasions are not surprising. But it is a mistake simply to ignore occasional, institutional poems, or to work so much with the model of writers achieving 'individual' voices in later life as to miss the evidence of their early work. The institutional identity is important here, and the configurations of early years are later not expunged, but renegotiated and rewritten. To put it another way, the fact that Milton was later to argue strongly against Andrewes on the question of episcopacy in *The Reason of Church-Government* does not mean that the evidence of the poem of 1626 has to be suppressed in the interests of the prose tract of 1641. Rather, there is some intervening negotiation waiting to be understood. The two poems express prevalent Jacobean ideas: one assumes that Protestantism needs vigilant leadership against the forces of Catholicism; the other embodies the example of the bishop as model minister, preaching the word, even beyond death. As it happens, these two aged survivors of the Elizabethan church had both been noted preachers in their dioceses, in London, and in Andrewes's case at court. Both had also been associated with the project of the King James Bible. For all the differences between them, they are cast, in effect, as role models.

As for James I, we might also take seriously young Milton's Latin celebrations of the role of the king, recently dead, as guardian of Protestant England. The four epigrams on James ('*In Proditionem Bombardicam*') were written in 1625 or 1626, that is, early in Milton's Cambridge years. There may be a set occasion for these verses, too, and they are probably associated with the epigram on the inventor of gunpowder ('*In Inventorem Bombardae*'), and the miniature epic '*In Quintum Novembris*', a memorial of the Gunpowder Plot. The providential saving of James from Catholic conspiracy in 1605 was celebrated annually on a public feast day, like the earlier providential defeat of the Armada in 1588 and the accession day of Elizabeth I. These events had become reference points in national Protestant mythology. (Later, 'Lycidas', which I shall invoke several times in this chapter, was to remember the Armada and to be built upon ideas of guarding the nation.) In the poems on James and the Plot, the King is given an unequivocal role as champion of true religion, likened to Elijah in the first epigram (lines 7–8) and celebrated for his anti-Catholic writings in the second (line 1). In all four epigrams the attempt to blow James to the skies is answered by his actual reception into heaven.

These poems attempt to preserve the orientations of the past as the guide to the present. '*In Quintum Novembris*' presents the devil as incensed against a godly king and prosperous godly island, seeking revenge for the past defeats of Catholic imperialism:

> Et memor Hesperiae disiectam ulciscere classem,
> Mersaque Iberorum lato vexilla profundo,
> Sanctorumque cruci tot corpora fixa probosae,
> Thermodoontea nuper regnante puella.
>
> (lines 102–5)

Remember and avenge the scattered Spanish fleet! Avenge the Iberian standards over-whelmed in the deep ocean and the bodies of so many saints nailed to the shameful cross during the late reign of the Amazonian virgin. (my translation)

This is an Elizabethan legacy remembered not in 1605 but at the beginning of the reign of Charles I. Changes of reign were often times for reminders and reassessments.

The influence of this pervasive national–Protestant mythology had in any case been readily visible in poems written by Milton in the last period of James's reign. The two Psalm paraphrases ('A Paraphrase on Psalm cxiv' and 'Psalm cxxxvi') written between December 1623 and December 1624, when Milton was only fifteen and still at St Paul's School in London, include phrases of high patriotic excitement. They may remind us of the thanksgivings of thousands of citizens lighting bonfires round England as Charles, the Prince of Wales, and Buckingham, the royal favourite, returned from Spain in October 1623 without a Spanish bride (Cogswell 1989: 6–53; Parker 1996: 31, 730). God has taken his people out of bondage, away from the control of Catholic Spain, and will perform further miracles – 'Shake earth, and at the presence be aghast / Of him that ever was, and ay shall last' ('A Paraphrase on Psalm cxiv', lines 15–16). God will support, now as before, the struggle against Catholic tyranny: 'O let us his praises tell, / Who doth the wrathful tyrants quell' ('Psalm cxxxvi', lines 9–10). As in the little epic, the lessons of the past must not be forgotten: 'And freed us from the slavery / Of the invading enemy' (lines 81–2). To remember the Armada is to remember the hand of God. By deciding to include these boyhood psalm paraphrases in his published collection of 1645, Milton seems to have been signalling to his readers his early connection with this pervasive Protestant mythology of the 1620s. Nor are traces of militant Protestant nationalism hard to find in the years immediately after the poems about the bishops and King James. I shall mention 'Elegy IV', of 1627, later in this chapter. At the end of 1629 'On the Morning of Christ's Nativity' announces that Milton's own sense of vocation is bound up with the completion of the fight against idolatry, since the era of Christ is presented as one of defeating false gods: 'Our babe to show his Godhead true, / Can in his swaddling bands control the damned crew' (lines 227–8). The poem is a zealously anti-Catholic Pindaric. On the occasion of Jesus's birth the poet dedicates himself and his writing, at his own coming of age, to the project of continuing reform, and later, in the collection of 1645, he chooses to put this idealistic poem at the beginning of his book.

Godly Bishops and Kings

In cultures of all periods, history is written in a selective way by concentrating on the acts of leaders. It is a way of subduing the mess of events to personal narratives and enabling them to be judged. The watching of great ones, living and dead, was endemic in early modern society and its literature, and it was authorized by master narratives, not only English chronicles but by the Old Testament. Milton grew up in a culture characterized by the vigilant watching of the various shepherds of the people, at court and in the church, testing them against the role models. With that in mind, I would like now to turn to some examples of evangelical bishops and their ministers that he would have known as a boy, and to assess his experience in London before his going up to Cambridge in 1625. Information about the Jacobean bishops and their policies is mainly drawn from Kenneth Fincham (1990).

When the 'preaching' Bishop of London, John King, close ally of the evangelically inclined Archbishop of Canterbury, George Abbot, lay on his deathbed in 1621, he was attended by Abbot himself (on King's Calvinist opposition to Arminianism, see Tyacke 1987: 15, 20–2, 63, 256–7), and Bishops Lake of Bath and Wells, Morton of Coventry and Lichfield, and Felton of Ely (whose elegy from Milton has been mentioned). This was a group of evangelical bishops resident in or near London at the time. To this circle in 1621, though not present at King's death, might be added Mountagu of Winchester, a frequent ally of Abbot and King and often at court, close to the king; Abbot's elder brother, Robert, of Salisbury; and Tobias Matthew, Archbishop of York. What they had in common apart from their Calvinist theology was a primary emphasis on the godly preaching function, 'feeding' the flock both by their own example and by their support of strong preaching ministers and extra lectureships. They worked to an agenda largely set in Elizabethan times and tended to see the chief dangers to the English church coming out of Rome rather than from the disruptive activities of zealous, nonconforming godly brethren (see Fincham 1990: 248–93).

The London in which Milton grew up was privileged in terms of the quality of its ministers, perhaps the best-provided place in England for well-educated and enthusiastically preaching clergy, during a reign which saw a better supply of able men than ever before. The Abbot–King alliance, able to exercise or influence much patronage, shaped churchmanship in many parishes. Abbot's appointment to Canterbury in 1611 was unexpected, because he had much less experience than many others, but it probably connected with the king's fears about Catholic conspiracy. 'What James was looking for in early 1611 was an archbishop who could police the Catholic community and unearth Catholic plots against his life' (Fincham 1990: 28–9). Abbott's tenure at Canterbury was also long, up to 1633, by which time his late Elizabethan style was well out of tune with the anti-Calvinism of the reign of Charles I, and he had lost much influence through the 1620s. King held London from 1611 also, to his death in 1621. Since he was well known for preaching in parishes in his diocese in most weeks (Fincham 1990: 253), it is quite possible that the young John Milton (aged thirteen by the time of the bishop's death) might have heard him in All Hallows, Bread Street, his parish church, or in one of the many other city churches. Whether he did or not, he would inevitably have experienced worship bearing the marks of the Abbot–King partnership.

To be more specific, the first rector of All Hallows whom Milton would have remembered, the Yorkshireman Richard Stock, took up his post also in 1611, having previously been curate there. Stock was Cambridge-educated and a stout, outspoken preacher, who had once – like Abbot and King – been a city lecturer. He based his thoughts on the bedrock of anti-Catholicism. Earlier, he had translated from Latin the anti-Jesuit controversial work of the famous Elizabethan divine, William Whitaker, *An Answere to the Ten Reasons of Edmund Campian*...(1606). He dedicated another work to the evangelical bishop Mountagu, and was a friend of the celebrated Calvinist teaching minister, Thomas Gataker of Rotherhithe, one of whose sons, incidentally, Milton must have known at St Paul's School. Curates at All Hallows were usually young scholars from Cambridge, and Stock showed many Cambridge connections, both within the church and with secular patrons (see Parker 1996: 9–10, 703–4; Fletcher 1956, I: 53–72). At his death in 1626, he was succeeded briefly by Samuel Purchas, chaplain to both Abbot and King (as well as a compiler of travel writings, which Milton would later engage with), and a passionate supporter in his sermons of the Protestant cause in Europe after the Palatinate crisis (Cogswell 1989: 28; Parker 1996: 31, 730). Then, at the end of the year, the 59-year-old Purchas also died and was replaced by the redoubtable Daniel Featley. Featley was chaplain to Abbot, too, and a noted Calvinist preacher and redoubtable controversialist, who shared his bishop's anti-Catholic stance and enthusiasm above all for the preaching function (Parker 1996: 36, 733–4). Featley's stoutly Calvinist and evangelical actions can be traced in Tyacke 1987 (pp. 64–5, 73, 78–9, 148–9, 151, 156, 212). There can be no doubt that as a boy Milton was surrounded by examples of stout preaching ministries of strongly anti-Catholic character.

The predominant character of the early Jacobean church was Calvinist in theology and evangelical in churchmanship, but by the 1620s the balance was beginning to swing towards the anti-Calvinist or 'Arminian' wing. This group put more emphasis upon ceremonial decency and disciplined order, and thought that an overemphasis on preaching led to as many troubles as benefits. Setting a balance between extremes in the church had always been a policy of James I. The king controlled appointments in the church at senior level and had bishops of various colours regularly in his court, increasingly using their administrative abilities there (Fincham 1990: 35–67). It was probably no accident that on the death of John King the new appointment to London was George Montaigne, who served until 1628, when he was translated to Durham and then again in the same year to York. Montaigne represented the anti-Calvinist group, which would become predominant, and in his concern for decency in church he scandalized his diocese in the year of his appointment by ordering the prosecution of all those who attended services with their hats on (Fincham 1990: 240). Having lost his ally Mountagu by death in 1618, Abbot was already weakened in his influence at court, and the loss of King reduced his position further.

Yet some traditions changed slowly, and the perception of change was very patchy throughout the country. Peter White (1992) and Ian Green (1996) challenge some aspects of Tyacke's account of the rise of Arminianism as overstated, and Green's account of catechism is based on practices in parishes nationwide, not on elite areas and institutions. The emphasis here is on places where awareness was high, and even so we shall see later that important presentations at Oxford and Cambridge were freed from Calvinist control only very late – into the Caroline period. The evidence which Nicholas Tyacke has analysed from the St Paul's Cross sermons in the Jacobean period shows much the same pattern. These sermons were the most high-profile series in England, with guest speakers drawn from all over the kingdom, and many of them were subsequently printed. Tyacke's analysis (1987: 248–65) clearly shows that these sermons, which took place just down the road from the Milton house, were monopolized by Calvinists until several years into the reign of Charles. Calvinist sermons ceased to be printed after July 1628, when Laud was translated to London; but the first Arminian sermon was not printed until 1632. These preachers were selected by the administration of the Bishop of London, and Canterbury and London together had overall authority over the licensing for print. In other words, the Abbott–King legacy still continued in these very public events for some years after King's death in 1621, despite the appointment of Montaigne, and not until the vigorous reforms of Laud were radical changes seen.

Looking at such evidence, we can see that the balance of the English church underwent shifts during Milton's boyhood, gradually moving away from a Calvinist, evangelical character. As we have seen, Milton's early years were probably spent in an environment created by the Abbot–King circle in London, but his later schooldays, in the early 1620s, were times of more confused leadership and great popular anxiety about possible betrayals of national Protestantism and the fate of the west European Protestant nations. Then, as he went up to Cambridge in early 1625, Milton would have been exposed to much debate about religion within the university. Nevertheless, the final attempt to impose a strict Arminian order in public worship did not come until the translation of William Laud to London in 1628 and to Canterbury in 1633, after the accession of Charles I in 1625. In much later years, following periods of private study and public controversy, Milton would develop strong individual opinions in matters of religion: liberal, erastian, antiprelatical and doctrinally unorthodox. But two assumptions remained central to his thinking: when he writes of the priesthood, he emphasizes as much as some of the ministers he heard in his early years the primary function of preaching, of 'feeding' the flock; and as central to his last works as to his first was an ideology which configured evil on the model of Catholic influence.

The role models of the leaders of the church are likely to have been particularly important to Milton as a boy destined himself for the ministry. But there are, of course, with the Calvinist/Arminian split, opposing models to consider in the early decades of the seventeenth century. In his useful survey of the Jacobean episcopate, *Prelate as Pastor*, Kenneth Fincham (1990: 248–9) illustrates this point by describing the contrasting symbolism of two episcopal memorial brasses. For the first model he chooses the brass of Henry Robinson, Bishop of Carlisle (d. 1616), showing the bishop as the good shepherd, with a candle in his right hand signifying the Gospel. Robinson is accompanied by a team of sheepdogs, who are the clergy under his command defending their flocks from the Roman wolf. This is the evangelical model of the bishop, highlighting the work of conversion and spreading the Gospel. Robinson himself had regularly preached in his diocese and built up a preaching ministry in the north-west of England.

In contrast, that of Samuel Harsnett, a Bishop of Norwich of the next generation (d. 1629), shows him wearing a mitre and an embroidered coat. This image was a challenge to those of Calvinist persuasion, for the mitre had been worn by abbots as well as bishops in pre-Reformation times, and was thus a tainted Romish object. Harsnett was one of the newer Arminian bishops. As Fincham says, 'These brasses exemplify the two conflicting images of the episcopal office in early Stuart England: the bishop as preaching pastor or as custodian of order' (1990: 249). By the 1630s the Arminian pattern was so much in the ascendancy that pastors of evangelical bent, stigmatized by the negative term 'puritan', were forced from the mainstream to the margins, or even into opposition. The fateful connection was then more regularly made, on the puritan side, between church governance and the taint of Catholicism. In the church satire of 'Lycidas' in 1637, St Peter is given a mitre as a sign of authority – he is the type of the bishop – but that is a laconic gesture at the Laudians who wore the hat but betrayed the true evangelical, preaching model: 'The hungry sheep look up, and are not fed' (line 125). Whatever his developing liberal theology, Milton's church politics ally him with the older evangelical model of preaching pastor and bishop, and against formalist discipline.

Turning to leadership of the state, there is an extraordinary archival record which gives a vivid sense of the ideological climate in which Milton lived as a boy in London and enables us to connect the picturing of the church with that of the monarchy. The so-called Milton Bible, in the British Library (Add MS 32,310), has been best known as a family Bible containing a few entries about births and deaths written in Milton's own hand in the 1640s, then continued by amanuenses after the onset of his blindness in the early 1650s. This 1612 King James Bible had once been annotated by someone else, presumably of the older generation. It contains a remarkable sequence of under-linings and marginal marks, apparently made in 1622–3, recording the agonized meditations of someone of ardent Protestant–nationalist persuasion about the directions of James in the last part of his reign (Brown 2000). The marks are made in the Old Testament historical books, minor prophets and some psalms. The method is to measure the performance of England's indecisive, elderly king against kings of Israel and Judah, judging the depth of resolve against the surrounding forces of idolatry. An instructive case is that of King Asa in 2 Chronicles 15. He is presented as a champion of true religion, replacing his idolatrous father Abijah, and commended for removing his mother from her throne as queen because of false religion, 'because she hath made an idol in a grove' (verse 16). Nevertheless, he stands in a moment of crucial judgement at the end of his reign, the reformation still not complete: 'the heart of Asa was perfit all his dayes' but 'the high places were not taken away out of Israel' (verse 17). So, too, Asa's son, Jehoshaphat, is noted where he is urged to follow his father's drive against idolatry, but again 'the high places were not taken away' (2 Chronicles 20: 33), and here as elsewhere the annotator puts the unambiguous letters in the margin 'KJ'. King James is measured in this way against many of the Old Testament kings, in the context of anxiety about his falling away from the zealous resistance of Catholicism wherever it may be found.

At the same time there is a noting of James's championing the true church in the past and of the need to purify the temple, especially of women with idolatrous tendencies. There is also a watching of a once providentially protected king, who seems to stand at some new crisis: 'For thou hast delivered my soul from death: wilt not thou deliver my feet from falling?' (Psalm 56: 13). James's role is to make clear, to the end of his days, his commitment to a vigilant anti-Catholic cause. It was in August 1622, amid hysteria about the fate of the Protestant Palatinate and the prospects of a Spanish match for Charles, that the king sought to curb criticism from pulpits by issuing 'Directions Concerning Preaching'. But he could not prevent wild rumours even about his own imminent conversion to Catholicism, an idea encouraged by notable conversions at court, including women in the household of his favourite, Buckingham (see e.g. Lockyer 1981: 58–9, 82–3, 114–15).

The concern of this annotator of the Milton family Bible was very widely shared. Nevertheless, at the same time as anxiety about the king's intentions was being expressed from pulpits, there was also a loyalty and an unwillingness to write him off as irredeemably fallen. Even as Samuel Purchas, soon to be one of Milton's London ministers, raised lurid fears in 1622 about the slaughter of Protestants –

> think what it is to see thy house fired; thy goods seized; thy servants fled; thy Wife ravished before your face and then hung up by the heels (modestie forbids the rest); thy Daughter crying to thee for helpe in one corner while thy little Sonne is tost on anothers Pike and the Sword at thy own throat

– he was also exhorting his audience to continuing loyalty, not 'to bee censorious of those whom God hath called Gods' (Cogswell 1989: 28; on Purchas and the patronage of the king, see Fincham 1990: 256).

So, too, the Milton family friend Thomas Myriell (see Parker 1996: 11, 18, 705, 718; Fletcher 1956, I, 393–4), music enthusiast and minister at St Stephen's, Wallbrook, tried to remind his congregation at St Paul's Cross in 1622 of the special place of England among Protestant nations (the sermon was printed the following year as *The Christians Comfort*). Then he sought to lessen fears of royal apostasy by advising that they 'should be very disloyal to his Majesty if we should needlessely feare [and] perplexe our selves with that wherein wee ought to beleeve him most firme and constant' (1623: 50). Myriell was another chaplain to Abbot, and may have been following the archbishop's own line (Fincham 1990: 255–6). What the biblical annotator and these preachers share is an agonized watching of court policy and a simultaneous re-assertion of the need to remain loyal to a monarch who had been cast by many in the role of Protestant champion. In this context Milton's own epigrams on James may easily be read: like Asa, James died as one who had not fallen to idolatry, but in a kingdom where much cleansing remained to be done. Dead, the king could be safely re-enrolled in Protestant national mythology, and the watching turn to new parties at court. When such texts were published at a later period, the example of an old king could be used as a reproach to newer kings.

The University of Cambridge in the Late 1620s

I have already made use of a number of texts belonging to Milton's early years at Cambridge. A full account of the development of Milton's religious, political and intellectual views during the whole of his long period at Cambridge (1625–32) forms a subject too large for the compass of this chapter. In any case, a good deal of fundamental work still needs to be done and there is a manifest need to update the accounts of Parker and Campbell (Parker 1996: 23–115) and Fletcher (1956, II). Here I shall simply outline some directions of change, connecting with the themes I have chosen. But assumptions about Milton's relationship with the university have, I think, often been overinfluenced by reading too literally the poem in which he seems to speak of a rustication from it: 'Elegy I'.

In this playful Latin verse letter written to his sophisticated, somewhat older friend Charles Diodati, Milton begins by talking of being in London and having his Cambridge rooms forbidden to him. This is a happy exile, because London offers him richer pleasures: leisure for books of his choice, theatre and lively society, especially watching all the girls go by. His friendship with Diodati, whom he had known at St Paul's School, was a good deal about literary matters, and the poem represents an ironic rewriting, in Ovidian measure, of Ovid's situation, banished by the emperor Augustus to boring Tomis on the Black Sea. Milton's exile is to his pleasant home, and it was probably vacation time. Some have wanted to take from the poem an idea of forcible rustication, because of words of somewhat dubious authority written in Aubrey's life indicating that Milton had been punished by his first tutor, William Chappell ('whipped him') and sent down, to return at a later time to a different tutor,

Nathaniel Tovey. Efforts have been made to fit the date and occasion of 'Elegy I' into this narrative (see e.g. Miller 1980).

This would not matter too much if other attitudes were not encouraged by these speculations. Put together with the various critical remarks made by Milton, both in his Cambridge years and much later, about the dry traditionalism of some of the studies there, this story has helped to encourage an assumption that Cambridge was not as formative on him as intellectual life fostered elsewhere. But the importance of the university must not be underestimated. Seen primarily as places for educating young men before they took orders in the church, Oxford and Cambridge were, potentially, the foremost debating places for theology, and they provided a concentration of intellectual ideas. Their influence on young minds was sufficient for both secular and ecclesiastical governments to want to keep some of their activities under control.

The political sensitivity of academic activity can easily be shown by the well-known story of what happened to Isaac Dorislaus, appointed to the first Professorship of History. Dorislaus began lecturing in 1627 on Tacitus. To lecture on Roman history, however, was always to be commenting by implication on contemporary politics. When he said that Tacitus cast doubts on the legitimate authority of the emperors, the lecture series was stopped, because of the reflection on the monarchy at a time of stress, during the Buckingham era at the beginning of Charles's reign (Norbrook 1999: 48; see also Sharpe 1989: 207–30). No bright young scholar could be at Cambridge in the late 1620s and early 1630s without accumulating some understanding of the mechanisms of political control.

Even within his own college, Christ's, Milton would have known Fellows of widely different religious and political sympathies. Chappell was sufficiently acceptable to the Arminian authorities in the 1630s to be promoted to senior ecclesiastical positions in Ireland. Tovey, who seems to have been a subtle, flexible man, was likewise beneficed in 1634 and showed Laudian sympathies in the 1640s and 1650s (Campbell 1987). Other Fellows were suspected of Romish views. Even within a college community, let alone the whole university, there was an education to be had about differences of alignment, especially to be noted during a period of difficult change.

In his university years Milton probably gathered an understanding of religious politics both from an observation of the university and from his closeness at home to godly communities and the centre of newsmongering and book publication around St Paul's, a mere stone's throw from the family house on the corner of Bread Street and Cheapside. In London, too, he could have observed a changing ecclesiastical climate with the appointment of an Arminian bishop, Montaigne, in 1621, followed by the more vigorous Laud in 1628. At Cambridge, the showpiece Commencement presentations were carefully monitored each year for doctrinal correctness, and appointments to two chairs of divinity were sensitive matters (see Tyacke 1987: 29–57). Late sixteenth-century Cambridge had famously been dominated by influential Calvinist theologians, but the reign of James saw a long contest between Calvinism and Arminianism. The anti-Calvinist Regius Professor of Divinity, John Overall, had to resign in 1606, and a later holder of the chair, John Richardson, seems also to have made a diplomatic resignation in 1617. In the early years of James's reign the Lady Margaret chair was held by Calvinists and the Regius chair by anti-Calvinists, who however often tempered their views in public. The king and the Archbishop of Canterbury were drawn into some disputes. Following the Synod of Dort in 1618, in which Cambridge theologians were involved and which sought to impose a Calvinist orthodoxy on the Dutch church, there seems to have been an attempt to impose conformity in England, too. But, as we have seen, the balance of 'court' bishops was in fact changing in the 1620s, and by 1624 more open Arminian arguments were possible: for example, the former Cambridge scholar Richard Montagu, in his *A New Gagg for an old Goose*, challenged central Calvinist tenets of the English church. Samuel Ward, Lady Margaret Professor, offered a correction to Montagu in the 1625 Commencement, but that was the last official act of Calvinist orthodoxy in the university. The next year an intended Calvinist thesis for the Commencement was blocked by the Arminian Bishop Neile acting on the instructions of the new king, Charles. The official Calvinism of Cambridge was over. The recently elected Chancellor of the university was Buckingham, chosen really as a cipher for the king. Milton was at Cambridge, under an anti-Calvinist tutor, during this transitional period. One year after he arrived, in 1626, the practice seems to have begun of smearing Calvinists as puritans; by the time he left, in 1632, the theological climate was quite different from that in which he had been brought up in London. Two years later, Archbishop Laud would be imposing uniformity of worship of a more sacramental kind, actively using the powers of discipline symbolized by the mitre and the keys.

We have a situation, then, in which Milton's theological views were to show the influence of Arminianism, but his religious politics were to resist the Laudian impositions of the 1630s and to preserve some of the political positions of the Calvinist culture in which he had largely grown up. This may be more comprehensible if we recall the extraordinary atmosphere of the early years of Charles's reign, especially in connection with the role of Buckingham and the disasters and unpopular expenses of the military expedition to the Isle of Ré.

As we have seen, Buckingham had for years been suspected with regard to the Protestant cause because of his involvement in the Spanish Match project and the high-profile conversions within his own family circle. He was, in any case, a much resented figure in many quarters as a result of his meteoric rise and monopoly on power and influence. Charles's marriage in 1625 to Henrietta Maria of France was one step better than a marriage to the Spanish royal house, but it was another Catholic alliance, and it brought a Catholic entourage, even a community of Capuchin monks, into the heart of London. The new reign began with renewed anxiety about a commitment to resisting Catholicism at home and on the continent in the religious wars. As we have seen, Milton's youthful Gunpowder Plot poems recuperate a Jacobean championship of Protestantism for the new reign. Hopes for intervention on the side of Protestantism in Europe were raised when war was declared both on Spain and France, and when an expedition was mounted to aid the Huguenots of La Rochelle. But the campaign, ambitiously but finally ineptly led by Buckingham, whom Parliament had already attempted to impeach, was an abject failure. The time round about 1627 was one of huge unpopularity for the court, as forced loans were needed to sustain the campaign (see Cust 1987; Cust and Hughes 1989). There was also great sensitivity in the government about popular dissent, and it is in this atmosphere that David Norbrook (1999: 43–51) charts one of the events in the emergence of an English republican literature, with the publication of Thomas May's translation of Lucan. The humiliation of Ré is signalled even in one of young Milton's academic exercises at Cambridge, the Vacation Exercise of 1628, which alluded to the ignominious flight by water of the English troops (*CPW* I: 285). It is worth considering how that reflected upon the Chancellor of his university. A matter of weeks later, however, Buckingham was dead, assassinated at Portsmouth. The authorities had much ado to control the popular celebrations.

Among those prosecuted for celebrating Buckingham's death was Milton's friend Alexander Gil, son of the high master of St Paul's School; fined and gaoled for two years, Gil only just escaped mutilation of the ears. This example is perhaps instructive. Gil had previously written a poem celebrating the sudden collapse, with huge loss of life, of a secret upstairs Catholic chapel in a London house in 1624; later, in 1629 or 1630, he was to celebrate a Protestant victory in the religious wars on the continent in his verses (Miller 1990; Parker 1996: 50–1, 76–7, 711–12, 754). Gil was no puritan, and we do not need to define too many doctrinal niceties here or differences in worship. There was a vast fund of Protestant–nationalist feeling, shared by most parties and supported by the familiar providential mythologies, the same fund which had been so spectacularly tapped in the celebrations in 1623 at the return of Charles from Spain without an Infanta (see Lake 1989). In 1628 most commentators still offered, in public at least, a defence of the king, casting Buckingham in the familiar role of bad counsellor. In later life, Milton was more likely to figure such relationships less protectively for the monarchy: in *Paradise Lost* Satan, a false prince, is not misled by, but connives with, his henchman Beezebub.

That Milton continued to think about the fight of Protestantism in Europe is clear also from his Latin verse letter, 'Elegy IV', written to his former teacher and friend, the Scots minister Thomas Young, in 1627. Without benefice in England, Young had accepted a post as minister to the English community in Hamburg. Milton celebrates his ministry in exile according to the primitive evangelical model:

> Vivit ibi antiquae clarus pietatis honore
> Praesul Christicolas pascere doctus oves;
> (lines 17–18)

A pastor lives there, famous for his esteem of the primitive faith and skilled at feeding his Christian flock. (my translation)

But, being in Germany, Young is near the wars of religion, and, apparently, not prosperous. Is this the way England should be treating those whom Providence has provided for its own spiritual care? Young is a true prophet exiled from his own people, like Elijah fleeing Ahab and Jezabel (lines 97–100). But that same Providence, he assured his former teacher, will eventually be your preserver [*custos*] and your champion [*pugil*] (line 112).

Here are some familiar co-ordinates. As in 'Lycidas', everything is about guardianship. The care of souls takes place amid dangers from the forces of tyrannous evil and idolatry; the role of the pastor is like that of the prophet, testifying to the truth, whatever the inimical circumstances; and the overarching story of guardianship is one of God's providential care. There is a heroic assumption beneath that narrative, of the need to recognize models of leadership in adversity and to keep faith with God's trusted design. Ideals of pastorship are inscribed in the discourses of militant resistance against the forces of false religion. All forms of Protestant thought emphasized the role of true pastors, and there were famous preaching bishops, like Andrewes, whom young Milton commemorated in death, of Arminian persuasion. But the co-ordinates of Milton's texts remain those of the Calvinist bishops and ministers under whom his family had grown up; as on Bishop Robinson's brass, the care of the flock means keeping the sheep from the clutches of the Roman wolves.

When he left university in 1632 and started to embark on yet another period of study, evidently of liberal arts, Milton had to justify his decision not to do as originally expected and take orders. To his own father he wrote the wonderfully turned *Ad Patrem*, mischievously pointing out that the love of poetry, which he could continue to pursue, was like his father's love of music, a sister art. Just as fascinating is the letter drafted to a friend in the Trinity Manuscript, which explicitly acknowledges that the disappointment the adviser is expressing is to do with the expectation of Milton becoming a priest (Milton 1972: 6–7). We do not have enough evidence to know whether his choice was motivated simply by a desire to have time to pursue other things. Milton's writings for aristocratic occasions in 1632 and 1634 suggest that he was content to model his instructive role as poet upon the pastoral example. But by 1637 in 'Lycidas' it is clear: the church authorities are indicted as having betrayed the cause of Reformation, the university is given an old-fashioned reminder of its duty to foster evangelism and fight the grim wolf, and the court is blamed for its lapses into false religion. Soon after (if the editor's dating is correct) Milton was writing into his Commonplace Book, from the early historian Sulpicius Severus, that 'the name of kings has always been hateful to free peoples' and the Hebrews are censured for choosing to exchange their freedom for servitude (*CPW* I: 440; cited in Norbrook 1999: 109). By the early 1640s an antimonarchical, anti-episcopal position is fully established: in *The Reason of Church-Government* Milton declares that if it is true that God designed episcopacy for the Israelites, then 'he did it in his wrath, as he gave the Israelites a King' (*CPW* I: 781; cited in Norbrook 1999: 112). By then, following the further radicalization of opinion, all the shepherds of the English people were condemned as false betrayers.

This is not to seek to trace back from the late 1640s and 1650s identical political positions for the late 1620s and 1630s. That has always been a problem in attempts to understand the 'radicalism' of Milton's earlier life. The co-ordinates of the revolutionary period simply cannot be the same as those of anxious authority-watching in the mid-1620s or even in 1637, whatever the ideological pressure on scholars to trace consistencies, or indeed to deny them. Some of the larger issues are reviewed, polemically, by Annabel Patterson in *Reading Between the Lines* (1993, esp. ch. 7). But there are earlier positions out of which later positions grow. It is the suggestion of this chapter that the zealous modelling of the evangelical pastor, so common and so ideologically charged in Jacobean times, provided the standard in the next generation for testing the fidelity of those in authority in church and state to the reformist cause. 'Some of the most characteristic features of the Jacobean Church', says Tyacke (1987: 186), were 'the stress on preaching and anti-Catholic polemic.' At the same time, the examples of Old Testament Hebrew kings provided the measure for zeal at court. Also, the powerful model of the true shepherd, the minister who would guard his flock from the pulpit, was extendable for a writer like Milton who could match that office with his own kinds of instruction. In 'Lycidas' shepherds of the people have to watch and guard the flock, the western approaches and the whole nation.

There may be a further benefit in this attempt to explain some of the preconditionings of Milton's later campaign against bishops and kings. It is possible that the habit of zealous watching of leaders, so embedded in late Jacobean culture and continuing into the 1630s, provided the necessary background for the achievement for which the mature Milton is so remarkable: his 'modern' ability to offer an analysis and critique of the manipulative powers of governments (see Sharpe 2000: 289–92; also Achinstein 1994; Zwicker 1993: 37–59; Corns 1992a: 194–220). The demystifying methods of *Eikonoklastes* and the many reductive exposures of the cultures of courts and churches in his later writings, splendidly compressed into the picture of the manipulations of court, religion and council in the first two books of *Paradise Lost*, may all have been primed by that zealous watching of the 1620s. One is tempted to use 'Lycidas' yet once more: what that poem also expresses, in its zealous watching of 1637, is a warning to his own university not to become the tool of its secular master, Charles, and all his formalist prelates.

BIBLIOGRAPHY

Writings

Milton (1972) [Trinity Manuscript].

References for Further Reading

Achinstein (1994); Brown (2000); Campbell (1987); Cogswell (1989); Corns (1992a); Cust (1987); Cust and Hughes (1989); Fincham (1990); Fletcher, Harris F. (1956); Green, Ian (1996); Hill (1958, 1977); Jameson (1981); Lake (1989); Lockyer (1981); Miller, Leo (1980, 1990); Morrill (1993); Myriell (1623); Norbrook (1999); Parker, rev. Campbell (1996); Patterson (1993); Sharpe (1989, 2000); Tyacke (1987, 1998); Walzer (1965); White (1992); Zwicker (1993).

8
Milton and Puritanism

N. H. Keeble

The 'ambiguous ill-made word'

The term 'puritan' became current during the 1560s as a pejorative nickname for Protestants who, dissatisfied with the Elizabethan settlement of the church by the Act of Uniformity of 1559, would have subscribed to the contention of the *Admonition to Parliament* of 1572 that 'we in England are so fare off, from having a church rightly reformed, accordingly to the prescript of Gods worde, that as yet we are not come to the outwarde face of the same' (Frere and Douglas 1907: 9). Puritans were distinguishable by their dissatisfaction with the rites and ceremonies of the Elizabethan church and by their desire to continue the process of Protestant reformation, halted in mid-career in England, they believed, in the compromise of an established church which retained government by bishops and a liturgy still modelled on that of Rome. They never, however, belonged to a single sect or constituted a clearly defined group within or without the episcopal Church of England. Drawing on native Lollard traditions which, despite sustained persecution, had survived in popular culture since the early fifteenth century, and fired by the zeal of exiles who, having fled during the reign of the Roman Catholic Queen Mary (1553–8), now returned inspired by their experience of the reformed practices of Jean Calvin (1509–64) at Geneva and Johann Bullinger (1504–75) at Zurich, puritanism had no one founder, no single recognized leader and no agreed policy. It embraced many forms and degrees of discontent with the *via media* of the Elizabethan church, from refusing to observe some of its rituals and ceremonial practices (such as, for ministers, wearing a surplice or, for worshippers, kneeling to receive the sacrament), to a refusal to attend the parish church and a rejection of the validity of episcopal orders. To realize their aspirations, puritans came to propose a variety of alternative models of church government and also, as they came into conflict with ecclesiastical institutions and the state authorities which supported those institutions, a variety of alternative constitutional political models.

The term 'puritan' is hence capacious and vague. Its scope has been much debated by modern historians who have sought to limit its connotations, but they are hampered by the looseness of its use in the seventeenth century. This was fully recognized at the time: 'the detested odious name of Puritan', remarked the anonymous *Discourse Concerning Puritans* (1641), probably the work of Henry Parker, so 'dilates itself' in ecclesiastical, political and moral senses that its 'vast circumference' encompasses a multitude of meanings (in Sasek 1989: 164, 167, 168); it is 'an ambiguous ill-made word', agreed the eminent puritan divine Richard Baxter (*Naked popery* [1677], 30). In a much cited chapter on 'The Definition of a Puritan' the modern historian Christopher Hill collected together a great many such citations illustrating the varied and conflicting senses of the word and the frustration of contemporaries with its elusiveness (Hill 1969b: 15–30; cf. Spurr 1998: 3–8, 17–27).

Nevertheless, while it is impossible to offer a precise definition of puritanism in ecclesiological, doctrinal or political terms, there is not, in practice, much difficulty in recognizing the puritan spirit (cf. the title of Nuttall 1967). While it manifested itself in a variety of ecclesiastical, theological and constitutional positions, its defining characteristic was a dissatisfaction with the present realization of Christian ideals and a consequent determination to reform practices and institutions. Its various strategies and platforms shared a desire to recover for individuals and for congregations the purity of doctrine, the simplicity of worship, the commitment of ministry and the integrity of faith which (it was believed) had characterized the early, or 'primitive', church of the first three centuries after Christ, before the growth of the ascendancy of Rome over western Christendom led (so it was held) to the corruption of the Christian Gospel and church. For all the revolutionary impetus of its politics, puritanism is hence marked by the backward glance, by a constant longing to return not only to the days of the early church, but even to the purity and innocence of Eden: the prospect of paradise regained haunts its imagination. Its moral and spiritual effort was directed to living as though 'strangers and pilgrims on the earth', natives of 'a better country, that is, an heavenly' (Hebrews 11: 13, 16). It was this repudiation of the world which led to characterizations of the puritan as a fanatic killjoy like Shakespeare's Malvolio in *Twelfth Night*. It led also to popular charges of hypocrisy and absurdity: the 'Stage-poets, Minstrels and the jesting Buffoons of the age, [made] them the principal subject of derision' (Parker, in Sasek 1989: 167), as in Ben Jonson's satiric representations of puritans in *The Alchemist* and *Bartholomew Fair*, or, after the political defeat of puritanism, in the protagonists of Samuel Butler's burlesque poem *Hudibras*. Those sympathetic to puritanism believed that, in popular usage, the term was no more than a convenient tag by which to insult anyone of 'honest strict demeanour, and civil conversation', an insult 'to cast dirt in the face of all goodness, Theological, Civil or Moral' (Parker, in Sasek 1989: 164, 167). Detailing the various senses of the term in the earlier seventeenth century, Baxter lamented that, *'among the vulgar'*, *'one that would speak seriously or reverently of God or Heaven, or of the scripture . . . or that would not swear . . . or that would not spend part of the Lords day in sports or idleness; or that would*

pray in his family...were called Puritanes and Precisians and hated and reviled openly'
(Keeble and Nuttall 1991, letter 448).

Since the culture of the time identified the well-being of the nation with uniform religious practice, any form of dissent or noncompliance was rigorously punished, by fines, imprisonment, mutilation or even (for persistent offenders) exile. For the greater part of its history, puritanism was in conflict with the law of the land and puritans were subject to various punitive legal measures and to persecution. The exception was the brief period during the 1640s and 1650s when men of puritan conviction gained political power. The loss of that power with the restoration of the Stuart monarchy in 1660 led to a period of sustained and determined persecution intended finally to suppress all dissident opinion. The attempt failed. The acceptance of toleration as a religious and civil duty was perhaps the most significant cultural development of the seventeenth century. It was a development driven by the courageous determination of generations of puritans not to submit their consciences to the dictates of ecclesiastical or state power. This resolution is nowhere more evident than in Milton's life and writing. He is a central figure in the cultural history of puritanism, a man whose life was shaped by commitment to its religious and political cause, whose writings were occasioned by their demands and whose creativity was inspired by their ideals. To read Milton is to know what it was to be a puritan.

Milton and Puritan Ecclesiology

The ecclesiastical history of puritanism is marked by the promulgation of, controversy over and rivalry among a succession of models of Reformed church government. Presbyterianism was the aim of the majority of early puritans, led by such Cambridge men as Walter Travers (*c.* 1584–1635) and Thomas Cartwright (1535–1603). This aspiration survived to become the official policy of the Long Parliament which, having abolished episcopacy in January 1643, summoned the Westminster Assembly of Divines in September 1643 to advise on a new church settlement. However, despite the publication of the Assembly's series of classic Presbyterian formularies – *Directory of Church-Government* (1644), *Directory of Public Worship* (1645), *Confession of Faith* (1648) and *Larger and Shorter Catechism* (1648) – its efforts were frustrated by opposition from within the puritan movement itself. The polity known originally as 'Independency', but in New England and subsequently in England as 'congregationalism' (cf. John Cotton, *The Way of the Congregational Churches* [1648]), was, under the patronage of Oliver Cromwell (1599–1658), successfully championed by the New Model Army with its watch-cry of 'Liberty of Conscience'.

While Presbyterians continued to think, like the episcopalians, in terms of a parish-based national church with a hierarchical government and a legally enforceable uniformity of belief and practice (with rigorous punishment of dissenters), Independency was based upon the autonomy of each separate congregation. Such congregations gathered themselves under ministers whom they elected and they ran their affairs in ways which were markedly democratic. While different churches might associate together, this system imposed upon no one church or region authority over the others, nor did it recognize a ministerial hierarchy. (These congregational principles were embodied in *The Savoy Declaration of Faith and Order* [1658], for which John Owen [1616–83] was largely responsible.) Though the resultant diversity of practice and belief horrified traditionalists committed to uniformity, Presbyterian no less than episcopalian, it is to Cromwell's lasting credit that as Protector he tolerated the widest possible range of Protestant opinion.

This divergence in ecclesiology is nicely illustrated by two early characterizations of puritanism: in his *English Puritanism* (1605), William Bradshaw (1571–1618) described an Independent, but John Geree (1601?–49) described a Presbyterian in his *The Character of an Old English Puritan* (1646) (see Sasek 1989: 78–94, 208–12). There was, furthermore, division within the Presbyterian ranks, between such strict Presbyterians as Thomas Edwards (1599–1647), who saw toleration as tending to religious and civil anarchy, and a significant group of so-called 'Presbyterians' who favoured ecclesiastical compromise based on the modified form of episcopacy (essentially a system of parochial bishops) proposed by James Ussher (1581–1656), Archbishop of Armagh. Their leader, Richard Baxter (1615–91), who preferred to be styled a 'Reconciler' rather than a 'Presbyterian', declared 'You could not (except a Catholick Christian) have truelier called me than an *Episcopal-Presbyterian-Independent*' (*A Third Defence of the Cause of Peace* [1681]: 110).

Cromwell's commitment to liberty of conscience, coupled with the hectic revolutionary temper of the Civil War years and Interregnum, saw, in addition to the Presbyterian and Independent traditions, the emergence of a great variety of radical sects which carried the Protestant principles of the Reformation to ever greater extremes. Since Elizabeth's reign there had been in existence small separatist congregations which had abandoned the legislative effort for national reform (cf. Robert Browne [*c.* 1550–1633], *Of Reformation without Tarrying for Any* [1582]). Variously condemned as 'Brownists', 'Barrowists' (after Henry Barrow, *c.* 1550–93), 'Anabaptists' and 'fanatics', their seventeenth-century successors, who included an unusually high representation of the socially disadvantaged and marginalized, espoused a range of disconcerting social and political aspirations which attracted opprobrium to themselves for tending all too literally to 'turn the world upside down' (Acts 17: 6; cf. Hill 1972). They included the Levellers of John Lilburne (1614?–57), the more radical and idealistic Diggers led by Gerrard Winstanley (fl. 1648–52), and a variety of short-lived and amorphous groups who scandalized contemporaries as Ranters and Familists. From this enthusiastic culture came the Baptists, who repudiated infant baptism (paedobaptism) in favour of the baptism of mature believers, and, in the 1650s, the Quakers, who, focusing on the illumination of the Spirit working within each believer, repudiated all the external ordinances and practices by which a church was traditionally defined. In the latter part of the century the charismatic George Fox (1624–91) emerged as their leader.

Milton, by his own account, was 'destin'd of a child' for a career in the church, but, convinced by the lordly high-handedness of the bishops (as it appeared to him) that 'tyranny had invaded the Church', he refused to 'subscribe slave' to secure ordination and so found himself, in a memorable phrase, 'Church-outed by the Prelats' (*CPW* I: 823). As it appears in a rhetorically charged polemical tract (*The Reason of Church-Government*, 1642), this passage may not be biographically reliable, but its accuracy matters less than the fact that Milton clearly wished to claim for himself a classic puritan's progress. He had been sufficiently conservative to write, in 1626, poems commemorating such pillars of the Jacobean church as Lancelot Andrewes, Bishop of Winchester ('Elegy III') and Nicholas Felton, Bishop of Ely ('*In Obitum Praesulis Eliensis*'); but by 1637, when he wrote 'Lycidas', there is a distinctly puritan edge to the scorn with which, in the voice of St Peter, he derides those ministers who 'for their bellies sake, / Creep and intrude, and climb into the fold' while 'The hungry sheep look up, and are not fed' (lines 114–15, 125). Outrage at such neglect of its pastoral duty was what fuelled puritan discontent with the Caroline church. When, a few years later, Milton returned from his continental tour in order to commit himself to the oppositional cause, it was this scorn which animated his first prose writings in the service of the Revolution. In a series of vituperative antiprelatical tracts (that is, tracts written against episcopacy) published in 1641–2 he excoriated the bishops: Andrewes was now a target of mockery (*CPW* I: 768–79).

In January 1643 the Long Parliament did abolish episcopacy, and convened the Westminster Assembly of Divines to advise on a national church settlement. It is a curiosity of Milton's antiprelatical tracts that, while they have a very great deal to say about bishops, and none of it good, they have almost nothing to say about what church polity should replace them. Hence, while Milton may be supposed in 1641–2 to have had Presbyterian sympathies, there is no evidence in him of any firm Presbyterian commitment, or even of much interest in ecclesiology *per se*. It is the prospect of the corrupt and tyrannical exercise of power which animates his writing, as it would do throughout his life. Before very long, he discerned this abuse in Presbyterians no less than in episcopalians. In *Areopagitica* (1644) he registered his disappointment at the determination of the Long Parliament, the majority of whose members were Presbyterians, to re-impose censorship and to stifle debate. Presbyterianism, it appeared, was quite as determined to outlaw dissent from its views as the episcopalians had been to enforce compliance with theirs. Of this, Milton had first-hand experience. He was deeply affected by the savagery of the response to his divorce tracts of 1643–5, three of them addressed to the Long Parliament and the first also to the Westminster Assembly. He was attacked in print by William Prynne, a leading lawyer and MP, and by Robert Baillie, a Scottish Presbyterian commissioner at the Westminster Assembly, and he found himself among the heretics and fanatics berated in Edwards's *Gangraena* (1646) as a libertine 'divorcer'. In two poems of 1646 (not published until 1673) Milton reacted bitterly to this outcry. In Sonnet XII he protested that he 'did but prompt the age to quit their clogs' (line 1) and, denying the authority of 'shallow Edwards and Scotch What-d'ye-call' to determine the limits of tolerable opinion, he concluded his extended sonnet 'On the New Forcers of Conscience under the Long Parliament' with resounding alliterative condemnation: 'New *Presbyter* is but old *Priest* writ large' (lines 12, 20).

Thereafter, Milton is to be counted among the Independents. It had been for 'crowding free consciences and Christian liberties into canons and precepts of men' that he had condemned the 'Prelaticall tradition' in *Areopagitica* (1644), and for 'the liberty to know, to utter, and to argue freely according to conscience, above all liberties' that he had argued passionately in that tract (*CPW* II: 554, 560). The uncompromising resolution with which Milton privileged conscience above all external authorities may have been unusual (though not unique: George Fox is his equal in this), but its general bias is distinctive of the individualism of puritanism. Inwardness and experiential immediacy are everywhere preferred in Milton. Throughout his writings there runs an authentically puritan opposition between the hollowness of habitual compliance with external forms and the integrity of inner commitment. The hypocrisy which Milton stigmatized in such phrases as 'a grosse conforming stupidity', 'this iron yoke of outward conformity', 'the ghost of a linnen decency', 'the gripe of custom' (*CPW* II: 563–4), was conceived as the single most serious obstacle to the spiritual life, whose highest virtue he took to be sincerity. It is as the 'Spirit, that dost prefer / Before all temples the upright heart and pure' that Milton characterizes the God whom he invokes at the opening of *Paradise Lost* (I. 17–18). It is with the sincerity of extemporary prayer, 'and other rites / Observing none', that Adam and Eve address God before retiring for the night (IV. 736–7). Above all, it is the attainment of an experiential 'paradise within thee, happier far' than the material bliss of Eden that Michael recommends to Adam, and *Paradise Lost* to its readers in the fallen world (XII. 587).

Puritanism associated this integrity with simplicity and plainness, in worship, in social manners and in aesthetics. The Quaker habit of using the familiar *thee* and *thou* to all, regardless of rank, epitomizes this preference for plain dealing over the dictates of social and cultural etiquette. That bias appears in Milton's statement that 'in matters of religion he is learnedest who is planest', and in his re-iteration of the puritan commonplace that 'in main matters of belief and salvation' the Bible is 'plane and easie to the poorest' (*CPW* VII: 272, 302). Though in his earlier prose and in *Paradise Lost* generic decorum required of him the rhetorical firecrackers of polemic and the grandeur of epic style respectively, plainness is nevertheless affirmed as virtue's style: the elaborateness of episcopal ceremonial marks down the bishops as surely as, in *Paradise Lost*, rhetorical dexterity declares Satan's duplicity; Adam and Eve dress up neither themselves nor their words.

Milton and Restoration Nonconformity

Following the restoration of the monarchy in 1660, the Act of Uniformity (1662) sought to secure a firmly episcopalian and traditional character for the re-established church by excluding from it all puritan opinion. It required episcopal ordination of every incumbent in the Church of England and his 'unfeigned assent and consent' to the entire Book of Common Prayer. Many of the 2,000 or so ministers, lecturers and university fellows ejected by 'Black Bartholomew Day', 24 August 1662, were unwilling nonconformists who hoped for eventual 'comprehension' (as the term was) within a broader national church. The restored regime, however, had other ideas. A series of punitive acts sought to deprive them of the means of livelihood, to prevent them holding services for worship, and to ostracize nonconformists and their followers from society. A period of persecution ensued during which they were at constant risk of beatings, fines and imprisonment, at the mercy of vicious neighbours, street gangs and paid informers. The campaign of intimidation failed. In 1689 the Toleration Act finally permitted worship in non-episcopal congregations. Nonconformity henceforth became an established fact of the nation's religious life: puritanism thus passed into dissent.

There is no evidence that either before or after the Restoration Milton was a member of any particular church. However, his continuing commitment to the puritan cause, and his sympathy for the suffering nonconformists, is clearly inscribed in his later writings. Most striking, perhaps, is the depiction in *Paradise Lost* of Abdiel, the one angel to resist Satan's blandishments. Unwavering commitment and indifference to adverse circumstances are his:

> Among the faithless, faithful only he;
> Among innumerable false, unmoved,
> Unshaken, unseduced, unterrified
> His loyalty he kept, his love, his zeal;
> Nor number, nor example with him wrought
> To swerve from truth, or change his constant mind
> Though single
>
> (V. 897–903)

Writing under the restrictions of Restoration prepublication censorship, Milton cannot explicitly identify the 'innumerable false' with the restored royalists and episcopalians, nor Abdiel's constancy with the witness of the persecuted nonconformist heirs of the puritans. However, two seemingly slight lexical choices do effect such an identification for the attentive reader. First, Abdiel describes as 'dissent' his refusal to join the angelic rebellion and as 'my sect' the heavenly host which confronts Satan (VI. 146, 147). At this date, *sect* and *dissent* are used exclusively of the nonconformists, and disparagingly, yet here is Milton so describing those loyal to God; the inference is plain. And secondly, in the proem to Book VII, Milton, in the person of the narrator, says of himself that, though 'fallen on evil days', he yet sings 'with mortal voice, unchanged / To hoarse or mute' (VII. 24–5). Abdiel would not 'change his constant mind' (V. 902); Milton is 'unchanged': Abdiel and the 'sect' of heaven retain their allegiance in despite of Satan, as Milton and the nonconformists keep theirs in despite of persecution (Keeble 1995/6: 11–12). If one would know the character of a puritan, it is here in the depiction of the Abdiel, with whom Milton identifies himself.

It is that unchanged voice which is heard when, in Book XII of *Paradise Lost*, Michael foretells the degeneration of the Christian church in the very tones of the Milton of the 1640s. The apostles, says Michael, will be succeeded by 'grievous wolves' who, abandoning the inspiration of the Spirit within, 'the truth / With superstitions and traditions taint'. Assuming to themselves 'names / Places and titles' and compelling obedience to their authority, they will 'force the spirit of grace itself, and bind / His consort liberty', with the result that 'heavy persecution' will fall on 'all who in the worship persevere / Of spirit and truth' and on those who refuse to accept that that 'in outward rites and specious forms / Religion [is] satisfied' (XII. 508–35). Milton's anticlericalism has not cooled since the antiprelatical tracts.

Samson Agonistes, almost certainly Milton's final poem (Worden 1995), is a study of imprisonment and despair consequent upon the loss, as it appears, of God's favour which, in many of its details, reproduces sympathetically the experience of nonconformists. When the Chorus exclaims at the suffering of God's chosen, dragged before 'unjust tribunals, under change of times, / And condemnation of the ungrateful multitude' (lines 695–6), it is impossible not to recognize the plight of nonconformists enduring the popular reaction against puritanism after the 'change' of the Restoration. Samson's description of what he endures, a 'prisoner chained', scarcely able to 'draw / The air imprisoned also, close and damp, / Unwholesome draught', delineates the plight of many an imprisoned nonconformist who, like Samson, found himself incarcerated for following what he took to be the divine will (lines 7–9). And the Chorus's bewilderment at the prospect of the chained Samson enacts the incomprehension of puritans who had thought themselves, like Samson, God's 'champion', led on 'to mightiest deeds' in the Civil War only to find themselves 'cast . . . off as never known' at the Restoration and left 'helpless' in the power of 'cruel enemies', the royalists, whom, by God's 'appointment', they had 'provoked' (lines 638, 641–4). And, in the passage in *Paradise Lost* just referred to, it is in this despised company that Milton situates himself, as one 'fallen on evil days / . . . In darkness, and with dangers compassed round, / And solitude' (VII. 25–8). For all the cultural authority of its classicism, *Paradise Lost* in fact speaks for the culturally deprived, for the marginalized and the despised: it speaks, in the decade of royalist triumphalism, for the nonconformist heirs of the puritans.

Milton and Puritan Politics

Although originally a religious movement, and always maintaining that character, puritanism quickly developed a political dimension. Under Elizabeth, a puritan party in the political sense had sought unsuccessfully to pass legislation reforming the national church. When, in 1603, James succeeded to the English throne, puritans

believed their time had come. This proved to be far from the case: James was only too
relieved to have left Presbyterian Scotland behind and had no inclination to import its
ecclesiastical ways into England. Puritan disappointment deepened when in 1625 his
son, Charles I, married the Roman Catholic Henrietta Maria and quickly showed
himself devoted to the ritualistic and liturgical – that is, in puritan eyes, to the
Romish – in religious practice. Charles's promotion of William Laud (1573–1645), a
suspected 'Romanizer' and a professed foe to all dissident and puritan opinion,
successively to the bishopric of London (1628) and the archbishopric of Canterbury
(1633), and his ruling without Parliament during the 1630s with Laud as a chief
minister, contrived to cement political opposition to his despotism with puritan
opposition to his religious policy. The cause of the crown became identified with
the cause of the episcopal church. The terms 'Presbyterian' and (subsequently)
'Independent' are henceforth descriptive of a political party as much as of a religious
denomination, and it becomes all but impossible to disentangle religious from
political motivation among those who opposed the Caroline regime. It was widely
believed that king and archbishop were complicit in a plot to introduce tyranny and
popery (the two indistinguishable in the eyes of most English people). The Grand
Remonstrance and accompanying petition, presented by the Commons to Charles I on
1 December 1641, warned the King that his bishops, 'who cherish formality and
superstitions', and ministers and members of his Privy Council, who 'for private ends
have engaged themselves to further the interests of some foreign princes', had been
corrupted by 'malignant parties' bent upon the return of popery into England. They
urged him to deprive the bishops of their voting power in the Lords, to relieve his
subjects of the need to comply with 'unnecessary ceremonies' and to remove from his
council all who promoted 'those pressures and corruptions wherewith [his] people
have been grieved' (Gardiner 1906: 203–7).

   The Remonstrance is couched in the very terms of Milton's antiprelatical tracts. In
the early 1640s Milton was speaking the language of the Long Parliament and
supporting its programme of reform. In his *Apology* (1642) he hailed its members as
'publick benefactors', 'reformers of the Church, and the restorers of the Commonwealth', 'Fathers of their countrey' (*CPW* I: 922, 924, 926). It is true that when, in his
Doctrine and Discipline of Divorce (1643), he praised their 'eminence and fortitude' and
'couragious and heroick resolutions' (*CPW* II: 226, 233), the commendation is in part
explicable by the occasion and purpose of his tract: Milton was looking for legislative
support for his proposals, and a little flattery of MPs would not go amiss. Nevertheless, it was in the Long Parliament that he placed his trust, and all too quickly it
proved to be misplaced. His subsequent support for the New Model Army, the Rump
and for Cromwell was founded in his disillusion at the Long Parliament's abandonment of the principles of reformed Protestantism, typified for Milton in the re-
imposition of prepublication censorship: 'Bishops and Presbyters are the same to us
both name and thing' he declared in *Areopagitica*, anticipating his 1646 poem (*CPW*
II: 539). He would henceforth be as bitter a political opponent of Presbyterians as of
any royalist or episcopalian.

If in the early 1640s Milton shared Parliament's contempt for bishops, he shared too its suspicion of courtiers and the court. In 1634, to typify moral turpitude, he picks the figure of a licentious courtier: when, in *Comus*, the Lady, who prefers the 'honest-offered courtesy' of 'lowly sheds' to the 'courts of princes', accepts the invitation to Comus's 'low / . . . cottage', it is to find herself trapped and threatened with rape in a 'stately palace' (lines 318–24, stage direction at line 657). It is in the accents of innumerable Caroline court poets that Comus attempts seduction: 'List Lady be not coy, and be not cozened / With that same vaunted name virginity' (lines 736–7). With fine generic irony, Milton chooses the masque, the form which was above all others identified with the Stuart court, through which to represent court culture as the source of temptation and evil. His opinion of courts never improved. In *The Readie and Easie Way* (1660), only a month before the Restoration, Milton foresaw a reactionary tyranny of decadent indulgence as its inevitable consequence: 'the old encroachments' would come on 'by little and little upon our consciences' within a culture of servile deference to a king who 'must be ador'd like a Demigod, with a dissolute and haughtie court about him, of vast expence and luxurie, masks and revels', while he has little to do but 'to pageant himself up and down in progress among the perpetual bowings and cringings of an abject people' (*CPW* VII: 423, 425, 426). Small wonder that in *Paradise Lost*, the monarchical is associated with the Satanic: it is 'High on a throne of royal state, which far / Outshone the wealth of Ormus and of Ind, / Or where the gorgeous East with riches hand / Showers on her kings barbaric pearl and gold' that Satan sits to conduct the council in hell (II. 1–4). In contrast, Adam walks out to meet Raphael 'without more train / Accompanied than with his own complete / Perfections, in himself was all his state'. He has no need of 'the tedious pomp that waits / On princes, when their rich retínue long / Of horses led, and grooms besmeared with gold / Dazzles the crowd, and sets them all agape' (V. 351–7). Ornament has become contamination in that 'besmeared': so much for the royal pageantry so beloved of the Stuarts!

Disdaining court culture, and disillusioned with the Presbyterians, Milton was immediately ready to defend the regicide in *The Tenure of Kings and Magistrates* (1649), a work whose especial venom is reserved not for the royalists but for the Presbyterians who, by seeking a negotiated settlement with the King in the late 1640s, in Milton's view lacked the courage of the convictions which had led them to embark on civil war. This denigration of those now purged from the Rump Parliament would have commended Milton to the military authorities quite as much as his defence of the regicide. The tract earned him a place in the government of the Commonwealth and of the Protectorate. As Secretary of Foreign Tongues he became the public voice of republican Britain, charged with defending its actions and with conducting its correspondence with foreign regimes. In this service, Milton had travelled beyond majority puritan opinion. The execution of Charles continued to be regarded with abhorrence by the majority of puritans, and republicanism, the consequence rather than the cause of the regicide, only ever enjoyed minority support. During the 1650s, those whose respect it did command grew disillusioned with the very man who had made it possible, Cromwell. The Protectorate was increasingly regarded as a monarchy in all but name, repudiated as fiercely by republicans for betraying the 'Good Old Cause' as by royalists for usurping Stuart power – but not, initially, by Milton. In 1652, in his sonnet 'To the Lord General Cromwell', written before the inauguration of the Protectorate, Milton, praising Cromwell as 'our chief of men', looks to him, not to Parliament, 'to save free conscience from the paw / Of hireling wolves whose Gospel in their maw' (lines 1, 13–14). In his *Pro Populo Anglicano Defensio Secunda*, published in 1654, a few months after Cromwell had become Lord Protector, Milton receives from his opponent the charge that he is 'worse than Cromwell' as 'the highest praise you could bestow on me' and he defends Cromwell's character, military prowess and exercise of power (*CPW* IV: 595, 662–9). However, during the final four years of Cromwell's life, Milton has nothing more to say of him, nor is there any elegiac tribute at his death. It appears that finally Cromwell, too, may have disappointed Milton, certainly so if mention of 'a short but scandalous night of interruption' in a 1659 tract written after the army had restored the Rump refers, as is likely, to the interruption of republican government by the Protectorate (*CPW* VII: 274; see further Woolrych 1974; Worden 1998).

In 1660 enthusiasm for the Restoration may not have been as universal as royalist propagandists claimed, but there is no doubting a general desire among puritans to return to traditional forms of authority. Milton, however, was pre-eminently possessed of the courage of his convictions. In the spring of 1660, when the Restoration of monarchy was evidently inevitable, he continued, at great risk to himself, to warn his countrymen against 'chusing them a captain back for *Egypt*' (*CPW* VII: 463). The man who, in *Eikonoklastes* (1649), had sought to destroy the sainted image of Charles I had lost none of his contempt for Stuart kings or their courts.

Looking back on his prose career in 1654, Milton constructed it as a systematic defence of religious, civil and domestic duty (*CPW* IV: 623–4). We may doubt that he had so coherent a programme at the time, but there is no denying that liberty is championed throughout the tracts. It continues to preoccupy the later poems: it is as a freedom fighter warring against a tyrannical God that Satan presents himself in *Paradise Lost*, and upon the discrediting of that claim that the poem's theodicy turns. The target of Milton's prose tracts reappears in Satan's totalitarian identification of freedom with power ('to be weak is miserable', I. 157); as Eve puts it in a marvellously Satanic rhetorical question, 'inferior who is free?' (IX. 825).

Milton and Puritan Doctrine

Puritan theology was as varied as puritan ecclesiology. Many puritans, such as John Owen and John Bunyan (1628–88), did retain the Calvinist allegiance of the puritan fathers, notably the 'English Calvin' William Perkins (1558–1602). This predestinarian theology exalted the sovereignty of God by attributing entirely to his inscrutable will the salvation or damnation of every person. It denied that corrupt humans have the capacity either to deserve, or even to choose to co-operate with, divine grace in effecting their salvation. Two apparent consequences perplexed critics of Calvinism: first, if God predetermines damnation, then he appears to be responsible for the sin which leads to damnation. And secondly, if salvation is owing solely to the imputation to the elect of the unmerited and unconditional free grace of Christ, then what role is there for morality in the Christian life? Antinomianism (the view that, since the salvation of the elect is immutably predetermined, they are not bound by the moral law) appeared to be the logical consequence of Calvinism. Among radicals, Titus 1: 15 ('Unto the pure all things are pure') might push such antinomianism into libertinism and amorality. However, while Calvinism continued to hold sway with many puritan divines, or to be carried to what might be regarded as its logical conclusion, others, such as the eminent republican Independent John Goodwin (1594?–1665), rejected Calvinism for Arminianism. This theology, derived from the Dutch Reformed theologian Jacob Arminius (1560–1609), rejected the predestinarianism of Calvinism and stressed the capacity of the human will to co-operate with, or to reject, divine grace. Other divines, notably Baxter, favoured the 'middle way' between these theologies developed by the French theologian Moise Amyraldus (1596–1664) and the theologians of the Protestant academy at Saumur. It allowed greater scope to the human will by maintaining that the Atonement was hypothetically universal (unlike the Calvinists, who limited its efficacy to the elect), but preserved the primacy of the divine role by maintaining election to salvation, though not to damnation. What matters more than the details of these theological positions, however, is the restless spirit of enquiry and passionate doctrinal debate which characterized puritanism.

Milton was certainly no Calvinist. In an example of the rhetorical figure polyptoton, the word 'free' and its grammatical variants echo through the Father's exposition of the divine plan in Book III of *Paradise Lost*. Humankind are created 'just and right, / Sufficient to have stood, though free to fall'; the fallen angels were 'formed free' and cannot for their rebellion blame 'Their maker, or their making, or their fate, / As if predestination overruled / Their will, disposed by absolute decree / Or high foreknowledge; they themselves decreed / Their own revolt': 'Freely they stood who stood, and fell who fell'. The homiletic purpose of the passage is perhaps at odds with its dramatic character as a divine pronouncement since its extended and repetitive structure creates a defensive and petulant tone unbecoming the divine; but its re-iterations are clearly designed to discountenance Calvinism and to leave the reader in no doubt that responsibility for moral acts lies squarely with the creature, not the creator: 'I formed them free, and free they must remain, / Till they enthrall themselves' (III. 95–128).

Milton is, then, committed to the freedom of the human will. Whether this puts him in the Arminian camp, or with the 'middle way' men, is debatable. God's pronouncement that some are 'chosen of peculiar grace / Elect above the rest; so is my will' but those who 'hear me call' in vain seal their own fate (*PL* III. 183–202), certainly sounds like the Amyraldian middle way (as argued by Thomas 1964: 49) but

Milton's theology is usually described as Arminian (as by Danielson [1982]). Whichever classification is preferred, however, Milton is characteristically puritan in the nature of his theological enterprise. 'Truth', he wrote in *Areopagitica*, referring to Psalm 85: 11, 'is compar'd in scripture to a streaming fountain; if her waters flow not in a perpetuall progression, they sick'n into a muddy pool of conformity and tradition' (*CPW* II: 543). The puritan mind does not declare itself in a particular sectarianism or dogmatism: Christian understanding is a continuing process of education and spiritual enlightenment rather than a goal ever finally achieved. We should indeed be grateful for the 'light of the Reformation' Protestants enjoy, but any 'who thinks we are to pitch our tent here, and have attain'd the utmost prospect of reformation...by this very opinion declares, that he is yet farre short of Truth' (*CPW* II: 548–9). What animates *Areopagitica* is not the revelation of truth but the excitement of its pursuit through interrogation and debate. That is why it is not heresy but conservatism, complacency and tradition which are the enemies, and why, for Milton, Christian faith carries with it the responsibility of independent intellectual endeavour: 'To be still searching what we know not, by what we know, still closing up truth to truth as we find it . . . is the golden rule in *Theology*' (*CPW* II: 551). Milton's claim to have formulated the arguments of his *Doctrine and Discipline of Divorce* with '*no light, or leading receav'd from any man*' but with '*only the infallible grounds of scripture to be my guide*' (*CPW* II: 433) is consistent with this. So, too, is the refusal of *De Doctrina Christiana* to rely upon commentaries and expositors. Even though the treatise may not be entirely of Milton's composition (Campbell et al. 1997), and though its heretical positions would have been fiercely contested, its intellectual ambition is entirely Miltonic and typical of the individualism of the puritan mind. Bunyan, for example, was taught by his pastor, John Gifford, to take 'not up any truth upon trust, as from this or that or another man or men, but to cry mightily to God that he would convince us of the reality therof'; his early publications were recommended to readers as inspired 'not by humane art, but by the spirit of Christ', and Bunyan himself, playing down the extent of his education, boasted that he had not 'borrowed my Doctrine from Libraries. I depend upon the sayings of no man' (Keeble 1987: 156–7).

This is another aspect of that privileging of self-determination and insistence on the duty of self-reflection which is so marked a feature of puritanism and which has left its legacy in the English lexicon: 'selfhood', and such other compounds in 'self' as 'self-command', 'self-confidence', 'self-esteem' are seventeenth-century coinages. It explains what may otherwise appear a distasteful, and inconsistent, feature of Milton's writing, namely his unwavering intolerance of Roman Catholicism. It is intolerable because, to Milton's way of thinking, it is impossible to be a sincere Roman Catholic. The stress in that tradition upon obedience to ecclesiastical authority reduces faith to subservience. Roman Catholics have what Milton, following theological tradition, calls an *implicit faith*, that is, a faith based upon an authority other than an individual's understanding of the Bible. Genuine, *explicit faith*, depends upon personal conviction. It is because, in his view, it is possible for its adherents to believe only 'as the Church believes' that, in *Of True Religion*, published in 1673 following the dispensation to worship privately granted to papists by Charles II's Declaration of Indulgence of 1672, Milton excluded popery, as 'the only or the greatest Heresie' (*CPW* VIII: 420–1) in Christendom, from the toleration he advocated for all holders of explicit faith, that is, Protestants of any persuasion. Saving faith involves more than submission to authority and deference to precedent; it requires personal conviction and commitment, maintained, if need be, in spite of authority and precedent. Hence, paradoxically but understandably, for Milton a person 'may be a heretick in the truth ... if he beleeve things only because his Pastor sayes so ... though his belief be true, yet the very truth he holds, becomes his heresie' (*CPW* II: 543). Conversely, no man should be condemned for sincerely held doctrine, no matter how erroneous. Milton argues in *Of True Religion* that though members of different Protestant denominations may in their various ways be doctrinally mistaken, they are yet 'no Hereticks. Heresie is in the Will and choice ... error is against the Will, in misunderstanding ... It is a humane frailty to err, and no man is infallible here on earth' (*CPW* VIII: 423). So it is that, in *Paradise Lost*, though 'credulous' and deceived by Satan, Eve remains 'sinless' until persuaded by her error to believe the serpent rather than to God (IX. 644, 659).

Milton and the Temper of Puritanism

Puritanism's opposition to conformity and to tradition, so powerfully articulated by Milton, with its consequent championing of individualism, generated a dynamic conception of the Christian life which was characteristically rendered in images of action and endeavour. For the many who had, in the 1630s, fled Laud's persecution in the 'Great Migration' to New England, or who, like Fox, had journeyed throughout England in search of spiritual assurance, or who had travelled far from home with the regiments of the New Model Army, journeying and combat had been spiritual experiences in biographical fact. There was a further incentive to the presentation of the Christian life in terms of warfare and itinerancy in the many historical battles and migrations through which God led his chosen people Israel, and in the Bible's many metaphorical deployments of warfare and of wayfaring, culminating in the great dominical assertion of John 14: 6 ('I am the way') and in the Pauline imagery of the race for salvation (e.g. 1 Corinthians 9: 24) and of the armour of faith (e.g. Ephesians 6: 11–13). This led to such titles as Arthur Dent's *The Plain Mans Path-way to Heaven* (1601) and John Downame's *The Christian Warfare* (1609) – and, most famously, to Bunyan's *The Pilgrim's Progress* (1678, 1684) and *The Holy War* (1682).

Milton conceived of the Christian life in just this way, habitually imaging its moral responsibilities and spiritual demands in terms of struggle and effort: 'our faith and knowledge thrives by exercise, as well as our limbs and complexion' (*CPW* II: 543). As early as the Nativity Ode (1629) he offers us a Herculean Christ-child, a 'dreaded infant' able 'in his swaddling bands' to see off the 'damned crew' of pagan deities (lines

222, 228). In a famous sentence, Milton, recalling Paul's image of the race, scorned monastic withdrawal: 'I cannot praise a fugitive and cloister'd vertue, unexercis'd & unbreath'd, that never sallies out and sees her adversary, but slinks out of the race, where that immortall garland is to be run for, not without dust and heat' (*CPW* II: 515). The correction by hand of 'the true wayfaring Christian' to 'the true warfaring Christian' in presentation copies of *Areopagitica* nicely illustrates the proximity and the potency of these images for the Christian life (II: 515 with n. 102). Every one of Milton's dramatic and epic designs is focused upon a contest with an adversary, upon trial, testing. The various senses of the polysemous *Agonistes* reach beyond Samson to encompass every Miltonic protagonist: athlete, contestant, champion, struggle and agony.

However, despite all this martial imagery, the puritan hero bore no resemblance to the questing knight errant of medieval chivalry. This is an ideal Milton explicitly rejected in the opening to Book IX of *Paradise Lost*, where, mocking the 'long and tedious havoc' of medieval and Renaissance chivalric romance, he asserts that he is 'Not sedulous by nature to indite / Wars, hitherto the only argument / Heroic deemed'. Having, in the previous eight books, demonstrated his mastery of epic structure and stylistic decorum, in this extraordinary self-reflexive moment he rejects the heroic values upon which the genre is based and announces as 'more heroic' than traditional epic subjects 'the better fortitude / Of patience and heroic martrydom' (IX. 14, 26–41). The European imagination had been captivated for two millennia by the heroic ideal; this epic's repudiation of the traditional epic subject is a key moment in our literary and cultural history. Michael's denigration of the heroic code as the worship of brute force, and of traditional heroes as 'Destroyers rightlier called and plagues of men' (XI. 689–97) is of a piece with this rejection, as is the attribution of the heroic 'virtues' to Satan. The strongly pacifist vein in Milton's later writing, especially in the Son's refusal of the 'ostentation vain of fleshly arm, / And fragile arms' as means to secure his kingdom (*Paradise Regained*, III. 387–8), is consistent with the bias of later seventeenth-century puritan writing (and particularly that of the Quakers) which, disillusioned by the collapse of New Model Army's achievements into military dictatorship, repudiated all use of 'carnal weapons'.

And so *Paradise Lost* recommends a new kind of hero, defined in the closing exchange between Adam and Michael in terms of self-denial rather than self-assertion, of patience, trust and suffering rather than aggression, cunning and triumph (XII. 561–87). This 'better fortitude' is not restricted to a privileged armigerous class. On the contrary, puritanism challenged every person to become a Christian hero in the context of their everyday domestic and commercial dealings. It is characteristic of puritan theology that it is practical in nature. Puritan treatises have no concept of the 'spiritual' or 'religious' life separate from everyday social life. Doctrinal debate could be heated and wonderfully intricate, and there are some minute analyses of soteriological issues, but there are no great systematic puritan theologians. The bias of puritan writings is homiletic and casuistical, concerned with the challenges of living a committed Christian life: 'It was never the will of God that bare *speculation* should be the end of his *Revelation* or of *our belief*. Divinity is an *Affective practical* Science' (Baxter, *Directions for Weak Distempered Christians* (1669), pt I, pp. 97–8). The puritan classics – works such as Baxter's *The Saints Everlasting Rest* (1650) – are exercises in what we would now call psychological analysis and counselling, remarkable for their clear-sighted address to fallible human nature. The preoccupations of Milton's great poems chime exactly with this puritan bias. They are inescapably homiletic, out to do us good. They set about this task in the traditional way of the preacher, by discoursing on examples of moral predicaments. From the Lady in *Comus*, through Satan, Adam and Eve in *Paradise Lost* and the Son in *Paradise Regained* to Samson's despair, all the great poems are focused upon the psychology of temptation, upon the demands of introspection and self-scrutiny, the challenge of remaining faithful in adversity. In this sense, Milton has only one subject, and it is a characteristically puritan choice.

So it is that, for all the grandeur and universal scale of *Paradise Lost*, its focus is upon ordinary humankind; and at its centre lies a peculiarly humdrum and domestic Eden. When, having followed Satan on his prolonged journey across the cosmos, we finally arrive in Eden, the centre of the universe and of the poem, it is to find very little going on: eating, drinking, gardening and making love. This is not other-worldly perfection, but the perfection of the world of the reader's everyday experience. Ordinariness is essential to Milton's conception of Eden. His Adam and Eve are people like us. Just so, puritanism rejected the exclusivity of the Roman Catholic use of the term 'saint' for exceptional and exemplary persons and adopted it democratically for all sincere believers. Nor is salvation gender-specific. It is true that misogyny is no less in evidence within puritanism than within other cultural traditions, and within Milton no less than in other writers, but what is remarkable is the strength of the contrary tendency in both puritanism and in Milton. *Paradise Lost* presents the creation of Eve not as an afterthought but as the completion and perfection of a paradise in which, without her, Adam is discontent: 'In solitude / What happiness...?' (VIII. 364–5). This had been the view of the early puritans' preferred Bible, the Geneva translation of 1560, which glossed Genesis 2: 22 with the comment 'mankind was perfect when the woman was created, that before was like an imperfect building'. Puritan writings have no patience with Roman Catholic notions of asceticism and abstinence ('who bids abstain / But our destroyer, foe to God and man?', *Paradise Lost*, IV. 748–9) and, accepting the legitimacy and propriety of sexual desire, they locate human happiness in loving relations between men and women, the 'sum of earthly bliss' (VIII. 522). This is the cultural context for Milton's moving wedding hymn for Adam and Eve (IV. 750–73), and for the poem's celebration of the experience of Adam and Eve 'Imparadised in one another's arms' as 'The happier Eden' (IV. 506–7).

It is this emphasis which allows *Paradise Lost* to be claimed, unexpectedly but not absurdly, as our first novel: it concerns a marriage which hits a sticky patch but pulls through in the end. (The other claimant to the title, *The Pilgrim's Progress*, is also a puritan classic which may be summarized in just this same way.) The final image of the poem is of a man and a wife restored to each other. Milton's epic culminates not in the judgemental image of the 'brandished sword' but in the scene of Adam and Eve walking together, 'hand in hand', to encounter the world beyond Eden, 'and providence their guide' (XII. 633, 647–8).

BIBLIOGRAPHY

Writings

Baxter (1669, 1677, 1681); Frere and Douglas (1907); Gardiner (1906); Keeble and Nuttall (1991); Sasek (1989).

References for Further Reading

Barker, Arthur E. (1942); Campbell et al. (1997); Collinson (1967); Danielson (1982); Durston and Eales (1996); Hill (1969b, 1972, 1977); Keeble (1987, 1995/6); Nuttall (1967); Paul (1985); Spurr (1998); Thomas, Roger (1964); Wallace (1982); Wolfe (1963); Woolrych (1974); Worden (1995, 1998).

9
Radical Heterodoxy and Heresy

John Rumrich

'Radical heterodoxy' suggests sharp divergence from orthodox opinions and promotion of change at the root level. Heterodoxy and orthodoxy are relative terms and, like obscenity, defy conclusive definition. Yet it is certainly safe to say that John Milton's characteristic response to social, political and religious authorities was adversarial, as this excerpt from *The Doctrine and Discipline of Divorce* indicates:

> Custome still is silently receiv'd for the best instructer...a certaine big face of pretended learning...which not onely in private marrs our education, but also in publick is the common climer into every chaire, where either Religion is preach't or Law reported: filling each estate of life and profession, with abject and servil principles; depressing the high and Heaven-born spirit of Man, farre beneath the condition wherein either God created him, or sin hath sunke him...Custome being but a meer face, as Eccho is a meere voice, rests not in her unaccomplishment, untill...shee accorporat her selfe with error, who being a blind and Serpentine body without a head, willingly accepts what he wants, and supplies what her incompleatnesse went seeking. Hence it is, that Error supports Custome, Custome count'nances Error. And these two betweene them would persecute and chase away all truth and solid wisdome out of humane life. (*CPW* II: 222–3)

Addressing an audience that embraced the then orthodox doctrines of predestination and total human depravity, Milton blithely asserts human dignity and counters custom with 'the industry of free reasoning' (*CPW* II: 224). The same conviction and disposition conspicuous in this passage are common features of Milton's many and various heterodoxies: an axiomatic belief in rational liberty and undaunted willingness to challenge merely customary authority.

As compared to 'radical heterodoxy', the term 'heresy' seems narrower, as if it pertained to religion only. The ostensible confinement of heresy to religious affairs is misleading, however. In the seventeenth century religion influenced, or at least was deployed to justify, every social and political institution. Hence, most of Milton's radically heterodox opinions were also susceptible to the charge of heresy. Such accusations, moreover, often carried an element of intimidation; grave heresy was subject to punishment ranging from torture and mutilation to spectacular, gruesome death. In this chapter, I will distinguish Miltonic 'heterodoxy' from 'heresy' somewhat arbitrarily, by what each tells us about his intellectual character. Milton's heterodoxies reflect a core belief in human liberty and a disposition to autonomy, while his proclivity for heresy manifests a corresponding, dynamic philosophy of knowledge – a fountain of thought crime. From this perspective, heresy is the broader category because in Milton's usage it implies an epistemology that underwrites every uncustomary opinion he expresses.

As Christopher Hill (1977) has demonstrated, Milton's irregular opinions reflect various seventeenth-century countercultural, politico-religious movements. In the 'Epistle Dedicatory' to *Heresiography*, first published in 1647, Ephraim Pagitt reprobates more than a dozen such sectarian heresies. Like other orthodox puritans writing in the mid-1640s – the caviling William Prynne in *Twelve Considerable Questions* (1644), Thomas Edwards in the monumentally vituperative *Gangraena* (1645) and Robert Baillie in *A Dissuasive from the Errours of the Time* (1646) – Pagitt was battling the heretical sects then proliferating in London. Milton featured on their lists because of his recently published and widely derided tracts advocating divorce, but he also endorsed or would eventually come to endorse other opinions they explicitly denounced as well as some, like polygamy, they overlooked. Pagitt's catalogue, for example, includes Arminianism, Arianism, Independency and toleration, all Miltonic deviations from orthodoxy that we will consider in some detail below. Additionally, Milton, like the 'Anabaptists', did not judge infants 'fit for baptism' and advocated 'immersion' not 'sprinkling' for adults undergoing the sacrament (*CPW* VI: 544, 550). With the 'Anti-Sabbatarians', he debunked observation of the sabbath, defining it as a commandment imposed on the post-Exodus Jews and therefore not binding on Christians (*CPW* VI: 705–14). Milton was also a thnetopsychist or mortalist, believing that, as Pagitt says, 'the soul is laid asleep from the hour of death, unto the hour of judgement', an opinion he deems '*Atheistical*' (1662: A3^v; see *CPW* VI: 399–414; *PL* X. 789–92, III. 245–9). The alarming tendency to cry down 'all Tythes, and set maintenances of Ministers', a heretical proposal to which Milton in 1659 devoted a modest pamphlet, Pagitt associates with both the Independents and the Anabaptists (1662: 101). Finally, with the 'Millenaries', Milton believed that Christ would reign on earth for a thousand years after his second coming, a heresy that in the late 1640s conformed to an independent and socially revolutionary, regicidal political profile (*CPW* VI: 624–5); Pagitt, in attacking the Millenaries, stresses that they await a time when Christ will bind '*their Kings in chains, & nobles in links of Iron*' (A3^r).

It may come as a surprise that Pagitt does not indict animist monism or creation *ex deo*, related metaphysical and ontological heresies that, as William Kerrigan (1983), Stephen Fallon and I have maintained, pervasively inform the epic cosmos of *Paradise Lost*. The notion that matter is instinct with life and motion seems to have attracted little polemical notice in the seventeenth century, probably because it was never identified with a particular sectarian menace. Such ideological perils as it may have held for orthodoxy were murky, indirect and hence largely unrecognized. Yet Milton's insistence that creation is vibrant with autonomous life and derives from God's own material potency befits his opposition to Calvinist determinism and to the mechanistic philosophies of Hobbes and Descartes (Fallon 1991: 194–243). The metaphysical conflicts embodied in *Paradise Lost*, moreover, especially concerning the first matter of chaos, reflect Milton's steadfast hatred of tyranny and characteristic espousal of individual freedom and autonomy (Rumrich 1995).

Milton's outspoken opposition to divine right monarchy and his service in Cromwell's foreign office owe more to his classically inspired republican politics than to his philosophy of matter. It is undiscriminating and anachronistic to account for the profoundly theocratic Milton as if he were an early exponent of classical liberalism; yet his specific views concerning the legitimacy of government certainly anticipate those of subsequent liberal political philosophers. *The Tenure of Kings and Magistrates: proving, that it is lawfull, and hath been held so through all ages, for any, who have the power, to call to account a Tyrant, or wicked King, and after due conviction, to depose, and put him to death, if the ordinary Magistrate have neglected, or deny'd to do it* . . . is a title noteworthy for more than its length. It introduces an innovative if not original version of the social contract – that the people or their representatives enjoy the right to end the tenure of their king or other government. The second half of the eighteenth century saw such principles articulated by revolutionaries on both sides of the Atlantic, not least Thomas Jefferson in the Declaration of Independence (Sensabaugh 1964; Shawcross 1991). Shortly thereafter, the framers of the United States Constitution institutionalized the right of the people or their representatives to change the government, by mechanisms both ordinary (like elections) and extraordinary (like impeachment). Popular sovereignty and the conditionality of a subject's allegiance have thus long since ceased to be radical notions, a historical disjunction between our time and Milton's that impedes recognition of his radicalism. We therefore do well to remember that during the Restoration period Milton's republican convictions piqued the powerful and were highly dangerous to maintain. Masson (1877–94) plausibly claims that *The Tenure of Kings and Magistrates* would have cost Milton his life had it not been ignored, perhaps deliberately, as evidence against him (6: 163–84). As late as 1870 the Reverend James Graham, in his edition of Milton's prose, could confidently declare that 'enunciation of this elaborate and wicked title is quite enough to deter any from wasting time in the perusal of the treatise itself' (1870: 230). In our time, however, the claims made in one of Milton's most politically daring and courageous publications have become, if not self-evident truths, then certainly common principles of government.

Three and a half centuries ago these claims were not bourgeois commonplaces, and the stakes involved in disagreements over the legitimacy of government were very high. In the present-day American polity, for example, impeachment is regularly described as the 'political equivalent of' capital punishment; but the verdict of guilty in Charles Stuart's trial led to the distinctly unmetaphorical removal of the head of the head of state, a stroke ultimately fatal to monarchical absolutism in England. Furthermore, unlike modern impeachment proceedings – much less elections or parliamentary votes of confidence – the trial of Charles Stuart was a procedure without legal precedent, occurring before a representative body that had been purged of those opposed to such a trial. Then and now, it is hardly possible to regard the proceeding as legitimate or properly democratic, which from the first made its justification precarious.

Milton was, if anyone could be, well suited by temperament, training and experience to take up such a cross-grained rhetorical challenge. As both a poet and a polemicist, he had already shown a peculiar, characteristic genius for arriving at shocking innovations and sometimes scandalous proposals by working from relatively ordinary conventions and premises. Although he had in preceding years exhibited a knack for such perverse ratiocination, it was his repeated justification of judicial regicide that led to a contemporary fame nearly as formidable and widespread as that enjoyed by the invincible Oliver Cromwell (Parker 1968: 386–9). Cromwell made it possible for Charles to be tried and executed; Milton articulated the rationale. We know Milton primarily as a poet, but during his lifetime few knew him as anything other than the regicides' 'goose quill champion' as the dramatist John Tatham named him in a satirical pamphlet first published just prior to the Restoration (1879: 289; *Character of the Rump* 1660). Perez Zagorin has observed of Milton, 'whereas his literary predecessors nearly always aligned themselves with wielders of power, the kings, courts, and nobility whose patronage they solicited, [he] chose the side of rebellion and made himself part of the insurgent forces of his age' (1992: 114). How was it that a would-be epic poet put himself in the midst of such things, at perhaps the most radical moment in English political history?

Prior to the regicidal events of mid-century, Milton gained notice mainly as a divorcer. His difficult first marriage, at the age of thirty-three, to Mary Powell, a maiden of seventeen, brought him to claim, in five separate publications between 1643 and 1645, that, as enlightened, reformed theologians agreed, meet companionship rather than procreation constituted the primary end of wedlock. On this basis, irreconcilable discord between husband and wife logically qualifies as a more just cause than adultery to void a marriage. To be forced by law to remain joined as one flesh in a spiritually dead union, Milton insisted, is like being a living person chained face-to-face to a corpse, a gruesome image borrowed from Virgil's account of outrages committed by the dreadful tyrant Mezentius (*CPW* II: 326–7). To persist in sexual relations within such a partnership, Milton further maintained, alluding to the blinded Samson's servitude under the Philistines, is 'to grind in the mill of an undelighted and servil copulation' (*CPW* II: 258). In short, to attribute to God the authorship of an escape-proof and potentially soul-killing institution was to write him down as being a tyrant as cruel as Mezentius, as brutalizing as the Philistines.

Milton's arguments for divorce had immediate as well as far-reaching consequences. A landmark in the history of the institution of marriage, they represent a pivotal moment in the development of his own politics, religious beliefs and, arguably, sexual identity.

The Lady of Christ's, as Milton was known at Cambridge, seems to have experienced only one profound attachment outside his family before the 1640s – to Charles Diodati, his boyhood friend at St Paul's School. His writings to and about Diodati indicate that they conducted their friendship according to the model of affectionate, aspiring, philosophical conversation exemplified in Plato's *Phaedrus*. In a letter to Diodati, Milton describes his love for his friend by resorting to a Greek phrase, *deinon erota*, that suggests the primal splendour of such love as well as its awesome and potentially threatening power – *deinon* as in dino-saur. The theory of wedded love articulated in the divorce tracts holds marriage to the same set of expectations and implicit fears, tailoring its conception of relations between husband and wife to fit the pattern of this previous homo-erotic bond. Hence in *The Doctrine and Discipline of Divorce*, Milton, to characterize matrimonial love, invokes the myth of Eros and his 'brother wondrous like him, calle'd *Anteros*', whom he seeks throughout the world as his ideal partner, suffering through erroneous choices 'till finding *Anteros* at last, he kindles and repairs the almost faded ammunition of his Deity by the reflection of a coequal & *homogeneal* fire' (*CPW* II: 254–5).

I am not concerned to address the question of whether or not Milton and Diodati were physically intimate. Such speculation tells us more about our preoccupations than about Milton or the historical significance of his heretical beliefs. The pertinent point is that his relations with Diodati seem to have led him to define matrimony as an ennobling, authentic, existential engagement of a kind that had previously been associated with the ideal of friendship between men. Had it not been animated by the divorce tracts' radical conception of wedded love, *Paradise Lost* as we know it could not exist. Justly admired for its epic realization of the conflict between Satan and God, his epic may also be read, perhaps more productively, as the story of a marriage. The Trinity Manuscript's sketch of *Adam Unparadised*, which likely dates from the late 1630s, portends nothing like the radical departures from the Genesis tradition found in Milton's epic, where Adam and Eve's erotic union is depicted as the peak of paradisal bliss and pressure point of human frailty – the domestic mainspring of the Fall.

Milton's arguments on behalf of divorce also had more immediate ramifications. In the mid-1640s insistence on the legitimacy of divorce for reasons other than adultery represented an outrageous departure from customary views. His five publications on the subject over two years distinguished Milton from the dominant religious and political faction of the 1640s, his former allies the Presbyterians. They took his tracts as evidence that press censorship, which in the previous decade they had themselves defied and suffered under, ought to be renewed. During the 1630s, under the hated Archbishop William Laud, Stuart control of the press had become especially harsh and included the public mutilation and branding of offending puritan authors. It was the predominantly Presbyterian Parliament in the early 1640s that loosened the Stuart stranglehold on the press. Indeed, the stalwart Presbyterian opposition to Charles's religious and ultimately his political authority, first in Scotland and then England, moved him to abandon London for Oxford in 1642 and begin preparations for civil war.

Taking advantage of the new freedom to publish, in 1641–2 Milton baptized himself as a polemicist, reinforcing the Presbyterian challenge to episcopalian church government. 'Episcopacy' derives from the Greek word for bishop – the opulent apex of the hierarchical pyramid – and much of the Presbyterian ire, and Milton's too, was ignited by the extravagance of 'canary-sucking and swan-eating' prelates (*CPW* I: 549). Milton's pamphlets of this period are therefore often referred to as antiprelatical or anti-episcopal. The Presbyterians, a faction whose name derives from the Greek word for elder, themselves comprised many moderate varieties of opinion, but generally advocated a less centralized and more representative form of church government, with elders selected by each parish convening in synods to establish church discipline. Having attained parliamentary ascendancy, in 1643 they convened a national representative body devoted to religious affairs – the Westminster Assembly, a grand synod indeed. After early efforts at compromise with the bishops failed, in October 1644 the Assembly recommended replacing the episcopacy with a thoroughly Presbyterian system (Masson 1877–94, 3: 172).

Now politically and religiously predominant, the Presbyterians soon found that not all those who had united to defy episcopacy and the king's authority supported the rest of their religious and political agenda. They pressed on, despite growing and varied opposition, mainly from the so-called 'Independents' or 'congregationalists'. This faction, Milton included, opposed imposition of a centralized and uniform national religion, whether episcopal or Presbyterian, and thought, as the aghast Ephraim Pagitt observed, 'that every particular Congregation ought to be governed by its owne particular Laws without any depending of any in Ecclesiastical matters' (1662: 95). Though a sizeable minority, the Independents never threatened Presbyterian sway in Parliament, which in 1645 moved to begin instituting Presbyterianism in London. This effort persisted into 1646 and coincided with a campaign to stifle heterodoxy and re-establish press controls – a campaign in which books like Pagitt's participated. Attacks on Milton's divorce tracts thus typically occurred within inventories of heresies that threaten public morality, a concern that went beyond the bounds of the Presbyterian faction. In approving the publication of a response to *The Doctrine and Discipline of Divorce*, licenser Joseph Caryl, himself a moderate Independent, accounted Milton's tract 'worthie to be burnt by the hangman' (Birch 1753, 1: xxviii). Caryl had many successors throughout Europe in decades to come, but pride of place in the drive to burn one or another of Milton's books belongs to the English.

As we have seen, divorce was only one of many opinions that orthodox puritans deemed heretical. Among the most obnoxious after 1642 was advocacy of toleration, which was understood to foster and categorically to encourage sectarian division. Roger Williams's *Bloody Tenet of Persecution for Cause of Conscience*, which recommended tolerance of all religious faiths, was published early in the summer of 1644 and burnt in accordance with a parliamentary order dated 7 August (Masson 1877–94, 3: 161–2). Pagitt classifies advocates of toleration under the catch-all rubric 'Atheists', which he applies to those who, like Williams or Milton the divorcer, 'preach, print, and practise their heretical opinions openly': 'for books *vide* the bloody Tenet; witnesse a Tractate of divorce, in which the bonds are let loose to inordinate lust' (1662: A3ᵛ). The irony is a familiar one. In seeking to reform church discipline and curb the spread of heterodoxy, those who a few years before had opposed episcopal oversight and driven Charles from his throne – the Presbyterians chief among them – now presumed to an authority over conscience similar to that asserted by the previous regime. 'New *Presbyter* is but old *Priest* writ large', Milton succinctly observed in about 1646 ('On the New Forcers of Conscience', line 20).

Milton's differences with the Presbyterians over church discipline and social policy expose more fundamental differences of theological and anthropological opinion. Calvinist soteriology, which predominated in late sixteenth- and early seventeenth-century England, held that neither the blessed nor the damned could do a thing to avert their fates. God shows mercy to some, effecting salvation by grace irresistible, and condemns the rest to perdition, either actively or simply by withholding mercy. Nicholas Tyacke (1987) has claimed that consolidation of an 'anti-Calvinist' heterodoxy in the early part of the seventeenth century critically influenced the course of political and religious events leading to civil war. Members of this anti-Calvinist minority manoeuvred themselves into highly influential positions within the ecclesiastical hierarchy – the most noteworthy and potent example being Archbishop Laud, who presided with Charles over the repressively 'thorough' government of the 1630s. These anti-Calvinists, however, were concerned with much more than soteriology. Like the Dutch clergyman James Arminius (who gave his name to 'Arminianism'), they did indeed reject Calvinist predestination; but, unlike Arminius and unlike Milton too, they rejected it from outside the Calvinist tradition (Fallon 1998: 94–5). Anti-Calvinists like Laud, regardless of their soteriological views, championed episcopacy, promoted sacramentalism and enforced a liturgical formality antipathetic to those like Milton, who, regardless of their soteriological views, rebuked the bishops, debunked sacraments, and sought plain spontaneity and authenticity in worship. As we have seen, prior to the mid-1640s Milton aligned himself politically with the Calvinists, though nowhere does he explicitly endorse predestination. *Comus* (1634) most clearly evinces Milton's comfort within Calvinist culture: the Lady behaves like one of the elect, and the threat of pollution through contact with the wicked animates the masque. Yet even Milton's aspiring lady is described as exercising free choice in 'synergy' with supernal power, as Thomas Corns has recently claimed, suggesting that Milton's early divergence from Calvinist soteriology may account for the doctrinal reticence of his antiprelatical tracts (1998a: 40–5).

Regardless of his opinion concerning predestination prior to 1640, young Milton stood firmly on the Calvinist side in the culturally broad-based clash between Calvinist and anti-Calvinist. This is not to deny, however, that disagreement over the means of salvation was a critical theological rallying point in the polemical battles between Calvinist and anti-Calvinist before the Civil War. With his usual accuracy and economy, Thomas Jefferson summarized the Arminian position adopted by the anti-Calvinists, one that he, like Milton a century before, found amenable for its emphasis on human liberty:

> They think . . . that there is an universal grace given to all men, and that man is always *free* and at liberty to receive or reject grace, that God creates man free, that his justice would not permit him to punish men for crimes they are predestinated to commit. They admit the prescience of God but distinguish between fore-knowing and predestinating. (Jefferson 1950–95, 1: 554)

Perhaps the defeat of episcopalian anti-Calvinists like Laud, in combination with the sanctimonious resort of the Presbyterian victors to their own coercive policies, opened a space for Milton to articulate an Arminian valorization of rational choosing and advocacy of free will. These tendencies become evident in the divorce tracts and explicit in *Areopagitica*'s exaltation of rational choice and support of toleration and individual accountability. After 1644 this epic poet of theodicy never wavers from his distinctive emphasis on human freedom and accountability, and Arminianism lies at the centre of the mature Milton's heretical theology (Kelley 1973; Danielson 1982; Fallon 1998).

The Presbyterians, on the other hand, construed the ethical categories of choice and responsibility as being, for fallen humanity, void, meaningless or wickedly delusional. The insistence in *Areopagitica* on a more expansive toleration than the Presbyterians would allow proceeds quite directly from Milton's conception of the human subject as an active moral agent, rather than as a passive vessel of divine wrath or mercy. The debate over church government was confined mainly to mid-century, and was decisively settled in favour of prelatical episcopacy after the Restoration. The struggle over toleration, by contrast, preceded this debate and continued until the passing of the Toleration Act in 1689, legislation that comes near to enacting what Milton had proposed in 1644 and again in 1673 – toleration for all Protestants. Far from being a transient issue in a developing dispute over ecclesiastical organization, the toleration controversy was a moment in which the most persistent and salient political and religious question of the century was explicitly articulated: how much and what sort of religious liberty is appropriate to the condition of fallen humanity?

Recently, some have debunked the status of *Areopagitica* as a landmark in the history of the struggle for freedom of the press and of religion. As George Orwell recognized in 1940, 'any Marxist can demonstrate with the greatest of ease that "bourgeois" liberty of thought is an illusion' (1957a: 39), a proposition that orthodox Presbyterians of the seventeenth century also found easy to demonstrate, as indeed do many academics of the present day. Not surprisingly, what Zagorin calls Milton's 'loyalty to the principle of liberty' (1992: 114) has lately been construed by some as an example of bourgeois false consciousness benefiting a particular class. The tactics of deconstruction and the hermeneutics of suspicion, furthermore, readily yield the conclusion that the ideal of free speech is similarly deceptive (Fish 1994). From this theoretically informed perspective, it would appear that Milton devoted much of his life to preparing a future for bourgeois illusions and in so doing inspired, or helped to delude, subsequent generations of liberty seekers. The final irony, however, rests in the realization that to account for Milton's stunning creative powers and lasting historical influence, even the most rigorous determinist must grudgingly return to his faith in liberty. For as Orwell also observes, such faith seems to be a psychological prerequisite of literary achievement: 'when [the Marxist] has finished his demonstration there remains the psychological *fact* that without this "bourgeois" liberty the creative powers wither away' (1957a: 39). Those attempting to come to terms with Milton's greatest poetry and its genesis may find this thesis worth pondering: regardless of whether or not human liberty is merely ideological and illusory, Milton could not have written the masterpieces of his maturity had he not been precisely the heterodox heretic that he was – an Arminian devoted to intellectual liberty and individual responsibility.

True enough, *Areopagitica* opposes pre-publication licensing, but not all forms of censorship, and proposes toleration only for Protestant Christians, not Roman Catholics – an exception also endorsed by John Locke. Milton's was a fairly extreme position at the time, but not the most extreme. Roger Williams's *Bloody Tenet of Persecution for Cause of Conscience*, the tract excoriated by Pagitt and burnt by order of Parliament, recommended complete toleration in matters of religion. Yet advocacy of even limited toleration provoked accusations of heretical conspiracy from the Presbyterians. Proposals of toleration were themselves deemed heretical in the mid-to-late 1640s, stirring suspicion and imputation of other forbidden opinions – especially Arminianism and Socinianism, an antitrinitarian heresy (McLachlan 1951: 9). If Milton's specific proposals seem crabbed by modern standards, they were certainly heterodox at the time. In seventeenth-century England, they also represented the limit of what might be achieved by way of religious toleration, and was indeed achieved *de facto* under Cromwell and by legislation in 1689 (Tyacke 1991: 30–1; Worden 1984). Freedom from prior censorship in combination with authorial liability post-publication has moreover been the prevailing principle of press law in England since the eighteenth century (Zagorin 1992: 55).

Milton's modern biographers have struggled to explain how the outraged critic of 'the new forcers of conscience' and proponent of toleration should so identify with the Cromwellian victors as to accept the post of licenser in 1649. Yet according to the contemporary testimony of a Dutch diplomat, Leo de Aitzema, Milton licensed the Socinian *Racovian Catechism* in accordance with his known tolerationist principles. Shortly after Aitzema arrived in England early in 1652, he reported that

> there was recently printed here the Socinian *Racovian Catechism*. This was frowned upon by the Parliament; the printer says that Mr. Milton had licensed it; Milton, when asked, said Yes, and that he had published a tract on that subject, that men should refrain from

forbidding books; that in approving of that book he had done no more than what his opinion was. (French 1949–58, 3: 206)

Stephen Dobranski has observed that Aitzema's report in itself does not certify Milton's integrity as a champion of toleration and reminds us that we know little for certain about Milton's activities as licenser, or about this particular case, even with Aitzema's report (1998: 142–4). We do know, however, that under Cromwell's government freedom to publish on religious matters was 'almost unbounded, approaching very near to the ideal advanced by John Milton in his *Areopagitica* of 1644' (Tyacke 1991: 31). The Cromwellian church, too, was notable for its inclusiveness: 'a loose confederation of Presbyterians, Independents, and some Baptists, with a great variety of permitted sectarian activity beyond its fringes' (Tyacke 1991: 30). Though it is perilous to argue from effect to cause, it seems safe to conclude that whatever licensing authority Milton may have wielded, he did so in a manner consistent with his argument in *Areopagitica*.

The licensing of the *Racovian Catechism* can be construed as the most concentrated and representative episode in Milton's career as a religious controversialist, a career that is itself exemplary of seventeenth-century religious controversy. The Presbyterians' association of loose church discipline and toleration with Arminianism and antitrinitarian heresy was not groundless. The connection looked real enough at mid-century. After debates over the means of salvation, which dominated the first part of the century, and then over church government, which erupted during the middle decades, the status of Christ represents the third major category of seventeenth-century theological controversy. Christological disputes become most prominent after the Restoration – when the Clarendon Code had obviated debate over ecclesiastical organization – but the effective introduction of antitrinitarian heresy into seventeenth-century religious discourse occurred in the 1640s, and the publication of the *Racovian Catechism* represents an obvious milestone (McLachlan 1951: 162–74).

Like most proponents of antitrinitarianism, the Socinians based their claims on scripture and reason. For Milton, the desirability of toleration follows from an authentically Protestant devotion to individual interpretation of scripture and, as we have seen, an Arminian emphasis on the dignity of human will and reason. Espousal of toleration on such grounds meant advocacy of an ecclesiastical organization capable of embracing any scripturally based sect – hence Milton's congregationalism – and any scripturally based departure from orthodoxy, including antitrinitarianism. Although we do not know precisely when Milton found himself convinced by antitrinitarian arguments, both *Paradise Lost* and *De Doctrina Christiana*, as Michael Bauman (1987) has persuasively argued, reveal him as a proponent of this 'archetypal' heresy (Wiles 1996: 4–5; Williams 1987: 1). Milton's heretical progression from 1640 to 1660 thus begins in anticlericalism, proceeds to an Arminian tolerationist stance which shuns the use of civil power in matters of conscience, and culminates in a specifically Arian endorsement of antitrinitarian tenets. As I maintain elsewhere (Rumrich 1996: 36–49), many late-century exponents of antitrinitarian heresy, Locke and Newton among them, follow a similar trajectory – as indeed would Thomas Jefferson.

Religious toleration was feared by the Presbyterians on the principle that tolerance propagates heresy. *Areopagitica* validates this fear. Its arguments articulate the epistemology of heresy to which I referred in beginning this chapter, a philosophy concerning the formation of knowledge and belief. To explain the epistemological condition of Protestant Christians, Milton claims that the truth expressed by Christ and his apostles became fragmented in subsequent generations. Christians are bound to seek the pieces and attempt to restore truth's original form, a task that will not be completed until the promised end: 'We have not yet found them all, Lords and Commons, nor ever shall doe, till her Masters second comming' (*CPW* II: 549). The ongoing search for truth, according to Milton, requires us 'To be still searching what we know not, by what we know, still closing up truth to truth as we find it', a process that inevitably entails 'much arguing, much writing, many opinions; for opinion in good men is but knowledge in the making' (*CPW* II: 551, 554). Perhaps the most telling adverb in Milton's poetry and prose, 'still' in this instance indicates that seeking and restoring the body of truth ought to be an incessant labour – an attitude or habit of being. This existential ethic Milton opposes to Presbyterian complacency and hypocrisy: 'It is not the unfrocking of a Priest, the unmitring of a Bishop, and the removing him from off the *Presbyterian* shoulders that will make us a happy Nation'; 'They are the troublers, they are the dividers of unity, who neglect and permit not others to unite those dissever'd peeces which are yet wanting to the body of Truth' (*CPW* II: 550–1).

As Janel Mueller (1998) reminds us, the etymologically minded Milton, though he recognized the pejorative sense of the term 'heresy', would ultimately claim that it properly indicates 'only the choise or following of any opinion good or bad in religion or any other learning' (*CPW* VII: 246). The formation of heresy in this neutral sense is the obligation of every true warfaring Christian. Writing in the midst of the Civil War, Milton refers to London as

> the mansion house of liberty...the shop of warre hath not there more anvils and hammers waking, to fashion out the plates and instruments of armed Justice in defence of beleaguer'd Truth, then there be pens and heads there, sitting by their studious lamps, musing, searching, revolving new notions and idea's wherewith to present...the approaching Reformation: others as fast reading, trying all things, assenting to the force of reason and convincement. (*CPW* II: 553–4)

In 'the mansion house of liberty', heresy implies no fault but represents a dynamic moment in a strenuous historical process, as David Loewenstein has claimed (1990: 35–50), a moment that produces conscientious belief and instigates further enquiry. Within a community of rationally and volitionally free individuals, this process inevitably produces new schools of thought, or deviations from existing ones – in short, sect and schism: 'there must be many schisms and many dissections made in the quarry and in the timber, ere the house of God can be built . . . [O]ut of many moderate varieties and brotherly dissimilitudes that are not vastly disproportionall, arises the goodly and the gracefull symmetry that commends the whole pile and structure' (*CPW* II: 555). Heresy evolves into orthodoxy, from which new heresies eventually depart, 'ev'n to the reforming of Reformation it self' (*CPW* II: 553). For Milton, moving by means of heresy towards still increasing awareness of the truth represents the only true orthodoxy – and would be the national orthodoxy, he claims, 'could we but foregoe this Prelaticall tradition of crowding free consciences and Christian liberties into canons and precepts of men' (*CPW* II: 554). The believer who knuckles under, following set doctrine without confirmation of conscience, 'only because his Pastor sayes so, or the Assembly so determins', becomes, in a celebrated phrase of marvellous compression, 'a heretick in the truth' (*CPW* II: 543). Thus turning the pejorative sense of heresy on its head, Milton presents the conscientious heretic as the only praiseworthy Christian and the complacent exponent of customary orthodoxy as a contemptible time-server. As Milton says in the Prefatory Epistle to *De Doctrina Christiana*, he still chose to follow '*the way which is called heresy*' (*CPW* VI: 124).

We have noted that Milton composed *Areopagitica* partly in response to the outcry over his divorce tracts and the subsequent drive to license books. The divorce tracts also prepared the way for memorable political arguments that came at the end of the 1640s, against the divine right of kings and their absolute authority over their subjects. As Milton remarks in *The Doctrine and Discipline of Divorce*, 'he who marries, intends as little to conspire his owne ruine, as he that swears Allegiance: and as a whole people is in proportion to an ill Government, so is one man to an ill mariage' (*CPW* II: 229). The connection was recognized at the Restoration and used to mock Milton, for example in Tatham's *Character of the Rump*: 'by his will [he] would shake off his governors as he doth his wives, four in a fortnight' (1879: 289). As Tatham rightly understood, Milton held that the people enjoy the right to divorce themselves from a tyrannical king, a right that many Presbyterians denied. Some indeed went so far as to argue that a subject people should endure the tyrannies of a Nero rather than rebel against a divinely sanctioned potentate.

The prose works Milton published in the 1640s thus track his increasing divergence from the Presbyterian orthodoxy with which he had allied himself early in the decade – an orthodoxy itself deemed heterodox under the episcopal system. Although subsequent generations would draw inspiration from them, these writings had precious little impact at the time. True, the bishops were undone, but only temporarily. Marriage law long remained unchanged, despite Milton's arguments for divorce. *Areopagitica*, composed as if it were an oration before Parliament, failed to persuade its members to repeal the Licensing Order. Also generally ignored was *The Tenure of Kings and Magistrates*; but at least its publication on 13 February 1649, two weeks after Charles's execution, drew the attention of the new government. Shortly thereafter, Milton was appointed its Secretary for Foreign Tongues, the Commonwealth's voice in Europe. In this role Milton at last made his mark.

Cromwell's council required Milton to defend the English regicides from their furious detractors at home and abroad. The first opponent was Charles I himself. After he perished, Charles published, justifying himself and divine right in a posthumous tract entitled *Eikon Basilike* ('The Image of a King'). Ghost-written by John Gauden and approved by Charles before his death, the king's book was well calculated to elicit public sympathy for the beheaded monarch. In the rigorous and occasionally mocking *Eikonoklastes* ('The Image Breaker'), Milton responded by exposing Charles's treacheries during the Civil War, most scandalously his willingness to open England to Roman Catholic powers in return for military assistance, an offence roughly comparable to a mid-twentieth-century American president inviting Soviet troops to help suppress domestic turmoil. Yet the sentimental posturing of Charles's pamphlet had both more immediate and more long-lasting success than Milton's factual exposure of the king's lies and treachery. For the next two hundred years and more, Charles's false outweighed Milton's true. S. Manning, a nineteenth-century clergyman-editor of Milton's prose, records his astonishment at finding 'how many of the calumnies against the Puritans, which are still current, are here [i.e. in *Eikonoklastes*] refuted, and how many eulogistic fictions touching the king's piety and devotion are disproved, but which, nevertheless, hold their place in our popular histories' (1862: 133). In hindsight, it is easy for us to see the poet's mistake: popular sympathy for even an occasionally abusive paternal figure under attack tends to neutralize logic and evidence. If the paternal figure is a king recently beheaded, silence would be a better reply than telling truths that will be perceived as arrogant cruelty towards a man no longer able to defend himself. Quite properly for a Christian king, Charles won by dying. The monarchy was soon resurrected in his son, and Milton for centuries thereafter was reviled for vilification of a king popularly considered a religious martyr – regardless of his crimes. If *The Tenure of Kings and Magistrates* was the more ideologically culpable work, *Eikonoklastes*, with its harsh disclosure of the dead king's malfeasance, long remained the more difficult to forgive.

No doubt the infamy Milton suffered at the Restoration pained him. He seems to have enjoyed public accolades and in the 1650s offered himself as an adviser to whom the English people and their leaders should attend. The vast celebrity he enjoyed during Cromwell's regime, moreover, came through his role as public defender of the English in the court of European public opinion. Shortly after Charles's trial and execution, the reigning intellectual heavyweight of mid-seventeenth-century Europe, the celebrated Claudius Salmasius, was hired to condemn the English regicides. He produced a massive Latin tract, *Defensio Regia pro Carolo Primo* ('Defence of Kings on Behalf of Charles I'), which portrayed the beheading of the Lord's anointed as an unspeakable crime that would inevitably bring God's wrath down on the English. Charged with replying quickly, Milton, virtually unknown in Europe, composed a light-footed, point-by-point refutation in superb neoclassical Latin, replete with devastating satiric abuse. *Pro Populo Anglicano Defensio* ('Defence of the English People') immediately exalted Milton's continental reputation and as late as 1753 was deemed Milton's 'most celebrated work in prose' (Birch 1753: 28). As Isaac Disraeli later remarked, 'all Europe took a part in the paper-war of these two great men', a paper-war in which 'the answer of Milton . . . perfectly massacred Salmasius' (1859: 237).

During the early 1650s counterattacks and renewed Miltonic defences ensued. In them Milton pushes the trope of the warrior for truth and liberty prominent in *Areopagitica* even further, portraying himself as a heroic champion, triumphant before all of Europe:

> I have in the *First Defence* spoken out and shall in the *Second* speak again to the entire assembly and council of all the most influential men, cities, and nations everywhere . . . It is the renewed cultivation of freedom and civic life that I disseminate throughout cities, kingdoms, and nations. But not entirely unknown, nor perhaps unwelcome, shall I return if I am he who disposed of the contentious satellite of tyrants [Salmasius], hitherto deemed unconquerable, both in the view of most men and in his own opinion. When he with insults was attacking us and our battle array, and our leaders looked first of all to me, I met him in single combat and plunged into his reviling throat this pen, the weapon of his own choice. (*CPW* IV: 554, 556)

If the 1650s was the decade in which Milton's warriorlike authorial spirit finally became apparent to an admiring world, it was also the decade of his greatest losses. The strain of composing the reply to Salmasius cost him what little was left of his already failing eyesight, a loss his enemies counted as a sign of divine displeasure at his impiety. In 1652 his troubled first marriage ended when Mary Powell succumbed to complications after the birth of her third daughter, Deborah. Their son, John, less than a year old, died a few months later. His wife, his only son, his sight – all gone in the same year. His second wife, Katherine Woodcock, whom he married in 1656 and with whom he seems finally to have found happiness, died only two years after their marriage, also because of complications from childbirth, so terribly dangerous to women at that period. By the end of the 1650s, in short, he was fast approaching old age as a lonely, blind, twice-widowed father of three daughters, and after the death of Cromwell in 1658 also endured the rapid disintegration of the English Commonwealth he had laboured so intensely to defend. In the first half of the 1650s, Milton proclaimed his own heroism and authorial integrity. It is for us to recognize the more remarkable display of these qualities in the decade's latter years.

In the end, the authorial capital he had accumulated defending the English people was squandered in repeated, futile publications that argued in favour of establishing a republic governed by an elected representative body. The one-time champion of the English people pleaded with his countrymen not to restore the monarchy, though he seems to have foreseen that his arguments would go unheeded: 'Thus much I should perhaps have said, though I were sure I should have spoken only to trees and stones; and had none to cry to, but with the Prophet, *O earth, earth, earth!* to tell the very soil it self, what her perverse inhabitants are deaf to' (*CPW* VII: 462–3). As the Restoration loomed, Milton's fame was quickly translated into calumny, and he became an object of scorn and insult among the people he had defended. Derided as a 'blind guide', he was mocked for having 'scribbled [his] eyes out' to no effect, berated for having 'thrown [his] dirty outrage on the memory of a murdered Prince as if the Hangman were but [his] usher' (Masson 1877–94, 5: 661). Royalist Roger L'Estrange commented that Milton had 'resolved one great question, by evidencing that devils may indue human shape'; or, allowing that Milton might indeed be human, observed that he gave 'every man a horror for mankind when he considers [Milton is] of the race' (Masson 1877–94, 5: 690). Another writer, congratulating Charles II on his return and condemning the regicides *en masse* for 'destestable, execrable murder, . . . never-before-paralleled nor ever-sufficiently-to-be-lamented-and-abhorred villainies', pauses to single out one culprit by name: 'this Murder . . . and these Villainies, were defended, nay extolled and commended, by one Mr. John Milton, [who] did . . . be-spatter the white robes of your Royal father's spotless life . . . with the dirty filth of his satirical pen' (Masson 1877–94, 5: 693).

It would be difficult to overstate the desire for bloody vengeance among some royalists at the Restoration, or the narrowness of Milton's escape from it. On the anniversary of Charles's execution in 1661, the corpse of Cromwell, dead three years, was disinterred and hoisted at Tyburn alongside those of his son-in-law Henry Ireton (d. 1651) and John Bradshaw (d. 1659). As reported in a contemporary newspaper account, the punishment of their corpses followed the same general protocol as that observed with living victims: 'they were drawn upon sledges to Tyburn. All the way . . . the universal outcry and curses of the people went along with them. When the three carcasses were at Tyburn, they were pulled out of their coffins, and hanged at the several angles of that triple tree, – where they hung till the sun was set; after which they were taken down, and their heads cut off, and their loathsome trunks thrown into a deep hole under the gallows' (Masson 1877–94, 6: 123). The carcasses' heads were then fixed on poles by the common hangman and set atop Westminster Hall, where they remained for many years.

Even more extreme punishment was eagerly anticipated by some for Milton, and was indeed inflicted on those regicides who lacked the sense to flee or die before the Restoration. John Egerton, Viscount Brackley, who in his youth had played the part of the elder brother in Milton's *Comus*, inscribed his opinion of Milton's deserts on the title page of *Pro Populo Anglicano Defensio*: 'Liber igni, Author furcâ, dignissimi', which is to say, 'The book is most deserving of burning, the author the gallows' (Parker 1968, 2: 975). How charming is divine philosophy! Not all the circling gallows birds were so austere and humourless. Derisively contemplating Milton's execution, John Tatham in 1660 wrote that 'he is so much an enemy to usual practices that I believe, when he is condemned to travel to Tyburn in a cart, he will petition for the favour to be the first man that ever was driven in a wheelbarrow' (1879: 289). Standard procedure, illustrated by the ritual abuse of the three corpses, called for the convict to be drawn from the Tower on a hurdle or in a cart through the city of London to Tyburn and then subjected to the rest of the usual sentence, which I quote here to give some sense of what Milton risked by staying in London and writing antimonarchical pamphlets to the bitter end: 'there to be hanged till he should be half dead; that then he should be cut down alive, his privy parts cut off, his belly ripped, his bowels burnt, his four quarters set up over the four gates of the city, and his head upon London bridge' (Thomas 1972: 40). This was the spectacularly allegorical sentence carved into the flesh of Englishmen convicted of treason up until the nineteenth century. As the regicides' penman, Milton's body presented an obvious surface for inscribing this sentence. Though theories abound, no one has ever been able to explain just how he managed to survive unscathed to complete and publish the poems for which he is now chiefly remembered. *Paradise Lost* was maybe half finished in 1660 and not published until 1667; *Paradise Regained* and *Samson Agonistes* were not published until 1671.

Zagorin observes that 'in exposing his antimonarchical opinions so outspokenly at such a moment, [Milton] stood virtually alone' (1992: 114). Many others associated with the regicides prudently fled the country. John Dryden, who keened in verse on the occasion of Cromwell's death in 1658, wrote poetry celebrating the arrival of Charles II in London in 1660. Those who claim that Milton did not genuinely advocate free speech, except perhaps as the victim of ideological delusion, or that his ideal of liberty evinces false consciousness, must consider his stubborn behaviour as the Restoration approached foolhardy, if not suicidal. It was, on the other hand, authentically Protestant behaviour. Orwell in 1946 traced the bourgeois heritage of intellectual liberty and integrity to the Protestant tradition and specifically cites Milton before offering this observation on heresy: 'a heretic – political, moral, religious, or aesthetic – was one who refused to outrage his own conscience. His outlook was summed up in the words of the Revivalist hymn:

> 'Dare to be a Daniel
> 'Dare to stand alone;
> 'Dare to have a purpose firm,
> 'Dare to make it known.'
> (1957b: 163)

By 1660 Milton had dared all of the above under circumstances seemingly designed to expose the slightest vacillation. He was heretical to the core.

BIBLIOGRAPHY

Writings

Baillie (1646); Edwards (1645); Locke (1689); Pagitt (1662); Prynne (1644); Williams (1644).

References for Further Reading

Bauman (1987); Birch (1753); Corns (1998a); Danielson (1982); Disraeli (1859); Dobranski (1998); Fallon, Stephen M. (1991, 1998); Fish (1994); French (1949–58); Graham (1870); Hill (1977); Jefferson (1950–95); Kelley (1941, 1973); Kerrigan (1983); Loewenstein (1990); McLachlan (1951); Manning (1862); Masson (1877–94); Mueller (1998); Orwell (1957a, 1957b); Parker, William R. (1968); Rumrich (1995, 1996); Sensabaugh (1964); Shawcross (1991); Tatham (1879); Thomas, Donald (1972); Tyacke (1987, 1991); Wiles (1996); Williams, R. (1987); Worden (1984); Zagorin (1992).

10
Milton and Ecology

Diane Kelsey McColley

'Ecology' may seem an anachronistic term for Milton's poetics of the natural world, since neither the word nor the science was invented until the nineteenth century. But its etymology suits the language of nature in Milton's poems better than its nearest early modern equivalent, 'economy'. Both come from the Greek οικοσ (*oikos*, household), but economy's other root is νομοσ (*nomos*, law), while ecology comes from λογοσ (*logos*, the expression of thought). Xenophon's *Economics* concerns prudent and profitable estate management; *Paradise Lost* concerns human responsibility for the shared habitat of earth, an organic sphere of interactive lives where only the renewable parts of edible plants are specifically designated for human use, and *A Masque* and *Paradise Regained* demonstrate renewals of justice to the household of nature after the violation of the 'one restraint' in Paradise. Milton represents a full spectrum of attitudes towards the natural world in his narrative and dramatic voices, but with a pervasive ecological consciousness in his poetics, his theology and his political philosophy. If, as Thomas Corns comments, 'Milton's ways of perceiving and representing the congruities between man and nature may have seemed a foolish excrescence to some intervenient generations ... to an age like ours, distressed by recognition of the human impact on global systems, Milton's characteristic idiom speaks with a new urgency' (Corns 1990a: 103–5).

Milton's environmental ethic is the more striking if we consider the intellectual tide against which he strove: Baconian and Cartesian proto-science, which made nature a storehouse of commodities to be extracted by technology; an expanding interpretation of the 'dominion' over nature given in Genesis as encouragement to shape all habitats for human use; the seemingly inexhaustible wilderness of the New World which colonizers advertised as both bountiful and in need of being subdued; and a Calvinist theology holding that the natural world was made exclusively for the earthly sustenance of the human soul. I shall read Milton's account of the human calling to dress and keep the garden – both to cultivate and to preserve the earth – in the contexts of Francis Bacon's ambition in the *Novum Organum* 'to extend the power and dominion of the human race itself over the universe' and 'recover the right over nature which belongs to it by divine bequest' (1857, 4: 114, 115) and of mineral, vegetable and animal experiments epitomized by Solomon's House, Bacon's model academy in the *New Atlantis*.

Milton's Ark of Language

In 1668 John Wilkins, Anglican cleric and founding Fellow of the Royal Society, published *An Essay towards a Real Character and a Philosophical Language*, intended to dismantle the Tower of Babel and give commerce, evangelism and experimental science a language perspicuous to all users. 'The reducing of all things and notions, to such kind of Tables as are here proposed', Wilkins suggests in his preface, 'would prove the shortest and plainest way for the attainment of real Knowledge, that hath been yet offered to the World'. 'Real Knowledge' depends on a definition of the visible world as a body of facts capable of translation by the rational intellect into a fixed language, 'not to be changed' (as Milton's Satan says of his own determination) 'by place or time' (*PL* I. 253).

To show that a rational catalogue of species is neither impossible nor contrary to scripture, Wilkins includes in his classification of animals a 'Digression' to prove mathematically that all air-breathing species and their provisions for a year's voyage could fit into the biblically prescribed dimensions of Noah's Ark (1668: 164). Although he thinks it 'most probable' that no animal was carnivorous before the flood (Genesis 1: 29, 30 and 9: 3), he agrees to suppose 'that those Animals which are now Praedatory were so from the beginning' and allots for the twenty pairs of carnivorous beasts 'five Sheep . . . to be devoured for food each day of the year, amounting to 1,825'. Animals would occupy the first and third levels of the ark, the birds stacked in cubicles and cages, with the sheep to be eaten packed into the second. Wilkins comments neither on the theological problem of original rapacity nor its satirical possibilities for the typology of the ark as the church. He does assure us that the stalls would be large enough for their occupants to lie down or turn around in and 'to receive all the dung that should proceed from them for a whole year'. After fitting the animals into the dimensions of ark architecture, Wilkins finds nearly 200 feet left over, but this excess is no defect of God's arithmetic; divine providence has left space for those few species still to be found in the 'undiscovered parts of the world', an exactitude providing 'rational confirmation of the truth and divine authority' of scripture (162–8).

Wilkins's ark is an excellent metaphor for his catalogue and his invented language. By installing 'all things and notions' in separate cells he hoped to make language hold still, or barely move, so that accurate global communication based on Western logic and desire for control could go on for ever. His 'Tables' require a high level of abstraction and a hierarchical arrangement dependent on dualistic oppositions.

Being is divided into God and the World; the World is divided into the Spiritual and the Corporeal; animals and plants are divided by method of reproduction, number and kind of feet, and other categorical features. Wilkins's abstract conception of species matches the static language he proposes.

Milton's ark of poetry, in contrast, is an inventive, organically constructed, polysemous, empathetic verbal habitat in which all creatures have space and liberty; an environment designed to expand the reader's consciousness of the household of earth at a time when the flood of commodification is rising. The root of the contrast is a different view of divine providence, as seen in the figure of Noah's Ark. Milton's Adam, mourning the suffering to all creation that his lapse has caused, sees this story in prophetic vision and renews his human vocation: 'I revive / At this last sight, assured that man shall live / With all the creatures, and their seed preserve' (*PL* XI. 871–3). Though Adam's prophecy rings ironic now, his understanding stands, that the continued existence of 'all the creatures' depends not only upon God's providence but also upon the stewardship of a race too prone to forget its calling. His joy in them and his sense of responsibility towards them provide the rudiments of an ecological ethic opposed to the principles of the Royal Society as represented by Bacon's quest for empire over nature and Wilkins's proposed facilitation of it by a sterilized language. Milton's language of nature is characterized by inclusiveness and affinitive form. His unfallen speaking characters are conscious of the whole circle of life that surrounds them, and his mimetic prosody draws us into muscular empathy with non-human beings. Adam and Eve in their morning prayer invoke 'all the creatures' as coworshippers and witnesses in language that imitates their sounds and motions; Raphael's creation story in Book VII lets us feel the kinetic and sensuous experience of each animal in its habitat, whether whale or oyster, eagle or swan, leopard or stag, ant or earthworm.

When, as Adam and Eve rest after gardening, 'the unwieldy elephant / To make them mirth used all his might, and wreathed / His lithe proboscis' (IV. 345–7), we must use our lingual might and wreathe our tongues lithely to pronounce the unwieldy line, creating a kinetic correspondence with the elephant's experience. Wilkins appeals to mercantile interests and has no empathy for elephants; they are designed for slavery and commerce: 'ELEPHANT, Ivory. Multifidous kind [with feet 'divided into many parts' (*OED*)]; having little prominencies at the end of the feet, representing toes, being of the greatest magnitude amongst all other beasts, used for the carriage and draught of great weights, and more particularly esteemed for tusks' (1668: 156). Edward Topsell, like Milton, comments on their entertainment value, but differently: the elephant's 'trunck called Proboscis and Promucis, is a large hollow thing hanging from his nose like skin to the groundward'; this 'trunck or hand is most easie to be cut off', as was done 'in the aedility or temple-office of Claudius, Antonius, and Posthumus being Consuls, and afterward on the Circus, when the Luculli were the commons officers. And when Pompey was Consul the second time, there were 17 or 20 which at one time fought within the Circus . . . with Spears and Darts'; one soldier crept between the legs of the elephants and 'cast up the Darts over his head into the beasts belly, which fell down round him, to the great pleasure of the beholders' (Topsell 1658: 153, 158). By comparing Adam and Eve in innocence – not-nocence, harmlessness – with Roman cruelty, one sees that Milton's passage contains more than humorous pleasure. It suggests a dangerous relation between empire over nature and empire over human beings and creates a kinetic empathy that lets us renew innocence in ourselves.

Milton's Theology of Nature

Aristotelian, Platonic, Thomistic, Calvinist and Cartesian dualism, Hobbesian mechanism, and the Baconian programme of empire over nature held, to varying extents, that the non-human world was created only for the use of the rational and immortal human soul. Milton was proto-ecological in his opposition to such dualism. He treats sentient creatures as worthy of their lives and does not classify them in terms of their usefulness to human beings. He acknowledges the damage to both the natural world and the human spirit wrought by penetrating and exploiting the body of Mother Earth: it is Mammon, the fallen angel who becomes the idol of wealth, by whose suggestion men 'Ransacked the centre, and with impious hands / Rifled the bowels of their mother earth / For treasures better hid' (*PL* I. 686–8).

The theological heresies of Milton's poetics of nature are monism, vitalism and the eternity of species. His monist materialism opposes dualism by holding that all things are made of the same matter, indivisible from spirit because spiritual and corporeal creatures are different only in degree. *De Doctrina Christiana* holds that matter cannot have existed independently from God, and therefore all matter, whether spiritual or corporeal, must have originated *in* God – not only its forms, but also its substance. In contrast to those who insist that nothing corruptible can ever have been a part of God, the tractate argues that 'it is a demonstration of supreme power and supreme goodness that such heterogeneous, multiform and inexhaustive virtue should exist in God, and exist substantially', and 'that he ... should disperse, propagate and extend it as far as, and in whatever way, he wills'. Virtue, or the power to act, is transmitted, then, to a heterogeneous and multiform creation. In answer to the question how created nature, if it is the substance of God, can become corruptible, he supplies liberty: 'it is not the matter nor the form which sins. When matter or form has gone out from God and become the property of another, ... it is now in a mutable state.' God grants his creatures liberty, along with its risks, so that they may be growing, diversifying, vital beings. A corollary is that 'since all things come not only from God but out of God, no created thing can be utterly annihilated.' Nor are body and soul separated in death; the whole person dies – body, spirit, and soul – and the whole person will be renewed in the general resurrection (*CPW* VI: 307–10 and Book I, ch. xiii).

In *Paradise Lost* the Archangel Raphael explains to Adam and Eve that

> one almighty is, from whom
> All things proceed, and up to him return,
> If not depraved from good, created all
> Such to perfection, one first matter all,
> Indued with various forms, various degrees
> Of substance, and in things that live, of life;
> But more refined, more spirituous, and pure,
> As nearer to him placed or nearer tending
> Each in their several active spheres assigned,
> Till body up to spirit work, in bounds
> Proportioned to each kind.
>
> (V. 469–79)

The emphatically repeated 'all' at the beginning of this statement, though biblical, is heretical to dualists who believe that only human souls can expect union with God. Here, body is not contrary to, but 'works' up to, spirit within the sphere of activity of each species or 'kind'. 'Each in their several active spheres assigned' retains some of the Aristotelian idea of a scale of nature ranked by degrees of capability; the more a creature can do, the higher it ranks. But 'several active spheres' also indicates, first, that all species retain their identities in the process of development; no entity will be lost. For maximum diversity all degrees of life receive being, and whether one is an angel, a lark or a sponge differently circumscribes one's 'active sphere'. But, second, all are 'active': not the mechanically determined things of Hobbes or Descartes, but beings whose activity springs from themselves. All bodies work 'up to spirit' (which is not immaterial) while retaining their special nature, 'in bounds / Proportioned to each kind'. (John Leonard discerns a pun in 'bounds': 'both "limits" and "leaps" . . . Milton's universe is both hierarchical and dynamic' (Milton 1998a: 781, n. to line 478, and above). All species, then, are kindred, made of the same 'first matter', are various in activity as well as form, and proceed from God and eventually return to him as 'spirit': not in a denigration of body or a separation from it, but through a process of refinement and increasing freedom without losing, indeed rather having actively participated in developing, the identities they have achieved.

The occult physician Robert Fludd agrees that God 'vivifieth all things' but disagrees that 'the creature can act of it self by a free-will' because God's virtue cannot be divided from his essence (1659: 16). His position approaches that of 'voluntarism', the doctrine that God's will is sovereign and inscrutable, held by royalists to justify the divine right of kings, who as God's representatives on earth are also sovereign and inscrutable. For Milton the spirit of God, though preferring to dwell in 'the upright heart and pure' (*PL* I. 18), is not a tyrant. He argues in *Areopagitica* that God gives freedom to rational creatures to learn and choose, and that governments should do the same. An implication of monism demonstrated in the government of nature by Adam and Eve is that although other animals lack the same degree of reason that is given to human beings, good government lets them live their lives without violent coercion or slavery. The two concepts of God can be aligned with the two concepts of government.

Vitalists opposed the mechanist belief that matter is distinct from spirit with the belief that nature is alive in all its parts. Poetically at least, Milton is of their party. At the beginning of creation the spirit of God 'vital virtue infused, and vital warmth / Throughout the fluid mass' (*PL* VII. 236–7), and that self-activating vitality remains in the forms differentiated during the subsequent days of creation. Since vitalists recognized the otherness of other beings as well as their kinship with humankind, vitalism in poetry does not promote the 'pathetic fallacy' of imagining that only human perceptions matter.

Seventeenth-century technology that relies on the doctrine of nature's instrumentality for human use extracts the granting of 'dominion' from Genesis 1 and ignores the vitality with which the earth brings forth in response to God's voice. Milton's sense of the earth's vitality is brought into relief by the instrumentalism of Gabriel Plattes's handbook on mining:

> Some have thought that the mighty Creator made the vast, deformed, and craggy Rocks and Mountaines in the beginning, but this appeareth to be an Opinion, whereby great dishonour may reflect upon the Creator, who . . . made nothing deformed or unfit for the use of which it was created: Now the earth being ordained to beare Fruits for the use of Men, and Rocks are not fit for that purpose, it plainely appeareth that they came by accident.

Though others thought them produced 'even as Warts, Tumours, Wenns, and Excrescences' on men's bodies, Plattes finds by experiment that 'Bituminous and Sulphurious substances are kindled in the bowells of the earth' and exposed by Noah's flood or the motion of the seas (1639: 5). This attitude fits with the love of regularity and utility we have seen in Wilkins's fervour to regularize language. Milton directly refutes it in his vitalist creation story: God says 'let dry land appear' and 'Immediately the mountains huge appear / Emergent, and their broad bare backs upheave / Into the clouds' (*PL* VII. 284–7). The responsive activity of the earth also produces each inhabitant from its habitat – waters generate, earth brings forth, clods calve.

Milton's belief that all beings will participate in the 'All in All' opposes the instrumentalist supposition that only human beings have souls. If Adam and Eve remain obedient, Raphael tells them, 'earth [will] be changed to heaven, and heaven to earth' (VII. 160); that opportunity lost, Michael affirms that the faithful will be received 'into bliss, / Whether in heaven or earth, for then the earth / Shall all be paradise' (XII. 462–4). That earth would be changed was orthodox; that heaven would reciprocally change 'to earth' or earth become 'all paradise' is a radical assertion. By analogy with Eden, the creatures would continue to delight the mind and senses and expand the imagination by their otherness, simply by being themselves and living their lives, even with a degree of uncarnivorous wildness. Satan for disguise usurps the lion's 'fiery glare' (IV. 402) and the serpent, while still innocent ('to thee / Not noxious') sports 'brazen eyes / And hairy mane terrific' (VII. 496–8). Original wildness, harmless because responsive to unfallen human virtue, is part of Edenic vitality.

The immortality of non-human beings is rooted in the biblical texts of Romans and Revelation. In Romans, 'the earnest expectation of the creature waiteth for the manifestation of the sons of God . . . Because the creature itself also shall be delivered from the bondage of corruption into the glorious liberty of the children of God' (8: 19–21). Doctrinal glossers rejected an inclusive reading of 'the creature', however. John Locke's *Paraphrase* renders verse 19, 'For the whole race of mankinde . . . waiteth in hope', and adds in a note, joining ethnocentrism to anthropocentrism, that '[ktisis] *creature* in the language of St Paul and of the New Testament signifies mankind espetialy the gentile world as the far greater part of the creation' (1987, 2: 557). The Calvinist and royalist Andrew Willet (1620) deploys a full range of opinion about the fate of other species after the apocalypse but in a leap of anthropocentric Aristotelian instrumentalism decides that 'it is not probable that, such kind of creatures beeing now appointed onely for the necessities of this life, for the foode, cloathing, and other seruices of man, which then shall be at ende, shall then bee restored to any such glorie.' Yet the Geneva Bible, published at the centre of Calvinism for English Protestant readers in 1560, makes clear the difference and plurality of the creatures that groan 'with us' and await the resurrection:

> The creatures shal not be restored before that Gods children be broght to their perfection: in the meane season they wait. [They are subject to vanity]: That is, to destruction, because of mans sinne. [By 'euerie creature'] He meaneth not the Angels, nether deuils nor men. (sig. TT.ii^r, nn. n, o, p)

The body also 'shalbe in the resurrection when we shalbe made conformable to our head Christ' (note r), sharing in the resurrection because Christ has become incarnate; and, for Milton, the rest of the corporeal creation, by virtue of its monistic kinship with humanity, will be included.

In the vision of heaven in Revelation 5: 13, 'every creature which is in heaven, and on the earth, and under the earth, and such as are in the sea, and all that are in them' praise the Lamb together. This verse too was usually interpreted as concerning only the elect, though the illustrator of the thirteenth-century Trinity College Apocalypse confutes its gloss by charmingly depicting land animals, birds, water birds and fish worshipping along with men and women – as Milton's Adam and Eve exhort them to do (V. 153–208). Perhaps Milton had this verse in mind in Michael's prophecy that the faithful will be received into bliss 'Whether in heaven or earth, for then the earth / Shall all be paradise' (XII. 463–4).

With respect to the ethical treatment of non-human beings, Milton's philosophy is nearly as heretical towards Aristotle as his theology is towards Aquinas and main-stream Calvinism. Aristotle in the *Politics* justifies the subjection of animals, women and slaves as 'servants by nature'. In the Pythagorean tradition, however, justice to all sentient beings was considered part of the *ethos* of a just community or a moral person. Pythagoras's moral repugnance at enslaving and slaughtering animals is powerfully rendered in Renaissance translations of Ovid's *Metamorphoses* by Arthur Golding and George Sandys, and justice to them is invoked by Plutarch, Diogenes Laertes, Porphyry and Michel de Montaigne, whose essay *Of Crueltie*, translated by John Florio in 1603, decries the presumption of 'that imaginary soveraintie that some give and ascribe to us above all creatures', and asserts that even if that supposed superiority should be true, 'yet is there a kinde of respect, and a generall duty of humanity, which tieth us not only unto brute beasts that have life and sense, but even unto trees and plants', and to whom we owe 'grace and benignity' (Montaigne 1893: 126). Milton embodies this ethic in unfallen Adam and Eve.

Ecological Justice in *A Masque*: Earth's Womb and King Solomon's Mines

Unlike most Elizabethan pastoral poems and allegorical masques, *A Masque presented at Ludlow Castle, 1634* locates the action in a real place, Ludlow Castle on the river Severn, on the border of England and Wales, where it was performed to honour a real event, the inauguration of the Earl of Bridgewater as Lord Lieutenant of Wales and the border counties. In the debate between Comus and the Lady (played by the Earl's young daughter), Comus, the lord of misrule, advertises Nature's offerings (much as promoters of colonization did) in an attempt to seduce the Lady to the luxury and display that characterized the Caroline court and its more ostentatious masques. To his claim that nature's abundance exists for human pleasure, the Lady replies that nature is a 'good cateress' (line 763) whose gifts are meant for those who use them temperately and distribute them justly, not those who waste them on a life of consumption. Although temperance in the use of nature's bounty has a long literary history, Milton's 'Lady' is perhaps the first advocate of justice to human beings founded on justice towards 'innocent Nature' (line 761). Her eloquent resistance prepares for her rescue from Comus, but the local genius of the river Severn effects it; grace works not through Platonic philosophy but through Sabrina, a descendent of the legendary founder of Britain, who 'Visits the herds along the twilight meadows, / Helping all urchin blasts' with 'precious vialed liquors' (lines 843–6) and who 'with moist curb sways the smooth Severn stream' (line 824). As a technological context for the ecology of Milton's masque, I propose another masque by a different kind of hydraulic engineer.

In 1636, shortly after the performance of *A Masque*, a mining engineer named Thomas Bushell presented a rock masque, together with the rock, to Henrietta Maria, Queen of England. Bushell was a votary and intellectual heir of Francis Bacon, and the masque took place on Bushell's estate of Road Enstone near Woodstock in Oxford-shire, where he had discovered a 'desolate Cell of Natures rarities' and turned it into a banqueting grotto with 'contemplative Groves and Walkes, aswell as artificil thunder and lightning, raine, haile showres, drums beating, organs playing, birds singing, waters murmuring, the dead arising, lights moving, rainbowes reflecting f[r]om the same fountain' (1659 *Abridgment*: 'Post-Script to the Judicious Reader', p. 7). Music for the masque was written by the accomplished composer Symon Ive and the verse by Bushell himself, whose application of what Ruskin would call the 'pathetic fallacy' brings into relief Milton's affinitive appreciation of a living earth: 'Harke, harke, how the stones in the Rocke / Strive their tongues to unlock, / And would show, / What they know, / Of the Joy here hath beene / Since the King and the Queen / Daigne to say / They would pay / A visit to this cell . . .' (1636: fos 5–5ᵛ). The artificial birds and musical waters also devote themselves to praise, an appropriation of nature's tongues for royal compliment frequent in royalist verse.

Deep ecology includes the principle that all forms of life exist for their own sakes and earth, water and air should be left as nearly as possible as nature made them. Finding an interesting rock formation and turning it into a mechanical grotto is not deep ecology. It illustrates the reluctance of 'Western Man' to leave anything alone. But Bushell was not an environmental villain. He proposed in his *Abridgment* to accomplish Bacon's plan to rehabilitate drowned mines in England and Wales in order to avoid importation of American minerals mined by slaves for the profit of Spain, to give felons who would otherwise be hanged or deported work suitable to mollifying stony hearts, to save the expense of transporting unrefined ores, and to replenish the king's coffers with silver coin without raising taxes. However, his conservation programme is not deep ecology either; he habitually calls mineable mountains 'barren' and never considers the convenience of any creature not human. He reveres the principles of Bacon's fable of Solomon's House, where, along with mineral and vegetable experiments, vivisection, poisoning of animals and genetic engineering are carried out to see 'what may be wrought upon the body of man' without pity for the bodies of animals, and heat is produced 'of bellies and maws of living creatures, and of their bloods and bodies' (1857 *New Atlantis*, 3: 159, 161). Both King James and Francis Bacon had been called 'England's Solomon', James for his peacemaking and Bacon after the Hebrew king's reputation as a naturalist derived from 1 Kings 4: 33, 'And he spake of trees, from the cedar tree that is in Lebanon even unto the hyssop that springeth out of the wall: he spake also of beasts, and of fowl, and of creeping things, and of fishes.' Bushell tells God in a 'Miner's contemplative Prayer' at the end of his *Abridgment* that 'Solomon beautified thine own Temple which he built with his far sought Mineral Treasure, and I would gladly erect a house to the honor of his name' (1659: 12).

Though allied to the crown and the programme that led to the establishment of the Royal Society, Bushell adjusted to the Protectorate and went even beyond Milton in professing a libertarianism 'so sensible of other mens suffering restraint for conscience sake, as I procured the liberty of many Jesuit Priests, Anabaptists, Brownists, Familists of love, Adamites, and one of the Rosie Crucians', conceiving that those who imprisoned their bodies 'could not warrant to save their souls, though they might protect their persons, which last is the only sauce of our allegiance to a soveraigne power' (1659 'Post-Script', p. 7). He learnt from Bacon not to punish offenders without 'a Jury of penitential soules of their own Tribe', for 'severity should never force a builder of his Solomons house, since it is barbarous for a Christian to behold the Image of God used like a Dog' ('Post-Script', p. 12). He falls short of Montaigne, who thought it barbarous to misuse dogs, but he does teach that work should be for the Glory of God and the relief of the poor, and that 'the Mistery of divine Phylosophy' will not give any who covet riches or perform wicked acts 'a sheare in such a blessing' ('Post-Script', p. 13).

In Milton's *Masque* at Ludlow, Comus, in agreement with Bushell at Enstone and the extravagances of the Caroline court, argues that Nature pours forth her bounty 'to please, and sate the curious taste' and – in commendation of mining – 'in her own loins / She hutched the all-worshipped ore, and precious gems / To store her children with' (lines 717–19). If Nature's benefits were not assiduously used, he claims, she would be 'strangled with her waste fertility' (line 728); if subterranean treasures were not mined,

> the unsought diamonds
> Would so emblaze the forehead of the deep,
> And so bestud with stars, that they below
> Would grow inured to light, and come at last
> To gaze upon the sun with shameless brows.
>
> (lines 731–5)

John Leonard explains that 'Gems were thought to grow and shine under the earth, so unsought gems would eventually illumine Hell' (Milton 1998a: 678, n. to 732–6). Mining lore suggests a further reading. Bushell writes that in Bacon's opinion 'subterranean Spirits hindered the perfect discoveries of the richest Mines ... by the mischievous gambols they plaid there, as by raising Damps, extinguishing the Miners lights, firing the sulphurous matter of the Mine, and scorching the greedy and faithless Workmen. For not only *Socrates*, *Plato*, and *Aristotle*' believed that 'multitudes of Evil Spirits' inhabited air, water, and 'the hollow Concaverns of the earth; but divers of our more modern learned Writers and Theologians are of the same perswasion'. He lists among these Thomas Aquinas and St Augustine, 'who conceive that God hath permitted their temporal habitations therein, partly for mens trial, as that of *Job*, and partly for the punishment of the wicked' (1659 *Abridgment*, 'To my Fellow-Prisoners for Debt, in Mind or Body', p. 10).

Comus tells the Lady that, by becoming inured to light, subterranean spirits could enlarge their scope for mischief. She retorts that far from over-producing to promote human consumerism, Nature, 'good cateress / Means her provision only to the good / That live according to her sober laws, / And holy dictate of spare temperance' (lines 763–6).

In *Sylva Sylvarum* Bacon writes, 'Stones have in them fine Spirits, as appeareth by their splendour: And therefore they may work by consent upon the spirits of men, to comfort and exhilarate them', especially diamond, emerald, 'jacinth oriental', and yellow topaz; 'light, above all things, excelleth in comforting the spirits of men', and 'light varied doth the same effect with more novelty' (1857, 2: 661). Other colourful possessions, such as feather paintings, also cheer the (human) spirits by bringing nature's beauty into private hands. Comus's reason for wearing jewels may be Milton's spoof on the idea of material commodities providing light: they inure us to a more divine light than the appropriative intellectual light of Solomon's House. Comus's notion of removing the jewels from the ceiling of the underworld to keep malicious spirits underground parodies the doctrine of human responsibility for nature and allies him with prospectors who, however well-intentioned, would ransack Earth's inner parts. Comus's advice to invade the earth matches his intent to invade the Lady, herself a figure of virgin nature. For him, Earth's loins, and hers, are storehouses of pleasures to be rifled, and his rhetoric of human empire over nature is a debased version of the brazen-age temptations of Solomon's House.

The Ecological Epic

In 1661, after an episode of acute air pollution at Whitehall, John Evelyn advised Parliament to pay attention to 'the State of the Natural, as the Politick Body of this Great Nation . . . since, without their mutual harmony, and well-being, there can nothing prosper' (23). *Paradise Lost* poetically debates issues concerning the health of the natural and politic bodies still present in ecological discourse today: the nature of the 'dominion' granted in Genesis; the implications of monotheism for human attitudes towards nature; the effects of Mammon on air, water and earth; and the need for human justice to other-than-human beings.

Milton's epic presents a creation in which all creatures emerge from and possess their habitats, and a garden, the epitome of global nature, which God gives to Adam and Eve to tend and keep. They and their future offspring, who, had there been no Fall, would have become a global family and visited the first garden as its 'capital seat' (XI. 343), are appointed caretakers of this 'fruitful earth' (VIII. 96) and of numerous species who are not for profit. Their prelapsarian management of the garden is minimal and draws forth its native fruitfulness. They eat fruits and grains which they can 'pluck' without destroying the plant (V. 321–49) and obtain knowledge and pleasure by observing animals without interfering with them (IV. 340–6). Animals are not made only to serve human beings; rather, human beings are responsible for their shared environment. One tree, withheld amid plenty, exercises their wills in self-restraint and reminds them to respect the Maker and not become exploiters and rampant consumers of what he has made.

Milton is so lavish in his presentation of Earth as generative and wounded mother that this ancient figure seems more than figurative; if it is poetic personification, it is also moral perception. The archangel Raphael tells how God creates matter from his own substance and withdraws his ordering will, leaving Chaos, a turbulent storehouse of materials from which self-motivating creatures can be made. The agent of creation is the omnific Word, who drives the chariot of paternal glory 'Far into chaos' and with golden compasses circumscribes the universe from 'Matter unformed and void' (VII. 220, 233). After the Son has brought peace to these noisy and lively materials, the accompanying androgynous Spirit acts:

> darkness profound
> Covered the abyss: but on the watery calm
> His brooding wings the spirit of God outspread,
> And vital virtue infused, and vital warmth
> Throughout the fluid mass, but downward purged
> The black tartareous cold infernal dregs
> Adverse to life: then founded, then conglobed
> Like things to like, the rest to several place
> Disparted, and between spun out the air,
> And earth self-balanced on her centre hung.
> (VII. 233–42)

This principle of self-balancing applies to each creature and results from that 'vital virtue' infused throughout the creation that the falls of Adam and Eve will wound.

After the creation of light, Raphael continues,

> The earth was formed, but in the womb as yet
> Of waters, embryon immature involved,
> Appeared not: over all the face of earth
> Main ocean flowed, not idle, but with warm
> Prolific humour softening all her globe,
> Fermented the great mother to conceive,
> Satiate with genial moisture, when God said
> Be gathered now ye waters under heaven
> Into one place, and let dry land appear.
> (VII. 276–84)

What follows is the activity of Earth herself, expressed in active verbs and onomatopoeic prosody. Mountains upheave their backs; valleys sink; waters haste 'with glad precipitance', rivers 'draw their humid train', the waters congregate in seas, Earth covers 'Her universal face with pleasant green' and makes gay her sweet-smelling bosom with herbs and flowers, 'That earth now / Seemed like to heaven' (VII. 291, 306, 316, 328–9).

When God says 'Let the earth bring forth soul living in her kind',

> The earth obeyed, and straight
> Opening her fertile womb teemed at a birth
> Innumerous living creatures, perfect forms
> . . .

> The grassy clods now calved, now half appeared
> The tawny lion, pawing to get free
> His hinder parts, then springs as broke from bonds,
> And rampant shakes his brinded mane
>
> (VII. 451, 453–66)

The alliteration of 'clods now calved' reinforces the link between the land and its offspring, and as we pronounce the counterpoint of verse line against syntax we experience the struggle and energy of the lion's liberation. Now, Raphael sums up, 'air, water, earth, / By fowl, fish, beast, was flown, was swum, was walked / Frequent' (VII. 502–4). The archangel describes each creature with delight and kinetic empathy, but without imposing angelocentric, much less anthropocentric, emotions.

The 'improvement' of nature for human use was an objective of seventeenth-century scientific societies, including the Hartlib circle and the beginnings of the Royal Society. Writers like Samuel Hartlib, Robert Hooke and John Ray connected scientific observation to spiritual as well as economic life and exclaimed at the beauty of divine craftsmanship. In contrast to Raphael's angelic empathy, however, some experimental scientists undercut respect for the lives and suffering of the very creatures that inventions like the microscope were helping them appreciate. Henry Power, for example, states of the fly that 'if you prick a pin through the eye, you shall finde more blood there, then in all the rest of her body', and of the horse-fly, 'Her eye is an incomparable pleasant spectacle … indented all over with a pure Emerauld-green, so that it looks like green silk Irish-stitch … Her body looks like silver in frost-work, onely fring'd all over with white silk …. After her head is cut off, you shall most fairly see (just at the setting on of her neck) a pulsing particle (which certainly is the heart) to beat for half an hour most orderly and neatly through the skin' (1664: 5–7).

In spite of their calling in Genesis to tend the garden, no previous literary or iconographic tradition showed Adam and Eve actually doing so. Animals paid fawning obeisance to Adam and the plants bloomed to adorn Eve, but God's idea that human beings should work before the Fall was allegorized or overlooked. Milton's Adam and Eve take earth-keeping in the state of original righteousness joyfully but seriously – especially Eve, who in the separation debate (IX. 205–384) argues that not even the threatening presence of the foe should deter them from following their vocation freely.

Edenic gardening requires only 'such gardening tools as art yet rude, / Guiltless of fire had formed, or angels brought' (IX. 391–2). After the Fall reduces the hospitality of nature, fire and craft become necessary, as Adam discerns (X. 1055–84). Milton foresaw the threats to nature and spirit of the intemperate technology incipient in the Baconian programme and recommended moderation. Raphael warns against a surfeit of scientific and speculative knowledge unintegrated with land and community – 'this Paradise / And thy fair Eve' – (VII. 111–30, VIII. 163–78), yet he provides a great

deal of it well integrated with moral wisdom. But the technocrats in *Paradise Lost* are
the fallen angels, both in the building of Pandæmonium and in the War in Heaven.
Milton may show knowledge of mining books like Plattes's in his description of
the infernal hill 'whose grisly top / Belched fire and rolling smoke; the rest entire /
Shone with a glossy scurf, undoubted sign / That in his womb was hid metallic ore, /
The work of sulphur' (I. 670–4). The obsolescent grammar of 'his womb'
avoids conflating the inward parts of hell with Earth's womb, and it is here that
Milton's narrator comments that it was on Mammon's suggestion that men 'Rifled
the bowels of their mother earth / For treasures better hid' (I. 687–8). When
Mammon's crew had 'Opened into the hill a spacious wound / And digged out ribs
of gold', the narrator adds, 'Let none admire / That riches grow in hell; that soil may
best / Deserve the precious bane' (I. 689–92) and ridicules the enterprise of monumental building.

During the War in Heaven, Satan invents cannons and gunpowder. The beautiful
things, 'plant, fruit, flower ambrosial, gems and gold' that adorn the surface of
heaven's 'continent', he explains, originate 'Deep under ground' from 'materials
dark and crude, / Of spiritous and fiery spume, till touched / With heaven's ray,
and tempered they shoot forth / So beauteous, op'ning to the ambient light' (VI. 474–
81). These same materials, cast and touched with fire, will shoot forth destruction.
What are we to draw from the typically Miltonic perplexity that heaven should have
such soil? First, I think, Milton's materialism: all things are from one first matter, and
heaven, Raphael says, may be more like to earth than we suppose. Second, Milton's
commitment to free will and ethical choice: that heaven should have ignitable
minerals corresponds with the principle of *Areopagitica* that the *matter* of good and
evil are the same. As in Eden, the same soil, depending on its use, can bring forth fruit
or death.

As with issues of gender and power, Milton incorporates complexities that invite
debate. For example, Adam, Eve and God express differing views of animal intelligence. Adam thinks that 'other Creatures all day long / Rove idle unemployed . . . And
of their doings God takes no account' (IV. 616–22). But when he complains (chrono-
logically earlier) of his loneliness, the Creator replies

> What callst thou solitude, is not the earth
> With various living creatures, and the air
> Replenished, and all these at thy command
> To come and play before thee, knowst thou not
> Their language and their ways, they also know,
> And reason not contemptibly;
>
> (VIII. 369–74)

The Creator is leading Adam to pursue his argument for a mate of his own kind, and
at the same time teaching him not to underestimate the beings in his domain. Eve,
surprised when the Serpent speaks to her, cries

> What may this mean? Language of Man pronounced
> By tongue of brute, and human sense expressed?
> The first at least of these I thought denied
> To beasts, whom God on their creation-day
> Created mute to all articulate sound;
> The latter I demur, for in their looks
> Much reason, and in their actions oft appears.
>
> (IX. 553–9)

Adam gives the animals too little credit, and Eve, in the case of the Serpent, too much credence; both are in the process of learning about their relation to the creatures for whose well-being they are responsible. Experimenters often disregarded the intelligence of animals and their capacity for happiness and suffering, which modern science is beginning to rediscover. The animals of Milton's Eden supply not meat, pulling power or advantage in war, but delight in otherness. The benign regard of Adam and Eve, Raphael and God for beings unlike themselves has social and political implications as well.

Satan's use of the natural world as engine against the Almighty and Mammon's as commodity, Raphael's empathy for every kind of 'living soul' (VII. 388) generated in the creation and Michael's discernment of God's presence in them, are incipient in the choices they make during that originary moment of Book V, the Son's appointment as vicegerent: a moment that preserves the Father's transcendence while making the Son a conduit of immanence. The conception of a transcendent deity in monotheism and the doctrine that man was made in God's image are sometimes held responsible, in some cases with good cause, for the arrogance of exploitative dominion over nature; but that arrogance is not intrinsic to monotheism. In *Paradise Lost* God the Father, because of his transcendence, is able to produce beings having selfhood and freedom and give them that experience of the holy that stretches the imagination beyond the assumptions of human reason. His invention of difference invites responsiveness to what is not oneself. God the Son, on the other hand, through his viceregency, mediates between the Father's transcendence and the beings he makes of his own substance through the Son's agency.

Because the Son is 'annointed' Raphael calls him 'Messiah', and his Messiahship is a kind of angelification. Without diminishing the Father's transcendence, which makes holiness and unhampered creativity possible, the Son brings divinity closer to, and eventually into, creaturehood. By this mediation, God's omnipresence can be in 'every kind that lives' (XI. 337) without being polytheistically confined within the natural world, subjected to vagary and necessity and producing idolatry.

Satan, rejecting the Son's appointment as head of the angels, denies that he himself is a creature at all (V. 853–63). By accepting creaturehood – refusal to do which is Satan's first sin – the Son has become worthy of his pre-eminence and able to be both the agent of the creation already prophesied and the redeemer of it after the Fall.

When first Eve and then Adam falls, 'Earth felt the wound, and nature from her seat / Sighing through all her works gave signs of woe . . . Earth trembled from her entrails, as again / In pangs, and nature gave a second groan' (IX. 782–3, 1000–1). The animals begin to devour each other and experience the suffering under which creation groans. Adam and Eve, desiring the transcendence Satan pretends the forbidden fruit will give, have become consumers of the sacred reminder of their responsibility to all creation, and *Earth* felt the wound; *all* – not just human probity – was lost. Ambition to transcend, rather than fulfil, their responsibilities has wounded Earth's very womb. The wound is not hopeless, however. The Archangel Michael assures Adam that God's 'omnipresence fills / Land, sea, and air, and every kind that lives' (XI. 336–7), and the process of reparation has begun when Adam exclaims after the vision of Noah's ark that 'man shall live / With all the creatures, and their seed preserve' (XI. 872–3).

Politics of Nature in *Paradise Regained*

In Milton's brief epic, Jesus in the wilderness refutes Satan's attempts to seduce him into either exploitation of the earth or idolatry of its goods. The temptations contain awareness of the costs to nature and spirit of empire, war, luxury and miraculous interventions in nature's processes.

Many royalist poets, though by no means all, were in the Baconian and Hobbesian camps, and wrote in closed couplets laden with verbs of human control and animal, vegetable and mineral servitude. In Edmund Waller's 'On St James's Park, As Lately Improved by His Majesty' the language of control over nature suits an absolute monarch or a Baconian projector: 'The sea, which always served his empire, now / Pays tribute to our prince's pleasure, too.' The young trees 'appear in even ranks' and 'thrust their arms so high, / As if once more they would invade the sky'; and 'All that can, living, feed the greedy eye, / Or dead, the palate, here you may descry; / The choicest things that furnished Noah's ark, / Or Peter's sheet, inhabiting this park'. Noah becomes the saviour of heaped boards; Peter's vision of unforbidden food (Acts 10: 9–13), which means to him that God is no respecter of nationality or social position, becomes the winding sheet of edible animals. Here the king 'resolves his neighboring princes' fates' and sees 'His flock subjected to his view below'. Like an agricultural projector, he will 'Reform these nations, and improve them more / Than this fair park, from what it was before' (Waller 1991: 397–400).

In *Paradise Regained*, Jesus in the wilderness confronts temptations to gastronomical, political and ecological domination. In the temptation of the banquet he contemns as 'pompous delicacies' Satan's invitation to consume 'meats of noblest sort / And savour, beasts of chase, or fowl of game, / In pastry built, or from the spit, or boiled, Grisamber-steamed; all fish from sea or shore' (II. 341–4, 390). Metallurgy, the exploitation of animals and the abuse of the land are effects of 'military pride' (III. 310–36) and prosodically deflated: steel armour and steel bows that 'shot / Sharp sleet of arrowy showers' – an onomatopoeic tongue-twister; horses clad in mail, 'the field all iron' – animals and vegetables mineralized – bearing the human 'flower' of provinces; elephants 'endorsed with towers' – an etymological literality that asks us to think literally; 'pioneers... with spades and axes armed / To lay hills plain, fell woods, or valleys fill, / Or where plain was raise hill' – the chiasmic reversal and internal rhyme mimicking the re-engineering of the land; rivers bridged 'as with a yoke'; mules, camels and dromedaries, also presumably yoked: nature throughout raided and enslaved by raiders and enslavers of nations. Satan tells Jesus that only by such military power can he expect to save his people and regain the throne of David; Jesus replies that the 'cumbersome / Luggage of war' is 'argument / Of human weakness rather than of strength' (III. 400–2).

In the concluding anthem, the angels recognize Jesus as the incarnate Son, who by 'vanquishing / Temptation, hast regained lost Paradise' (IV. 607–8). *Paradise Regained* picks up ecological strands from both *A Masque* and *Paradise Lost* as Jesus rejects the temptations to display miracles, conquer kingdoms or obtain wealth, knowledge and power, even for what seem to be good causes. He systematically rejects pursuits that are costly to nature: war, imperial power, wealth for personal advancement and display. His simplicity of life, though not of mind, and his spiritual readiness will be the source of plenitude, however, figured in the banquet with which the poem concludes; and he will later stretch a small amount of bread and fish to feed thousands both physically and spiritually. At the summit of the poem, perfectly balanced on the pinnacle, reversing the Fall, he stands; may we think of this balance as including the temperance by which the health of nature, as well as of the spirit, can be regained?

BIBLIOGRAPHY

Writings

Bacon (1857); Bushell (1636, 1659); Corns (1990a); Evelyn (1661); Fludd (1659); *Geneva Bible* (1560); Locke (1987); Milton (1998a); Montaigne (1893); Plattes (1639); Power (1664); Topsell (1658); Waller (1991); Wilkins (1668); Willet (1620).

References for Further Reading

Bennett, Joan S. (1987); Donnelly (1999); Du-Rocher (1993, 1994); Edwards, Karen (1999); Fallon, Stephen M. (1991); Leslie and Raylor (1992); Low (1985); Marjara (1992); McColley (1999a, b); Rogers (1996); Rudrum (1989); Theis (1996).

11
The English and Other Peoples

Andrew Hadfield

Colonies and Ethnic Theology

John Milton, as David Armitage has so cogently argued, was a poet against empire (Armitage 1995). He associated a drive for imperial expansion with the worst excesses of a dying and corrupt political culture. In fact, in his view the two are inextricably linked, the one necessitating the other. An extended critique of the evils of the late Stuart regime is made throughout *Paradise Lost*, a work which can no longer be read as an expression of Milton's quietism and withdrawal from political thought and political life (Hill 1977, ch. 29; Norbrook 1999, ch. 10). Satan, a figure in keeping with the politics of Charles I as well as Oliver Cromwell, once he has manipulated the Parliament of devils to allow him to implement his plan of corrupting humankind, sets off for the New World like an explorer, merchant or colonist seeking out exotic lands. Milton describes Satan resembling

> a fleet descried
> Hangs in the clouds, by equinoctial winds
> Close sailing from Bengala, or the isles
> Of Ternate and Tidore, whence merchants bring
> Their spicy drugs: they on the trading flood
> Through the wide Ethiopian to the Cape
> Ply stemming nightly toward the pole. So seemed
> Far off the flying fiend:
>
> (*PL* II. 636–43)

The significance of this epic simile, of course, is that the vehicle and object of the comparison can be reversed. European merchants are, in a fundamental way, Satanic, a point reinforced by the repetition of the comparison between Satan and epic voyagers near the start of Book IV (lines 159–71).

Satan's journey ends when he finally reaches the innocent New World of the Garden of Eden. As has often been pointed out, explorers represented the Americas so frequently in terms of the Garden of Eden that the comparison became a stultifying cliché (Sheehan 1979). Milton, perhaps following John Donne's revitalization of a tired image when he referred to his mistress's body as 'my America, my new found land', narrates Satan's corruption of Eve in terms of a voyeuristic European bringing sin into Paradise. Satan approaches Eden as a sex-starved seducer and the landscape, once innocent, now resonates with a glut of pornographic imagery:

> So on he fares, and to the border comes,
> Of Eden, where delicious Paradise,
> Now nearer, crowns with her enclosure green,
> As with a rural mound the champaign head
> Of a steep wilderness, whose hairy sides
> With thicket overgrown, grotesque and wild,
> Access denied; and over head up grew
> Insuperable highth of loftiest shade,
> Cedar, and pine, and fir, and branching palm,
> A sylvan scene, and as the ranks ascend
> Shade above shade, a woody theatre
> Of stateliest view.
>
> (*PL* IV. 131–42)

Given that Milton places such importance on the corruption of sex as a central indication of the Fall, so that what was once pure and lovely becomes a prefiguration of the burning fires of hell, it is appropriate that Satan should be seen to bring a depraved form of sexuality into the Garden. The first half of the description contrasts markedly with the second. The first seven lines depict the boundary of Eden, which Satan has just reached. The description of a 'rural mound' with overgrown 'hairy sides', denying access, cannot but resemble a virginal vagina resisting male advances, especially when balanced against the specifically unsexual imagery of the 'sylvan scene' in the last six lines. Satan appears as a rapist, a potent male ready to ravish and exploit the untouched lands before him, imagery which recalls Sir Walter Ralegh's description of Guiana as a 'countrey that yet had her maydenhead, never sackt, nor wrought, the face of the earth hath not bene torne' (Ralegh 1997: 196; Montrose 1991: 12–13). By implication, the reader who understands the connotations of these lines (and which reader could not?) becomes complicit with Satan's act through the misfortune of their own fallen nature. The innocence of Eden's inhabitants is, as yet, untouched, a contrast symbolized in the difference between the two balanced halves of the description. But we all know what will happen.

Once again, the vehicle and message of the allegory demand to be reversed and read the other way round. Imperial designs, which stem from a corrupt rigging of the democratic mechanisms of the state, are Satanic (Armitage 1995: 221). Adam and Eve stand for the innocent peoples of the Americas, just as they are seen to stand for Adam and Eve. As before, this identification went back to the early days of English colonial history, most strikingly represented in the first plate provided by Theodor De Bry of the series that accompanied his edition of Thomas Harriot's *A Briefe and True Report of the New Found Land of Virginia* (1590), produced as the first part of his massive multivolume series of the same year, *America* (Harriot 1972). As we travel with Satan, we have the choice whether to repeat the greed and envy which inaugurated the Fall, or to try to oppose a fundamental injustice.

Milton's strong feelings about colonial oppression and the corruption of the innocent may well have stemmed from his friendship with Roger Williams, the dissident who founded the colony at Plymouth Bay after he had fallen out with the governors of the Massachusetts Bay Colony. Williams was sharply critical of assumptions of colonial superiority to the natives of the New World. His work, *A Key into the Languages of America* (1643), a guide to the Algonquian language, tried to represent the natives as sophisticated and humane people who were being exploited and oppressed by their European counterparts. Williams's critique is precisely the same as Milton's in *Paradise Lost*: that 'the Massachusetts colonists, much like the King and the clerical hierarchy within England, have succumbed to their own desire for power' (Scanlan 1999: 127). Just as Satan (Cromwell, Charles I) moves from the metropolitan centre of hell to the pastoral idyll of the Garden of Eden, so did the governors of the Massachusetts colony. Given that Williams taught Milton Dutch in 1652 when he had returned from New England, it seems that Williams's ideas probably formed the basis for Milton's representation of Satan's epic voyage (Parker 1996: 410).

Milton's representation of Adam and Eve as peoples of the New World is, on one level, quite laudably enlightened and anti-ethnocentric (although it should be pointed out that there is a long history of opposition to colonialism as an exploitative practice: see Hadfield 1998; Scanlan 1999). But it is also, in the words of Jacques Derrida analysing the identical sentiments of Claude Lévi-Strauss, 'an ethnocentrism *thinking itself* as anti-ethnocentrism' (1974: 120; Derrida's emphasis). Milton represents the people of the Americas as innocent prelapsarians abroad in the mire of the postcolonial world, forcibly joined to the sophisticated postlapsarian peoples of Europe through intercontinental contact. The perceived time lag between the two continents and the obvious question as to why God had not let the native Americans advance at the same rate as their European counterparts had led many Spanish theologians of the previous century to question their humanity (Pagden 1982). *Paradise Lost* affirms the humanity of the natives and attacks the inhumanity of Europeans, but indicates that it is the latter who must protect the former in the fallen world. After all, it is only sophisticated, guilty readers who will be able to decipher the wiles of those who have fallen under the spell of Satan. Prelapsarian man will be unable to comprehend the low cunning of the devil. It is one of the central paradoxes of *Paradise Lost* that only the fallen can actually read it right.

There are further consequences arising from Milton's establishment of a dichotomy between the corruption of the Old World and the innocence of the New, which in turn have serious repercussions for the peoples of Europe and, specifically, the British

Isles. It follows that if the inhabitants of the Americas are prelapsarian creatures, then all those who have had access to the word and mercy of God must be deemed responsible for their actions and, therefore, guilty, if they fail to choose the right path. In other words, the innocence of the New World serves to emphasize the guilt of the Old. Milton's harsh judgement of Catholics is unsurprising and well documented. *Areopagitica* is quite explicit that 'Popery' and 'open superstition' cannot be tolerated, partly because Catholicism itself was a religion which demanded 'a fugitive and cloister'd vertue' by prohibiting a wide range of books via the papal index (*CPW* II: 565, 515). Notwithstanding his notable affection for his many friends and connections in a Catholic country such as Italy, visited when he performed his 'Grand Tour' (1638–9), while there Milton refused to keep silent when asked about his religious convictions, and condemned what he regarded as erroneous, tyrannical beliefs (Parker 1996, ch. 6).

Colin Kidd has recently demonstrated that early modern conceptions of national identity cannot be separated from theological belief. We cannot return to the past and expect the same categories that we take for granted today to operate as systems for organizing intellectual ideas. Kidd points out that 'the primary value of ethnicity was not ethnological in the modern sense, but lay within the theology of "evidences", where it functioned as a vital weapon in the defence of Christian orthodoxy and the authenticity of scripture from heterodox assaults' (1999: 10). This would appear to describe Milton's ethnology exactly. In *Paradise Lost*, peoples are divided in terms of their state of theological awareness (fallen versus unfallen people; evil versus good fallen people), and the justification of the ways of God to men involves explaining, carefully and exactly, how each nation or race fits into God's overall plan. Kidd points out that it was only with the decline of 'ethnic theology' that conceptions of secular national identities and a concomitant scientific racialism could develop (72). Indeed, it was a division of the peoples of the world into the Mosaic categories of sons of Ham, Shem and Japhet which, paradoxically, provided a hope of tolerance and ultimate integration, in contrast to the overt racism of later means of understanding and the division of peoples into their constituent nations.

However, for Milton, at least, 'ethnic theology' could lead not only to severe judgements of those who failed to follow God's word, but to support for the brutal suppression of God's enemies. Nowhere is this more marked than in Milton's writings on the four nations of the British Isles.

'In Quintum Novembris'

Milton's interest in the four nations was marked at an early stage and finds its earliest expression in a Latin poem on the failure of the Gunpowder Plot, *'In Quintum Novembris'*, written while he was still a student at Cambridge (November 1626). The poem divides people into categories on the basis of 'ethnic theology', prefiguring themes and subjects that were to occupy Milton throughout his mature writing career. Milton describes how England, united with Scotland under the rule of James, enjoys a period of peace and prosperity. Such happy stability incites the envy of Satan and the Catholic hordes he controls. For Milton's Satan, Englishness and Protestant virtue are inseparable:

> Atque pererrato solum hoc lacrymabile mundo
> Inveni, dixit, gens haec mihi sola rebellis,
> Contemtrixque iugi, nostraque potentior arte.
> Illa tamen, mea si quicquam tentamina possunt,
> Non feret hoc impune diu, non ibit inulta,
> Hactenus; et piceis liquido natat aere pennis;
> Qua volat, adversi praecursant agmine venti,
> Densantur nubes, et crebra tonitrua fulgent.
>
> (lines 40–7)

'I have wandered over the whole world', he says, 'and this is the only thing that brings tears to my eyes; this is the only nation I have found which rebels against me, spurns my government and is mightier than my crafts. But if my efforts have any effect, these people will not get away with it for long: they will not go unpunished.' (*CSP*: 40, 47)

Milton is again writing within a tradition; this time, one which regarded England after the Reformation as 'the elect nation' chosen by God to be the new Israel and show the true way forward to the rest of the world (Haller 1963). While other nations have succumbed to the wiles of Satan and immersed themselves in sin, falling prey to the evils of Catholicism, England has stood alone in preserving God's message. England's national identity is defined by its superior religious virtue. Milton's early version of Satan refers back to events in the last century to inspire the Catholics to vengeance. He urges them to 'memor Hesperiae disiectam ulciscere classem, / Mersaque Iberorum lato vexilla profundo, / Sanctorumque cruci tot corpora fixa probrosae, / Thermodoontea nuper regnante puella' (Remember the past! Avenge the scattered Spanish fleet! Avenge the Iberian standards overwhelmed in the deep and the bodies of so many saints nailed to the shameful cross during the Amazonian virgin's reign' (lines 102–5). Post-Reformation religious divisions have established the character and nature of the English and battle lines have been drawn up. Elizabeth's reign stands directly behind the legitimate authority of James's Parliament – in contrast to the violent opposition of the Catholics, who will destroy proper rule in order to support their own undesirable dynasty. Satan appeals to a different legacy which can be re-established: 'Saecula sic illic tandem Mariana redibunt, / Turque in belligeros iterum dominaberis Anglos' ('Thus the Marian regime will at last be re-established in that land, and you will have the warlike English under your thumb again') (lines 127–8).

Milton's conception of the nature and character of government in England refers us back to the building of Pandæmonium, the false Parliament in hell in *Paradise Lost*. '*In Quintum Novembris*' indicates that, for Milton, the monarch rules as the monarch in Parliament and needs the elected chamber to authorize his or her authority: a hotly contested issue in early seventeenth-century England, especially given James's belief in the sanctity of his own right to govern without executive support. Attempts to diminish or overthrow that authority are the work of papist devils, as the poem makes clear. In making such connections, Milton places the tradition of Parliament as central to an English identity, indicating that opposition to its existence or proper functioning is the work of foreign, antireligious and antipatriotic forces. One of the tragic messages of *Paradise Lost* is that the Restoration has broken an English democratic tradition as the English failed, when they had the chance, to institute God's proper government on earth, undermined their elected government and opted instead for a 'foreign' form of rule.

Milton preserved his sense of England's inherent righteousness and superiority to other nations when he visited Italy. '*In Quintum Novembris*' contains a long description of Satan flying to Italy, where he rouses the devils and pagan kings to forge a Catholic alliance and tempts the Pope when he is asleep (lines 48–89). Milton, like any English traveller, found much to admire in Italy, and the journey stimulated him culturally and intellectually (Chaney 1998, ch. 12; Parker 1996, ch. 6). He made a number of Italian friends, and was later vociferous in his condemnation of atrocities against Italian Protestants in the sonnet 'On the late Massacre in Piedmont' (1655; *CSP*: 341–3). But he had to be warned on numerous occasions that his outspoken defence of English Protestantism could lead him into trouble with the ubiquitous Jesuits. As his biographer has noted, 'Travel inspired Milton's patriotism' and he discovered that there was 'an English culture worth respecting' (Parker 1996: 179). The tour undoubtedly helped to inspire Milton to follow his calling to become 'the greatest of English poets' (180).

The History of Britain

Soon after his return from Italy Milton began work on a never-produced Arthurian British epic, presumably a first attempt to realize his ambition to become the pre-eminent poet of the British Isles. He began serious work on a wide range of British historians from the early middle ages to recent contemporaries, including Bede, Gildas, Geoffrey of Monmouth, William of Malmesbury, Raphael Holinshed and Samuel Purchas (Parker 1996: 190, 841–2). It is likely that Milton abandoned his work because he felt that he was too much in thrall to his major poetic precursor, Edmund Spenser, whose major poem, *The Faerie Queene*, was also an Arthurian epic, albeit an oblique one (Lacy 1986: 521–2; Quilligan 1983). In *Areopagitica* (1644), written soon afterwards, Milton praised *The Faerie Queene* as a true guide to virtue (perhaps making it a peculiarly *English* work?), and Spenser as 'a better teacher then *Scotus* or *Aquinas*' (*CPW* II: 516). This might indicate that Milton saw no need to duplicate work already done, which could only cramp his lofty ambition.

But if there was less mileage in a specifically British or English epic than might at first have appeared, Milton's assiduous reading nevertheless led to *The History of*

Britain, probably written in the late 1640s, but not published until 1670 (*CPW* V: xix–xxxvii; von Maltzahn 1991, ch. 2). History was central to Milton's conception of himself as a poet, because it could reveal the truth of a nation's identity: only if history is properly conceived and understood can legitimate poetic labours flourish. Milton was working with two types and styles of historical writing and two historiographical traditions. His notion of history was heavily influenced by Roman and Greek historians such as Herodotus, Thucydides, Polybius, Livy, Plutarch and Tacitus; but his favourite historian was Sallust (*CPW* V: xliv–v). Milton was also interested in Italian history (*CPW* V: xxvi). In short, he admired such historians for their dispassionate attempts to analyse complex historical situations and produce an objective, rational narrative. He aspired to a lucid and economical style of writing, shorn of rhetorical excesses. Equally, he admired the republican stance which many of the historians in question advocated as they exposed the corruption and weaknesses of oligarchic and monarchic government.

However, Milton was also influenced by the homiletic, moralistic tradition of much British history, notably in Geoffrey of Monmouth, Gildas and Bede. These writers saw a providence at work in the universe, whereby the Britons enjoyed their greatest success, most notably during Arthur's reign, when they were in tune with God's desires and, consequently, behaved most virtuously. Conversely, corruption, civil strife and oppression led to the abasement of the Britons and, eventually, their expulsion from the island which their ancestor, Brutus, had named.

The two traditions were not necessarily in conflict. Gildas's *De Excidio et Conquestu Britanniae* was an acerbic commentary on the sins of the Britons which had led to their spectacular downfall in the fifth century. It had been edited just over a hundred years earlier by Polydore Vergil, the most sceptical and Italianate of British historians, who elsewhere led the case against the historical existence of Arthur. Milton's aim in *The History of Britain*, I would suggest, was to combine the merits of Sallust and Gildas in a sophisticated narrative which would also provide a hard-hitting moral lesson.

As has long been recognized, Milton's work needs to be read in the context of the late 1640s, specifically the events of February–March 1649, and his frustration at the opportunities lost by the country's leaders (*CPW* V: 426–31; von Maltzahn 1991, chs 3–5). Milton, significantly enough, was particularly exercised by the willingness of Parliament to squander 'the republican *occasione* . . . within a month of the execution of Charles I' (von Maltzahn 1991: 31). Despite Pride's Purge (December 1648) and the execution of the King in January 1649, Parliament was starting to re-admit MPs who had opposed the decisive action of the republican elements within the parliamentary forces (Bennett 1997, ch. 12). Milton clearly felt that the possibility of establishing the true historical legacy of the English Reformation was being lost; and, once again, one notes how central to his conception of the English nation was a properly functioning Parliament.

The parallel is made absolutely secure through the discovery of 'The Digression', a passage of direct commentary linking the history of Britain after the Romans left to events in England in the late 1640s, which was omitted from the text of *The History of Britain* published in 1670. 'The Digression' appeared as a twelve-page quarto in 1681, with its full title, *Mr. John Milton's Character of the Long Parliament and Assembly of DIVINES in 1641*. The passage was clearly not relevant in the context of the 1670s, and may have served to distort rather than clarify the significance of the work (*CPW* V: 423–4). Besides, Milton's actual service in the Interregnum government and his remaining hopes for future change in the British Isles would also have militated against including a harsh analysis of the Britons as a people.

Milton suggests that the Parliamentarians have assumed the wrong historical mantle through their inadequacies and prevarication. The 'New Magistracy' have put their own 'private Ends before' and

> Hence Faction, thence Treachery, both at home and in the Field: Every where Wrong, and Oppression: Foul and Horrid Deeds committed daily, or maintain'd, in secret, or in open. Some that thir enimies were not stronger then they: when as one legion drove them twice out of the Ile at first encounter. Nor could the Brittans be so ignorant of warr whome the Romans had then newly instructed; or if they were to seeke, alike were thir enimies, rude and naked barbarians . . . they had armies, leaders and successes to thir wish; but to make use of so great advantages was not thir skill. (*CPW* V: 442–3)

Milton's comparison is exactly tailored and barbed. The Britons were not lacking in courage and they did not lose their land to the Saxons, Scots or Picts through straightforward military defeat. In fact, the *History* goes out of its way to praise the martial prowess of the Britons. Hence their failure must be put to other reasons, namely, 'the ill husbanding of those faire opportunities, which migh[t] seeme to have put libertie, so long desir'd, like a brid[le] into thir hands' (*CPW* V: 443). True liberty is there waiting, but the Britons simply fail to seize the day, as do their English counterparts over a thousand years later. Milton shows here that, once again, he perceives English/British history as a story of two traditions, or paths to be taken. The Britons failed to inaugurate a period of great liberty and virtue when the opportunity presented itself, and, so the *History* forcefully points out, history is repeating itself with the failure of the English to establish the godly republic in the aftermath of the King's execution.

In fact, the best have become the worst as they have betrayed the hopes of the people:

> Thus they who of late were extoll'd as our greatest Deliverers, and had the People wholly at their Devotion, by so discharging their Trust as we did see, did not only weaken and unfit themselves to be dispensers of what Liberty they pretended, but unfitted also the People, now grown worse and more disordinate, to receive or to digest any Liberty at all. For Stories teach us, that liberty sought out of season, in a corrupt and degenerate Age, brought *Rome* itself into a farther Slavery. (*CPW* V: 448)

In this passage, we can see Milton making a careful link between a history of the decline of the Roman empire written by Sallust or Tacitus, with the moralistic history of the decline of the Britons of Gildas or Geoffrey of Monmouth. From the combination of the scientific and the homiletic, Milton deduces a general law of human history, that it is better for nations not to have tried to establish true liberty than to have tried and failed through sinful behaviour. Being God's chosen nation, as the Bible amply illustrates, was as much a curse as a blessing. The consequences of the failure of the British led to greater oppression than had occurred before; and the same will happen again if the lessons of Milton's *History* are not heeded.

The very mention of the city of Rome illustrates Milton's point. Rome was the great city of the pre-medieval world, having risen from the ashes of the Old World. It was founded by Aeneas, a refugee from Troy after that great monument of ancient civilization was destroyed. According to Geoffrey of Monmouth, Brutus, a descendant of Aeneas, was expelled from Rome and went on to found the race of Britons, whose progeny ruled as kings 'to the entrance of *Julius Caesar*'. Milton repeats Geoffrey's narrative – acknowledging his source (*CPW* V: 9) – and, although he has some scepticism about the authenticity of Geoffrey's claims, acknowledges the usefulness of the connections made. The Britons 'lighting on the *Trojan* Tales in affectation to make *Britain* of one Original with the *Roman*, pitch'd there' (*CPW* V: 8). Rome was therefore inextricably linked to the fate and future of the Britons as its precursor and originator. Just as Rome went through periods of democratic success when liberty was preserved and overbearing tyranny when liberty was banished, so did Britain. More seriously still, Rome shadowed seventeenth-century England as the fountain of tyranny because it was the seat of the papacy, as '*In Quintum Novembris*' had demonstrated. If Rome had once been the foundation of European civilization, the best that the pre-medieval world had to offer, it had now become the worst, a Satanic city, which had turned its back on its ancient traditions of democracy, liberty and virtue.

Milton used the image of Rome as the centre of a corrupted and degenerate civilization throughout his work. As has been pointed out, Pandæmonium, the gaudy building built by Mammon that houses the devil's Parliament, has quite specific Roman features:

> Anon out of the earth a fabric huge
> Rose like an exhalation, with the sound
> Of dulcet symphonies and voices sweet,
> Built like a temple, where pilasters round
> Were set, and Doric pillars overlaid
> With golden architrave; nor did there want
> Cornice or frieze, with bossy sculptures graven,
> The roof was fretted gold. Not Babylon,
> Nor great Alcairo, such magnificence
> Equalled in all their glories, to enshrine
> Belus or Serapis their gods, or seat
> Their kings, when Egypt with Assyria strove
> In wealth and luxury.
>
> (*PL* I. 710–22)

The building itself undoubtedly resembles St Peter's in Rome: 'The pilasters, the carved roof, the guilding, the brazen doors and the adjacent council chamber: all these details fit' (Milton 1968: 503). Moreover, Rome was commonly perceived by Protestants as the second Babylon, the centre of the still powerful forces of the old, pagan world, a connection Milton highlights and develops in this passage. Milton extends the chain of ancient, pagan cities and edifices back to the Egyptian pyramids and the Tower of Babel, built by Nimrod as a means of connecting man back to God (an action parodied when the fallen angels build a highway between hell and earth in Book X). The typology of the chain needs to be reversed. Pandæmonium may be compared to Rome, Babylon, the pyramids and Babel, but it is the Parliament building of the fallen angels, which serves as the model that the others copy. Milton adopts the same process when he has the fallen angels discussing problems of classical philosophy and reciting ancient epics while Satan travels to discover earth. A line of falsehood is retrospectively established as a means of defining the true and the good. The excesses and weaknesses of the English Parliament during the Interregnum show that its members became the inheritors of a Roman tradition of lies and tyranny, rather than an English tradition of truth and democracy. The best has become the worst.

Such perversion develops but does not fundamentally alter the oppositions established in '*In Quintum Novembris*'. They re-appear in Milton's last major poem, *Paradise Regained*. One of Satan's last temptations of Christ is that of world government, a bad means of imposing the good, that will negate the decision to grant humankind freedom of choice outlined in the discussions between God and Christ in *Paradise Lost*, Book III. Satan transports Christ to a magnificent city, which he reveals to be Rome. Although Satan does describe in some detail the impressive architecture and opulent ornamentation of the buildings, as well as the wealth of Rome's possessions and territories, these are not the substance of the temptation. Satan tells Christ that the emperor Tiberius has no heir and has retired to Capri, 'His horrid lusts in private to enjoy' (*PR* IV. 94), and has promoted instead a wicked favourite, Sejanus, 'Hated of all, and hating' (IV. 97) (the history of Tiberius's reign is taken from Tacitus and Suetonius). The temptation is that Christ himself might seize control and reform the empire:

> with what ease
> Endued with regal virtues as thou art,
> Appearing, and beginning noble deeds,
> Might'st thou expel this monster from his throne
> Now made a sty, and in his place ascending
> A victor people free from servile yoke!
> And with my help thou mayst; to me the power
> Is given, and by that right I give it thee.
> Aim therefore at no less than all the world,
> Aim at the highest, without the highest attained
> Will be for thee no sitting, or not long
> On David's throne, be prophesised what will.
> (*PR* IV. 97–108)

Satan has confused and combined two traditions of government in equating David's rule with that of Rome. This fundamental error helps Christ to establish his sense of his own identity and he finds it nearly as straightforward to reject the political temptation as he does to dismiss the lure of luxury and wealth. Christ makes the familiar link between godless government and Satan when he responds to the suggestion that he could free the empire of its ruler: 'what if I withal / Expel a devil who first made him such?' (IV. 128–9). Satan has tempted Christ to correct the symptoms, not the real disease, as Christ now explains. Christ sees the malign development of the Roman empire as the responsibility of the people who made it, not simply the fault of a vile and corrupt leader who can be left to his 'tormentor conscience' (IV. 130). The Romans are not his responsibility either, having become 'vile and base' and 'Deservedly made vassal' who were 'once just, / Frugal, and mild, and temperate' (IV. 132–4). Satan's perception of politics as either enlightened or tyrannous despotism helps Christ to articulate his own more democratic understanding of the political process. Change must come from below:

> What wise and valiant man would seek to free
> These thus degenerate, by themselves enslaved,
> Or could of inward slaves make outward free?
> Know therefore when my season comes to sit
> On David's throne, it shall be like a tree
> Spreading and overshadowing all the earth,
> Or as a stone that shall to pieces dash
> All monarchies besides throughout the world,
> And of my kingdom there shall be no end:
> Means there shall be to this, but what the means,
> Is not for thee to know, nor me to tell.
>
> (*PR* IV. 143–53)

It is clear that Christ is not withdrawing from politics, but re-asserting the need to keep politics clean and pure. One must never lose sight of the fundamental division of the peoples of the world into the enslaved and the godly. The Roman empire has imposed its designs on its citizens and subjects, willing and unwilling, so that all have been sullied by its corrupt nature. In essence, those who, whether through conscious evil or ingrained habit, do not want to be made free, cannot be liberated from the wiles of Satan. The new just rule of Christ, as his sacrifice for humankind in *Paradise Lost*, Book III, indicates, can only be inaugurated by willing followers. It cannot be imposed from above. Although no one can know how this transformation will take place, we can know what political forms will be brushed aside: namely, monarchy and other types of oppressive government from above. Christ can only operate through peoples who follow his teachings and are prepared to establish proper democracy. The English have singularly failed to do so, which is why Milton turns against them with such force in his later writings. But it would be an error to assume that Milton had made a clean break with his earlier political ideas.

Milton describes the Romans in *Paradise Regained* as a people who 'govern ill the nations under yoke' (IV. 135). This phrase reminds readers of the heated debates over the Norman Conquest which took place throughout the seventeenth century. On the one side were those who argued that the Normans had destroyed good Saxon laws and imposed a tyrannous 'Norman yoke' on the previously free-born English; on the other were those who argued that the Normans had in fact codified a chaotic legal system and introduced good, workable laws (Pocock 1987: 318–20).

In *The History of Britain* Milton comes down firmly on the first side. He establishes Ethelbert as 'the first Christian King of *Saxons*, and no less a favourer of all civility in that rude age'. Ethelbert 'gave Laws and Statutes after the example of *Roman* Emperors, written with the advice of his sagest Counsellors'. He makes it his business 'to punish those who had stoln ought from Church or Churchman, thereby shewing how gratefully he receiv'd at thir hands the Christian faith'. Ethelbert is adopting the good legacy of Rome by combining sensible laws with the true – democratic – Christian faith (a pointed contrast to Satan's efforts in *Paradise Regained*). Unfortunately, his son Eadbald 'took the course as fast to extinguish; not only falling back to Heathenism, but that which Heathenism was wont to abhor, marrying his fathers second wife'. The people, correspondingly, abandon their Christianity and return 'eagerly to thir old Religion' (*CPW* V: 195–6).

This episode reveals how volatile the history of a people can be and how rapidly the shift from virtue to vice generally is, a lesson Milton evidently hoped readers of his *History* would learn. The Saxons establish the rudiments of good, Christian government, but, as often as not, they fail to learn from the disasters the Britons inflict on themselves through their bad behaviour. By the end of Book IV Milton shows that history is repeating itself. In the middle of the eighth century the Danes are about to invade a corrupt and enfeebled people, a fact signalled by a portent when the north roof of St Peter's church in York was seen to rain blood. Alcuin, 'a learned Monk', attributes the sign to:

> thir neglect of breeding up youth in the Scriptures, the spruce and gay apparel of thir Preists and Nuns, discovering thir vain and wanton minds, examples are also read, eev'n in *Beda*'s days, of thir wanton deeds: thence Altars defil'd with perjuries, Cloisters violated with Adulteries, the Land polluted with blood of thir Princes, civil dissentions among the people, and finally all the same vices which *Gildas* alleg'd of old to have ruin's the *Britans*. (*CPW* V: 255–6)

In short, the Saxons, like the Britons before them, have betrayed their Christian, democratic heritage and fallen prey to the worldly sins of Rome. The union of the merging Saxon kingdoms does not have the desired or anticipated effect:

men might with some reason have expected from such Union, peace and plenty, greatness, and the flourishing of all Estates and Degrees: but far the contrary fell out soon after, Invasion, Spoil, Desolation, slaughter of many, slavery of the rest, by the forcible landing of a fierce Nation. (*CPW* V: 257)

The inhabitants of mainland Britain suffer a series of invasions: from the Saxons, the Danes and then the Normans. But each invasion is preceded by a spiritual invasion of the false principles of Rome. The use of the term 'union' undoubtedly refers the reader to James I's attempted union of the kingdoms of the British Isles and his assumption of the mantle of the 'King of Britain'. The implication, of course, is that the same problems are now plaguing the English, who will head for a fall if they do not mend their ways.

Like the Britons before them, the Saxon kingdom degenerates into civil war, with 'the lesser Kingdoms revolting from the *West-Saxon* yoke' (*CPW* V: 259). Again, the use of a key term is pointed: 'yoke' suggests that the behaviour of the West-Saxons mirrors that of the later invaders (Pocock 1987: 318–20). Milton does indeed take a strong line against the Norman invasion, praising Harold Godwin as a good king who established 'good Laws, repeal'd bad, became a great Patron to Church and Church-men, courteous and affable to all reputed good, a hater of evill doers' (*CPW* V: 394). Despite the internal dissension and poor behaviour of the Saxons/English, enough that is worthwhile of their rule remains to make the Norman invasion an event to regret. The English 'were constrein'd to take the Yoke of an out-landish Conquerer' who 'promis'd peace and defence; yet permitted his men the while to burn and make prey' (*CPW* V: 402).

The English brought tyranny upon themselves and 'gave to *William* thir Conqueror so easie a Conquest' (*CPW* V: 402–3). One of the central morals of the *History* is that imperial conquest is to be condemned, as it leads to tyranny, oppression and an attack on the true word of God. Nations can only prosper if they treat their own citizens well and respect the rights of others (which does, of course, include the right of showing them God's true word). This is the lesson the English/British must heed if they are finally to throw off the legacy of the past. As the 'Digression', *Paradise Lost* and *Paradise Regained* demonstrate, it is one they find all too easy to ignore, with dire consequences.

Observations on the Articles of the Peace

If Milton showed admirable foresight and even-handed principles in respecting the autonomy of Christian nations in many of his writings and arguing the case for godly democracy, he showed little tolerance for the other peoples within the British Isles. The Picts, Scots and Irish play minor roles on the fringes of *The History of Britain*, which is really about the English. An early key to Milton's sense of the peoples neighbouring England is given in a comparison made while narrating the Roman invasion of Britain: 'For it seems that through lack of tillage, the North-ern parts were then, as *Ireland* is at this day; and the inhabitants in like manner wonted to retire, and defend themselves in such watrie places half naked' (*CPW* V: 101). The Irish are a primitive people who need to be integrated more care-fully into the rest of Britain under the government of the civilized English. Just as the Northern Britons have been transformed into reasonable and at least partially civilized citizens, so, the pointed comparison implies, must the Irish be.

Milton's views are unexceptional for Englishmen in the mid-seventeenth century, who generally regarded the Scots, Irish and Welsh as threats to civilization, religion and liberty (Kidd 1999; Bennett 1997, pt 1). The stereotype of the Celtic peoples presented them as brutal, emotional, lacking proper homes and towns, possessed of a low cunning, more often naked than clothed, dependent on primitive forms of agriculture for survival, superstitious and primitive in religion, and prone to destructive dissension (Kidd 1999, ch. 7). One of Milton's earliest works, *Comus* (first acted 1634), set on the border of England and Wales, is clearly about the need to control and exclude the wild Celtic threat of the sensual Comus, who, like Circe, can imprison men within the brutish bounds of their senses and so exclude reason. As Philip Schwyzer has pointed out, 'Comus exhibits many of the evil features of the wild Irish (the degrading eloquence of the bard, the rootless roving of the kern)' (1997: 35). Sabrina, the nymph who leads the dance that ends the masque, has often been seen as 'a sort of salute to special cultural resources of Wales and the borders'. However, she should more accurately be regarded as 'an alternative *to* local tradition', a means of imposing an English cultural purity on resistant forms of identity and a 'paranoid recoiling form the hybrid' (39, 42). In short, Milton's masque dramatizes a conflict between the English Protestant forces of reason, order and the rule of the spiritual, and a composite Celtic figure representing unreason and anarchy, under the control of the wild body.

The text in which Milton most cogently expressed his views on the Celtic peoples within the British Isles was his polemical tract *Observations on the Articles of the Peace* (1649). *The Articles of the Peace* were an agreement that had been signed between the Earl of Ormonde, Charles I's Lord Lieutenant in Ireland, and the Confederacy led by Owen Roe O'Neill, thirteen days before the execution of the King on 30 January 1649. The document appeared to promise independence for the Irish and had resulted from a series of desperate moves by Charles to cement an alliance capable of opposing the growing power of the parliamentary forces as the war grew into the War of the Three Kingdoms. Indeed, the articles were in essence a dead letter even as they were signed, because neither Charles nor Ormonde had the power or indeed the will to keep the promises made. They were 'bargaining for Irish support with pledges that they hoped never to have to keep' (*CPW* III: 168–9). As a means of counteracting Charles's pledges after his execution, Parliament employed Milton to publish an edition of the treaty and some related documents, including his own thoughts on the *Articles*. This work was duly published on 16 May 1649.

The *Articles* consisted of thirty-five items which agreed, among other things, to dismiss past treason (an act of oblivion); to allow the Irish Parliament to establish its own independent laws; to allow Ireland to run its own maritime affairs; to abolish the rent increases recently introduced by Thomas Wentworth, Earl of Strafford; to allow the Irish judiciary to hear complaints of mistreatment; to suspend outstanding attainders and indictments against Catholics, repeal all acts against them, and allow Catholics to stand for Parliament; and, most significantly, to allow freedom of worship by abolishing the Oath of Supremacy to the English monarch as head of the church – a promise Milton and most other Parliamentarians did not believe was his to make (*CPW* III: 170–1). Such items went against Milton's attempts throughout his life to preserve a clear distinction between the godly Protestants and the subversive and evil Catholics, admitting, as he saw it, a Trojan horse undermining the state. Moreover, Milton was able to vent his spleen against the Ulster Presbyterians, who, supported by their Scottish brethren, had been party to the *Articles*. As Merritt Y. Hughes has pointed out, there is a 'painful irony' in Milton's attempt to repudiate an alliance between Catholics and Presbyterians in the name of 'wider principles of religious toleration' (*CPW* III: 173; Bennett 1997, ch. 4). The poet against empire was blind to the possibility that Britain itself might be an imperial concept (McEachern 1996, ch. 7); or that, after the revolution of the saints, religion might actually have become less rather than more tolerant.

Milton, like many of his contemporaries, regarded the *Articles* as a treasonable surrender (*CPW* III: 171). His *Observations* attempt to answer the thirty-five items of the *Articles*, often with a withering sarcasm. In commenting on the twenty-second article, which repealed the prohibition on traditional Irish agricultural practices of oat burning and ploughing using horses' tails, Milton argues that the English have surrendered to the obstinate Irish and neglected their duty of drawing an inferior culture towards civilization. Although this particular article is 'more ridiculous then dangerous', it serves:

> to declare in them a disposition not onely sottish, but indocible and averse from all Civility and amendment, and what hopes they give for the future, who rejecting the ingenuity of all other Nations to improve and waxe more civill by a civilizing Conquest, though all these many yeares better shown and taught, preferre their own absurd and savage Customes before the most convincing evidence of reason and demonstration: a testimony of their true Barbarisme and obdurate wilfulnesse to be expected no lesse in other matters of greatest moment. (*CPW* III: 303–4)

In contrast to the compromises – however insincere and self-serving – made by Charles, the Catholics and the Presbyterians, Milton looks back to a more straightforward distinction between the civil and the savage (Protestant and Catholic). Milton argues that 'no true borne *English-man*, can so much as barely reade them [the *Articles*] without indignation and disdaine' and he refers the reader back to the 'mercilesse and barbarous Massacre of so many thousand *English*' (*CPW* III: 301) during the Rebellion of 1641. Milton, relying on the exaggerated account of the atrocities carried out in Sir John Temple's *True Impartial History of the Irish Rebellion* (1644), is referring the English reader back to a historical moment when battle lines were clearly drawn and re-affirming the familiar opposition between the English Protestant and the Irish Catholic. Attempts to obscure and complicate such divisions may seem appealing to those understandably tired of prolonged conflict. It is Milton's task to expose the superficiality of such reasoning and demonstrate that liberty is better served in the long term if a secure basis is established for mutual co-operation and toleration. The *Articles*, so appealing to the naïve reader, in fact undermine ancient English liberties. The Irish are now 'grac'd and rewarded with such freedomes...as none of their Ancestors could ever merit by their best obedience...to be infranchize'd with full liberty equall to their Conquerours' (*CPW* III: 301), despite the fact that they have spent their history threatening the very liberties they now enjoy.

While he might have deplored certain forms of colonial exploitation in *Paradise Lost*, in the *Observations* Milton strongly supports a benevolent and beneficial conquest by a superior power as a means of bringing an inferior people closer to the standards of the civilized. The epic similes which place Satan's voyages in context (see above, pp. 174–5) all connote the exoticism of the barbarous East or the New World of the Americas, indicating that Milton did not have his experience of politics within the British Isles in mind when writing his major poem.

It is easy to deplore the Anglocentrism of the *Observations*. The text ends with a stinging attack on the Presbyterians in their 'Pontificall See of *Belfast*'. Not only does Milton suggest that they have effectively become Catholics by association – thus preserving the clear distinctions Milton cherishes – he berates them for daring to defy 'the sovran Magistracy of *England*, by whose autoritie and in whose right they inhabit there' (*CPW* III: 333). The sentence indicates that for Milton sovereignty has passed from the monarch to the land (England). In the process, loyalty to the nation rather than the monarch has become paramount and, consequently, more rather than less exclusive. It was no historical accident that the royalist forces were able to enter into alliances with Scots, Welsh and Irish more readily than their Parliamentarian counterparts (Bennett 1997, ch. 9). Allegiance to a single figure of authority allowed for a flexibility which membership of a nation did not. Milton dismisses the Presbyterians as 'a generation of High-land theevs and Red-shanks [Scottish mercenaries in Ireland]', admitted 'by the courtesie of *England* to hold possessions in our Province, a Countrey better then thir own' (*CPW* III: 333–4). He contrasts them to the Saxons who came to England, at least ostensibly, to help the Britons fight their enemies. The Presbyterians, who were all of Scots descent, have come to assist the Irish rebels. Milton is able to link the Celtic enemies of England together.

While acknowledging the charge of Anglocentrism, one ought to note that Milton produced this text to order for a specific historical purpose, as he did *The History of Britain* (Corns 1990b). The views expressed within the work are not necessarily ones dear to Milton's heart. Nevertheless, if Milton's hostility towards the Irish and the Scots does not fit easily with his criticisms of the imperial exploitation of other cultures elsewhere in his writings, they do square neatly with his sense of England's Protestant mission and his keen sense of 'ethnic theology'.

BIBLIOGRAPHY

Writings

Harriot (1972); Milton (1968, 1974); Ralegh (1997).

References for Further Reading

Armitage (1995); Bennett, Martyn (1997); Chaney (1998); Corns (1990b); Derrida (1974); Hadfield (1998); Haller (1963); Hill (1977); Kidd (1999); Lacy (1986); McEachern (1996); Montrose (1991); Norbrook (1999); Pagden (1982); Parker, William R. (1996); Pocock (1987); Quilligan (1983); Scanlan (1999); Schwyzer (1997); Sheehan (1979); von Maltzahn (1991).

12

The Literature of Controversy

Joad Raymond

Fresh Woods, and Pastures New

In July 1639 the thirty-year-old John Milton stepped down on to the safe shores of his native land. During his fourteen- or fifteen-month tour of the continent he had conversed with philosophers, divines and poets and had found himself welcome; he had been inspired by the cultural life of Italy, particularly in the Florentine *accademia*, where appreciation of his poetic and philological abilities had puffed his ambition; he had refined his languages, and witnessed scholars and intellectuals participating in civic life. Fifteen years later he wrote that he had returned because 'the sad tidings of Civil war in England summoned me back' (Milton 1998b: 1116). The sentiment suggests that in 1639 Milton already sensed that there was a public role for him to play at his country's moment of crisis. Familial respects called him first to tranquil Horton, but he soon turned to London.

In the autumn and winter of 1639 the streets of the metropolis were alive with news and debate. The events of the preceding two years had done much to disturb the peaceful surface of the Personal Rule, and discontent was registered in the realm that would later come to be known as 'public opinion'. In July 1637 Charles had imposed a revised Book of Common Prayer upon the Scottish Kirk, provoking resistance that resulted in the invasion of England by a Covenanting army, and the surrender of the King's forces. Charles signed a peace treaty, the Pacification of Berwick, in June 1639. Yet the Covenanters' first invasion was not in arms but in print, in thousands of copies of pamphlets printed initially in the Netherlands and subsequently in Scotland, then exported to and distributed in England. These presented the justness of the Covenanting cause in simple and direct language. Thus one 1638 pamphlet, entitled *A Short Relation of the State of the Kirk of Scotland since the reformation of Religion, to the present time for information, and advertisement to our Brethren in the Kirk of England, by an hearty Well-wisher to both Kingdomes*, reported:

In the yeare 1636 the Bishops framed a booke of Canons and constitutions for governing the kirke of Scotland. Which did quite subvert the order and forme of discipline established, contained many errours, and opened a doore for many moe [sic] both in doctrinall and disciplinarie points of Religion, whensoever the Kings Majestie upon the Bishops recommendation would ordaine the same. (B1^v–B2^r)

These pamphlets provoked a stir on the streets of London, in towns on the main routes stretching out from it, and between Scotland and the metropolis. They were read alongside tracts written in England and printed in the Low Countries, which criticized the religious policy of Charles I for its allegedly popish tendencies. Most famously, *Newes from Ipswich* (1636), a pseudonymous satirical pamphlet probably written by William Prynne, attacked the innovations of Archbishop William Laud and the restrictions under which London presses operated. Prynne was one of the scourges of Caroline church government, severely punished, along with John Bast-wick and Henry Burton, for seditious publications. The sufferings of this godly triumvirate elicited much public sympathy. Their pamphlets and their punishment, and the co-ordinated campaign of covenanting propaganda addressed to an English audience, fostered a receptive reading public, keen to hear news and, perhaps, to witness political change.

The reading public had been growing in the three kingdoms of England, Scotland and Ireland, and in the principality of Wales, since the late sixteenth century, when literacy rates began a long-term rise. Yet the extent to which it constituted a public in the stronger sense of the word – a body of people with similar sets of beliefs and expectations, whose interpretations of events were co-ordinated by dynamic and shared news media – is debatable. Prior to the late 1630s there were several sub-stantial channels for communicating news and opinion, of which the foremost was gossip and word of mouth. Manuscripts played an important part in spreading relatively reliable news, in a spectrum extending from private epistolary communica-tion, through professional and semi-professional writers of periodical news, to the scribal production of manuscript 'separates', short tracts on particular matters of interest. Since the reign of Henry VIII the printed page had been used to persuade readers, and a few short books reporting news had appeared, usually advising an official point of view. News also circulated in ballad form, thus reaching a wide audience, though the news itself was far from detailed or reliable. During the 1580s pamphlets began to emerge in significant numbers: inexpensive and short books, written in a vernacular or demotic style, addressed to a wide readership, intended to inform and/or persuade, and concerning some topical event or argument. By the mid-seventeenth century the pamphlet was an important means of conducting political debate and influencing public opinion, but in its early decades its influence was limited. An examination of the (extant) output of printing presses during periods of crisis or public scandal suggests that the culture of print was not particularly responsive to the kinds of circumstances and events that would later become integral to the commercial practices of the book trade. Later in the century, years of crisis – 1642, 1649, 1660, 1679–81 – would be marked by significant increases in the number of printed items coming from the presses. Prior to the 1640s no such phenomenon can be traced. The year of the Addled Parliament, 1614, witnessed no expansion of print, and neither the proceedings of the Parliament nor the central issues debated in it, appeared in print. The 1631 trial of the Earl of Castlehaven for sodomy with his servants and assisting the rape of his wife was one of the greatest scandals of Stuart England. Though graphic sexual details circulated in manuscripts, the allegations, trial and executions were not reported in printed media. The popular press was not yet a primary vehicle for political controversy or current affairs.

This essay explores Milton's position in the changing contexts of print in the seventeenth century, and particularly his participation in the raucous and rapidly expanding pamphlet culture. By placing Milton in this world – a world of which his writings show him to be acutely conscious – it is possible to understand more intimately the nature of his prose writings, his decision to put aside his poetic ambitions for so long, and, perhaps, the shape that those late, great poetic works assumed when they did appear. To this end I consider both local contexts and the broader movements of change and continuity; but I begin with some quantitative perspectives on the seventeenth-century book trade.

Dangerous and Suspicious Fruit

Gauging press output by counting the number of surviving titles has its limitations. Survival rates were low and varied considerably; in the long term they probably increased, as a number of diligent enthusiasts, among them the London bookseller George Thomason, began to establish their collections. Catalogues of surviving seventeenth-century books are not yet exhaustive, nor always reliable on the matter of reprints and reissues. Title-counts do not take into account the size of impressions: a seditious book imported from the continent in the 1630s might be printed only in 200–250 copies, and many pamphlets of the early 1640s were probably printed in runs of between 250 and 1,000; 1,500–2,000 was the normal maximum for an officially sanctioned work, whereas some of the Covenanters' pamphlets produced in Scotland appeared in much larger numbers, one in a remarkable edition of 10,000. Correlated with contemporary perceptions and other evidence, however, statistics do offer a useful impression of real changes in the book trade. The number of titles produced during the 1610s, 1620s and 1630s, while showing a very slight gradual increase, remained between 400 and 700 per annum. In 1641 it topped 2,000, and in 1642 it peaked at 4,000 before declining sharply. Except in 1666, when the conflagration that razed London simultaneously consumed the survival rates of books and the productive capacity of the London presses, annual press output remained between about 1,000 and 3,000 titles for the next half-century. Productive capacity never declined to anything like 1630s levels. The cultural and political significance of the printing press changed permanently during the 1640s.

During the years of increased output the presses produced a greater number of short works in quarto format. Books printed as more prestigious folios were likely to be learned; more sumptuously presented, they were certainly more expensive. A quarto of few sheets was the form for works of controversy or news; short, inexpensive, easily sold and distributed, convenient for the street, alehouse or (from the 1650s onwards) coffee-house, as opposed to the library or study. The supply of the raw materials of books was not highly flexible. No white paper (suitable for printing) was manufactured in Britain and therefore it had to be imported. The number of presses remained fairly stable from year to year, and the number of skilled master printers and compositors was limited. Therefore we should not expect that the number of sheets coming from the presses increased in the same proportion as the number of titles; nor should we assume that the multiplication of words was as great, though more words were usually squeezed on to a quarto sheet than appeared on a folio. What these figures reveal is that in years of increased numbers of titles the emphasis of the printing and publishing trade shifted away from large volumes towards short and topical works. Pamphlets and sermons displaced histories and bulky theological books.

In addition to the role of the Covenanters and Covenanting propaganda, six short-term causes of the transformation of English print culture in 1640–2 can be identified; all were to leave a lasting impression upon Milton as well as upon British history. First was the meeting of the Short Parliament of April to May 1640 and the Long Parliament from November 1640 onwards. Parliament became the centre of popular discontent with the king and church. Among its first proceedings were the indictments of Laud and Thomas Wentworth, Earl of Strafford, the king's closest advisers. A series of satirical pamphlets attacked these figures and others associated with them. Second was the pressure of public opinion. In the metropolis, and perhaps elsewhere, the interests of the reading public were increasingly sharply focused on domestic politics. These were not necessarily readers who had felt deprived of these materials previously; the changing nature of the news transmuted appetites as well as publications. The feeding of these appetites was certainly facilitated, however, by the weakening of control over the presses, a third cause of the revolutions in print media. The mechanisms of prepublication licensing faltered with the Parliament's abolition of the Courts of High Commission and Star Chamber in the summer of 1641. Stationers (all those working in the book trade) were able to flout the regulations that nominally lay in place, and, apart from occasional outcries over some pirated or spurious reports of parliamentary speeches and the like, Parliament turned a blind eye to the excesses of the press. Opinion was too divided, and political crisis too imminent, to make effective censorship possible, even if it was desired in some quarters. Fourth, the Irish Rebellion of October 1641 electrified public interest in the crisis, enhanced both support for Parliament and expectations of its performance, and stimulated a growing appetite for ever more frequent news updates. Fifth, the Parliament's Grand Remonstrance of November 1641, a history of the king's reign and a bitter series of complaints, published as a pamphlet and widely publicized, polarized already divided public opinion. After its hotly contested approval by the Commons, attempts to seek political consensus were undermined by the turbulent language of political exchange. Sixth, and consequent upon the above factors, was the appearance of newsbooks in November 1641. These early 'newsbooks', so-called because they were printed as quarto pamphlets rather than the folio format usually associated with the term 'newspaper', were weekly periodicals of news – the immediate predecessor of the modern newspaper. They had themselves been preceded by the series of 'corantos' of foreign news, which appeared irregularly in the 1620s and some of the 1630s. Yet the newsbooks were new beasts: regular, consistent in format and appearance, more heterogeneous and much more numerous. Whereas only a handful appeared in late 1641, subsequent years saw hundreds of issues and many competing titles. They became a staple of the book trade, not only providing a regular income for many stationers at the lower end of the market, but powerfully influencing popular conceptions of the nature of print and the printed voice. These six main factors – there were other, lesser influences at play too – precipitated fierce pamphlet controversies and transformed the role of print, the nature of writing and, by implication, the arena of political encounters.

Sclanderous Libels, Bitter Pasquines, Railing Pamphlets

Milton's first engagement with the pamphlet wars, in an exchange between Bishop Joseph Hall and the pseudonymous 'Smectymnuus', in some ways typified the byways of controversy. Hall precipitated the encounter with his anonymous *An Humble Remonstrance to the High Court of Parliament* (1640[/1]), a defence of the Book of Common Prayer and of episcopal church government. He complained of the recent excesses of the press:

> how many furious and malignant spirits every where have burst forth into sclanderous libels, bitter Pasquines, railing Pamphlets? (under which more presses than one have groaned) wherein they have endeavoured, through the sides of some misliked persons, to wound that sacred Government [of the church]. (6–7)

Smectymnuus's response, *An Answer to a Booke Entituled, An Humble Remonstrance* (1641), was written by five Presbyterians whose initials spelled their tongue-twisting pseudonym: Stephen Marshall, Edmund Calamy, Thomas Young (a former tutor of Milton's), Matthew Newcomen and William Spurstowe. Hall responded with *A Defence of the Humble Remonstrant Against the frivolous and false exceptions of SMECTYM-NUUS* (1641), provoking the Smectymnuans' *A Vindication of the Answer to the Humble Remonstrance, from the Unjust Imputations of Frivolousnesse and Falsehood* (1641), in turn inducing Hall's *A Short Answer to the Tedious vindication of Smectymnvvs. By the Author of the Humble Remonstrance* (1641). Other texts by other writers sprang from the heat of this exchange. Milton's participation may have begun with a postscript appended to the Smectymnuans' *Answer*; during 1641–2 he wrote five tracts criticizing Hall and prelacy, beginning with *Of Reformation* in May 1641. From this moment Milton was deeply engaged in polemical exchanges, and despite his showy dismissal of these as a left-handed exercise, he was to remain primarily committed to prose controversy and the practicalities of radical politics for the next fifteen years.

The titles produced in this exchange illustrate the means by which printed debate multiplied words. Hall and the Smectymnuans frequently employed animadversion, a form of exchange rooted in theological controversy, in which the opponent was quoted, selectively or unabridged, in order to repudiate him or her. This became common even in less exalted forms of discourse, including polemical journalism. Old words were repeated and new ones added: thus exchanged tracts tended to increase in length. Pamphlets and longer tracts were both responsive to current affairs and reactive to other publications, and one short work could set off a chain reaction leading to many longer ones. This can also be seen in less direct modes of response or imitation – such as the burgeoning of play-pamphlets in 1641–2, or the epistle to a public figure in 1659–60 – which were in part fashions for genres precipitated by successful works. The learned animadversion of Hall and the Smectymnuans was the high end of a tendency characteristic of a wide range of controversial publications. This capacity to multiply by repetition, recycling and splitting – of words, pages, books, voices, genres – is probably the most central aspect of the polemical and news publications that proliferated from the 1640s onwards. Words, pages, books, voices and genres were repeated, anatomized and reconfigured.

The press sought not only to persuade, but also to inform. One of the signal shifts of the years surrounding 1641, and especially of that year itself, was the revolutionary supply of detailed domestic political news in printed media, hitherto partially obstructed. Parliamentary proceedings and speeches had circulated in restricted manuscript forms prior to the Long Parliament. Though transcripts of the 1628 parliament, for example, were commercially available as scribally produced separates, these were very expensive and reached a fairly limited audience. The audience expanded when these were printed – at about the same time as the first printed domestic news weeklies – as *The Diurnall Occurrences of every dayes proceeding in Parliament . . . 1628* (November 1641). During 1641 weekly transcriptions of parliamentary proceedings, known as 'diurnal occurrences', could be purchased in manuscript, for about a shilling and sixpence. Readers were increasingly able to supplement them with printed parliamentary speeches, which cost around a penny. These were sometimes authorized by the speakers, who wished to disseminate their reason and eloquence 'without doors'; some speeches were transcribed by onlookers and printed, often inaccurately, without authorial permission; in a few cases what purported to be speeches in Parliament were fabrications commissioned by unscrupulous booksellers. From November 1641 the weekly diurnal occurrences were made available in printed form, at a fraction of the former cost and probably in considerably greater numbers. These newsbooks soon diversified to include much more than parliamentary proceedings; an increasing breadth of political matter was available in print, and in turn print played an ever more important part in politics.

Other kinds of news entered the newsbooks, commonly those available in occasional pamphlets: accounts of sieges and eye-witness reports of battles; of crimes and misdemeanours, executions and scaffold speeches; sensational descriptions of malformed babies and miraculous apparitions, of witches and seers; human interest stories; overseas news, frequently military, but sometimes reflecting on the political or cultural life of distant nations, and sometimes intimating the perception of British politics and habits through foreign eyes; travel writing, particularly from the New World; reports of disasters, domestic and overseas; reports on trade, such as the cargoes of recently arrived merchant ships, or business opportunities; stories of the behaviour and strange doctrines of religious enthusiasts; advertisements, initially for books, but subsequently for a diversity of other products, particularly medicines and cures, and also for runaway criminals, missing property and for various services; summaries of the weekly bills of mortality, counting deaths in London parishes; book notices; astrological predictions; perhaps most importantly, political editorials. The newsbook was a fundamentally heterogeneous form, defined by bibliographical and formal characteristics more than by content, and it could successfully incorporate any number of miscellaneous features: Hebrew anagrams; woodcut portraits of soldiers and statesmen; pornographic poetry; commentaries on Aristotle and Suetonius. The newsbooks of the 1640s were paradoxical, in that they frequently combined transparently polemical and persuasive objectives with this uncontrollable diversity of informative matter. They cannot be reduced to 'mere' propaganda, but neither were they simply an extension of previous news media. The combined effect of a revolution in form and content, and the quantities in which they became available, was considerable, and they consequently began to perform a different kind of function.

New and hitherto unheard voices were made audible in print, encouraged by the unprecedented openness of the press during the 1640s. Among the speeches of these new voices were petitions, from artisans, apprentices and women, that became a feature of parliamentary political life. Petitions suggested an incursion of a greater part of the population into governmental practices previously imagined (and still assumed by many) to be beyond common reach. Printed petitions appealed to Parliament, but did so by standing before a public, the readership; they implied that the latter constituted an authority in themselves, whose views they might seek to represent. Some voices newly adopted fresh styles, brimming with inspiration and eloquent and unfamiliar expressions of selfhood. Other voices brought innovation in the beliefs they expressed, including radical and inspired attitudes to religion. More generally the number of printed writings by women increased significantly during the 1640s, though actual quantities remained very low; as a percentage of total publications the figure rose from about 0.4 per cent to about 1 per cent.

The burgeoning of news and controversial publications provided a platform for political and religious movements, most famously the Levellers, Diggers and Quakers. The Leveller leaders managed a brilliantly conceived public relations exercise in print that fostered widespread understanding of and sympathy for the movement. This involved less the articulation of preformulated policies than an exploration of controversial religious and political proposals in a public medium. For a while the voice of the movement flourished in the face of opposition from Parliament and the army; when the Leveller leaders were in prison they continued to write, or to find substitute authors, and presented themselves as sufferers for the cause of truth. The successful organization of the Leveller movement relied as much on the use of print to communicate to an audience as on specific networks between citizens and soldiers; without books they would have been an entirely different kind of movement, and they acknowledged this by foregrounding books and reading in their visual iconography. While itinerant preaching was the basis of the early success of the Quaker movement, printed texts soon assumed an importance equal to that in the Leveller movement. The output of Quaker authors, male and female, grew to imposingly high levels, and caused concern to the Cromwellian regime of the 1650s, as well as to Charles II's 1660s government. The Quakers, anxious to forge a positive public image and to counter the widespread attacks on them in pamphlets and newsbooks, established regular meetings to supervise not only the publication but the content of works written by Friends. This amounted to institutionalized self-censorship, and represents perhaps the most concrete, if not the earliest, example of a religious or political movement introducing formal regulation of its appearance in a mass medium.

Among the most unconventional and anticonventional new voices were those of individual religious and political radicals. These were writers who were unlikely to have been able to have their works published before 1641 even had they wanted to; though probably more important to their novelty was the inspiration available in the vigorous intellectual and confessional milieu of the 1640s. Not only did the radicals explore startling expressions of spirituality; they had their explorations placed before the reading public, in modes of writing that challenged literary decorums. The prophetess Anna Trapnel, who relied on a male amanuensis to transcribe her ecstatic visions, spoke in extraordinary, richly biblical though often opaque passages of poetry and prose; her 'writings' ranged from pamphlet-sized autobiographical narratives, were wryly satirical of political and patriarchal authority, to a vast spiritual odyssey in verse. The Behmenist pantheist Thomas Tany, alias Theauraujohn, combined dramatic public gestures, including Bible-burning, with a series of nine intensely witty pamphlets published between 1650 and 1654. In these he repudiated religious orthodoxies and condemned secular authority, yet did so in a mystical, obscure and rhyme-laden prose that mocked the logical structures of language. Abiezer Coppe, probably the most notorious of the radical antinomians labelled 'Ranters', also challenged the rational patterns of language to considerable poetic effect, and presented spiritual experiences in narrative form, anticipating Blake, that resist being reduced to reportage or allegory:

> 1. Follow me, who, last Lords day Septem. 30. 1649. met him in open field, a most
> strange deformed man, clad with patcht clouts: who looking wishly on me, mine eye

pittied him; and my heart, or the day of the Lord, which burned as an oven in me, set my tongue on flame to speak to him, as followeth.

2. How now friend, art thou poore?

He answered, yea Master, very poore.

Whereupon my bowels trembled within me, and quivering fell upon the worm-eaten chest, (my corps I mean) that I could not hold a joynt still.

And my great love within me, (who is the great God within that chest, or corps) was burning hot toward him; and made the lock-hole of the chest, to wit, the mouth of the corps, again to open: Thus.

Art poor?

Yea, very poor, said he.

Whereupon the strange woman who, flattereth with her lips, and is subtill of heart, said within me.

It's a poor wretch, give him two-pence.

(Smith 1983: 101–2)

Driven by a rich biblicism, Coppe and others sought to express an inspired sense of the sublimity of their being, its unity with God, and an (anti-Calvinist) sense of human perfectibility. Coppe's writing is heterogeneous in the extreme, but in this passage, and in other pamphlets including the Leveller Robert Overton's *The Araignement of Mr. Persecution* (1645), biblical parable is blended with dramatic dialogue and interior reflection, anticipating the narrative surety of the novel.

The press also bore a new strain of popular political writing, committed to plainer styles. In editorials prefaced to his influential newsbooks, *Mercurius Britanicus* (1643–6), *Mercurius Pragmaticus* (1647–9), and especially *Mercurius Politicus* (1650–60), Marchamont Nedham (a friend of Milton's from *c.*1650) tried to disseminate political theory through its practical application to current news. Emphasizing that the roots of human motivation lay in rational self-interest, Nedham's writings struck many of his contemporaries as startlingly secular, leading to accusations of atheism. The opportunities offered by the new media – pamphlets and newsbooks – enabled Nedham and others to draw on the writings of Machiavelli, Guicciardini and on the elaborate political thought of late humanism, epitomized in the writings of Justus Lipsius, and to popularize them by cultivating a mode of simple and lucid political prose accessible to a less educationally privileged readership. Once within the literary culture of the pamphlet, these ideas could be turned with considerable perspicuity to critiques of political authority. Just as writers such as Nedham, Milton, John Hall of Durham and John Canne could deploy *ragione di stato* to establish the authority of the revolutionary regimes of the 1650s, others, including John Warr and James Harrington, exploited the same language and ideas to challenge this authority: such was the consequence of bringing this intellectual apparatus before the public, in the form of inexpensive controversial literature.

Many pamphlets were strikingly 'literary' in the broad sense: their authors self-consciously deployed rhetorical and generic devices and patterns in order to create large-scale imaginative effects to make their points more forcefully. Controversial pamphlets would commonly invent fictional scenarios, and present a dialogue or letter emerging from them. Recently deceased figures would appear in hell and talk of recent news with the long dead. Tortured with a guilty conscience, ghosts might return from the shades to engage in conversation with the living. Mock trials, such as Overton's *Araignement of Mr. Persecution*, descended from Trajano Boccalini's *De' Ragguagli di Parnasso* (1612), combined forensic dialogue with news reporting and wish fulfilment (a guilty verdict). A series of play-pamphlets published in the spring of 1648, beginning with *Mistris Parliament Brought to Bed of a Monstrous Childe of Reformation* and concluding with *M^rs. Parliament Her Invitation of M^rs. London, To a Thanksgiving Dinner*, described the struggles in Westminster and the City in a crude allegorical dialogue. Such low-grade literary productions were sometimes little more than buffoonery, entertainment commercially produced for the alehouse, but usually a deeper purpose is evident: they used satire to persuade or to state a case. They shared an audience and a design, sometimes a political vocabulary, with more earnest works, and were not discrete from the realm of political controversy. Milton engaged in just such satirical dialogue in *Animadversions upon the Remonstrants Defence against Smectymnuus* (1641).

Letters of advice, a pamphlet genre perhaps deriving from humanist public expressions of friendship or counsel to princes, offered an opportunity for creative manipulation or re-invention of polemical circumstances. Letters could be forged in an opponent's voice, in order to unmask the opponent's hypocrisy or lack of moral fibre. When *Mercurius Aulicus*, the royalist newsbook, printed a spurious letter from 'Susan Owen', wife of a soldier in the Parliament's army, mocking her lack of verbal, social and moral sophistication, *Mercurius Britanicus*, the parliamentarian newsbook, responded in like kind with a spoof letter from the Earl of Caernarfon:

> He jeers us with an intercepted Letter of Mistresse *Susans* the Citizens wife, complaining for her husbands company, which she utterly disavowes; we will show you one of your Cavaliers Epistles intercepted about the same time, to a friend in *London*, onely you must excuse me, I printed not the oathes, but left spaces.
>   Jack,
> WE *have not left*   *one* Woman   Lady   Gentlewoman
> *Waytingmaid*   or other   honest   *we have now some*
>   Irish   *and Frenchwomen come to us*   we intend not to leave till
>   we have   sinned with all Nations as well as our owne,
>
>   thine
>   Carnavan

Nedham used the spurious letter genre to spectacular effect in *Newes from Brussels. In a Letter From a Neer Attendant On His Majesties Person* (1660), a pamphlet written in the fictional persona of a Cavalier anticipating the Restoration of Charles II, and the revenge that he and others would enjoy upon those who had co-operated with the republican regimes. Nedham provoked both serious and satirical responses: the grave

political implications of this devious fiction were evident enough. The most celebrated published letters of the Civil War were not fictional at all, but were stolen
from the author and published in order to effect a very different kind of speech-act
from that which he had intended. These were private letters from Charles I to his
French Catholic wife, Henrietta Maria, captured at the Battle of Naseby in 1645, and
published in a short tract entitled *The Kings Cabinet opened*. They exposed the King's
duplicity, and, according to parliamentarian commentators, showed that his wife had
an influence over him incompatible with the good of Protestantism. The publication
marked a turning point in popular sentiment for and against the king.

Other, minor pamphlet genres of note included satirical 'characters', derived from
the gentlemanly literary exercise and perhaps from the Elizabethan stage. National
stereotypes of the Irish, Scots and Welsh entered into print, each with orthographic
conventions to represent their accents. Conventional perspectives on contested political and religious issues were challenged in the form of 'queries', a series of numbered
questions formulated to undermine conventions and proffer alternatives. Pamphlets
also provided a suitable vehicle for political proposals, blueprints for improved
governance, even utopias, accounts of ideal or ironically marred communities that
reflected upon the imperfections of the present world. Reports of wonders and
monstrous births furnished the reader with evidence that a disturbance in the wider
order of nature had occurred, that God had offered a providential warning to man, or
to the English, and were used to delineate a vision of the undisturbed, pre-inversion
order of nature and society. Parodic genres, such as mock-prognostications, had been
around for some decades. Likewise, for every kind of pamphlet there was its satirical
inverse: the mock-newsbook, the mock-speech, the mock-parliamentary proceedings
(including accounts of parliaments of women), the mock-letter, the mock-sermon, the
mock-almanac, the mock-gallows-speech, the mock-prophecy. Inversion was a characteristic pattern of representation and thought, and it extended to the reformulation
of genres.

Milton, it hardly needs to be said, did not write in all these genres. His first
pamphlets were extended, sophisticated pieces that intentionally bridged the boundaries, such as they were, between pamphlet polemic, scholarship and philosophical
reflection. He used satire, animadversion, printed laughter, colloquialisms, the pan-
oply of fleering reflections; but he did not trouble himself with the most demotic of
pamphlet genres or styles. This was in part because he observed the boundaries of the
debate in which he was engaged: in order effectively to persuade the public who were
reading the controversial works on church government in 1641–2 of the lack of
scriptural justification for episcopacy, Milton focused on the arguments, supplement-
ing them with satire. This is not to say that the tracts are earnestly blunt; in fact,
Milton probably had unexpressed reservations about the Presbyterian model of church
government even at that point, and allied himself with the Presbyterians largely for
strategic purposes. Rather, it is to suggest that he was more engaged with the
persuasive force of reason than with the possibilities of extravagant and unguarded
speech. Later, in the divorce tracts of 1643–5, he focused even more closely on

detailed scriptural arguments, though his virtuoso rhetorical performances manifested a dangerously self-conscious pleasure in producing unexpected readings of biblical texts. While sincerity and divine inspiration purported to be at the heart of the works – and we have no reason to believe that for Milton they were not – the sheer ingenuity of the arguments, and the rhetorical flair with which he presented them, threatened to cut across this grain. Later he was to regret having written them in the English language, thus making them available to a wide and therefore less uniformly educated audience; though at the time that was probably the precise objective of his language choice. The tracts written under the Commonwealth and Protectorate – excepting the workmanlike, though troubled and troubling, *Observations upon the Articles of Peace* (1649), a commissioned justification of a reconquest of Ireland – represent the elite end of the pamphleteer's spectrum. As such they suggest an unusual respect for the reading public, who are expected to interpret with patience, integrity, superior reason and spiritual enlightenment. In a flurry of shorter pamphlets in 1659–60 which defended liberty of conscience, spoke against the possibility of a Stuart restoration and imagined alternatives to this likelihood, Milton became his most explicitly polemical, and his writing turned to engage with the numerous pamphlets which flew from the presses expressing contrary views and hopes. Milton's writings of 1658–60 were paper bullets, written with an immediate audience in mind. Yet unlike his ally Marchamont Nedham, he did not toy with the most vituperative forms – fictional epistles or satirical poetry. Milton chose the cerebral over the sly or non-sensical, and the pamphlet remained for him the means of extending his speech, not of making it hollow. He continued to prefer as the best means of persuasion the reasoned word – or its semblance – reinforced with coercive eloquence.

This is True Liberty

The controversy fostered by pamphlets and polemics shook the foundations of the literary world. It is therefore all the more remarkable that Milton should have sought to defend these publishing practices in *Areopagitica; A Speech of Mr. John Milton For the Liberty of Unlicenc'd Printing, To the Parlament of England* (1644). Yet Milton singled out small books as precisely the medium through which truth could unpredictably emerge, guided both by providence and by the force of human reason. Milton censured the attempt by Parliament to re-introduce prepublication licensing in an Ordinance of 1643, and by the Stationers' Company – the guild which regulated and looked after the interests of those working in the book trade – to secure a tight monopoly over the commodities of print. Truth and falsehood entered the world through a single apple rind: to establish institutional means to expunge one was to risk the emergence of the other. This is a double argument. No human mechanism could successfully filter truth and error with certainty. Moreover, it is in the individual's experience of reading and wrestling with falsehood that she or he is purified by truth. Belief cannot be handed out, spooned like food to a child.

Milton was by no means alone in his defence of unfettered reading. In a series of tracts published during the 1640s the Leveller William Walwyn offered an eirenic and pro-toleration view of human society. His *The Compassionate Samaritan* (1644) criticized the 1643 Ordinance, claiming it had 'stopt the mouthes of good men'. Licensers, like the recently abolished bishops, sought to monopolize the truth, 'yet if the people would but take boldnes to themselves and not distrust in their owne understandings, they would soon find that use and experience is the only difference, and that all necessary knowledge is easie to be had, and by themselves acquirable' (Walwyn 1989: 101, 109). A free press empowered readers. A few months before Walwyn's pamphlet appeared, Henry Robinson's *Liberty of Conscience* (1644) had criticized all forms of coercion exerted over the conscience or understanding. Though a free press might introduce more erroneous doctrines into the world, it also permitted the public repudiation of them, and thus the re-education of the deceived, as truth would vanquish error; and, as any Protestant knew, all serious truths entered the world under the hateful name of heresy.

What is peculiar to Milton is his careful evocation of the world of cheap print. Milton's metaphors in this forty-page pamphlet are as rich and vertiginous as in any of his writings. Their opulence disposes readers to misconstrue the argument, mistaking the specific for the universal, the abstract for the historically grounded. In a famous passage that rolls one trope into another, Milton makes books animate:

> For Books are not absolutely dead things, but doe contain a potencie of life in them to be as active as that soule was whose progeny they are; nay they do preserve as in a violl the purest efficacie and extraction of that living intellect that bred them. I know they are as lively, and as vigorously productive, as those fabulous Dragons teeth; and being sown up and down, may chance to spring up armed men. And yet on the other hand unlesse warinesse be us'd, as good almost kill a Man as kill a good Book; who kills a Man kills a reasonable creature, God's Image; but hee who destroyes a good Booke, kills reason it selfe, kills the Image of God, as it were in the eye. Many a man lives a burden to the earth; but a good Booke is the pretious life-blood of a master spirit, imbalm'd and treasur'd up on purpose to a life beyond life. (*CPW* II: 492–3)

The image of the dragon's teeth sown by Cadmus is so strong that we are disposed to overlook that small books were indeed sewn up and down, being stitched together instead of bound; and that in 1642 stitched books did indeed 'spring up armed men'. Other allusions to the presence of books are less arch. Milton repeatedly refers to typography, allowing it to pervade the brusque satire of Catholic licensing practices: 'Sometimes 5 *Imprimaturs* are seen together dialogue-wise in the Piatza of one Title page, complementing and ducking each to other with their shav'n reverences, whether the Author, who stands by in perplexity at the foot of his Epistle, shall to the Presse or to the spunge' (*CPW* II: 504). The sight, feel and smell (537) of books permeate the prose: he alludes to 'a hand scars legible' to the 'fairest print' (530), to 'wet sheets' (528) of print, to a press standing still (532), to 'interlinearies, breviaries, *synopses*, and other loitering gear' and 'the multitude of Sermons ready printed and pil'd up' at booksellers' stalls (546). He is particularly sympathetic to small books, encouraging the reading of 'all manner of tractats' (517), and cautioning that 'a wise man will make better use of an idle pamphlet, then a fool will do of sacred scripture' (521). In speaking 'For the Liberty of Unlicenc'd Printing', Milton defends not large folio volumes, scholarly or devotional works, restricted by economic circumstances to the educational or social elite, but small, vernacular writings, which reached the widest community of readers possible. Though the pamphlet wars of the 1640s engendered a cacophony of voices, scurrilous, frenzied and even politically dangerous, *Areopagitica* defended them as possible contributions to the providential progress of Truth. Milton thus spoke out on behalf of the Levellers, Diggers and Quakers, of play pamphlets and anti-Laudian satires, speeches and newsbooks, as each could be a dragon's tooth from which might germinate a metamorphosed and militant Truth.

Disputing, Reasoning, Reading

Areopagitica imagined a world of dynamic readers, wrestling with material books, as well as with the substance of their words. These are the circumstances into which Milton pitched all of his subsequent writings, both prose and poetry. In a sonnet written *c*.1647, he reflected on the publication of *Tetrachordon* (1645), one of his divorce tracts, and imagined the circumstance in which a reader encountered it:

> it walked the town awhile,
> Numbering good intellects; now seldom pored on.
> Cries the stall-reader, bless us! what a word on
> A title-page is this! And some in file
> Stand spelling false, while one might walk to Mile-
> End Green.
>
> (*CSP*: 308; 'Sonnet XI', lines 3–8)

The readers that Milton construed in *Areopagitica*, and less trustingly here, carried their experiences into their encounters with other kinds of texts. The controversies contested in pamphlet literature spilled over onto other kinds of pages, and moulded the expectations and practices of readers of poetry as well as of prose. Around 1580 Sir Philip Sidney had aired, in order to dismiss it, a purportedly common view that poetry was a harmless exercise. A hundred years later poetry was clearly embedded in political culture, and a powerful tool within it. Dryden's *Absalom and Achitophel* (1681) is an extreme example of a poetic allegory published in pamphlet form and functioning as effective political propaganda; but other poems shared in the very charged political atmosphere of the popish plot, other literary works participated in political debate, not only commenting on it from a distance, but seeking to influence readers. The practices and perceptions of readers shaped authorial performances;

writers anticipated the readers' critical strategies. All kinds of writing had been not only politicized, but *polemicized*. In a sense writing had also been *pamphletized*: writers were sensitive to the condition of their public speech, the printed medium in which they encountered their readers, and commonly alluded to the bibliographic details of printing, distribution and reading. The pamphlet had entered the literary imagination as the most public, and thus influential, form of speech, with all the advantages and ills that this entailed.

Parallel to the revolution in print was a transformation in readership and in the exercise of reading: readers became more numerous and more querulous. The potential audience of the pamphlet embraced anyone who could read. This was overwhelmingly the 'middling sort', and especially but not exclusively London-dwellers. Between 1600 and 1700 the population of England rose from about four million to about five million; as a consequence of inward migration London's population growth was considerably greater. By the end of the century London was the metropolis of the western world, and also its bibliopolis. Literacy was more common in the capital, encouraged by population density, by the presence of books and printed texts, by the education given to apprentices, and perhaps by access to godly congregations. Literacy rates changed during the seventeenth century, though lack of evidence precludes definitive measurement of either literacy or illiteracy, and any general estimate conceals substantial regional variation and simplifies the complex and shifting social dynamics. Figures can be inferred from the curricula of various educational provisions, and the numbers of those who made a mark when subscribing their name. Writing was taught after reading, and signing one's name was probably the first piece of penmanship conned by most; thus those who were able to write their name had probably learned to read. Estimates from these sources suggest that in 1600 at least one in ten women could read; in 1700, at least three in ten. In 1600 at least three in ten men could read; by the end of the century that figure had risen to almost half of all men. Literacy among women was closely related to social status (few outside the aristocracy or gentry could read) and exhibited less geographical variation than among men; literate women in London were probably not much more common than elsewhere. For men, however, London citizenship offered significant learning opportunities; there perhaps seven out of ten men were able to read around the middle of the century. Of course, the reality was more complicated than percentages can reveal: on the margins of literacy many possessed partial skills, including the ability to read print but not handwriting, or the ability to descry a few words.

Though London was the main centre of printing, books and pamphlets were distributed throughout the three kingdoms, either by provincial booksellers or individually, using the post or carriers. Seventeenth-century correspondence among the gentry, and to a lesser extent the middling sort, is littered with references to books accompanying letters. In London books were sold at bookseller's shops, positioned in a cluster around St Paul's, with many vendors of pamphlets in Paternoster Row, and at stalls in the streets, lining Paul's walk and in the churchyard itself. St Paul's was already the recognized centre of the book trade when the Stationers' Company established their hall there in 1554; and at least from the mid-sixteenth century it was a focus for the exchange of news and gossip. Also involved in the distribution of ballads and chapbooks were itinerant chapmen; from 1640 street hawkers, often known as 'mercuries' (a term which would soon subtly shift meaning, to indicate a wholesale vendor), played an increasingly important role in selling small books and pamphlets on the London streets. These were a particular irritation to the authorities as they were difficult to monitor, and thus provided a suitable outlet for surreptitious and forbidden books, both radical and royalist. The cries of these street vendors, their low manners and morals, haunt satirical writings of the 1640s.

Satires of controversial pamphlets, and anxious comments in diaries and correspondence, suggest fears among the elite that the 'vulgar' or 'common sort' were being given access to matters that were properly above their reach. The common sort might be persuaded, by news or polemic, to disrupt social, political and religious hierarchies. To the apprehensive, movements like the Levellers and Quakers seemed to be the realization of these fears. Not everyone among the elite adopted such an ungenerous view of the abilities of readers. In *Areopagitica* Milton attributes to readers a profound and conscientious independence, or at least the capacity for such a stance. He describes a reader's impatience with the state's intervention in the reading experience: 'every acute reader upon the first sight of a pedantick licence, will be ready with these like words to ding the book a coits distance from him, I hate a pupil teacher, I endure not an instructer that comes to me under the wardship of an overseeing fist' (*CPW* II: 533). Readers must be capable of making up their minds, he suggests, as godliness requires belief, and belief involves understanding and choice, the free exercise of reason. Readers must be trusted, he urges, 'for if we be so jealous over them, as that we dare not trust them with an English pamphlet, what doe we but censure them for a giddy, vitious, and ungrounded people' (*CPW* II: 536). Recent research on the history of reading suggests that many readers, not just the highly educated, were able to construct elaborate interpretations, to twist texts to their own interests and needs, to measure one argument against another, to read against the grain. Propaganda could be effective, not because it made readers the pawns of centrally administered publicity, but because it made them active participants in a public sphere of political debate.

Milton's expectations were high. Despite – or perhaps because of – the egalitarian vision of *Areopagitica*, his sophisticated arguments, Latin and Greek epigrams, and sure-footed allusions placed great demands upon his readers. His intended readers were not merely literate, but learned and reflective; he anticipated diligent reading, attention to minute details and broad sweeps of reasoning, and an improbable open-mindedness to unconventional beliefs; an ideal reader perhaps not unlike himself. *Eikonoklastes* (1649), his commissioned response to *Eikon Basilike* (1649), has been regarded as a practical failure, despite its brutal rhetorical and logical superiority, because it confronted popular sentiments. Milton's intent in *Eikonoklastes* was to disabuse the people, to smash the false image created in *Eikon Basilike* and to replace it with the truth, to strip away false, glozing names and discover the things underneath, to devise a republican renarration of the royalist romance. He over-estimated his audience – though we simultaneously find him describing the readers of the king's book, and thus implicitly the readers of his own refutation, as an 'inconstant, irrational, and Image-doting rabble' (*CPW* III: 601). After the unfavourable reception of the first edition of *Eikonoklastes* he added to this phrase: 'that like a credulous and hapless herd, begott'n to servility, and inchanted with these popular institutes of Tyranny, subscrib'd with a new device of the Kings Picture at his praiers, hold out both thir eares with such delight and ravishment to be stigmatiz'd and board through in witness of thir own voluntary and beloved baseness' (601). Milton's prose, from the antiprelatical tracts to the anti-Restoration pamphlets, was repeatedly fractured by this conflict between a desire to speak to an empowered readership, benefiting from a universal covenant of grace, and a sense that the English are ultimately obstinate, stupid, and lacking in civic-mindedness.

Milton did not make enough compromises to be an entirely successful pamphleteer. One German reader of *Areopagitica* suggested in 1647 that it would have been more persuasive if it had been made less abrasive and supereloquent: he wrote that it was 'rather too satyrical throughout...and because of his all too highflown style in many places quite obscure' (Miller 1989; Norbrook 1999: 124). While Nedham sought to seduce his readers, and sway their judgements by tickling their humours, Milton sweetened his prose only with the brilliance of rhythm, elaborate and dense rhetorical devices, and sinewy metaphors. Milton's writings participated in the response, counter-response, and anti-counter-response culture of the pamphlet, but he fashioned himself as standing apart from it.

More Publick then Preaching?

From 1641 to 1660 Milton's public vocation was as a writer of polemical prose. He did not know this in 1641 when he decided to engage for the first time in a pamphlet controversy, any more than he knew that one day he would write an epic of enduring eminence. Yet Milton's decision was symptomatic of a momentous change in British culture. In some respects Milton's career as a writer can be seen as representative of the transformations, noted by many contemporaries, taking place in 1638–42, and of longer-term changes occurring in the half-century on either side of these years.

A slow growth in the public circulation of print for the purposes of news and controversy can be traced as far back as the Henrician Reformation. The Elizabethan Privy Council sensed the possibility of using print for propaganda purposes. The first real increase in topical and controversial items occurred in the 1580s and 1590s with a flurry of commercially produced news publications. There was widespread political debate during the 1620s, and, perhaps, the beginning of a political opposition located in the spaces where debate occurred: taverns and manuscript coteries. Yet during the 1640s mass protests began to affect institutional political debate, and print became an important element in coordinating the understanding and motivation of these collective movements. The increased quantity of cheap, topical print increased the shared element of political culture, introducing national and metropolitan political issues to members of the middling sort whose horizons had previously been more confined to the local community. By this means a public was created; and perhaps a realm of critical political debate like that characterized by the German social theorist Jürgen Habermas as a 'public sphere'. The pamphlet wars of the 1640s clearly grew out of earlier controversial literature – and many pamphleteers recognized this by acknowledging the Elizabethan controversialists Thomas Nashe and Martin Marprelate as their predecessors – but the sheer transformation in quantity also involved a revolution in quality. Print began to acquire new functions, as reading began to acquire new practices.

Readers who discovered new reading experiences during the 1640s were reluctant to relinquish their heightened expectations of the availability of news and debate. Any government seeking entirely to frustrate these would be risking disaffection. Political controversy 'without doors' thus survived repeated changes in government. Parliament made several lukewarm attempts to reinforce licensing practices during the 1640s, but none had much effect, at least until the September 1649 Act, which was predominantly concerned with periodical newsbooks. Under the Commonwealth and subsequent Protectorate the government used propaganda more than outright suppression to quell the voices of many critics. Such a course of action had been advised by Marchamont Nedham on several occasions, though Nedham was not averse to advising the government on press control, nor to taking advantage of a monopoly when one was offered. Milton himself displayed similarly complex motivation when he accepted employment by the Council of State in March 1649, as Secretary for Foreign Tongues. His remit was from the first much broader than translation. Experienced in the practicalities of the book trade, he liaised with stationers on behalf of the Council, arranging publication of official works, as well as contributing his own to the effort. In March 1651, for about a year, he became licenser to Nedham's *Mercurius Politicus*, an official government mouthpiece, albeit one that was at times more outspoken and radical than most of its sponsors. Since the nineteenth century scholars have looked quizzically upon this volte-face from the position regarding licensing advocated in *Areopagitica*. Yet little can be learnt about Milton's motivation: there is no evidence of him interfering in the content of *Politicus*, nor in the other works he licensed. When the Council of State seized the heretical Racovian catechism in 1652, Milton was interrogated, apparently in connection with licensing it; he noted that he had acted according to his principles. Yet the mere fact of licensing, accepting a role that potentially empowered him to infringe the intellectual liberty of others, would seem to contradict both *Areopagitica* and Milton's more general case for a positive understanding of liberty. The compromises of Milton and Nedham point to a pragmatic interest in encouraging debate, while applying the maximum polemical pressure on its outcome. This, and the attitude of 1650s governments more generally, recognized, and consolidated, the role the reading public had to play in politics. Despite particularly swingeing orders concerning printing in 1655, neither

Commonwealth nor Protectorate entirely suppressed oppositional voices. Visitors to London expressed surprise at the burgeoning print culture in the area around St Paul's, and at the quantity of anti-Cromwellian writing that was freely available on the streets.

The restoration of monarchy did not entirely reverse the changes in the uses of print. Charles II, and his faithful bloodhound of the press Roger L'Estrange, did clamp down on the space available for political controversy. Licensing legislation of the 1660s, combined with the careful monitoring and control of nonconformists, succeeded in quietening debate, and thus depleted the resources of public opinion. Despite this late appearance of hope for social conservatives, however, Pandora's box had been opened; no subsequent legislation or other intervention was to prevent a significant part of the populace from reading and debating news and politics. During subsequent moments of political crisis – notably 1678–81 and 1688–9 – the press, with Parliament's encouragement, escaped control, and a polemical mêlée broke out, resembling civil war hostilities. When pushed, as in 1681, the king, his Council and their intelligence service were able to dampen practical antigovernment pamphleteering; but the government sought to assert its position at least as much through asserting its own case as through blanket censorship. The *London Gazette*, the bi-weekly, subsequently tri-weekly newspaper founded in 1665, was closely supervised from the office of the Secretary of State, and for long periods of its existence was restricted to offering foreign news, like the corantos of the 1620s. Yet during these times foreign news could constitute a focus for opposition to the king or Parliament, and the coffee-houses remained vibrant. The freedom within debate became attenuated in some periods, while flourishing in others, the place of the public in the formulation of parliamentary policy shifted, the energy of the prose and the arguments conducted in cheap print waxed and waned; but for all this printed controversy had achieved a new and enduring social status.

This is related not by way of an apology for the oppressive tendencies of the regime of Charles II, but to suggest that the conditions of controversy had been permanently changed. The first controversy about church government in demotic, vernacular prose presented in inexpensive printed form took place in 1588, with a series of pamphlets presented under the pseudonym Martin Marprelate; a century later it was axiomatic that a government or its opponents wishing to manipulate or to appeal to public opinion would present their case in printed pamphlets. Within this broader sweep, the years 1638–42 represent a momentous shift, realizing earlier potentials and setting enduring precedents. Thus Milton's decision to become a pamphleteer was part of a watershed in the history of print and of political culture in Britain.

Milton committed himself to pamphleteering for twenty years because he thought that this civic vocation mattered. Printed controversy offered a way for the writer to engage in public life; whereas earlier humanists would present counsel to princes as the means of combining a life of thought with political participation, in Britain by the late 1630s a writer could offer counsel to the reading public. During his frustration with this practical career in the mid-1650s he returned to his dormant poetic ambitions, and crafted the masterpieces for which he is celebrated today. For readers of the first editions of these works in the 1660s and 1670s Milton was primarily a controversialist. The apparent incongruity between these two vocations soon developed after the poet's death, as he became himself a figure in polemical controversy. Tory writers tried to smear the Whigs by associating Whig politics with Milton's republicanism. Whigs accordingly distanced themselves from him on grounds of polemical prudence. 'That grand Whig, Milton' was of course the incendiary prose-writer. The poetry flourished, was acknowledged, annotated, illustrated, published in folio; the prose remained uncollected until two editions in 1697 and 1698, one without imprint, the other with a false Amsterdam imprint. The poetry was read with admiration, and, by English readers, with pride, as evidence of the hearty sinews of the native tongue. The prose was an embarrassment, a reminder of real and ongoing conflict. Not until the 1830s were the two re-united in a single edition. In this way the polemical controversies that caused Milton to re-orient his literary ambitions in 1638–42 have been embedded in the history of his reception ever since.

BIBLIOGRAPHY

Writings

Hall (1640[/1]); Milton (1998b); Raymond (1993); Smith (1983); Walwyn (1989).

References for Further Reading

Achinstein (1994); Corns (1992a); Cressy (1980); Dobranski (1999); Hill (1977); Knoppers (1994); Loewenstein and Turner (1990); Love (1993); Miller, Leo (1989); Norbrook (1999); Potter (1989); Raymond (1996a); Skerpan (1992); Smith (1989, 1994); von Maltzahn (1995); Watt (1991); Weber (1996); Wolfe (1963); Zwicker (1993).

PART III
Texts

The Early Poetry

13

'On the Morning of Christ's Nativity', 'Upon the Circumcision' and 'The Passion'

Thomas N. Corns

Poetry and the Liturgical Calendar

Milton chose to place his Nativity Ode first in his first collection of poems, published in 1645. It is by no means the earliest he wrote, though among the vernacular poems which, with a handful of Italian sonnets, make up the first part of that two-part collection (his Latin and Greek poems come later), only 'A Paraphrase on Psalm 114' certainly antedates it. Still, chronology of composition probably pays little part in the organization of the volume, and the precedence he attributes to the poem invites interpretation. He avowedly wrote it in the December following his twenty-first birthday, the legal age of majority in early modern England, and it has sometimes been claimed as a declaration of a newly acquired poetic maturity. Quite probably, its location indicates the poet's assessment of its quality. Milton's collection was published by the most important publisher of creative writing in the mid-century, the bookseller Humphrey Moseley, towards the beginning of a glittering career. His preface to the collection shows his shrewd understanding of the work he was launching. We cannot know whether it was he or Milton who thought of the policy, but he would certainly have seen the sense of putting a work of obvious assurance and distinction at the start of the collection, where a browsing customer would surely see it.

In terms of its subsequent critical reception, the ode has generally been recognized as Milton's first manifestation of poetic genius and, qualitatively, a poem to be set alongside 'Lycidas' and *A Masque presented at Ludlow Castle, 1634* as his most significant poetic works before *Paradise Lost*. That judgement has much to support it, and the poem has certainly generated a rich and diverse critical appreciation and a level of response analogous to his masque and his pastoral elegy (see, for example, Allen 1970: 24–40; Barker 1940–1; Belsey 1988: 1–5, 19–23; Broadbent 1960: 12–31; Burnett 1981: 34–41; Demaray 1968: 31–40; Leishman 1969: 51–67; Prince 1954: 58–63; Tuve 1957: 37–72, all of which remain very useful). Yet the association is in other respects misleading, for within *Poems (1645)* the ode generically forms a group, arguably a series, with two other works, 'The Passion' and 'Upon the Circumcision', the former tentatively dated by Carey 1630, the latter 1633 (*CSP*: 122, 172). Like those poems, the Nativity Ode eschews the revived Spenserian pastoralism of 'Lycidas' and *A Masque*, taking early Stuart literary baroque as its informing cultural ideal.

All three are poems commemorating dates within the Christian year: Christmas Day; 1 January (the feast of the Circumcision); and Good Friday. As such they belong to a seventeenth-century literary preoccupation, which, while already established in the Jacobean period, developed considerably after the accession of Charles I. John Donne's 'Goodfriday, 1613', arguably the best of this subgenre, establishes some of its characteristic presentational forms (including at least one that radically shapes the Nativity Ode), though as the tradition later develops a more celebratory and sacerdotal quality becomes dominant. Major poets including Robert Herrick, George Herbert and Richard Crashaw wrote such poems; so, too, did William Drummond of Hawthornden, among Scottish poets probably the most influential on English readers and writers, as well as many minor figures. The first part of this chapter contextualizes Milton in this tradition. It is not a source study, though occasionally specific debts will be investigated. However, we deal here with a literary culture in which poems often circulated in manuscript for decades before appearing in print. Milton published some of his earliest poems ten or fifteen years after he wrote them. What he was reading in manuscript – and who was reading his poems in the same medium – are matters of speculation, but are largely irrelevant to my project, which aims at a larger, more generalized account of his work in relation to the literary sensibility and the aesthetic predilections and assumptions of his own age.

Religious poetry for the most part reflects, sometimes in complex ways, other aspects of the religious experience and practice of the culture that produces it. In this case, the commemorative impulse mirrored a growing emphasis within the Anglican church (and one which Drummond would have understood and probably sympathized with – he was a royalist supporter in the political crises of the late 1630s and the 1640s). Throughout the 1620s Arminian ceremonialism became increasingly influential within the church and state. At its core lay assumptions about the salvation that stood open to all believers who cooperated with the action of a widely extended grace under the prompting and influence of the clergy and the ceremonies and offices of the church. By the end of the decade William Laud, successively promoted to the see of London and then the archiepiscopate of Canterbury, had developed a theological style that chimed well with the predilections and priorities of Charles I. In place of the preaching ministry favoured by Calvinists, especially those of a puritanical leaning, Laud developed an ecclesiastical style that promoted ritual and 'the beauty of holiness', emphasized the special status and role of the clergy, and revalued the holy days and Christian festivals of the English liturgical year. Peter Lake, drawing here on the words of an anti-Calvinist divine, describes Laudian piety vividly:

The great festivals of the Christian year both figured and extended to all believers the benefits conferred on fallen humanity by Christ's life, passion and resurrection. 'They which come to God's house upon the day of Christ's nativity (coming in faith and love as they ought) are', argued Robert Shelford, 'partakers of Christ's birth; they which come upon the day of circumcision are with him circumcised from the dominion of the flesh' . . . Shelford [concluded] that the keeping 'of the holy feasts of the Church' was one of the main offices of holiness. (Lake 1993: 175, quoting a tract of 1635)

Of course, one may wish to argue that, since the maturer Milton most certainly opposed the Laudian domination of the Church of England with an implacable hostility, he may in his version of 'holy day' poems be developing a critique. It is a hypothesis to which I shall return. But let us at least begin by recognizing the striking congruence between what he is producing and the work of straightforwardly ceremonialist writers like Crashaw and Herrick. The common ground, in terms of thematic and ideological concerns and in terms of poetic idiom, between Milton and the mainstream, is very considerable, as we shall see.

Passion Poetry

Apart from the Nativity Ode, this group of Milton's poems has been deprecated or dismissed, but they sit interestingly alongside other early Stuart poems on the same topics. Milton never engaged extensively with Christ's Crucifixion anywhere in his œuvre. In Michael's narrative of the future course of world history that ends *Paradise Lost*, the event receives less than four lines:

> he [the Son] shall live hated, be blasphemed,
> Seized on by force, judged, and to death condemned
> A shameful and accursed, nailed to the cross
> By his own nation, slain for bringing life;
>   (XII. 411–14)

Moses and Nimrod receive much fuller treatment. Again, in *Paradise Regained* Milton elected to turn his and the readers' gaze from the crucial phase of the Atonement. 'The Passion' (*CSP*: 123–5), then, offers a unique example of Milton's poetic engagement with a scene he evidently found difficult to depict.

His informing strategy is one of averting his attention from the scene of suffering to a consideration of its impact on himself and of the inadequacy of his poetic idiom. It is a stratagem which accords in part with John Donne's much greater poem, 'Goodfriday, 1613. Riding Westward' (Donne 1968: 306–8). There, literally and symbolically, the poet writes as one travelling away from the site of Golgotha and 'That spectacle of too much weight for mee' (line 16). Donne's poem defines the nature of the poet's guilt, which disables him from looking on the tortured body, and expresses the hope that, through a penitential process and 'by thy grace', he may turn his face to Christ. Milton's poem, while it too rehearses a studied evasiveness, an aversion from the scene at Golgotha, explores the theme less in terms of personal regeneration and more in terms of the writer's development as Christian poet.

He begins by pondering the change of idiom he must make from the celebration of the Nativity: 'For now to sorrow must I tune my song, / And set my harp to notes of saddest woe' (lines 8–9), a reflection which occupies the first two stanzas. In the third he considers Christ, but explores the mysteries of the Incarnation rather than the sacrifice of the Atonement. His Christ remains a 'sovran priest', though one who stoops his 'regal head' to enter the 'Poor fleshly tabernacle' of human form. Not blood, but the 'odorous oil' that anointed him in heaven, drops from his head (stanza III). Stanza IV has the poet pondering the difficulties of hitting the right tone for the task. Stanza V has the most memorable conceit, though one that has received some censure for its self-conscious preciosity: 'The leaves should all be black whereon I write, / And letters where my tears have washed a wannish white' (lines 34–5). The lines are not without some interest, however. As critics and editors have observed, funeral elegies were occasionally printed in white letters on black pages, and more commonly they were printed with a thick band of black around the page edge (Woodhouse and Bush 1972a: 159). But the conceit relates to a larger motif of the baroque idiom in which the medium literally assumes a form that symbolizes its theme, as in those funeral and commemorative plaques of Bernini that seem to melt in distress at the message they carry (Wittkower 1955: 203, 204 and pl. 64). Even Herbert, much more accomplished than Milton would ever be in this idiom, has a conceitful confusion of literal and metaphorical writing, though of a gorier kind:

> Since blood is fittest, Lord, to write
> Thy sorrows in, and blood fight;
> My heart hath store, write there, where in
> One box doth lie both ink and sin
> ('Good Friday', lines 21–4, Herbert and Vaughan 1986: 34)

Of course, where Milton's idiom is tentatively hypothetical ('*should* all be black'), Herbert's direct imperative ('*write* there') reflects a greater assurance in his command of the conceit.

Stanza VI describes a kind of poetic ecstasy, in which the poet's soul, 'In pensive trance' (line 42), traverses to Jerusalem at the time of the Crucifixion; again, though, his regard does not engage with the tortured Christ but turns in stanza VII to his sepulchre, where the poet '*would* score' on it – note again the mood of the verb – his 'plaining verse' (lines 46–7), etching the words with a well-directed flow of tears. The last stanza rehearses the image of the poet lamenting in 'mountains wild' or in 'The gentle neighbourhood of grove and spring' (lines 51–2) the grief he feels. This sort of intrusion of the poet into the narration or description of the biblical events which he is commemorating is quite commonplace in early modern devotional verse. Herrick, for example, presents two poems as if addressed by the poet to Christ on the way to the cross ('His words to Christ, going to the Crosse' and 'Another, to his Saviour', Herrick 1956: 399). Among the examples of early seventeenth-century poems on the Passion I have considered, only Richard Crashaw, a convert to Catholicism, describes the physicality of suffering with a precision beyond the familiar list of the wounds of Christ, and he does so with an alarming vividness at once disturbing and surreal:

> They 'have left thee naked, LORD, O that they had
> This garment too I would they had deny'd.
> Thee with thyself they have too richly clad,
> Opening the purple wardrobe in thy side.
> ('Upon the Body of Our Bl. Lord, Naked and Bloody', lines 1–4,
> Crashaw 1957: 290)

The English Protestant tradition is reluctant to look so closely or think and feel so deeply about the physical suffering of Christ. Certainly, it is utterly alien to Milton's religious sensibility, and that of his Anglican contemporaries.

Then Milton's poem ends, and the poet, publishing it for the first time in 1645, added the note, 'This subject the author finding to be above the years he had when he wrote it, and nothing satisfied with what was begun, left it unfinished' (*CSP*: 125). The critical tradition has taken a poor view of this, plainly affronted by a poem that, though not good enough to satisfy the poet, is supposed to be good enough for his readers. (For a variety of pithy indictments, see Woodhouse and Bush 1972a: 152–5.) But its incomplete state is wholly consonant with the principal themes of the poem. For this is a poem about the inadequacy of the poet's idiom to capture the enormity of Christ's sacrifice. It is a poem about what the poet would like to do, but cannot, and just as Milton as believer cannot really bring himself to contemplate the tortured Christ, so Milton as poet cannot commemorate the event. There is no reason to doubt his assertion that the work is incomplete and abandoned; but that in itself confirms the limitations of the young poet's abilities, the definition of which lies at the centre of the work.

The Feast of the Circumcision

The feast of the Circumcision, 1 January, finds surprisingly frequent celebration among early Stuart poets. Circumcision was very infrequently practised in seventeenth-century England, and then only as a surgical procedure, rather than a religious rite. However, the feast falls within the traditional feasting period of Christmas, which ended on Twelfth Night. Devotionally, it allowed an interlude of sombre reflection into the festive mood. For court poets, it provided an opportunity to contrast with the exhilaration of a society perhaps in the grip of preparations for a Twelfth Night masque (the traditional day for such performances). Indeed, Herrick explicitly links the two:

> let no Christmas mirth begin
> Before ye purge, and circumcise
> Your hearts, and hands, lips, eares, and eyes.
> ('Another New-yeeres Gift, or Song for the Circumcision', lines 7–9,
> Herrick 1956: 367)

The ritual serves as a sort of sorbet to cleanse the spiritual palate before the next course of feasting.

Herrick's poems were often set to music by court composers, among them Henry Lawes, Milton's collaborator in *A Masque*. He has two Circumcision poems in *His Noble Numbers*. The first is endorsed 'Composed by M. *Henry Lawes*', and its title indicates the circumstances of its performance, 'The New-yeeres Gift, or Circumcisions Songs, sung to the King in the Presence at White-Hall' (Herrick 1956: 365–6), that is, in the presence chamber, one of the more public rooms of the royal suite, no doubt by choristers associated with the King's Music. It is a part-song, in five parts with a chorus. 'Another New-yeeres Gift, or Song for the Circumcision' (Herrick 1956: 366–7) has the same structure. Since New Year's Day was the traditional occasion for giving presents, the feast also allowed court poets and musicians to make a gift for the king. William Cartwright, a younger, quite talented university poet with aspirations towards court patronage, produced another performance poem, 'For the Kings Musick', 'On the Circumcision', approximating closely to an oratorio with two voices singing the parts of Levites (Cartwright 1651: 318–19).

Milton's 'Upon the Circumcision' (*CSP*: 172–3), while certainly showing no obvious potential for musical setting, is the most conventional of his devotional poems, the one that sits most squarely within contemporary practices and concerns. Milton's poem links the circumcision of Christ, a first effusion of blood accepted by him as part of the human nature he has assumed, with the act of Atonement: this 'wounding smart' (line 25) anticipates the Passion:

> O ere long
> Huge pangs and strong
> Will pierce more near his heart.
> (lines 26–8)

The sentiment is commonplace in poems commemorating this liturgical feast. Thus Cartwright has his first Levite show a surprising prescience in observing, 'this young loss / Only preludes unto his Riper Cross' (lines 11–12, Cartwright 1651: 318). Similarly, Francis Quarles writes,

> The drops this day effused, were but laid
> For his Good-Frydayes earnest, when he paid
> For our Redemption blood in full summers,
> Now it but drops, then in a tempest comes,
> ('Of our Saviours Circumcision, or New-yeares day', lines 11–14,
> Quarles 1969: 9)

Other poets sometimes show a greater interest in the infant Christ. For example, Herrick, with a characteristic lightness of touch he usually achieves in describing children, notes 'His whimpering, and His cries' ('The New-yeeres Gift, or Circumcisions Songs', line 14), and commends the child to the 'warm bosome' of his mother (line 29). Cartwright, delicately playing on the mysteries of Incarnation, notes 'His Bloud was but his Mothers Milk erewhile' (line 4, Cartwright 1651: 318). Milton makes no mention of the Virgin Mary.

Nativity Poetry

'On the Morning of Christ's Nativity' (*CSP*: 101–16) rises in many ways above the rather commonplace achievements of Milton's other devotional poems and stands out from the mass of other early Stuart poems about Christmas. But it is essential that we recognize the common ground and the familiar repertoire of motifs and conceits that he shares with his contemporaries, and which provide the framework for his first great poem.

Milton critics sometimes remark that his is a poem not about the Nativity but about the Incarnation. In fact, it is about both, for Milton, of course, recognized that the latter is manifest in the former; so, too, did his contemporaries, and, as in Milton's poem, the Nativity and the Crucifixion are frequently connected. Doctrinally, the issues are straightforward; the Nativity has Christ enter into human form to take upon himself the guilt of fallen humankind, and to atone for that guilt through the sacrifice of the Crucifixion. Indeed, as Diane McColley has observed, 'The readings for the communion service on Christmas Day, Hebrews 1 and John 1, concern the identity, exaltation, and kingship of the Son as creating Word and Redeemer' (1997: 186). In this vein, an accomplished little poem by the minor poet William Hammond, 'Upon the Nativity of our saviour and Sacrament then received', makes the connections very explicitly:

> None but two-fac'd *Janus* can be guest
> And fit himselfe unto this double feast.
> That must before joyntly the Manger see,
> And view behind the execrable Tree.
> (lines 7–10, Hammond 1655: 83–4)

Or, in Ben Jonson's rather more robust expression,

> What comfort by him doe wee winne,
> Who made himselfe the price of sinne,
>   To make us heires of glory!
> To see this Babe, all innocence;

A Martyr borne in our defence;
Can man forget this Storie?
('A Hymne On the Navitie of my Saviour', lines 19–24,
Jonson 1947: 130)

When Milton observes that the baby Jesus is the tortured Jesus of the Atonement he reflects not a morbid obsession or a resistance to the festive spirit of Christmas; rather, he makes the usual connections:

The babe lies yet in smiling infancy,
That on the bitter cross
Must redeem our loss;
(lines 151–3)

Again, Milton connects the baby born in Bethlehem with the creation of the world. Though of course the Genesis account makes no mention of the Trinity, it was a theological commonplace, following Hebrews 1: 10 and acknowledged in the communion service for Christmas Day (see above), to identify the Son as the agency responsible for the Creation, a process depicted in those terms by Milton in his narrative in *Paradise Lost* Book VII, where he is sent 'with glory and attendance of angels to perform the work of creation in six days' ('The Argument', *PL*: 388). In the Nativity Ode, 'Nature' and the poet recollect that the music heard at the Incarnation was heard at the Creation (lines 117–24, more fully considered below). Milton builds a rather oblique chain of association in comparison with Ben Jonson's declarative, 'I sing the birth, was borne to night, / The Author both of Life, and light' ('A Hymne', lines 1–2). The minor poet Thomas Philipot explores the paradox of the maker of earth being made of earth, the maker of humankind assuming mankind's form:

... God who mans fraile house of earth compos'd
Himselfe in a fraile house of earth enclos'd,
Who did controule the Fire, Aire, Sea, and Earth,
Was clad with all these foure, and had a birth
In time, who was begotten before time,
.   ('On the Nativitie of our Saviour', lines 5–9, Philipot 1646: 46–7)

Jeremy Taylor, a minor poet though a distinguished Anglican divine and prose writer, perhaps comes closest to Milton's representation of the process of creation by a godhead now incarnate in a neonate:

He that begirt each zone.
To Whom both poles are one,
Who grasp't the Zodiack in's hand
And made it move or stand,

Is now by nature man
By stature but a span
('[The Fourth] Hymn for Christmas Day', lines 19–24,
Taylor 1870: 23)

William Drummond of Hawthornden sets the achievements of the Creation against the greater 'amazement' occasioned by the Incarnation. Spreading 'the azure Canopie of Heaven' and giving 'strange motions to the Planets seven' define one aspect of the godhead, but at the sacrifice of that power in taking on human weakness 'Angels stand amaz'd to muse on it' (Sonnet x, 'Amazement at the Incarnation of God', Drummond 1976: 93).

Other topoi link Milton's Nativity Ode with broadly contemporary poems on the same subject: the insertion of the poet into the setting of the poem; the poem as gift; and the connection between the incarnate Christ and the rising sun. Of course, the first relates ideologically to renewed Anglican interest in the pastoral value of the festivals of the liturgical calendar, and is also a feature of Passion poems. As the festival returns, its celebration becomes a kind of contemporary re-enactment of the original event, an ectype of that archetype, and the celebrants recapture the sensations of authentic witnesses of the scene. For Milton, that process is represented explicitly as a conscious spiritual exercise, as his Muse, the 'heavenly Muse' (line 15; presumably Urania) is targeted on Bethlehem on the morning after the birth of Christ. Other poets simply assume their own presence, though there are charming and ingenious variants, the best of them from Herbert, who brings the Bethlehem stable into rural England:

> All after pleasures as I rid one day,
> > My horse and I, both tired, body and mind,
> > With full cry of affections, quite astray,
> I took up in the next inn I could find.
> There when I came, whom found I but my dear,
> > My dearest Lord, expecting till the grief
> Of pleasures brought me to him, ready there
> To be all passengers' most sweet relief?
> ('Christmas', lines 1–8, Herbert and Vaughan 1986: 70–1)

Milton suggests premeditated intrusion into the scene – indeed, his Muse is to beat the Magi to their objective – 'O run, prevent them with thy humble ode' (line 24). In Herbert's elegantly understated poem, the encounter seems both serendipitous and inevitable.

The poem-as-gift topos is widely adopted. In Milton, it figures in the meditational preface in which his Muse is released: the intended outcome inspires both the poet to complete the poem and the Muse to deliver it, rather competitively. John Collop, a minor and rather shadowy writer but, like Milton, published by Humphrey Moseley, spends much of his 'On the Nativity' pondering quite what he can give Christ on his birthday: 'Shall I the shepherds Musick take? / Or to thine Angels tune my voice?' He concludes that all he has to offer is the 'Odours of an heart that's broke', which are expressed in the poem that he writes (Collop 1656: 110). Herrick writes some delicate little poems about and for children (see, for example, his 'Graces for Children' and 'Another Grace for a Child', Herrick 1956: 355–6). In 'To his Saviour, a Child; a Present, by a child', he imagines the poem he is writing is a flower, a gift, to be carried by a child-believer to the Christ child:

> Go prettie child, and beare this Flower
> Unto thy little Saviour;
> And tell Him, by that Bud now blown,
> He is the *Rose of Sharon* known:
> When thou hast said so, stick there
> Upon his Bibb, or Stomacher:
>   (lines 1–6, Herrick 1956: 354)

Of course, the topos allows an element of reflexivity to enter as poems contain references to themselves as gifts or products to be bestowed, which suits well the characteristic aesthetic of early Stuart poetry, which values such accomplished, controlled elegance combined with a lightly sustained faux-naïveté.

Finally, there is the association of Christ with the sun. In Milton's poem this supports two conceits. The real sun is represented as being unwilling to rise:

> The sun himself withheld his wonted speed,
> And hid his head for shame,
> As his inferior flame,
> The new enlightened world no more should need;
> He saw a greater sun appear
> Than his bright throne, or burning axle-tree could bear.
>   (lines 79–84)

Later, the Christ-child dismisses 'Each fettered ghost' and 'yellow-skirted fays' as shadows are dismissed when

> the sun in bed,
> Curtained with cloudy red,
> Pillows his chin upon an orient wave,
>   (lines 229–36)

Once more, the topos recurs widely. Philipot uses it in pedestrian if persistent fashion, initiating the trope with a singularly unpromising line:

> Who can forget that ne're forgotten night,
> That sparkled with such unaccustom'd Light?
> Wherein when darkness had shut in the day,

> A Sun at midnight did his beams display;
>
> …
>
> And though this Sun of Righteousnesse did lie
> Wrapt up in Clouds of darke Obscurity,
> Yet he could such a stock of light allow,
> As did the Heavens with a new Star endow,
> ('On the Nativitie of our Saviour', lines 1–4, 31–4,
>   Philipot 1646: 46)

Drummond opens his sonnet ix, 'For the Nativitie of our Lord', using essentially the same paradox – the Christ-Sun rising at night more brightly than the sun itself rises to bring in day:

> O than the fairest Day, thrice fairer Night!
> Night to best Dayes in which a Sunne doth rise,
> Of which that golden Eye, which cleares the Skies,
> Is but a sparkling Ray, a Shadow light
>   (lines 1–4, Drummond 1976: 92)

Drummond, however, turns the figure with far greater conviction and precision and offers the resonant and enigmatic image of a sun devalued in the comparison. Crashaw has a shepherd sing:

> Gloomy night embrac't the place
> Where the noble Infant lay.
> The Babe lookt up and shew'd his face,
> In spight of Darknesse it was Day.
> It was thy Day, Sweet, and did rise,
> Not from the East, but from thy eyes.
> ('A Hymn of the Nativity, sung as by the Shepherds',
>   lines 17–22, Crashaw 1957: 106)

There is no reason to suppose that, in theological terms, any of these poets disputed the principle of kenosis, the notion that at the Incarnation Christ set aside all attributes of a supernatural kind. The doctrine rests on Paul's words in Philippians 2: 7, 'But [Jesus] made himself of no reputation, and took upon him the form of a servant, and was made in the likeness of men.' The translation in the Authorized Version weakens the force of the Greek original, which speaks of an emptying out of the godhead, a phrase better reflected in Milton's 'Upon the Circumcision': Christ 'Emptied his glory, even to nakedness' (line 20) (see Lieb 1970). All celebrations of the paradox and mystery of the Incarnation are premised on kenosis. Yet repeatedly the Nativity is represented in terms of Christ's glory, manifest in his outshining the sun, as though the birth marks a sort of transitional stage in which Christ is manifest in his residual powers which are in the process of being set aside.

The Achievement of 'On the Morning of Christ's Nativity'

Thus far, I have sought to demonstrate Milton's close involvement with early Stuart devotional verse, examining and illustrating the continuities of strategy, of topoi and of idiom, between his three early celebrations of liturgical feasts and the practices of his contemporaries. My concerns have not been to demonstrate specific debts, but rather to place Milton firmly in context. Milton's great Restoration poems in some ways break the mould of English vernacular verse, seeking out comparison with the timeless classics of Homer, Virgil and the Greek tragedians. His early poetry, though no doubt bearing discernible continental influences, shares a lot of common ground with his immediately contemporary cultural milieu. Yet his Nativity Ode is an extraordinary achievement that takes so many of the building blocks, the prefabricated parts, of Caroline religious poetry and makes from them a challenging, ambitious and original verse. Young Milton never had the sustained argumentation and robust expression of Donne, nor the assurance of Herbert, nor the deftness of Herrick, nor the imaginative vividness of Crashaw; yet here he gives clear evidence of a different voice in English poetry.

As I have hinted, this is a decidedly competitive poem. Milton, like his contemporaries, thrusts himself into the frame of the events he commemorates. But most are happy to ponder whether the gift they bring, their poem, is really fitting or appropriate, whether it can stand comparison with the gifts of the Magi; and they often conclude that it ranks as a simple song alongside the rustic acclamations of the original peasants. The self-image Milton produces within the poem appears both sterner and more confident, as he urges his Muse to beat the Magi to the stable door. Though his ode is explicitly termed 'humble' (line 24), its humility is little in evidence. His Muse speeds it towards the Christ-child like a tea-clipper bringing home the first of the harvest, and is besought, not to second the efforts of the lowly shepherds, but to 'join thy voice unto the angel quire, / From out his secret altar touched with hallowed fire' (lines 27–8), which sounds a rather more majestic Christmas present than the material gifts of the wise men.

Milton's real competition, however, is not with New Testament Magi but with contemporary poems. By stepping into a subject area as frequently visited as this, he is inviting – perhaps insisting on – comparison with the rest, from the swagger of the first line to the assured closure of the last. Just look at that opening, which is, of course, the opening to the whole volume of his early poetry: 'This is the month, and this the happy morn'. Note the metrical irregularity, the stressed first syllable that announces a prosodic master wholly in control of his medium. But the challenge is a specific one, as well as generalized to his generation of poets. Early seventeenth-century verse often has a pseudo-dialogic quality. Poems often function as ripostes to other poems, answering them, capping them or qualifying them. One could point, for example, to Edmund Waller answering Sir John Suckling's 'Against Fruition 1', or Suckling answering William Davenant's 'Madagascar', or Thomas Carew answering Aurelian

Townshend's elegy for Gustavus Adolphus. Poems frequently engage other poems in this period (Corns 1998b: 56–7, 62–3). H. Neville Davies has convincingly demonstrated that Milton's Nativity Ode is in an intricate relationship to a poem by Drummond of Hawthornden, 'An Hymne of the Ascension' (Davies 1985). Drummond's poem (Drummond 1976: 104–7), a ringingly confident and declarative masterpiece of baroque literary art, depicts Christ's ascent to heaven after the Resurrection. There are numerous connections between the poems. These include striking verbal echoes listed by Davies: Drummond's 'Edens leprous Prince' (line 42) and Milton's 'And leprous sin' (line 138); Drummond's 'And archt in Squadrons bright' (line 103) and Milton's 'Keep watch in squadrons bright' (line 21); and more (Davies 1985: 8–10). There are thematic connections too: the defeat of the powers of evil, the destruction of the pagan cults, the redemption of man and his retrieval of a lost heritage, and cosmic flights graced by the assistance and homage of the heavenly bodies (Davies 1985: 12). Davies's account extends also to structural and prosodic features. He concludes that, at the least, 'Milton found the Ascension Hymn worthy of the most detailed scrutiny' (22). All that, I find convincing. But, given the characteristic tendency of early Stuart poets to progress through the process of riposte, we may see something more challenging, perhaps more aggressive, about Milton's intent: a matching poem charting Christ's movements in the opposite direction in an idiom more declarative, even, than Drummond's own. At the time that Milton wrote his poem, Drummond was an author of considerable standing and reputation. Famously visited by Ben Jonson, and a friend, too, of Michael Drayton, he published a second edition of his most significant collection, *Flowres of Sion*, the first to contain his Ascension hymn, in 1630. (As Davies argues, Milton must have been familiar with the poem in manuscript.) By the time Charles I visited Scotland in 1633, Drummond was 'the unofficial Scottish poet laureate' and was commissioned to write the official entertainment for the King (Drummond 1976: x–xii): Milton had published nothing. Milton consciously sets himself in direct comparison with a writer of status and accomplishment. Though literary history has treated their reputations rather differently, in 1629–30 Milton's actions represented a bold assertion of his own poetic ambition.

The poetic persona produced within the poem is distinctive (and perhaps disturbing) in other ways. We see it in the religious sensibility and values implied in his depiction of the Christ-child. This is a matter both of omission and of explicit celebration. It has often been observed that Milton's Nativity scene excludes both shepherds and the Nativity animals from proximity to the child. Certainly, the former are left outside the stable, albeit with souls 'in blissful rapture' (line 98); and allusion to the animals is only infrequently a feature of contemporary analogues. But the omission of any reference to the weakness taken on at the Incarnation is much more significant. Milton's Christ may wear 'swaddling bands' but he displays the power of an infant Hercules, who strangled serpents sent to kill him while in his cradle; Christ himself masters no mere serpents but 'Typhon', either an Egyptian god or a monster of Greek mythology (lines 226–8). Perhaps most strikingly, Mary is a marginal figure. In the final stanza she 'Hath laid her babe to rest' (line 238), but we see her maternalism in no detail. In Crashaw, Christ's 'cheek' is gone to bed "Twixt Mother's breasts' ('A Hymn of the Nativity, sung as by the Shepherds', lines 49–50, Crashaw 1957: 107). While his Marian enthusiasm may seem explicable in terms of his conversion to Catholicism, it should be noted that the Virgin's milk and breasts recur as frequent objects of allusion in Nativity poems by Protestant writers. Milton, who never invites his readers to consider the suckling Christ and who studiedly eschews the intimate dependencies of infancy, is the exception.

Indeed, those omissions accord perfectly with his long description of the impact of the Incarnation on the gods of pagan religions. The theme is to be found in contemporary analogues. For example, in Thomas Philipot we find, 'Now Truths great Oracle it selfe was come, / The Faithlesse Oracles were strucken dumb' (lines 25–6, Philipot 1646: 46). Philipot had matriculated at Cambridge the year after Milton left, and his collected poems were published after *Poems (1645)*. So he may be echoing Milton's lines, which he could have encountered in a (non-surviving) university manuscript or in print:

> The oracles are dumb,
> No voice or hideous hum
> Runs through the arched roof in words deceiving.
>
> (lines 173–5)

But it is just as likely that the coincidence of phrase has its origins in the widespread tradition, which commentators trace to Plutarch, that the pagan oracles fell silent at the time of Christ's early ministry (Woodhouse and Bush 1972a: 95). Drummond has his ascending Christ leave behind Satanic temples 'sackt and torne': 'what ador'd was late, now lyes in Scorne' ('An Hymne of the Ascension', lines 62–5, Drummond 1976: 105). But only Milton develops the expulsion of the gods into a protracted ceremony of power based on spectacular punishment. The passage extends from stanza XVIII to stanza XXV, and each deity or group is dismissed with an apposite humiliation. Nymphs are turned off from the locations they haunt like camp-followers stripped and shorn in the rough justice of liberation, 'With flower-inwoven tresses torn' (line 187). Some gods or their attendant acolytes are merely left desolate and bemused, though a sterner fate awaits several of the zoomorphic deities of the Middle East. Ram-headed Hammon, in a resonant and suggestive phrase, 'shrinks his horn' (line 203), while Osiris, in the manifestation of a bull, is blinded by 'The rays of Bethlehem' (line 223). Like an antimasque fleeing at the appearance of noble masquers, the creatures of the pagan creeds offer no resistance.

There is a certain savage delight in the sadistic reverie about the effortless control exercised by the Christ-child. It anticipates, in some ways, the violent fantasy of bishops squirming in the lowest circle of hell with which, over a decade later, Milton concludes *Of Reformation*, his first antiprelatical pamphlet (*CPW* I: 613–17). But Christ's control, while it reflects and projects a religious sensibility awed by the power of the godhead, matches the sort of control the young poet demonstrates in organizing the larger themes of his poem. Among analogues, the Nativity scene is often accompanied by the music of the spheres. Thus, for example, Cartwright's 'On the Nativity' has the performers sing:

> 3.
> The Spheres are giv'n us as a Ring; that Bliss,
> Which we call Grace is but the Deitie's Kiss,
>
> Ch[orus].
> And what we now do hear Blest Spirit sing,
> Is but the happy Po'sie of that Ring
>   (lines 3–6, Cartwright 1651: 317)

Again, as noted above, the Nativity is frequently linked with the Creation, the Atonement and occasionally the Last Judgement. Masterfully, Milton fashions from the music-of-the-spheres topos a controlling and informing image that links those three events on the time-line of world history with each other and with his own age.

A complex number symbolism informs the structuring of the poem (see Røstvig 1975; Davies 1975; and, for a straightforward introduction, Moseley 1991: 113–14). Only one principle concerns me here: the principle of centrality. Here part of Davies's argument is highly pertinent. If the poem is considered as thirty-one stanzas long (that is, the four stanzas of the proem plus the hymn), then stanza XII of the hymn is the central stanza; if we take just the twenty-seven stanzas of the hymn, then stanza XIV is central. Together they frame 'the magnificent stanza which most readers rightly and instinctively identify as the effective centre of the poem' (Davies 1975: 105). In *Paradise Lost* the very centre of the epic celebrates the moment in which the Son enters into the chariot of the Father to sweep the fallen angels from heaven, effectively exalted to the apocalyptic throne of judgement (*PL* VI. 749–59; for a summary of the arguments, see Fowler's comments, *PL*: 26); it is a moment of transcendence, fittingly served by its centrality. In the Nativity Ode, stanza XIII, flanked by two stanzas, each a centre in its own right, in Davies's phrase, appears 'like an emperor with kings as attendants', occupying 'a position of sovereign honour' (Davies 1975: 105–6):

> XII
> Such music (as 'tis said)
> Before was never made,
> But when of old the sons of morning sung,
> While the creator great
> His constellations set,
> And the well-balanced world on hinges hung,
> And cast the dark foundations deep,
> And bid the welt'ring waves their oozy channel keep.
>
> XIII
> Ring out, ye crystal spheres,
> Once bless our human ears,

(If ye have power to touch our senses so)
And let your silver chime
Move in melodious time;
And let the base of heaven's deep organ blow,
And with your ninefold harmony
Make up full consort to the angelic symphony.

XIV
For if such holy song
Enwrap our fancy long,
Time will run back, and fetch the age of gold,
And speckled vanity
Will sicken soon and die,
And lep'rous sin will melt from earthly mould,
And hell itself will pass away,
And leave her dolorous mansions to the peering day.
                                                    (lines 117–40)

Brilliantly, Milton juxtaposes the immediate present with recollection of the Creation and anticipation of the second coming. He has carefully dated the hymn for his readers with a specificity rare in Caroline literary practice; a headnote to the first edition states clearly 'Compos'd 1629'. The poet inserts into his narrative his own invocation to the music of the spheres that will accompany Christ when he comes in judgement as surely as it accompanied him at the Creation and at his birth on the first Christmas; simply, Milton calls in 1629 for the end of the world, and the millennium of Christ's reign with his saints on earth in a kind of golden age, which will be followed by 'a new heaven and a new earth: for the first heaven and the first earth were passed away' (Revelation 20: 3–4, 21:1). Of course, it is his own voice, *in propria persona*, we hear in the middle of the poem.

Most in the early twenty-first century think of the history of the world in terms of vast aeons of time; educated Europeans in the early modern period took a strictly finite view. Indeed, scholars believed the age of the world to be calculable from the evidence of the Bible, and their efforts placed the Creation only a few thousands of years before the Incarnation. The endeavour culminated in the work of James Ussher, Archbishop of Armagh, whose estimate that the Creation was in 4004 BC was published in the 1650s (Knox 1967: 105–7). But the early Stuart period also saw great interest in calculating the end of the world, and there was frequent speculation that it was imminent. While belief that Christ's second coming would be soon was widespread among religious radicals, it extended across the ideological spectrum. James I thought he could sense 'the latter dayes drawing on' (Hill 1969a: 313). Joseph Mede, probably the most distinguished academic at Christ's College, Cambridge, in Milton's day, published his great work on the prophecies of the Revelation of St John the Divine in 1627.

Milton's poem certainly reflects the assumption that the whole history of the world may well last only a few thousand years, but he is certainly not proclaiming the imminence of the second coming, though he celebrates that event as something dearly wished for by the young poet — and vividly imagined. This central passage accords with the imperatives which open John Donne's Holy Sonnet vii:

> At the round earths imagin'd corners, blow
> Your trumpets, Angells, and arise, arise
> From death, you numberless infinities
> Of soules ...
>
> (lines 1–4, Donne 1968: 296)

But Donne's sonnet turns into a meditation on the poet's unreadiness to meet a Christ returned in judgement, and ends with a penitential prayer. The poet of the Nativity Ode, in contrast, is utterly and triumphantly confident of his own readiness and of his own salvation.

Milton's poem is a devotional act wholly compatible with the emphases of the Anglican tradition in general and the specific and immediate imperatives of Laudian ceremonialism. Yet there are a tone and a self-image that surely distinguish this poem from those of Herrick, who is ejected from his living in the Civil War, from Carew, who is to die in exile, a convert to Rome, from Drummond, a reclusive royalist, or from Cartwright, a victim of camp fever in embattled, loyalist Oxford. Milton's poem asserts his own self-worth and his own individualism. Though he shares so much of the poetic idiom of his contemporaries, he has nothing of their self-effacement, nothing of their priestliness, nor of their collective, rather corporate voice. He speaks for himself in celebration of a Christ-child represented in terms of his real and potential power, which eclipses worldly dominion. This is not a radical or puritan or oppositional poem, but it reflects a religious sensibility which, as we know, will become radicalized as the crises of the late 1630s develop. 'Christ the only King!' was a favoured slogan on the standards of radical regiments in the New Model Army. In a sense, it is the theme of Milton's first work of genius.

BIBLIOGRAPHY

Writings

Cartwright (1651); Collop (1656); Corns (1998b); Crashaw (1957); Donne (1968); Drummond (1976); Hammond (1655); Herbert and Vaughan (1986); Herrick (1956); Hill (1969a); Jonson (1947); Knox (1967); Lake (1993); Philipot (1646); Quarles (1969); Taylor (1870); Wittkower (1955).

References for Further Reading

Allen (1970); Barker, Arthur E. (1940–1); Belsey (1988); Broadbent (1960); Burnett (1981); Davies, H. Neville (1975, 1985); Demaray (1968); Leishman (1969); Lieb (1970); McColley (1997); Moseley (1991); Prince (1954); Røstvig (1975); Tuve (1957); Woodhouse and Bush (1972a).

14

John Milton's *Comus*

Leah S. Marcus

If poetic offspring can be said to possess gender, then John Milton's *A Masque presented at Ludlow Castle*, more frequently (if erroneously) known as *Comus*, is a daughter who has traditionally been prized for her delicacy and beauty. The first published version (1637) featured a letter dedicatory from Henry Lawes, the court musician who had arranged and participated in its 1634 performance at Ludlow Castle, to John Egerton, who had played the part of the Elder Brother on that occasion, describing the masque as not openly acknowledged by its author, yet 'a legitimate offspring, so lovely, and so much desired' as to have tired Lawes's pen in making copies – hence his decision to bring it into print (Milton 1957: 86). The second published version (in Milton's 1645 *Poems*) includes a letter from Sir Henry Wotton to Milton praising the masque as 'a dainty piece of entertainment' perused by Wotton with 'singular delight': 'Wherein I should much commend the Tragical part if the Lyrical did not ravish me with a certain Doric delicacy in your Songs and Odes, whereunto I must plainly confess to have seen yet nothing parallel in our Language' (cited from Milton 1937: 216–17).

This much-desired Miltonic daughter was not only dainty and lovely, but also chaste: much twentieth-century critical discussion centred on the poem's celebration of the twin virtues of virginity and chastity, and its exploration of the relationship between them. Featuring as its chief protagonist a Lady lost in a wild wood and made captive by a lascivious enchanter, the masque is Milton's only major work to centre on a woman's experience, and the only one in which the poet seems to have identified unabashedly with that experience. There are many important connections between the Lady's emphasis on chastity and virginity and Milton's own. He had, we will recall, been known during his Cambridge years as 'the Lady of Christ's', and from that period onward was sedulous in defending himself against the least suspicion of sexual licence. In 'Elegy VI' to his boyhood friend Charles Diodati (1629) he had argued that one who would be a poet must live a life 'chaste and free from crime', itself a true poem. He expressed the same sentiment even more vigorously in the self-justificatory passages of *An Apology for Smectymnuus* (1642). The gender implications of Milton's unusual emphasis on male chastity would merit further study, but for our purposes here it suffices to note that, like most middle- or upper-class women of his period, he tied the possession of chastity to the proper exercise of his life's vocation – in their case marriage, in his, poetry.

The form of Milton's masque, furthermore, allied it with literary forms that were particularly associated with women during the period. The *Masque's* deep immersion in motifs from pastoral and romance may well have lent it a feminized aura in the perceptions of a contemporary audience. Delicate pastorals were the particular speciality of Queen Henrietta Maria and her court; indeed, the year before Milton's masque the Queen had been attacked – at least by implication – in William Prynne's *Histrio-Mastix* as a 'notorious whore' for her acting in pastorals at court. The genre of romance was even more strongly associated with women: well before and far beyond *The Countess of Pembroke's Arcadia* and Spenser's *Faerie Queene*, whose primary dedicatee had been Queen Elizabeth I, romances were considered particularly attractive to, and appropriate for, female audiences. Milton's masque has particularly deep and strong affinities with *The Faerie Queene* and, like Spenser, Milton was willing, at least in this one instance, to 'maken memorie' of a woman's 'braue gestes and prowesse martiall' (*Faerie Queene* III. ii. 1, lines 4–5), even if the 'gestes' and 'prowesse' of Milton's Lady are a matter of courage and forbearance, clad in the 'complete steel' of chastity, rather than the more actively militaristic adventures of Spenser's heroine Britomart. What happens if we take seriously the masque's apparent status as the 'daughter' in Milton's canon, as a poem particularly attentive to women?

The occasion of Milton's masque was an important one: it was, according to its 1637 title page, 'Presented at Ludlow Castle 1634: on Michaelmas Night, before the Right Honourable John, Earl of Bridgewater, Viscount Brackley, Lord President of Wales, and One of His Majesty's Most Honourable Privy Council'. Michaelmas was traditionally the date on which newly elected or appointed officials took office, and this particular Michaelmas was the night of the Earl of Bridgewater's formal installation as Lord Lieutenant of Wales and the border counties, though he had been performing many of the functions of the office since 1631. We are not certain how Milton got the commission to write the entertainment for this occasion – most likely through Henry Lawes. But it seems almost certain that he knew the date of the masque's projected performance, for at several points he employs subjects particularly associated with the date of Bridgewater's installation, the Feast of St Michael and All Angels, 29 September. As the archangel Michael was imagined as a special guardian over human affairs; so Milton supplies an 'Attendant Spirit', performed by Henry Lawes, and appearing in the guise of a shepherd, Thyrsis, to guide the Lady and her two brothers (performed by the Earl of Bridgewater's youngest children: Alice, aged fifteen, John, aged eleven, and Thomas, aged nine) to the very celebration taking place that night at Ludlow. There are a number of liturgical echoes between the masque and the lessons proper for the holiday (see Taaffe 1968–9; Hassel 1979: 157–61; Marcus 1986: 201–3). One of the features of Michaelmas, which marked the beginning of the

autumn law term, was a period of 'misrule' during which legal and other governmental hierarchies were briefly flouted and turned upside down; Kidderminster, for
example, which was a scant thirty miles from Ludlow, celebrated a 'lawless hour' in
honour of the holiday. This festive misrule is arguably reflected in the masque
through the person of Comus, the foul enchanter who dances a 'wavering morris'
(line 116) and carouses in the dark forest outside Ludlow with his cohort of
humans made beasts as a result of his powerful magic. As President of the Council
of Wales and Lord Lieutenant of Wales and the counties on the Welsh border,
Bridgewater was King Charles I's regional deputy and surrogate; he was charged
with keeping order and presiding over the Council, an important court of law that
had been granted special jurisdiction over 'unlawful games', adultery and other sexual
offences. So it was particularly appropriate for a masque celebrating Bridgewater's
installation to show his children in victory over the local intemperance of Comus and
his crew. On the level of its public occasion, Milton's masque shows the Earl's children
struggling and finally triumphing over 'sensual Folly, and Intemperance' – that is,
displaying just the mental strength and equipoise that would be required of those
who would sit in judgement in the Council of Wales over the vices of others.

As has been frequently noted of late, however, the masque's theme of victory over
unchastity may have held a more personal meaning for the Earl of Bridgewater and his
family, and here we return to the question of the poem's particular attention to
women. As early as 1960, Milton scholars began to notice a curiously expiatory
quality in *A Masque presented at Ludlow Castle*: David Wilkinson interpreted the
performance as enacting a communal, family 'escape from pollution'. But why,
apart from the matter of the Earl's prominent judicial position, would *this* particular
family have been interested in expiatory ritual? In 1971 Barbara Breasted set the
world of Miltonists abuzz by providing an answer in her '*Comus* and the Castlehaven
Scandal', which argued that Milton's artistic choices, and even some of the likely cuts
for performance, were deeply influenced by a family scandal of three years before. In
1631 the Countess of Bridgewater's brother-in-law, Mervin Touchet, second Earl of
Castlehaven, was beheaded for the crimes of rape and sodomy. It was extremely rare
for a peer of the realm to be executed for sexual offences, but Castlehaven's were
particularly notorious. He was alleged to have regularly committed sodomy on his
male servants, and to have helped one of them rape his own wife, Anne Stanley
Brydges, Lady Chandos, eldest of three daughters of the fifth Earl of Derby and his
wife Alice, the Dowager Countess of Derby in whose honour Milton had written his
brief entertainment *Arcades*, probably in 1631 or 1632. One of the rape victims in the
Castlehaven scandal had therefore been the Countess of Bridgewater's own sister.

Nor had Castlehaven's crimes stopped with his sodomy and alleged encouragement
of the rape of his wife. According to the trial testimony, he was also responsible for the
pollution of his daughter-in-law Elizabeth Brydges, who was married to his son and
heir Lord Audley and living in the same house, and who was fifteen years old at the
time of Castlehaven's trial – the same age as her cousin Alice Egerton at the time of
the performance of Milton's *Masque* at Ludlow. The Earl of Castlehaven was alleged to

have encouraged his most highly favoured servant to have a protracted affair with his own daughter-in-law Elizabeth in hopes of producing baseborn offspring that he intended to make his heirs in place of his estranged son, Lord Audley.

The Earl of Castlehaven steadfastly denied most of the charges against him, and at least some of them may indeed have been manufactured by Audley, who stood to inherit at least some of his father's lands upon the latter's execution. But the reputations of both Lady Castlehaven, the Countess of Bridgewater's sister, and her daughter Elizabeth, Alice's cousin and the Countess's niece, were irredeemably besmirched by the trial and its attendant notoriety. The Castlehaven scandal in all of its lurid seaminess was the talk of the nation during 1631 and for several years thereafter. Indeed, the Dowager Countess of Derby refused to allow either her ruined daughter or her ruined grand-daughter to enter her house until they had been pardoned by the King. The Earl of Bridgewater and his family were not directly implicated in the scandal, but they were certainly caught up in its aftermath, and the records show that Bridgewater offered material support for his wife's sister. Indeed, as Breasted argues (1971: 222 n. 18), it is possible that Bridgewater's formal installation as President of the Council of Wales was delayed at least in part as a result of the Castlehaven affair, which was such a prolonged nightmare for his family. It would be impossible to overestimate the public knowledge of the affair: Milton certainly knew of it, and so, we may be sure, did the audience of the *Masque* at Ludlow, which included court and town officials as well as members of the family. In taking on the subject of chastity in an entertainment for a family that had so recently been clouded by public shame, Milton was taking on a topic of enormous contemporary interest, and requiring the utmost tact.

The masque as performed on Michaelmas Night 1634 was not precisely the masque as Milton had written it, and he would make further revisions before its publication in 1637. In particular, some of Comus's and the Lady's lines alluding most directly to sexual jeopardy were apparently excised from the performance text as represented in the formal presentation copy, the 'Bridgewater manuscript' given to the family after the event. Almost half of the Lady's first speech is missing from the Bridgewater manuscript, including a passage which welcomes 'pure-eyed Faith, white-handed Hope... / And thou unblemished form of Chastity' and expresses the belief that God 'Would send a glistering guardian if need were / To keep my life and honour unassailed' (lines 212–19). Barbara Breasted has argued that this passage was cut by Henry Lawes and/or Milton because they thought it 'indecorous to require a young unmarried noblewoman to talk in public about sex and chastity, particularly when her cousin's loss of honour was probably still one of the most scandalous stories in England' (1971: 207). Similarly, later on in the exchange between Comus and the Lady, her lines referring to the ease with which Comus has deceived her were cut:

> Hast thou betrayed my credulous innocence
> With vizored falsehood, and base forgery,

> And wouldst thou seek again to trap me here
> With liquorish baits fit to ensnare a brute?
>
> (lines 696–9)

Also cut were the most explicitly sexual lines of Comus's response – those referring to 'that same vaunted name virginity' and urging the Lady to sexual indulgence in the usual terms of *carpe diem* poetry: 'If you let slip time, like a neglected rose / It withers on the stalk with languished head. / Beauty is Nature's brag, and must be shown . . .' (lines 737–44).

Of course, there were good dramatic reasons for cutting some of the masque's longer speeches. Many more recent audiences of performances of Milton's masque have no doubt wished for greater brevity as well. But Breasted is surely right to see the masque's relationship with the Castlehaven scandal as one reason for the excision of these particular lines. Milton or Lawes, or perhaps a member of the Egerton family, wanted the more explicitly sexual references toned down, not in the vain hope of rendering invisible any connection between the masque and the family's recent ordeal, but rather out of a recognition that too open reference to the ordeal would come across as strident and overdone. But they evidently did not see any reason for cutting some of the most sexually disturbing lines of the masque. After the Lady's verbal sparring with the enchanter, he proffers his cup in an apparent attempt to force her to drink, but is interrupted by the entrance of the Lady's two brothers, who 'wrest his glass out of his hand, and break it against the ground' (*CSP*: 222). But the rescue is incomplete because their sister is still immanacled, 'In stony fetters fixed, and motionless' in a chair that her saviour Sabrina later describes as a 'marble venomed seat / Smeared with gums of glutinous heat' (lines 818, 915–17).

Milton scholars have had a field day attempting to discover just what Milton meant by this peculiarly disgusting, vaguely sexualized chair in which the Lady is physically imprisoned, despite what she referred to earlier as the unassailable 'freedom of my mind' (line 663). Surely, on the level of topical interpretation we have been considering, the Lady's predicament recalls that of innocent victims of sexual violation – knowing their own guiltlessness and 'free' in their minds, yet besmirched and immobilized by the seamy glue of public sexual innuendo. Unlike her ruined aunt and cousin, the Lady is pure in body as well as mind, yet even that purity does not allow her to escape unscathed. Indeed, her predicament – mental freedom and denial, but some measure of physical jeopardy – links her with victims of rape: not only with her aunt and cousin, but also with a specific fourteen-year-old rape victim for whom her father had spent many hours during the previous years striving to achieve justice (Marcus 1983). The Lady's brothers had debated the power of virginity at considerable length before discovering her predicament, the Elder Brother contending for the radiant power of her virtue, and the Younger Brother fearing her helplessness in the dark wood at night. Both brothers are right. The sorcerer has not 'touched her mind', but her body is no longer under her own power. She requires the aid of Sabrina, a mythographic figure associated with the river Severn in Wales who, according to the standard accounts, was also an innocent victim-by-association of family sexual crimes: the product of a rape, thrown into the river to drown and instead transformed to a healing goddess. (Indeed, rape was a very common problem in the Welsh border country through which the Lady and her brothers are imagined as passing in the masque.)

Through the imprisonment of the Lady, Milton's masque offers an important, healing message about human powerlessness and the possibility of redemption and renewal. The fact that the Lady is released by another woman is also significant, suggesting the healing power of networks of women like the extended family of the powerful and imperious Dowager Countess of Derby, her daughters and her numerous grand-daughters, especially those in the Bridgewater household, seven of whom were already married by the time of the masque's performance. Milton's Lady, her mother and her sisters had their own strongly Protestant religious culture within the Bridgewater household, and I shall have more to say about that later on. Because of its portrayal of survival and transcendence of sexual innuendo, Milton's masque surely carried a powerfully resonant message for the women in the Bridge-water family.

After the appearance of Breasted's work on the Castlehaven scandal, a number of critics took a position made clear in John Creaser's representative title, 'Milton's *Comus*: The Irrelevance of the Castlehaven Scandal' (1984): namely, that the Castle-haven material could safely be set aside on grounds that Milton probably did not intend the connections, that the Bridgewater family would certainly not wish to have been reminded of their painful recent past, and that such bothersome specificities do not, in any case, enrich our understanding of Milton's work. In the words of Cedric Brown, 'To centre on the generally instructive idea of the *komos*, which is also to see the particular relevance of chastity, gives us one way, too, in which we can escape too specific a topical reference to the infamous Castlehaven scandal' (1985: 4). These critical attempts to evade the scandal's relation to Milton's masque have not proved generally persuasive, since the matter remains an important subject in scholarly discussion and even more in teaching of the *Masque*. In fact, they represent special pleading. On some deep level, by brushing the scandal aside these critics wish to preserve the chastity of Milton's poetic 'daughter' and, by extension, the poet's power to control the afterlife of his creative offspring. But authorial and patriarchal values cannot always be transmitted with such pristine intactness, as Milton himself well knew. Much of the power of his treatment of chastity in the Ludlow masque comes from the recognition that chastity is actually a very complicated layering of ideals and one that is on some levels, for all its steel-clad power, quite vulnerable, especially in the lives of women.

Of course Creaser and Brown are right to insist that Milton's masque is about much more than the Castlehaven scandal alone. Once we broaden our range of vision to include a wider seventeenth-century debate on the meaning of chastity within a climate of official tolerance for sports, holiday observances and various forms of artistic 'licence', we can identify myriad ways in which the masque's treatment of the strength and fragility of chastity resonate with a national debate. Milton's *Masque* is an astonishingly rich showcase of music, dance, poetry, and masquing disguise and ceremony, but it questions the value of all of its component arts in a way that is ingenious and original. As has frequently been noted, the *Masque* contributes to the national controversy surrounding the Book of Sports, first issued by James I in 1618 and re-issued by Charles I in 1633. The Book of Sports attempted to negotiate between strict puritan sabbatarianism and judicial attempts to restrain Sunday and holiday pastimes on the one hand, and Catholic and ceremonial Anglican love of ritualism and old pastimes – like 'good cheer' at Christmas, morris dancing and maygames, and festive church wakes – on the other hand. The Book of Sports carefully defined the circumstances under which Sunday and holiday festivities should be lawful within the English church. Opponents of the Book pointed out, among many other arguments, that the practice of old customs like going into the woods a-maying was scarcely an innocent pastime. For example, they asserted a connection between the practice of maying customs and a rise nine months later in the rates of bastard births. In 1633 and the ensuing years, attempts to enforce tolerance for what was derisively known in hostile circles as the 'dancing book' encountered fierce opposition. Dancing, festivity and even masquing itself became strongly politicized activities.

Milton's Ludlow entertainment, composed only a year after Charles I's re-issue of the Book of Sports, bears some resemblance to Ben Jonson's *Pleasure Reconciled to Virtue*, which had been performed at court on Epiphany 1618, in honour of James I's first publication of the Book of Sports. Jonson's masque was not yet in print, but Milton could have encountered it in manuscript or through contemporary descriptions. Like Milton's, Jonson's masque is poised between competing varieties of pleasure; and, like Milton's, it features an 'antimasque' of Comus. Jonson's Comus, however, is a much cruder fellow than Milton's: he enters at the masque's very beginning and offers his boisterous delights in a 'Hymn' that begins like a typical mummers' play: 'Room, room, make room for the bouncing belly' (Orgel and Strong 1973, 1: 285). Jonson figures the reconciliation of pleasure and virtue through a series of tests of Hercules, who on one level represents James I in his 'mortal body' as a fallible human leader, who has to vanquish first excess (in the person of Comus) and then dearth (a menacing throng of mean-spirited and seditious pygmies), in order to discover virtue. But given Hercules's well-known mythic status, the outcome of his struggles is fairly predictable; similarly, the later parts of the masque are suffused with another, more transcendent representation of royal reforming energies in the form of Hesperus, a force of nature rather than a person, who gives an aura of relentless inevitability to the masquers' choice of virtue.

Milton's masque, by contrast, is open-ended. Despite the Earl of Bridgewater's close ties to the court, there is no figure within the masque that can be reliably identified with a Stuart monarch. The Earl himself is introduced by the Attendant Spirit as 'A noble peer of mickle trust, and power' who bears a 'new-entrusted sceptre' over an 'old, and haughty nation proud in arms' (lines 31–6), but Milton is remarkably reticent about who has entrusted Bridgewater with this 'sceptre' (see Marcus 1986: 179–87). The saving magic of the masque comes not from the Earl or from the distant monarch, but from Sabrina, an indigenous figure associated with the Welsh landscape rather than with court or king. Milton's masque is cartographic in the same sense as Michael Drayton's *Poly-Olbion* and other seventeenth-century treatments of the British landscape that marginalize royal authority by charting the land as a network of competing local affiliations rather than as spokes radiating out from a central hub of power and influence (see Helgerson 1992: 105–47). The Earl of Bridgewater is celebrated as an independent locus of authority, not as an agent of royal power.

Moreover, the placement of Milton's Comus, so much more refined and aristocratic than Jonson's, is interesting. The enchanter does not appear 'up front' at the beginning of the masque, as would be expected of the typical courtly antimasque, where vice can be readily and safely identified. Instead, he is enfolded deep within a 'drear wood', and within a series of lies and disguises that are impenetrable even to the virtuous except through sad experience. Unlike Jonson's Hercules, Milton's Lady is not readily legible as a mythic figure, though she has frequently been likened to Spenser's Una from *The Faerie Queene* and to the Woman in the Wilderness in the Book of Revelation (see Scoufos 1974). The Lady plays herself, Alice Egerton, and stands in for every virtuous woman who has ever been thrown into a situation for which nothing in her past could prepare her. By comparison with Jonson's production and most other court masques, Milton's masque is frighteningly devoid of markers by which virtuous conduct can be measured collectively and defined in advance. Even Thyrsis, its guardian angel figure, has to improvise and take risks to get things to come out right for his charges. *Comus*'s long lyrical passages and debates, its uncharacteristic emphasis on dramatic tension and narrative, break through the usual masque's sense of closure and mastery into a more strenuous moral space that requires constant individual vigilance and careful judgement of every human encounter.

If masquing seems a rather difficult pursuit in *Comus*, this may be in part because the choice whether or not to be a masquer was an active issue within the Egerton family. It is well known that each of the three children who performed in *Comus* had previously danced in masques at court, but it is perhaps less well known that one of Alice Egerton's sisters had refused to participate in court masques, and another sister had wished she had the courage to refuse. The Countess and her daughters appear to have had strong affiliations with contemporary puritanism, while the Earl and at least the elder son were more orthodox, though probably anti-Arminian and anti-Laudian. The heir, John Egerton, was a strong royalist and Church of England man during the English Civil War, writing in his copy of Milton's *Pro Populo Anglicano Defensio* 'Liber igni, Author furcâ, dignissimi' ('The book is most deserving of burning, the author of the gallows'); several of his sisters, on the other hand, ended up as nonconformists (Marcus 1986: 173; see also Collinges 1669). Many of the differing opinions in the Book of Sports controversy existed within the Earl's own family, and Milton's challenge was to create an entertainment that could accommodate and challenge their diverse opinions about the moral valuation of the cornucopia of arts and pastimes incorporated within it.

Milton's masque not only reworks elements of *Pleasure Reconciled to Virtue*; it also incorporates echoes of more recent masques in which family members had participated, and interestingly enough, some of the clearest echoes of these entertainments are embedded in the language of the necromancer Comus. Like the court masque, his realm is of the night and the wee hours of the morning. His beckoning of his followers to nocturnal delights strongly recollects the invitations to dancing and revelry in the Stuart court masque. So does his later use of the *carpe diem* motif to cajole his audience to be receptive to his enchantments, though those lines were cut from the actual performance at Ludlow. More tellingly, his speech welcoming revelry and likening the masquers to stars in the heavens recalls two masques in which members of the Egerton family had recently danced. Comus banishes 'Strict Age, and sour Severity' (line 109), and sets up a typically Stuart dichotomy between lesser mortals and the high-minded masquers themselves:

> We that are of purer fire
> Imitate the starry quire,
> Who in their nightly watchful spheres,
> Lead in swift round the months and years.
> (lines 111–14)

Similarly, in Aurelian Townshend's *Tempe Restored* (1632), Alice Egerton had played the part of one of the 'influences of the stars' who presaged the appearance of the main masquers, all of whom descended from the heavens in imitation of astral bodies. Townshend's masque also features Comus's mother Circe, along with her brutish crew of victims, in his antimasque. Milton's Comus is Circe's immediate offspring, but in Milton's masque it is Comus, the antimasque figure, who takes on the astral imagery (Orgel and Strong 1973, 2: 479–83).

Comus's self-descriptive reference to 'purer fire' also comes from a recent Caroline masque, Thomas Carew's extravaganza *Coelum Britannicum*, enacted in February 1634, less than a year before Milton's masque. In *Coelum Britannicum* Thomas and John Egerton had played the role of torchbearers to main masquers clad with 'purer fire' tempered by Jove (Charles I) to fit them for their roles in the heavens as 'new stars' (Orgel and Strong 1973, 2: 567–80; quotation from p. 578). The reference suggests a strange congruence between the Egertons as torchbearers in Carew's masque, and the beasts attendant upon Milton's Comus, the attendants in both cases partaking of their masters' 'purer fire'. Comus's invitation to revelry in Milton's version has just enough echoes of recent Caroline entertainments to suggest a strong affinity between his tipsy, decadent and finally menacing solemnities and the masquing ideology of the court. Initially disguised as a simple shepherd, he eventually reveals himself as a libertine courtier and proponent of Charles I's Book of Sports, inviting all comers to seemingly innocent games – a 'wavering morris', and 'merry wakes and pastimes' (lines 116, 121) – that modulate almost imperceptibly into sexual seduction and spiritual death.

Given Milton's care in associating courtly entertainment with dangerous revelry, we might suppose that he would stand unequivocally behind the Lady's scornful rejection of Comus's blandishments, and indeed, in successive revisions of the text the poet gradually strengthened and extended her arguments against Comus's case in favour of epicurean indulgence. Comus contends for revelry with an argument with subterranean connections to the biblical parable of the talents – a text to which Milton returned again and again over the years. Natural abundance, the enchanter contends, was granted for human enjoyment, and failure to 'spend' and use what was offered so freely would represent a churlish denial of divine praise: '[I]f all the world / Should in a pet of temperance feed on pulse, / Drink the clear stream, and nothing wear but frieze, / The all-giver would be unthanked, would be unpraised' (lines 719–22). To this clever defence of conspicuous consumption, the Lady responds with a proto-ecological, and even proto-communist, argument: Nature, 'good cateress', does not want her children to be 'riotous / With her abundance' but rather favours 'spare temperance' through her 'sober laws':

> If every just man that now pines with want
> Had but a moderate and beseeming share
> Of that which lewdly-pampered Luxury
> Now heaps upon some few with vast excess,
> Nature's full blessings would be well-dispensed
> In unsuperfluous even proportion,
> And she no whit encumbered with her store,
> And then the giver would be better thanked,
> His praise due paid,
>
> (lines 762–75)

This is good, sober puritan doctrine of the type that might well have appealed to the more precise among the Egerton women; but it is not necessarily the masque's final word.

To us in the early twenty-first century, an argument based on a sense of the relative scarcity of natural resources is compelling, and it has at least some effect on Comus, who claims to 'fear / Her words set off by some superior power' (lines 799–800). Yet the Lady's powerful rhetoric cannot keep her free from the more powerful rod of the enchanter. If Comus's arguments had implicated the culture of the Stuart court masque in the rites of Hecate, the Lady's replies leave her immobilized and immanacled – incapable of the active energy against vice that led her to spar with Comus in the first place. The purpose of the debate is not to show good in triumph against evil, but to demonstrate the complexity of the problem – as it was disputed, no doubt, within the Bridgewater household, and at length in the nation at large: advocates of the Book of Sports pleaded for the essential innocence of traditional pastimes and for the 'freedom to be merry'; opponents felt obliged to oppose the 'freedom' and the merriment in order to preserve their innocence; neither position was altogether satisfactory. How could one be free and still chaste?

As I suggested initially, Milton identifies strongly with the Lady, and her dilemma was his as well. In his early works, we frequently find him awkwardly poised between a desire to experience life's pleasures and a fear of self-pollution. On a psychological level, the immobility of the Lady in the enchanter's chair can be seen as representing a psychological stalemating that Milton himself sometimes felt. As a remedy, the Attendant Spirit suggests Haemony (line 637), a mysteriously allegorical herb whose meaning has puzzled critics and led to many ingenious and notorious interpretations. It has been claimed to represent 'Platonic philosophy', or Christian grace, or temperance, or Christian knowledge, or the blood of Christ, or skill-combined-with-truth, or the holy scripture – to mention only some of the possibilities (see Woodhouse and Bush 1972c: 932–8; Brown 1985: 104–15). In the Ludlow performance of the masque, the seemingly allegorical lines describing Haemony's transformed appearance 'in another country' from 'small unsightly root' to 'a bright golden flower' were cut, so that, as Brown has complained, 'the audience seems to have been taken straight from the darkish, prickly leaves to the name Haemony' (1985: 113). If ever there was a crux to demonstrate that no single interpretation will ever satisfy everyone, the meaning of Haemony is that crux. My own inclination is to think botanically rather than allegorically, and the closest botanical match to Milton's Haemony is, as Charlotte Otten has shown, hypericum or andros-aimon (haemony), a plant now found on every pharmacist's shelves and called St John's Wort. In Milton's time, hypericum was strongly associated with the sun and gathered on Midsummer Eve, the Feast of St John the Baptist. Fittingly, since it had connections with light and regeneration, it was believed to have special powers over the demonic: 'a plant whose botanical features, stamped with the signature of the sun, enabled it to quell the forces of darkness; whose efficacy as a device able to detect sorcerers and thereby protect a virgin's chastity was universally acknowledged; and whose potency as a demonifuge was established from antiquity by herbalists and theologians and attested to by Milton's collaborator Henry Lawes', who had used the plant more than once against demons (Otten 1975: 95). In our own culture, the demon of depression has replaced the Satanic hordes, and hypericum is a widely used and frequently effective remedy against depression. Was it used against 'melancholy' in the seventeenth century? Did Milton try it himself? Would it be utterly irresponsible to suggest that he, and perhaps others, employed the plant against the debilitating and imprisoning effects of too much study or too much self-denial? He had recently written a complaint about the effects of too much solitary devotion to learning, by which 'a man cuts himselfe off from all action & becomes the most helplesse, pusilanimous & unweapon'd creature...either to defend & be usefull to his friends, or to offend his enimies' (*CPW* I: 319; see also Norbrook 1984a: 256). Hypericum's strong associations with the sun (which for many people also acts as an antidepressant) and with the banishing of the demons of darkness makes all of these speculations about Milton's interest in haemony highly attractive, if incapable of proof.

Significantly, in the masque the two brothers employ Haemony successfully to break the enchanter's cup and disperse its contents harmlessly on the ground. The herb at least temporarily defeats Comus's ability to recruit more humans to his beastly crew by appealing to their 'fond intemperate thirst' (line 67); but intemperate thirst was never the Lady's problem. Nor, so far as we know, was it Milton's. And so we have circled back to the saving power of Sabrina, this time in a wider context that includes the tarnish on the Bridgewater family as a result of the Castlehaven scandal, but also the problem of sexual vulnerability more generally and the reconciliation of chastity and freedom. On this broader level, the Lady's imprisonment seems to relate to the repression of desire: her strenuous efforts to preserve her chastity against a powerful – and courtly – enchanter leave her immobilized and empty, unable to extricate herself under her own power. Almost as much ink has been spilt in an effort to determine Sabrina's allegorical significance as in the decoding of Haemony. Here, as in discussing the herb, I am less interested in the abstract principles with which she can be associated – though she surely functions as a bearer of divine grace – and more interested in articulating what she brings to the Lady's situation. With the invocation of Sabrina, an intense poetic lyricism combined with playfulness and festivity enter the masque for the first time in an innocuous form. Sabrina is in many ways the counterpart of Comus: as he carried a soothing cup, she carries vials of healing liquors; she, like him, is associated with music and dancing, surrounded by lovely, dancing 'Nymphs' by night, and grateful shepherds by day, who 'at their festivals / Carol her goodness loud in rustic lays, / And throw sweet garland wreaths into her stream' (lines 847–9). With the invocation of Sabrina, all of the beauty and arts that appeared to have been contaminated in their essence by Comus and his courtly crew flood back into the masque in a new, wholesome setting that re-invents them and presents them to the Lady and her brothers as utterly fresh and uncorrupted. Comus is still at loose somewhere in the forest: his foul blandishments can still ensnare other hapless travellers. But the children are released from his power, and can proceed to the court of their parents at Ludlow, and participate without fear of taint – and to whatever degree each finds individually acceptable – in the dancing and festivities surrounding the Earl's installation.

As we have already noted, Milton's masque has many Spenserian echoes, and those become particularly rich and evocative in the entertainment's final scenes: the drowning Sabrina's revival in 'aged Nereus' hall' (line 834), and his attendant daughters the Nereides (*Faerie Queene* III. iv. 34–44); the references in the masque's epilogue to the Hesperian gardens, to the dancing graces, and to Venus and Adonis paired with Cupid and Psyche, as in Spenser's Garden of Adonis (*Faerie Queene* III. vi. 29–50), where their erotic joy in each other is rendered perpetual, the source of Adonis's astonishing creativity as the 'Father of all formes' and also of enduring '*Pleasure*, the daughter of *Cupid* and *Psyche* late'. These final segments of the masque are also particularly evocative of the writings of the so-called seventeenth-century Spenserians like

Drayton, who told the story of Sabrina 'in her imperial Chair' of shining crystal in his *Poly-Olbion*, and William Browne, who provided a pattern for the Attendant Spirit's blessing of Sabrina's stream in *Britannia's Pastorals* (see notes to Milton 1937, pp. 264, 266). As David Norbrook has pointed out, poets writing in Spenser's highly wrought allegorical and apocalyptic Elizabethan style under the Stuart monarchs tended to look back upon the reign of Elizabeth as a time of appropriate militancy against Catholicism and against 'lukewarmness' within the English church. In terms of seventeenth-century policy, the Spenserians tended to be alienated from the main-stream of court culture, and to identify with the 'hotter sorts of Protestants' who deplored the nation's dominant policy of pacifism *vis-à-vis* threats to reformed religion at home and abroad (Norbrook 1984a: 195–266). By reviving the Spenserian mode so effectively in *Comus*, Milton aligned the Earl of Bridgewater and his family with this literary current of estrangement from the dominant trend of Caroline politics and courtly culture. As we have seen, the alignment worked particularly well in terms of the reforming allegiances of women in the family; indeed, the aged Dowager Countess of Derby, its matriarch, was a surviving remnant of the heroic Elizabethan age of Protestant militancy.

Many critics have seen particularly strong echoes of Spenser in the final lines of the masque, where the Attendant Spirit counsels his auditory,

> Mortals that would follow me,
> Love Virtue, she alone is free,
> She can teach ye how to climb
> Higher than the sphery chime;
> Or if Virtue feeble were,
> Heaven itself would stoop to her.
> (lines 1017–22)

Spenser expresses a similar sentiment in Book III of *The Faerie Queene*, after Florimel's rescue from the lustful fisherman:

> See how the heauens of voluntary grace,
> And soueraine fauour towards chastity,
> Doe succour send to her distressed cace:
> So much high God doth innocence embrace.
> (III. viii. 29, lines 2–5)

By ending his masque on a strongly Spenserian note, Milton underlines the strongly Spenserian quality of his work, and its emphasis in common with the earlier poet on militancy in defence of truth and chastity. But Milton's conclusion, as we might suspect, takes on particular resonance in light of the specific controversies over chastity that fermented during his own time – most especially the Castlehaven scandal, and the polarization of opinion that surrounded Charles I's republication of the Book of Sports, by which elements of the court and conservative Anglicans sought to promote traditional holiday sports and pastimes on grounds that the people deserved the 'freedom to be merry'. The conclusion of the Ludlow masque turns the formulation around: 'Love Virtue, she alone is free,' and when virtue is loved, freedom will follow, though not, perhaps, without the aid of heaven.

As I have been arguing throughout, Milton's masque has a special status among his works because of its attention to, and sympathy for, women. At a time when mainstream puritan opinion tended to be highly patriarchal, Milton's entertainment espouses a freer and more aristocratic sense of women's enablement and potential cultural impact. At a time when most imaginative literature still promulgated the ethos that a violated or sexually compromised woman had to commit suicide in order to prove her chastity, Milton shows a woman in some of the same jeopardy being healed and restored to her family through the ministrations of another woman. Shortly after William Prynne had been punished for calling women actors 'notorious whores', Milton places an aristocratic woman at the centre of an important dramatic and political event. Indeed, the masque's many intimations of alliance between the Lady lost in the drear woods, Spenser's Una representing true faith or the true church, and Revelation's Woman in the Wilderness place Milton's Lady in the position of spokeswoman for a cause well beyond her own chastity. She speaks for a militant Protestantism that is not content to rest with half measures, and that will, the poet suggests, carry forward into the next generation the strenuous values inherited from the Dowager Countess of Derby and the tradition she represented. Indeed, the Lady's particular emphasis on virginity represents an interesting link with the Virgin Queen Elizabeth: reformers who were alienated from court values and policy during the early Stuart era often invoked the image of the dead queen as a silent rebuke to the present, and there may be elements of that idealization in Milton's portrayal of the virgin Lady. However we choose to interpret its specific resonances, it is clear that Milton's masque represented a tribute to the Earl of Bridgewater, but also a perhaps even warmer tribute to the zeal and virtue of women in the Bridgewater family. At a time when they were still recovering from the seamy revelations of the Castlehaven scandal, Milton reaffirmed their spiritual strength through his portrayal of the Lady, and forged a strong imaginative alliance between their 'reformed' spirituality and his own hopes for the nation's future.

BIBLIOGRAPHY

Writings

Milton (1937, 1957, 1973); Orgel and Strong (1973).

References for Further Reading

Breasted (1971); Brown (1985); Christopher (1976); Collinges (1669); Cox (1977); Creaser (1984a); Diekhoff (1968); Fletcher, Angus (1971); Hassel (1979); Helgerson (1992); Herrup (1999); Lindley (1984); Marcus (1983, 1986); McGee (1976); McGuire (1983); Mundhenk (1975); Norbrook (1984a); Otten (1975); Scoufos (1974); Taaffe (1968–9); Walker (1988); Wilkinson (1960); Woodhouse and Bush (1972c).

15
'Lycidas'

Stella P. Revard

Milton's pastoral monody 'Lycidas' records a moment in history – 1637 – when a young pastor-poet and learned college friend, Edward King, met an untimely death by drowning, and when Archbishop Laud was imposing an oppressive programme of censorship and ecclesiastical reform on England. 'Lycidas' begins with a shaking, the shattering of the poet's laurel crown, as well as a shaking of the religious and national hopes of England: 'Yet once more, O ye laurels and once more / Ye myrtles brown, with ivy never sere' (lines 1–2). Included within the personal crisis, the necessity of a young poet taking on a poetic task that he feels unready to shoulder, to compose a song to lament Lycidas, 'dead ere his prime' (line 8) is also the shadow of national crisis. God is shaking the nation, 'yet once more', as the prophetic text in Hebrews proclaims: 'Yet once more I shake not the earth only, but also heaven. And this word, Yet once more,' explains the apostle, 'signifieth the removing of those things that are shaken, as of things that are made, that those things which cannot be shaken may remain' (Hebrews 12: 26–7).

'Lycidas' is an apocalyptic vision set in the woods and pastures of an Arcadian England, a lament for a nation enclosed within a personal statement of grief, loss and disappointment. It is also a pastoral song, begun at dawn as a shepherd-poet wanders imaginatively across the landscape of his country and concluded at sunset as he fixes his eyes upon the western bay where Edward King, the Lycidas of the title, drowned. Yet 'Lycidas' also moves beyond the geographic borders of Britain, from the furthest Hebrides to St Michael's Mount in Cornwall, where the apocalyptic angel who guards the shores of Protestant England looks towards Catholic Spain. Although situated in the present, the poem glances backward in time to the mythic pastoral past and forward to the promised fulfilment of all time in the biblical heaven of Revelation. Imitating the ancient pastoral of Theocritus, Virgil, Bion and Moschus and the more modern pastoralism of Mantuan, Spenser and other Renaissance poets, Milton introduces a biblical vein into a predominately Greco-Latin poetic form. Thus, while adopting for himself the voice of a simple shepherd swain, he includes within 'Lycidas' the solemn tones of classical authority and the thunder of biblical prophecy.

A draft manuscript of 'Lycidas' that records the stages of composition and revision exists in the Trinity College Library in Cambridge. The poem was printed three times in Milton's lifetime: first in the 1638 Cambridge volume that commemorated Edward King, next in a revised version in Milton's own *Poems* (1645), and finally in the expanded *Poems* (1673), re-issued in the penultimate year of Milton's life. Each printing presents the reader with a different context for the poem. In 1638 'Lycidas' is part of an official commemorative publication put out by Cambridge University, which is, like Milton's own 1645 and 1673 *Poems*, a double book, comprising twin volumes with separate title pages. The first volume – *Justa Edovardo King naufrago* – consists of a group of twenty poems in Latin and three in Greek; the second, *Obsequies to the Memorie of Mr. Edward King* (with its own title page), a collection of twelve poems in English addressed to Edward King and two to his sister, with 'Lycidas' the last poem both of the English collection and of the double book. Milton's decision to write in English is a deliberate one; he might just as well have joined the more numerous university poets in the Latin volume. He also makes a deliberate choice of pastoral monody for his form, hearkening back perhaps to a genre that university poets had used in the volumes of commemorative verse that came forth after the death of Sir Philip Sidney. Sidney was commemorated both as Daphnis and as Lycidas in volumes published by Oxford University. As a university poet Milton may have remembered the pastoralism of the Oxford volumes and the honorary pastoral name given to England's poet-patriot who had died defending Protestantism in the Netherlands.

Like many of the poems in the 1638 volume, Milton's 'Lycidas' is heavily classical in reference. Allusions to Apollo, the muses, Orpheus, the gods of the sea Neptune and Thetis, and even the dolphins are not rare in the poems of the King collection. Unlike the other poems, however, 'Lycidas' uses these classical references to construct a fictive narrative, in which Edward King assumes the character of a shepherd-poet, pastor to his flock and a would-be lover, who died young. As poet Lycidas is connected to Lycian Apollo, the patron god of poets; as pastor to St Peter, the head of the Christian church, which King would have served. In its 1638 version there is no headnote to the poem. 'Lycidas' begins without the usual pastoral frame that introduces poem, speaker, and occasion. We must surmise from what he says who the speaker is and what is his relationship to the title character, who must not 'flote upon his watry bear / Unwept' (lines 12–13). The speaker is not identified until the closing frame, when he is called the 'uncouth Swain', who has been singing to the oaks and rills. Yet from the beginning it is clear that he shares with Lycidas the roles of poet, pastor and lover, as the laurel, ivy and myrtle, the emblems of the gods Apollo, Bacchus and Venus plucked in the opening lines, indicate. He shares also a past as a scholar-shepherd at Cambridge. In coming to terms with Lycidas's death and in singing for him, the poet-speaker is exorcizing his own doubts about his calling as poet-pastor as well as justifying his trust in the 'god' who struck Lycidas down in an untimely fashion and who permits unworthy pastors to serve in his place.

In 1645 and in 1673, Milton provides a headnote to 'Lycidas', in which he identifies the genre of the poem as monody – an ode for a single voice, as Renaissance critics such as J. C. Scaliger defined it. He also identifies himself as author-speaker and describes the circumstances that brought it forth: 'In this monody the author bewails a learned friend, unfortunately drowned in his passage from Chester on the Irish Seas, 1637' (*CSP*: 243). While Milton names himself as author, he leaves Edward King unnamed, rendering him only as a 'learned friend'. He had signed 'Lycidas' in the 1638 *Obsequies* only with his initials, J. M., whereas King, by context, was clearly identified as subject. The 1645 version reverses the situation, with Milton claiming authorship, but leaving King anonymous. The headnote concludes by claiming that the poem also 'by occasion foretells the ruin of our corrupted clergy then in their height'. In 1645 Milton places the stamp of fulfilled prophecy on his pastoral monody.

Having introduced speaker, occasion and subject in the opening section, Milton begins the dirge proper with an invocation to the muses that imitates a refrain used by Theocritus, Bion and Virgil: 'Begin then, sisters of the sacred well' (line 15). By echoing his predecessors, Milton informs us how deeply rooted in classical tradition this poem is – and how consciously so. Most of the principal characters are classical ones: the muses the poet invokes, the satyrs and fauns who dance to the pastoral pipes, old Damoetas who hears their song, and the ever-present nymphs of wood and water. The archetypal poet of classical literature, Orpheus, is alluded to and his poetical father Apollo makes an appearance. When he denies that the natural elements destroyed Lycidas, Milton does so by bringing on the gods of wind and water that represent them: Neptune's herald Triton and the god of the winds, Aeolus, whom he calls by his elegant Greek patronymic, Hippotades; the nymph Panope plays upon the sea with her sisters while Lycidas drowns. Moreover, Cambridge University appears in pastoral dress as the river god Camus. The fringes of his mantle and bonnet are inwrought with figures that are 'like to that sanguine flower inscribed with woe' (line 106), the hyacinth, into which the grieving Apollo transformed another youth untimely plucked.

Throughout 'Lycidas' Milton practises the craft of a pastoral shepherd-poet; he even refers obliquely to the most famous practitioners of that art by apostrophizing the Syracusan fountain Arethuse of Theocritus's Sicily and the river Mincius that flows near Virgil's Mantua: 'O Fountain Arethuse and thou honored flood, / Smooth-sliding Mincius' (lines 85–6). In their idylls and eclogues, Theocritus and Virgil depict pastoral work and pastime, and in Idyll 7 and in Eclogue 9 respectively introduce us to two countrymen named Lycidas. The nymphs Neaera and Amaryllis also belong to this tradition, although it is more probable that Milton is also imitating Renais-sance models here, such as Joannes Secundus's cruel Neaera of his Orpheus eclogue and *Basia*, and Giambattista Amalteo's fair Amaryllis of his own pastoral 'Lycidas'. Although ancient and Renaissance pastoral do not fully define the pastoral for Milton, they are the touchstones by which he measures his art. Pastoral provides Milton with a well-defined poetic tradition that exploits a closeness to the natural world, an immediacy of human contacts and a universality of human values; it is also a medium that permits reference to political and social complexities under the guise of speaking of rural life. This classical tradition had its counterpart in the Bible – in the Psalms, the Book of Ezekiel and the Gospels, where good shepherds, false hirelings and threatening wolves are spoken of. Renaissance pastoral sometimes brought the two traditions together, as with the sixteenth-century Italian poet-monk Mantuan and the English poet Spenser, who use pastoral to criticize the abuses of the Roman and the English churches.

Despite its many classical references, however, 'Lycidas' is a profoundly English poem. It is not just the classical muses and Apollo who are invoked, but the native Druid bards and the nymphs of Anglesey, who play on the steep ridges of their holy island, Britain's Parnassus. The Welsh river Dee spreads its 'wizard stream' (line 55) alongside the swift Hebrus, which bore the gory head of the dead Orpheus to the Lesbian shore, and the Arcadian river Alpheus, who followed his beloved Arethusa to Sicily. Milton continually reminds us that we are in a Britain that in the past has nurtured its Druid bards and Protestant pastors. While classical allusion makes 'Lycidas' international, Milton roots his poem in place with references not to far-off Helicon or Aetna but to locales on the British map.

Early in the poem Milton remembers an idyllic Cambridge by portraying its landscape in terms that recall ancient pastoral. This is the part of 'Lycidas' that Samuel Johnson most vociferously objected to as unskilful and improbable. Each day the shepherd-students metaphorically drive afield and feed their flocks, and at evening play their 'rurall ditties . . . / Tempered to the oaten flute' (lines 32–3). In this picture of idealized shepherd life, the followers of Bacchus – the rough satyrs and fauns – join with the poet-shepherds in song and dance. Yet only a little later, with Lycidas's death, the landscape turns barren, and the shepherds can only bewail his absence. Now the poet refers to different followers of Bacchus: not to his merry fauns and satyrs, but to the Bacchantes, who savagely destroyed the poet Orpheus, whom universal nature lamented even as it now laments the young poet Lycidas. The loss of Lycidas not only leaves nature desolate but also produces an alteration in the so-called shepherd life that threatens the calling both of poet and pastor.

'Lycidas' is a poem that asks questions, the first of which is the innocent query, 'Who would not sing for Lycidas?' (line 10) – answered immediately with the imperative that one poet must sing for another. We know that Theocritus's Thyrsis sang for the mythic Daphnis in Idyll 1; Bion for Moschus; Virgil for his friend Gallus in Eclogue 10. So too, Milton must sing for Lycidas/King in hopes that hereafter a future poet, 'some gentle Muse', may 'favour [his] destined urn' (lines 19–20). The next question comes after the intervening passage of pastoral mourning. Although nature joins with the shepherds in grieving for the poet whose song will no more be heard in wood or copse, the deities of nature, the local nymphs of grove and stream, did nothing to save Lycidas from his untimely death. In Idyll 1 Theocritus had asked the nymphs of Greece and Sicily where they were when Daphnis died, whether they were on Pindus or Aetna or by the side of Peneus. Replacing these with Mona and

Deva, the Latin names for Anglesey and the river Dee that flowed near Chester, King's embarkation point for Ireland, Milton queries the local nymphs. But it is a futile question to which he himself replies: 'Had ye been there . . . for what could that have done?' (line 57). Moreover, this question gives way to the still more futile inquiry, only half articulated, 'What could the Muse herself that Orpheus bore' (line 58). All these questions relate intimately to the so-called reasons for Lycidas/King's death. The poets of *Justa Edovardo King* had also asked why Apollo had not saved the poet or divine Providence the young pastor; most of Milton's fellow poets responded by urging pious submission to fate or to the will of heaven. Milton, however, will not be so easily answered. The next question he poses is a curious *non sequitur*, but one so natural that it seems almost inevitable. He shifts from questioning why Lycidas died to asking why he himself should continue to serve a calling, 'the homely slighted shepherd's trade' (line 65), which offers scant reward.

That the poet-speaker of the monody should identify closely with the dead Lycidas is to be expected. He had stressed in the Cambridge section the mutual pursuits that joined them, as he repeated the words, 'Together both . . . both together' (lines 25–7). The *I–he* of the opening lines gives way to *we* and *our*, as he describes their Cambridge experience, and finally to *thou*, as he laments Lycidas's absence: 'But O the heavy change, now thou art gone, / Now thou art gone, and never must return!' (lines 37–8). None the less, it is with a little surprise that we note that the poet seems less concerned that Lycidas has died without fulfilling his potential than that he himself might also die early and unfulfilled. Forgetting the dead man, he is impelled by the urgency of his own demands. Is it worth it to continue to 'meditate' the thankless Muse? Is it not better to do, he asks, as others do: 'To sport with Amaryllis in the shade, / Or with the tangles of Neaera's hair?' (lines 68–9), here making explicit the amatory dimension hinted at with the plucking of Venus's myrtle in the opening lines. Is it worth it to live laborious days (in hopes of the fulfilment of fame) when the 'blind Fury' may come suddenly and slit 'the thin-spun life' (lines 75–6)?

At its centre 'Lycidas' poses questions without clear answers. To reply to them Milton adopts a particular poetic strategy. The poet changes from the singer of a pastoral lament to the speaker of a dramatic narrative, as several poetical voices, different from his own, from Apollo to St Peter, in sequence take centre stage. This section of 'Lycidas' has often been described as digressive, and so it is – in a way that Pindaric ode, a genre of lyric poetry that was becoming popular in the seventeenth century, also is digressive.

Pindaric ode was famous not only for its digressions, but also for its abrupt shifts of subject, its unusual junctures, its use of illustrative myth and its multiple poetic voices. The influence of Pindaric ode may account in fact both for the unusual metrics and the unusual poetic strategies that Milton adopts in 'Lycidas'. Pindar's metrics had influenced Italian canzone, and either directly or indirectly influenced Milton, as he sought for a new lyric model for 'Lycidas' that would permit unusual rhyme schemes, unrhymed lines, and alternate long and short lines. Structurally, 'Lycidas' also has some affinity to Pindaric ode, which, as Renaissance critics explain, consists of interlinking sections, following a basic five-part pattern – exordium, proposition, confirmation, digression and epilogue. 'Lycidas' adheres roughly to a similar pattern. In the epilogue, moreover, Milton calls 'Lycidas' a 'Doric lay' (line 189). Both the odes of Pindar and the idylls of Theocritus were composed in Doric dialect. The swain who sings the Doric lay 'touched the tender stops of various quills' (line 188), these 'quills' being the different modes of composition he employed, Pindaric ode and pastoral eclogue among them.

Like Pindar's odes, 'Lycidas' is an occasional poem in which so-called digression plays a major role. Pindar's own odes were produced to celebrate athletic victory, but Pindaric ode had been imitated during the Renaissance by continental and English poets alike to celebrate many kinds of victories as well as to lament the dead. In his Pindaric ode for Cary and Morison, for example, Ben Jonson both celebrates the living and commemorates the dead. Even when celebrating one occasion, moreover, Pindar frequently 'digresses' in order to probe questions basic to human life – the meaning of victory and defeat, joy and sadness, life and death, good and evil. He questions human beings' relationship to the divine, and he also queries the reasons for the gods' favour towards and censure of human beings. In the so-called digressions of his odes, Pindar often alludes to mythic figures, sometimes briefly, sometimes in longer interpolated narratives. Sometimes he even brings mythic figures forth and permits them to speak for themselves. Milton's compressed retelling of the Orpheus story, for example, resembles a brief Pindaric myth. As with Pindar's brief myths, Milton does not tell the whole of Orpheus's story, only its horrific conclusion. We do not see the poet who could move trees and rocks with the sound of his voice; only the 'gory visage' (line 62) of the decapitated head sent down the swift Hebrus. The mythic allusion serves as a bitter reply to the poet's helpless querying; neither nature nor the Muse saves the poet. It also anticipates the more rigorous questioning of fate that follows.

Milton uses another 'Pindaric' tactic to answer the shepherd-swain's demands, bringing Phoebus Apollo forth to reply. As the patron god of poetry, he is one of the figures most frequently invoked in the poems of *Justa Edovardo King*, usually in a *pro forma* manner to pay tribute to King as a Cambridge poet. Milton, however, summons Phoebus Apollo neither to compliment King nor to lament his death. Milton could not help remembering that Phoebus Apollo makes personal appearances in two of Virgil's eclogues. In Eclogue 6 Phoebus takes hold of Tityrus by the ear – just as he touches the poet's trembling ears in 'Lycidas' – to offer the poet literary advice: to keep his sheep fat, but his verse slim. In Eclogue 10 Phoebus again appears, now to regret Gallus's recklessness in dying for Lycoris. Neither situation quite applies to the one before us, for Milton's Phoebus is neither speaking poetics nor comforting the speaker for the death of Lycidas. But as poetic father to the Muse's son Orpheus, he has some stake in vindicating himself as well as the Muse.

In 'Lycidas' Phoebus Apollo interrupts the swain's angry indictment of divine justice to assert 'Jove's' justice, just as Apollo or Zeus or Poseidon often interrupts the narrative in Pindar's myths to assert the justice of divine ways. In 'Lycidas' the poet says that 'Fame is the spur that the clear spirit doth raise' (line 70), a fame prematurely dashed to disappointment; Phoebus replies, 'Fame is no plant that grows on mortal soil' (line 78), correcting the swain's vision as he repeats the key word, 'fame'. With a simple rejoinder Phoebus changes the perspective from mortal to immortal. His speech has the ring not only of Pindar's dramatic utterances, but also of Pindar's *sententiae* – the often praised aphorisms that Pindar so frequently employs to assert the moral and the divine purpose of his odes. When the critics Warton and Jerram comment on Phoebus's speech in 'Lycidas', they both point to Pindar, Jerram citing specifically *Nemean 7. 45*: 'Honor comes to those whose fame the god increases, magnifying them, even though they are dead.' In this ode Pindar is reminding his audience that both life and potential fame are uncertain. Like Milton, he asserts that true fame can exist only in the divine, not in the human dimension.

Both the questioning of the poet-speaker and the reply of Phoebus particularly fit a classical rather than a Judeo-Christian context. Milton very carefully avoids either phrasing the demand as a Jobean question or permitting the latitude of a Jobean answer. He touches on, but skirts the issue of divine providence. Yet, in a similar situation, the poets of *Justa Edovardo King* demand why King, who was devoted to service of a God higher than the god of poetry, was cut off. Asking the Jobean question they return, perforce, the Jobean reply: that the wisdom of God is unknowable and unsearchable. By alluding to the 'thankless Muse' and to the Fury with the fatal shears, however, Milton has kept the context classical, excluding (for the moment) the inevitable question of the Christian God's ultimate design. Some critics complain that Phoebus's reply is a little too pat. But Phoebus has focused on only one aspect of the many questions that the poet has raised. He replies to the issue of 'earthly' versus 'eternal' fame, making the approbation of 'all-judging Jove' (line 82) the gauge by which deeds should be judged. Although this gauge might easily be applied as a Christian standard, only Jove, God's classical stand-in, is invoked: 'As he pronounces lastly on each deed, / Of so much fame in heaven expect thy meed' (lines 83–4). The neat couplet advises the poet to wait for heavenly arbitration; it allays no anxieties about the blind Fury-Fate, still present with her shears. Indeed, this classical *sententia*, offered mid-poem, is not a final pronouncement and extends no further than the bounds of a classical Olympus. Milton's Phoebus is quieting poetic anxieties, just as Virgil's Phoebus had offered advice on pastoral poetics.

When Milton resumes his pastoral song with allusions to Arethuse and Mincius, he continues in the narrative vein, suspending still further the lament proper of the monody. As though in reply to the earlier query, why the nymphs did not assist their 'loved Lycidas', he brings on stage the herald of the Sea, Triton, and the guardian of the winds, Aeolus. Triton interrogates the waves and winds, the usual culprits in shipwreck, asking whether they caused Lycidas's mishap. Aeolus brings the answer, that the air was calm, the sea level, and the sea goddesses, Panope and her sisters, at play. According to reports of the shipwreck (printed in the Latin summary at the beginning of *Justa Edovardo King*), the sea indeed was calm, and the wreck caused by the ship going aground on a rock. But Milton chooses to blame neither the dangerous sea-coast nor the unskilful pilot of the vessel, but the ship instead: 'that fatal and perfidious bark / Built in the eclipse, and rigged with curses dark' (lines 100–1). No crux, aside from that of the 'two-handed engine', more puzzles readers of the poem than this one. Does the 'perfidious bark' have a specific allegorical significance? Is it the fatal body of man himself, cursed with original sin since the Fall? Is it the body of state, perfidious and dark, that entangles the innocent in its machinations? Or is the poet simply laying the ultimate blame for King's death on the man-made ship that bore him from the shore and not on the forces of nature that threaten such vessels? On the one hand it is a turn away from nature to man and society, which rigged and cursed the ship; on the other it is one further testament that the reasons for Lycidas/King's death are unknowable. A higher fate ruled the fatal bark, condemned by its construction during the eclipse, even before it set sail.

The procession of mourners for Lycidas – another traditional feature of the classical lament – consists of two father figures only: Camus and St Peter. Peter appears not in his pastoral aspect as the great shepherd, but as the pilot of the Galilean lake and as the keeper of the keys to heaven. The ordinary shepherds and shepherdesses, who are mourners in *'Epitaphium Damonis'*, Milton's Latin lament for Charles Diodati, take no part in the procession, even though it is to them, presumably, that the poet addresses his pastoral song. Camus, the river god, represents Cambridge, which earlier had been represented by the community of poet-shepherds who knew Lycidas/King. At the time of his death, King, who had been a fellow undergraduate with Milton, was still resident at Christ's College, having been the recipient of a fellowship. Father Camus laments him as his 'dearest pledge' 'reft' from him (line 107). At this time Cambridge, if not specifically Christ's College, was a stronghold of puritans; King's tutor had been the puritan William Chappell, who for a while had also been Milton's tutor. Even so, King did not challenge Laud's authority and had received his fellowship by royal mandate. His extant poems commemorate royal occasions, such as Charles I's recovery from a sickness and the birth of his children. But in contributing to royal collections, King did no more than many Cambridge poets did.

As a poem, the 1638 'Lycidas' avoids direct historical or biographical reference. Beyond alluding to his death by drowning, Milton supplies few biographical details about Edward King. He does not tell the tale that others told of the young minister kneeling and praying, Bible in hand, as the ship went down. He lets King represent the type – the good pastor and the good poet – without worrying too much whether King filled both roles completely. While he identifies himself as friend and fellow poet-pastor, he leaves unrecorded his credentials as poet. His ambition to grow wings and mount with Pegasus, which he confides in a letter to Charles Diodati only months earlier, he does not mention here. Similarly, he leaves ambiguous his status as pastor. Had he at this point already made a final decision not to take holy orders? Further, he does not dwell – even when he brings the representatives of the university and the church on the scene – on the controversies that were shaking church and state at this very time. He had probably already formulated many of the views on bishops that he expounds in *Of Reformation* in 1641. Even so, he adorns Peter's head with the bishop's mitre, a symbol he was later to scorn, and merely has Peter shake his 'mitred locks' (line 112), perhaps in disapproval of Laud and his fellows. He declines, however, making Peter a spokesman for his views on bishops. Instead he engages the universal issues that were facing Christians, issues that had been taken up not so much by church reformers as by the poets. Hence we find common ground between Milton and Dante as they use St Peter to denounce the corrupt clergy, or Milton and Mantuan, or Milton and Spenser, as they use the pastoral poem as a means to call the venial clergy to account.

Like Father Camus, Peter claims Lycidas as one of his own, a shepherd who served his flock: 'How well could I have spared for thee, young swain' (line 113). But Milton's focus is not upon the loss of the faithful shepherd, but upon the unchecked corruption of the bad shepherds. In 1637 Archbishop Laud had tightened the laws of censorship. In August that year, shortly before Edward King's drowning, the doctor John Bastwick, the clergyman Henry Burton and the lawyer William Prynne, having been tried by the Star Chamber and convicted of seditious libel, were punished by branding and by having their ears cropped. The public execution of these sentences was attended by a crowd sympathetic to the victims, and support for the men was expressed in tracts published later that described the proceedings. Some readers of 'Lycidas' wish to see in the rhyming of 'shears' and 'ears' in the Phoebus section reference to that punishment (lines 75, 77), pointing to Milton's use of a similar rhyme in 1646 in his tailed sonnet, 'On the New Forcers of Conscience' (lines 16, 17). It is an understandable gesture, but a mistaken one. Even in the long section of the poem devoted to the denunciation of the bad shepherds, there is no clear reference to the famous three that Laud had made an example. Maybe Milton was chary of his own ears. But I think another explanation is more likely; he was concerned in this passage less with the sufferings of the faithful than with the outrages of the guilty.

Rather than referring to Prynne's punishment, Milton echoes what the lawyer had said about the guilty clergy. In his 1637 tract *A Breviate of the Prelates intolerable usurpations*, Prynne had chosen his epigraph from Ezekiel 34: 2–10, the very biblical text that Milton uses to underpin the Peter passage:

> Thus saith the Lord God unto the Shepheards of Israell that doe feed themselves: Should not the Shepheards feede the Flock? Yee eate the fat, and yee cloath you with the wooll, yee kill them that are fed, yee feede not the Flocke. The diseased have yee not strengthned, neither have yee healed that which was sicke, neither have yee bound up that which was broken, neither have yee brought againe that which was driven away, neither have yee sought that which was lost, but with force & with cruelty have you ruled them, & c. Therefore, O yee Shepheards, heare the word of the Lord. Thus saith the Lord God, Behold I am against the Shepheards, and will require my Flocke at their hand, and cause them to cease from feeding the Flocks, neither shall the Shepheards, feede themselves any more, for I will deliver my Flock from their mouth, that they may not be meat for them.

Milton makes the gist of St Peter's denunciation of the corrupt clergy simply a restatement of these verses from Ezekiel, indicting those clergy who 'for their bellies' sake, / Creep and intrude, and climb into the fold' (lines 114–15), those who feed themselves rather than the sheep. But he has also made this passage join with one that affirms by implication the worth of the 'faithful herdsman's art' (line 121). Earlier the shepherd-speaker had questioned the reward of service to the 'homely slighted shepherd's trade' (line 65), as well of devotion to the Muse. Phoebus had affirmed the value of poetry; now St Peter affirms the value of the pastoral calling. Milton takes the opportunity, moreover, to link once again the calling of pastor and poet. He had praised the integration of pastoral and poetic life in the Cambridge passage. The good shepherds were also good poets. Now such integration has failed. The bad pastors also prove to be bad poets: 'their lean and flashy songs / Grate on their scrannel pipes of wretched straw' (lines 123–4). Poetry distracts the bad shepherds from fulfilment of their pastoral duties: 'The hungry sheep look up, and are not fed' (line 125). Summarizing the degradation of religious life in England, Milton turns once more to the metaphors of disease. As the loss of Lycidas brought a premature blight to the flowers, now the neglect of the sheep makes a foul contagion spread: 'swoll'n with wind, and the rank mist they draw, / Rot inwardly, and foul contagion spread' (lines 126–7). The year 1637 saw a major visitation of the plague, and many thought that the pestilence was a judgement of God upon the people of England and their unworthy clergy. Moreover, Milton joins the reference to plague with an allusion to the 'grim wolf with privy paw' who 'Daily devours apace and little said' (lines 128–9). Only here does he point the finger at the dangers of doctrinal malfeasance. Yet so subtly has he done so within the pastoral context that critics cannot agree whether the 'grim wolf with privy paw' is the Archbishop himself, who was permitting Catholicism to spread, or the Jesuits, who with covert stealth were making converts in England. However, when Milton changes 'little said' of the 1638 text to 'nothing said' in 1645, he strengthens the doctrinal warning.

Although Prynne reminded the prelates of God's great day of judgement, he did not call down a 'two-handed engine' upon them. The lawyer Prynne had a judicial solution. He hoped that 'our present Gracious Soveraigne' would deem worthy some suitable punishment for those who 'suspend, excommunicate, fine, imprison the living persons of his faithfull Ministers and Subjects, (contrary to all Law and Iustice)'. He had in mind – in accord with the judgement demanded in Ezekiel – stripping them of their 'Bishoprickes, Archdeaconries, Chauncellourships, and other offices, as forefaited by their severall abuses, extortions, and oppressions committed in them' (1637: 257–8). Milton's engine is far more threatening. In keeping with the opening and close of 'Lycidas' the tones we hear are apocalyptic: 'But that two-handed engine at the door, / Stands ready to smite once, and smite no more' (lines 130–1). When Milton added the headnote in 1645 that he had 'by occasion [foretold] the ruin of our corrupted clergy then in their height', was he referring specifically to the judgement of the engine that Peter called down upon them? Some have argued that he was, and that the engine should be identified, accordingly, as the axe that struck Laud or the judicial orders of Parliament that deprived the established clergy of their livings. Yet, given the apocalyptic fervour of these lines, it would be a mistake to limit them to such historical outcomes, unforeseen in 1637 even by a prophetic poet. That the most logical solution to the controversial engine remains to connect it with the two-handed sword of the angel of the apocalypse – Michael – is not surprising. In 1645 as in 1638 the lines resound with a kind of apocalyptic finality. In Book 12 of Revelation Michael wages a war against Satan and his angels, a war that, some commentators said, would result in the binding of Satan in hell. This binding, described in chapter 20, would usher in the thousand-year reign on earth of Christ and his saints – the so-called millennium. Like many men in the seventeenth century, Milton thought, as he said several times in his antiprelatical tracts, that the mild reign of Christ on earth was near. But mild though this reign would be, it would begin with a judgement on the wicked. However Milton might exult in 1645 in the fall of the corrupt clergy, he continued to make St Peter's words resound with an apocalyptic warning of a final and even greater reckoning.

With an invocation to Alpheus, Milton resumes his pastoral strains. For some critics the references to Arethuse at line 85 and to Alpheus at line 132 are simply compliments to Theocritus's native pastoral. But when Milton joins Alpheus to the Sicilian Muse, 'Return *Alpheus*, the dread voice is past, / That shrunk thy streams; return Sicilian Muse' (lines 132–3), he turns our attention to the Greek myth in a more expansive way. The Arcadian nymph Arethusa had fled from the river god Alpheus, who pursued her undersea and mingled his waters with hers as she was transformed in Sicily into a fountain. The story was alluded to in antiquity by Pindar, Theocritus, Virgil and other writers, and in the Renaissance by mythographers who often interpreted it as a resurrection myth. In their undersea voyage both Arethusa and Alpheus are transformed, leaving behind their pastoral identities in Arcadia and receiving new life in another realm. Pindar alludes to their story at the beginning of *Nemean 1* when he names Sicily the holy breathing place of Alpheus, the site where the river god attained his second breath as the immortal husband of Arethusa. Milton apostrophizes Arethusa immediately after Phoebus has pronounced his words on fame; Alpheus after Peter has denounced the bad shepherds. At each point the invocation of one or the other of these mythic figures signals a change in the direction of the pastoral song.

The use of the name 'Muse' for Arethusa also has some unmistakable implications, for the Muses collectively and singly have been dealt with harshly by the poet. At his first invocation he sweeps aside the Muses' 'denial vain, and coy excuse' (line 18); he accuses Calliope of impotence in saving her poet-son; he regards the Muse as thankless and service to her unrewarding. But at this point in the monody, the Muse has become a gentle mother who calls 'the vales, and bid them hither cast / Their bells, and flowrets of a thousand hues' (lines 134–5); she is the returning maiden who brings with her the spring. Milton seems to have conflated Arethusa with Proserpina, and, as Pindar tells us in *Nemean 1*, Sicily is home to them both. Imitating the flower catalogue of Spenser's 'Aprill' and of Shakespeare's *A Winter's Tale*, Milton implicitly recalls the vernal flowers that Proserpina let fall, those very flowers that will bloom again in the spring when she returns to the earth.

The presence of feminine comfort at this juncture in the poem is important, for up to now 'Lycidas' has been a poem of masculine loss and abandonment, from which the strong feminine figures and supporting goddesses of Milton's earlier poems are absent. The shepherd-swain wanders alone in a desolate landscape where the masculine figures who come – even the 'fathers' Phoebus, Camus, and Peter – offer excuse, or moral sentence, or express regret or anger, but do not comfort. Up to now the feminine too is impotent. The nymphs have not heard Lycidas's dying cries; the unnamed Muse Calliope does not appear; the pastoral mistresses – Neaera and Amaryllis – have been regretfully cast aside, unable to provide distraction or moment- ary pleasure. The shadow of the mother's death is everywhere; the surviving son searches, but cannot find her, the feminine having been extinguished in his life. Milton's own mother Sarah had died in April 1637. A sense of helpless bereavement accompanied by a fear of death and dissolution breathes throughout Milton's monody. Then the words sound, 'Return Alpheus'; and, along with Alpheus, the returning lover, comes the restored Muse – 'return Sicilian Muse' – the nurturing mother, who strews flowers, who has not abandoned the poet after all. Although the flowers do not bring Lycidas back to life, they bestow the comfort that up to now has been missing from the poem.

Early in the monody the poet links Lycidas to the tragic Orpheus whose 'divine head' was destroyed and brought down the Hebrus river to the sea (Trinity MS; *CSP*: 247). Now, he links him with another classical demigod, the river Alpheus, who in pursuing Arethusa undersea enacts the pagan version of the Christian resurrection, anticipating in fact Lycidas's 'second breath' and redemption in heaven. Milton indirectly alludes to Alpheus's undersea voyage as he describes how the dead Lycidas visits 'the bottom of the monstrous world' (line 158). Then, closing the circle, he alludes to still another classical figure – the poet Arion who was not drowned, but came safely through the seas to shore, saved by the dolphins. Milton never names Arion; he doesn't have to. Merely by referring to the dolphins, as J. Martin Evans has observed (1978, 1998b), he recalls the Arion story and also other mythic accounts of salvation by dolphins. Ultimately, however, it is not the dolphins that save Lycidas, even though Milton has metaphorically linked them with him. The myths of resurrected Alpheus and the rescued Arion are stories of salvation that parallel, but do not replicate, the Christian story. Missing from their accounts of rescue is the one who alone can effect Lycidas's resurrection. The angel of the guarded mount may call Lycidas homeward, but it is only through Christ that he is saved.

The allusion at this point in the poem to Michael, the angel who defeated Satan in the apocalyptical War in Heaven and holds the scales of judgement, is significant. Like the other Christian figures in the poem, he is unnamed, being identified only as 'the great vision of the guarded Mount', St Michael's Mount in Cornwall. The visionary angel holds the heights of the promontory where perhaps the lost Lycidas 'Sleep'st by the fable of Bellerus old' (line 160). Milton endows the angel with an almost mythic quality, connecting him implicitly with the fabled giant Bellerus as though he too were part of the landscape of Cornwall and were defending the shores of Britain by merely fixing his eyes on the strongholds of Catholic Spain, Namancos and Bayona. Michael neither speaks nor seconds Peter's harsh sentence against the corrupt pastors. Instead he is urged to turn his gaze from Spain to 'Look homeward' and 'melt with ruth', pitying the lost Lycidas, whose body has not been and will not be recovered until he is resurrected in heaven. With the anticipated turn of the apocalyptic angel, we too are looking homeward, but not towards Britain; rather towards other shores.

The real consolation in 'Lycidas' begins as abruptly as the spurious consolation of the previous section. Yet, the poet could not now say: 'Weep no more, woeful shepherds weep no more' (line 165), if he had not first summoned them to the laureate hearse, empty of Lycidas's body, and strewn it with 'every flower that sad embroidery wears' (line 148). For a funeral – even a ceremonial one – is the first step to coming to terms with the unchangeable aspect of death with which this poem has struggled from the beginning. Nature renewing its beauty and recovering from the desolation experienced at Lycidas's death assists the mourning with the sense of new beginning that must come after every loss. To effect that renewal Milton couples the daffodils that come before the swallows dare with the amaranth that blooms only in paradise: 'Bid amaranthus all his beauty shed, / And daffadillies fill their cups with tears' (lines 149–50).

No real consolation can come in 'Lycidas' without a transformation of its classical pastoral to Christian pastoral – at least symbolically. Not even the presence of Peter, the keeper of the keys, can open heaven for the dead shepherd; only Christ, with his saving power, can do this. But not even Christ appears by name in this classical monody; only by his mythic name, the 'day-star' (line 168), and only through allusion to the Gospel story of his walking the waves (Matthew 14: 25–33). By naming Peter, 'the Pilot of the Galilean lake' (line 109), Milton has prepared for the subsequent use of a story so crucial to the concluding movement of the poem. The Gospel of Matthew tells how Peter, sailing the ship on the sea of Galilee with the other disciples, sees Jesus walking on the water. He first expresses his faith by asking Jesus to bid him come to him, but then falters and begins to sink in the water. Only when Jesus takes him by the hand does Peter recover and declare his belief in Jesus as the Son of God. The poet-speaker, like Peter, has doubted and has faltered, questioning the very grounds of Christian belief. Yet when the vision of Michael points him homeward, he can at last affirm his faith, as he tells the other shepherds: 'Lycidas your sorrow is not dead' (line 166).

The statement that Lycidas is alive in heaven is made through the use of a natural metaphor that in no way disturbs the pastoralism of the monody. Though Lycidas is 'Sunk...beneath the watery floor', it is only as the sun – the day-star – sinks in the ocean bed, and yet rises once again the next day, 'repairs his drooping head, / And tricks his beams, and with new spangled ore, / Flames in the forehead of the morning sky' (lines 167, 169–71). 'So', the poet proclaims triumphantly, 'Lycidas sunk low, but mounted high' (line 172). But are we being treated to one more false surmise, one more hopeful analogy? Lycidas is no 'day-star', who can rise and renew himself. However, Christ is, and his resurrection is figured in the rising of the sun. Through him and through the might that he evinced as he walked the waves, Lycidas may rise and walk with him. With the introduction of the metaphor of day-star and the recollection of the incident that tried Peter's faith, Milton raises his pastoral to a new level. We are ready for the 'other groves' and 'other streams' (line 174) in the 'blest kingdoms meek of joy and love' (line 177). This line referring to these 'blest kingdoms' was inadvertently omitted from the 1638 'Lycidas', but supplied in a Cambridge University copy in a hand thought to be Milton's.

The vision of Lycidas resurrected in heaven, hearing the 'unexpressive nuptial song' of the Lamb (line 176) is biblical. Yet the language differs not at all from that used throughout this pastoral monody. Lycidas still walks in groves beside streams, as his fellow shepherds do, but he is no longer entertained by shepherd pipes and shepherd dances. His community is still a fellowship, but one of saints 'In solemn troops, and sweet societies / That sing, and singing in their glory move, / And wipe the tears for ever from his eyes' (lines 179–81). Milton had begun the final section of the poet-shepherd's song with an injunction, 'Weep no more, woful shepherds weep no more'. Astute critics have noticed how the repetition of 'no more' picks up the opening refrain of the poem, 'Yet once more', with its double message of biblical prophecy and resumed pastoral song. The announcement, 'Now Lycidas the shepherds weep no more' (line 182), has a similar effect. The poet has achieved the aim of his pastoral song; he is able once more to address Lycidas directly, assuring him that he has brought comfort to his fellow mourners. But the resonant 'no more' also raises our eyes to the achievement of an apocalyptic moment. The society that Lycidas will inhabit will not be established until the final chapters of Revelation when the Judgement is past and the New Jerusalem has come down to earth.

> And I saw a new heaven and a new earth: for the first heaven and the first earth were passed away . . . And I John saw the holy city, new Jerusalem, coming down from God out of heaven, prepared as a bride adorned for her husband. And I heard a great voice out of heaven saying, Behold, the tabernacle of God is with men . . . And God shall wipe away all tears from their eyes; and there shall be no more death, neither sorrow, nor crying, neither shall there be any more pain: for the former things are passed away. (Revelation 21: 1–4)

The words from Hebrews with which 'Lycidas' began – 'Yet once more' – promised that God would shake the nations, removing those things that are shaken so that 'those things which cannot be shaken may remain'. The verses from Revelation that underlie its penultimate section confirm that promise.

Yet having affirmed that Lycidas is living among those who listen to the song of the Lamb, Milton turns his attention once more to earth. While the Christian pastor-poet is entertained in heaven, he retains a numinous aspect on earth in the form of a pagan 'genius'. But he is not a genius of the wood or the meadows, haunting those places where he lived, having left a part of himself behind to console his fellow shepherds. No; he becomes a genius of the very element that destroyed him – the perilous flood, almost as though the poet were having a last word with those water deities who did not protect Lycidas: 'Henceforth thou art the genius of the shore, / In thy large recompense, and shalt be good / To all that wander in that perilous flood' (lines 183–5). Lycidas becomes a guardian spirit to pilot others and bring them safely to land, yet serving as the model of the good pastor, who leads those to salvation who trust in 'him that walked the waves'.

Much has been written about Milton's use of a closing frame – the eight lines of octosyllabic verse – in which he identifies 'the uncouth swain' as the singer of the Doric lay we have just heard. Is Milton deliberately distancing himself from the song and the unknown singer who has been singing it, perhaps disclaiming them both? The adoption of a conventional frame and regular metre at the conclusion of a poem that began abruptly without frame and unevenly without a clear rhyming pattern has made some critics suspicious. By doing the obvious, even the conventional, was Milton setting one last puzzle for his readers? Yet he was to use a frame and adopt a pastoral *persona* three years later in his Latin pastoral, '*Epitaphium Damonis*', and few critics have for that reason called his credibility into account. Should we not accept the pastoral frame and metrical regularity in 'Lycidas' for what they are, the simplest of signals, that with them Milton is turning from a world disordered by grief and doubt to a natural world finally returned to its accustomed order? In this he is faithful to the genre he has adapted. Bringing us down from the apocalyptic heights, he lets the fictive swain rise, take on once more his blue mantle and, returning to pastoral commitment, be gone. Even as the swain departs, however, Milton leaves his readers to wonder at the meaning of the final line of the monody and also whether the swain or John Milton speaks the words: 'Tomorrow to fresh woods, and pastures new' (line 193).

Writings

Milton (1638, 1645, 1673).

References for Further Reading

Alpers (1996); Austin (1947); Berkeley (1974); Binns (1972); Brooks and Hardy (1951a); Campbell and Postlethwaite (1994); Dietz (1997); Elledge (1966); Evans (1978, 1998b); Forrest (1974); Grant (1965); Hanford (1910); Harrison (1939); Hunt (1979); Kirkconnell (1973); Labriola (1984); Leonard (1991); Lieb (1989); Lipking (1996); Lloyd (1958); Martz, (1972, 1980/1986); Nichols (1973); Norbrook (1984a); Patrides (1983); Pecheux (1976); Prince (1954); Prynne (1637); Quint (1983); Rajan (1978–80); Revard (1997b); Shumaker (1951); Tayler (1978, 1979); Wittreich (1979); Woodhouse (1952).

The Prose

16

Early Political Prose

Elizabeth Skerpan Wheeler

By 1641 Milton had established a definite, if minor, public identity: he was a poet. 'An Epitaph on the Admirable Dramaticke Poet W. Shakespeare' had appeared in 1632 in the Second Folio of Shakespeare's plays. *A Masque Presented at Ludlow Castle* (*Comus*) had been performed in 1634 and published in 1637. 'Lycidas' closed the memorial volume *Justa Edovardo King naufrago* in 1638. And yet, according to his own account in 1654, he abandoned a year of travels in Italy, undertaken for the 'improvement of my mind' (*WJM* 8: 125), to return to England in 1639, eventually to 'be of use' (*WJM* 8: 129) writing prose works, first in pamphlet wars against episcopacy, and finally in service to the state.

Certainly, by 1654, in his *Pro Populo Anglicano Defensio Secunda*, when he was styling himself 'John Milton, Englishman', Milton chose to present his entry into public controversy as part of a grand design. From this perspective, his early political prose works become evidence for how he understood himself in his historical moment. As he explained in 1654, in wanting to 'be of use', he intended to join those already putting themselves at risk, 'fighting for their liberty' (*WJM* 8: 125). His actions would thus be part of a collective enterprise to restore the English people to their ancient liberties. Accordingly, he began by taking part in the growing attack on the episcopal governance of the Church of England, writing five works that have come to be known as the antiprelatical tracts. Considering these pamphlets a success, Milton writes,

> [I] began to turn my thoughts to other subjects; to consider in what way I could contribute to the progress of real and substantial liberty; which is to be sought for not from without, but within, and is to be obtained principally not by fighting, but by the just regulation and by the proper conduct of life. (*WJM* 8: 131)

And so, his explanation continued, the design took shape. He came to see that liberty had three 'species': religious, domestic and civil. Realizing that his antiprelatical tracts addressed the first variety, and that Parliament was engaging with the third, he next undertook an investigation into the second – domestic or private liberty, itself divisible into three parts. His enquiry into the first part – the regulation of marriage – yielded four tracts on divorce, examined in this volume by Annabel Patterson (chapter 17). His consideration of the second was summed up in the tract *Of Education*. Study of the third – 'freedom of opinion' (*WJM* 8: 131) – culminated in *Areopagitica*, his great attack on the licensing of books. His grand design thus resulted in eleven tracts between 1641 and 1645, an achievement Milton himself commemorated in 1646 when he presented them in a bound volume to the Bodleian library (Milton 1998b: 874).

From his own perspective, then, Milton's early political tracts represent a signifi- cant stage in his development, an element in the construction of a carefully cultivated public self. From a modern, scholarly perspective, an understanding of exactly what that self is becomes essential to our reading of Milton's later political thought and activity. Until recently, study of the early prose centred on *Areopagitica*, its vivid arguments against censorship, and Milton's subsequent if brief career as a censor, attempting to determine, among other questions, whether Milton was a precursor of modern liberalism, defending freedom of speech (the 'tolerationist' thesis), or a covert authoritarian tyrant, dedicated to the suppression of truly opposing views in defence of a repressive theocracy ('anti-tolerationist'). Since 1990, however, scholars have expanded their study of the prose in two major directions. First, historical investiga- tion into the intellectual contexts of Milton's ideas, exemplified by the work of Martin Dzelzainis, David Norbrook and Nigel Smith, has come to understand Milton as a classical republican rather than a modern liberal, a person who, following Aristotle, sees the human being as a political animal rather than an individual seeking freedom from the state. Second, investigation of his social contexts and views on writing, conducted by such scholars as Stephen B. Dobranski, Elizabeth Magnus and Sandra Sherman, has presented a Milton for whom the whole enterprise of knowledge- making was a collaborative process, an insight that challenges the conventional view of Milton as the epitome of the individualistic, independent author. This work calls for a re-evaluation of Milton's self-representation and the aims of his arguments, positioning him as we now see him at the nexus of classical republicanism and iconoclastic Christianity.

This model is proving highly fruitful. It frees Milton of the burden of having to be one of us. It also frees him from the imposed dialectic of 'public versus private'. Nevertheless, as we shall see, there remain many tensions and contradictions in the early prose works that the new model does not fully resolve. These tensions arise from the very notion of public participation and the intersection of the often conflicting traditions of classical republicanism and Christianity: a Miltonic vision that perceives both the need for and the danger of verbal exchange. Such exchange is necessary because, following classical republican principles, it is the manner in which the public citizen fulfils himself. It is dangerous because, following Milton's understanding of Christianity, the self is also the expression of the image of God within and includes an immortal soul in need of saving. One's perception of that self, however, is contingent, so that the self as well as ideas may be shaped or altered by the confrontation with opposing voices. The self exists – and must exist – in exercise, but it also exists independently, so that exercise puts the self at risk. In the course of his early prose works, Milton explores the implications of his vision of verbal exchange. While he finds no means of resolving the tensions inherent in that vision, Milton presents verbal exchange as a necessary act of courage.

The Antiprelatical Tracts

In joining the attack on the bishops, Milton affiliated himself with the major political movement of the day. Opposition to the two Scottish wars – the Bishops' Wars – in 1639 and 1640 led to the formation of a true opposition party, which coalesced around dissatisfaction with governance of the Church of England and the high church policies of the Archbishop of Canterbury, William Laud. In December 1640 the Root and Branch Petition, calling for the abolition of bishops, was presented to the Long Parliament, which impeached Laud on 18 December. These successes predictably bred a backlash. As David Norbrook has shown (1999: 110), by the early months of 1641 a royalist party was forming around the defence of the church. This party found its best expression in the voice of the great Anglican controversialist Joseph Hall, Bishop of Exeter. His works and the responses they provoked provide the immediate context of Milton's tracts.

Hall's first salvo, published in January 1641, was *An Humble Remonstrance to the High Court of Parliament*, defending the liturgy and the apostolic succession of bishops. The work prompted several answers, including, in late March, *An Answer to a Booke Entituled, An Humble Remonstrance*, by 'Smectymnuus', an acronym formed from the initials of five moderate puritan clergymen, including Thomas Young, a former tutor to Milton. The work concluded with a postscript, which may be Milton's. Hall responded on 12 April with *A Defence of the Humble Remonstrance against the Frivolous . . . Exceptions of Smectymnuus*, which provoked the Smectymnuuans' *Vindication of the Answer to the Humble Remonstrance, from the Unjust Imputations of Frivolousnesse and Falsehood* on 26 June. When Milton wrote his antiprelatical tracts, he engaged in a lively and ongoing conflict.

Milton's chief purpose is to attack those of Hall's arguments that derive from custom and the writings of the church fathers. But, as Kranidas (1982, 1983) shows, the issue in this debate – for both Milton and Hall – increasingly becomes the credibility of the speaker. In the world of printed argument, the verbal representation of the self becomes tenuous, an image projected to an anonymous audience without the mediation of that audience's response. Milton's concern with that image finds embodiment in his five tracts in a preoccupation with form and its lack: forms of worship, forms of argument, and both Milton's and Hall's forms of self-presentation. Most notably, the tracts contain a series of interrupted or unresolved stories that suggest an internal questioning of the integrity of Milton's own narratives. This questioning occurs as Milton presents ideas and themes that will prove to be constant in his work, ideas that arise from the delicate balance between truth and the contingencies of public exchange.

Of Reformation: May 1641

In his first independent performance (if we regard 'A Postscript' as his), Milton presents his words carefully in writing to the anonymous print audience. Its dual character is reflected in the appearance of the tract itself. The title page gives the full title as *Of Reformation Touching Chvrch-Discipline in England: And the Cavses that hitherto have hindred it*. The first page retains the subtitle, but alters the main title to 'Of Reformation in England'. While the context is overtly religious, the alteration suggests that 'reformation' could be a much more extensive project than the elimination of bishops. Indeed, Milton's argument focuses on *form*. 'Reformation' goes beyond simple change to reshape and restructure not only the church but the way we think: what proofs we accept, how we read, what is essential and what indifferent to Christians and their communities.

Throughout *Of Reformation*, Milton represents his argument through the governing metaphor of the body. The history of the church is the story of corruption of its body politic. The 'Doctrine of the *Gospel*' was once

> refin'd to such a Spirituall height, and temper of purity, and knowledge of the Creator, that the body, with all the circumstances of time and place, were purifi'd by the affections of the regenerat Soule, and nothing left impure, but sinne; *Faith* needing not the weak, and fallible office of the Senses, to be either the Ushers, or Interpreters, of heavenly Mysteries, save where our Lord himselfe in his Sacraments ordain'd. (*CPW* I: 519–20)

The body was so pure that it was in effect disembodied. Without a body, doctrine is immediately accessible to the soul. There is no possibility of error or miscommunication that may occur when doctrine passes through the mediation – the interpretation – of the senses. Moreover, the disembodied body is free of corruption; it cannot decay. It thus has complete, formal integrity, unaffected by its interaction with the soul. Such an interaction is perfect because it is completely safe.

Corruption is loss of form, deformation. But here corruption occurs because those entrusted with the protection of doctrine force it to take tangible form:

> that they might bring the inward acts of the *Spirit* to the outward, and customary ey-Service of the body, as if they could make *God* earthly, and fleshly, because they could not make themselves *heavenly*, and *Spirituall*: they began to draw downe all the Divine intercours, betwixt *God*, and the Soule, yea, the very shape of *God* himselfe, into an exterior, and bodily forme. (*CPW* I: 520)

'Form' is not synonymous with 'body'. God has a 'shape' without 'bodily forme', which is why he has existence independent of the body's ability to perceive him. In logic, the form of something is the thing itself. Bodily form is that which is apparent to the senses: statues, vestments, incense, rituals, traditions. And bodily form, in Milton's discussion, is a result of spiritual failure, the inability to make oneself 'heavenly'. Reformation is nothing less than restoring form – the original shape – to doctrine, and that process requires the removal of 'bodily forme'.

Milton's programme for reform calls for the defence of truth through reading the scripture. We understand scripture through reading, a process inevitably mediated through the senses. Hence Milton's attention to right reading. Axiomatic to its practice is the conviction that it is possible to have a proper, direct correspondence between words and things; that, properly understood, words will express truth and will therefore mean exactly what they say. As Milton explains, 'The very essence of Truth is plainnesse, and brightnes; the darknes and crookednesse is our own. The *Wisdome* of *God* created *understanding*, fit and proportionable to Truth the object, and end of it, as the eye to the thing visible' (*CPW* I: 566). The understanding is the mind's eye. Right reading is reading with the disembodied mind's eye, the eye that, being purely intuitive, is synonymous with spirit. Right reading frees the spirit from the body. Because it is incorporeal, its actions do not alter but restore true form. Conversely, reading with the body's eye, responding to the physical manifestations of human authority, returns our spirit to the physical body and the mutable world. Because episcopacy has no support from scripture, which is truth, bishops are part of the bodily form that mediates between Christian reader and scripture, and part of the corrupting process that impedes the soul from joining with the spiritual form. Because the source of corruption is known, Milton has every confidence that it may be removed, and doctrine restored to its true form.

However, there is a strong countercurrent in *Of Reformation*: one that suggests some anxiety about the public stance that Milton takes by virtue of having written the tract, even though the words appear mediated because, as the title page declares, they are 'Written to a FREIND'. Writing a pamphlet is obviously not analogous to the spirit speaking with God. Even if the friend is God, the medium of print in which the ideas are transmitted gives the words themselves bodily form and subjects them to the 'ey-Service' of readers. Moreover, words that are the most persuasive to readers are those that make the most effective appeal to the physical, sensual world: the manner of speaking that Lana Cable characterizes as 'carnal rhetoric' (1995: 2). To accomplish his goal of re-formation, Milton must give his ideas exactly the bodily forms he most suspects.

His ambivalence towards this process finds expression in the peculiar Tale of the Wen in the second book of the tract. In this fleshly tale, the Body calls a meeting of all the members to pursue the common good. The Head appears and, attached to it, 'a huge and monstrous Wen little lesse then the Head it selfe, growing to it by a narrower excrescency' (*CPW* I: 583). To the consternation of the other members, the wen insists on its own importance, 'second to the head', and demands special privileges. A 'wise and learned Philosopher' is called in to consult, and he identifies the wen as a parasitical growth, full of 'folly' and 'filth' (584) that will be exposed as such 'when I have cut thee off'. But the threatened surgery does not occur. The tale breaks off immediately after the Philosopher's speech. The narrative is interrupted with the wen still present, ugly and vociferous. Because the Philosopher does not act, readers are left with the question of whether the head's original form will ever be restored. The wen survives as a competing, if monstrous, alternative to Milton's vision.

The wen casts its shadow on the entire tract. Throughout *Of Reformation* Milton employs the language of disease, tumour and deformity. Episcopacy 'gives a Vomit to [GOD] himselfe' (*CPW* I: 537). The bishops' arguments are based on the writings of the church fathers, produced when '1. The best times were spreadingly infected. 2. The best men of those times fouly tainted. 3. The best writings of those men dangerously adulterated' (549). True re-formation will occur only when we 'begin roundly to cashier, and cut away from the publick body the noysom, and diseased tumor of Prelacie' (598). The body politic regains health by having its true form restored.

But the process of healing is more complex than Milton's surgical metaphor suggests. The language he chooses to describe the healthy body politic renders ambiguous the traditional metaphors of balance and harmony. He explains, 'a Commonwealth ought to be as one huge Christian personage, one mighty growth, and stature of an honest man' (*CPW* I: 572). While the *OED* does not record a meaning of 'growth' as 'a morbid formation' before 1847, nevertheless Milton's use may suggest just that. The wen is 'growing to' the head; the commonwealth is a 'growth'. The similar actions render the two things similar. Moreover, as Milton explains, health does not mean lack of difference:

> And because things simply pure are inconsistent in the masse of nature, nor are the elements or humors in Mans Body exactly *homogeneall*, and hence the best founded Commonwealths, and least barbarous have aym'd at a certaine mixture and temperament, partaking the severall vertues of each other. (*CPW* I: 599)

The Yale editors of *Of Reformation* point out that here Milton paraphrases one of his commonplace book entries from Sir Thomas Smith; however, Milton makes some significant alterations. The entry reads, in part, 'no more then the elements are pure in nature', that is, the elements are not pure (*CPW* I: 442), whereas Milton's revision makes pure things 'inconsistent'. Even purity itself has no consistent being: no pure, single form. Its true form, then, is to be subject to change.

So if even a healthy body is subject to change, it is constantly in danger of imbalance, of excessive and even monstrous growth, and thus of alteration sufficient to change from one thing into another (from 'healthy' to 'sick'). In Milton's history of corruption in the church, the healthy, pure soul, subject to the 'bodily forme' of prelatical rituals, experienced 'over-bodying', which caused a change in her nature: she 'forgot her heavenly flight'. Worse, 'out of question from her pervers conceiting of *God*, and holy things, she had faln to beleeve no *God* at all' (*CPW* I: 522). The church passed from being the spouse of Christ to being a whore (557). Growth and change provide for transformation, but transformation into what?

Milton's 'debatement with my selfe' (*CPW* I: 525) over the possibility of reformation – a preliminary two-mindedness – resolves itself into the form of *Of Reformation*. If 'A Postscript' is Milton's, he begins his polemical career as an excrescence to someone else's work, taking on his own form in *Of Reformation*. His opposition to mediation by bishops – an opposition to excrescence and shape-shifting – leads to his full health and form as a polemicist. And yet Milton is not alone in giving form to his tract, for his anticipating a hostile reception causes it to alter its form: 'Here I might have ended, but that some Objections, which I have heard commonly flying about, presse mee to the endevour of an answere' (601). To exist is to take form, but to take form is to risk corruption. The proper, healthy 'growth' of the body, or body politic, can become a 'tumour'. To enter into verbal exchange is to acknowledge the tenuousness of form.

Of Prelatical Episcopacy: June or July 1641

The briefest of the antiprelatical tracts bears the longest title: *Of Prelatical Episcopacy, and Whether it may be deduc'd from the Apostolical times by vertue of those Testimonies which are alledg'd to that purpose in some late Treatises: One whereof goes under the Name of Iames Arch-Bishop of Armagh*. As the title says, the tract is a specific response to several works, including *The Judgement of Doctor Rainoldes Touching the Originall of Episcopacy* (25 May 1641) by James Ussher, Archbishop of Armagh. Because it is a response, its form is mediated by others, and yet Milton uses his exchange with hostile interlocutors to demonstrate the need for freedom from mediation. *Of Prelatical Episcopacy* becomes an enquiry into the nature of authority, especially that of words and texts. As both Thomas Kranidas (1982) and Stanley Fish (1990) have argued, authority begins and ends with scripture. Further, Kranidas shows that Milton also examines the question of how we must judge both scriptural and nonscriptural texts. *Of Prelatical Episcopacy* demonstrates how both authority and sound judgement, as well as error, arise from reading.

Milton defines reading as he did in *Of Reformation*. We are to make 'first the Gospell our rule, and Oracle' (*CPW* I: 650), testing the words of the church fathers and others against them. In reading, we are to be guided 'either by plaine Text, or solid reasoning' to learn, for example, that there is no 'difference betweene a Bishop, and a Presbyter' (625). As in *Of Reformation*, the proper words of a true text may communicate their truth directly to readers, or else readers may employ their understanding to discern the truth in the text. Problems arise due to lack of integrity in some texts and to 'credulous readers', misled by the allure of 'old *Martyrologies*, and *legends*' (627). Words in old texts may be used in ways inconsistent with scripture:

Now for the word προεςώς [proestos], it is more likely that *Timothy* never knew the word in that sense: it was the vanity of those next succeeding times not to content themselves with the simplicity of Scripture phrase, but must make a new Lexicon to name themselves by. (632)

The texts themselves may be 'adulterat' 'forgeries' (639), or else their history may appear so close to legendary stories – as is Photius's account of the Treatise of Timothy, appearing with his story of the Seven Sleepers (633) – as to be unreliable. When and how, then, can readers trust themselves to read, especially when, as Fish argues, the scriptures themselves contain parables and narratives that require the 'supplement' of the readers' reasoning?

The process of proving all things by the authority of scripture and 'solid reasoning' is necessary but dangerous. Human authority is untrustworthy; scriptural authority may need the periodic application of 'solid reasoning', but it is the word of God and therefore the only authority that is truly reliable. Fish points out that, in a tract concerned with reading scripture, Milton never quotes any scriptural texts, contending that Milton is therefore acting protectively towards them, keeping them free from violation by human eyes. But in refusing to quote scripture, Milton keeps its form intact and ready for the independent test of readers. His own careful reading and reasoning provide an object lesson in the methods appropriate for the study of both hazardous and salutary materials. And yet readers must ultimately practise for themselves, a practice that should include reading Milton's tract. *Of Prelatical Episcopacy* reminds readers that truth is attainable, and that all nonscriptural authority – including their own – is fallible. Truth is the prize, but confusion and distraction will be the risks one encounters along the way.

Animadversions: July 1641

In the third of his antiprelatical tracts, Milton shifts his attention from authentic texts to the authentic self. *Animadversions upon The Remonstrants Defence Against Smectymnuus* challenges Bishop Hall to determine who had the more effective public persona. As Thomas Kranidas argues, the 'chief argument was not in fact "Believe *this*", but rather "Believe *me*"' (1983: 248). Milton puts his public self to the test in direct confrontation with the words of Hall, which in turn shape Milton's tract and persona. Following the conventions of the satirical, Marprelate tradition (see Egan 1976), Milton isolates words, phrases and sentences from Hall's *Defence*, deracinating his opponent's text to make it lose its form and therefore its textual integrity. Further, the famous vehemence of Milton's words mocks and de-forms the opponent's persona; the bishop's presumed dignity may be deflated by simple laughter: 'Ha, ha, ha' (*CPW* I: 726). In this verbal exchange, Milton examines Hall's ideas and arguments and shows the limits of proving all things. In *Animadversions* Milton challenges Hall's vision of church government by contrasting the values of mediation, tradition and liturgy to those of reading, scripture and composed prayer. At stake is the question of which shall have primacy: outer or inner authority. Freedom of speech returns as a major issue, as it was in *Of Reformation*; but here Milton qualifies it specifically as freedom to follow the 'light of grace' (*CPW* I: 702) in interpreting scriptures and inventing prayers, to give full expression and therefore form to the spirit within.

In Milton's argument, the spirit may be given form by both words, whether in reading or in prayer, and action, both speaking and listening. In reading, we gain knowledge of ourselves and our spirits by studying the Bible, the best 'instrument of necessary knowledge' (*CPW* I: 699). The Bible may function as such because it is both the word of God and entirely self-contained. The writers of antiquity, however, require much more extensive evaluation:

> But hee that shall bind himselfe to make Antiquity his rule, if hee read but part, besides the difficulty of choyce, his rule is deficient, and utterly unsatisfying; for there may bee other Writers of another mind which hee hath not seene, and if hee undertake all, the length of mans life cannot extend to give him a full and requisite knowledge of what was done in Antiquity. (699)

To reject the authority of antiquity in favour of that of the scriptures is 'to free ingenuous minds' (698) from servitude to other human authority, and to grant that authority to individual readers when, guided by the light of grace, they read the Bible and judge for themselves.

If one's own interpretation of the Bible has greater authority than the writings of antiquity, so also does a minister's individual, composed prayer have greater value than a liturgy. The set prayers and forms of the liturgy are nothing more than 'the vain babble of praying over the same things immediatly againe', while composed prayer is the 'patheticall ejaculation rays'd out of the suddain earnestnesse and vigour of the inflam'd soul, (such as was that of *Christ* in the Garden)' (*CPW* I: 682). Composed prayer is thus more *authentic* than liturgy: it gives form to something actually felt by the person praying. Set prayers in a liturgy give merely 'bodily forme' (*Of Reformation*, *CPW* I: 520), and may not correspond at all to the intent or state of mind of the speaker. Without intent, the words have no meaning because they do not give form to the spirit. Thus it is futile for Hall to defend the words of the liturgy by claiming that they are good in themselves. When Hall asks, 'If the Devils confest the Son of God, shall I disclaime that truth?' (*CPW* I: 687), Milton answers, ' 'Tis not the goodnesse of matter therefore which is not, nor can be ow'd to the *Liturgie*, that will beare it out, if the form, which is the essence of it, be fantastick, and superstitious, the end sinister, and the imposition violent' (688). In such a situation, there can be no valid worship.

The essence of worship is the collaborative relationship between people and preacher. When the preacher gives voice to the spirit within him, he offers that spirit to his congregation. When people hear 'the free utterances of privat brests' (*CPW* I: 670), as princes have sometimes done when they have gone 'under disguise into a popular throng', they are likely to hear 'the precious gemme of Truth'. Composed prayer allows the minister to fulfil his calling, giving form to the essence that is within, and permitting true *ministering* to the people. This is the point of Milton's interrupted narrative of the strange gardener (*CPW* I: 715–17). In this fictitious 'Law case' an 'honest and laborious servant' (716) tends the garden of a rich man, nurturing the plants and helping them to grow. The work is suddenly interrupted by a 'strange Gardener' who has no experience whatever with gardening, but who claims the right to tend the garden. The true gardener smiles and shakes his head at the absurd claims of the stranger, but offers no verbal response. Milton provides no resolution either, concluding that he cannot reveal the outcome 'till the end of this Parliament' (717). Rudolph Kirk notes (*CPW* I: 717 n. 31) that Milton anticipates the end of the prelates' power at that time, and yet in his tale this resolution is not a *fait accompli*. Like the pamphlet battle with Hall, the outcome is uncertain. Milton's words may be more authentic than Hall's, his public persona more credible, and yet Milton here acknowledges that he cannot guarantee a particular resolution. The righteousness of the true gardener is not enough to carry the day.

The Reason of Church-Government: January or February 1642

After a hiatus of six months, Milton returned to public controversy with *The Reason of Church-Governement Urg'd against Prelaty*, in part a response to personal attacks levelled against him in the omnibus tract *Certain Briefe Treatises, Written by Diverse Learned Men, Concerning the Ancient and Moderne Government of the Church*. In this tract, the first to bear Milton's name, self-expression is intimately linked to the pursuit of truth. Both are processes that demand interaction with others and that give form – and therefore existence itself – to the spirit within. And both processes are potentially dangerous: Milton's own personal narrative is the interrupted story of *The Reason of Church-Government*.

The principal subject of the first of the two parts of the tract is the question of what is to be given form. This is the first overt statement – to be developed extensively in *Areopagitica* – that verbal exchange is the process that gives form to truth. Verbal exchange is the means of accomplishing that discipline, which is

> not only the removall of disorder, but if any visible shape can be given to divine things, the very visible shape and image of vertue, whereby she is not only seene in the regular gestures and motions of her heavenly paces as she walkes, but also makes the harmony of her voice audible to mortall eares. (*CPW* I: 751–2)

In such exchange, human beings fully exercise their powers of discernment, which were given them by God and which makes them 'his rationall temple' (758).

The need for public verbal exchange leads Milton to a detailed defence of religious sects. The prelates, he argues, are the true schismatics, because they break away from the practices of reforming churches abroad. The sects, on the other hand, continue the tradition of past reformers, who themselves were accused of fomenting schism: 'the

Primitive Christians in their times were accounted such as are now call'd Familists and Adamites, or worse' (*CPW* I: 788). The sects are, then, a sign of religious health, and also the reason why intellectual freedom is needed for the pursuit of truth. The verbal exchanges prompted by sectarian argument, like the counsels of the apostles, provide the opposition that creates truth. Such vigorous exchanges are:

> the throws and pangs that go before the birth of reformation . . . For if we look but on the nature of elementall and mixt things, we know they cannot suffer any change of one kind, or quality into another without the struggl of contrarieties. (795)

If reformation is the goal, then the verbal exchanges of the sects are the means. Milton argues with confidence that, in 'the fierce encounter of truth and falshood' (796), truth will emerge victorious.

Milton writes with less confidence when his defence of the sects becomes, in the second part of the tract, a defence of himself. Milton presents his entry into public life as a response to a risk: what he does, or fails to do, will shape people's perception of what he is. If he truly believes free speech to be a 'treasure' (*CPW* I: 804), and 'the cause of God and his Church' (805) to be in need of advocates, he cannot possess integrity if he neglects to join the controversy. Such a failure would render him 'worthlesse'. And yet, this participation is an interruption of his overall declared purpose in life, causing him to 'write . . . out of mine own season, when I have neither yet compleated to my minde the full circle of my private studies' (807). There follows an autobiographical narrative, widely noted by scholars to be Milton's first explanation of his calling as poet. The narrative provides an extended comparison of poetry and preaching. Both are public callings. Both are 'the inspired guift of God' (816), given only to a few in any nation; both 'celebrate in glorious and lofty Hymns the throne and equipage of Gods Almightinesse, and what he works' (817). Both were Milton's earliest chosen careers. And both have been interrupted by the 'urgent reason' (820) of public controversy. Devoted now to polemics – works 'of my left hand' (808) – and 'Church-outed by the Prelats' (823), Milton has no idea whether his own story will ultimately continue, or whether it too will change form in the course of reformation. Confident of the triumph of truth, Milton is less so about his own future: will he achieve what he believed to be his calling, or will the process of exchange prove him wrong and give form to something he cannot anticipate? What *is* the nature of Milton's spirit?

An Apology Against a Pamphlet: April 1642

Milton's final foray into the antiprelatical controversy moves from the self interrupted to the self composed. In his response to yet another attack on himself and his character in a tract possibly composed by Bishop Hall and his son Robert, Milton expresses a clear sense of the self at risk. Defence of truth requires public action and yet it renders the individual combatant vulnerable, exposing him to the possibility that he may be proved wrong, mistaken in himself, inadequate to the task. *An Apology Against a*

Pamphlet Call'd A Modest Confutation of the Animadversions upon the Remonstrant against Smectymnuus undertakes the defence of truth by means of a defence of personal integrity. Milton writes 'as a member incorporate into that truth whereof I was perswaded' (*CPW* I: 871) and yet he also seeks to articulate his essential self, completing the narrative interrupted by the necessity of the times.

Recent scholarship has emphasized the highly rhetorical nature of the Miltonic self. Paul Stevens, for example, argues that 'Milton's self is produced in the process of writing', and that, to achieve his ultimate goal of subsumption by God (a '*vertical* transformation'), that self undergoes 'a series of culturally approved *lateral* transformations' (Stevens 1988: 268). Certainly, *The Reason of Church-Government* and *An Apology* do contain self-representations that are not entirely consistent, but throughout Milton is in search of a deeper authenticity, a revealing of the self that, while adaptable to circumstances, nevertheless gives form to an internal truth. Hence Milton's expositions on true and false uses of rhetorical figures (*CPW* I: 877) and on 'miming' (879–82) as false representation. In *An Apology*, there is an essential self to be defended; autobiography becomes combat – a 'hazardous' process (888) and a 'tryall' (889), because it is a test of whether one truly *is* as one *says*.

This assertion is the ground of Milton's famous affirmation of integrity in writing:

> he who would not be frustrate of his hope to write well hereafter in laudable things, ought him selfe to bee a true Poem, that is, a composition, and patterne of the best and honourablest things; not presuming to sing high praises of heroick men, or famous Cities, unlesse he have in himselfe the experience and the practice of all that which is praise-worthy. (*CPW* I: 890)

This sentiment, while not original, emphasizes that the self is not entirely rhetorical. There is an inner self that must be aligned with the outer. What some may perceive as multiple outer selves are in fact manifestations of various facets of the inner self – not 'produced' as such, but shaped and expressed. These outward expressions may be attacked, questioned, edited, altered; but this process should finally bring a writer to the point where his own mind may provide justification for his arguments (901).

Milton's own autobiography thus becomes the confirmation of his arguments in favour of proper reading, composed prayer and action. In his previous tracts, as we have seen, these three subjects enable the search for truth. Here, they are the means of testing the validity of the ways in which the self is expressed. Public expression is therefore a necessity for the development of all Christian souls, and Milton praises the current government for listening to the petitions of 'the meanest artizans and labourers, at other times also women, and often the younger sort of servants' (*CPW* I: 926). As Milton understands it, there is a link between eloquence and character:

> that indeed according to art is most eloquent, which returnes and approaches neerest to nature from whence it came; and they expresse nature best, who in their lives least wander from her safe leading, which may be call'd regenerate reason. (874)

As one becomes eloquent by exercising the reason, so the spirit itself develops through its expression: 'For not only the body, & the mind, but also the improvement of Gods Spirit is quicken'd by using' (937–8). This is the reason why one must put oneself at risk through the trial of public action. It is Milton's understanding of Aristotle's definition of man as a political animal. Heroism lies in the risk of changing and being changed in verbal exchange.

The underlying tension in the antiprelatical tracts results from Milton's lack of resolution about the stability of the self. One may be tried by contraries, developed and improved, but one may also be interrupted and altered. The interruptions could be the result of Milton's eschatological perspective – the process of exchange will continue until the end of time. But they could also be the result of an inescapable worry about the nature of the responses generated by participation in public conversations. To every public utterance there will be a reply. The wen may burst forth with a response that cannot be entirely contained. The possibility of an uncontainable response prompts this anxiety: not that the response asserts yet another falsehood to be refuted, but that it may be right. To participate in public, verbal exchange is to subject the self to hostile editing, a 'reading' that is not entirely within one's control. This anxiety provides a subtext for Milton's justly most famous political tract – *Areopagitica*.

Areopagitica: November 1644

In many respects, *Areopagitica; A Speech of Mr. John Milton For the Liberty of Vnlicenc'd Printing, To the Parlament of England* is Milton's most brilliant articulation of ideas he first expressed and developed in the antiprelatical tracts. He shapes those ideas, giving them a new and more powerful meaning. Again, the tract concerns itself with the conception of form, whether that of Truth, books or the self. It is also a crucial text for scholarship, a vital piece of evidence for determining the form of Milton – his own character and political views.

Milton himself presents readers with multiple possibilities for interpretation. His own account of his composition of *Areopagitica*, presented in his *Pro Populo Anglicano Defensio Secunda*, emphasizes his belief that the determination of truth and falsehood should not be left 'in the hands of a few' (*WJM* 8: 133), especially if those few are intellectually deficient. Milton thus suggests that *Areopagitica* is a defence of principle. The tract is also a response to yet another personal attack – this one a harsh criticism of the second edition of *The Doctrine and Discipline of Divorce* (published 13 August 1644), delivered by Herbert Palmer in a sermon before the House of Commons (see Blum 1987: 82–3; Hill 1978: 149–50). So *Areopagitica* is another example of the self on trial. This personal perspective has led many scholars, from the editor Ernest Sirluck (*CPW*) to Stanley Fish (1987) and Francis Barker (1984), to see Milton defending the private self against the interests of the state, or vice versa (Illo 1988), and thus as a champion of individual freedom or religious authoritarianism.

But, more directly, *Areopagitica* is a harsh critique of the Licensing Order of 1643 – an Order of Parliament in a time of great political instability (see Norbrook 1999: 119–20; Smith 1990: 104). This Order was issued explicitly to protect the monopoly on printing held by the Company of Stationers. It also defined 'books' by all those involved in their production: authorities were to 'apprehend all Authors, Printers, and other persons whatsoever imployed in compiling, printing, stitching, binding, publishing and dispersing of the said scandalous, unlicensed, and unwarrantable papers, books and pamphlets as aforesaid' (*CPW* II: 798). As Stephen Dobranski argues (1999: 105), when Milton defends unlicensed printing, he is supporting the book trade itself and envisioning the process of knowledge-making as a collaborative enterprise (see also Kolbrener 1997: 25–7; Magnus 1991: 95–6). This Milton is a republican public citizen.

This newer view of Milton is highly persuasive, but, as I have argued at the beginning of this chapter, he cannot fully participate in Aristotle's definition of the political animal. Classical theorists did not confront the issue of a political animal with an immortal soul in need of salvation, or a truth equated with some kind of Christian revelation. Milton clearly did. So for Milton, truth must be both a process and an absolute, the self both constructed and essential, and reading both transformative and 'indifferent' to the soul. The power of *Areopagitica* comes from the irreconcilability of the two positions, and Milton's movement between the competing but equally positive values.

As in the antiprelatical tracts, Milton's central issue is the advancement of truth through public, verbal exchange. He employs the structural metaphor of Solomon's Temple to explain the process of reformation: this 'Temple of the Lord' is a 'gracefull symmetry' arising 'out of many moderat varieties and brotherly dissimilitudes that are not vastly disproportionall' (*CPW* II: 555). This analogy is in keeping with his vision of the multiform nature of truth. Like Proteus, she can change into many shapes before assuming her true one, and it is 'not impossible that she may have more shapes then one' (563). Also, God may be 'decreeing to begin some new and great period in his Church, ev'n to the reforming of Reformation it self' (553). All of these processes embody the principle of *discordia concors* (see Norbrook 1999: 137–8; Kolbrener 1997: 11–13), conflict giving rise to a greater harmony. Though the body of truth has been mangled, yet the search for its parts continues, and shall continue to the second coming (*CPW* II: 549); it is the duty of public officials to allow the search – the conflict of verbal exchange – to continue, as it does whenever books are published.

And yet Milton does place limits on this search, limits that amount to damage control on the risk of public exchange. The reasons why such controls should be necessary become clear when we see that Milton identifies the book with the self. First, books appear as living entities, brought to life by Milton's prose. They are 'not absolutely dead things, but doe contain a potencie of life in them to be as active as that soule was whose progeny they are' (*CPW* II: 492); the 'living labours of publick men' (493) and 'intellectuall off spring' (505). Moreover, just as a book may be living, a human being may be a book. Milton speaks of an author 'print[ing] his mind' (531) and argues that one's experiences may be considered a book: 'what ever thing we hear or see, sitting, walking, travelling, or conversing may be fitly call'd our book, and is of the same effect that writings are' (528; see Sherman 1993). Finally, both book and self are products of collaboration. In the act of reading, readers learn to shape their character. Even 'bad books', when read properly, can help readers 'to discover, to confute, to forewarn, and to illustrate' (*CPW* II: 512–13). And such encounters are a requirement of expressing the form within. As we have seen in the antiprelatical tracts, discipline gives shape (*Reason of Church-Government*), and use brings us closer to our nature (*Apology*); so, in *Areopagitica*, 'that which purifies us is triall, and triall is by what is contrary' (515). One ensures that one's beliefs are true by testing them. Books are important tools in the process.

But we must ask what Milton means by trial. A suggestion appears in his description of writing a book: 'When a man writes to the world, he summons up all his reason and deliberation to assist him; he searches, meditats, is industrious, and likely consults and conferrs with his judicious friends' (*CPW* II: 532). Books, both good and bad, test the potential author's ideas. The author reasons with himself and develops his arguments by practising them with friends. Trial and collaboration are one; collaboration is a sociable process, not a struggle. In this version of trial, risk to the self is minimal because of the context in which the trial takes place. In this trial, all the contestants know the ground rules, whether they are friends, rival sectarians or even prelates of the Church of England.

Ironically, the risk is also minimal because, in *Areopagitica*, the self is simultaneously malleable and immutable. Milton argues in favour of unlicensed printing because at the core of the individual is a substance that cannot be changed. A fool will be a fool, whether with the best book or no book (*CPW* II: 521), and no person's essence can be changed by outside interference: 'Banish all objects of lust, shut up all youth into the severest discipline that can be exercis'd in any hermitage, ye cannot make them chaste, that came not thither so' (527). The kind of trial Milton advocates here is limited. It can shape and discipline, but it cannot alter one's essence. Hence, government licensers actually have nothing to fear from the free printing of books. No book will corrupt those who are not already corrupt. However, the kind of books Milton has in mind will be a vital help in producing the public citizens upon whom the state depends for its preservation and maintenance.

Milton's powerful optimism in *Areopagitica* rests on his careful suppression of the alternative interpretation of public trial – the kind that periodically emerges in the antiprelatical tracts. In the earlier tracts, Milton does acknowledge the possibility of being changed in ways one cannot anticipate and may not like. This kind of trial may become *agon*. The alternative reading appears in *Areopagitica* in Milton's almost parenthetical remarks about the suppression of Catholic books and works of 'open superstition' (*CPW* II: 565), and the punishment of 'mischievous and libellous' books by 'the fire and the executioner' (569). Recent defenders of Milton's position point out that he was writing in wartime, when Catholicism was perceived as a real threat, and that works which present themselves as truth have no place in a context in which truth is a process. These arguments are valid. Nevertheless, I want to suggest here that Milton's objections may lie deeper: if truth is a process and the self collaborative, then both may be re-formed by differences that are neither 'moderat' nor 'brotherly'. Truth may become error, the self revised. One may be persuaded – erroneously – that one is wrong. Hence, Milton perceives the need to set and maintain the limits of public discourse. He both courts the process and public, verbal exchange and resists it.

*

Even in *Areopagitica*, form is ultimately tenuous. Truth has many forms, but if there are too many, then there is no form because form gives essence. Without form, there is no tangibility. In Milton's early pamphlets, there is always the possibility that the wen will not be cut off, that truth's body will not be reassembled. Milton's last prose work, *Of True Religion, Heresy, Schism, Toleration* (1673), continued the anti-Catholic arguments of *Areopagitica* while advocating collegial toleration of all other Christians. Truth still needed defenders.

But Milton did envision an alternative. In the great works of the Restoration, central figures realize themselves through unrestricted collaboration. In *Paradise Lost* and *Paradise Regained*, Satan himself becomes a significant interlocutor. In *Samson Agonistes*, Dalila, Harapha and other enemies of the Israelites interact with Samson. In these works, the heroes actualize themselves by interacting with 'brotherly' and hostile – and evil – figures alike. In the prose works, 'popery' must be suppressed; in the late poetry, Satan speaks. Milton also willingly subjects himself to trial by putting his own creative powers into authentically wicked figures. Milton thus eventually confronts the issue of genuine and necessary risk, the self in *agon*, by resolving it poetically. But, as *Of True Religion* shows, Milton could not resolve the issue politically in his historical moment.

BIBLIOGRAPHY

Writings

Milton (1967, 1974, 1998b).

References for Further Reading

Barker, Francis (1984); Blum (1987); Cable (1995); Dobranski (1999); Dzelzainis (1995a); Egan (1976); Fish (1972, 1987, 1990); Hill (1978); Illo (1988); Kolbrener (1997); Kranidas (1982, 1983); Loewenstein (1990); Magnus (1991); Norbrook (1999); Sherman, Sandra (1993); Smith (1990); Stevens (1988).

17

Milton, Marriage and Divorce

Annabel Patterson

It is a grave irony, none the less grave for being slightly comic, that Milton left us his thoughts on marriage primarily in four pamphlets advocating divorce. And though he was later to claim, in his *Pro Populo Anglicano Defensio Secunda*, that these pamphlets were merely part of a disinterested analysis of the 'three varieties of liberty without which civilized life is scarcely possible', religious, domestic and civil (*CPW* IV: 624), we know that the primary motivation for at least the first, the painful and revealing *Doctrine and Discipline of Divorce*, was the early collapse of Milton's late-begun marriage. This personal humiliation was a great intellectual catalyst. It led first to his discovery of the thought of the continental reformers, especially Martin Bucer, on the topic of divorce; then to his involvement in verbal flytings with those who had complained in print about his advocacy of 'divorce at pleasure'; then to his insertion of a definitive and radical definition of marriage into the Picard manuscript of *De Doctrina Christiana c.* 1660, and finally (though the compositional priority of these last two stages might be debated) to a poetic and imaginative representation of the first of all marriages, in the far from ideal but none the less heartwarming drama of Adam and Eve in *Paradise Lost*.

In the twenty-first century this aspect of Milton's experience is likely to remain a magnet for his modern readers, for at least two reasons. After thirty or so years of feminist criticism, most of which has assumed that Milton was a misogynist, we are now in a position to reassess the long-term interest of his theory of marriage for generations for whom the feminist battles are now receding as more or less won – within the academy, that is. And from a narrower scholarly perspective, revisiting in a scrupulously textual way how Milton *expressed* his marriage theory has pertinence to another struggle over his soul – between those who deny that Milton's Christianity was heterodox and therefore dispute his authorship of *De Doctrina Christiana*, and those, myself included, who for all sorts of different reasons are confident he wrote it. This chapter will deal more extensively with the former than the latter, in part because the evidence adduced about the value and interest of his thought will serve the second purpose also, to show that his marriage theory was, if not logically consistent, psychologically and linguistically coherent. It all carries his bold and indomitable signature.

So let us now go back to the beginning of the story and see how Milton found himself engaged in rethinking the nature of matrimony. In seventeenth-century England, the legislation governing marriage was in limbo, thanks to the Reformation. Technically, it was still governed by canon law, which decreed, since marriage was a sacrament, that there could be no divorce with right of remarriage (*a vinculo matrimonio*), undoing the chain completely. What was possible was legal separation (*a mensa et thoro*): freedom to eat and sleep alone. The grounds, however, were narrow, being limited in England to adultery and cruelty. Canon law permitted nullification on the grounds of a prior cause unknown to one of the partners, such as consanguinity, a prior contract, impotence or female impenetrability.

Why, you may ask, did canon law still pertain in a Protestant country like England, when in Europe most Protestant states, denying that marriage was a sacrament, had legalized remarriage for the innocent party after divorce for adultery? In fact, in 1552 Edward VI had appointed a commission to bring England into line with continental practice; the commission had included Archbishop Thomas Cranmer and Sir John Cheke, and the product was the *Reformatio Legum Ecclesiasticarum*, a set of proposals for reform which included divorce for desertion and for 'capital hatreds' (*CPW* II: 717 [and passim]). The proposals were defeated in the House of Commons, and under Elizabeth and James the Anglican hierarchy reinforced the position of canon law. Yet privately puritan ministers ignored the canons and recognized remarriages of the innocent party in cases of adultery or desertion; so that a man, like Milton, who thought he needed his freedom could have taken this semi-official route to obtain it.

Milton thought he needed his freedom because, in June 1642, he had made what by all accounts was a hasty and imprudent marriage with the eldest daughter of a royalist family, Mary Powell, a girl about half his age. So we were told by Milton's nephew, Edward Phillips, in 1694:

> About Whitsuntide it was, or a little after, that he took a Journey into the Country; no body about him certainly knowing the Reason, or that it was any more than a Journey of Recreation: after a Month's stay, home he returns a Married-man, that went out a Batchelor. (Darbishire 1932: 63)

Phillips's story is so well told that it bears extensive quotation. After the marriage festivities in Milton's house in London, the bride's family went back to Oxfordshire, leaving her alone with Milton and his students:

> By that time she had for a Month or thereabout led a Philosophical Life (after having been used to a great House, and much Company and Joviality). Her Friends, possibly incited by her own desire, made earnest suit by Letter, to have her Company the

remaining part of the Summer, which was granted, on condition of her return at the time appointed, Michaelmas, or thereabout: . . . Michaelmas being come, and no news of his Wife's return, he sent for her by Letter; and receiving no answer, sent several other Letters, which were also unanswered; so that at last he dispatch'd down a Foot-Messenger with a Letter, desiring her return; but the Messenger came back not only without an answer, at least a satisfactory one, but to the best of my remembrance, reported that he was dismissed with some sort of Contempt. (Darbishire 1932: 64–5)

Phillips speculated that the cause of Mary's failure to return was in part political; the royalist Powells, with the King's party established at Oxford, imagined that the Civil War would soon be ended in their favour, and that the marriage would become 'a blot in their Escutcheon' (65). But he also recorded Milton's state of mind at this treatment:

It so incensed our Author, that he thought it would be dishonourable ever to receive her again, after such a repulse; so that he forthwith prepared to Fortify himself with Arguments for such a Resolution, and accordingly wrote . . . Treatises, by which he undertook to maintain, That it was against Reason, and . . . not proveable by scripture, for any Married Couple disagreeable in Humour and Temper, or having an aversion to each other, to be forc'd to live yok'd together all their Days. (65)

Here then, and not in any disinterested overview of the vital human liberties, lay the motive for both editions of *The Doctrine and Discipline of Divorce* (1 August 1643 and 2 February 1644) – followed by the series of follow-ups and self-justifications that Milton felt he needed, given the hostile response his arguments had received: *The Judgement of Martin Bucer* (15 July 1644) and *Tetrachordon* (4 March 1645) with their supplemental diatribe against Milton's critics on this issue, *Colasterion*, also given the same date by George Thomason. (Thomason was a great private collector of Civil War tracts who dated each acquisition, thereby enhancing the historical value of his collection.)

Milton may have begun, as Phillips most intriguingly suggests, collecting arguments about divorce in order 'to fortify himself' psychologically for the formal separation to which, on the grounds of desertion, he would have been entitled. But by the time he had worked through the arguments, he apparently believed he could persuade the Long Parliament and the Westminster Assembly to change the law – to legislate the right to divorce *a vinculo* for both parties, not only on the old grounds, but also for incompatibility. Should Parliament have been persuaded, the effect, of course, would have been to transfer the control over marriage from the church to the state and reconstitute it as a civil contract. In this Milton was hopelessly unrealistic. Such legislation would not be fully enacted in England until more than halfway through the twentieth century. Perhaps by the time he wrote the ill-tempered *Colasterion* he had grasped how unseasonable and unpopular his proposal was in the 1640s. Perhaps by then, hoping to marry 'one of Dr Davis's daughters, a very handsome and witty gentlewoman', he was considering taking the back-door route of finding a rebellious minister sympathetic to such cases. The personal unyoking, however, was not to happen. Phillips also related how, given 'the declining state of the King's Cause', efforts were made by the Powells and their friends to effect a reconciliation between the Miltons, efforts that were rewarded by a scene of domestic tragicomedy prophetic of *Paradise Lost*, Book X. As Eve, after the Fall and the couple's bitter mutual recriminations, initiated their emotional recovery on her knees, 'with tears that ceased not flowing' (*PL* X. 910), Milton was unexpectedly confronted by his wife 'making Submission and begging Pardon on her Knees before him' (Darbishire 1932: 66). This must have happened some time in the summer of 1645, for by October Mary was living with her husband in his large new house in the Barbican, and immediately became pregnant with their first daughter. If *Paradise Lost* is their story also, the Miltons left the garden of innocence together, in a mood at least of amicable resolution, and hand in hand.

What happened in Milton's head between Michaelmas 1642 and the summer of 1645 is recorded in the four divorce pamphlets, or five if we count the two different versions of *The Doctrine and Discipline*, the second of which contains significant additions. Roughly speaking, he begins with an ill-concealed personal bitterness, moves towards formal high-mindedness by citing a vast chorus of authorities for his position, and ends with renewed personal bitterness, and coarseness – but now redirected to his 'answerers'. More importantly, I believe, Milton *discovered* for himself the principle of companionate marriage as Protestantism was still inventing it, and the engine of his discovery was humiliation and disappointment. That is to say, by finding Mary Milton wanting (and missing), he imagined in the hole she had made in his feelings what a good marriage might be. Consequently he could see for himself, and with acid clarity, what was wrong with a legal system that encouraged hypocrisy, stressed the dynastic and physical aspects of marriage over the psychological and sociable, and did not allow for second chances.

The Doctrine and Discipline of Divorce is, more than any of the other tracts, a plea for second chances, and its language is unintentionally revelatory of its author's own appeal for such respite. In the supplementary address to the Long Parliament that Milton added for the second edition he seemed to disclaim the possibility of being 'the agent of his owne by-ends, under pretext of Reformation' (*CPW* II: 225), yet a few paragraphs later admitted that sometimes self-interest works for the public good: '[W]hen points of difficulty are to be discusst, appertaining to the removall of unreasonable wrong and burden from the perplext life of our brother, it is incredible how cold, how dull, and farre from all fellow feeling we are, without the spurre of self-concernment' (226). This is as far as Milton goes, however, in admitting the auto-biographical nature of his argument, which is everywhere supposed to be disguised by the use of the third person. In Book I, Chapter III, Milton seeks to refute the argument that divorce would be unnecessary if people carefully considered the 'disposition' of their mates before locked into wedlock. *Caveat emptor.* Look before you leap. 'But let them know again', Milton responded, that for all the warinesse can be us'd, it may yet befall a discreet man to be mistak'n in his choice: and we have plenty of examples. the soberest and best govern'd men are lest practiz'd in these affairs; and who knows not that the bashfull mutenes of a virgin may oft-times hide all the unlivelines & naturall sloth which is really unfit for conversation; nor is there that freedom of accesse granted or presum'd, as may suffice to a perfect discerning till too late: and where any indisposition is suspected, what more usuall then the perswasion of friends, that acquaintance, as it encreases, will amend all. And lastly, it is not strange though many who have spent their youth chastly, are in some things not so quick-sighted, while they hast too eagerly to light the nuptiall torch; nor is it therfore that for a modest error a man should forfeit so great a happines, and no charitable means to release him. (249)

Despite the presence of all these implied plurals – the soberest men, who 'oft-times' mistake mental apathy for maidenly modesty, the 'usuall' interference of friends, the 'many' who are inexperienced because, unlike their peers, they have spent their youth chastly, and most of all that phrase inserted in the second edition about 'plenty of examples' – despite all these screens, Milton himself in his shame and isolation stands naked before us in the very phrases he thought he had so carefully chosen to hide behind.

The two phrases balanced against each other in the last cited sentence suggest that reform is required by human fallibility, expressed exclusively as *masculine* fallibility, a point to which we must return. But there is more here than a mere concession to short-sightedness. Milton disputes the justice of weighing 'a modest error' against 'so great a happines', and deciding that the former, so small, must cost one the latter, so imaginably generous in scale. What is this 'so great a happines' he has now forfeited? The next chapter attempts to define it, by rewriting St Paul's ungenerous concession, '*It is better to marry then to burne*' in terms of the book of Genesis. 'What might this burning mean?' asks Milton. 'Certainly not the meer motion of carnall lust, not the meer goad of a sensitive desire'.

What is it then but that desire which God put into *Adam* in Paradise . . . that desire which God saw it was not good that man should be left alone to burn in; the desire and longing to put off an unkindly solitarines by uniting another body, but not without a fit soule to his in the cheerfull society of wedlock. Which if it were so needfull before the fall, when man was much more perfect in himself, how much more is it needfull now against all the sorrows and casualties of this life to have an intimate and speaking help, a ready and reviving associate in marriage . . . Who hath the power to struggle with an intelligible flame, not in Paradise to be resisted, become now more ardent, by being fail'd of what in reason it lookt for. (251–2)

Deprivation increases desire by explaining the nature of desire to itself, thus making loneliness theoretically intelligible. It is not the Fall, however, that deprives us of the ideal marital scenario, according to this first appeal to Genesis. On the contrary, the Fall made it essential to us. It is Milton's personal fall into the erratic choice of a mate that has taught him, too late, what he really 'lookt for'.

Out of misery comes poetry in prose: 'Who hath the power to struggle with an intelligible flame, not in Paradise to be resisted'. One has only to compare this sentence with other English Protestant definitions of companionate marriage to perceive Milton's originality and complexity. Thus John Dod and Robert Cleaver, in their *Godly Forme of Housholde Governement: For the Ordering of Private Families according to the directions of Gods word*, which appeared in many editions from 1598 onwards, used scripture to assert a much plainer ideal – and with it, a warning *against* divorce:

> Wedlocke or Matrimonie, is a lawfull knot, and unto God an acceptable yoking & joyning together of one man, and one woman, with the good consent of them both; to the end that they may dwell together in friendship and honesty, one helping & comforting the other, eschewing whoredome, and all uncleannesse, bringing up their children in the feare of God: or it is a coupling together of two persons into one flesh, according unto the ordinace of God; not to be broken, but so to continue during the life of either of them, Gen. 2.2, Malachi 2.14, Rom. 7.31. (Dod and Cleaver 1612: F8^r)

Dod and Cleaver, moreover, specifically warn against the kind of imprudent marriage choice that, Milton had argued, resulted from incomplete knowledge of the intended. All the qualifications or disqualifications, they warned, may not be 'spied at three or four commings, and meetings of the parties':

> for hypocrisie is spunne with a fine threed, and none are so often deceived as lovers. He therefore which will know all his wives qualities: or she that will perceive her husbands dispositions, & inclinations, before either be married to the other, had need to see one the other eating, and walking, working, and playing, talking, and laughing, and chiding too. (G6^v)

Note how the practical tone of this puritan handbook is marked by a concern for reciprocity, here for the wife's pre-understanding of the contract also, and later for the kind of realism that will make for sensible adjustments. 'Let the husband think, that he hath married a daughter of Adam, and all her infirmities; and likewise let the woman thinke, that she hath not married an Angell, but a child of Adam, with his corruption' (M6^r).

Milton, however, here as perhaps in *Paradise Lost*, saw himself as an angel. And it is his unrealistic, flaming idealism that leads directly, by implied syllogistic reasoning, to his scandalous paradox, that the would-be divorcer is actually the best upholder of marriage:

> if that mistake have done injury, it fails not to dismisse with recompense, for to retain still, and not to be able to love, is to heap up more injury... He therfore who lacking of his due in the most native and humane end of mariage, thinks it better to part then to live sadly and injuriously to that cherful covnant (for not to be belov'd & yet retain'd, is

the greatest injury to a gentle spirit) he I say who therfore seeks to part, is one who highly honours the married life, and would not stain it. (*CPW* II: 253)

This conclusion is scandalous not only in its reversal of societal assumptions, but also in its political unconscious – the sexual political unconscious, that is. The revealing slippage from the high-minded 'to retain still, and not to be able to love' to the querulous 'not to *be* belov'd & yet retain'd' admits the personal motives that Milton elsewhere disclaimed. Who, this syntax asks, is doing the divorcing? Who injures whom?

In fact, Milton answered this question for us, and to his own discredit, when he added to the second edition (Book II, Chapter XV) an attack on the opinion of Beza and Paraeus that divorce was permitted in Jewish law for relief of wives, rather than husbands. 'Palpably uxorious!' exclaims Milton at this point (in February 1644), in one of the most dramatic utterances of the entire work:

Who can be ignorant that woman was created for man, and not man for woman; and that a husband may be injur'd as insufferably in mariage as a wife. What an injury is it after wedlock *not to be belov'd*, what to be slighted, what to be contended with in point of house-rule who shall be the head, not for any parity of wisdome, for that were somthing reasonable, but out of a female pride. (*CPW* II: 324; italics added)

The return of the theme of injury, and especially of the phrase 'not to be belov'd', sorts out the ambiguities of the earlier passage. And Milton actually glossed this outburst by alluding to the book of Esther and the story of Vashti, 'whose meer denial to come at her husbands sending lost her the being Queen any longer' (325). Somewhat over a year later Mary Milton's 'denial to come at her husbands sending' was, however, to be forgiven.

Before moving on to the other three divorce pamphlets, there is another aspect of *The Doctrine and Discipline* that needs to be confronted, however disconcerting it may be. This is the language that Milton used to denote the sexual, as distinct from the sociable, aspects of marriage. His object, of course, was to demote the sexual, or what he calls the carnal, because that was what canon law regarded as central and determinative of the relationship. But the language in which this demotion was effected seems in excess of its purpose. In 1978 Edward Le Comte, in *Milton and Sex*, examined Milton's vocabulary in this pamphlet, and concluded that it registered personal disgust with his sexual experience, caused, perhaps, by its being so new to him. He noted that Milton equated heterosexual activity not only with animalism, a 'bestial necessity', 'bestial burning', 'animal or beastish meeting', 'a brutish congress', but also with physical labour or slavery (29–30; cf. James Turner [1987: 203], who judiciously recognizes Milton's ideas of sexuality as 'many-layered'). Central to Le Comte's perception is a sentence of Milton's that must, in its almost unmediated physicality, give nearly every reader pause:

O perversnes!... that to grind in the mill of an undelighted and servil copulation, must
be the only forc't work of a Christian mariage, oft times with such a yokefellow, from
whom both love and peace, both nature and Religion mourns to be separated. (258)

We should also group around the grinding in the mill the following phrases from
elsewhere in the pamphlet: 'bondmen of a luckles and helples matrimony' (*CPW* II:
240); 'sowe the furrow of mans nativity with seed of two incoherent and uncombining
dispositions' (270); 'the disparity of severall cattell at the plow' (277); and especially
'God loves not to plow out the heart of our endeavours with over-hard and sad
tasks... by making wedlock a supportles yoke... to make men the day-labourers of
their own afflictions' (342). Sex is hard work when the heart is not in it.

On the other hand, Milton cannot quite bring himself to talk straight to the issue.
Metaphors and euphemisms abound, and, as they so often do, only make things seem
worse than they really are. Archaic allegories of the body, complete with alliteration,
connote embarrassment: 'the vessell of voluptuous enjoyment' or 'the channell of
concupiscence' (*CPW* II: 248–9). But the libidinal narrative cannot decide whether
failure or success is more depressing. 'The impediment of carnall performance', the
'stopt or extinguisht... veins of sensuality', and the 'disappointing of an impetuous
nerve' alternate with the 'impatience of a sensuall desire... reliev'd' and the 'pre-
scrib'd satisfaction of an irrationall heat'. The canon law prescribes that 'the contract
shall stand as firme as ever', however 'flat & melancholious' the emotional relationship. Above all, in the notorious 'quintessence of an excrement' (248), his periphrasis
for semen, Milton rather highlighted than solved the problem of which euphemism is
the signpost or the symptom. Abstract thought and philosophical idealism (expressed
in a classicizing and pseudoscientific vocabulary) reveal their connections to a venerable tradition of misogynistic distaste.

In sum, then, *The Doctrine and Discipline of Divorce* presents a logical case for the
reform of the divorce law, superimposed on a subtext of emotional chaos. Milton
could apparently not decide whether his wife deserved to be divorced primarily
because of her desertion and disobedience, or because she had disappointed him by
her lack of intellectual substance; 'if not with a body impenetrable, yet... with a
minde to all other due conversation inaccessible' (*CPW* II: 250). And all the signs (in
his writing) were that the physical relationship, which had obviously been established, made him mightily uncomfortable. These textual tics and grimaces were to
disappear, almost completely, from his later pamphlets on the subject of divorce; and
part of the reason for this change is that Milton was diverted from his resentment
against his wife to indignation about the hostile responses to *The Doctrine and
Discipline*, in whose reception he now perceived his honour to inhere.

We know that his first divorce pamphlet had generated a hostile reaction, especially
among the clergy, because Milton himself presented that reaction as the motive for his
next one, the translation of part of Martin Bucer's *De Regno Christi*. The choice of
Bucer's advocacy of divorce as a bulwark for his own was probably made, in part,
because of Bucer's own history as a reformer who had been invited to England and

offered a chair of divinity at Cambridge. As *'a man call'd from another Countrey to be the instructer of our nation'* (*CPW* II: 437) Bucer therefore had more authority, Milton might have supposed, on the subject of English marital law than would the other continental reformers who shared his opinions. Bucer, moreover, had written *De Regno Christi* for Edward VI in 1550, so that it was intimately connected with that commission appointed by Edward which had *almost* accomplished the reforms for which Milton had been arguing. In the preface 'To the Parlament' that preceded *The Judgement of Martin Bucer*, as also on the title page, Milton foregrounded this connection with the Edwardian Reformation; and in the preface he explains both his motives for returning to the subject, and the sequence of events that has made this new publication necessary.

First, he explains, when the first edition of *The Doctrine and Discipline* appeared anonymously, *'some of the Clergie began to inveigh and exclaim on what I was credibly inform'd they had not read'* (*CPW* II: 434). He therefore determined *'to shew them a name that could easily contemn such an indiscreet kind of censure'*, and revised and expanded the first pamphlet for its second edition, which appeared over his name, but without a licence. Three months after its appearance he discovered the Bucer treatise, and decided to re-educate English readers in the thought of so important an authority:

> For against these my adversaries, who before the examining of a propounded truth in a fit time of reformation, have had the conscience to oppose naught els but their blind reproaches and surmises, that a single innocence {his own} might not be opprest and overborn by a crew of mouths for the restoring of a law and doctrin falsely and unlernedly reputed new and scandalous, God . . . hath unexpectedly rais'd up as it were from the dead, . . . one famous light of the first reformation to bear witnes with me . . . And O that I could set him living before ye in that doctoral chair, where once the lernedest of England *thought it no disparagement to sit at his feet! (CPW* II: 437, 439)

With this seemingly incontrovertible ally in hand, Milton may have thought that all he had to do was to translate Bucer's Latin. And so he did, omitting what did not serve his purpose (such as the chapter on the merits of the single life!). Unsurprisingly, therefore, the tone of this pamphlet, once the belligerent preface is past, is sedate, impersonal and, on the subject of sexuality, reticent. Married couples are urged to 'love one another to the height of dearness', and enjoined 'that they defraud not each other of conjugal benevolence' (*CPW* II: 466), a phrase very different in resonance from 'carnal concupiscence'. There is only one small sign of recent personal investment, where Milton added a strange phrase extending the reasons for divorce: 'Who sees not that it is a wickednes so to wrest and extend that answer of [Christ's to the Pharisees], as if it forbad to divorce her who hath already forsak'n, or hath lost the place and dignitie of a wife by deserved infamy, *or hath undertak'n to be that which she hath not naturall ability to be'* (473).

As so often, Milton was mistaken in his confidence, or at least his hopes. One week after the appearance of *Martin Bucer*, on 13 August 1644, the Presbyterian divine

Herbert Palmer preached a sermon before the Long Parliament and the Westminster Assembly in which he urged both bodies to move against heresy and schism. Among several examples of recently published opinions that ought to be suppressed, Palmer urged them to act

> if any plead Conscience...for divorce for other causes then Christ and his Apostles mention; Of which a wicked booke is abroad and uncensured, though deserving to be burnt, whose Author hath been so impudent as to set his Name to it, and dedicate it to your selves. (1644: 54)

The sermon was published later in the year: it was entered in the Stationers' Register on 7 November. In the interim, that Stationers' Company attempted to take action against some of the most scandalous publications, presenting a petition to the House of Commons which led them to instruct its Committee for Printing 'diligently to inquire out the Authors, Printers, and Publishers of the Pamphlet against the Immortality of the Soul, and concerning Divorce'. Finally, on 19 November, there appeared an anonymous *Answer to a Book, Intituled, The Doctrine and Discipline of Divorce*, carrying a special endorsement by the licenser, Joseph Caryl. We know that all but the last of these events combined to motivate Milton to write the most famous of his pamphlets, *Areopagitica*, in appeal against the revived tyranny of licensing. But by 4 March 1645 he had also written a full-scale rebuttal of the attacks on *The Doctrine and Discipline of Divorce*, to be published, unlicensed and without the name of his printer, as *Tetrachordon*, a four-stringed appeal to scripture.

The stated motive for *this* pamphlet was that some of the more 'judicious' readers of *The Doctrine and Discipline* had 'requir'd...that the scriptures there alleg'd, might be discuss'd more fully' (*CPW* II: 582); that is to say, that the disparity between the Mosaic law of divorce, as based on Deuteronomy 24: 1–2, and Christ's own seeming prohibition of it, in Matthew 5: 31–2 and 19: 3–9, be explained in a more rigorous and consecutive manner. Hence the structure of the pamphlet as an extended commentary on the four main scriptural texts on the issue of marriage and divorce: Genesis, Deuteronomy, Matthew and 1 Corinthians. Massively buttressed by biblical and legal scholarship, Milton's argument has the impersonal manners of a bulldozer. But again it is prefaced by an attack on the *'furious incitements'* which have been issued by Palmer's sermon to Parliament, which despite the fact that they have had no deleterious consequences for him so far, have demanded this further *'defence of an honest name'* (*CPW* II: 579, 581). Outraged that the pulpit has been deployed, against canon law itself, to denounce an individual, Milton matches abuse with abuse:

> *The* impudence *therfore, since he waigh'd so little what a gross revile that was to give his equall, I send him back again for a* phylactery *to stitch upon his arrogance, that censures not onely before conviction so bitterly without so much as one reason giv'n, but censures the Congregation of his Governors to their faces, for not being so hasty as himself to censure.* (*CPW* II: 582)

He had thus moved once again, as in the later stages of his campaign for reforms in church government, from intense and incendiary idealism to hand-to-hand warfare and satire.

Once again, however, there is an aspect of *Tetrachordon*'s thought on marriage that we need to face, despite its deleterious effect on Milton's reputation among modern readers. This was not predicated on the need to reconcile the seemingly more liberal Old Testament with the apparently more restrictive New. Rather, it stemmed from Milton's meditation on the enigmatic words of Genesis 1: 27: 'So God created man in his owne image, in the image of God created he him.' If, wrote Milton, we wish 'an impartial definition, what Mariage is, and what is not Mariage; it will undoubtedly be safest, fairest, and most with our obedience, to enquire . . . how it was in the beginning' (*CPW* II: 586–7). This enquiry is not, however, to be conducted with any sense of the scriptural text as problematic, but with a literalism whose results were convenient. 'It might be doubted why he saith . . . *him*, not them . . . especially since that Image might be common to them both. . . . But *St. Paul* ends the controversie by explaining that the woman is not primarily and immediatly the image of God, but in reference to the man . . . *he the image and glory of God, she the glory of the man:* he not for her, but she for him' (589). This appeal to 1 Corinthians 11 permits Milton to import St Paul's other thoughts on the inferiority of the woman. It is true, and not to be overlooked, that Milton builds in a qualification to Pauline misogyny: 'Not but that particular exceptions may have place, if she exceed her husband in prudence and dexterity, and he contentedly yeeld'. But in the particular case he has in mind, the Pauline interpretation holds:

> But that which far more easily and obediently follows from this verse, is that, seeing woman was purposely made for man, and he her head, it cannot stand before the breath of this divine utterance, that man the portraiture of God, joyning to himself for his intended good and solace an inferiour sexe, should so becom her thrall, whose wilfulnes or inability to be a wife frustrates the occasionall end of her creation, but that he may acquitt himself to freedom by his naturall birthright, and that indeleble character of priority which God crown'd him with. (*CPW* II: 589–90)

The crucial phrases here are 'an inferiour sexe', 'the occasional end of her creation', and 'that indeleble character of priority', which subsumes both a chronological priority of creation and an ontological priority of value. Man was created as valuable in himself; woman, only by occasion of his loneliness.

The final stage of Milton's thoughts on marriage, however, only refers to such arguments as already on record and not requiring restatement. Though produced simultaneously with *Tetrachordon*, *Colasterion* is almost exclusively Milton's personal attack on the anonymous author of *An Answer to a Book, Intituled, The Doctrine and Discipline of Divorce, or, A Plea for Ladies and Gentlewomen, and all other Maried Women against Divorce* (1644). Milton had complained bitterly in his preface to *Martin Bucer* that his opponents '*have stood now almost* [a] *whole year clamouring a farre off, while the*

book hath bin twice printed, twice bought up, & never once vouchsaft a friendly conference with
the author, who would be glad and thankfull to be shewn an error, either by privat disput, or
public answer' (*CPW* II: 436–7). Now that he had his public answer, he was outraged.
Calling his adversary a 'wind-egg', that is, an addled egg, 'an actual Serving-man', 'a
conspicuous gull', 'this Pork', 'this fleamy clodd of an *Antagonist*', to mention but half
of the insults, he claimed that the whole process of animadverting (point-by-point
rebuttal) is beneath him. This is another version of his claim, in *The Doctrine and*
Discipline, to have found himself, though burning with an intelligible flame, bound to
'an image of earth and fleam' (*CPW* II: 254). And, as in his desire to be free of Mary,
Milton ends *Colasterion* (an instrument of punishment) with the urge to separate:

> At any hand I would bee ridd of him: for I had rather, since the life of man is likn'd to a
> Scene, that all my entrances and *exits* might mixe with such persons only, whose worth
> erects them and their actions to a grave and tragic deportment, and not to have to doe
> with Clowns and Vices. (*CPW* II: 756–7)

This was not, in the circumstances, a persuasive posture.

How would Milton redeem himself from this 'scowring and rubbishing' (*CPW* II:
756) as he himself called it? In part, because his circumstances changed, and Mary
went down on her knees before him, 'Creature so fair his reconcilement seeking' (*PL*
X. 943); in part, by passing through the fires of a greatly more important controversy
than this, and engaging in the verbal battles of the Commonwealth and regicide
pamphlets; in part, by eventually taking the largest possible view, and at the
Restoration putting his thoughts on marriage in the context of human experience
and history at large, and an entire system of divinity. Let us deal first with the place of
marriage and divorce in *De Doctrina Christiana*, where it assumes a position and
proportion far larger than it ever would have done without these encounters of 1642–
1645.

Current views of the compositional history of *De Doctrina Christiana* are too vexed
to be canvassed here. Here we are concerned only with Book I, Chapter X, whose title,
originally in Latin, reads: 'Of the special government of man before the Fall: dealing
also with the sabbath and marriage'. Yet this seeming afterthought, marriage, in fact
takes up virtually the whole chapter, and itself falls into two radical halves, a defence
of polygamy and a defence of divorce in cases of incompatibility. Despite the fact that
Milton, as Edward Phillips reported in his early *Life* of his uncle and as the text
confirms, used as his starting point the Protestant theologies of William Ames and
John Wolleb, in this chapter he both contradicts them on the question of polygamy
and abandons them on the subject of divorce. While directly quoting Wolleb's
Compendium on the *forma* and purpose of marriage, Milton quickly proceeds to add a
section on the *forma ipsa*, that is, the essential or quintessential form, which consists in
'goodwill, love, help, solace and fidelity'. If these are missing, then marriage is so far
from being indissoluble that it must necessarily, logically, thereby be dissolved. In
effect, Milton at this point substitutes for Wolleb as his base text his own earlier

arguments from *Tetrachordon*, with such closeness as to suggest that he had the text in front of him. The textual analysis here is complicated by the fact that Milton's Latin, which often quotes Wolleb exactly, is differently translated in the Columbia and Yale editions. The much older translation by Charles Richard Sumner, which the Columbia edition prints, is sometimes more reliable in this chapter (vol. 15, esp. 152–78), but for the analogies with *Tetrachordon* the reader should consult the excellent notes accompanying John Carey's translation (*CPW* VI, esp. 368–81). There are other echoes too. When Milton wrote, 'Malum itaque tam importunum atque intestinum quid est cur non liceat amoliri?' it was translated by Carey as 'What is there, then, to prevent us from getting rid of an evil so distressing and so deep-seated?' (*CPW* VI: 372) but by Sumner, more accurately, as 'Why then should it be unlawful to deliver ourselves from so pressing an intestine evil?' (*WJM* 15: 157); but it is Carey's notes that draw our attention to the Chorus's complaint in *Samson Agonistes* about how deceptively women appear, even to 'wisest men and best / Seeming at first all heavenly under virgin veil, / Soft, modest, meek, demure, / Once joined, the contrary she proves, a thorn / Intestine' (lines 1034–8). The telling reappearance of this word 'intestine', so much more painfully physical than 'deep-seated', so typical of Milton's reliteralization of Latinisms, might alone prove that this chapter in *De Doctrina Christiana* and *Samson Agonistes* have a single author.

On the other hand, it is Carey who translates Milton's 'matrimonii . . . servitutis pistrinum' with the appropriate literalism, as 'the slavish pounding-mill of unhappy marriage', which appropriately recalls the indignity Milton added to *The Doctrine and Discipline of Divorce* in its second edition: 'that to grind in the mill of an undelighted and servil copulation, must be the only forc't work of a Christian mariage' (*CPW* II: 258).

More interesting still, perhaps, than these textual links between *De Doctrina Christiana* and the divorce pamphlets (links more indissoluble, perhaps, than marriage) is the fact that Milton here revisits the question of whose experience of being unloved is primarily in question. Whereas in *The Doctrine and Discipline*, as I have shown, his syntax suggested gender instability, here in a powerful and still personally inflected passage he casts his vote for the woman as the unloved, and hence the one who will most benefit from being released from the relationship:

Quae enim durities, quam amare suo merito non possis, eam honeste ac liberaliter dimittere? non amatam nec injuria neglectam, fastiditam, exosam, servitutis gravissimae sub iugo (tale enim est conjugium si abest amor) a viro neque amante neque amico acerbissima lege retineri, ea demum durities est omni divorto durior. (*WJM* 15: 164)

In this case the Carey translation (*CPW* VI: 375) is closer to what we need, but it requires a little amending, as in the following suggested retranslation:

For where is the hard-heartedness in sending away honorably and generously she who, by her own desert, you cannot love? That a woman who is not loved nor neglected unjustly, who is an object of distaste and hatred, should by a most cruel law be retained beneath the yoke of the most heavy slavery (for that is what marriage is if love is absent) by a man neither her lover nor her friend, that is a hardship harder than any divorce.

And even this emendation fails to do justice to the framing of this passage by the double appearance of *durities*, which, like his other proof-texts, Milton is redefining to suit his purpose. But to translate *retineri* as 'to be retained' creates, as it should, the connection back to *The Doctrine*'s second revelation '(for not to be belov'd & yet retain'd is the greatest injury to a [male] gentle spirit)' (*CPW* II: 253), while the first, and competing one, 'for to retain still, and not to be able to love, is to heap up more injury' can now be seen as the earlier stage of 'quam amare . . . non possis', whom you (not he, not you out there in the audience, but you, second person singular) cannot love. Rewriting this dilemma in the context of theological disputes over marriage, Milton restored the concept of victimage to the woman, which is where, in Hebraic law, it belonged.

If the Picard manuscript of *De Doctrina* dates, as seems most likely, from the opening years of the Restoration, Milton still had time to clarify his thinking on the subject of marriage and divorce. In some respects, though readers might look forward to a discussion of the great poems as the proper consummation of this argument, to reiterate here what Milton 'said' on this topic in *Paradise Lost* and *Samson Agonistes* is an anti-climax, so heavily has this territory been ploughed by those with a stake in proving or disproving Milton's anti-feminism. Here are some of the things he certainly did. First, it must be acknowledged that in *Samson Agonistes* he experimented with a different scenario from that so persuasively enacted in *Paradise Lost*, a scenario in which the returning, erring wife is not to be received again by her husband, despite her remarkable beauty and, a telling word, 'importunity' (line 397); Samson has now substituted a literal grinding in the mill for the metaphorical one in which he made himself Dalila's 'bond-slave' (line 411), and finds the later state an improvement over the former. Into the episode of his rejection of Dalila Milton was able to insert the contentious issue of the wife who belongs to another religion or party from her husband, and to give to the frequently tiresome Chorus the Pauline view that 'God's universal law / Gave to the man despotic power / Over his female' (lines 1053–5).

In *Paradise Lost* the story is much less simple. First, Milton transferred to his poem his earlier meditations on Genesis, and inserted into Book IV the Pauline doctrine of original inequality, that Adam was made 'for God only, she for God in him' (IV. 299). On the other hand, Milton had incontestably changed his mind on the subject of Genesis 1: 27; 'for in their looks divine / The image of their glorious maker shone' (*PL* IV. 291–2). *Both* Adam *and* Eve have been formed in the image of God, which implies the revision of the biblical text: 'in the image of God created he *them*'. Third, he allowed his poem to express, and in his own authorial voice, his mature and comfortable view of marital sexuality, which is now equated with 'the rites / Mysterious of connubial love' (IV. 742–3), rites which neither partner refuses. In part, Milton is responding to patristic arguments that sexuality did not precede the Fall; but in part he is also conflating good sex with love, a remarkable advance from his attempts in *The Doctrine and Discipline* to separate the two. 'Hail wedded love, mysterious law, true source / Of human offspring' cries the narrator (IV. 750–1):

> Far be it, that I should write thee sin or blame,
> Or think thee unbefitting holiest place,
> Perpetual fountain of domestic sweets,
> Whose bed is undefiled and chaste pronounced,
>
> . . .
>
> Here Love his golden shafts employs, here lights
> His constant lamp, and waves his purple wings,
>
> (IV. 758–64)

It was in that new knowledge that he could also reconceive that 'indeleble character of priority' that in *Tetrachordon* (*CPW* II: 590) he had assigned to Adam by making Eve the initiator of their reconciliation after the fallen quarrel; as also, more ingeniously, by having her recount the story of her creation *before* Adam is allowed to remember his. And Eve, of course, gets to speak the last human words of the poem, articulating a new paradox to undo, finally, the scandalous claim that 'he . . . who . . . seeks to part, is one who highly honours the maried life, and would not stain it' (*CPW* II: 253). Instead, Eve says simply, with the departure from Paradise upon them, 'with thee to go, / Is to stay here; without thee here to stay, / Is to go hence unwilling' (XII. 615–17).

BIBLIOGRAPHY

Writings

References for Further Reading

Darbishire (1932); Dod and Cleaver (1612); Palmer (1644).

Le Comte (1978); Turner (1987).

18

Republicanism

Martin Dzelzainis

Republicans and Regicides

Thomas Hobbes signs off the Review and Conclusion appended to *Leviathan* by invoking a superstition of exactly the kind that the work was intended to dispel. He fears that the moment of *Leviathan*'s publication – late spring 1651 – is inauspicious since 'in the revolution of States, there can be no very good Constellation for Truths of this nature to be born under, (as having an angry aspect from the dissolvers of an old Government, and seeing but the backs of them that erect a new;)'. Just as *Leviathan* literally enters the world under the sign of Gemini, so metaphorically the birth of the English republic is a time when politics faces two different ways. To dismiss the metaphor as merely an ironic flourish, however, would be to overlook the fact that Hobbes had surveyed 'divers English Books lately printed' before concluding that 'much of that Doctrine, which serveth to the establishing of a new Government, must needs be contrary to that which conduced to the dissolution of the old' (Hobbes 1996: 484, 489, 491).

Modern scholars have often followed Hobbes's lead in assuming a fundamental difference of outlook between the regicides and the republicans. For them too it seems that gazing upon the 'angry aspect' of the regicides means only seeing the back of the republicans, while looking the republicans in the face means occluding their view of the regicides. Thus John Morrill insists that 'the English revolution saw a violent act carried out by a fairly isolated band of well-placed soldiers and civilians, mainly driven by religious fanaticism (the regicides) which gave rise to a political programme supported by a wider and more pragmatic group (the republicans)' (Morrill 1993: 23). This takes Hobbes's point about the two separate cadres and superimposes a further antithesis (also to be found in Hobbes) between reason and passion. And the same contrast between republican rationality and regicidal irrationality is implicitly being invoked when Blair Worden explains that many republicans opposed the regicide because they saw in it 'the victory not of their principles but of brute force' (Worden 1991: 456).

Another characteristic highlighted in these accounts is the republicans' tendency to react to what others did rather than take the initiative themselves. The prime example is the regicide. According to Perez Zagorin, if republicanism is defined as 'a doctrinaire antagonism to all forms of kingship', then those 'who created the revolutionary government were not, for the most part, republicans. They put Charles I to death, not out of an antagonism to kingship, but because they had concluded that no other alternative was left them' (Zagorin 1954: 146, 148). Although republicans such as Sir Henry Vane the younger and Algernon Sidney were prepared to join the Rump – the Commonwealth regime that was in power from 1649 until dismissed by Cromwell and the army in April 1653 – their achievements were limited. As Worden points out, the Rump

> was the remnant of the ancient constitution, not a replacement of it. In so far as it introduced a republican form of government it did so by default, not by design. There was no king in the Rump period, but no republican constitutional architecture either. English republicanism of the 1650s is consequently more often a criticism of the English republic than an endorsement of it. (Worden 1995: 169)

The republicans thus forged their political identity in opposition to the coup that dissolved the Rump, to Cromwell's engrossing of power to himself as Protector from December 1653 onwards, and to the continued domination of politics by the army. Only in 1656, when Cromwell summoned the second parliament of his Protectorate, did the republicans find their collective political voice.

It is generally agreed that republican ideology too was shaped by events more than it shaped them. 'English republican theory', we are told, 'was far more the effect than the cause of the execution of the king in 1649' (Pocock and Schochet 1993: 147). Even after the event, the theory was slow in developing. Jonathan Scott has drawn up a list of 'key republican texts' from Milton's *The Tenure of Kings and Magistrates* (1649) to Algernon Sidney's *Discourses Concerning Government* (published posthumously in 1698), but finds that none of those in the first wave, such as Milton's *Tenure* or Marchamont Nedham's *The Case of the Commonwealth of England Stated* (1650), 'amounts to much as a positive statement of republicanism. In this respect they are limited, defensive. Their objectives are justification and submission' (Scott 1992: 37, 40). Only when the Rump's apologists felt emboldened by the defeat of the royalists at Worcester in September 1651 did they switch from defending the regime in *de facto* terms to asserting republican principles (see Pocock and Schochet 1993: 160). However, the main spur to the 'republican speculation' of the 1650s was not so much the struggle against the Stuart monarchy as the 'impermanence of the successive improvised regimes of the Interregnum' which replaced it (Worden 1990: 226). Here too the consensus is that republican thought finally came of age only with a wave of anti-Cromwellian works in 1656 which included Nedham's *The Excellencie of a Free State*, Sir Henry Vane's *A Healing Question Propounded* and James Harrington's *Oceana*.

Looked at in this light, Milton's republican credentials appear less than convincing. Whenever republicans were driven into opposition by events – the army's purge of the Long Parliament in December 1648, the regicide, the dissolution of the Rump, Cromwell's elevation to Protector – Milton would cleave to the powers that be. When the Rump needed support immediately after the regicide, Milton urged adherence 'to the present Parlament & Army' in *The Tenure* (*CPW* III: 194). When it required defending on the international stage, he produced *Pro Populo Anglicano Defensio* (1651). And when the Protectoral regime was establishing itself early in 1654, he furnished a panegyric upon Cromwell in *Defensio Secunda* (see Worden 1998). Only in the last few months of Cromwell's rule did he begin to distance himself from the Protectorate, disowning it altogether once Cromwell was dead (see Woolrych 1974; Worden 1995; Dzelzainis 1995b; Armitage 1995; and Knoppers, ch. 19 in this volume). And only in a flurry of published and unpublished works shortly before the Restoration did he express opposition to monarchy in terms approaching the unequivocal.

However, the extreme belatedness of Milton's conversion to doctrinaire republican-ism is merely one part of the problem. The other is how he managed to make this conceptual leap at all if, as Thomas Corns claims, there is 'little in his vernacular writings of 1649 and almost nothing in his Latin defences to show that Milton actively sought to argue for the English republic in terms derived either from classical models or from Machiavellian political theory' (Corns 1995: 26). Before addressing these questions, however, we need to consider two further points. The first is that there is in fact no consensus among students of the early modern period about what if anything constitutes the core of republicanism, only a number of competing defin-itions. The second is that our view of Milton's republicanism will vary according to which of these definitions we adopt; for this choice will determine whether the task of understanding Milton's republicanism is, say, one of establishing the exact moment at which Milton subscribed to some crucial piece of dogma, rather than, say, one of tracing how a commitment to republicanism in some broader sense manifested itself in his writings over time.

Milton and Republicanism

The most important and clear-cut of the competing definitions is the doctrinaire view that to be a republican requires nothing less than outright opposition to the institu-tion of monarchy as such. Milton's more usual position of maintaining that what he opposes is not kingship *per se*, but tyranny, falls short of this requirement in that it theoretically leaves the door open to non-tyrannical monarchy (see Worden 1990: 228; Corns 1995: 33). But in the sequence of published and unpublished works he wrote between the autumn of 1659 and the spring of 1660 Milton expresses hostility not only to Stuart tyranny in particular but to monarchy in general, and not only to monarchy but also – adopting the republican jargon for kings, protectors, dictators and the like – to the rule of any 'single person' whatsoever. Thus in *A Letter to a Friend* (October 1659) he insists on 'the Abjuracion of a single person', or, as he puts it by way of rhetorical variation, 'the abjuracion of Monarchy' (*CPW* VII: 330, 331). In *Proposalls of Certaine Expedients* (October–December 1659) he urges the Parliament and army to declare themselves 'against single government by any one person in cheif' (VII: 336). And in the first edition of *The Readie and Easie Way to Establish a Free Commonwealth* (February 1660) he proclaims his confidence that 'all ingenuous and knowing men will easily agree with me, that a free Commonwealth without single person or house of lords, is by far the best government' (VII: 364–5; see also 332, 337, 361, 362, 368, 393, 427, 429, 432).

Milton's new-found intransigence extends to reproving other republics for failing to exorcise every vestige of a single person from their bodies politic. The Venetians still retained a Doge as the pinnacle of their republican constitution, while the Dutch, despite having abolished the supreme office of Stadholder, traditionally reserved for the head of the House of Orange (Nassau), were still overshadowed by the Orange dynasty itself. In the first edition of *The Readie and Easie Way*, Milton accordingly urges the English to reject 'the fond conceit of somthing like a duke of *Venice*, put lately into many mens heads, by som one or other suttly driving on under that prettie notion his own ambitious ends to a crown'. This is the only way to ensure that, unlike the United Provinces, 'our liberty shall not be hamperd or hoverd over by any ingag'ment to such a potent family as the house of *Nassau*, of whom to stand in perpetual doubt and suspicion, but we shall live the cleerest and absolutest free nation in the world' (*CPW* VII: 374–5; also 446).

It is striking, however, that while Milton urges pure republicanism upon others, some of his own thinking still appears unreconstructed. The clearest instance is the passage in the first edition of *The Readie and Easie Way* where he declines to rule out the possibility of a monarch governing in the public interest:

> I denie not but that ther may be such a king, who may regard the common good before his own, may have no vitious favourite, may hearken only to the wisest and incorruptest of his Parlament: but this rarely happ'ns in a monarchie not elective; and it behoves not a wise nation to committ the summ of thir well-being, the whole of thir safetie to fortune. And admitt, that monarchy of it self may be convenient to som nations, yet to us who have thrown it out, received back again, it cannot but prove pernicious. (VII: 377–8)

The suggestion is framed in terms of a string of conditions likely to be met, if at all, only by an elective monarch, who is convenient, if at all, only for some nations, though not the English. However, even if we allow that Milton is only raising the possibility in theory to show that it is out of the question in practice, it still runs counter to his main argument. Reviewing the passage for the second edition (April 1660), Milton decided it was too concessive and effectively cancelled it by wedging an addition of more than 350 words between the two sentences. The new material warns against becoming 'the slaves of a single person' and culminates in the remarkable assertion that 'a single person, [is] the natural adversarie and oppressor of libertie, though good' (VII: 448, 449). That is to say, even if the single person by whom you are ruled happens to be someone who is 'good' (in the sense of regarding the public interest, dispensing with vicious favourites, and so on), he will nevertheless endanger your liberty simply by virtue of being *what* he is: a single person.

This may sound like rhetorical overcompensation, but it is arguable that Milton means exactly what he says; if so, it represents the high-water mark of his republicanism. Equally, it demonstrates how exacting the doctrinaire definition is. For there are several figures usually thought of as republicans – Henry Neville and Sidney, for example, as well as Milton – who cannot strictly be counted as such because of their willingness at times to contemplate some form of accommodation with monarchy. Even Machiavelli, the key figure in the Renaissance revival of republican thought, occasionally suggests that it may be possible for a community to live a free life under the rule of a king (see Skinner 1998: 54–5).

Those who prefer a less exclusive definition suggest that what forms the core of republicanism is not outright opposition to monarchy but a commitment to mixed government, in which a monarchical element is combined with aristocracy and democracy. Originally formulated by Plato and Aristotle, and popularized by Polybius, the classical theory that the best form of government consists of a balance between the one, the few and the many had achieved the status of a commonplace by the early sixteenth century, from which time it was frequently rehearsed by English humanists (see Peltonen 1995). Milton was completely familiar with the theory. In *Of Reformation* (May 1641), he drew on Polybius and Sir Thomas Smith's Aristotelian account of mixed government in *The Commonwealth of England*, to declare that

> the best founded Commonwealths, and least barbarous have aym'd at a certaine mixture and temperament, partaking the severall vertues of each other State, that each part drawing to it selfe may keep up a steddy, and eev'n uprightnesse in common.
>
> There is no Civill *Government* that hath beene known, no not the *Spartan*, not the *Roman*, though both for this respect so much prais'd by the wise *Polybius*, more divinely and harmoniously tun'd, more equally ballanc'd as it were by the hand and scale of Justice, then is the Commonwealth of *England*: where under a free, and untutor'd *Monarch*, the noblest, worthiest, and most prudent men, with full approbation, and suffrage of the People have in their power the supreame, and finall determination of highest Affaires. (*CPW* I: 599; and see I: 442)

Ten years later, when Milton's royalist opponent, Salmasius, suggested that the theory was a novelty espoused by the 'parricides', he again cited Aristotle and Smith to underline how orthodox it was (*CPW* IV: 476).

The model referred to most often in discussions of mixed government was Venice. A succession of republican theorists applauded the exquisite balance the Venetians had achieved among the Doge, the Senate and the Consiglio Grande, as well as the elaborate constitutional machinery by which it was preserved (see Pocock 1975). The English republican most interested in the model was undoubtedly James Harrington, but Milton too thought Venice was one of the 'greatest and noblest Commonwealths' (*CPW* VII: 370; also 436). Indeed, Zera S. Fink has suggested that the theory of the mixed state was 'the guiding principle', from which Milton never deviated 'throughout the whole period from 1640 to 1660'. The first question Milton asked of any political arrangement was how well it realized the ideal of a mixed state. Thus, when he eventually rejected not only monarchy but 'all single-person magistracies', the reason why he did so in the first instance was because they had proved not to be 'a satisfactory representative of the monarchial or magisterial element in the state', a role Milton now thought should be performed by a council of state (Fink 1962: 103–4, 109, 120).

However, the proposition that Milton saw politics entirely through the lens of this theory is unconvincing. It would mean, for example, that when Milton turned against the Protector for displaying monarchical tendencies, it was actually because these tendencies made him less suitable to represent the monarchical element in the state. Nor can the claim that Milton was unwavering in his attachment to the mixed state be maintained except by special pleading. Fink admits that, having rejected 'even mere figureheads', the 'one thing Milton would not borrow from Venice was the doge', but maintains that this did not lead him to abandon the Venetian model altogether. Milton was able to avoid taking this step, he suggests, because the council of state proposed in *The Readie and Easie Way* bears 'a striking general likeness to the Venetian council', and that this body, not the Doge, 'was the real magistracy of the state' – obviously a case of forcing the model to conform to Milton rather than demonstrating how Milton conformed to it (Fink 1962: 110n).

The theory of the mixed state was, moreover, so widely disseminated that it cannot be identified exclusively – or even especially – with the republicans. According to Sir Robert Filmer in *The Anarchy of a Limited or Mixed Monarchy* (1648), even the 'meanest man of the multitude' believed that 'the government of the kingdom of England is a limited and mixed monarchy', attributing this to the fact that both 'the pulpit and the press do tend and end in this confusion' (Filmer 1991: 133). Similarly, when examining the rights of the sovereign in *Leviathan*, Hobbes declared that, but for the 'opinion received of the greatest part of *England*, that these Powers were divided between the King, and the Lords, and the House of Commons', there would never have been a civil war (Hobbes 1996: 127). When writing *Behemoth* in 1668, he was still blaming 'the whole nation' for having been 'in love with *mixarchy*, which they used to praise by the name of mixed monarchy, though it were indeed nothing else but pure anarchy' (Hobbes 1990: 116–17).

Revealingly, however, Hobbes is not attacking the parliamentarians here but responding to a question about the culpability of the King's advisers. His targets were Sir John Colepepper and Viscount Falkland, who in June 1642 issued *His Majesty's Answer to the Nineteen Propositions* in which – astonishingly – they accepted that England was governed by a mixture of 'absolute monarchy, aristocracy and democracy' that combined 'the conveniences of all three, without the inconveniences of any one, as long as the balance hangs even between the three estates' (Kenyon 1976: 21). Their aim in adopting the opposition's idiom was to re-establish the King and his veto as part of the legislative process and so prevent the practice of issuing ordinances in the name of the Lords and Commons alone. The price of this *démarche* was accepting that the King was no longer above three estates consisting of the commons in one house and the lords and bishops in another, but merely co-ordinate with the commons and the lords (minus the bishops, who had been excluded earlier in the year). In the *Anarchy*, Filmer was attacking Philip Hunton, whose *Treatise of Monarchie* (1643) became 'the *locus classicus* for the idea of a mixed monarchy in England during the 1640s and 1650s' (Tuck 1993: 235). However, Hunton was no republican but a Presbyterian. From the start of the conflict, the aim of the English Presbyterians and their Scottish allies had been twofold: to establish a Calvinist system of church government, and then, by establishing a mixed monarchy, to lock the system into place politically. Hunton was a systematic thinker, unlike Milton, but *Of Reformation* emerged from broadly the same ideological milieu, and so constituted a demonstration of Presbyterian sympathies rather than any republican leanings.

Given these complications, it is hardly surprising that several commentators have concluded that republicanism eludes any attempt at formal definition. The tradition, they argue, is essentially 'a moral one, opposing the moral qualities of virtue to vice, reason to passion, liberty to tyranny' (Scott 1992: 47). What republicans cleave to is not some or other doctrine but, more broadly, 'a politics of virtue' (Worden 1994: 46). Milton is typical in displaying 'a high degree of indifference with regard to constitutional forms' (Dzelzainis 1995a: 19). For him, 'form counts for much less than spirit' (Worden 1995: 170). His republicanism is in consequence 'more an attitude of mind than any governmental configuration', and manifests itself in the 'eloquent rehearsal, not of republican argument, but of republican values' (Corns 1995: 27, 41).

However, if the key to understanding Milton's republicanism is his commitment to a politics of virtue, then it is hard to see 1649 as a watershed. For the outline of this politics is already visible in the pamphlets he wrote in the mid-1640s. *Of Education* (June 1644) draws on the analysis of fortitude in Cicero's *De officiis* as the foundation of a curriculum designed to produce students who will be 'stedfast pillars of the State', while *Areopagitica* (November 1644) is in one sense an essay on temperance, by which Milton means the responsibility for 'managing' one's own life – especially 'the dyeting and repasting of our minds' – which God commits to 'every grown man' (*CPW* II: 398, 513). But Milton's thinking had taken this turn even before the Civil War broke out, to judge from an entry in the Commonplace Book citing Machiavelli's *Dell'Arte della Guerra*:

> Respub. regno potior. perche delle repub. escano piu huomini eccellenti, che de regni. perche in quelle il piu delle volte si honora la virtù, ne regne si teme.

[A republic is preferable to a monarchy: 'because more excellent men come from republics than from kingdoms; because in the former virtue is honoured most of the time and is not feared as in monarchies'.] (*WJM* 18: 164; see *CPW* 1: 421 [adapted])

As Milton was aware, however, Machiavelli owed this insight to the classical historian Sallust, whose *Bellum Catilinae* opened with a moral analysis of Rome's rise to greatness. The crucial moment was 'when the rule of the kings, which at first had tended to preserve freedom and advance the state, had degenerated into a lawless tyranny' ('ubi regium imperium, quod initio conservandae liberatatis atque augendae rei publicae fuerat, in superbiam dominationemque se convortit'), since this prompted the Romans to expel them and change their government to a republic. As soon as the city had gained its liberty it began to flourish, because the citizens were now willing and able to place their talents at its disposal whereas previously they were inhibited from doing so by kings, who 'hold the good in greater suspicion than the wicked, and to whom the virtue of others is always fraught with danger' ('Nam regibus boni quam mali suspectiores sunt semperque eis aliena virtus formidulosa est') (Sallust 1995: 12–13 [VI. 7; VII. 2]). For Sallust, as for Machiavelli and Milton (who placed both these sentences from *Bellum Catilinae* on the title page of *Eikonoklastes* [October 1649]), liberty was the key to a flourishing state.

This stratum of Milton's thought stands in particular need of further excavation; for it holds out the best hope of recovering the values and concepts that connect his early writings to his later ones and that also form a link between him and other supporters of the Commonwealth like Nedham and Sidney. Perhaps the most important of these shared assumptions are those relating to what Quentin Skinner has recently called the neo-Roman theory of liberty.

Milton and the Neo-Roman Theory of Liberty

Although the formula 'neo-Roman' is obviously anachronistic, there are good reasons for persisting with it. The first is that it serves to underline the point that the theory was not associated exclusively with any of the versions of republicanism we have just been examining, but was espoused both by doctrinaire republicans and by those willing to contemplate an accommodation with monarchy (see Skinner 1998: 55 n. 177). The second is that it straightforwardly registers the fact that this theory was a revival and adaptation of one originally developed by classical moralists and historians working within the conceptual framework of the Roman law of persons (see Skinner 1998: 38–44). The legal literature relating to private law was eventually codified by order of the Emperor Justinian in the sixth century – comprehensively in the *Digest* and in simplified textbook form in the *Institutes*, the latter being the version in which Milton studied it.

The opening titles of the first book of the *Institutes* set out what it means to be free and unfree (see Justinian 1975: 13–26). According to the law, you are either free and therefore possess a natural ability to do what you please unless prohibited in some way, or you are a slave and therefore subject to the dominion of – which is to say you are owned by – someone else (I. 3, 'De iure personarum' ['On the law of persons']). There is no intermediate status: 'all persons are slaves or free' ('omnes homines aut liberi sunt aut servi'). In the latter case, this is either because they are free born and so have never been slaves (I. 4, 'De ingenuis' ['On free born persons']), or because they are freedmen or freedwomen who were once slaves but have been released from servitude by manumission (I. 5, 'De libertinis' ['On freedmen']). However, the slave's lack of freedom cannot simply consist in being physically coerced by the master whose property he or she is; after all, a slave working as a secretary might never receive the kind of ill treatment routinely inflicted on a farmhand. Their lack of freedom should rather be seen as a corollary of their legal condition, as set out in the title 'On those who are independent and dependent' (I. 8: 'De his qui sui vel alieni iuris sunt'). This makes the important distinction between those who are 'within their own jurisdiction' ('sui iuris sunt'), and those who are 'subject to the jurisdiction of another' ('alieno iuri subiectae sunt'). Again, there is no intermediate position: either you have jurisdiction over another (or at least over yourself), or you are within the jurisdiction of someone else. Thus the children of Roman citizens are at all times 'in the power of their parent' ('in potestate parentum'), while slaves are at all times 'in the power of their master' ('in potestate dominorum'). As Skinner points out, this allows us to resolve 'the apparent paradox of the slave who manages to avoid being coerced'; since they are nevertheless in their master's power, they 'remain subject to death or violence at any time'. 'The essence of what it means to be a slave, and hence to lack personal liberty, is thus to be *in potestate*, within the power of someone else' (Skinner 1998: 41).

This understanding of freedom and slavery informs the work of all the writers we have been considering so far, whether they were republicans in the strict sense or not. In Milton's case, this dates (at least) from his reading of Roman law in the early 1640s. The Commonplace Book has several entries from the *Institutes* on 'what lawyers declare concerning liberty and slavery' (*CPW* I: 470; and see 410, 411, 471). But he appears also to have worked his way carefully through the rest of Book I, paying particular attention to later titles dealing with persons who, although *sui iuris*, were nevertheless deemed incapable of managing their own affairs for one reason or another. Thus 'De tutelis' (I. 13, 'On guardianships'), considers the case of those who, though 'not within someone else's power' ('in potestate non sunt'), are 'under a guardian' ('in tutela') or 'under a curator' ('in curatione'). Boys and girls 'below the age of puberty' ('impuberes') can be designated the 'wards' ('pupilli' or 'pupillae') of a tutor who supervises their affairs, while, as is explained in 'De curatoribus' (I. 23, 'On curators'), those who have reached puberty but nevertheless lack the mental capacity to manage their own lives can have a curator appointed to act as their substitute (Justinian 1975: 43, 53, 56).

The clearest evidence for Milton's interest in these legal arrangements, in addition to the broader topics of freedom and slavery, is found not in the Commonplace Book but in *Areopagitica*, his attack on the parliamentary Licensing Order of June 1643. Halfway through the work, Milton changes his angle of attack on the Order 'from the no good it can do, to the manifest hurt it causes'. Its most damaging effect is the 'discouragement and affront' it offers 'to learning and to learned men', by which he means 'the free and ingenuous sort of such as evidently were born to study' (*CPW* II: 530–1). Milton's choice of terms is precise; his primary concern is with the impact of the Order on those who are not slaves but *ingenui*: free-born adult men. What he predicts is that a system of licensing prior to publication will turn these *ingenui* into *servi* (slaves).

It is true that Milton does not begin by putting the point in these stark terms. Rather, he suggests that authors fall into the category of those who are nominally *sui iuris* but are actually treated as if they were under age (*impuberes*) or otherwise incompetent to exercise their rights. Certainly, those in favour of licensing do not 'count him fit to print his mind without a tutor and examiner'. But in this case, he asks,

> What advantage is it to be a man over it is to be a boy at school, if we have only scapt the ferular, to come under the fescu of an *Imprimatur*? if serious and elaborat writings, as if they were no more then the theam of a Grammar lad under his Pedagogue must not be utter'd without the cursory eyes of a temporizing and extemporizing licencer. (*CPW* II: 531)

Like a schoolboy, the author is 'not trusted with his own actions'. Although he may be prepared to take full responsibility for his work by 'standing to the hazard of law and penalty', he will not be allowed to do so and in consequence will have no reason 'to think himself reputed in the Commonwealth wherin he was born, for other then a fool or a foreiner'. Under this regime, no writer can hope to produce 'proof of his abilities' sufficient to be elevated to 'that state of maturity, as not to be still mistrusted and suspected'. Instead, he is far more likely to be forced to 'appear in Print like a punie with his guardian', bearing a licence from the censor to prove 'that he is no idiot' (531–2). Nor can any serious reader respect writings produced 'under the tuition, under the correction of his patriarchal licencer'. What Milton hates most of all is 'a pupil teacher', a figure who in terms of Roman law embodies a complete paradox – a would-be 'instructer' who is himself still 'under the wardship of an overseeing fist' (533). In short, what the Order systematically brings about is the infantilization of the author, leaving him in a condition of legal disability which is little short of 'servitude like that impos'd by the Philistims', an 'undeserved thraldom upon lerning' and a 'second tyranny over' it (536, 539).

It is important to stress, however, that no actual censoring of texts need take place for the system to have this enslaving effect. Our liberty is of course diminished to the extent that we are interfered with or coerced, but this is not the only way in which we can become unfree: we also forfeit our liberty whenever we find ourselves dependent on the continued goodwill of others for the enjoyment of our rights. Accordingly, as

Skinner remarks, 'it is the mere possibility of your being subjected with impunity to arbitrary coercion, not the fact of your being coerced, that takes away your liberty and reduces you to the condition of a slave' (Skinner 1998: 72). The reason why Milton objects so strongly to prepublication censorship, therefore, is that it leaves the author's freedom to publish entirely at the discretion of the licenser. How that discretion may happen to be exercised is beside the point. While it is of course deplorable if your work is altered against your wishes, you are actually no better off if the licenser passes your text unchanged, because the fact that you are still dependent on his will, even if he shows no inclination at present to exert his powers and may never do so, is in itself enough to nullify your freedom. For the danger is that such a condition of dependency will inevitably constrain your behaviour, leading to self-censorship and the production of what Milton (citing Francis Bacon) calls *'such authoriz'd books'* that speak nothing *'but the language of the times'* (*CPW* II: 534).

Milton in 1649

We can now approach some of Milton's writings in 1649 with an eye to unearthing whatever continuity they exhibit with his neo-Roman theorizing earlier in the decade. This admittedly runs counter to the usual procedure, which is to begin in 1649 with Milton the regicide and then chart his progress on the road to republicanism over the following decade. But while this procedure undoubtedly chimes with the theme of belatedness which features so strongly in many accounts of republicanism, it does little to explain why Milton should have been in the revolutionary vanguard in 1649.

In the space of twenty-four months between 1649 and 1651, Milton wrote four works: *The Tenure of Kings and Magistrates, Observations upon the Articles of Peace, Eikonoklastes* and *Pro Populo Anglicano Defensio*. However, he was an inveterate reviser, and they eventually yielded no fewer than eight texts between them (ten if you include French and Dutch translations). Surprisingly, however, the precise sequence in which these texts were published has still not been established: in particular, we do not know whether the second edition of *The Tenure* came before or after the first edition of *Eikonoklastes*, or whether the second edition of *Eikonoklastes* came before or after the *Defensio*. To complicate matters further, there is the vexed question of the date of the Digression to the third book of *The History of Britain* (first published in 1670, although the Digression itself remained unpublished in Milton's lifetime). Milton later claimed that he wrote most of the first four books of *The History* (and hence presumably the Digression) between publishing *The Tenure* in February 1649 and taking up his post as one of the secretaries to the Council of State the following month. Although the Digression has been dated to 1660, there is a strong case for taking Milton's account at face value (see Woolrych 1993; von Maltzahn 1993a). Assuming therefore that the Digression does belong to the weeks between the execution of the King and the Acts abolishing the office of king and the House of Lords in mid-March, what does it tell us about Milton's perspective on the revolution in progress?

At the start of Book III of *The History*, Milton took up the story of what happened to the fifth-century Britons in the aftermath of the Roman withdrawal and the end of 'imperial jurisdiction' over them. With recent events in mind, he saw an opportunity for comparing 'that confused Anarchy with this intereign', and the parallels he found between 'two such remarkable turns of State' formed the basis of the Digression (*CPW* V: 129–30). The problem he set himself was

> to consider what might bee the reason, why, seeing other nations both antient and modern with extreame hazard & danger have strove for libertie as a thing invaluable, & by the purchase thereof have soe enobl'd thir spirits, as from obscure and small to grow eminent and glorious commonwealths, why the Britans having such a smooth occasion giv'n them to free themselves as ages have not afforded, such a manumission as never subjects had a fairer, should let it pass through them as a cordial medcin through a dying man without the least effect of sence or natural vigor. (V: 441)

For sheer richness and density of historical reflection, this is a passage which is almost unequalled anywhere in Milton's prose. Worden rightly sees in it an allusion to Machiavellian *occasione* – the opportunity that must be seized if liberty is not to be lost (Worden 1990: 233–5). However, Milton also draws upon Sallust and the Roman law for his analysis. His account of the ennobling effects of liberty is clearly derived from Sallust's account of the birth of the Roman republic, when the expulsion of the Tarquins freed men of virtue from the suspicions under which they had laboured: 'the free state once liberty was won, waxed incredibly strong and great in a remarkably short time, such was the thirst for glory that had filled men's minds' ('Sed civitas incredibile memoratu est adepta libertate quantum brevi creverit; tanta cupido gloriae incesserat') (Sallust 1995: 12–15; VII. 3). Another of Milton's phrases, 'from obscure and small to grow eminent and glorious commonwealths', appears to be taken directly from Sallust's rendition of a speech by Cato in which he tells the Senate not to 'suppose that it was by arms that our forefathers raised our republic from obscurity to greatness' ('Nolite existumare maiores nostros armis rem publicam ex parva magnam fecisse') (Sallust 1995: 104–5; LII. 19). Cato's message that martial spirit counts for less than moral virtues such as industry and justice is echoed later in the Digression when Milton's despairingly analyses the failure of the ancient and modern Britons to make the most of liberty:

> To other causes therefore and not to want of force, or warlike manhood in the Brittans both those and these lately, wee must impu[te] the ill husbanding of those faire opportunities, which migh[t] seem to have put libertie, so long desir'd, like a brid[le] into thir hands. (*CPW* V: 443)

Finally, it is also clear from the reference to 'manumission' that Milton's account of these 'remarkable turns of State' is partly framed in terms of the private law of persons. The Britons, ancient and modern alike, are thus *libertini*, freedmen who have been released from servitude and are now 'masters of thir own choise' (V: 441). Milton spells out the point at the end of Book II when he cites a letter from Honorius which 'acquits' the Britons 'of the *Roman* jurisdiction', and again at the start of Book III when he emphasizes that 'the imperial jurisdiction departing hence left them to the sway of thir own Councils' (V: 126, 129). In short, the Britons were no longer *alieni iuris* ('within the jurisdiction of another') but *sui iuris* ('within their own jurisdiction'), and hence free.

The great theme of the Digression – that 'the gaining or loosing of libertie is the greatest change to better or to worse that may befall a nation under civil goverment' (*CPW* V: 441) – is also central to the neo-Roman project, and it is therefore hardly surprising that Milton should bring so much of its conceptual arsenal to bear. Does this also set it apart from his other works? Although Worden may be right in saying that Milton 'could express himself more freely in his unpublished writings', it would be a mistake to suppose that there is a categorical separation between these writings and those he published under the Commonwealth (Worden 1990: 231). For example, in the *Defensio* he again observes that 'after the Romans departed, for about forty years the Britons were *sui iuris*, and without kings' ('Post Romanorum ex insula discessum sui juris Britanni circiter annos 40. sine regibus fuere') (*WJM* 8: 434–6). This is, if anything, even more pointed in its assertion that to be *sui iuris* is simply to be without kings. Moreover, the conceptual arsenal was largely in place before Milton broke his four-year silence with *The Tenure*, a work that in any case precedes and informs the Digression. Thus Milton opens *The Tenure* by paraphrasing Sallust: tyrants do not fear 'bad men, as being all naturally servile', but direct 'all thir hatred and suspicion' against those 'in whom vertue and true worth most is eminent' (*CPW* III: 190). He also invokes the moment when the Romans 'quitted and relinquishd what right they had' to the Britons who were thereby 're-invested with thir own original right' (III: 221). And, finally, he elects to analyse public issues in terms of private law:

> they that shall boast, as we doe, to be a free Nation, and not have in themselves the power to remove, or to abolish any governour supreme, or subordinat, with the goverment it self upon urgent causes, may please thir fancy with a ridiculous and painted freedom, fit to coz'n babies; but are indeed under tyranny and servitude; as wanting that power, which is the root and sourse of all liberty, to dispose and *oeconomize* in the Land which God hath giv'n them, as Maisters of Family in thir own house and free inheritance. Without which natural and essential power of a free Nation, though bearing high thir heads, they can in due esteem be thought no better then slaves and vassals born, in the tenure and occupation of another inheriting Lord. Whose goverment, though not illegal, or intolerable, hangs over them as a Lordly scourge, not as a free goverment; and therfore to be abrogated. (III: 236–7)

The distinction underlying the passage is the familiar one between those who are *sui iuris* ('a free Nation', 'Maisters of Family') and those who are *alieni iuris* ('babies', 'slaves' and 'vassals'). On this occasion, however, Milton's commitment to the neo-

Roman theory of liberty leads him on to a remarkably subversive conclusion. As we saw earlier, no actual coercion but the mere possibility of being subjected to it is sufficient to enslave you. This thesis can, however, be turned back upon the master; for, no matter how benign he may be in practice, it is impossible for him to erase the stigma of enslaving those whom he has in his power. Milton follows the same manoeuvre. What is crucial, he says, is being able to change your government, or any aspect of it, at will. For if you cannot do this, then the fact that it is 'not illegal, or intolerable' is irrelevant; you are in its power, and hence enslaved by it, and this alone is sufficient grounds for it 'to be abrogated'. At this point, therefore, Milton's quarrel is no longer with actual coercion in the form of tyranny but with the potential for enslavement which appears to be inherent in monarchical government as such.

Admittedly, the argument in *The Tenure* is far from transparent, and this may explain why Milton returned to it in *Eikonoklastes* when replying to the king's assertion that the subject's liberties solely consist 'in the enjoyment of the fruits of our industry, and the benefit of those Laws to which we our selves have consented' (*CPW* III: 574). The view of liberty invoked here is a negative one, according to which liberty is purely a matter of not being interfered with or coerced by others. The point Milton seizes on, and satirizes, is that if not being interfered with in the enjoyment of your property is all that counts, then it becomes impossible to differentiate between political regimes:

> First, for the injoyment of those fruits, which our industry and labours have made our own upon our own, what Privilege is that, above what the *Turks, Jewes,* and *Mores* enjoy under the Turkish Monarchy? For without that kind of Justice, which is also in *Argiers,* among Theevs and Pirates between themselvs, no kind of Goverment, no Societie, just or unjust could stand; no combination or conspiracy could stick together. (III: 574)

The king's offer was inadequate from the neo-Roman point of view because, in order to remain free, it is not enough to avoid being interfered with; we must also avoid being dominated by the capacity for arbitrary power. This is what Milton means by his reply to the king: 'We expect therfore somthing more, that must distinguish free Goverment from slavish' (574). The 'somthing more' involves nothing less than the surrender of all the discretionary powers which, in the view of the neo-Roman theorists, had allowed Charles to coerce his subjects with impunity and hence reduce them to the status of slaves. Chief among them was the power of the veto which, Milton complains, Charles had arrogated to himself 'as the transcendent and ultimat Law above all our Laws; and to rule us forcibly by Laws to which we our selves did not consent' (575).

Milton made his point rather more crisply on the title page of *Eikonoklastes* in the form of a third epigraph from Sallust (the first edition in fact failed to specify the work and quoted loosely, but Milton had corrections made for the second edition). It was taken from a speech by the tribune Gaius Memmius in *Bellum Iugurthinum,* where he sums up a series of outrageous abuses of power with the observation that 'to do with impunity whatever one pleases is to be a king' ('Nam impune quae lubet facere, id est regum esse') (Sallust 1995: 204–5 [XXXI. 26]). The crucial thing here is that acting with impunity is being held out not as a perversion of kingship but as the very essence of it. The upshot is that in *Eikonoklastes*, even more clearly than in *The Tenure*, Milton's quarrel is with integral aspects of monarchy as such.

It does therefore appear that there are fundamental continuities in Milton's thought which mean that the radicalism he displays in 1649 is not the altogether unheralded phenomenon it is sometimes taken to be. Nor does he seem conceptually impoverished in the (alleged) absence of a republican ideology. Nor is there an unbridgeable gap between what he was saying in 1649 and what he was saying in 1659. For when we turn to *The Readie and Easie Way*, we find him advancing familiar arguments in a familiar idiom. Twenty years after he began to study the law of persons, he found the definitive form of words to express the view that any adult must be impatient with monarchy:

> And what madness is it, for them who might manage nobly thir own affairs themselves, sluggishly and we[a]kly to devolve all on a single person; and more like boyes under age then men, to committ all to his patronage and disposal, who neither can performe what he undertakes, and yet for undertaking it, though royally paid, will not be thir servant, but thir lord? how unmanly must it needs be, to count such a one the breath of our nostrils, to hang all our felicity on him, all our safetie, our well-being, for which if we were aught els but sluggards or babies, we need depend on none but God and our own counsels, our own active vertue and industrie; (*CPW* VII: 427; see also 362)

For those who are *sui iuris* and so 'might manage nobly thir own affairs' to 'devolve' the responsibility 'on a single person' would be 'unmanly', to act 'more like boyes under age then men', in fact to regress to being 'babies'. A republic, Milton is saying, is the only form of government fit for adults.

BIBLIOGRAPHY

Writings

Filmer (1991); Hobbes (1990, 1996); Justinian (1975); Sallust (1995).

References for Further Reading

Armitage (1995); Corns (1995); Dzelzainis (1995a, b); Fink (1962); Kenyon (1976); Morrill (1993); Norbrook (1999); Peltonen (1995); Pocock (1975); Pocock and Schochet (1993); Scott (1992); Skinner (1978, 1998); Tuck (1993); von Maltzahn (1991, 1993a); Woolrych (1974, 1993); Worden (1990, 1991, 1994, 1995, 1998); Zagorin (1954).

19
Late Political Prose

Laura Lunger Knoppers

On 24 October 1667 Samuel Pepys reflected with some asperity on the taciturn, tobacco-chewing general who had helped to make possible the restoration of Charles II. In Pepys's view, George Monck (now Duke of Albemarle) was a 'block-head' who 'hath strange luck to be beloved, though he be, and every man must know, the heaviest man in the world' (1974, 8: 499). None the less, Pepys conceded, Monck was 'stout and honest to his country' (499). With the latter point, Milton would have strongly disagreed. The extent to which, in 1659–60, Milton placed his hopes in Monck as the one person able to preserve civil and religious liberty has not been fully recognized; undoubtedly his disappointment was bitter. Hindsight can distort our view of the last days and months of the republic, which are often discussed as if the march back to kingship were inexorable and inevitable. But contemporaries, including Milton, recognized other possibilities. Resituating Milton's late political prose in a detailed historical context that takes fuller account of Monck's important role complicates recent assessments of both Milton's classical republican-ism and his alleged repudiation of another military strong man, Oliver Cromwell. Milton's hopes in Monck also illumine the rhetorical complexity of *The Readie and Easie Way to Establish a Free Commonwealth* and its use of the language of the Good Old Cause – especially biblical language – to persuade as well as prophesy.

Scholarly Issues

Milton's political prose of 1659–60 has become an important and contested site for key issues in recent scholarship, particularly the relation between Milton's poetry and prose, the nature and significance of his republicanism, and his attitude towards the Protectorate, especially towards the figure of Oliver Cromwell. Questions under debate include: To what extent does Milton hold to consistent principles and to

what extent does he accommodate to or change with shifting circumstances? Is the
late prose, especially the two editions of *The Readie and Easie Way*, politically engaged
and activist, genuinely designed to affect current events, or is it utopian or prophetic?
To what extent is Milton's attack aimed not only at monarchy but also at Oliver
Cromwell and the Protectorate? How important are the biblical references? What
changes did Milton make between the two editions of *The Readie and Easie Way* and
why are they significant? How do the values of this tract carry over into the poetry,
especially *Paradise Lost*?

Scholars agree that *The Readie and Easie Way* needs to be read in close relation to the
complex and shifting politics of 1658–60. Austin Woolrych, Godfrey Davies, Ronald
Hutton and others provide valuable details of the historical context. At stake for
Milton are questions of consistency and of political engagement. In an early study,
Barbara Lewalski argues that Milton is 'an extremely practical, able, and realistic
polemicist' (1959: 202), who shows 'principle, not mere expediency' (198) in advocating, albeit through varied means, the ends of religious and civil liberty. Thomas
Corns places more emphasis on Milton's inability to keep up with the rapidly
changing political scene, as 'the tempo of political polemic could not match the
tempo of political change' (1992b: 280).

Scholars discussing *The Readie and Easie Way* as a jeremiad – or as linked with the
prophet Jeremiah – have looked less at the details of the political scene and more at
the literary and performative aspects of the work. These critics differ in their
emphases on prophecy versus practicality. James Holstun suggests that in the second
edition of *The Readie and Easie Way*, 'Milton as Jeremiah pleads almost suicidally for
his own execution, which will verify his prophecy about his nation's expiring liberty'
(1987: 262). Reuben Sanchez argues, in contrast, that Milton in fact 'finds the
exemplary model of hope in Jeremiah' (1997: 71). My own earlier study (Knoppers
1990) characterizes Milton's tract as dual, employing emotive language of persuasion,
while the repeated images of backsliding none the less indicate a headlong rush back
to the bondage of kingship.

More recent scholarship on *The Readie and Easie Way* has returned to political
engagement with less attention to literary form. In these studies, the tract evinces
Milton's long-held and core republicanism and attacks not only impending monarchy
but Oliver Cromwell and the Protectorate. The attack on Cromwell is said to be
located in the epigraph to Sulla, in the emphasis on a 'single person', and in the
denunciation of the court, obliquely referring to the increasingly monarchical Protectorate (Dzelzainis 1995b; Armitage 1995). This repudiation of Cromwell
is, however, contested. Robert Fallon observes that, given the immediate political
context, Milton would not have been gratuitously attacking the long-dead Protector
but aiming at the real and immediate threat of impending monarchy (1981; 1993:
202–5). Paul Stevens (2001) argues that evidence for between-the-lines repudiation of
Cromwell in the late prose is highly circumstantial and speculative, and that Milton's
attitudes were shaped more by the Protestant nationalism that he shared with
Cromwell than by doctrinaire republicanism.

The debate over Milton's target – explicit and implicit – and the degree of his political engagement or withdrawal in *The Readie and Easie Way* is significant in relation to political readings of the poetry, in particular *Paradise Lost*. Earlier readings had aligned Satan with Charles I, or juxtaposed shared concerns with tyranny, liberty and authority in the texts and their Restoration contexts. More recently, however, David Norbrook (1999) has argued that Milton's repudiation of an ambitious and monarchical Cromwell extends into the figure of Satan – who appropriates and misuses republican language – in *Paradise Lost*, and Blair Worden (1998) links Milton's Satan and the 'great dissimulator Cromwell'.

This chapter will contend that *The Readie and Easie Way* shows much about Milton's late republicanism, but that such 'republicanism' is more complex and conflicted than has been recognized and does not entail a bitter repudiation of Cromwell. Rather, Milton's appeal to George Monck, as a military general who might, paradoxically, force the people to be free, evokes rather than contrasts with his earlier appeals to and faith in Cromwell. A fuller sense of Milton's republicanism attends to the biblical as well as the classical sources, so that figurative language, rhetorical techniques and Milton's self-presentation as a prophet are not a turning away from politics but a powerful tool of political persuasion. The prophetic, emotive language works to persuade, although, in the second edition of *The Readie and Easie Way*, it also works to tell the story, to witness to and record the failures of the chosen people.

Earlier Writings and Political Context for *The Readie and Easie Way*

Revisionist historiography has for some time argued for the contingent, short-term causes of civil war and regicide. But the fall of the Protectorate, the subsequent shifts in governing bodies, and the return of the monarchy in May 1660 still tend to be read through hindsight, in light of the restoration that did occur but by no means seemed inevitable to contemporaries. By resituating Milton's texts in a less determined and more volatile political context, we can better recognize the full rhetorical resources that he brings to bear in texts intended to persuade as much as to prophesy, and, indeed, to persuade through biblical and prophetic, as well as vernacular, language.

The accession of Richard Cromwell as Lord Protector, upon his father Oliver's death in September 1658, was warmly received by a broad section of the gentry as evinced in an outpouring of addresses and letters. By no means the foolish 'Tumbledown Dick' of popular history, Richard met various initial challenges – such as the republican backlash in the Parliament that met in January 1659 – with a combination of tact and forcefulness. None the less, from January to April the position of the Protectorate deteriorated under a barrage of propaganda for the 'Good Old Cause' that temporarily united sectarians, republicans and politically active elements of the army. Forceful against earlier threats, Richard lost his nerve in April, when he was pressured by the army grandees, including his brother-in-law Charles Fleetwood, into dissolving the Parliament; the grandees were in turn pressured by junior officers into recalling the purged or, as it came to be known, 'Rump' Parliament that Oliver had dismissed in April 1653. Richard resigned peaceably, and the Protectorate came to a close.

Despite his having acquiesced in, indeed lauded, Oliver Cromwell's dissolution of the purged Parliament in April 1653, Milton now welcomed them back. In *Considerations Touching the Likeliest Means to Remove Hirelings* (August 1659; *CPW* VII: 273–321), written largely on the issue of tithes and advocating the separation of church and state, Milton praised the Parliamentarians as 'the authors and best patrons of religious and civil libertie, that ever these Ilands brought forth', and he applauded their return after 'a short but scandalous night of interruption' (*CPW* VII: 274). Commentators disagree sharply on the meaning of this latter phrase. Some powerful voices – Austin Woolrych (1974; *CPW* VII: 85–7), Barbara Lewalski (1959) and, more recently, Martin Dzelzainis (1995b) – take the phrase as referring to and hence repudiating the whole of the Protectorate. Thomas Corns (1992b: 274) and Robert Fallon (1981; 1993: 183–5), however, point out that 'short' is more in keeping with the two-week period between the dissolution of Richard's Parliament and the return of the Rump.

But the republic that was restored struggled for stability. The summer and early autumn of 1659 found a tense and tenuous relation between the civilian Rump and the army that had restored it. Joined against a common royalist enemy during 'Booth's rebellion' in August, army and Parliament were soon again at odds. The cashiering of nine senior army officers proved the last straw. In October 1659 John Lambert expelled the Rump by force, and England was ruled by a Committee of Safety, consisting of army officers and civilians nominated by the Council of Officers.

Although he had continued to serve the various councils under Richard and under the restored republic, the blind Milton had not been at the centre of things for some time. After a conversation with an unnamed friend who informed him of the most recent parliamentary purge, Milton wrote (although he did not publish) a response that shows a struggle to maintain certain broad ideals in the face of a complex and fragmented situation. In *A Letter to a Friend, Concerning the Ruptures of the Commonwealth* (20 October 1659; *CPW* VII: 322–33), Milton rejects Lambert's forcible dissolution as 'most illegall & scandalous, I fear me barbarous, or rather scarce ~~not~~ to be exampled among any Barbarians, that a paid army should for no other cause, thus subdue the supreme power that sett them up' (*CPW* VII: 327). Milton saw ambition and self-interest in the army, urging them to find the one among them who, like Achan after the battle of Jericho (Joshua 7), sought forbidden riches for himself at the risk of bringing divine wrath upon the nation. But how could the crumbling republic be settled? Milton now proposed an early version of the 'senate or generall Councell of State' (329) that would be the centrepiece of *The Readie and Easie Way*. Although the means were shifting, the ends of preserving civil and religious liberty remained, and Milton thus proposed two qualifications for the councillors: 'Liberty of conscience to all professing scripture the rule of their faith & worship, And the Abjuracion of a single person' (330). With the political situation still in flux, Milton left it open whether the council would be elected annually or be perpetual: in the more extreme circumstances of *The Readie and Easie Way*, he would no longer trust the electorate to make the proper choice.

The crisis deepened in late October when General George Monck – leader of the army of occupation in Scotland – weighed in on the side of the Rump Parliament and the army began to divide against itself. A career soldier and former royalist, Monck had loyally served the republic and Protectorate in Ireland, in Scotland and in naval combat during the first Dutch war. Plain-spoken, taciturn and moderately Presbyterian in his religious sympathies, Monck had acquiesced in the overthrow of Richard Cromwell, but his belief that the military should be the servant of civil authority finally prompted his intervention after Lambert's coup. Having pledged to 'stand by and assert the Liberty and Authority of Parliament', Monck remained poised in Scotland, seemingly ready to do battle with the forces under Lambert that were making their way northwards. Monck's declared objection was against rule by the sword, and he wrote to Lambert that 'the Nation of ENGLAND will not endure any Arbitrary Power, neither will any true English-man in the Army, so that such a Design will be ruinous and destructive.' He entreated Lambert to restore Parliament to its former freedom, 'that we may not be a scorn to all the world, and a Prey to our Enemies' (Monck 1659).

Once again Milton composed, but did not publish, a response: *Proposalls of Certaine Expedients for the Preventing of a Civill War Now Feard, & the Settling of a Firme Government* (CPW VII: 334–9). In language close to Monck's own, Milton outlined the 'scorne' that England would evoke by continual changes, and the associated dangers both at home and abroad. Hence, he proposed the settling of a 'firme & durable government', an act of oblivion for army actions and the conditions of 'full liberty of conscience to all who professe their faith & worship by the scriptures only, & against single government by any one person in cheif & house of Lords' (CPW VII: 336). Unlike Monck, however, Milton proposed that in the present chaos and trouble, the council 'sitt indissolubly' and that those chosen for the Parliament 'do retaine their places during life' (336). Milton's recognition that 'no government is like to continue unlesse founded upon the publick autority & consent of the people' (336) led him to argue for parliamentary government, rather than siding with the military coup; but at the same time, he severely qualified the meaning of 'the people', to those 'well affected' (337), or, in other words, already sympathetic, to a republican form of government. That Milton did not mention Monck, or make any particular suggestions for his subsequent role, indicates that he simply took Monck's adherence to the Parliament at face value and accepted his professed aim of a Commonwealth form of government.

The last days of 1659 and the early days of 1660 showed a chaotic and shifting political scene in which the single point of continuity and stability was the figure of George Monck. The Committee of Safety, faced with apprentice riots, the decline of trade and calls for a free Parliament, was losing its tenuous grip on power. On 24 December, London army regiments declared for the Rump Parliament, who resumed their seats on 26 December. None the less, on New Year's Day 1660 Monck crossed the Tweed at Coldstream and began to march southwards. Although the Rump had replaced the much-disliked Committee of Safety, its unrepresentative and oligarchic rule in turn evoked hostility. County petitions – many of which were presented to Monck – demanded the return of the members secluded in December 1648, pre-liminary to elections of a free and full Parliament. Public hostility to the Rump found expression in a spate of doggerel satire. In late December Thomas Rugge described a 'jeering printed sheet that jeered the Parliment, and called it the rump and the Speaker the fart, and many abusey bookes to all that was in power under the Parliment, it beeing called the Rump Parliment' (1961: 23). By February, Pepys was writing that 'boys do now cry "Kiss my Parliament" instead of "Kiss my arse", so great and general a contempt is the Rump come to among all men, good and bad' (1970, 1: 45). The Rump had to reconcile its 'rule for the people' with the likelihood that, given a choice, most of the people would have rejected them and brought back the king.

As Monck approached London, tensions only increased, as both the City and the Rump seemed to believe that Monck would side with them. On 18 January Pepys wrote that 'all the world is now at a loss to think what Monke will do: the City saying that he will be for them, and the Parliament saying he will be for them' (1970, 1: 22). Rugge wrote that everyone expected that 'the Citty would suffer for theire offronts to the souldiery', and that 'these fouer lines were in almost everybodys mouth':

> Monck under a hood, not understood,
> The Citty pulls in theire hornes;
> The Speaker is out and sick of the goute
> And the Parliment sitts upon thornes.
>
> (1961: 30)

John Viscount Mordaunt, a royalist agent in London, wrote that he found Monck 'a black monk' (1945: 153) and could not see through him.

Yet Monck continued his public support of the Rump. In a printed letter of 26 January he rebuked the Devon gentry for their petition in support of the secluded members, expressing his fear that re-admitting these members might 'obstruct our peace and continue our War', given how many of them assert 'Monarchical interest' (1660a: 5–6). As for the monarchy, Monck wrote that it 'cannot possibly be admitted for the future in these Nations, because its support is taken away, and because it's exclusive of all the former Interests both Civil and Spiritual' (5). The government that does 'comprehend and protect' the various civil and religious interests, he affirmed, 'must needs be Republique'. Much of the alleged opacity of Monck at this time comes from a simple refusal to accept his continuing support of republicanism. Hence, Pepys writes in late January that 'the news this day is a letter that speaks absolutely Monkes concurrence with this Parliament and nothing else, which yet I hardly believe' (1970, 1: 30). But Milton, as we shall see, took Monck's professions at face value.

As Milton set out to write *The Readie and Easie Way*, the Rump Parliament still sat, with an apparent supporter in Monck. Arriving in London on 3 February, Monck had initially supported the Rump against the City. Despite some mixed signals, Monck's demonstrations of astonishment at being thought capable of infidelity to Parliament and his exhortations to the deputies of the City to submit seemed to point towards his continuing republicanism. But during Milton's composition of his tract, most of which was probably written between 18 and 21 February, the political scene shifted rapidly. Relations between the City and Parliament deteriorated sharply, as the City now refused to pay taxes to an unrepresentative Parliament. On 9–10 February, upon the orders of Parliament, Monck carried out the distasteful task of destroying the posts and chains erected for defence in the City and arresting eleven members of the Common Council. But after experience of public hostility, the opposition of his officers, chaplain and wife, and the Rump's own intransigence and ingratitude, he apparently had a change of heart. On 11 February Monck sent a letter to Parliament excusing himself from using further force against the City and urging them to fill up their vacancies and set a date for their own dissolution. Pepys records that as Monck was openly reconciled with the City elite, bonfires burned and rumps were roasted: 'But the common joy that was everywhere to be seen! The number of bonefires, there being fourteen between St. Dunstan's and Temple-bar... and all along burning and roasting and drinking for rumps – there being rumps tied upon sticks and carried up and down' (1970, 1: 52). Before Milton could publish his work, the Rump had in fact been supplemented by Monck's re-admission on 21 February of those members secluded by Pride's Purge in December 1648 as a prelude to the trial of Charles I. None the less, Milton added a prefatory paragraph and rushed into print his denunciation of monarchy and his plan for a constitutional settlement of the republic.

The First Edition of *The Readie and Easie Way*

In the introductory paragraph of *The Readie and Easie Way to Establish a Free Commonwealth*, which appeared some time between 23 and 29 February (*CPW* VII: 340–88), Milton writes that although 'the face of things hath had some change' since the writing of the body of his treatise, he finds himself 'not a little rejoicing to hear declar'd, the resolutions of all those who are now in power, jointly tending to the establishment of a free Commonwealth' (*CPW* VII: 353–4). And, in fact, Monck had re-admitted the secluded members only under strict conditions and after adjuring them to remain faithful to a Commonwealth. In a speech to the members of Parliament, Monck insisted that 'I have nothing before my eyes but Gods Glory, and the settlement of these Nations, upon Commonwealth *Foundations*' (1660b: 3). He spoke out against kingship, reminding the members that 'the old Foundations are by Gods

Providence so broken, that in the eye of Reason, they cannot be restored but upon the ruines of the people of these Nations' (4). Restoring the king, he maintained, would bring arbitrary power, as well as the return of prelacy, 'which these Nations I know cannot bear, and against which they have so solemnly Sworn' (4–5). Milton's denunciation of kingship and his plea for the Commonwealth thus has an important and powerful contemporary audience in Monck.

The Readie and Easie Way deploys the multifaceted language of the Good Old Cause, invoking biblical as much as classical language and models. Indeed, the most developed parallel is between England and the kingdom of Judah at its time of greatest crisis, just before the fall of Jerusalem. Milton defers to the authority of the prophet Jeremiah to establish his own authority, speaking out on the past, present and future. But in doing so, Milton does not turn away from politics; rather, the emotive, prophetic language is itself a powerful instrument of persuasion.

Drawing on biblical history and the analogy between England and Judah as two chosen nations, Milton provides an overall framework within which to interpret England's present political dilemma: past blessings, present sins, and future blessing or judgement depending upon the people's actions. In present-day terms, however, the desire of the people to return to kingship is more than a political mistake – it is a moral and spiritual sin, an act of idolatry comparable to that of the backsliding Jews who desired to return to Egypt. Milton declares his aim to be persuasion: 'to remove if it be possible, this unsound humour of returning to old bondage, instilld of late by some cunning deceivers, and nourished from bad principles and fals apprehensions among too many of the people' (*CPW* VII: 354–5). The 'unsound humour' begins the language of disease, corruption and contagion marking the body politic that permeates the tract. Set alongside the language of disease is the language of bondage, enthralment and slavery, as Milton goes on to castigate the desire 'to fall back, or rather to creep back so poorly as it seems the multitude would, to thir once abjur'd and detested thraldom of kingship' (356). Such backsliding 'not only argues a strange degenerate corruption suddenly spread among us, fitted and prepar'd for new slaverie, but will render us a scorn and derision to all our neighbours' (357). Vivid, overlapping metaphors build emotional resonance: Milton heightens the effect with repetition: synonymous or near-synonymous verbs, adjectives and nouns. The images cluster densely, linking disease, bondage and backsliding.

Despite the aim of persuasion, the imagery and rhetorical force of the tract imply the difficulty of persuading the backsliding people. To underscore further the necessity for action, Milton thus turns to the future to spell out the full implications of the disaster. Moving from the glorious past marked by 'mercies and signal assistances from heaven in our cause' to an inglorious future under monarchy, the English are never likely to attain 'as we are now advanc'd, to the recoverie of our freedom, never likely to have it in possession, as we now have it' (*CPW* VII: 358). If 'God in much displeasure gave a king to the *Israelites*, and imputed it a sin to them that they sought one' (359), how much worse will be the sin of the English in *returning* to kingship, once delivered?

As in *Eikonoklastes*, Milton in *The Readie and Easie Way* links kingship with idolatry. If in his earliest political prose he had argued against tyranny, and justified the trial and execution of a king who had broken his covenant with God and the people, Milton now aims more directly at kingship as an institution: 'a king must be ador'd like a demigod, with a dissolute and haughtie court about him, of vast expence and luxurie, masks and revels, to the debaushing of our prime gentry both male and female' (*CPW* VII: 360). A king will 'pageant himself up and down in progress among the perpetual bowings and cringings of an abject people, on either side deifying and adoring him' (360–1), however undeserved such attentions might be. At best, a king 'sits only like a great cypher'; at worst he is 'a mischief, a pest, a scourge of the nation' (361). Milton heightens his ridicule of kingship by doublets and accumulating detail that convey the accumulating trouble of the court. Repetition – 'bowings and cringings'; 'deifying and adoring' (360–1) – underscores the servitude, indeed the idolatry of the people.

In his work on Milton's prose style, Thomas Corns has noted that *The Readie and Easie Way* is an exception to the plain style and 'spare functionalism' of Milton's other middle-to-late prose tracts. Rather, figurative language, sets of synonyms and high adjectival use link the tracts with Milton's early antiprelatical prose, possibly as an effort to recapture the fervour and excitement of the Good Old Cause (1982: 65). The dense and allusive language of *The Readie and Easie Way* not only recaptures the fervour of the 'Good Old Cause', but resonantly interprets particular events in the context of sacred history. Biblical references frame and permeate the tract. The title itself seems to allude to the 'good way' to which Jeremiah urges the people to return: 'Thus saith the Lord, Stand ye in the ways, and see, and ask for the old paths, where is the good way, and walk therein, and ye shall find rest for your souls' (Jeremiah 6: 16a). Yet the people's response in Jeremiah's time (as in Milton's) is ominous: 'But they said, We will not walk therein' (6: 16b).

At the heart of *The Readie and Easie Way*, Milton shows 'with what ease we may now obtain a free Commonwealth, and by it with as much ease all the freedom, peace, justice, plentie that we can desire'; and he sets out, on the contrary, 'the difficulties, troubles, uncertainties nay rather impossibilities to enjoy these things constantly under a monarch' (*CPW* VII: 379). The tract thus proposes 'a readie and easie way' to such a Commonwealth through the establishment of a perpetual senate, presumably the Long Parliament itself, its numbers filled up by the election of additional members who are 'not addicted to a single person or house of lords' (368). The senate would have broad authority over law, finances, the military and foreign affairs, although if desirable, there might be a limited rotation of members, and its powers would also be qualified by the devolution of certain responsibilities to the counties. The broad ends of this government remain what Milton has envisaged throughout his prose career: spiritual and civil liberty. While Milton is clearly addressing his proposal to the immediate political situation, biblical allusion and resonance give that plan broader significance, showing the spiritual and moral implications of particular political actions: restoring the king or, conversely, preserving the republic.

In the passionate peroration which closes the first edition of *The Readie and Easie Way*, Milton identifies more closely with the prophet Jeremiah and makes more clear the dual purpose of his tract: to persuade but also to witness, to speak the words that will make the people accountable and help to interpret their achievement – or failure. To underscore the extremity of the situation in England, Milton points to a dark time in the history of Judah, the fall of Jerusalem to the Babylonians and the return of some of the people to what they saw as the protection and plenty of Egypt:

> if lastly, after all this light among us, the same reason shall pass for current to put our necks again under kingship, as was made use of by the *Jews* to return back to *Egypt* and to the worship of thir idol queen, because they falsly imagind that they then livd in more plenty and prosperitie, our condition is not sound but rotten, both in religion and all civil prudence. (*CPW* VII: 386–7)

Jeremiah lived in a period of religious nationalism, during which the people of Judah intrigued with Egypt and other anti-Babylonian forces, believing that Jerusalem – the site of the Temple – would never be captured or destroyed. But Jeremiah, rebuking the people for their backsliding, derided the false security of the Temple and preached that God had given them over to the Babylonians as instrument of punishment. Considered a traitor, mocked, excoriated and imprisoned, Jeremiah was vindicated, ironically, only by national disaster: the fall of Jerusalem. None the less, the people continued to defy Jeremiah and put their faith in false gods. Some returned to Egypt, forcing the old prophet to accompany them. Back in Egypt, they continued to reject Jeremiah's judgements:

> As for the word that thou hast spoken unto us in the name of the Lord, we will not hearken unto thee. But we will certainly do whatsoever thing goeth forth out of our own mouth, to burn incense unto the queen of heaven, and to pour out drink offerings unto her, as we have done . . . for then had we plenty of victuals, and were well, and saw no evil. (Jeremiah 44: 16–17)

Milton's reference to the idol queen, puzzled over by commentators, evokes this queen of heaven or *l° malkat haššaāmayim*, mentioned only in Jeremiah, and hence points to this extreme situation of the return to Egypt. Those Judahites who returned to Egypt bring upon themselves the covenant curse: 'Behold, I will watch over them for evil, and not for good: and all the men of Judah that are in the land of Egypt shall be consumed by the sword and by the famine, until there be an end of them' (Jeremiah 44: 27). Although Jeremiah holds out hope for a return of the exiles in the distant future, the present generation has wrought its own destruction. Milton thereby underscores the very dangerous position of the English nation, even while insisting that the backsliding to Egypt still can – and must – be stopped.

In concluding the first edition of *The Readie and Easie Way*, Milton makes more explicit his prophetic attitude and mission, although these are never wholly divorced from the end of persuasion. Echoing the words of Jeremiah, Milton both defers to biblical authority and establishes his own. And he claims that, even if he had no real audience, like the prophet Jeremiah, he would still have spoken: 'Thus much I should perhaps have said, though I were sure I should have spoken only to trees and stones, and had none to cry to, but with the Prophet, O *earth, earth, earth*: to tell the verie soil it self what God hath determined of *Coniah* and his seed for ever' (*CPW* VII: 388). Here Milton bitterly aligns Charles II with Coniah, son of the wicked king Jehoia-kim, exiled in Babylon, and denounced by Jeremiah as a 'despised broken idol' and 'a vessel wherein is no pleasure', cast out never to return (Jeremiah 22: 28). In the second edition, Milton would excise this potentially treasonous reference and turn the threatened curse against the people as a whole.

In his closing sentences, Milton looks both for human action and divine aid, as he hopes to 'have spoken perswasion to abundance of sensible and ingenuous men' but also 'to som perhaps, whom God may raise of these stones, to become children of libertie' (*CPW* VII: 388). Attempting to 'give a stay to these our ruinous proceedings and to this general defection of the misguided and abus'd multitude' (388), Milton draws on the monitory failures of an earlier chosen people and the impassioned language and stance of their disregarded prophet, Jeremiah.

Recent scholarship on republicanism and *The Readie and Easie Way* tends to disregard this biblical language, or to treat the prophetic framework defensively, as derogating from political engagement. But Milton's self-fashioning as a Jeremiah and his deployment of biblical allusion to frame, interpret and universalize current events is not a move away from politics but a powerful tool in the current debate. And Milton need not be a Jeremiah, if his words are heard by the children of liberty – or by their erstwhile Protector, General George Monck.

Milton and General Monck

Having completed and rapidly published *The Readie and Easie Way*, Milton turned to the man at the centre of power, General Monck, to appeal for help in ensuring that the electorate returned a Parliament still committed to the maintenance of a Common-wealth form of government. Such an appeal made more sense at the time than might now appear. Monck's republicanism in 1658 and early 1659 has been obscured by hindsight and knowledge of his eventual role in the Restoration. Post-restoration biographers were concerned to date Monck's shift to royalism as early as possible, and certainly contemporaries were suspicious and uncertain. But Monck's public adherence to the republic appeared unwavering, even, as we have seen, just after his re-admittance of the secluded members of Parliament.

In *The Present Means, and Brief Delineation of a Free Commonwealth* (*CPW* VII: 389–95), most likely written between 23 February and 14 March, Milton writes under the apparent misapprehension that the strict qualifications for candidates for the upcoming elections have not been repealed. (In fact, on its restoration, the Long

Parliament had almost immediately annulled all the previous legislation of the
Rump, including the writs that included strict qualifications for elections.) Taking
at face value Monck's continued public adherence to the Commonwealth, Milton
offers advice on how to shape both the electorate and the outcome, with the threat of
military force if co-operation is not forthcoming. Citing Monck's 'publish'd Letters to
the Army, and your Declaration recited to the Members of Parlament' that showed the
'Danger and Confusion of readmitting Kingship in this Land' (*CPW* VII: 393),
Milton advises Monck to call the leaders of the localities to London, educate them
in the necessity of avoiding single-person rule, and then let them return to their own
locales to shape elections for local councils and members of the 'Grand or General
Council' (394).

As in *The Readie and Easie Way*, Milton praises this grand council – which will sit
perpetually – as a 'a firm foundation and custody of our Public Liberty, Peace, and
Union' (394). None the less, Milton implicitly recognizes the popular sentiment in
favour of a return to monarchy in a final, thinly veiled suggestion that, if necessary,
Monck resort to military force: if the gentlemen convened by Monck 'refuse these fair
and noble Offers of immediate Liberty, and happy Condition', others should be found
'who will thankfully accept them, your Excellency once more declaring publickly this
to be your Mind, and having a faithful Veteran Army, so ready, and glad to assist you
in the prosecution therof' (395). If Milton continues to adhere to republicanism, it is
republicanism backed with a military sword.

Milton's appeal was not without some foundation. As we have seen, in his speech to
the restored Parliament, Monck explicitly supported the republic and warned against
the return of kingship and prelacy. Similarly, in his published letter to the army
regiments upon re-admitting the secluded members, Monck insisted that he had 'no
Intentions or Purposes to return to our old Bondage' and 'since the Providence of God
hath made us free at the Cost of so much Blood, we hope we shall never be found so
unfaithful to God and his People, as to lose so glorious a Cause.' Rather, he vowed to
'adhere to you in the continuing of our dear-purchased Liberties, both Spiritual and
Civil'. The restoration of the secluded members was the only remedy for a 'broken and
divided People, ready to run into Blood and Confusion' (Monck 1660c).

Yet Monck clearly looked for an end to the Parliament, and the 'putting the
Government into Successive Parliaments'. A 'free state', Monck maintained, 'cannot
be consistent with the perpetual sitting of these Members'. Milton was either unaware
of or pointedly ignored Monck's dictum on successive parliaments. And Monck, above
all, opposed the rule of the sword. These crucial differences, in the end, might well
have rendered Milton's advice pointless; but in fact, it seems highly probable that
Milton's letter – which survives only in draft form – was never sent.

A close look at the tumultuous months leading up to publication of *The Readie and
Easie Way* thus shows Milton continuing to foreground religious and civil liberty, but
less than particular about the constitutional means. By early 1660 he was putting his
faith in a military strong man – as he had earlier with Cromwell – to preserve liberty
in church and state against the wishes of the backsliding majority. Although con-

temporary speculation was rife, there is no hard evidence that Monck intended to diverge from his support for the Rump Parliament until after his arrival in London, when he found the city in turmoil and, from the Common Council down, disowning the authority of the remnant of a Parliament elected nearly twenty years earlier. Having urged the Parliament to fill up its vacancies preliminary to its own dissolution, Monck professed to envision the same ends when restoring, under strict qualifications, the secluded members. Milton's direct appeal to Monck – or at least his draft of the form that such an appeal would take – was not, under the circumstances, unreasonable or unrealistic. Milton could not have known that after restoring the secluded members, Monck would invoke another long-held principle, that the soldiery should be servant to, not master of, the civil government, and that he would not again intervene by force.

The Second Edition of *The Readie and Easie Way*

Political events in March 1660 were by no means moving in the direction that Milton had hoped. On 5 March the Presbyterian majority in the Long Parliament revived the Westminster Confession of Faith and reinstated the Solemn League and Covenant, originally taken in 1643, which pledged not only adherence to Parliament, but defence of the King's Majesty's person and authority. On 13 March the Engagement to remain faithful to a Commonwealth without a king or House of Lords was annulled. The Act by which the Long Parliament was dissolved on 16 March included writs for new elections that did not disqualify royalists from voting, or from standing for candidacy, if since the Civil War they had shown good affection to the Parliament.

Contemporaries saw not only the end of Parliament, but the return of the king. But Monck, as commander-in-chief of the armed forces, kept the remaining republican sympathizers in the army under control, preventing a remonstrance by his officers against Charles Stuart or any single-person rule, on the grounds that they should not meddle with the civil authority. By mid-March, Monck seems to have bowed to the popular will to bring back the king. Indeed, on 19 March Monck accepted a letter from the king himself and was secretly dispensing advice that would lead to the Declaration of Breda and the Restoration. None the less, Milton corrected and revised *The Readie and Easie Way*, and managed, under more difficult circumstances, once again to get the tract into print.

By the time he revised and republished *The Readie and Easie Way*, which appeared in its second edition some time during the first ten days of April (*CPW* VII: 396–463), Milton must have realized that Monck would not act to save the Commonwealth. A new epigraph to Sulla, adapted from Juvenal, almost surely points to Monck: *et nos consilium dedimus Syllae, demus populo nunc* (we have advised Sulla, now let us advise the people) (*CPW* VII: 405). The analogy between Monck and Lucius Cornelius Sulla (138–78 BC) was apt if bitter. A military general, Sulla twice marched with his army on Rome. Although Sulla implemented a number of constitutional reforms – including re-establishing the supremacy of the Senate – in an attempt to strengthen the Roman republic, his bloody military dictatorship ultimately paved the way for the monarchy of Caesar. Whereas early Miltonists identified the intended target of the epigraph as Monck, more recent readings assert that it points to Cromwell (Armitage 1995; Dzelzainis 1995b). Yet in early 1660 Milton's concern was not Cromwell, but Monck and what he could do – or could have done – to save the republic.

Monck remained part of a real if dwindling audience for the second edition of *The Readie and Easie Way*. Stanley Stewart (1984) argues for a shift to prophecy in the second edition, as the work becomes less concerned with the immediate political situation and more concerned with literary and mythological ends. This same disjunction between persuasion and prophecy is espoused by those scholars who argue, on the contrary, that Milton remains committed to republican activism to the end. But prophecy in *The Readie and Easie Way* is not opposed to but rather a powerful tool of rhetoric and persuasion. Even in the second edition, Milton has not entirely despaired. Rather, his purpose is dual: to persuade and to prophesy; to interpret, record and tell the story of a chosen nation, now backsliding beyond even the precedent of backsliding Judah.

Seemingly in response to the criticisms of the first edition, Milton elaborates on the perpetual senate in more detail, including safeguards and justification for keeping the vote away from the 'noise and shouting of a rude multitude' (*CPW* VII: 442). The contradiction between the will of the people and the end of liberty Milton now takes on directly. '[O]f freedom they partake all alike, one main end of government' (455); if, however, the majority of voices are against freedom, the lesser can compel the greater: 'More just it is doubtless, if it com to force, that a less number compell a greater to retain, which can be no wrong to them, thir libertie, then that a greater number for the pleasure of thir baseness, compell a less most injuriously to be thir fellows slaves' (455). The implicit threat of force suggests that Milton had not given up altogether – not even on Monck.

Milton also expands on arguments that might appeal to the Presbyterians – or their sympathizer in Monck – explaining why the Solemn League and Covenant did not extend to preserving a king who had violated its ends, dropping his earlier emphasis on separation of church and state, and heightening the dangers of monarchy, including retribution against the 'new royaliz'd presbyterians' (*CPW* VII: 451). The evils of kingship multiply, indeed breed, in the second edition: hence, to the adoration of a king as a demigod, Milton adds a papist queen, 'then a royal issue, and ere long severally thir sumptuous courts; to the multiplying of a servile crew, not of servants only, but of nobility and gentry, bred up then to the hopes not of public, but of court offices; to be stewards, chamberlains, ushers, grooms, even of the close-stool' (425). As in the first edition, Milton skilfully uses vivid imagery and specific, accumulating details to heighten the sense of danger and persuade his readers into action.

The second edition of *The Readie and Easie Way* elaborates even more on the backsliding people, particularly through the metonymic language of the yoke. Milton repeats his earlier denunciation of the desire of the people 'basely and besottedly to run their necks again into the yoke which they have broken, and prostrate all the fruits of thir victorie for naught at the feet of the vanquishd' (*CPW* VII: 428). But his prose now becomes even more vehement: 'Is it such an unspeakable joy to serve, such felicitie to wear a yoke?' (448). Milton warns that they will not 'obtain or buy at an easie rate this new guilded yoke which thus transports us' (450). And he deploys vivid language of sexual impurity, disease, animal yoking and vomit to castigate the 'zealous backsliders' whose necks are 'yok'd with these tigers of Bacchus, these new fanatics of not the preaching but the sweating-tub' (452–3). Then, even this description he retracts as too optimistic: 'yet shall they not have the honor to yoke with these, but shall be yok'd under them; these shall plow on their backs' (453).

The language of Jeremiah, intermittent but persistent, becomes especially crucial in the expanded peroration to the second edition, as Milton pleads with the back-sliding nation 'to bethink themselves a little and consider whether they are rushing' (*CPW* VII: 463). But as he urges his listeners to attempt to 'stay these ruinous proceedings; justly and timely fearing to what a precipice of destruction the deluge of this epidemic madness would hurrie us' (463), Milton employs reiterated imagery of backsliding that undermines any easy assurance of correction or change. The proposed 'readie and easie way' was rapidly becoming more of an act of faith. None the less, in the very act of speaking out Milton makes clear that he is not without hope that the English may still not be doomed to go back.

Milton's Last-ditch Appeal

Even after the second edition of *The Readie and Easie Way*, Milton once again spoke out against the Restoration, and he once again appealed to George Monck. In *Brief Notes Upon a Late Sermon* (10–15 April 1660; *CPW* VII: 464–86), Milton responded to a sermon preached by Matthew Griffith, former chaplain to Charles I, that not only was vindictively royalist, but, in printed form, was dedicated to Monck himself. Griffith went too far, and was imprisoned by order of the Council of State. Milton took the opportunity not only to rebuke Griffith for his royalism but to clear the name of the man he still professed to see as defending the republic. Indeed, the dedication of the sermon to Monck seems particularly to have enraged Milton, who rebukes Griffith for his 'impudent calumnie and affront to his Excellence' in urging Monck '*to carry on what he had so happily begun in the name and cause* not of God onely, which we doubt not, but *of his anointed*, meaning the late Kings son' (*CPW* VII: 470–1). To write such a dedication to Monck, Milton retorts, 'is to charge him most audaciously and falsly with the renouncing of his own public promises and declarations both to the Parlament and the Army' (471). None the less, Milton's words constitute an implicit challenge to Monck to follow up his republican words with appropriate action: 'and we trust his actions ere long will deterr such insinuating slanderers from thus approaching him for the future' (471). What actions Milton has in mind he does not specify: perhaps he was still hoping for the military intervention that he had envisioned in his drafted letter to Monck. But he continues to look to Monck as a military strong man who might help the backsliding nation avoid the return of Stuart kingship.

Complicating any argument for Milton's doctrinaire republicanism, he also puts forward – in the course of rebuking Griffith – the suggestion that if the nation will indeed insist on kingship, better King George than the return of the Stuarts. Hence, as in *The Readie and Easie Way*, Milton avows that 'Free Commonwealths have bin ever counted fittest and properest for civil, vertuous and industrious Nations' (*CPW* VII: 481), while monarchy, in contrast, is 'fittest to curb degenerate, corrupt, idle, proud, luxurious people' (481–2). If the backsliding nation will 'condemn' itself to kingship, the Stuarts could and should be avoided: 'yet chusing out of our own number one who hath best aided the people, and best merited against tyrannie, the space of a raign or two we may chance to live happily anough, or tolerably' (482).

Milton's apparent advocacy of kingship for Monck complicates views of his return to the republican fold in 1659–60. True, the suggestion of 'King George' was a desperate, last-minute expedient. But Milton's continued responsiveness to a single figure who could guarantee civil and religious liberty makes it less likely that he was utterly disappointed with Oliver Cromwell. As late as mid-April 1660, Milton seemed still to hope for military intervention or a new Protectorate backed by the threat of the sword. But Cromwell was long dead and 'honest' George had other plans.

The election returns in April brought in a strong royalist majority. Monck, having professed to royalist agents that he had long intended to do the King service, now presented to the Parliament the conciliatory letters from Charles that helped ensure an unconditional restoration. Widely lauded in popular print as the 'Saint George' who had saved England, Monck was one of the first to greet the King upon his arrival at Dover in May. Rugge describes the scene of 'the Generall kneelinge at his Majestys feete', as the King 'embraced and kissed him' (1961: 88). Subsequently reaping numerous honours, including being created Duke of Albemarle, Monck served Charles II as an adviser and in naval service until his death in 1671, when he was buried in Westminster Abbey.

Monck's role in the Restoration has overshadowed his republican past, purged by early biographers who strove to date his royalism as early as possible. In turn, histories of republicanism have likewise purged Monck or viewed him as a covert royalist all along. But in 1659 and early 1660, Monck's continued public adherence to the republic kept open possibilities to which Milton responded in his late prose. *The Readie and Easie Way* exhibits *both* literary aims *and* political engagement; its biblical references not only universalize and interpret but persuade. And in the immediate circumstances there was more cause for Milton to hope than afterknowledge of the collapse of the republic and the restoration of kingship might suggest. But Monck bowed to popular sentiment, for perhaps conflicting reasons, and Milton's hopes in him were dashed. If Satan's specious use of the republican language of liberty in *Paradise Lost* reflects on any particular contemporary, it might well be not Cromwell, but the former republican turned kingmaker, 'honest' George Monck.

BIBLIOGRAPHY

References for Further Reading

Armitage (1995); Ayers (1974); Barnaby (1990); Corns (1982, 1992b); Davidson (1993); Davies, Godfrey (1955); Dzelzainis (1995b); Fallon, Robert T. (1981, 1993); Holstun (1987); Hutton (1985); Knoppers (1990); Lewalski (1959); Monck (1659, 1660a, b, c); Mordaunt (1945); Norbrook (1999); Pepys (1970/1974); Raymond (1996b); Rugge (1961); Sanchez (1997); Stevens (2001); Stewart (1984); Woolrych (1957, 1974); Worden (1998).

The Late Poetry

20

Paradise Lost in Intellectual History

Stephen M. Fallon

While acute readers from Milton's time to our own – notably John Toland, William Blake, Denis Saurat, Maurice Kelley, Christopher Hill and John Rumrich – have recognized Milton's intellectual unconventionality and even heterodoxy, others have built the popular myth of Milton as spokesperson for orthodox Christianity. Attention to the relevant theological and philosophical contexts, however, indicates that a fiercely individual vision lies behind Milton's epic. Knowledge of the intellectual context reveals, for example, that the project of justifying the ways of God to men, while it might strike us as tamely pious, is audacious, presumptuous and, from the prevailing Calvinist perspective, even damnable. In nearly all of his works, furthermore, Milton not only charts his own course through the questions animating intellectual debate in his day, he also writes about himself. Auden remarked that, despite his bawdry, Shakespeare is the most chaste of writers, in that he does not write about himself. By comparison, the autobiographically promiscuous Milton, as in Hamlet's simile, unpacks his heart like a whore.

This chapter will approach *Paradise Lost* through intellectual history. It will highlight the questions that Milton addressed and the originality of his responses – as well as his presentation of himself as heroically singular. For the sake of analysis, I divide the poem into several parts. I will consider Milton's idiosyncratic engagement with the theological context in Books I–III, the books of heaven and hell, and with the philosophical context in Books IV–VIII, the books of Eden. Regarding Books IX–X, I will focus on the uneasy apprehension of error and danger that follows almost inevitably on the confident iconoclasm of earlier books. Turning to Books XI–XII, I will look at the manner in which Milton's unusual views are integrated into an explicitly fallen context, a context that he now shares with readers from whom he had earlier separated himself. These divisions are of course artificial and heuristic; Milton is engaged theologically and philosophically throughout the epic, and anxiety emerges before Book IX.

Books I–III: Asserting Eternal Providence and Theological Debate

> what in *me* is dark
> Illumine, what is low raise and support;
> That to the height of this great argument
> *I* may assert the eternal providence,
> And justify the ways of God to men.
> (I. 22–6; my emphasis)

The assertion of eternal providence is obligatory in religious works of Milton's time, but by claiming that he will justify God's ways, Milton throws down a gauntlet. Theodicy, or the defence of God, was suspect from the Calvinist perspective dominant among English Protestants of a puritan or dissenter inclination. Calvinists held that the justice of God's actions is not subject to the scrutiny of limited human reason. Where, to paraphrase the Book of Job, was Milton when God laid the foundations of the earth? Can Milton draw out Leviathan with a hook (Job 38: 4, 41: 1)? Calvin, quoting Romans 9: 20 ('Who are you, O man, to argue with God? Does the molded object say to its molder, "Why have you fashioned me thus?"'), sternly comments that 'such depth underlies God's judgments that all men's minds would be swallowed up if they tried to penetrate it . . . Monstrous indeed is the madness of men, who desire thus to subject the immeasurable to the puny measure of their own reason' (*Institutes* [1556], 1960, III. xxiii. 4). Thus the 'assertion' behind Milton's project is as much an assertion of human reason, and of Milton's role as defender of actions that many would see as above defence, as it is an assertion of God's prerogative.

The anti-Calvinist stance on theodicy, so countercultural within the puritan tradition, is characteristic of Milton in two ways, which taken together are paradoxical. First, it minimizes a gap between divine and human reason that most saw as nearly infinite. Milton in *Paradise Lost* repeatedly collapses hierarchical distinctions and figurative distances, between heaven and earth, between angels and human beings, and – more fitfully – between man and woman. Second, the stance foregrounds Milton's singularity, his assertive and unique self: 'what in *me* is dark / Illumine'; 'That.../ *I* may assert'. Milton, as many have observed, assumes the mantle of prophet, a status shared with several figures in his epic – notably Abdiel, Enoch, Elijah – who stand out from the miscellaneous crowd. Milton the collapser of hierarchical distances confronts Milton the man who stands out from the crowd. The poet, in a paradox that replays his career as a political theorist, is a leveller, an equalizer of hierarchies, who needs to think of himself as uncommon, as gifted and blessed above his peers. The tension generated by this paradox will lead to a sharp recoil in the epic, as the spectre of alienation and distance haunts the poet-narrator.

The theology of *Paradise Lost* opposes that of Calvin, according to which God gratuitously and arbitrarily chooses to predestine fallen individuals either to salvation or to damnation. Calvin's God saves by an irresistible grace that is unmerited by those to whom it is granted. Only those elect individuals granted such grace can be saved, and they are inevitably saved. Emphasizing God's omnipotence, Calvinists insisted that God alone determines who is saved, and that his choices are not guided or constrained by the choices of creatures. They defended the justice of this doctrine by pointing to the fact that all deserve damnation, and by the more sweeping voluntarist position that God's choices cannot and should not be measured against any prior or external standard of justice, because those choices define justice. According to the *supralapsarian* branch of Calvinist doctrine, even the Fall is predestined and necessary; according to the other, *infralapsarian*, branch, Adam and Eve were free until they forfeited that freedom in choosing to disobey.

Milton's defence of God counters the arbitrariness of the Calvinist model. Even fallen creatures are, with the help of grace, free to stand or fall, to obey or disobey. Grace sufficient for salvation, Milton maintains, is offered to all, not merely to a predestined elect, and it is resistible. One's salvation or damnation depends on whether one freely accepts or rejects universally offered grace.

In *Paradise Lost* Milton grasps authority for his anti-Calvinist theodicy by placing it in the mouth of God. In a pair of speeches early in Book III (lines 80–134, 168–216) the Father, after announcing that Satan will succeed in tempting Adam and Eve, lays out a plan of salvation:

> so will fall,
> He and his faithless progeny: whose fault?
> Whose but his own? Ingrate, he had of me
> All he could have; I made him just and right,
> Sufficient to have stood, though free to fall.
> Such I created all the ethereal powers
> And spirits, both them who stood and them who failed;
> Freely they stood who stood, and fell who fell.
> . . .
> if I foreknew,
> Foreknowledge had no influence on their fault,
> Which had no less proved certain unforeknown.
> So without least impulse or shadow of fate,
> Or aught by me immutably foreseen,
> They trespass, authors to themselves in all
> Both what they judge and what they choose; for so
> I formed them free, and free they must remain,
> Till they enthrall themselves:
>
> (III. 95–102, 117–25)

The concluding lines refer to the fall of the angels, but, as the context makes clear, they refer by extension to the fall of the human race. The statement also fits Milton's understanding of the postlapsarian human condition.

Is the Father, as some have claimed, querulously defensive? One answer, proposed by Stanley Fish, is that the defensive tone is a projection of the reader's fallen perspective on to God's dispassionate statement of fact (1998: 62). But Fish's ingenious argument, explicitly grounded on a Calvinist aesthetic, imports an inappropriate Calvinist perspective, according to which God's actions are essentially above defence and rational evaluation. A more appropriate context is the theology of James Arminius, who recognizes that, given the omnipotence of God and the presence of evil choices, it is crucial, if one is to establish God's justice, to acquit God of malicious manipulation of hapless creatures. He writes that the Calvinist view of predestination, according to which God (1) ordains the fall of the human race (from which 'the fall of man necessarily followed') and (2) chooses to deprive many, prior to any choices on their parts, of the grace without which they cannot avoid sin, 'is injurious to the glory of God' and entails the conclusion that 'God is the author of sin' (*Declaration of Sentiments*, in Arminius 1956, I: 228). On account of this position, congruent at every point with Milton's, Arminius was forced to spend much of his time defending himself against charges of heresy from fellow Protestants. Milton makes the same arguments in *De Doctrina Christiana*. He rejects offhandedly the argument that God ordains the fall of the race: 'Everyone agrees that man could have avoided falling' (*CPW* VI: 174), and, like Arminius, he draws the logical conclusion of God's culpability from the doctrine of absolute predestination:

> If God decreed unconditionally that some people must be condemned, and there is no scriptural authority for such a belief, it follows from this theory of unconditionally decreed reprobation that God also decided upon the means without which he could not fulfill his decree. But the means are sin, and that alone. (*CPW* VI: 191)

The Calvinist would object not to Milton's (or Arminius's) logic but to the propriety of using logic to test divine justice in the first place. Both Milton and Arminius insist that divine foreknowledge has no effect on human freedom. The Father's insistence in *Paradise Lost* that no hint of fate or foreknowledge causes the Fall echoes the Milton of *De Doctrina Christiana*, who insists that 'From the concept of freedom, then, all idea of necessity must be removed . . . even . . . that shadowy and peripheral idea of necessity based on God's immutability and foreknowledge' (*CPW* VI: 161–2).

If Fish's argument, with its condemnation of anything but a passive acceptance of divine claims, does not allow for any significant questioning of divine justice, William Empson's reading is problematic for the opposite reason. Empson's God is defensive because he is guiltily passing the buck. He manipulates his creatures shamelessly and then sadistically tortures them for the actions that he makes inevitable (1981: 115–16, 204–10). Fish doesn't allow for meaningful theodicy – God is simply assumed *a priori* to be just and above defence; Empson's view is no less closed to theodicy, for in his version Milton's God is simply indefensible.

In asserting the freedom of Adam and Eve, Milton's God resolutely denies the supralapsarian doctrine that he ordained the fall of humanity. In his next speech he contradicts the more generally accepted infralapsarian Calvinist view of absolute predestination (i.e. predestination regardless of foreseen merit) after the Fall. For Milton, as for Arminius, individuals, though heirs to the 'mortal sin / Original' (IX. 1003–4) are not condemned arbitrarily, without reference to their own free choices. Milton, or Milton's God, carefully distinguishes between the divine grace that alone can save sinners, and the individual's responsibility to choose to accept offered grace:

> Man shall not quite be lost, but saved who will,
> Yet not of will in him, but grace in me
> Freely vouchsafed; once more I will renew
> His lapsèd powers, though forfeit and enthralled
> By sin to foul exorbitant desires;
> Upheld by me, yet once more he shall stand
> On even ground against his mortal foe
>
> (III. 173–9)

Through the Father, Milton endorses human freedom without making the Pelagian claim that fallen human beings can choose to believe and obey without divine help. The power behind faith is God's, but by virtue of universally offered, sufficient grace human beings are free, as they are not in the Calvinist model, to accept or reject belief and thus to be saved or not. The fine balance is evident in the formula 'saved who will, / Yet not of will in him, but grace in me'.

The lengths to which the Father goes to explain the relations between sin, freedom and grace testify to Milton's conviction that the justice of God is explicable to reason. In Milton's epic the unbridgeable gap between divine and created reason characteristic of Calvinism is a feature of hell. The speeches of Satan and his followers are marked by incomprehension and contradiction, as they wander wide of the truth in their efforts to understand and improve their hopeless situation. The very environment of hell is compounded of confusion; the visual murkiness – 'darkness visible' (I. 63) – signals an intellectual murkiness. Immense distance separates the devils from their former home: 'As far removed from God and light of heaven / As from the centre thrice to the utmost pole' (I. 73–4). Intellectually they flail and flounder toward an infernal version of the Calvinist doctrine of absolute predestination, blaming God for their choices, and suggesting that the system was rigged. For the devils, God, like the Calvinist deity as viewed by Milton, is the author of sin, who set up a system leading inevitably to a fall. When Satan, in a lucid moment – which, significantly, occurs outside hell – accepts responsibility for his free rebellion (IV. 66–7), he quickly veers from this unpalatable recognition to the absurd credo 'Evil be thou my good' (IV. 110).

The devils' predicament is painfully evident in the Council in Hell in the second book, where it becomes obvious that no solution is open to them. Mammon's and

Belial's counsels are arguably the best available given the circumstances. If, as the Father announces in Book III, there is no chance of redemption, why not seek ways to find some semblance of good in hell (Mammon) or to appease God and thus partially assuage his wrath (Belial)? But which way they fly, intellectually as well as morally and physically, is hell. After the Council, the fallen angels break up, some to pursue epic games, some to sing, some to the dismal task of exploring the infernal world, and some to puzzle out providence and divine justice:

> Others apart sat on a hill retired,
> In thoughts more elevate, and reasoned high
> Of providence, foreknowledge, will, and fate,
> Fixed fate, free will, foreknowledge absolute,
> And found no end, in wandering mazes lost.
> (II. 557–61)

In the chiastic structure of lines 559–60 free will disappears into the tight knot it shares with fixed fate and absolute foreknowledge. Milton here portrays as an infernal punishment the confusion and puniness of reason confronted with such questions. The immense distance that Calvin sees between divine and human reason is in *Paradise Lost* a function not of an inescapably fallen nature but of the obstinate ignorance of the devils.

Commitment to freedom thus drives the theology of *Paradise Lost*. Free agents make choices that govern their fates. The Son volunteers freely, and therefore meritoriously, to redeem fallen humankind. The devils freely choose to fall, but afterwards, significantly, refuse to acknowledge that freedom and seek to shift responsibility to God.

Books IV–VIII: Degrees of Substance and the Materialism Debate

Milton's insistence on freedom also helps to account for what many have seen as an anomaly in *Paradise Lost*: the idiosyncratic, animist materialist universe in which the epic action is set. Less than a century after the poem's composition as acute a critic as Samuel Johnson was puzzled by it:

> Another inconvenience of Milton's design is that it requires the description of what cannot be described, the agency of spirits. He saw that immateriality supplied no images, and that he could not show angels acting but by instruments of action; he therefore invested them with form and matter. (Johnson 1905, 1: 184)

Johnson complains of the poem's 'confusion of spirit and matter' because he assumes that angels must be purely immaterial. The assumption and its consequence are embedded in Johnson's confident assertion that Milton 'saw that immateriality supplied no images'. One assumption leads to another: that Milton 'invested' immaterial angels 'with form and matter'. An anonymous letter to the *Gentleman's Magazine* in March 1738, while harsher, may have more accurately reflected Milton's project, accusing Milton of 'corrupting our Notions of spiritual Things, and sensualizing our Ideas of Heaven' (Shawcross 1972: 101). In Milton's universe, everything is both material and alive: angels are not incorporeal, and what we think of as inanimate matter is animate. As Raphael tells Adam and Eve, angels do not merely make a show of eating, as in the tradition (V. 433–43), but actually eat and digest. The difference between the angelic and human realms is not, as conventionally thought, an unbridgeable gap between the purely incorporeal and the corporeal. Instead, they are 'Differing but in degree, of kind the same' (V. 490).

Milton's angels are corporeal not merely for narrative convenience, but because Milton believed they were bodily creatures. Johnson's orthodox assumptions regarding the immateriality of angels seemed less self-evident in the philosophical climate of the mid-seventeenth century. Milton's materialism is an original contribution to a debate with profound implications for freedom of the will, and thus for ethics and religion.

The implications for ethics of the seventeenth-century debate over substance are clear in Thomas Hobbes, whose secular Calvinism was as unacceptable to Milton as his political opinions. Hobbes argued that whatever is, is bodily, and that all events are caused by physical motion, including mental events. He finds the phrase 'incorporeal substance' nonsensical and an 'abuse of speech' (1986: 108, 113, 171). Physical motions in the brain produce mental activity; thought is a corporeal 'tumult of the mind' (119). Like other mental phenomena, choice is a corporeal motion in the brain determined by prior corporeal motions. To one who claimed that the will is free, Hobbes 'should not say he were in an Errour; but that his words were without meaning, that is to say, Absurd' (113).

The illusion of freedom arises from our inability to trace the long and complex chain of causation, a chain that Hobbes at least nominally links at the far end to God:

> because every act of man's will and every desire and inclination proceedeth from some cause, and that from another cause in a continual chain (whose first link is in the hand of God the first of all causes), they proceed from *necessity*. So that to him that could see the connexion of those causes, the *necessity* of all men's voluntary actions would appear manifest. (1986: 137)

Hobbes's long chain is another version of the distance between divine and human perspectives that Milton counters in *Paradise Lost*. The omnipotent factor for Hobbes, despite the conventional piety of the passage here quoted, might be less the decisions of a personal God than an unbreakable chain of materialist and mechanist causation, a chain he anatomizes in his *Leviathan*.

The revolutionary and regicide Milton would find little comfort in *Leviathan*, as its determinist argument prefaces and underwrites an argument for passive acceptance of sovereign power. (The republican implications of Milton's animist materialism are examined by John Rogers [1996: 112–22].) Moreover, Hobbes's determinist argument scandalized not only republicans, but the many who saw in it the death of morality or ethics. One alternative was offered by René Descartes, who attempted to locate a home for free will in an incorporeal soul. For Descartes the visible, corporeal universe operates, as it does for Hobbes, mechanically; but incorporeal substance is freed from mechanism. Descartes famously grounded his argument for incorporeal substance in the indubitable experience of an 'I' that thinks: 'I think, therefore I am.' Having secured a foothold in incorporeal substance, Descartes assigns to that substance self-activity and freedom.

Descartes for a time was promoted by the Cambridge Platonists, philosophers often associated with Milton (Henry More was a fellow of Christ's, Cambridge, Milton's college), and fierce opponents of Hobbes. Ralph Cudworth's massive attack on mechanism and his articulation of a dualism of active incorporeal substance and inert corporeal substance, the confidently titled *True Intellectual System of the Universe* (1678), announces on the opening page its intention to defend freedom of the will, which he perceived as under attack by the mechanist materialism of Hobbes, the pervasive but unnamed antagonist of Cudworth's book. More and Cudworth were initially drawn to Descartes as an advocate of free will, the incorporeal soul and the existence of an incorporeal God, but eventually they concluded that Descartes's dualism and incorporealism constituted a blind for a fundamental mechanism. They argued that, matter being essentially dead and inert, *nothing*, including what we think of as merely physical phenomena, could occur in the world without the activity of incorporeal substance. Their own defence of free will was tied to this argument that incorporeal substance lay behind every action in the world, and that apparently mechanical phenomena were traceable to the activity of a low-level, unconscious, but still incorporeal and active substance that More termed the 'spirit of nature' and Cudworth 'plastic nature' (i.e. shaping nature).

More's and Cudworth's arguments committed them to endless defences of occult phenomena (including the activity of witches) as well as improbable demonstrations of the incorporeal causes of apparently mechanical phenomena. Their dualism, and thus their defence of free will, faced an uphill battle given the growing prestige and explanatory power of the new (and mechanical) natural philosophy. In this context Milton's philosophical model begins to seem central and relevant to his epic, despite Johnson's opinion of its private and quixotic character. In the middle books of his epic, Milton, like Descartes and the Cambridge Platonists, advances an alternative to Hobbes's mechanist determinism. But here Milton characteristically swims against the tide, for he does not subscribe to Descartes's dualistic view of an incorporeal substance circumscribed in God and human souls or minds, nor does he follow the Cambridge Platonists' dualism with its pervasive incorporeal substance extending from God to an occult plastic nature. At a time when the reality of

incorporeal substance is under attack, Milton finds a home for freedom in a recon-
ceived, animate and *corporeal* substance. This conception, like his insistence on freedom of the will, has the effect of minimizing distances and closing formerly
unbridgeable divides.

Instead of an ontological gulf between body and incorporeal spirit, Milton imagines a continuum of matter, with tenuous matter at one end and gross matter at the
other. What we think of as incorporeal – souls, angels – is in fact subtly corporeal.
Our souls are not different in kind from our bodies, but only in degree. Our corporeal
bodies and souls can move up or down the continuum depending on moral status. As
one chooses the good, one becomes relatively less corporeal, but still material;
conversely, evil coarsens substance. Raphael employs a plant metaphor to make this
plan concrete for Adam:

> O Adam, one almighty is, from whom
> All things proceed, and up to him return,
> If not depraved from good, created all
> Such to perfection, one first matter all,
> Indued with various forms, various degrees
> Of substance, and in things that live, of life;
> But more refined, more spirituous, and pure,
> As nearer to him placed or nearer tending
> Each in their several active spheres assigned,
> Till body up to spirit work, in bounds
> Proportioned to each kind. So from the root
> Springs lighter the green stalk, from thence the leaves
> More airy, last the bright consummate flower
> Spirits odorous breathes: flowers and their fruit
> Man's nourishment, by gradual scale sublimed,
> To vital spirits aspire, to animal,
> To intellectual, give both life and sense,
> Fancy and understanding, whence the soul
> Reason receives, and reason is her being,
> Discursive, or intuitive; discourse
> Is oftest yours, the latter most is ours,
> Differing but in degree, of kind the same.
> Wonder not then, what God for you saw good
> If I refuse not, but convert, as you,
> To proper substance; time may come when men
> With angels may participate, and find
> No inconvenient diet, nor too light fare:
> And from these corporal nutriments perhaps
> Your bodies may at last turn all to spirit,
> Improved by tract of time, and winged ascend
> Ethereal, as we, or may at choice

Here or in heavenly paradises dwell;
If ye be found obedient,
                              (V. 469–501)

The opening, with its evocation of neoplatonist emanation and return, would sound reassuringly familiar to early modern ears. But what follows is audacious and speculative. The dynamic of ontological ascent is figured in the schematic and synchronic portrait of the plant. As one moves from earthy root to stalk to leaves to flowers, one moves towards more delicate and less gross matter. The fruit of the plant becomes our food, whereupon the sublimation towards tenuous matter continues 'by gradual scale' in the production of corporeal spirits. Milton modifies the familiar Galenic triadic hierarchy of spirits – the natural, the vital and the animal – by omitting the first and adding 'intellectual' spirits. What we might (and Milton's contemporaries certainly would) think of as a divide between the corporeal and the incorporeal vanishes, as these subtle but corporeal spirits 'give . . . life and sense, / Fancy and understanding', from which the soul 'receives' reason, and 'reason is her being'. We have travelled from plant to soul without meeting an ontological gap.

Milton closes the gap from both sides: souls are corporeal, and phenomena long thought inanimate are alive. Just before the speech on the one first matter, Raphael describes cosmic respiration and nutrition: the earth feeds sea, the sea the air, the air the moon and other celestial bodies, and all these the sun, which 'at even / Sups with [i.e. on] the ocean' (V. 425–6). Milton employs a subtle interlace of what we normally think of as the material and the immaterial in his descriptions of Eden, which is a great organism. In the Garden 'trees wept odorous gums and balm' (IV. 248); this is a conventional enough trope, but things become more interesting when Milton turns to bird song in Eden: 'The birds their choir apply; airs, vernal airs, / Breathing the smell of field and grove, attune / The trembling leaves' (IV. 264–6). Their song animates the wind, but at the same time the wind is animated by the field and grove. The airs that are at once the breath of birds, their songs, and songs of spring, meet the airs 'breathed' by the landscape. Milton's Eden is an extraordinary place, not only for the arresting beauty of his descriptions (see, for example, IV. 236–63), but for the literal animation of the landscape. This interpenetration of corporeal and incorporeal is shared with heaven, where gates move by themselves, for 'within them spirit lived' (VII. 204), and where angels eat as heartily as Raphael does when he visits earth (V. 630–8). Hell, by contrast, is a land of death, less refined, spiritous and pure than any other location, its very grossness and lifelessness an ironic index of the moral significance of animate matter in Milton's epic.

In repudiating the dualistic separation of soul and body, whether in the ancient Platonic and or the modern Cartesian sense, Milton draws together the animate and the inanimate, the incorporeal and the corporeal, heaven and earth. When Adam asks about the War in Heaven, Raphael explains that some accommodation of different realms, some 'likening spiritual to corporal forms, / As may express them best', will be necessary, but he quickly backtracks: 'though what if earth / Be but the shadow of heav'n, and things therein / Each to other like, more than on earth is thought?' (V. 573–6).

The closing of ontological distances serves the same end as the narrowing of the gap between divine and human reason in the early books: Milton's insistence on significant creaturely freedom and moral autonomy. If Hobbes reduces thought to a mechanical phenomenon, Milton ascribes to what we usually consider 'inanimate' matter attributes we normally associate with mind, will or soul. In *Paradise Lost* it is not only sentient creatures who choose their mode of being; Milton's monism extends this choice to matter as well. Belial advises against continued armed opposition to God, because 'the ethereal mould [the stuff of heaven] / Incapable of stain would soon expel / Her mischief, and purge off the baser fire / Victorious' (II. 139–42). After the devils fall from heaven, 'heaven rejoiced, and soon repaired / Her mural breach, returning whence it rolled' (VI. 878–9). When Eve falls, 'Earth felt the wound, and nature from her seat / Sighing through all her works gave signs of woe, / That all was lost' (IX. 782–4). The continuity of the chain of being described by Raphael in Book V suggests that we take these passages as more than figurative. The reactions of the matter of heaven and earth are moral and ontological simultaneously; in this they mirror the choices of the poem's rational creatures. Moral choices in *Paradise Lost* have implications for one's place along the continuum of the one first matter.

The visible universe, moreover, is not a prison from which we must escape, but a fabric woven by God from his own 'material potency', as John Rumrich terms it (1996: 144). Milton's unique perspective is written into his depiction of Chaos, the realm traversed by Satan in Book II and the material of creation in Book VII. The Father acknowledges his complex relation to the realm of Chaos:

> Boundless the deep, because I am who fill
> Infinitude, nor vacuous the space.
> Though I uncircumscribed myself retire,
> And put not forth my goodness,
>
> (VII. 168–71)

Chaos is that region from which God retires, refraining from putting forth his goodness. The distance won by this restraint accounts not only for the formlessness of Chaos, but also for the freedom of the universe created from the body of God, including the freedom of creatures (Rumrich 1996: 144–5).

The rehabilitation of matter in *Paradise Lost* is reflected in Milton's revaluation of the passions, his violation of the Renaissance truism that passion, typically gendered feminine, must be held in check by the reason. Raphael voices this truism while admonishing Adam about his passionate love of Eve (VIII. 561–94), but Milton's epic sees where Raphael is seen least wise. The great erotic poetry of the epic, the insistence on prelapsarian and even angelic sexual activity, breaks the precedent set by the 'crabbed opinion' of Augustine (*Tetrachordon*, *CPW* II: 596). The poetry endorses Adam's celebration of 'vehement [mindless] desire', of 'Transported touch', and of

'Commotion strange' (VIII. 526–31), and undermines Raphael's priggish and entirely conventional warning.

Books IX–X: The Dampened Wing and the Anxiety of Singularity

Whatever some might make of the current relevance of Milton's speculations on salvation and substance, *Paradise Lost* is hardly, in Walter Raleigh's notorious phrase, a 'monument to dead ideas' (1900: 88). Careful attention to these speculations reveals the audacity of Milton's ideas on divine and human freedom. In the words of *Areopagitica*, 'embalmed' in these supposedly dead ideas is the 'pretious life-blood of a master spirit', revealing, poststructuralist truisms notwithstanding, Milton's living singularity. And written into *Paradise Lost*, along with the idiosyncratic construction of matter and spirit and the audacious claims for human freedom, is the almost inevitable anxiety attendant on public singularity and iconoclasm. This anxiety emerges most clearly in the invocation to Book IX, the book of the Fall, as Milton can be caught contemplating, despite his claims for heroic singularity and virtue, the possibility of his own alienation from God. Traces of this anxiety also appear in earlier invocations.

In the invocations Milton takes occasion, as he had so often in his career, to write about himself. The political prose is punctuated with autobiographical passages, even when Milton acknowledges, as he does in *The Reason of Church-Government*, that autobiography is out of place or untimely. His own marriage in ruins, he writes not one but four books on divorce. *Areopagitica* is the anguished cry of an author who can't bear to think of censors pawing through his own works. Despite his readiness to write about himself, Milton, the puritan writer *par excellence*, did not leave us the autobiography almost obligatory for seventeenth-century puritan writers. While the endlessly repeated puritan story, derived from Augustine's *Confessions*, revolves around sin, conviction and repentance. Milton never openly acknowledges his own sinfulness in his autobiographical digressions. It is easy to imagine the cumulative strain on Milton; though the product of a culture in which confession of sin is both mandatory and a mark of conversion and salvation, he repeatedly claims for himself innocence and singular virtue.

In the opening invocation, Milton gestures toward an intimate and heroic relation with God:

> And chiefly thou O Spirit, that dost prefer
> Before all temples the upright heart and pure,
> Instruct me, for thou knowst; thou from the first
> Wast present, and with mighty wings outspread
> Dovelike satst brooding on the vast abyss

And mad'st it pregnant: what in me is dark
Illumine, what is low raise and support;

(I. 17–23)

The Spirit (not the trinitarian Holy Spirit but the spirit of the one God) prefers the pure heart to 'all temples'. Placing hearts before temples, Milton shares the Protestant emphasis on the direct relation with God as opposed to one mediated by a priesthood and institution. But the juxtaposition of singular and plural is significant and not merely conventional. '[U]pright heart[s]' would also have been consonant with a Protestant vision of a community of the godly, each of whom forges a relationship with God. The emphasis on the singular heart fits Milton, who sets himself apart, as specially gifted and chosen to follow in the tradition of Moses and John, invoked a few lines earlier.

The Spirit both broods on and impregnates the Abyss, thus combining male and female roles. At the same time, it is invoked to fill Milton, and he becomes pregnant with the story that he will inscribe with his pen. Milton, who dictated his poem early in the mornings, would wait impatiently for his amanuensis, complaining that he 'wanted to be milked' (Parker 1996: 1090). Milton will be both mother and father of his text, the passive receptacle of inspiration and the active assertor of eternal providence. Significantly, he shares this gender confusion, or perhaps gender appropriation, with the God of *Paradise Lost*.

As the epic progresses, traces of doubt and anxiety intrude. In addressing 'holy light' in Book III's invocation, Milton asks 'May I express thee unblamed?' (III. 1, 3). This intimation of presumption is short-lived, as Milton turns his attention to a more contrived concern, the danger of the 'obscure sojourn', left in the past now that the author-narrator has 'Escaped the Stygian pool' (III. 15, 14). This danger depends on the fiction that the author-narrator has in fact visited the infernal world of the first two books. The invocation moves to a more lasting anxiety when Milton contemplates his blindness, but despair is transformed into triumph as the blindness becomes the (ironically, visible) marker of Milton's inclusion in the prophetic line of vision connecting Homer and Tiresias.

Anxiety mounts in the invocation to Book VII: 'Up led by thee [Urania] / Into the heav'n of heav'ns *I have presumed*, / An earthly guest, and drawn empyreal air, / Thy tempering' (VII. 12–15; my emphasis). Milton is poised between confidence in heavenly invitation and an uneasy sense that he is overreaching or presumptuous; is he a guest or a gate-crasher? The degree of his concern is evident in his prayer:

with like safety guided down
Return me to my native element:
Lest from this flying steed unreined (as once
Bellerophon, though from a lower clime),

> Dismounted, on the Aleian field I fall
> Erroneous, there to wander and forlorn.
>   (VII. 15–20)

The simile of Bellerophon generates a complex allusive context, with elements both of foolish presumption and of preternatural virtue (Fallon 1994). In the remainder of the invocation Milton famously sings of his having 'fallen on evil days, / ... and evil tongues', and of finding himself 'In darkness, and with dangers compassed round, / And solitude' (VII. 25–8). Milton refers to the hostile Restoration climate; as a defender of the regicide and spokesperson for champion of the Commonwealth and Protectorate, he was gaoled for a time and in danger of his life. But the fear of a fall after presumptuous flight suggests also anxiety aroused by intellectual unconventionality.

Milton hesitates between a heroic self-conception, as unparalleled spokesperson of God, and the fear occasioned by that self-conception, that by overreaching he has forfeited God's favour. The anxiety, not surprisingly, colours the invocation of the book in which the favoured first-born of creation falls. While Milton has everywhere collapsed the distance between the human and the angelic (and even the divine), Book IX narrates events that widen the distance. No more will angel sit with Adam, 'permitting him the while / Venial discourse unblamed' (IX. 4–5). The finality here responds to the open-ended questioning of the moment six books earlier when the poet had wondered if he could express divine wisdom 'unblamed'. The disobedience and overreaching of Adam is met with decisive and immediate repudiation,

> on the part of heaven
> Now alienated, distance and distaste,
> Anger and just rebuke, and judgment given,
> That brought into this world a world of woe,
> Sin and her shadow Death,
>   (IX. 8–12)

As the opening lines echo the invocation to Book III, so these lines bring us back to the very beginning of the epic, when sin 'Brought death into the world, and all our woe' (I. 3). The distance invoked is intellectual as well as physical: the distance between what God and human beings can know and the distance between heaven and hell.

The yoking of 'distaste' with 'distance' evokes the epic's many reminders that knowledge of good and evil comes with the taste of the fruit. After his fall, Adam plays punningly with the links between taste and knowledge:

> Eve, now I see thou art exact of taste,
> And elegant, of sapience no small part,
> Since to each meaning savour we apply,
> And palate call judicious;
>   (IX. 1017–20)

The distaste of heaven for Adam and Eve's sin of forbidden knowledge is liable to be renewed in distaste for Milton's own presumptuous speculations. The key here as elsewhere is whether Milton is acting on his own or with divine guidance. If the latter, then his song is more heroic than any in history (he alludes specifically to Homer's and Virgil's); if the former, he has much to answer for. He contemplates both success and its alternative if

> an age too late, or cold
> Climate, or years damp my intended wing
> Depressed, and much they may, if all be mine,
> Not hers who brings it nightly to my ear.
>
> (IX. 44–7)

If his wing is damped and depressed, if with Bellerophon he falls to the plain 'Erroneous, there to wander', then he is back in the position of the devils in Book II, with elevated thoughts, 'reason[ing] high / Of providence, foreknowledge, will, and fate, / Fixt fate, free will, foreknowledge absolute, / And [finding] no end, in wandering mazes lost' (II. 558–61). He falls, that is, into the sin and presumption against which Calvin inveighed, that of measuring the things of God by human reason. In Adam and Eve's sin and its punishment Milton sees the image of the risk that he himself takes. If anything, he is potentially closer to the danger of Eve, to her susceptibility, illustrated in the dream in Book V, to the temptation of singularity. With the obscure vision of his own potential fall, the distance between himself and God that he has been attempting to close not only throughout the epic but also throughout his entire career threatens to expand infinitely. The prospect of falling from the sky with damped wing is uncomfortably close to the free fall of Satan in a vacuum of chaos: 'all unawares / Fluttering his pennons vain plumb down he drops / Ten thousand fathom deep' (II. 932–4). Milton is poised over the abyss in *Paradise Lost*. He has answered a summons to heroic action; but was it a divine summons, like that prompting the Son in Book III to volunteer for his mission, or a self-summoning, like that prompting Satan to his own mission in Book II?

Books XI–XII: The Subjected Plain and Milton's Ambivalence

In the final books Milton bridges the gap between the world we know and the worlds for which we require revelation or prophecy. We have not visited heaven or hell, nor have we experienced the life of the unfallen, but the experiences narrated in the final books are familiar to us. At the beginning of the epic the Miltonic narrator 'intends to soar / Above the Aonian mount' (I. 14–15); twelve books later, we accompany him as he brings Adam and Eve 'down the cliff... / To the subjected plain' (XII. 639–40). The mountain and plain images, ascent and descent, bracket the epic. For this concluding narration, one does not need the inspired visionary; a fallen son of

Adam and Eve is now sufficient, and Milton is again one of us (even if a particularly talented one of us).

Books XI and XII have been considered by many the product of diminished energy and inspiration. C. S. Lewis famously described them as an 'untransmuted lump of futurity' (1942: 125). I imagine that Lewis would accept one or another of the many defences of the final books that his criticism has provoked, but would still echo Hamlet's 'O what a falling off was there'. However ingeniously structured, the biblical history recounted in Books XI and XII does seem pedestrian after the flights of the earlier books. A more direct reply to Lewis's concern would be that in switching to a more pedestrian register in the final books Milton is matching form to meaning. The weariness that Lewis notes may be a thematic weariness, not flagging authorial achievement. The gap between the characters' experience and shared human experience narrows in the final books, and with it the gap between narrator and readers. Michael explains to Adam that, by remaining sinless, he would have dwelled for ever in Eden as capital and received delegations of descendants from around the world; 'But this pre-eminence thou hast lost, brought down / To dwell on even ground now with thy sons' (XI. 347–8). If we experience a falling off as *Paradise Lost* rounds to its conclusion, it may be because the poem and its narrator come to dwell on even ground with us.

The attenuation is echoed and epitomized in the education of Adam, the slow learner of the final books. The palpably flawed Adam learns lesson after lesson in intellectual humility as the exacting angel Michael corrects him. The education begins with vision, made possible because Michael removes from his eyes the 'film' left by sin (XI. 412) and instils in them drops from the 'well of life', which 'pierced, / Even to the inmost seat of mental sight' (XI. 416–18). This moment parallels that passage in the invocation to Book III, when Milton prays that the 'celestial light' might 'Shine inward', so that he may 'see and tell / Of things invisible to mortal sight' (III. 51–5). If Adam has film removed from his eyes, Milton has 'mist from thence / Purge[d]' (III. 53–4). The survey of the world granted to Adam (XI. 377–411) corresponds to Milton's access to an entire universe in the epic.

But vision fails Adam halfway through his education, for, as Michael explains, 'objects divine / Must needs impair and weary human sense' (XII. 9–10). Milton, claiming to see 'things invisible to mortal sight' (III. 55) without benefit of Michael's eye-drops (XI. 414–15), is either greatly blessed or damnably presumptuous. Adam, on the other hand, is guided by Michael carefully between extremes; Adam is to be sent out of the Garden 'though sorrowing, yet in peace' (XI. 117) and 'sad, / With cause for evils past, yet much more cheered / With meditation on the happy end' (XII. 603–5). When Michael tells Adam at the end of his education, 'Let us descend now therefore from this top / Of speculation' (XII. 588–9), one can imagine on Adam's part both disappointment and relief: disappointment in loss of visionary privilege and relief to be again on firm ground. The flawed but saved Adam of the end of the epic must raise ambivalent feelings in Milton. The possibility of sin forgiven and a vision less adventurous than his own must on some level be attractive to one living with the strain of singular and possibly deluded vision. There is safety in less exalted status, less distance to fall. Milton in the invocation to Book VII notes the transition from the song of the invisible heavens to the song of the visible earth, 'More safe I sing with mortal voice' (VII. 24). At the same time, Milton invariably throughout his career presents himself as singular in both virtue and achievement. The most clearly Miltonic male figures at the end of the epic are not Adam but Abraham and, especially, Enoch, a latter day Abdiel figure.

The final books evince Milton's own ambivalence on this score, most pointedly in the contrast between the roll-call of singular heroes of faith and the proud figure of Nimrod. Book XI ends with the story of Noah, the one just man in a wicked world; Book XII opens with Nimrod, the giant whose 'proud ambitious heart, . . . not content / With fair equality, . . . / Will arrogate dominion undeserved / Over his brethren' (XII. 25–8). If the epic condemns usurpation of political authority over equals, it also celebrates those who by merit of virtue stand out from their colleagues. Before Noah came Enoch,

> The only righteous in a world perverse,
> And therefore hated, therefore so beset
> With foes for daring single to be just,
> And utter odious truth,
>
> (XI. 701–4)

This figure, clearly one with whom the outspoken and zealous Milton identifies, is raised to heights to which Nimrod vainly aspired with his ill-fated and presumptuous tower: 'him [Enoch] the most high / Rapt in a balmy cloud with wingèd steeds / . . . to walk with God / High in salvation and the climes of bliss' (XI. 705–8).

Milton's preoccupation with questions of legitimate spiritual and visionary aspiration on the one hand and prideful presumption on the other persists in the final books. As it must be in a materialist and monist system such as Milton's, visual impairment is as much a function of physical constitution as it is of spiritual status. Milton's 'mortal sight' fails (XII. 9). The Father makes clear that the banishment of Adam and Eve from Eden is not only an appropriate punishment but also a corporeal necessity:

> Those pure immortal elements that know
> No gross, no unharmonious mixture foul,
> Eject him tainted now, and purge him off
> As a distemper, gross to air as gross,
> And mortal food, as may dispose him best
> For dissolution wrought by sin,
>
> (XI. 50–5)

The danger in Nimrod's presumptuous ascent is expressed by Adam again in physical terms:

>   wretched man! What food
>   Will he convey up thither to sustain
>   Himself and his rash army, where thin air
>   Above the clouds will pine his entrails gross,
>   And famish him of breath, if not of bread?
>   (XII. 74–8)

With the Fall, we have become less mobile. Gone is the freedom of the prelapsarian couple, who, like the devils, 'gross by sinning grown' (VI. 661), have forfeited the chance to 'winged ascend / Ethereal' as angels (V. 498–9). In the final books Milton brings us back down to earth, to the world we have always inhabited but from which Milton for the time seems to have escaped. The descent is both a recapitulation of the beginning of history and, for the author, a lamentable decline, a decline measured by the limitations of Adam.

But there is another model for the poet that embraces the paradoxes of humility and aspiration in which Milton toils. Even as Adam becomes at the end a pupil, and not an especially apt one, Eve sleeps. Eve, whose exclusion from the divine tutorial has sometimes been taken as yet one more of Milton's misogynist slights, turns out to have been differently and, arguably, more highly privileged. Having received a vision in sleep, she forestalls Adam's eager recounting of what he learned in the angel's school that day:

>   Whence thou returnst, and whither wentst, I know;
>   For God is also in sleep, and dreams advise,
>   Which he hath sent propitious, some great good
>   Presaging, since with sorrow and heart's distress
>   Wearied I fell asleep:
>   (XII. 610–14)

The direct and mysterious education of Eve, not marked it would seem by the false starts and erroneous wanderings of Adam's responses to Michael, bears an uncanny resemblance to Milton's description of the inspiration of the epic, offered by a

>   celestial patroness, who deigns
>   Her nightly visitation unimplored,
>   And díctates to me slumbering, or inspires
>   Easy my unpremeditated verse:
>   (IX. 21–4)

Milton, as we have seen, spoke of his desire to be 'milked' after these visits. The site of inspiration as described in the invocations is maintained at the end of the epic in Eve. It is feminized, perhaps a final gesture of the levelling that has been Milton's hallmark in philosophical and theological speculation. One might speculate that the levelling here serves the purpose of protecting Milton from the threat of presumption and its punishment. Nevertheless, Eve the subordinate woman receives a vision higher and more direct than Adam's (in terms of the comparison of angelic and human intellects in Book V, it is 'intuitive' like the angels' rather than 'discursive').

In the end, as attention to the intellectual contexts helps us to see, the great adventure of *Paradise Lost* is as much Milton's adventure as it is the adventure of the creation, fall and redemption of humankind. Wordsworth is often credited with taking Miltonic epic and recasting it, according to the Romantic ethos, as an epic of the inner self. He himself makes that claim in the opening pages of *The Prelude*, amid a cloud of allusions not only to *Paradise Lost* but to Milton's prose recountings of his epic aspirations. But Milton was there before Wordsworth, for *Paradise Lost* is as much an epic of an inner self as anything that Wordsworth wrote. The stakes are high, for Milton is out on his own matching and measuring God's justice with his reason, inventing a way of looking at the composition of the world that clashes with all systems available in his time, making theological claims singled out for reprobation by leading theologians of his time and place. Looking at Milton's speculations against their intellectual context does not explain them away, or give us reason to ignore them as the quaint but common coin of his time. Instead, it helps us to see just how unusual, oppositional, creatively conflicted and volcanic Milton was, notwithstanding his appropriation as a conservative cultural icon. An iconoclast in his lifetime, Milton, if we will listen to him, will break the icon that he has become.

BIBLIOGRAPHY

Writings

Arminius (1956); Calvin (1960); Cudworth (1964); Descartes (1984); Hobbes (1986); Milton (1998c); More (1978).

References for Further Reading

Abraham (1998); Bauman (1987); Danielson (1982); Dobranski and Rumrich (1998); Edwards, Karen (1999); Empson (1981); Fallon, Stephen M. (1991, 1994); Fish (1998); Guibbory (1986); Haskin (1994); Hill (1977); Johnson (1905); Kelley (1941); Kerrigan (1974, 1983); Lewis (1942); Parker, William R. (1996); Raleigh (1900); Rogers (1996); Rumrich (1996); Saurat (1925); Shapin and Shaffer (1985); Shawcross (1970, 1972); Toland (1699).

21

The Radical Religious Politics of *Paradise Lost*

David Loewenstein

Milton most likely composed *Paradise Lost* between 1658 and 1663, a period of great political turmoil and transition during which this godly republican writer strenuously resisted the oncoming Restoration and lamented its inevitable realization. In the second edition of *The Readie and Easie Way* (April 1660), published just weeks before King Charles II entered London, Milton daringly cried out with prophetic fervour against his countrymen for 'chusing . . . a captain back for *Egypt*', especially after 'all this light among us' during the revolutionary decades; and he characterized, with a sense of alarm, the reckless popular rush towards monarchy, warning 'to what a precipice of destruction the deluge of this epidemic madness would hurrie us' (*CPW* VII: 462–3). The impending Restoration returned not only the king, but the Church of England, and with this came a great wave of militant Anglicanism, strict censorship and religious persecution. Radical as well as orthodox puritans (including Presbyterians) suffered (Baxter 1696: Parts I and II). Conventicles or unauthorized meetings for religious worship were suppressed and godly ministers ejected (Matthews 1934). The so-called Clarendon Code enacted by the Cavalier Parliament (1661–5) consisted of a series of repressive, savage acts aimed at all those who refused to conform to the established church. Milton himself was arrested and imprisoned during these dark times, quite possibly in November 1660, the same month the uncompromising nonconformist writer John Bunyan was imprisoned for preaching to a conventicle (Parker 1968; Parker 1996: 575–6). Michael's prophetic, grim lines at the end of *Paradise Lost* powerfully convey the severe conditions of the Restoration for all who dared to dissent: 'Whence heavy persecution shall arise / On all who in the worship persevere / Of spirit and truth' (XII. 531–3).

To what extent, then, did Milton's radical religious voice in *Paradise Lost* remain 'unchanged / To hoarse or mute', especially given the cold political climate of the Restoration when the solitary, blind poet had 'fallen on evil days' and 'evil tongues' (VII. 24–6)? Does the great spiritual epic, written by a visionary poet who seeks inner illumination, reveal the godly republican writer of the English Revolution renouncing his daring political convictions and retiring like Truth 'Bestuck with slanderous darts' (XII. 536)? One distinguished historian has recently argued that as Milton was composing *Paradise Lost* he realized more acutely 'the lesson of the measureless difference of proportion between temporal politics and eternal verities' and that during these years the poet 'withdraws from politics into faith' (Worden 1990: 244). While rightly calling attention to the poet's concern with 'eternal verities' in *Paradise Lost*, this formulation, however, may strike us as unsatisfactory: it fails to account for the ways in which politics and religious convictions remain interconnected in Milton's great spiritual poem and for the ways in which it remains sharply polemical after the collapse of the English Revolution. Milton presents *Paradise Lost* as a poem of restoration in the provocative sense that religious radicals understood it: the 'one greater man' who will 'Restore us' (I. 4–5), the poet prophesies, is no Stuart king but the Messiah himself. We need not agree, then, that politics and faith were exclusive alternatives for the poet 'fallen on evil days', or that the politics of *Paradise Lost*, illuminated well by recent commentators (Radzinowicz 1987; Quint 1993; Achinstein 1994; Corns 1994; Knoppers 1994; Norbrook 1999), should be separated from Milton's radical religious concerns. This chapter argues that the radical spiritual and political dimensions of the poem are more closely interconnected than readers have sometimes allowed, and that this gives the poem a notably polemical edge.

Politics in Milton's Hell

Milton daringly begins his narrative in hell with Satan's Titanic challenges to heaven's power. Satan is not only a courageous military leader, rousing his rebel angels from their abject state; he is also a skilful politician, employing the fierce language of resistance as he continues, unrepentant, to defy God, having been defeated in celestial warfare. Moreover, Book II opens with a major political debate – a Parliament in hell – as the devils consider whether to battle God, make the best of their situation in hell, or destroy God's newest creation: humankind.

Given the religious politics of the English Revolution, how precisely should we interpret the political language and posturing in hell? Here the poem's reader needs to be particularly discerning – indeed, vigilant – for at moments Satan's fiery language sounds remarkably close to that of Milton the controversialist. In hell, speaking 'with bold words', Satan assaults 'the tyranny of heaven' (I. 82, 124), scorning (much like the fiercely antimonarchical Milton) the very idea of assuming the idolatrous posture of a sycophantic courtier who must 'bow and sue for grace / With suppliant knee' and 'deify' a king's 'power' (I. 111–12) whose reign he and his followers disdain. And in his rhetorically impressive speech that finally rallies the 'Grovelling' fallen angels (I. 280), a defiant, sarcastic Satan asks: 'in this abject posture have ye sworn / To adore the conqueror?' (I. 322–3). This ardent language, as Satan repudiates the bondage of hell and the tyranny of heaven's king, does indeed seem close to Milton's just weeks before the Restoration. Flaunting his godly republican convictions and showing his own dauntless 'courage never to submit or yield' (I. 108) to the bondage of a regal power he scorned, Milton did not hesitate to spurn 'the base necessitie of court flatteries and prostrations' and 'the perpetual bowings and cringings of an abject people ... deifying and adoring' a new Stuart king (*The Readie and Easie Way* [second edition], *CPW* VII: 428, 426), as many of his servile countrymen had done before the seductive image of the King projected in *Eikon Basilike* (1649), the immensely popular royalist text Milton attempted to demolish in *Eikonoklastes*.

Satan's political language, however, is neither stable nor consistent; at one moment he sounds like a bold revolutionary, at another like a conservative royalist. At the beginning of Book II we find him sitting 'High on a throne of royal state' as he appeals to 'the fixed laws of heaven', which made him leader of the fallen angels, and urges his princes and potentates to 'return / To claim [their] just inheritance of old' (II. 1, 18, 37–8). These are hardly the rousing words of a defiant political revolutionary – a 'Deliverer from new lords' (VI. 451) – who repudiates the old social or political order. As the Leveller writer William Walwyn warned about artful politicians 'in these warping times', they are 'Satan's chief agents' and begetters of all discord 'made up of Contradictions ... In a word, observe them well, and you shall see Christ and Belial, God and Mammon in one and the same person' (*The Fountain of Slander* [1649], Walwyn 1989: 381–2). Walwyn's warning captures essential qualities in Milton's Satan: his contradictions are no less evident in his uses of political vocabulary and his ambiguous behaviour. As Milton had observed in the apocalyptic climax to *Eikonoklastes*, antichristian powers and European monarchs who rebel against the King of Kings and derive their power from the eschatological Beast of Revelation (as in Revelation 17), shall be 'doubtfull and ambiguous in all thir doings' (*CPW* III: 598–9), which included their equivocal uses of language, artifice and dissimulation. Moreover, in the late 1640s, Milton had become further alerted to political ambiguity in his polemical confrontations with the Presbyterians who had once zealously promoted war and revolution against King Charles and then treacherously attempted to reinstate him: these were 'prevaricating Divines' who exploited verbal ambiguities and scriptural hermeneutics ('fitted for thir turnes with a double contradictory sense') to pursue their shifty politics (*CPW* III: 232, 195). Ambiguous in all his doings, Satan too is a master of verbal and political equivocation himself, as he usurps and manipulates the rhetoric and ideology of political resistance and skilfully simulates the role of radical revolutionary. If, as John Toland suggested in his life of Milton, 'the chief design' of *Paradise Lost* is 'to display the different Effects of Liberty and Tyranny' (Darbishire 1932: 182), then Milton's poem dramatizes how malicious and tyrannical designs manifest themselves through artifice, as well as through subtle forms of verbal and political equivocation.

While Milton shows us the power of Satan's political rhetoric, he also qualifies the splendour and heroic posture of the devils in ways that reveal his continuing polemicism with regard to religious politics. Thus the impressive epic catalogue of fallen angels in Book I (lines 376–522) highlights themes of idolatry and pagan practices (as well as themes of lust and violence) as it looks forward to the decline of the church narrated in Book XII. Milton's reference to 'gay religions full of pomp and gold' (I. 372), in the midst of this narrative of idolatry and idolatrous cults, evokes Roman Catholic as well as Laudian religious ceremonialism during Milton's own age; Milton the polemicist had blasted 'these gaudy glisterings' of ceremonial religion (encouraged by Archbishop William Laud in conflict with the English Reformed tradition) when 'altars indeed were in a fair forwardnesse' and prelates 'were setting up the molten Calfe of their Masse againe' (*CPW* I: 828, 771). Indeed, the godly continued to fear the revival of pagan and idolatrous practices at the time of the Restoration (when, for example, maypoles, prohibited by the Long Parliament, prominently returned with Charles II). Ironically, when the devils complain about the religious rituals of heaven – their having 'to celebrate his throne / With warbled hymns, and to his Godhead sing / Forced alleluias; while he lordly sits / Our envied sovereign' (II. 241–4) – they make themselves sound like victims of religious conformity and Laudian ritualized worship.

Furthermore, the description of Belial who 'reigns' in 'courts and palaces' and 'in luxurious cities' (note the poet's use of the present tense), as well as 'the sons / Of Belial, flown with insolence and wine' (I. 497–502), evokes a world of misrule and riot associated with aristocratic deviancy in Restoration England: the 'Sons of Belial' was a phrase regularly used by puritan sermon writers to refer to the Cavaliers. In *Eikonoklastes* Milton complained of 'thousands of blaspheming Cavaliers about' the King and 'those Carouses drunk to the confusion of all things good or holy' (*CPW* III: 452); and in *Of True Religion* (1673), a pamphlet Milton published the year before the second edition of *Paradise Lost* appeared, he complained of 'this Nation of late years...grown more numerously and excessively vitious then heretofore; Pride, Luxury, Drunkenness, Whoredom, Cursing, Swearing, bold and open Atheism every where abounding' (*CPW* VIII: 438). Two years into the Restoration, Thomas Ellwood (a young Quaker who came to study with Milton) observed that 'a sense of the prophaneness, debaucheries, cruelties, and other horrid impieties of the age, fell heavy on [him], and lay as a pressing weight upon [his] spirit' (Crump 1900: 116). Milton was haunted by a similar sense of Restoration profaneness. Fallen on 'evil days' and 'evil tongues' during Restoration England, the daring but vulnerable poet of *Paradise Lost* poignantly yearns for protection from 'the barbarous dissonance / Of Bacchus and his revellers' (VII. 32–3).

The 'great consult' (I. 798) of fallen angels, however, may at first suggest to readers that politics in hell are closer to those of revolutionary England, where liberty of political debate and dispute often flourished and conflicting viewpoints were aired – a political nation with 'much arguing, much writing, many opinions' (*Areopagitica*, *CPW* II: 554). But the vigilant reader can see that the Parliament in hell too is a dramatic study in 'the different Effects of Liberty and Tyranny'. Its first speaker, the fierce and blunt Moloch, is motivated especially by a desire for revenge after infamous defeat in the celestial civil war; his aggressive warrior ethic recalls Satan's drive for revenge (see I. 35, 107, 604), as well as the outmoded heroic ideology of classical epic which sanctioned revenge. But given the political contexts we have been invoking, it is worth recalling that godly republican writers also associated the pursuit of revenge with royalist defeat and bitterness: in his pro-regicide tracts Milton frequently refers to the unrepentant King Charles I's furious desire 'to be reveng'd on his opposers' as 'he seeks to satiat his fansie with the imagination of som revenge upon them' (*CPW* III: 563); such is 'the lust or vengeance of the embittered king who acknowledges no master' (*CPW* IV: 532). Writing in the Restoration, the godly republican Edmund Ludlow observed that Charles II's looks 'were full of revendge, as if he would have the cittizens to see that he reteyned in his memory the injuryes which his father and he had received from them' (1978: 157). In the War in Heaven Moloch is described as a 'furious king' (VI. 357) who blasphemes God; and in the debate in hell, the poet notes his campaign of 'Desperate revenge' (II. 107) as he, through open war, 'seeks to satiat his fansie with the imagination of som revenge' upon the powers of heaven.

Other fallen angels, however, dismiss Moloch's call for open war and revenge, so that the Parliament in hell quickly becomes a study in the art and dangers of political rhetoric. The poet's sharpest condemnation is reserved for Belial – under his seductive rhetoric ('he pleased the ear', II. 117), he counsels 'ignoble ease, and peaceful sloth, / Not peace' (II. 227–8) as he dismantles Moloch's arguments and suggests that his compatriots refrain from the use of force or guile against heaven. The vigilant, fit reader of the poem, Milton's warning reminds us, needs to discriminate with care; seductive political rhetoric can easily disarm its listeners, as the response of the fallen angels to Mammon next illustrates. His argument that they can indeed create a magnificent empire in hell is greeted with a groundswell of immediate applause – which is dramatically countered by the mighty figure of Beelzebub, Satan's strongman: rising up with his 'Atlantean shoulders' (II. 306), he silences the applause while acknowledging the powerful effect of Mammon's political speech ('so the popular vote / Inclines', II. 313–14), even as he undercuts it. Beelzebub's malicious proposal to destroy or conquer earth and its 'puny inhabitants' originates of course with Satan, 'the author of all ill' who 'first devised' it (II. 367, 381, 379); in his antimonarchical tracts, Milton used similar terms to characterize the divisive Charles I, 'the impenitent author of all our miseries' and 'the first beginner' of England's civil wars (*CPW* III: 328, 451). The long political debate has been carefully rigged and Beelzebub flatters the fallen angels as soon as they vote 'with full assent' (II. 388). Quickly taking advantage of the political situation, Satan, moreover, will allow no further dissent; once he accepts his heroic role as emissary to earth, he stifles debate: 'Thus saying rose / The monarch, and prevented all reply' (II. 466–7). Significantly, the other fallen angels do not dare to dissent: 'they / Dreaded not more the adventure than his voice / Forbidding' (II. 473–5). Pandæmonium, 'the high capital / Of Satan and his peers' (I. 756–7), then, is hardly a 'mansion house of liberty', as Milton had once characterized revolutionary London (*Areopagitica*, II: 554), a city thriving on ideological warfare and the ferment of political debate.

Moreover, when the emissary from hell begins his 'bold enterprise . . . against God and man' (the Argument to Book IV), Milton uses language that likewise recalls his polemical writings and commitment to the Good Old Cause. Thus the poet unmasks Satan – 'Artificer of fraud' – as he responds to the devil's initial soliloquy, delivered as he first views Eden and concluding (after expressing his internal anguish and the hell he carries within him) by asserting his imperial ambitions. The poet's commentary exposes the 'counterfeit' Satan as 'the first / That practised falsehood under saintly show, / Deep malice to conceal' (IV. 117, 121–3). Likewise, Milton the controversialist had exposed the seductive theatricalism of Charles I – his 'saintly show' masking 'his arbitrary wilfulness, and tyrannical Designes' – by observing that 'the deepest policy of a Tyrant hath bin ever to counterfet Religious' (*CPW* III: 397, 361). Milton's portrait of Satan thus dramatizes the origins of such saintly counterfeiting. Moreover, when Satan soon invades Eden with ease (reminding us of its vulnerability and the need for watchfulness), Milton's language explicitly evokes the discourse of the Good Old Cause as the poet links hell's malicious emissary with the 'hirelings' of contemporary England: 'So clomb this first grand thief into God's fold: / So since into his church lewd hirelings climb' (IV. 192–3). The issue of hirelings in the church supported by tithes was one of the most contentious in the English Revolution, and inflamed religious radicals. Here in *Paradise Lost* Milton continues to wage his polemical warfare against the insatiable hirelings or salaried clergy whom he had attacked in *The Likeliest Means to Remove Hirelings out of the Church* (1659) and in his 1652 sonnet to Cromwell (where he calls them 'hireling wolves whose Gospel is their maw'). Such polemical, anticlerical language will reverberate sharply in the grim historical account of the church's decline later in the poem ('Wolves shall succeed for teachers, grievous wolves', XII. 508).

Politics and Faith in Milton's Heaven

The tense encounter between Satan and the angel Abdiel in heaven, narrated in Books V and VI, further dramatizes the religious politics of the poem. Once Satan begins his rebellion, 'fraught / With envy' (V. 661–2) at the elevation and anointing of the Son of God, he employs secrecy and speaks 'Ambiguous words' (V. 703) to fuel his resistance, reminding us of Milton's depiction of European monarchs who rebel against the King of Kings and derive their power from the Beast of Revelation as 'doubtfull and ambiguous in all thir doings' (*CPW* III: 598–9). Indeed, as Satan addresses the rebel legions, the poet notes that he speaks 'with calumnious art / Of counterfeited truth' (V. 770–1); however rousing it may sound, Satan's political rhetoric is slippery and equivocal. His powerful opening speech to his legions is fraught with contradictions.

Thus he begins by appealing to the authority of 'these magnific titles' which should remain 'merely titular' and concludes by claiming that 'those imperial titles . . . assert' their 'being ordained to govern' (V. 773–802). The idea that inherited titles of honour mean the very right to power is one to which either a royalist apologist or a Presbyterian polemicist might appeal: William Prynne, who defended the Presbyterian church and rights of kings in 1648, wrote that '*Titles* of Honour and Nobility (as *Kings, Princes, Dukes, Lords, &c.*) are as ancient almost, as the world itselfe' and honoured 'with special *priviledges*' (Prynne 1648: 68); moreover, when King Charles was tried by the High Court of Justice in early 1649, the King, recalls the republican Edmund Ludlow, insisted 'that the kingdome was his by inheritance . . . that being the originall of his title' (1978: 131). In *The Tenure of Kings and Magistrates*, however, Milton asserted that 'the Titles of Sov'ran Lord, natural Lord, and the like, are either arrogancies, or flatteries' (*CPW* III: 202); and in the *Pro Populo Anglicano Defensio Secunda* (as he praised Cromwell's political and military achievements), he scorned 'the popular favor of titles' which 'seem so great in the opinion of the mob' (*CPW* IV: 672). As Satan's rousing speech progresses, he nevertheless sounds more like a revolutionary puritan: he scorns the notion of paying 'Knee-tribute' to the anointed Messiah, abhors worshipping 'his image now proclaimed', and urges his compatriots 'to cast off this yoke' (V. 782, 784, 786), as though they were mid-century English radicals resisting the bondage of the Norman yoke. In *The Readie and Easie Way*, Milton, resisting the popular rush towards renewed monarchy, himself had scornfully wondered: 'Is it such an unspeakable joy to serve, such felicitie to wear a yoke?' (*CPW* VII: 448). Satan, of course, is inciting rebellion against the Son, who has been elevated by 'merit more than birthright' (III. 309) – a crucial detail reminding us that the politics of Milton's heaven differ from the hereditary divine right politics of Stuart kingship. A rhetorical *tour de force*, Satan's 'bold discourse' (V. 803) needs to be watched carefully by the poem's reader, vigilant to its equivocations and contradictory political discourses.

Milton's angel Abdiel (meaning 'servant of God') responds to Satan's political rhetoric with fiery zeal and the scorn of the righteous, solitary Miltonic prophet who dares to utter the 'odious truth' in the midst of 'a world perverse' (XI. 704, 701; cf. VI. 36–7). In characterizing Satan's inciting speech as 'argument blasphémous' (V. 809), Abdiel's words evoke the Beast of Revelation (13: 5–6) who opens 'his mouth in blasphemy against God . . . and them that dwell in heaven' and makes war with the saints (as God's loyal angels are later called in the War in Heaven: VI. 47, 767, 801, 882). Moreover, Abdiel challenges Satan's account of heavenly politics, not on a theoretical level, but on the basis of experience: 'Yet by experience taught we know how good, / And of our good, and of our dignity / How provident he is, how far from thought / To make us less' (V. 826–9). In his very first soliloquy, Satan recalls that God's mild monarchy was no state of tyranny and arbitrary power: 'all his good proved ill in me', Satan observes, 'nor was his service hard' (IV. 48, 45). Indeed, Abdiel's response reminds the poem's discerning readers of heaven's special political circumstances – God's kingship is unlike any other kind of kingship and certainly does not resemble an earthly Stuart monarchy. Abdiel thus attempts to restrain Satan's dangerous rhetoric and to counter his astonishing (if exhilarating) assertion – an expression of unbridled individualism – that he and his legions are 'self-begot, self-raised' (V. 860): Satan's primal sin is his desire to exist on his own and to create an identity for himself not created by God.

The close affinity between Abdiel, scornfully rejected by Satan's camp, and the daring visionary Miltonic poet, 'with dangers compassed round, / And solitude' (VII. 27–8), is underscored by Milton's description of 'The flaming seraph fearless, though alone / Encompassed round with foes' (V. 875–6). Like the poet whose radical voice remains 'unchanged / To hoarse or mute' in the midst of the evils days of the Restoration, Abdiel will not 'swerve from truth, or change his constant mind / Though single' (V. 902–3) and reviled with reproach and judged perverse. Like the solitary Jesus in *Paradise Regained*, who finds himself repeatedly harassed and tempted by Satan in the wilderness, the faithful seraph remains unmoved, unshaken and unseduced.

Indeed, in the context of the poem's tense Restoration milieu, Milton's Abdiel, who maintains 'the cause / Of truth' against 'revolted multitudes' (VI. 31–2) embodies, in an imaginative way, the fierce nonconformist who has endured the highly charged slander of sedition by the potent tongues of political or ecclesiastical authorities. Abdiel is the only character in the poem called 'seditious' – Satan reviles him by calling him 'seditious angel' (VI. 152) – an inflammatory epithet that evokes the religious and political controversies of the Revolution and its aftermath. Sectaries, heretics and contentious political radicals were regularly called 'seditious'. Thus John Lilburne the Leveller complained in 1653 (in his *Just Defence*) that it was common to be labelled 'factious and seditious, men of contentious and turbulent spirits . . . for no other cause, but for standing for the truth' (Haller and Davies 1944: 452). William Walwyn likewise complained that the 'faithfull puritan' was reviled 'under pretence of herisie, schisme, faction, sedition, and the like' (Walwyn 1989: 175). During the Restoration, when fears of sectarian insurrection continued, the Conventicles Act of 1670 sought 'more speedy remedies against the growing and dangerous practices of seditious sectaries and other disloyal persons, who under pretence of tender consciences have or may have at their meetings contrive insurrections' (Kenyon 1986: 356). There is much pointed irony, indeed, when the rebel Satan himself reviles the faithful, fiery seraph as 'seditious'.

Moreover, when Satan, in response to the 'seditious' Abdiel, characterizes himself and his rebel host as meeting 'in synod' (VI. 156), his language likewise evokes Milton's world of religious controversy. The term 'synod' itself links Satan and his compatriots, whom he elevates above angels by calling 'Gods', with more orthodox clerical powers of Milton's day, notably the Presbyterian Assembly of Divines who attempted to determine and reinforce spiritual laws and matters of religion (including the suppression of heresies) by their synods or ecclesiastical courts, part of their system of jurisdiction or 'classic hierarchy' (see 'On the New Forcers of Conscience under the Long Parliament', line 7) that Milton could write about with biting satire. In the Parliament of hell the rhetorically skilful Beelzebub likewise addresses the fallen angels as 'Synod of gods', an address meant to flatter them once he has proposed the 'bold design' of Satan against humanity and they, easily swayed, have shown their 'full assent' (II. 391, 386, 388). Like other religious radicals, Milton scorned the idea of a national synod and its association with a national church and theological hegemony, observing in *Eikonoklastes* that 'Synods from the first times of Reformation' are 'liable to the greatest fraud and packing' so that they offer 'no solution, or redress of evil, but an increase rather' (*CPW* III: 535; cf. 492). In *A Remonstrance of Many Thousand Citizens* (1646), Richard Overton (along with William Walwyn) had criticized the 'Synod in judgement . . . countenancing only those of the presbytry, and discountenancing all the Separation, Anabaptists and Independents' (Sharp 1998: 43). Referring to the other godly angels – those loyal 'saints' (VI. 47) – Abdiel speaks ironically to his adversary on the battlefield, throwing the language of sectarianism back in the face of the rebel Satan:

> but thou seest
> All are not of thy train; there be who faith
> Prefer, and piety to God, though then
> To thee not visible, when I alone
> Seemed in thy world erroneous to dissent
> From all: my sect thou seest, now learn too late
> How few sometimes may know, when thousands err.
>   (VI. 142–8)

Abdiel's polemical words fuse the discourse of radical religion and nonconformity with the tense political events of Milton's heaven – a dramatic reminder that the political upheavals of the 1640s and 1650s, as well as the fierce backlash after 1660 against dissidents, had been fuelled by religious ferment and acute fears of radical sectarianism. In the poem's mythic heaven, where rebellion leading to the 'horrid confusion' (VI. 668) of civil war is not generated by the faithful puritan dissenter, as it were, Milton is also prompting his fit godly readers to reconsider the relations between political rebellion, sectarianism and civil confusion which orthodox authorities were keen to link in previous decades (Loewenstein 2001).

Politics and Faith in Postlapsarian History

We find much evidence of Milton's polemical religious politics in the poem's final books, where we also discern poignant tensions in his responses to postlapsarian history. The tragedy of the Fall, Milton's poem shows, has disturbing consequences for human history and politics. The last two books of the poem, in which archangel Michael presents often dispiriting visions and narratives of human history characterized by 'sharp tribulation' (XI. 63), are full of political themes that often evoke the turbulent world of Milton's revolutionary England and the religious tensions of the Restoration. These books depict a handful of faithful individuals – the righteous few – emerging in the midst of dark periods of lawless tyranny, warfare and heavy religious persecution 'in a world perverse'.

The formidable, warlike archangel Michael (as opposed to the 'sociable' archangel Raphael, V. 221, earlier in the poem) fittingly presents the hard lessons in postlapsarian history. The first tragic scene presented to Adam – that of the murder of the meek,

gentle and obedient Abel, the man of 'faith' (XI. 458; see Hebrews 11: 4), by 'the
unjust' Cain (XI. 455) – would have had poignant resonance for religious radicals in
Milton's age. They often interpreted the slaying of the righteous Abel in terms of the
spilling of the innocent blood of the saints. Thus Sir Henry Vane, to whom Milton
addressed a famous sonnet, observed that the apocalyptic conflict between the forces of
Christ and Antichrist 'first discovered itself in the two brothers, *Cain* and *Abel*' (Vane
1655: 173); and in a work published in the Restoration, Vane described Abel as the
first martyr (Vane 1662a: 64). The slaying of Abel of course is the first of many shapes
of death Adam will now learn about; but it also dramatizes the persecution and
struggles of the faithful throughout history – persecution that many religious radicals
considered no less acute in mid-seventeenth-century England.

The final books of history contain solitary 'just men' who rise up in the midst of
dark moments in history, much as the zealous Abdiel speaks out and finds himself in
the midst of universal reproach from rebellious legions 'for daring single to be just, /
And utter odious truth, that God would come / To judge them with his saints' (XI.
703–5). In the fourth tragic pageant of Book XI, Milton introduces another figure of
faith – Enoch – amid a world perverse who is 'therefore hated' (702) and beset with
enemies. In Hebrews 11: 5 Enoch is 'By faith...translated that he should not see
death'; here we see the lone 'just man' (XI. 681) rising up in a world of Homeric strife
and destruction, as he speaks 'much of right and wrong, / Of justice, of religion, truth
and peace, / And judgment from above' (XI. 666–8), before being rescued by heaven
'to walk with God / High in salvation and the climes of bliss' (XI. 707–8). Michael's
vision of the godly Enoch illustrates what the radical martyr Henry Vane observed
about the battered, despised saints at the time he was tried (and subsequently
executed) in the Restoration: 'Here is nothing in this world...but reproaching and
despising God's precious Saints; but in Heaven there is a good reception for them'
(Vane 1662b: 81). Indeed, as the case of Enoch shows, these lone, vehement prophets
in history may not be successful in renovating their fallen or backsliding world
afflicted by oppression and violence. Milton's Noah himself is a zealous preacher
and just man, 'the only son of light / In a dark age' rising up in a sybaritic, ungodly
time of 'luxury and riot' and vainly preaching 'Against allurement' and 'custom' while
'fearless of reproach and scorn, / Or violence' (XI. 715, 808–12); Milton the controversialist depicted himself in similar terms as he combated 'the gaudy allurements'
of the prelatical church and complained of 'these enormous riots of ungodly mis-rule
that Prelaty hath wrought' in church and state (*CPW* I: 557, 861), while later
attacking the allurement and custom of royal tyranny supported by 'vast expence
and luxurie' (*CPW* VII: 425).

As Michael switches from visions to narratives in Book XII (since 'faith cometh by
hearing...the word of God': Romans 10: 17), the poet's religious politics continue to
be highlighted, though again in the more universal context of his sacred epic.
Michael's first narrative here concerns the political tyranny and aggressiveness of
Nimrod, the builder of Babel, the primal monarchic tyrant in human history, and a
type of Satan, Antichrist and Charles I:

> one shall rise
> Of proud ambitious heart, who not content
> With fair equality, fraternal state,
> Will arrogate dominion undeserved
> Over his brethren, and quite dispossess
> Concord and law of nature from the earth.
>   (XII. 24–9)

The hunting of 'men not beasts shall be his game', the angel adds (XII. 30), a reminder that Milton had depicted the wilful, proud Charles I precisely in these terms: Nimrod, 'the first that hunted after Faction', was 'reputed, by ancient Tradition, the first that founded Monarchy; whence it appeares that to hunt after Faction is more properly the Kings Game' (*CPW* III: 466). Warning against a tyrannical leader 'from heaven claiming second sovereignty' (XII. 35), Milton in his pro-regicide tracts had justified resistance. Moreover, for religious radicals in Milton's England, proud Nimrod was identified as the first persecutor of the saints: as one of the leading radical army chaplains, William Erbery, wrote, Nimrod was the first earthly king, the first oppressor of the world, and 'a hunter of the best Men, as our kings have also been, hunting the saints up and down all the land over' (Erbery 1648: 33). In his pro-regicide tracts Milton argued that it was an honour for puritan saints to engage in a fierce apocalyptic struggle to destroy antichristian kings, including Charles I, the builder of 'that spiritual *Babel*' (*CPW* III: 598) in Milton's age. Just like Satan, who accuses the faithful, zealous Abdiel of being 'seditious', Nimrod accuses those who resist him of being rebellious, much as Charles Stuart ('the first beginner' of England's Civil War) accused parliamentarians and puritan saints: 'And from rebellion shall derive his name, / Though of rebellion others he accuse' (XII. 36–7). Or, in the words of a radical Restoration commentator writing in the Miltonic tradition of political resistance and popular sovereignty, Nimrod is the first of 'those Traitors and Rebels, who would make you believe that it is Treason and Rebellion to call them to account for the *Treason* and *Rebellion* they are guilty of' ([Jones] 1663: 41). At least one contemporary reader of *Paradise Lost* immediately recognized the provocative republican implications of the Nimrod episode: commenting on this passage in a letter to John Evelyn in 1669, John Beale, a royalist reader, accurately concluded that 'Milton holds to his old Principle', only to add a year later that one of the 'great faults of his *Paradyse Lost*' is 'his Plea for our Original right' (von Maltzahn 1993b: 189–90).

Adam's passionate critical response to the narrative of Nimrod is itself highly revealing: 'Oh execrable son so to aspire / Above his brethren, to himself assuming / Authority usurped, from God not given' (XII. 64–6). Seventeenth-century commentators on patriarchal power (including Lancelot Andrewes and Sir Robert Filmer) had frequently claimed that the first fathers – particularly Adam – had been kings (Sommerville 1986: 30–1). But in Milton's poem, Adam's rejection of Nimrod's usurping politics ('man over men / He made not lord', XII. 69–70) reveals his instinctive republican values rather than kingly ones – in accordance with Milton's antimonarchical polemics against arbitrary powers – and Michael promptly confirms the rightness of Adam's judgement: 'Justly thou abhorr'st / That son, who on the quiet state of men / Such trouble brought' (XII. 79–81). Adam, with his republican instincts, has provocatively targeted the first earthly king himself as a 'usurper' (XII. 72). In this respect, this episode in *Paradise Lost* can be seen as an imaginative polemical response to the seventeenth-century view that kingly power and politics originated with Adam.

Michael's narrative addresses a sad consequence of the Fall in human history: earthly monarchy and tyranny, along with the loss of inward and outward liberty. Here too we can discern the voice of the more polemical Milton. Throughout his pro-regicide and republican tracts, Milton had warned and reminded his countrymen (as well as European readers) of unbridled tyranny such as Charles I's; and in the *Defensio Secunda* he warned citizens of the Commonwealth to remain especially vigilant against the danger of tyranny within: 'many tyrants ... will from day to day hatch out from your very vitals' (*CPW* IV: 680–1). The political tyranny Michael describes is likewise an inward state – of rule dangerously turned upside down – that results in outward servitude, the kind that had more recently beset Caroline and Civil War England:

>   upstart passions catch the government
> From reason, and to servitude reduce
> Man till then free. Therefore since he permits
> Within himself unworthy powers to reign
> Over free reason, God in judgment just
> Subjects him from without to violent lords.
>   (XII. 88–93)

The history of humankind under Satan–Nimrod offers a few glimpses of political hope – heroic individuals of faith like Abraham (XII. 111ff.) or Moses, God's 'saint' (XII. 200ff.), who displays God's 'wondrous power' and instructs his people typologically about spiritual deliverance (XII. 232–5). The narrative of Pharaoh itself has apocalyptic overtones as Michael compares an obdurate, rageful Pharaoh to 'the dragon, that old serpent, which is the Devil, and Satan' (Revelation 20: 2; see XII. 191). Milton himself compared an obstinate Charles I with Pharaoh (see e.g. *Eikonoklastes*, *CPW* III: 516), so that Michael's description of the Israelites wandering 'Through the wild desert' (XII. 216) likewise potently evokes the unsettled Civil War years when the English endured 'a second wandring over that horrid Wilderness of distraction and civil slaughter' (*CPW* III: 580). But notably the 'race elect' in Michael's narrative choose 'not the readiest way' – an unmistakable allusion to Milton's famous anti-Restoration political tract – lest they be returned 'back to Egypt' (XII. 214–19). Here Milton's polemical voice indeed remains 'unchanged'.

Ultimately Moses, a type of the law, could not lead the children of Israel into the land of eternal rest and, in accord with the increasingly inward thrust of this radical Protestant poem, Michael explains how the Mosaic law will be superseded by a law of faith written in the hearts of believers (XII. 300–6). Michael's narratives of later biblical history likewise evoke the circumstances of Milton's England. Thus, following the Babylonian captivity, factions soon arise contaminating the Temple of the Lord: 'first among the priests dissension springs, / Men who attend the altar, and should most / Endeavour peace: their strife pollution brings / Upon the Temple itself' (XII. 353–6). The emphasis on the altar here may remind us of the religious tensions of Laudian England, when ceremonialism fuelled bitter conflicts; but the emphasis on 'dissension' among the priesthood may recall as well Milton's hatred of the orthodox puritan clergy who with 'clov'n tongues of falshood and dissention' (*CPW* III: 235) aggravated political tensions in Civil War England when they equivocated in their behaviour towards an unrepentant King Charles.

Michael's final, haunting narrative about the faithful few and the spirit within also evokes, though without specific topical reference, the embattled religious world of Restoration England, in which dissenters especially were fiercely persecuted and the established church conflicted with the religion of the Spirit. There are many echoes of the Pauline epistles here (including Ephesians 6: 11–17) as Michael describes the apostles who, armed with 'spiritual armour', are fervent martyrs who 'shall amaze / Their proudest persecutors' (XII. 491, 496–7). Indeed, religious radicals in Milton's turbulent age, including the spiritually inward-looking but indomitable Quakers, frequently compared their afflictions and trials in the wilderness of the world to those of Christ's apostles who lived by the inward Spirit and the law of faith and who were persecuted, mocked and reproached.

The narrative of post-apostolic history, however, turns particularly grim as Michael describes periods of darkness and superstition when men will 'seek to avail themselves of names, / Places and titles, and with these to join / Secular power, though feigning still to act / By spiritual' (XII. 515–18). The Restoration seemed like such a spiritually dissipated age to Milton and his radical religious contemporaries. On the eve of the Restoration Charles II, on what sounded like a more conciliatory note, had declared 'a liberty to tender consciences, and that no man shall be … called in question for differences of opinion in matter of religion' (Declaration at Breda, April 1660, in Kenyon 1986: 332); nevertheless, religious radicals who believed that liberty of conscience was fundamental, rightly feared that it would be severely constrained under the King's Cavalier Parliament and the Anglican church. Writing on behalf of the Quakers, the largest radical sect, the pamphleteer and prophet Margaret Fell observed in 1660: 'so we *desire* and also *expect* to have the *liberty of our Consciences* and *just Rights*, and *outward Liberties* as other people of the Nation, which we have promise of *from the word of a King*, that we may not be made a prey upon by *the prophane envious People and Priests*' (Fell 1660: 7). In the last years and months of the Interregnum, Milton himself claimed not only that 'liberty of conscience … above all other things ought to be to all men dearest and most precious' (*CPW* VII: 456), but that state coercion was 'not to be us'd in matters of religion' (VII: 277). In Michael's account of post-apostolic history, however, 'Spiritual laws by carnal power shall force / On every conscience' and 'heavy persecution shall arise / On all who in the worship

persevere / Of spirit and truth' (XII. 521–2, 531–3) – as it had done during
Restoration England when nonconformists were living under siege. Here, too, Milton's radical religious voice is 'unchanged'. Despite the general tenor of his lines,
which mention no specific Restoration events or persecuted dissidents, they nevertheless evoke a godless, antiheroic age when many of his contemporaries had rejected
the religion of the Spirit and deemed 'in outward rites and specious forms / Religion
satisfied' (XII. 534–5). Michael's prophetic narrative has a sharp polemical edge to it
as it condemns religion expressed through 'specious forms'. Yet the depiction of Truth
retiring 'Bestuck with slanderous darts' in the midst of a world perverse without any
reforming individuals conveys tension in the poet's response as he laments this dark
period in history when 'works of faith / Rarely be found' (XII. 536–7) – and curses it.
True, the archangel concludes this haunting prophecy with an apocalyptic vision of
'New heavens, new earth' (XII. 549), but it does not fully offset the darker narrative of
spiritual decline, secular power and 'heavy persecution': 'so shall the world go on, / To
good malignant, to bad men benign' (XII. 537–8).

At the end, after the often sorrowful lessons of postlapsarian history, Adam can
nevertheless speak of a subversive weakness that would have had pointed resonance for
the besieged godly of the 1660s: 'by things deemed weak / Subverting worldly strong,
and worldly wise / By simply meek' (XII. 567–9). So Adam understands as he leaves
Paradise to become an exile in the fallen world, promising 'ever to observe / [God's]
providence, and on him sole depend' (XII. 563–4). For followers of the Spirit within
during an age of 'heavy persecution', such lines would have conveyed much more than
simple resignation.

Paradise Lost, moreover, offers the consolation of the 'paradise within' (XII. 587), a
replacement for the lost earthly Paradise (certainly 'happier far' than the wreckage of
fallen Eden that Adam and Eve leave behind them) and a reminder that the only true
church – like '[God's] living temples, built by faith to stand' (XII. 527) – lies within
the self. The 'paradise within' reminds us how radically inward Milton has made the
epic poem. Indeed, some religious radicals believed that heaven and hell did not exist
at all as external places, but were manifestations only of internal states: 'Heaven and
hell, light and darknesse, sorrow and comforts is all to be seen within', wrote Gerrard
Winstanley in 1649 (Winstanley 1941: 215). Milton never goes quite this far: his
heaven and hell are physical places (and richly imagined), though Satan carries hell
'within him' (IV. 20), just as Adam and Eve will now carry 'a paradise within' them.
Nevertheless, paradise at the end of Milton's visionary epic is not so much a place as a
symbol, located within the heart of the individual Protestant believer and exile. And
in a crucial sense the poem's emphasis on the 'paradise within' the individual believer
speaks movingly to a generation of religious radicals whose unorthodox and polemical
writings had challenged all forms of external and institutionalized religion as they
sought guidance instead from the inner Spirit or light: 'the Kingdom of God is within
you, and the way to the Kingdom is within you', wrote the Quaker prophet James
Nayler, and thus 'it is not to be found in Forms and Customs' (Nayler 1656: 1).
Milton himself never belonged to a sect or gathered church (though he befriended

Quakers later in his life), yet in the 'evil days' of the 1660s, when the Anglican church
sought to stifle dissent, he could show in this polemical spiritual epic what it meant
to reject 'outward rites' and 'specious forms' of religion and derive instead spiritual
strength from a paradise within the godly believer.

   Yet that internal impulse and Milton's tragic vision, we have seen, did not mean
that the radical godly poet and republican simply withdrew from politics into faith
when the Revolution collapsed. In *Paradise Lost* Milton's responses to the politics of
postlapsarian history are more deeply conflicted than that, and these tensions contribute to the poem's richness as a Restoration nonconformist text. His religious poem
expresses at its darkest moments the solitary visionary poet's urge to withdraw like
the martyred Truth from a world perverse; but it also counters and complicates this
response by means of the poet's sharply polemical voice which remains 'unchanged /
To hoarse or mute'. Writing in an age when the godly suffered fierce persecution for
daring to 'persevere / Of spirit and truth', the vulnerable poet strived, like his fiery
seraph, to remain 'unterrified' among 'faithless' and 'innumerable false' (V. 897–9).

BIBLIOGRAPHY

Writings

Baxter (1696); Crump (1900); Darbishire (1932);
   Erbery (1648); Fell (1660); Haller and Davies
   (1944); [Jones] (1663); Kenyon (1986); Ludlow
   (1978); Matthews (1934); Nayler (1656); Parker, William R. (1968, 1996); Prynne (1648);
   Sharp (1998); Vane (1655, 1662a, b); Walwyn
   (1989); Winstanley (1941).

References for Further Reading

Achinstein (1994); Benet (1994); Bennett, Joan S.
   (1989); Buhler (1992); Corns (1992a, 1994);
   Davies, Stevie (1983); Fallon, Robert T. (1995);
   Hill (1977, 1984); Keeble (1987); Knoppers
   (1994); Loewenstein (1993, 1998, 2001); Norbrook (1999); Quint (1993); Radzinowicz
   (1987); Rogers (1996); Shifflett (1998); Sommerville (1986); von Maltzahn (1993b); Wilding (1987); Worden (1990).

22
Obedience and Autonomy in *Paradise Lost*

Michael Schoenfeldt

If only we too could discover a pure, contained, human place, our own strip of fruit-
bearing soil between river and rock.

Rilke, Duino Elegies

Milton's epic famously opens decrying 'man's first disobedience'. But obedience, the
conduct corollary to the first human sin, is a particularly difficult virtue for twenty-
first-century readers to appreciate. As William James observed at the beginning of the
last century,

> The secular life of our twentieth century opens with this virtue [of obedience] held in no
> high esteem. The duty of the individual to determine his own conduct and profit or
> suffer by the consequences seems, on the contrary, to be one of our best rooted
> contemporary Protestant social ideals. So much so that it is difficult even imaginatively
> to comprehend how men possessed of an inner life of their own could ever have come to
> think the subjections of its will to that of other finite creatures recommendable.
> (*Varieties of Religious Experience*, 1902: 305)

Under the spell of a post-Romantic suspicion of the virtue of obedience – a suspicion
which the history of the last century has only enhanced – and influenced deeply by a
Protestant belief in economic self-reliance, James assumes that the existence of a
rational inner life is necessarily in conflict with the overt demands of obedience.

This is not an assumption that John Milton would share. For him, both before and
after the Fall, moral authenticity and psychological autonomy emerge from the practices of obedience. What changes at the Fall is not so much the moral status of
obedience as its political trajectory. Where before the Fall, obedience involves the
relatively simple attention to a single prohibition, after the Fall it entails the performance of a range of uneasily graduated and interpretively elusive virtues. After the Fall, in
other words, the object of obedience changes from a single imperative to whatever

conduct a rigorous exercise of right reason determines. Obedience, then, demands rather than denies the active engagement of the inner life of reason.

In *The Invention of Autonomy: A History of Modern Moral Philosophy*, J. B. Schneewind argues that the curve of ethical philosophy in the seventeenth century moves from 'an older conception of morality as obedience' to 'the conception of morality as self-governance' (1998: 4). He demonstrates how the Jamesian opposition between obedience and autonomy emerged in eighteenth-century moral philosophy. Milton, by contrast, articulates autonomy in the language of obedience. Lacking a moral vocabulary that would signal the political distinctiveness of his project, Milton sometimes sounds ethically rather traditional as he generates a revolutionary morality and politics out of the potentially conservative virtue of obedience. The Fall entails not the trajectory that one might anticipate, from formal obedience to self-determination, but rather a move from prelapsarian autonomy achieved by obedience to a single command to postlapsarian autonomy attained through obedience to the inner prompting of rigorous reason. This unexpected articulation of inner guidance in the vocabulary of external compulsion produces the complex ethics of obedience that Milton depicts. For Milton, then, obedience epitomizes rather than opposes the inner life of the subject.

But after the Fall, as *Areopagitica* reminds us repeatedly, the truth one is enjoined to obey is not easy to discover; it is at best partial, and demands the provisional reconstruction of a mangled and decaying corpse. The truth-seeker is like Isis who searched

> for the mangl'd body of *Osiris*, went up and down gathering up limb by limb. . . . We have not yet found them all, Lords and Commons, nor ever shall doe, till her Masters second comming; he shall bring together every joynt and member, and shall mould them into an immortall feature of lovelines and perfection. (*CPW* II: 549)

Between the Fall and the second coming, virtuous action involves the rational if inevitably incomplete reconstruction of a higher order which one struggles to apprehend in order to strive to be obedient to it. It demands the full resources of intellect and will.

Discovering the proper course of virtuous action is even more demanding because reason is enfeebled at the Fall. As Michael tells Adam,

> Since thy original lapse, true liberty
> Is lost, which always with right reason dwells
> Twinned, and from her hath not dividual being:
> Reason in man obscured, or not obeyed,
> Immediately inordinate desires
> And upstart passions catch the government
> From reason, and to servitude reduce
> Man till then free.
>   (*PL* XII. 83–90)

Humans suffer an internal revolt among their appetites and passions; this revolt entails a microcosmic and physiological version of the disobedience they have performed. The passions that should obey right reason instead assault it, blurring the very capacity necessary to apprehend even a partial truth.

Milton, moreover, emphasizes that virtuous conduct in a postlapsarian epistemology must be forged in the absence of particular laws or taboos. In *Areopagitica* Milton confutes censorship by indicating that God requires that each individual become 'his own chooser' (*CPW* II: 514). Rather than imposing such external prohibitions as censorship, Milton's God demands the performance of such internal virtues of degree as temperance. 'How great a vertue is temperance' Milton asks in *Areopagitica*,

> how much of moment through the whole life of man? yet God committs the managing so great a trust, without particular Law or prescription, wholly to the demeanour of every grown man. . . . For those actions which enter into a man, rather then issue out of him, and therefore defile not, God uses not to captivat under a perpetuall childhood of prescription, but trusts him with the gift of reason to be his own chooser. (*CPW* II: 513–14)

Paradise Lost tells the story of humanity's progress from the 'perpetuall childhood of prescription' that is prelapsarian obedience to the anxious adulthood of rational autonomy. Before the Fall, Adam and Eve must obey only 'This one, this easy charge, of all the trees / In Paradise that bear delicious fruit / So various, not to taste that only Tree / Of knowledge' (IV. 421–4). But after the Fall, they must exercise a relentless ethical casuistry, continually applying clouded reason to the confounding clamours of desire and the confusing imperatives of graduated virtues and contradictory authorities.

For, as Milton argues, again in *Areopagitica*, God 'command[s] us temperance, justice, continence, yet powrs out before us ev'n to a profusenes all desirable things', so that our apprehension of, and obedience to, these ethical commands can be tested (*CPW* II: 528). God, then, surrounds us with plenty not as a blessing but rather as a test; he then expects us to figure out the moment when sustenance becomes excess, and partake temperately. The tarnished but necessary tool by which these judgements are to be made is reason. '[L]earn to obey right reason', Milton urges his compatriots in *Defensio Secunda*, 'to be masters of yourselves' (*WJM* 8: 251; *CPW* IV: 684). For Milton, finally, self-mastery emerges from rather than being opposed to obedience. 'When God gave [Adam] reason', Milton writes,

> he gave him freedom to choose, for reason is but choosing; he had bin else a meer artificiall *Adam*, such an *Adam* as he is in the motions. We our selves esteem not of that obedience, or love, or gift, which is of force: God therefore left him free, set before him a provoking object, ever almost in his eyes; herein consisted his merit, herein the right of his reward, the praise of his abstinence. (*CPW* II: 527)

Where we might think of obedience as occurring amid coercive political structures, for Milton obedience which is coerced is no virtue at all, and even ceases to be obedience. In *Paradise Lost*, the Father wonders aloud 'What pleasure' he could take from forced obedience, 'When will and reason ... had served necessity, / Not me' (III. 107–11). Milton, then, wishes to gear the achievement of liberty to the performance of obedience.

This is no easy task. In the opening of *The Reason of Church-Government*, Milton invokes the example of Plato to the effect that 'persuasion certainly is a more winning, and more manlike way to keepe men in obedience then feare' (*CPW* I: 746). Conceding that fear can perhaps produce the shadow of an indecorously gendered obedience, Milton proceeds to urge the example of Moses, 'the only Lawgiver that we can believe to have been visibly taught of God', who 'began from the book of Genesis, as a prologue to his lawes' (747). This narrative and poetic preamble to the laws is significant because it was designed so

> That the nation of the Jewes, reading therein the universall goodnesse of God to all creatures in the Creation, and his peculiar favour to them in his election of *Abraham* their ancestor, from whom they could derive so many blessings upon themselves, might be mov'd to obey sincerely by knowing so good a reason of their obedience. (*CPW* I: 747)

Milton continually idealizes just this state, where subjects are moved by reason to sincere obedience. For Milton, obedience is not a function of servility but rather the highest form of ethical autonomy. While blind, unthinking obedience to authority is in many ways worse than disobedience, willed obedience to the higher authority of reason is an unequivocal good. Opposing both the shackles of rigorous legalism and the release of unbridled licentiousness, Milton posits willed obedience as the essence of moral life.

Milton then imagines obedience not as a static condition but rather as active, even heroic conduct. As a demonstration of just how dynamic obedience is, Raphael links the possible conversion of human matter into spirit to successful and continued obedience:

> time may come when men
> With angels may participate, and find
> No inconvenient diet, nor too light fare:
> And from these corporal nutriments perhaps
> Your bodies may at last turn all to spirit,
> Improved by tract of time, and winged ascend
> Ethereal, as we, or may at choice
> Here or in heavenly paradises dwell;
> If ye be found obedient,
>
> (*PL* V. 493–501)

Adam responds incredulously, not to the stunning possibility of human bodies becoming progressively ethereal, but rather to the prospect of human disobedience:

'Can we want obedience then / To him, or possibly his love desert / Who formed us
from the dust' (V. 513–16). He seems unable to conceive of the very concept that God
has so deliberately and visibly planted in his paradise. Adam's surprise elicits from
Raphael a long gloss on the concept of obedience, emphasizing its immense ontological distance from lordly coercion or circumstantial compulsion:

> God made thee perfect, not immutable;
> And good he made thee, but to persevere
> He left it in thy power, ordained thy will
> By nature free, not over-ruled by fate
> Inextricable, or strict necessity;
> Our voluntary service he requires,
> Not our necessitated, such with him
> Finds no acceptance, nor can find, for how
> Can hearts, not free, be tried whether they serve
> Willing or no, who will but what they must
> By destiny, and can no other choose?
> Myself and all the angelic host that stand
> In sight of God enthroned, our happy state
> Hold, as you yours, while our obedience holds;
> On other surety none; freely we serve,
> Because we freely love, as in our will
> To love or not; in this we stand or fall:
>   (*PL* V. 524–40)

The very length of the speech, and its repeated trope of definition by negation,
indicates the difficulty that Milton experiences in the articulation of freely willed
obedience.

Adam remembers God admonishing him soon after he was created about the
crucial importance of obedience:

> Of every tree that in the garden grows
> Eat freely with glad heart; fear here no dearth.
> But of the tree whose operation brings
> Knowledge of good and ill, which I have set
> The pledge of thy obedience, and thy faith,
> Amid the garden by the tree of life,
> Remember what I warn thee, shun to taste,
> And shun the bitter consequence: for know,
> The day thou eatst thereof, my sole command
> Transgressed, inevitably thou shalt die;
>   (*PL* VIII. 321–30)

Adam recalls, moreover, a surprising and uncharacteristic austerity infusing God's
words here, as if the Creator, like a parent, intended tonally to underscore the

importance of the warning: 'Sternly he pronounced / The rigid interdiction, which resounds / Yet dreadful in mine ear' (VIII. 333–5).

Obedience, then, is the marrow of prelapsarian autonomy. But the very ontology of God's last best gift to Adam – Eve – suggests the immense difficulty of theorizing or sustaining a fully autonomous prelapsarian existence. When he first glimpses Eve, Adam declares: 'I now see / Bone of my bone, flesh of my flesh, myself / Before me; woman is her name, of man / Extracted' (VIII. 494–7). Psychological autonomy is in severe tension with such literally visceral bonds. The language exudes interdependence, not self-reliance. Eve, moreover, describes her obligation in relation to Adam in terms of a mode of obedience to external authority that disputes the imperatives of autonomy:

> My author and disposer, what thou bidst
> Unargued I obey; so God ordains,
> God is thy law, thou mine:
>> (IV. 635–7)

Here obedience has a clear object – the words of another human being, whose prior creation sanctions his presumed superiority.

In the relationship of Adam and Eve, the strictures of obedience begin to chafe against the claims of autonomy. Eve's wish to work apart on the morning of the Fall exhibits an autonomy the text otherwise licenses, but not when it is in tension with obedience to her companion. Milton allows Eve to cite some of the most compelling arguments of *Areopagitica* in defence of her wish to work alone:

> And what is faith, love, virtue, unassayed
> Alone, without exterior help sustained?
> Let us not then suspect our happy state
> Left so imperfect by the maker wise,
> As not secure to single or combined.
> Frail is our happiness, if this be so,
> And Eden were no Eden thus exposed.
>> (IX. 335–41)

Eve here specifically articulates a compelling account of the moral autonomy of prelapsarian existence. For Eve, this autonomy can be tested, and does not demand the constant presence of another human in order to stay vigilant.

Adam responds by giving Eve a lesson in prelapsarian moral psychology, reminding her that because their will is free, it can be misled. He articulates at once their autonomy and their vulnerability to deception, as he tells her that the real danger to a prelapsarian human is not external but internal:

> within himself
> The danger lies, yet lies within his power:
> Against his will he can receive no harm.

> But God left free the will, for what obeys
> Reason, is free, and reason he made right,
> But bid her well beware, and still erect,
> Lest by some fair appearing good surprised
> She dictate false, and misinform the will
> To do what God expressly hath forbid.
>
> (IX. 348–56)

Adam suggests that remaining virtuous amid temptation is a matter of obedience; here, though, the object of obedience is not the stern command of God but rather the more elusive dictates of reason within the individual subject. Adam feels that they have a better chance of attending to these dictates when together than apart: 'Not then mistrust, but tender love enjoins, / That I should mind thee oft, and mind thou me' (IX. 357–8). 'Mind' is a rich word here; a verb deriving from the very rational faculty whose function is to attend to reason, 'mind' means not 'obey' but 'remind', and suggests through the parallel syntax a mutuality that would trouble both the gendered obedience that Adam's words adumbrate, and the longing for autonomy that Eve's wish to work apart whispers. Adam feels they would be stronger together; Eve feels that her strength cannot be manifested unless they are apart. Adam even characterizes his separation from Eve with a surprisingly violent verb – sever – suggesting the near-physical pain it causes him:

> Seek not temptation then, which to avoid
> Were better, and most likely if from me
> Thou sever not: trial will come unsought.
> Wouldst thou approve thy constancy, approve
> First thy obedience;
>
> (IX. 364–8)

Adam again invokes obedience as a check on behaviour, but obedience here significantly has no object. Is it to Adam? Is it to God? Is it to an inner voice of reason? Are these three authorities in complete synchronization? Adam's parting words to Eve surrender the larger point, but in the syntax of command:

> Go; for thy stay, not free, absents thee more;
> Go in thy native innocence, rely
> On what thou hast of virtue,
>
> (IX. 372–4)

Ironically, Adam's acquiescent mandate precipitates a homily on the intricate relationship among freedom, self-reliance and inner virtue.

Indeed, when Adam relates to Raphael the depth of his feeling for Eve, Raphael becomes progressively concerned that what Adam feels for Eve is not ennobling love

but rather unruly passion. Adam experiences with Eve a depth of pleasure that
transports and alters his very being; he

> must confess to find
> In all things else delight indeed, but such
> As used or not, works in the mind no change,
> Nor vehement desire,
>
> . . .
>
> but here
> Far otherwise, transported I behold,
> Transported touch; here passion first I felt,
> Commotion strange, in all enjoyments else
> Superior and unmoved, here only weak
> Against the charm of beauty's powerful glance.
>   (VIII. 523–33)

Adam can only explain his profound passion for Eve through a surmise about their
respective ontogeny:

> Or nature failed in me, and left some part
> Not proof enough such object to sustain,
> Or from my side subducting, took perhaps
> More than enough;
>   (VIII. 534–7)

Adam's feelings for Eve, in other words, run counter to the rational autonomy that
humans are expected to exercise in Paradise. Adam knows he is supposed to be
superior because he was created first and so is theoretically closer to God –

> For well I understand in the prime end
> Of nature her the inferior, in the mind
> And inward faculties, which most excel,
> In outward also her resembling less
> His image who made both, and less expressing
> The character of that dominion given
> O'er other creatures;
>   (VIII. 540–6)

– but he also knows that his experience of passion for her creates a powerful undertow
to the current of male superiority that runs through the epic:

> yet when I approach
> Her loveliness, so absolute she seems
> And in herself complete, so well to know
> Her own, that what she wills to do or say,

> Seems wisest, virtuousest, discreetest, best;
> All higher knowledge in her presence falls
> Degraded, wisdom in discourse with her
> Loses discount'nanced, and like folly shows;
> Authority and reason on her wait,
> As one intended first, not after made
> Occasionally;
>
>   (VIII. 546–56)

It is fascinating that Adam's erotic attraction for Eve should be stated in a vocabulary underscoring her autonomy; she is 'absolute . . . And in herself complete'. It is as if the physiology of creation belies the priority that is thought to underpin male superiority. Adam cannot be complete without Eve, since a piece of him was used to make her, but Eve possesses a physiological integrity that underwrites her psychological autonomy.

Raphael is not pleased at Adam's ardent passion for Eve, and responds with the 'contracted brow' of concerned disapproval. Raphael suggests that Adam is 'attribúting overmuch to things / Less excellent' (VIII. 565–6). Raphael fears, furthermore, that the fervency of this love will conflict with Adam's obedience to God, and his corollary obedience to internal reason. Raphael in response offers Adam a quick lesson in the virtue of self-esteem, hoping that Adam will assume the pre-eminence that all seem to think the priority of his creation bestows upon him:

> weigh with her thyself;
> Then value: oft-times nothing profits more
> Than self-esteem, grounded on just and right
> Well managed;
>
>   (VIII. 570–3)

Raphael is careful to indicate that the problem is not so much the emotion of love *per se* as the covert challenge that passionate love presents to right reason:

> What higher in her society thou findst
> Attractive, human, rational, love still;
> In loving thou dost well, in passion not,
> Wherein true love consists not; love refines
> The thoughts, and heart enlarges, hath his seat
> In reason, and is judicious, is the scale
> By which to heavnly love thou may'st ascend,
> Not sunk in carnal pleasure,
>
>   (VIII. 586–93)

But it is difficult to comprehend the force and the location of the distinction between love and passion in prelapsarian subjects. Raphael indeed suggests the distinction is best registered in the ultimate effects of such feelings. If it leads one up a Platonic ladder of love, it is a licensed affection; but if it inaugurates a descent into the carnal passion of prelapsarian beasts, it is irrational emotion. This curiously experiential account of the hierarchy mirrors in miniature the troubling epistemology of the Fall: just as one can only know good from evil once one has tasted from the tree of disobedience, so can one know whether a particular passion is licit or illicit only by seeing where it takes one.

Raphael's parting words to Adam attempt to articulate just the kind of rational passion he has been describing, urging Adam to cultivate towards God an affection which synchronizes the fervour of love with the performance of obedience:

> Be strong, live happy, and love, but first of all
> Him whom to love is to obey, and keep
> His great command; take heed lest passion sway
> Thy judgment to do aught, which else free will
> Would not admit;
>
> (VIII. 633–7)

Where Adam's love for Eve must be distinguished from a potentially subjugating passion, Adam's love for God should flower in obedience to God. What emerges in prelapsarian social existence is a complex triangle of love and obedience among God, the first man and the first woman.

The Fall is imagined at the beginning of Book IX as a complete distortion of these intricate relations. The central term among Milton's many 'dis' words describing the new social dispensation between humans and God is of course *disobedience*:

> foul distrust, and breach
> Disloyal on the part of man, revolt,
> And disobedience: on the part of heaven
> Now alienated, distance and distaste,
> Anger and just rebuke, and judgment given,
>
> (IX. 6–10)

In the temptation scene, the issue of obedience takes on a curious charge. When the serpent leads Eve to the forbidden tree, Eve reiterates the sole command that God has given them, and then uses an echo of Paul to describe the degree to which prelapsarian life is otherwise free from prohibition:

> But of this tree we may not taste nor touch;
> God so commanded, and left that command
> Sole daughter of his voice; the rest, we live
> Law to our selves, our reason is our law.
>
> (IX. 651–4)

In the passage to which Eve's speech refers (Romans 2: 14–15), Paul had brilliantly incorporated the Stoic ideal of natural law into a Christian ethics to produce a model of inner virtue available to the Gentiles: 'For when the Gentiles, which have not the law, do by nature the things contained in the law, these, having not the law, are a law unto themselves: Which shew the work of the law written in their hearts, their conscience also bearing witness, and their thoughts the mean while accusing or else excusing one another.' Eve suggests here that she and Adam practise a kind of preternatural obedience to an inner law that resembles the single overt prohibition of paradisal existence. In this regard, they are a law unto themselves.

The serpent's response is to pick apart the illogic implicit in the blend of licence and prohibition that is prelapsarian existence:

> Indeed? Hath God then said that of the fruit
> Of all these garden trees ye shall not eat,
> Yet lords declared of all in earth or air?
>
> (IX. 656–8)

The serpent then converts the divine prohibition into a test of her 'dauntless virtue' (IX. 694) rather than the proof of obedience that God desires. Eve is in fact able to convince herself that God's 'forbidding / Commends' the tree 'more', that ultimately 'Such prohibitions bind not' (IX. 753–4, 760). At the moment of falling, God becomes for her 'Our great forbidder' (IX. 815), known for his single prohibition rather than the bounteous gifts she and Adam had praised profusely in Book IV.

Adam in turn falls because he feels a physiological and emotional link to Eve that belies the moral autonomy that would allow him to stand. He soliloquizes:

> How can I live without thee, how forgo
> Thy sweet converse and love so dearly joined,
> To live again in these wild woods forlorn?
> Should God create another Eve, and I
> Another rib afford, yet loss of thee
> Would never from my heart; no no, I feel
> The link of nature draw me: flesh of flesh,
> Bone of my bone thou art, and from thy state
> Mine never shall be parted, bliss or woe.
>
> (IX. 908–16)

He then reiterates his own lack of autonomy when he tells Eve that he has chosen to fall with her because he cannot imagine existence without her:

> So forcible within my heart I feel
> The bond of nature draw me to my own,
> My own in thee, for what thou art is mine;
> Our state cannot be severed, we are one,
> One flesh; to lose thee were to lose myself.
>
> (IX. 955–9)

Here obedience and autonomy are absolutely linked; or rather, disobedience is made a function of Adam's failure to conceive of himself as a separate and autonomous being. He feels that Eve's status and actions are his own. As James Turner argues, Adam's 'craving for partnership...seems to define his whole being; he is unfinished without Eve' (1987: 283). But by making Eve so crucial to Adam's existence, the poem excites a tension between the philosophical autonomy it overtly endorses and the marital sociability it also admires. 'Wedded love', the bond the poem praises eloquently as the 'mysterious law, true source / Of human offspring', and the foundation of all social relations, thus threatens the moral autonomy the poem enjoins (IV. 750–1). Uxoriousness, the poem suggests, at once fulfils the social imperatives of Paradise and challenges the obedience that sustains paradisal existence.

After the Fall, Milton explains the internal affects of their disobedience using the familiar lexicon of Renaissance faculty psychology:

> not at rest or ease of mind,
> They sat them down to weep, nor only tears
> Rained at their eyes, but high winds worse within
> Began to rise, high passions, anger, hate,
> Mistrust, suspicion, discord, and shook sore
> Their inward state of mind, calm region once
> And full of peace, now tossed and turbulent:
> For understanding ruled not, and the will
> Heard not her lore, both in subjection now
> To sensual appetite, who from beneath
> Usurping over sovereign reason claimed
> Superior sway:
>
> (IX. 1120–31)

Mortal disobedience liberates the internal affections and appetites from congenital obedience to reason.

Milton brilliantly represents this inner turmoil in the subsequent argument between Adam and Eve, suffused with discordant passion and self-exculpatory rationalization. In a bitter irony, Eve blames Adam for not ordering her to remain with him: 'why didst not thou the head / Command me absolutely not to go' (IX. 1155–6). Adam rejoins by asking exasperatedly, 'what could I more? / I warned thee, I admonished thee, foretold / The danger...beyond this had been force, / And force upon free will hath here no place' (IX. 1170–4). When Adam tells the Son that Eve 'gave me of the tree, and did eat', the Son asks: 'Was she thy God, that her thou didst obey / Before his voice'? (X. 143–6). Obedience here entails neither the autonomous attention to right reason the poem praises nor the careful following of God's single command but rather the polemical occasion for blaming another human for one's own foibles. The Son in turn pronounces a twofold curse on Eve: 'children thou shalt bring / In sorrow forth, and to thy husband's will / Thine shall submit, he over thee shall rule' (X. 194–6). Obedience here is not the autonomous exercise of reason that Milton values but the enforced subjugation of one will to another.

We also meet in the epic a curious perversion of the signal virtue of obedience to one's progenitor when Sin offers to open the gates of hell despite the 'command of heavens all-powerful king' which tells her she is 'forbidden to unlock / These adamantine gates' (II. 851–3). Adjudicating the demands of competing authorities, as postlapsarian ethical subjects continually must do, Sin reasons to Satan that

> Thou art my father, thou my author, thou
> My being gav'st me; whom should I obey
> But thee, whom follow?
>
> (II. 864–6)

Filial piety here underwrites a hellish version of the obedience that the epic repeatedly enjoins.

In *Paradise Regained* Satan similarly attempts to claim the virtue of obedience for himself by arguing that 'What [God] bids I do' (I. 377). The Son responds by asking, 'Wilt thou impute to obedience what thy fear / Extorts, or pleasure to do ill excites?' (I. 422–3). For Milton, acting in consonance to God's will out of cowardice or perverse pleasure is not obedience. Obedience entails an actively willed response to the dictates of reason and proper authority. Neither the 'Knee-tribute' by which Satan mocks heavenly adoration (*PL* V. 782) nor the authoritarian effort 'to bind with laws the free' (*PL* V. 819) by which Satan characterizes God's announcement of the Son, Miltonic obedience involves the deepest commitments of the free self.

In the War in Heaven Satan likewise aspires to appropriate the language of liberty for his own will to power. The debate between Abdiel and Satan in the middle books is in many ways a quarrel over contradictory definitions of obedience, and their relationship to autonomy. Abdiel is introduced as the angel 'than whom none with more zeal adored / The Deity, and divine commands obeyed' (*PL* V. 805–6). After hearing Satan's proposals, Abdiel asks indignantly, 'Shalt thou give law to God' (V. 822), critiquing one version of the façade of autonomy. Abdiel declares to Satan that his political ambitions entail not revolutionary postures but rather vulgar disobedience. Satan responds by appealing to a mythology of self-creation:

> who saw
> When this creation was? Rememberst thou
> Thy making, while the maker gave thee being?
> We know no time when we were not as now;
> Know none before us, self-begot, self-raised
> By our own quickening power
> . . .
> Our puissance is our own,
>
> (V. 856–64)

Abdiel responds not by disputing Satan's mythology but rather by arguing that Satan will soon experience a sea change in his relationship with God. Satan and his troops will no longer flourish amid the 'indulgent laws' of heaven; rather, 'other decrees / Against thee are gone forth without recall; / That golden sceptre which thou didst reject / Is now an iron rod to bruise and break / Thy disobedience' (V. 883–8). In the ethical metallurgy of heavenly rule, disobedience transforms a gentle government into a repressive regime.

The heavenly throngs that welcome Abdiel back to heaven describe Satan and his troops as those who 'reason for their law refuse, / Right reason for their law, and for their king / Messiah, who by right of merit reigns' (VI. 41–3). Despite their claims to autonomy ('self-begot, self-raised' [V. 860]), their rejection of God is also a repudiation of reason and merit, the crucial media of ethical autonomy. When they subsequently meet on the battlefield, Satan tells Abdiel that he had formerly perceived consonance between the experience of liberty and the order of heaven, but now sees 'that most through sloth had rather serve' (VI. 165–70). He suggests, in other words, that heavenly obedience is a matter of lethargy and comfort, rather than the active, willed, rational choice that God demands. Abdiel replies by arguing that obeying God is a more rational and heroic pursuit than ruling in other realms could ever be: enjoy 'in hell thy kingdom', he says, 'let me serve / In heaven God ever blest, and his divine / Behests obey, worthiest to be obeyed' (VI. 183–5). When the Son enters the fray on the third day, he tells the Father that he will send to hell those 'That from thy just obedience could revolt, / Whom to obey is happiness entire' (VI. 740–1). Raphael concludes the narration by telling Adam the reason for the story of the War in Heaven: '[L]et it profit thee to have heard / By terrible example the reward / Of disobedience' (VI. 909–11). Like Adam and Eve, Satan is guilty of disobedience. He confuses the heroic exertions of willed service with the slothful comforts of servility, and the happiness of obedience with the hell of purported command.

When God announces the creation of humanity, he makes obedience a central element of his plan. 'I will create', he says,

> Another world, out of one man a race
> Of men innumerable, there to dwell,
> Not here, till by degrees of merit raised
> They open to themselves at length the way
> Up hither, under long obedience tried,
> And earth be changed to heaven, and heaven to earth,
>
> (VII. 155–60)

Had humans not fallen, obedience would have been not a static but a transformative virtue, allowing them ultimately to enter heaven. The act of creation itself exemplifies the obedience of the matter of the universe to the voice of its maker: 'Let there be light, said God, and forthwith light / Ethereal, first of things, quintessence pure / Sprung from the deep' (VII. 243–5). Raphael, moreover, explains to Adam that he would like to hear Adam's account of his own creation because he was away on a mission from God that day; God indeed, he relates, regularly sends angels 'upon his high behests / For state, as sovereign king, and to inure / Our prompt obedience' (VIII. 238–40). Such missions give the angels the chance to exercise an obedience which is perhaps too easy to perform in heaven.

Obedience, moreover, will ultimately be the virtue that will restore humans to God, typologically repairing what was broken in the first act of disobedience. Michael tells Adam that the Saviour will regain Paradise not by battling Satan heroically, but rather

> by fulfilling that which thou didst want,
> Obedience to the law of God, imposed
> On penalty of death,
>
> . . .
>
> The law of God exact he shall fulfil
> Both by obedience and by love, though love
> Alone fulfil the law;
>   (XII. 396–404)

Milton here paraphrases Paul, who writes in Romans 5: 19 that 'as by one man's disobedience many were made sinners, so by the obedience of one shall many be made righteous.' *Paradise Regained*, of course, depicts not the typical story of Jesus's corporeal suffering but rather the inert drama of 'one man's firm obedience fully tried / Through all temptation' (I. 4–5). Continually, Milton nudges the central messages of the Judeo-Christian faith in the direction of the obedience he so values.

This profound valuation of obedience makes the situation of Mosaic law particularly interesting to the development of Miltonic ethics. Designed to govern all aspects of human conduct, Mosaic law is applied, according to Milton, not so much to induce an impossible obedience as to produce a conviction of the full effect of that original sin that ensues from that first act of disobedience. 'So many and so various laws are given' to the Israelites, Michael argues, 'to evince / Their natural pravity, by stirring up / Sin against law to fight' (*PL* XII. 282–9). Michael here paraphrases Paul, who writes: '[T]he law entered, that the offence might abound' (Romans 5: 20). After the Fall, law elicits not obedience but transgression. When the Israelites find that they cannot 'the moral part / Perform', they will know that 'Some blood more precious' than that 'of bulls and goats . . . must be paid for man' (*PL* XII. 292–9). For Milton, this is the sacrifice of Jesus, which will inaugurate 'a better covenant' (XII. 302) between mortal and God than that available under Hebraic law. Michael describes the transition from Hebraic to Christian ethics as a move

> From shadowy types to truth, from flesh to spirit,
> From imposition of strict laws, to free
> Acceptance of large grace, from servile fear
> To filial, works of law to works of faith.
>   (XII. 303–6)

Yet this 'free acceptance of large grace', although supplanting the 'imposition of strict laws', does not so much abrogate as fulfil the demands of obedience. Near the end of *Paradise Lost*, Adam sums up the lesson he has learned from the narration of biblical history; he now knows 'that to obey is best, / And love with fear the only God, to walk / As in his presence' (XII. 561–3). It is telling that the infinitive 'to obey' here has no direct object, since that is precisely the quandary confronting mortal ethics. Michael grants that Adam has thus 'attained the sum / Of wisdom' (XII. 575–6) but suggests that Adam must also 'add / Deeds to thy knowledge answerable, add faith, / Add virtue, patience, temperance, add love' (XII. 581–3). With this necessary supplement of active but ineffable virtue, Adam will 'not be loath / To leave this Paradise, but shalt possess / A paradise within thee, happier far' (XII. 585–7). By allowing their acquired knowledge of the bewildering complexities of postlapsarian obedience actively to enter the muddle of quotidian ethical practice, Adam and Eve will discover something deep within themselves that distils the essence of the garden they must leave. Although prelapsarian paradisal existence was sustained by obedience to a single external directive, postlapsarian paradisal interiority emerges not from blind obedience to external directives but rather from the rigorous exercise of moral autonomy achieved through periodic and profound introspection. Such introspection, and its concomitant ethical practices, locate the recovery of the moral essence of the lost Paradise amid the inner chambers of the human subject.

It is telling that in this epic so concerned with the tensions between human sociability and divine obedience, between the demands of affective bonds and the ethics of autonomy, the penultimate word is 'solitary': 'They hand in hand with wandering steps and slow, / Through Eden took their solitary way' (XII. 648–9). The ethical path of humanity after the Fall is to turn inward, and seek the muddled guidance of fallen reason. Tellingly, Adam and Eve leave Paradise in a posture of consent rather than one exhibiting submission. The Fall, then, entails not a transition from obedience to autonomy but rather a resituation of the virtue of obedience in terms of internal autonomy. No longer performed in relation to a single prohibition given from above, obedience must now respond to myriad laws, partial truths and gradual virtues, all glimpsed at best through the darkened glass of reason. In *Queen Mab*, Shelley writes that Christianity

> inculcates the necessity of supplicating the Deity. Prayer may be considered under two points of view; as an endeavour to change the intentions of God, or as a formal testimony of our obedience. But the former case supposes that the caprices of a limited intelligence can occasionally instruct the Creator of the world how to regulate the universe; and the latter a certain degree of servility analogous to the loyalty demanded by earthly tyrants. Obedience indeed is only the pitiful and cowardly egotism of him who thinks he can do something better than reason. (1853: 101)

Shelley here clearly shows himself very much of the devil's party, articulating a suspicion of the relative virtue of obedience which is still very much with us. For

Milton, though, obedience involves not the cowardly egotism of one who thinks he or she can do something better than reason but rather the laborious and rigorous exercise *of* reason. Milton certainly knew that obedience could parade as political servility or a foolish formalism, two forms of behaviour he abhorred; but he also knew that it could manifest the highest good of which humans are capable.

Obedience, moreover, became for Milton a principle of political resistance; it involves not just doing what you are told, but using reason to figure out what authority you are supposed to follow, and to ascertain what you are supposed to do according to a higher moral code. 'The free man's mind', argues Northrop Frye, 'is a dictatorship of reason obeyed by the will without argument: we go wrong only when we take these conceptions of kingship and service of freedom as social models' ('The Garden Within', *The Return of Eden*, 1965: 111). The political liberty Milton prized is manifested most meaningfully and extensively in the quotidian regulation of self by reference to an interiorized sense of moral obligation – a process which he defines as obedience. The author of *De Doctrina Christiana* defines obedience as 'that virtue whereby we propose to ourselves the will of God as the paramount rule of our conduct, and serve him alone' (*WJM* 17: 69; see also *WJM* 14: 25; 17: 19, 51; *CPW* VI: 663–4, 129, 644, 656–7). The radical blend of volition and submission implicit in this definition produces behaviours that employ the principle of divine authority to reject the arbitrary commands of terrestrial power. Samson's violent obedience to 'rousing motions' (*Samson Agonistes*, line 1382), for example, licenses his aggressive disobedience of Philistine commands. The fact that the voice of divine authority must be heard at best as an 'inner prompting' means that the lines of force, in Milton's poems and his culture, meet ultimately in the clouded heart of the autonomous subject. If, as Schneewind argues, the seventeenth century is the period in which an older conception of morality as obedience begins to give way to a conception of morality as self-governance, we can see in *Paradise Lost* and throughout Milton's corpus how an emergent notion of political autonomy could be articulated in the venerable language of political obedience.

BIBLIOGRAPHY

Writings

Rilke (1984); Shelley, Percy Bysshe (1853).

References for Further Reading

Frye (1965); Hoopes (1962); Hunter (1989); James (1902); Schneewind (1998); Schoenfeldt (1993); Sennett (1980); Turner (1987).

23

Paradise Lost and the Multiplicity of Time

Amy Boesky

Paradise Lost is a poem deeply interested in time. It is hard to turn to a passage in Milton's epic without finding references to time as an abstraction or a principle – we learn, for example, that Satan falls for 'Nine times the space that measures day and night' (I. 50), that the fallen angels spend 'irksome hours' in hell (II. 527), and that there is night as well as day in heaven. Time matters in the epic not only in general ways but also as a specific limit or boundary: Eve reaches for the forbidden fruit at noon, Raphael is permitted to spend a set number of hours with Adam and Eve, the War in Heaven lasts for three days, and the moment that Adam and Eve must leave Eden is determined by 'the hour precise' (XII. 589). The anachronistic presence in Eden of time as measure (so that 'noon' marks a specific moment in a world where spring and autumn co-exist) is contrasted with the importance in the epic of ritual time – set times of day and night for nourishment, lovemaking, prayer, labour and rest. Milton's epic traces the shift from what Walter Benjamin has described as Messianic or sacred time to an accepted sense of time as 'homogeneous, empty' (1969: 261, 263). But sacred time is not confined to the past for Milton; for, though time in *Paradise Lost* is crucially involved with falling and fallenness, it is also instrumental in Milton's vision of the attainment of grace.

The Temptation of Sequence

Counting and telling, as Stuart Sherman has suggested, are etymologically linked phenomena. 'O[ld] E[nglish] *tellan*, to narrate, is cognate with Middle Low German *tellen*, to count, reckon' (1996: ix). To recount, in narrative terms, is to enumerate, to put events into a sequence made sensible through chronology. According to Frank Kermode, narrative plotting is a means of countering the potential emptiness of time by filling it up with successive events. In narrative, Kermode argues, 'that which was conceived as simply successive becomes charged with past and future: what was *chronos* becomes *kairos*'. Kermode distinguishes the Greek *chronos* (which he construes as empty or merely successive time) from *kairos* ('times which are discordant and full' (1966: 46). But as Sherman observes, the sheer 'successiveness' of narratological reckoning creates its own kind of fullness and meaning (1996: 11). The fullness of such 'successivity' resonates for readers as well as writers. For readers, sequentiality (What happened first? What next?) has a powerful allure.

The possibility of this kind of chronological order is at once enabled and impeded by Milton's epic. In the opening twenty-eight lines the Bard uses the word 'first' four times, emphasizing the sense of a beginning which links the origins of narrative to the origins of creation. Through the repetition of 'first', Moses (who 'first taught the chosen seed') is linked to the Muse (who 'from the first / Wast present') to the Bard (who is beginning his poem) and to the reader (who is just beginning to read it). When the Muse is twice exhorted to 'say first' what caused Adam and Eve to fall (I. 28–9), all of these 'firsts' converge in the poem's principal subject: the origins of disobedience. This layering of 'firsts' initially seems to assure readers that we are starting not just at the beginning, but at the *first* beginning. Yet even as the possibility that the poem can be understood sequentially is being established, the idea of sequence is tested and exposed as flawed.

A striking example of this occurs after the narrator's description of Satan's fall. Initially this is given in the past tense; but at line 54 of Book I the reader is dropped into the present tense of the epic through the word 'now', a word which shoots us down into hell, into Satan's perspective, and into a temporal moment that defies sequence. The reader, who has been following a description of Satan's fall set in the past tense, tumbles through this 'now' into the midst of things, as well as into a narrative present which presumes that the narrator, the reader and Satan all occupy the same temporal moment. '[B]ut his doom / Reserved him to more wrath; for now the thought / Both of lost happiness and lasting pain / Torments him' (I. 53–6). This 'now', however brilliantly it forges an identification between the reader and Satan, troubles the intrinsic idea of chronology. 'Now' opens a gap in temporal sequence, betraying the impossibility of counting and recounting through customary measures. Sequence is belied, and the reader is suddenly made aware that time does not work in a linear fashion, but instead in dazzling circuits, flashbacks and repetitions.

In a similar way, allusions in *Paradise Lost* do not adhere to temporal unity. Instead, they layer or compress time. To allude in literature is often to refer back to a previous event or image, but Milton's allusions make history and narrative multivalenced and multitemporal. When Satan arrives in his odyssey at the gates of heaven at the end of Book III, for example, the gates are described with a splendour that holds the reader with Satan outside of their bounds, looking in. Descriptions of the gorgeous gem-stones of the portal give way to the rendering of its inimitable gleam, and then to an analogy comparing the stairs to those seen by Jacob fleeing Esau in the field of Luz (III. 505–15). This allusion complexly crowns the binary trope of open and shut that has been repeated throughout Book III. But the allusion is also intriguingly anachron-istic. The way in which Satan sees the unmountable stairs to the heaven he has lost gets compared to a point in a future which has not yet occurred, but one that is nevertheless posited in the past tense: Satan *sees* these stairs as Jacob, Adam's descendant, *saw* angels ascending and descending. Satan's vision does not precede Jacob's, but proleptically comes after it, suggesting that we are once again occupying a special 'now' in which classical, biblical and early modern events slide backwards and forwards, enriching and estranging each other.

It could be argued that there is no time in *Paradise Lost*, as Samuel Johnson objected that there is no nature in Lycidas: rather, there is no fixed chronological time in which the artifice of history ('and then and then and then') is understood to move in a linear, one-directional fashion. In another sense time is everywhere in *Paradise Lost*, but it is richer and more multifaceted than modern readers might expect. Miltonic allusions are not atemporal but extratemporal, conjoining and compressing the classical and the Christian. The future for Milton's narrator, to borrow a phrase from Ursula K. LeGuin, is a metaphor. Milton makes continuous comparative use of the future to shade his representations of unfallen Eden; Eve's naked innocence, for example, is first presented in Book IV contrasted by a flashforward to its eventual degradation:

> Nor those mysterious parts were then concealed,
> Then was not guilty shame, dishonest shame
> Of nature's works, honour dishonourable,
> Sin-bred, how have ye troubled all mankind
> With shews instead,
>
> (IV. 312–16)

The narrator here bends time to suggest that history is more meaningful when layered, prior innocence best (or only) seen through the distorting lens of its loss. 'Were then', 'was not' get elided in this passage into the narrative present tense: 'how have ye troubled all mankind'. Eve's perfection, in other words, is represented in a multidimensional temporal space that circumnavigates past, present and future.

If time is often layered or deflected in the epic, why are we still so compelled by the temptation of sequence? Chronology (and its denial) are continually linked in the epic to the process of narrating. This is made especially clear in a passage near the end of Book I. The narrator, remarking on the construction of Pandæmonium, gives an account of its architect, Mulciber, whose fall is described in a sequence in which descent is temporally calibrated. Mulciber, we are told, was 'thrown by angry Jove / Sheer o'er the crystal battlements: from morn / To noon he fell, from noon to dewy eve / A summer's day' (I. 741–4). The slowly drawn out brilliance of this passage makes the reader experience Mulciber's fall in a kind of slow motion, from 'morn' to 'noon' to 'eve', as if these temporal designations were plateaux bounced off one by one in a long and eerie descent. Then abruptly the narrator interrupts this narrative to denounce it: 'thus they relate, / Erring' (I. 746–7). Mulciber and his crew, the narrator advises, had in fact fallen long before this, and the evocative image of that initial fall (from morn to noon to eve) is now invalidated. This is an unsettling moment, working to trouble the categories established by the Bard in the opening proem. Can there really be a 'first' that we can understand, and if so, how can we determine it? What if that 'first' is an error, like the timing of Mulciber's fall? How can designations like 'mean while' or 'when' or 'when as' or 'after' or 'before' make sense without becoming flattened out or reductive? Stanley Fish has argued that this is part of an overall tendency to invalidate the reader's apprehensions in *Paradise Lost*:

> This distrust extends to all the conventional ways of knowing that might enable a reader to locate himself in the world of any poem. The questions we ask of our reading experience are in large part the questions we ask of our day-to-day experience. Where are we, what are the physical components of our surroundings, what time is it? (1967/1971: 22)

But the Mulciber passage is amended by the narrator in very specific ways. It is not wrong in substance (Mulciber did fall, after all). It is the timing that is inaccurately reported – Mulciber fell earlier than they say, and it appears that the error is less strategic than it is a consequence of narrating. Saying creates a desire for sequence, and the sequence it elicits is wrong. Counting and recounting, then, are interinvolved, but also strikingly at odds.

It is important that Mulciber's fall and its chronology are linked to the process of narrating and of understanding narration. Narration is continually linked in *Paradise Lost* to the temptation of sequence and its impossibility, and the issue seems to inhere in the process of narrating rather than in the ethical status of the narrator. Even God, who sees all time at once ('past, present, future he beholds', III. 78) relies on chronological conventions when he narrates or is himself narrated. He 'first beheld', he 'then surveyed' (III. 64, 69); and in Raphael's account in Book V, God suggests a chronological sequence not only for the promotion of the Son ('this day I have begot whom I declare / My onely Son') but also for potential subversion ('him who disobeys / Me disobeys, breaks union, and that day / Cast out from God and blessed vision, falls / Into utter darkness' (V. 611–14). Despite the inadequacy if not the danger of the careful sequence God ascribes to future events, God (at least through the Bard's narration) counts as he recounts.

Narration requires (and confounds) chronology in part because it is only an approximation of events that cannot be bound by time. Raphael worries about this when he begins to describe to Adam and Eve the events of the War in Heaven. He worries that he may be narrating events that they may not understand, and that the discursive structures he employs will only be the shadow of the experiences behind them. 'I shall delineate so, / By likening spiritual to corporal forms, / As may express them best' (V. 572–4). Raphael's narrative begins both with a rhetorical position in time, and with an immediate suggestion of its inutility: 'when on a day / (For time, though in eternity, applied / To motion, measures all things durable / By present, past, and future' (V. 579–82). Time exists in heaven, as Raphael explains later, for pleasure and diversion, but also to enable counting and recounting. As God says to the Son after the second day of fighting: 'two days are past, / Two days, as we compute the days of heaven' (VI. 684–5). Such computation works to delineate, to create boundaries, suspense and fulfilment. When Adam asks Raphael in Book VII to relate things closer to his world, Raphael replies that he may answer his desire of 'knowledge within bounds' (VII. 120). Time is one of these 'bounds', a measure both for relaying and for ending relation. The long dialogues which span Books V–VIII of the epic frame a series of embedded narratives, each of them complexly and delicately time-bound: Raphael's account of the three-day War in Heaven; Adam's corresponding account of his own emergence into life, his dialogues with God and the subsequent creation of Eve. Not only does each element of each narrative depend on the underlying question 'when', but the unfolding of each story is constrained for all of its participants by what Frank Kermode has called the 'sense of an ending'. Raphael's visit itself is confined to 'half this day' (V. 229), a temporal limit which works, like genre, to shape discourse. Raphael's approach in Book V is greeted by Adam with urgency: he instructs Eve to 'Haste hither' to behold the approaching angel, and then to 'go with speed' to gather bounty from nature to entertain him (V. 308, 313). But once engaged in dialogue with Raphael, Adam labours to slow him down – 'How subtly to detain thee I devise' (VIII. 207) – repeatedly suggesting that the day which they have been allotted has not yet been spent. As long as there is time allotted, Adam wants to fill it.

Delay and Desire

Narration is unique in the ways that it slows time down through mimesis: by retelling events, narration makes its auditors pause, reliving past or future experiences while breaking out of the customary and restricted practices of ordinary time. While Adam is listening to Raphael, he feels displaced, spatially and temporally; he feels himself to be in heaven, experiencing events beyond his ken. He is in this sense outside of time. But he is also acutely sensitive to time's passage, to the ebbing away of the 'large day' granted for the dialogues. He wants both to savour Raphael's account and to slow it down. This desire to detain Raphael is linked to another kind of desire in the poem, one that is associated with Eve and with what the epic represents as a kind of erotics of delay.

Time and pleasure are linked in the epic by Raphael, who makes clear that temporal changes exist in heaven, not for utility but for enjoyment. The day's 'seasons' referred to in Eve's love sonnet to Adam in Book IV ('With thee conversing I forget all time', line 639) find an echo in Raphael's description of heaven's 'seasons' in Book V (lines 629–30): 'For we have also our evening and our morn / We ours for change delectable, not need.' For the unfallen, change is experienced as pleasure. The fluctuations of light and dark create a cycle that Raphael locates 'fast by' the throne of God, as if such mutability were intrinsically associated with godhead itself:

> There is a cave
> Within the mount of God, fast by his throne,
> Where light and darkness in perpetual round
> Lodge and dislodge by turns, which makes through heaven
> Grateful vicissitude, like day and night;
>
> (VI. 4–8)

Not only does Milton's heaven know darkness (as his hell knows light), this fluctuating darkness is an essential part of heaven's dynamism and its beauty. This point is worth noting because readers sometimes assume that change (such as the advent of seasons) is introduced only after Adam and Eve fall. While time is indeed experienced differently after the Fall, it is not mutability that dictates this. 'Grateful vicissitude' is an intrinsic part of Milton's vision of grace.

Critics have long noted that Adam and Eve's experience before the Fall is distinctive in Milton's poem. Unfallen experiences include lovemaking, arguing, having nightmares, oversleeping and feeling frustrated by the pressures of labour. Perhaps not surprisingly, then, Adam and Eve are also aware of time before the Fall, and even experience time as shortage or lack. Not only do Adam and Eve labour in Eden, feeling the want of 'more hands' (IV. 629) to help them with the burden of their gardening, they also 'haste'. When Raphael arrives, Adam exhorts Eve not only to 'haste' to come and see him, but to 'go with speed' (V. 313) to gather fruits for their lunch. Urgency is not unfamiliar in prelapsarian Eden, nor is the sense of the day as a space for labour, even for labour that is perceived as not quite sufficient. But it is also possible in unfallen Eden to linger, to savour time, to pray expansively and sensuously, to enjoy ease made 'more easy' by the labour it recreates. The unfallen experience of time has its 'seasons', its times for labour and for recreation. Those 'seasons' appear to unfold organically, dictated by the rhythms of the 'grateful vicissitude' of day and night. Before the Fall, it is possible to experience time through sensuous resistance. For Milton, this is summed up by the word 'delay'. To delay in Eden before the Fall is not to resist time so much as to savour it, as Adam and Eve savour the delicious fruits given to them for their enjoyment. Delay, like narrative, becomes a delicate release from time, even a form of praise or wonder.

Here, as so often, Eden and Eve are closely affiliated. Eve is marked by time in unique ways because of the promise she offers of future generation. Her beauty and innocence are heightened by her status as the fulfilment of future promise: she is hailed by Raphael as 'mother of mankind' (V. 388), a title that positions her even in prelapsarian Eden as signifying less now than she will later, after the Fall. But if on the one hand she is always ahead of herself – a sign for what is to come – Eve also savours time in ways that distinguish her from other characters. She is both ahead of and behind herself, temporally displaced. For Adam, her beauty is crowned by her 'sweet reluctant amorous delay' (IV. 311), a phrase that emphasizes *delay* both by freighting it with three distinct modifiers and by associating it with the word 'sweet', one of the signal words used to describe Eden.

Why should unfallen Eve's blazon conclude with 'delay'? This reluctance, this sense both of holding back and of hesitating, connects Eve to a rich and complex tradition of classical and Renaissance erotic poetry in which time and desire are understood to be intricately related. Such poetry, often categorized by its dominant motif of *carpe diem*, enjoyed a strong revival among English lyric poets in the middle of the seventeenth century. In the most famous of these poems, such as Robert Herrick's 'To the Virgins to Make Much of Time' or 'Corinna's Going a-Maying', or Andrew Marvell's 'To His Coy Mistress', the speaker (male) exhorts his lover (female) to seize the day, to enjoy her beauty, youth and sexuality before they fade. Though *carpe diem* poems almost always employ a rhetoric of persuasion, part of the compliment of praise they offer is structured around the woman's continued resistance. Her perfection is partly determined by her hesitation; were she to acquiesce, her enjoyment would alter her perfection as surely as would her eventual submission. Only in deferral does the lady of the *carpe diem* lyric retain her perfection.

Eve's delay is different, for the narrator assures us not only that she has already acquiesced to Adam, but also that their lovemaking has augmented rather than decreased her perfection. Eve holds a special position; she is innocent without being a virgin. Yet Eve's association with delay, with temporal withholding, continues to associate her with the virginal perfection of the lady of *carpe diem* poetry. Moreover, Eve's hesitation positions her subtly but distinctly in a different temporality from that of Adam. She comes later; her creation follows on Adam's, and she is formed both to complement Adam and to follow him. 'Heaven's last best gift' (V. 19). Eve retains the logic of the supplement: she is that which comes last. It is this temporal otherness that makes Eve hold back when Adam is ready and makes her ready when Adam holds back. Often she is associated with the sense of lateness or futurity, as when she absents herself from the dialogue with Raphael in order to resume her gardening, preferring to hear Adam relay Raphael's message to her alone, later. This quality of hesitation or temporal estrangement prompts other characters in the poem (particularly Adam and Satan) to hurry her. In Book V, when Adam finds Eve still asleep, he leans over her and urges her to awake in terms that replicate the exhortation of *carpe diem*:

> Awake
> My fairest, my espoused, my latest found,
> Heaven's last best gift, my ever new delight,
> Awake, the morning shines, and the fresh field
> Calls us, we lose the prime, to mark how spring
> Our tended plants, how blows the citron grove,
> What drops the myrrh, and what the balmy reed,
> How nature paints her colours, how the bee
> Sits on the bloom extracting liquid sweet.
>
> (V. 17–25)

Satan, too, addresses Eve in her troubling dream by urging her to awake, though his is a *carpe noctem*, a lyric that urges her to seize the night and the fruit of the forbidden tree: 'Why sleepst thou Eve? Now is the pleasant time,' Satan says 'with gentle voice' close at Eve's ear, a voice she mistakes for Adam's – perhaps in part because she knows so well its structure of exhortation (V. 36–8).

Eve's continuous withholding and hesitation are part of what renders her overly complete to Adam, and part of what makes Adam suspect himself to be slightly incapacitated in her presence. When Eve recounts her coming into being at the pool, the narrative she offers underscores the depth of her affinity with delay: it is not that she denies Adam, but rather that she defers her submission to him. Eve remembers waking to find herself 'reposed', dilating rather than eschewing slumber. She recalls laying down 'to look into the clear / Smooth lake', and the sleepy, almost narcotic attraction she feels for her own image. Her passive pursuit of the guiding voice ('what could I do, / But follow strait, invisibly thus led?') and subsequent withdrawal ('back I turned') further suggests the dreamy 'not yet' of the resistant lady of the *carpe diem* tradition (IV. 449–80).

Eve's attraction to her own image, as various critics have pointed out, is at once more complicated and more suggestive than any mere replication of the Narcissus story it overwrites. It is not merely that Eve's delay intensifies Adam's desire, but rather that desire and delay are here mutually instantiated. For Adam, desire is expressed as urgency: twice in the poem (once in this passage and once just after the Fall) he seizes Eve's hand, a verb that deepens the sense that Milton is revising the *carpe diem* tradition. For Adam, as for the male speakers of the *carpe diem* poems, seizing is associated with loss, as well as with its denial.

For Eve, by contrast, desire is expressed not as urgency, but as delay. Her hesitation opens up a space in the epic (like narrative) that confounds the linearity of time, doubling experience and making it circular rather than moving it forward. This sense is emblematized by the circular image of the pool in Eve's narrative. Eve's reflection, like her memory of it, doubles and repeats her sense of identification by slowing narrative down, elaborating and repeating rather than moving forward. The dilatory pleasure of Eve's lingering is, like so many aspects of unfallen Eden, appreciated more fully once we have witnessed its loss. After the Fall, delay becomes painful rather than pleasurable, the drawing out of sorrow rather than of joy. When Eve comes to Adam in Book XII, prepared for the expulsion and soothed by God in her dream, she announces her readiness to join him by declaring: 'In me is no delay' (line 615). Critics have rightly appreciated Eve's maturity here: like Hamlet, Eve by the end of the poem has earned the state of 'readiness' by abjuring delay. But she has earned it at a cost, for the loss of delay is a loss of a particular state of being in time, a sense of each moment as so full that only lingering can open up its pleasures.

Time and the Fall

In what ways is the experience of time altered by the Fall in Milton's epic? Like so many aspects of *Paradise Lost*, the experience of time is subtly rather than radically changed by fallenness, emphasizing the internal and psychological state of disobedience rather than its external or punitive consequences. Edward Tayler (1979) has suggested that after the Fall *kairos* is replaced by *chronos*, meaningful, sacred time replaced by time that is merely chronological. But Tayler's helpful distinction presumes a more logical kind of representation than Milton will allow. Where, given the density and complexity of Milton's temporal aesthetic, can we locate such ideas as 'before' or 'after' the Fall? I have been suggesting, however, that Milton weaves *kairos* and *chronos* together both before and after the Fall, representing a pleasure in successivity as well as a tragic meaningfulness infused into fallen time. Rather than experiencing fallen time as newly empty, Adam and Eve perceive time after the Fall as charged with new (and painful) meaning. Only after the Fall does time begin to count, in the sense of mortality; only now do 'seasons' become distinct (and fragmented) periods rather than fluctuating phases of each pleasurable day.

One consequence of the Fall for Adam and Eve's experience of temporality is that time begins to be felt as a measure in a new way. Their sense of hours as 'fruitless' at the end of Book IX suggests not only the possibility of guilt associated with time's passage but a new recognition of a new valuation of time, a sense of hours bearing or not bearing 'fruit'. This new association between time and fruitlessness suggests that time and labour have been conjoined by the Fall, and that labour, rather than nature, will now bear time's stamp.

The most subtle consequence of the Fall is the most important in terms of the experience of time. The Fall cleaves a previously continuous experience of time into 'past', 'present' and 'future'. In essence, the construction of the present depends on this rupture. The present (experienced as isolated from past and future) is a fallen temporal space. Satan's example is instructive. Satan refuses to acknowledge such a thing as 'first' – there are no origins that he can remember, or that he will allow himself to remember. His fantasy of autogenesis is a refusal of both time and memory. He does not remember coming to know what Abdiel knows. 'We know no time when we were not as now', he tells Abdiel in defiance (V. 859). Satan exists in a continual present, locked in the 'now' that first introduces him to the reader. For Satan, this 'now' determines him. Because he does not remember his own creation, he will not acknowledge it. Memory and knowledge are circular: Satan refuses to know what he cannot remember, and cannot know what he refuses to remember. His 'present' is a refusal of time. In this context, Satan's rhetorical position before the troops of fallen angels in Books I and II stigmatizes change, positing the 'mind' as the site of defiance. Satan boasts that he brings to hell 'A mind not to be changed by place or time' (I. 253). The apparent bravado of this statement is complicated by his refusal to be altered by time. At the beginning of Book IV, Satan struggles with the possibility of seeking God's forgiveness. But it is impossible for him to liberate himself from the 'now' that is his prison. Hating God, he cannot imagine not hating God. The more trapped he is by the present of his hell, the less possible it becomes for him to articulate either past or future.

The word 'present' has multiple meanings in *Paradise Lost*. When the Bard addresses the Muse in the opening proem ('thou from the first / Wast present'), he uses the word to mean 'beside, with, or in the same place as'. One cluster of meanings of the word 'present' have to do with space, and another with time. According to the *OED*, the use of the word to refer to 'the present time, the time that now is' as opposed to the past or future was an early seventeenth-century usage. (We think of the opening line of Donne's sonnet, 'What if this present were the world's last night?') In *Paradise Lost*, the word 'present' is used to refer to time in particular ways only after the Fall. Adam, first recognizing his nakedness, implores the trees to cover him. In a passage that details the emergence of shame, and the simultaneous realization that his body has parts that are 'unseemly', Adam first refers to the present as a condition:

> cover me ye pines,
> Ye cedars, with innumerable boughs
> Hide me, where I may never see them more.
> But let us now, as in bad plight, devise
> What best may for the present serve to hide
> The parts of each from other, that seem most
> To shame obnoxious, and unseemliest seen,
> (IX. 1088–94)

The use of 'now' before 'the present' signals not only that Adam has seen his own shame, made material in his naked and (now) unseemly body, but that he has emerged into a new awareness of temporality, one that has broken 'the present' off from the past that has now been lost. The enormity of this rupture is hard to fathom, given the multiple losses that the passage sustains – Adam and Eve have lost their mutual sense of each other's perfection; they have gained knowledge of death; they have first experienced shame.

The initiation into the postlapsarian present has important consequences. Only here, seeing the 'now' into which Adam is expelled, do we recognize the fluidity of unfallen temporal boundaries. Before the Fall, past, present, future were seamless, fluid, indivisible for Adam and Eve. They lived with presence, not with the isolated present cut off from the circuit of grace. When Adam and Eve are led out of Eden, the pathos of their new experience of time is encapsulated in the juxtaposition between their last attempt to delay and its new impossibility: 'In either hand the hastening Angel caught / Our lingering parents, and to the eastern gate / Led them direct, and down the cliff as fast / To the subjected plain' (XII. 637–40). 'Lingering' here is the tragic corollary of the 'delay' they have abjured. Bracketed by the angel's haste, they move as slowly as possible out of a space that will for ever after be temporalized for them ('behind'). The world that lays 'all before' Adam and Eve (XII. 646) is a world where the spatial and temporal have been flattened out into a linear plain, and where the relation between 'present' and 'presence' will have to be rediscovered.

Time and Grace

Milton's epic makes the reductive quality of time as measure a consequence of the Fall. But to conclude that the loss of time's 'fullness' is progressive and linear is to misunderstand the prominence temporality is given in the attainment of grace. God's redemption is repeatedly described as his 'day', a temporal space that will bring together *chronos* and *kairos*, plenitude and successivity. The complexity of Milton's vision in this regard is apparent even in the opening lines of the proem to Book I. Lines 1–5 establish the subject matter of the epic through a series of clauses layered one after another:

> Of man's first disobedience, and the fruit
> Of that forbidden tree, whose mortal taste
> Brought death into the world, and all our woe,
> With loss of Eden, till one greater man
> Restore us, and regain the blissful seat,
> Sing heavenly Muse,

At line five ('Restore us, and regain the blissful seat') the past tense of disobedience ('brought death') is elided into words whose tense is more elastic ('restore', 'regain'), and the capacity of the Muse to project herself backwards and forwards in time enables the reader to consolidate the tragedy of what has been lost with the glory of what will be restored. This is achieved partly by Milton's layering of tenses, and partly by his use of the present tense ('restore') to suggest a future free of time that is chronological. This tense, one that Milton often employs, elides the fallen present with the salvaged future.

When Michael comes to prepare and to console Adam and Eve in Books XI and XII, he tells them that they are to lose Paradise. Eve greets this news with an expression of unspeakable pain:

> Oh unexpected stroke, worse than of death!
> Must I thus leave thee Paradise? Thus leave
> Thee native soil, these happy walks and shades,
> Fit haunt of Gods? Where I had hope to spend,
> Quiet though sad, the respite of that day
> That must be mortal to us both.
>   (XI. 268–73)

The consolation that Michael offers is centred on space and topography. Adam and Eve must understand that God is found not only in Eden ('surmise not then / His presence to these narrow bounds confined / Of Paradise or Eden', XI. 340–2). Though they have lost their geographic 'pre-eminence' (XI. 347), even beyond the bounds of Eden they will still know God. But the sorrow of Eve's response to their displacement suggests a temporal dislocation as well. The flowers, which have been her provenance, represent to her the loss of a ritualized cycle of time:

> O flowers,
> That never will in other climate grow,
> My early visitation, and my last
> At ev'n, which I bred up with tender hand
> From the first op'ning bud, and gave ye names,
> Who now shall rear ye to the sun, or rank
> Your tribes, and water from the ambrosial fount?
> (XI. 273–9)

Michael's visions in Books XI and XII poignantly confirm Eve's understanding of the Fall as a temporal diaspora. Paradise, which would have been a centre ('from whence had spread / All generations', XI. 343–4) is closed off to them, and the future becomes a narrative that is both emotionally and intellectually impenetrable. Adam's experiences of the visions prior to the example of Noah make him experience the future as a curse: 'Oh visions ill foreseen! Better had I / Lived ignorant of future, so had borne / My part of evil only' (XI. 763–5). Adam's horror at what the future holds is redeemed, however, by the vision of Noah, the 'one just man' (XI. 818) whose perfection and justness Adam recognizes as more important than the whole world of wicked sons destroyed.

Aptly, the rainbow that stands as covenant from God is meant to remind humankind both of time and of its eventual redemption, as Michael explains at the end of Book XI:

> day and night,
> Seed-time and harvest, heat and hoary frost
> Shall hold their course, till fire purge all things new,
> Both heaven and earth, wherein the just shall dwell.
> (XI. 898–901)

Adam's greatest lesson in Books XI and XII is to understand not future events themselves, but their context in 'God's day', that moment when time as it is now known shall be redeemed. Michael makes clear to Adam that the present is always an imperfect shadow of this future, for example in the case of law:

> So law appears imperfect, and but given
> With purpose to resign them in full time
> Up to a better covenant, disciplined
> From shadowy types to truth, from flesh to spirit,
> From imposition of strict laws, to free
> Acceptance of large grace, from servile fear
> To filial, works of law to works of faith.
> (XII. 300–6)

What needs emphasis, however, is the extent to which this future-as-grace is rendered conditional. On the one hand, it is certain that after the Fall, grace in Milton's epic is a future condition. If the present is shameful and impoverished, the future is granted the possibility of perfection, of an internal paradise 'happier far' than the Paradise Adam and Eve have lost. But this grace is by no means guaranteed. Michael's description of the 'paradise within' has led some readers to argue that Milton is arguing for a 'fortunate fall'. In fact, Michael's promise is based on a challenge he sets to Adam. Having attained 'the sum / Of wisdom' (XII. 575–6), he must now

> only add
> Deeds to thy knowledge answerable, add faith,
> Add virtue, patience, temperance, add love,
> By name to come called charity, the soul
> Of all the rest: then wilt thou not be loath
> To leave this Paradise, but shalt possess
> A paradise within thee, happier far.
>   (XII. 581–7)

Michael's vision of the paradise within is posited in a temporal space ('then') which has not yet happened. Only *then*, once Adam has added to his present knowledge all of these things, will a kind of paradise be restored.

BIBLIOGRAPHY

Writings

Milton (1971a).

References for Further Reading

Benjamin (1969); Cirillo (1962, 1969); Colie (1966); Dohrn-van Rossum (1996); Fabian (1983); Fish (1967/1971); Grossman, (1987); Guibbory (1986); Kermode (1966); Le Goff (1980); Leonard (1990); Mumford (1934); Quinones (1972); Rogers (1996); Sherman, Stuart (1996); Tayler (1979); Thompson (1991).

24
Self-Contradicting Puns in *Paradise Lost*

John Leonard

A bracing sense of oppositeness enlivens much of Milton's wordplay. English is rich in words that mean the opposite of themselves, and Milton often avails himself of the energizing spark that exists within or between such words. Sometimes he plays contrary senses against each other in an antanaclasis (a figure of speech in which a word is repeated in a different meaning). A famous instance occurs when Satan entering Paradise 'At one slight bound high overleaped all bound / Of hill or highest wall' (IV. 181–2). Here the two senses of 'bound' come into a jarring collision. But there are also quieter effects, as when Raphael tells Adam that created things ascend to God 'in bounds / Proportioned to each kind' (V. 478–9). 'Bounds' again means both 'leaps' and 'limits', as Raphael's next words confirm: 'So from the root / Springs lighter the green stalk' (V. 479–80). The pun implies that Milton's universe is both hierarchical and upwardly mobile.

Puns of this kind are frequent in Milton. *Paradise Lost* affords many examples, and it will be the main focus of this chapter. But I shall begin with an illustrative instance from *Samson Agonistes*. The chorus is voicing a warning about wives:

> Seeming at first all heavenly under virgin veil,
> Soft, modest, meek, demure,
> Once joined, the contrary she proves, a thorn
> Intestine, far within defensive arms
> A cleaving mischief,
>
> (lines 1035–9)

Most editors tell us that 'cleaving' means 'clinging'. Merritt Hughes (Milton 1957) and John Carey (1997; *CSP*) detect an allusion to the poisoned shirt that Deianira sent her husband Hercules. The shirt clung fast to Hercules's flesh and killed him. 'Cleave' can mean 'cling to' (*OED* v.[2] 4), but it can also have the opposite sense 'separate by dividing' (*OED* v.[1] 2). Milton of all men knew that wives can inflict pain by leaving their husbands. The presence of 'defensive arms' even invites the violent sense: 'divide by a cutting blow' (*OED* v^1 1). Dalila has been a 'cleaving mischief' in all three senses. She has cleaved to Samson, she has cleaved from him, and she has shorn him like 'a tame wether' (line 538), a castrated ram. Milton was certainly alive to the semantic fissures in 'cleave'. In his divorce pamphlet *Tetrachordon* (1645), published three years after his first wife had left him, he wrestles with the biblical injunction that a man 'shall cleave unto his wife' (Genesis 2: 24). '*Cleav to a Wife*', he concurs, 'but let her bee a wife, let her be a meet help, a solace, not a nothing, not an adversary, not a desertrice' (*CPW* II: 605). An unhappy marriage cries out to be cloven, not clung to; but even as he pleads for divorce, Milton cleaves to wounded love. 'Cleaving mischief' is not *just* witty. The phrase captures the imagination because it declines to commit itself on the thorny question of which is worse, an intestine thorn or a desertrice. It is often difficult, with Milton's wordplay, to distinguish caustic irony from anguished sincerity. His self-contradicting puns usually evoke the sense of oppositeness that we associate with the word 'irony', but the irony seldom lapses into sarcasm, for both senses mean exactly what they say. William Empson has offered a valuable formulation of irony in *Some Versions of Pastoral*. 'An irony', he writes, 'has no point unless it is true, in some degree, in both senses' (1935: 56). This chapter will try to show how Milton's self-contradicting puns are ironic in Empson's sense.

One can imagine a deconstructive approach to this topic. One might talk, for example, of how Milton's wordplay reveals the 'trace' of Derridean *différance* and so shows language to consist of nothing but differences without positive terms. But Milton's self-contradicting puns matter because they present differences *with* positive terms and so give readers the freedom and the responsibility of choice. Deconstruction all too often deprives readers of this valuable freedom and responsibility by foreclosing interpretation with a pre-emptive 'always already'. The term 'always already' has of late become a shibboleth in literary criticism. Critics place faith in it because they think that it opens texts up, but in practice it usually closes them down. At the end of this essay I shall argue that 'always already' does special violence to Milton, for he, more than any other poet, challenges us to throw off the shackles of peremptory pre-emption with an emancipating 'not yet'.

Let us turn, then, to *Paradise Lost*. The War in Heaven – a civil war – causes many words to cleave asunder. Here is Raphael on the novelty of hate in heaven:

> strange to us it seemed
> At first, that angel should with angel war,
> And in fierce hosting meet, who wont to meet
> So oft in festivals of joy and love
> Unanimous,
>
> (VI. 91–5)

'Fierce hosting' is a tautology for the fallen reader, but an oxymoron for Raphael. We readily hear the military sense 'hostile encounter' (*OED* 'hosting'), but this sense is 'strange' to Raphael, for whom the verb 'host' has hitherto meant 'entertain as a guest' (*OED* v² 1a) or 'be a guest' (*OED* v² 2). 'Hosting', for Raphael, implies 'festivals of joy and love', and he hankers after the old meaning even as he steels himself to the new one. There is nothing trivial about this pun, which is based on a real etymological connection. *Hostis* in Latin can mean either 'enemy' or 'stranger'. *Hospes* (the root of 'hospitality') means 'he who entertains a stranger'.

Hospitality is a recurrent theme in *Paradise Lost*, where it inspires some of Milton's richest – and most perplexing – wordplay. One soliloquy is so divided against itself that critics are divided against each other as to its meaning. Satan, seeing Adam and Eve for the first time, is moved to offer them everything he has:

> league with you I seek,
> And mutual amity so strait, so close,
> That I with you must dwell, or you with me
> Henceforth; my dwelling haply may not please
> Like this fair Paradise, your sense, yet such
> Accept your maker's work; he gave it me,
> Which I as freely give; hell shall unfold,
> To entertain you two, her widest gates,
> And send forth all her kings;
>
> (IV. 375–83)

Most critics see only sarcasm here, but William Empson in *Some Versions of Pastoral* (and again in his later works on Milton) has famously argued that 'Satan might mean it as a real offer.' Satan 'need not know' that human beings are incapable of living comfortably in hell, so 'the irony is that of Milton's appalling God' (1935: 168). Clearly, the question of Satan's intentions is central to our ethical appraisal of him at this moment. One way of approaching the problem is to examine the wordplay in these lines, and to ask whether it indicates gloating malice or real generosity.

Here we encounter a surprise. One might suppose that it would be Empson who would tease benevolent meanings out of Satan's words. It is Empson who wants Satan to be benign. Empson does find 'ruined generosity' in the last three lines. He claims that Milton 'does not use *all*, his key word, for any but a wholesale and unquestioned emotion' (169). But this is not a compelling argument for Satan's generosity. Sceptical readers might doubt (as many have doubted) whether 'all' really is Milton's 'key word'. Even if we allow it to be that, we might still object that 'send forth all her kings' indicates 'wholesale and unquestioned' malice. Empson would be hard pressed to refute the objection, for he himself has just conceded that malice is the dominant feeling in the immediately preceding lines:

The cuddling movement of *mutual amity*, with the flat mouth of the worm, in *am-*, opening to feed on them, the insinuating hiss of *so streight, so close*, full of the delicious softness of the tormentor, belong to the Satan who will have his guests tortured by

incongruous Furies (ii. 596); so the voices whispered to Bunyan, and he thought his
bowels would burst within him. (168)

This is pertinent, but it does not help Empson's claim (made just three sentences
earlier) that 'Satan might mean it as a real offer.' Empson's argument for Satan's
generosity has turned into the opposite of itself and become an argument for Satan's
cruelty.

But orthodox critics should not smile too soon. If Empson finds himself producing
evidence for the adverse party, so too does Empson's mighty opposite, Alastair Fowler.
Fowler has published two editions of *Paradise Lost*, one in 1968 and one in 1998. Both
contain a long note on Satan's soliloquy and Empson's reading of it. Fowler insists on
Satan's wickedness, and cites Empson only to refute him. But even as he does so, he
unearths some benign meanings that threaten to corroborate Empson's case. We are
faced then with something of a riddle. Empson and Fowler read the soliloquy in
diametrically opposed ways, yet each cites evidence that helps the other. Empson
concedes that 'so strait, so close' is spoken with the torturer's 'insinuating hiss';
Fowler, glossing those same words, ruefully admits that they can bear a benevolent
meaning. I cite his 1968 edition:

> *strait*] intimate (*OED* 14); but also with the sinister overtone 'involving privation' (*OED*
> 6b). The *Ed I* and *Ed II* spelling 'streight' allows a play with *straight* = honest; but this
> must be considered very secondary in view of the continuation *so close*. (635)

There is a touch of nervousness in those 'but's. It is to Fowler's credit (and characteristic of his own honesty as a critic) that he should admit meanings that militate
against his view of Satan. But even as he admits them he hedges them with the sober
warning that they 'must be considered very secondary'. Fowler's first definition repays
closer scrutiny, for the one word 'intimate' does not quite do justice to this now
obsolete sense. The full entry for *OED* 'strait' 14 reads: 'Of friendship, alliance, etc.:
Close, intimate.' Some instances, with dates: 'streicte amitie' (1561), 'streight friend-
shippe' (1568), 'a most neer and strait union among the faithful' (1617), and 'strait
alliance and confederacy' (1647). 'Strait' can convey real, open-hearted warmth, so
Empson might have conceded too much when he gave the word over to 'the
tormentor'. 'Close' is also hospitable to benevolence. The *OED* cites the phrase
'close friends' from as early as 1577 under the definition 'closely attached, intimate'
(*OED* 'close' 17). *Pace* Fowler, a play on 'straight' meaning 'honest' need not be
suppressed 'in view of the continuation *so close*'. 'Strait' and 'close' can both be taken
straight.

But it would be foolish to deny that devilish cruelty also stakes a claim to these
words. Fowler draws attention to one sinister meaning when he informs us that 'strait'
could have the now obsolete sense 'involving privation' (*OED* 6. b). Another ominous
(and obsolete) meaning is 'affording little room, narrow' (*OED* 2). This sense was
often applied to prisons (*OED* 2. b), as when Sir Walter Ralegh speaks of captives

confined 'in streight places, loden with yrons'. Together with 'close', this operation of 'strait' hints that hell's human inhabitants will be kept in close confinement, even though Satan at once goes on to promise that 'there will be room' (IV. 383). As Roy Flannagan (Milton 1998b) notes, 'while he seems to be offering them more room, he is really replacing the openness of Paradise with the claustrophobia of Hell.' Another relevant sense of 'strait', now obsolete, but common in the sixteenth and seventeenth centuries, when it was used of 'sufferings, punishment', is 'pressing hardly, severe, rigorous' (*OED* 6. a). Spenser uses 'strait' in this sense when he tells how Radigund bound Artegall with 'hard bands / Of strong compulsion, and streight violence' (*Faerie Queene* V. v. 33). Both 'strait' and 'close' also convey the idea of ungenerous giving: 'close, stingy' (*OED* 'strait' 15. a), 'close-fisted, stingy' (*OED* 'close' 8). The hint of grudgeful giving is all the more effective for coming right after a phrase that suggests the opposite idea. 'Mutual amity' ought to involve reciprocal beneficence, but on Satan's lips 'mutual amity, so strait, so close' claws back what it gives. The idea of generous giving nevertheless re-asserts itself just two lines later when Satan boasts of his bounty:

> my dwelling haply may not please
> Like this fair Paradise, your sense, yet such
> Accept your maker's work; he gave it me,
> Which I as freely give;
>
> (IV. 378–81)

Editors have long recognized that this is a blasphemous echo of Matthew 10: 8 ('freely ye have received, freely give'). The travesty becomes all the more pointed if the distinction between Satanic munificence and miserliness is collapsed. There is more wordplay in 'haply may not please' and 'sense'. 'Haply' means 'perhaps', but the proximity of 'please' invites a play on 'happily' to suggest our lost joy and Satan's gloating glee. 'Sense' glances at Adam and Eve's physical 'liability to feel pain' (*OED* 5).

   For many readers, the sheer abundance of malevolent meanings will tell decisively against Empson's generous argument for Satan's generosity. It must be admitted that malevolence usually predominates when cruel and kind meanings compete for the same semantic space. Cruelty is often crueller for being couched in kind words; kindness is seldom kinder for being couched in cruel ones. But we cheapen Satan's soliloquy if we follow the example of most critics and write it off with the blunt word 'sarcasm'. The soliloquy is ironic, not sarcastic, and the irony has point because it is 'true, in some degree, in both senses'. Satan's speech traces and enacts a real struggle of conflicting emotions. Empson rightly acknowledges this flow of feeling, but he makes it flow in the wrong direction. He thinks that the tormentor's 'insinuating hiss' gradually gives way to 'generosity'. But it is at the beginning, not the end, of his soliloquy that Satan delivers his great tribute to humankind:

> Creatures of other mould, earth-born perhaps,
> Not spirits, yet to heavenly spirits bright

> Little inferior; whom my thoughts pursue
> With wonder, and could love, so lively shines
> In them divine resemblance, and such grace
> The hand that formed them on their shape hath poured.
>
> (IV. 360–6)

'Little inferior' echoes Psalms 8: 5 and Hebrews 2: 7 on man's excellence: 'thou hast made him a little lower than the angels, and hast crowned him with glory and honour.' This biblical allusion, unlike that to Matthew 10: 8 a few lines later, is not a travesty. For once Satan *is* willing to give. As his heart opens, so does his vocabulary. Satan's word 'pursue' at first seems to be consonant with his mission. His whole reason for being in Paradise is 'to follow with hostility or enmity; to seek to injure' (*OED* 'pursue' 1). But now, as he catches his first sight of his intended victims, his thoughts 'pursue / With wonder, and could love' (lines 362–3). 'Pursue' is disarmed of its enmity. Love is still a possibility thirteen lines later in 'so strait, so close', but Satan's finer feelings are progressively straitened and closed as the soliloquy continues.

Empson speaks of the 'grandeur' of Satan's climactic offer, and this feeling is there. But it is strangled by strait-heartedness: 'hell shall unfold, / To entertain you two, her widest gates, / And send forth all her kings' (IV. 381–3). Empson claims that 'all' is the 'key word' in these lines, but the word that really matters is 'entertain'. It is 'entertain' that brings together and resolves the bracing contradictions that have animated the entire speech. 'Entertain' does have a positive side. It can mean 'receive', 'show hospitality to' (*OED* 12, 13), as in the apotheosis of Lycidas:

> There entertain him all the saints above,
> In solemn troops, and sweet societies
> That sing, and singing in their glory move,
> And wipe the tears for ever from his eyes.
>
> (lines 178–81)

Satan's 'entertain' plays on this sense, but his primary meaning is 'admit and contain' (*OED* 11). Satan means exactly what he says when he promises that the *gates* will entertain Adam and Eve. He is making an etymological pun on Latin *intertenere*, 'to hold among' or 'hold between'. It is easy to get *in* through hell's gates. It is not so easy to get out.

Satan's 'entertain' is darkly ominous even if we ignore its etymology. In modern English 'entertain' always implies some kind of pleasant diversion, but this was not the case when Milton wrote. Several instances cited under the neutral sense 'treat in a (specified) manner' (*OED* 8) describe acts of cruelty. We hear of one person being 'entertained with all variety of persecution' (1608–11) and another being 'disgracefully entertained by Sir Amias Powlet, who clapt him in the stocks' (1630). 'Entertain' was also a military term used of hostile engagements on the battlefield (*OED* 9. c). Satan plays on this sense during the revolt in heaven, when he invites his followers 'to prepare / Fit entertainment to receive our king / The great Messiah' (V. 689–91). Later, when the devils fire their artillery, he puns more openly and aggressively:

> O friends, why come not on these victors proud?
> Erewhile they fierce were coming, and when we,
> To entertain them fair with open front
> And breast, (what could we more?) propounded terms
> Of composition, straight they changed their minds,
> Flew off, and into strange vagáries fell,
> As they would dance, yet for a dance they seemed
> Somewhat extravagant and wild, perhaps
> For joy of offered peace:
>
> (VI. 609–17)

This is both like and not like Raphael's 'fierce hosting'. Both puns involve an igniting collision between generosity and aggression, but the attitudes of the two speakers could not be more different. Raphael laments lost friendship; Satan relishes his new pugnacity.

Critics have often deplored the poor quality of the devils' puns on the battlefield. The crudity and obviousness of these puns can nevertheless be defended. Dramatically, the coarse sarcasm of the jests is there to express the coarse jubilation of the devils. We should also remember that the puns are not at first obvious to the loyal angels, for whom the invention of artillery comes as a surprise. The devils' puns are appropriate to their context, even though they are not among Milton's wittiest endeavours. ('Peace' in the lines just quoted probably includes a bad pun on 'piece of ordnance'). Most of the devils' puns are crude, but there are some instances of finer wit. One excellent (and unjustly neglected) pun occurs in the second half of the line we have just been considering: 'To entertain them fair with open front'. Editors rightly inform us that 'open front' means both 'candid face' and 'divided front rank'. But there is more to it than that. Satan does not just play innocent candour against guilty deceit. He also plays one kind of candour against another. 'With open front' recalls the now obsolete phrase 'with open face', meaning 'brazenly' (*OED* 'open' 5. b). This locution was commonly used of those who brazenly defied God. An *OED* instance from 1650–3 refers to 'Men . . . who . . . did . . . with open face, as they say, vent Blasphemies and Impieties'. This defiant sense is exactly right for Satan, who is too proud merely to hide his hostility. He prefers to flaunt it, gleefully, comically, with open face, in the good angels' faces, knowing that they will not understand him.

This gleeful flaunting of a malevolence that is at once open and hidden is an important part of Milton's conception of Satan. Satan delights to mock the good angels with ambiguity – especially when they ask stupid questions. At the end of Book IV Gabriel asks Satan to explain why he is violating Eve's sleep in Paradise when he should be burning in hell. Satan's sardonic reply seems to give nothing

away. But on closer inspection it is all the more contemptuous for giving everything
away:

> Gabriel, thou hadst in heaven the esteem of wise,
> And such I held thee; but this question asked
> Puts me in doubt. Lives there who loves his pain?
> Who would not, finding way, break loose from hell,
> Though thither doomed? Thou wouldst thyself, no doubt,
> And boldly venture to whatever place
> Farthest from pain, where thou mightst hope to change
> Torment with ease, and soonest recompense
> Dole with delight, which in this place I sought;
> To thee no reason; who knowst only good,
> But evil hast not tried:
>
> (IV. 886–96)

Satan is not lying. He really has come to Paradise to 'recompense / Dole with delight'.
Gabriel hears only the innocent meaning 'replace sorrow with joy', but Satan's darker,
truer meaning is 'delightfully deal out death'. 'Recompense' includes 'mete out in
requital' (*OED* 3), while 'dole' includes 'dealing out of gifts' (*OED* sb.[1] 5), especially
the 'dealing of death' (*OED* sb.[1] 5. b). 'Recompense to no man evil for evil' says St
Paul (Romans 12: 17). Satan deals death to all humankind in requital for his
sufferings. He recompenses dole 'with delight', because that is what he delights to
do. Lest this be thought too ingenious, let me briefly recall some other places where
Milton makes play with 'dole' and 'recompense'. In *Samson Agonistes* the chorus speak
of Samson 'dealing dole among his foes' (line 1529). In *Paradise Lost* 'recompense' is
corrupted at the moment of Adam's Fall:

> she embraced him, and for joy
> Tenderly wept, much won that he his love
> Had so ennobled, as of choice to incur
> Divine displeasure for her sake, or death.
> In recompense (for such compliance bad
> Such recompense best merits) from the bough
> She gave him of that fair enticing fruit
> With liberal hand:
>
> (IX. 990–7)

Christopher Ricks in *Milton's Grand Style* notes that 'recompense' is here 'darkened
and infected' before our eyes (1963: 116). The first 'recompense' means 'compensation
for some loss or injury' (*OED* 2). Eve gives Adam the apple 'in recompense'
because she is grateful that he has chosen to share her fate. But when 'recompense'
reappears in the next line it has the more ominous sense: 'retribution for an offence'
(*OED* 5). Sin brings its own harsh recompense, as an embittered Adam will soon

discover: 'Is this the love, is this the recompense / Of mine to thee, ingrateful Eve?' (IX. 1163).

Satan is a master of sardonic wordplay, but not all of the verbal wit in *Paradise Lost* is on his side. Milton often mocks Satan by aggressively withholding the desirable meaning of a self-contradicting word. 'Success' repeatedly frustrates Satan. Modern readers are accustomed to hear only the positive sense 'prosperous achievement', but throughout the seventeenth century that meaning existed side by side with the older sense 'result', which might be used of any outcome, 'favourable or otherwise' (*OED* 1). Milton often punctures Satan's pretensions by playing the two senses against each other. A memorable instance occurs in the opening lines of Book II. I quote the whole sentence to capture its bathos:

> High on a throne of royal state, which far
> Outshone the wealth of Ormus and of Ind,
> Or where the gorgeous East with richest hand
> Showers on her kings barbaric pearl and gold,
> Satan exalted sat, by merit raised
> To that bad eminence; and from despair
> Thus high uplifted beyond hope, aspires
> Beyond thus high, insatiate to pursue
> Vain war with heaven, and by success untaught
> His proud imaginations thus displayed.
>
> (II. 1–10)

Irony enters with 'merit', which could mean 'desert of either good or evil' (*OED* 2). Satan thinks that he deserves good, but 'bad eminence' suggests otherwise. 'High uplifted beyond hope' strives to mean 'lifted higher than he had hoped' but cannot quite escape the alternative construction: 'lifted high, but in a place so low as to be beyond all reach of hope'. After this, 'success' must mean 'ill success', 'failure'. But the positive sense is not just absent. Milton aggressively withholds it – dangles it, as it were, under Satan's nose. Satan is 'by success untaught' because he has learned nothing from defeat, and because he has had no victory from which to learn. The twist of the knife is 'imaginations', which here means 'schemes, plots' (*OED* 2. a), but also hints at Satan's proud delusions.

Satan's greatest delusion is that he can thwart God:

> If then his providence
> Out of our evil seek to bring forth good,
> Our labour must be to pervert that end,
> And out of good still to find means of evil;
> Which oft-times may succeed, so as perhaps
> Shall grieve him, if I fail not, and disturb
> His inmost counsels from their destined aim.
>
> (I. 162–8)

Here 'succeed' has the neutral sense 'ensue' (with 'evil' as subject). 'If I fail not' means 'unless I am mistaken' (*OED* 'fail' 11). But the sequence 'succeed . . . fail' awakens the modern meanings of both words to suggest that Satan's successes will turn to failure. When he speaks of God's 'destined aim', Satan uses 'destined' in the weak sense 'intended' (*OED* 2). He claims that he can circumvent God's will, but the strong sense 'appointed by a divine decree' (*OED* 1) gives him the lie. Satan's grasp on 'success' proves slippery even when he faces a lesser opponent. When, in the War in Heaven, the good angel Abdiel challenges him to single combat, Satan accepts the challenge with confident contempt:

> well thou com'st
> Before thy fellows, ambitious to win
> From me some plume, that thy success may show
> Destruction to the rest:
>
> (VI. 159–62)

'Thy success' means 'thy failure'. Satan is using 'success' in the old sense 'fortune (good or bad)' (*OED* 2), and he takes it as given that Abdiel will meet with *ill* success. Abdiel's inevitable defeat will then 'show / Destruction to the rest' of the *good* angels. But Milton's voice behind Satan hints that Abdiel will enjoy more success than Satan has bargained for.

Fowler finds another suggestive pun when Satan claims that God created us to spite the devils. According to Satan, God

> to spite us more,
> Determined to advance into our room
> A creature formed of earth, and him endow,
> Exalted from so base original,
> With heavenly spoils, our spoils:
>
> (IX. 147–51)

By 'spoils' Satan simply means 'spoils of war'. But the word might have a secondary meaning unintended by Satan. Fowler in 1968 notes that Satan 'unwittingly . . . prophesies . . . the exaltation of human nature through the Incarnation and Christ's second victory over Satan, in which human nature was very often referred to as "spoil" ("the armour or body of the slain": *OED* II. 5).' Some might think this far-fetched, but Fowler pertinently cites the Son's prophecy of the Resurrection, in which 'spoil' clearly does refer to exalted human nature: 'I shall rise victorious, and subdue / My vanquisher, spoiled of his vaunted spoil' (III. 250–1). Fowler's pun is also made plausible by the verb 'exalt' ('Exalted from so base original'), which Milton uses elsewhere of the Incarnation, as when God tells the Son: 'thy humiliation shall exalt / With thee thy manhood also to this throne' (III. 313–14). The mud-man Adam will be more 'Exalted' even than Satan imagines.

There might be more to 'spoils' than this, for the word can imply Satan's degradation as well as man's exaltation. 'Spoil' could mean 'the skin of a snake' (*OED* 6. a). Satan speaks of 'spoils, our spoils' (IX. 151) just a few lines before he enters the serpent – an act that he explicitly describes as an Incarnation:

> Oh foul descent! That I who erst contended
> With gods to sit the highest, am now constrained
> Into a beast, and mixed with bestial slime,
> This essence to incarnate and imbrute,
> That to the height of deity aspired;
>
> (IX. 163–7)

The contrast with man could not be more complete. Christ's Incarnation elevates human 'spoil' to God's throne; Satan's Incarnation constrains his angelic essence into a serpent's spoil. Ricks has shown that the pun on 'incarnate' caught the eye of Milton's earliest editors. As early as 1695, Patrick Hume remarked: 'as *our blessed Saviour's* taking our Nature upon him, is styled, *His Incarnation*'. A pun on 'spoil' would work very well with the pun on 'incarnate'. In both cases, the wordplay is richer for being muted. As Ricks notes of 'incarnate', 'it is the silence of the context which makes the word effective – any nudge from the poet would have been fatal to the Grand Style' (1963: 73). So with 'spoils'. As Satan speaks of 'heavenly spoils', he thinks only of humanity's present gain and his present loss. But the future gains and losses will be greater even than he imagines.

Imaginative precision with words is a characteristic feature of Milton's satire. We need to be especially vigilant with words that have narrowed in meaning between Milton's time and our own. Such words can sound discordant or incongruous to the modern reader, and for that reason they warrant a closer look. Consider the following lines from the description of the Paradise of Fools. The satire is aimed at those who take monastic vows on their deathbeds ('Dying put on the weeds of Dominic', III. 479) so as to gain surreptitious entrance into heaven. At first the trick seems to work. The impostors 'pass disguised' (480) through the planets and fixed stars,

> And now Saint Peter at heaven's wicket seems
> To wait them with his keys, and now at foot
> Of heaven's ascent they lift their feet, when lo
> A violent cross wind from either coast
> Blows them transverse ten thousand leagues awry
> Into the devious air;
>
> (III. 484–8)

'Wicket' is an odd word to use of heaven's gate. We might have expected a grander word, and Milton fulfils our expectations just twenty lines later when he describes 'a kingly palace gate / With frontispiece of diamond and gold' (III. 505–6). So why call it a 'wicket'? Fowler in both of his editions conjectures that Milton chose a 'low word' so as to ridicule 'the Romanist doctrine' that St Peter controls heaven's keys. This is plausible, but we should not assume that 'heaven's wicket' is identical with the 'kingly palace gate'. A 'wicket' is 'a small door or gate made in, or placed beside, a large one, for ingress and egress when the large one is closed' (*OED* 1). This sense works beautifully with Milton's satirical purpose. Heaven's gate is closed to religious hypocrites. But no matter – a wicket is open, and St Peter stands at it, jangling his keys. The monks had always planned to creep in, as we would say, 'through the back door'. Now it seems that they can stride boldly in through the front door, even though it is locked fast in their faces. They eagerly press forward – only to be blown into 'the devious air'. 'Devious' means 'off the main road' (*OED* 1), but also hints at the unscrupulousness and insincerity of those who seek to enter heaven by devious means.

Devious intrusion is a recurrent theme in Milton's anti-ecclesiastical satire. Describing Satan's leap over the walls of Paradise, Milton writes: 'So clomb this first grand thief into God's fold: / So since into his church lewd hirelings climb' (IV. 192–3). 'Lewd' here means 'ignorant', 'worthless' (*OED* 4, 5), but also glances at the original sense 'not in holy orders' (*OED* 1). The pun implies that a stipendiary clergy is no clergy. Milton plays on the same etymology when Abdiel confronts Satan on the battlefield. Answering Satan, who has just dismissed the good angels as 'Ministering spirits' (VI. 167), Abdiel says:

> This is servitude,
> To serve the unwise, or him who hath rebelled
> Against his worthier, as thine now serve thee,
> Thyself not free, but to thyself enthralled;
> Yet lewdly dar'st our ministering upbraid.
>
> (VI. 178–82)

'Lewdly' means 'wickedly' (*OED* 2) and 'ministering' means 'serving', but together the two words imply a division between those who humbly serve as God's ministers (*OED* 'minister' v. 9) and those who 'lewdly' place themselves outside his church. 'Lewd hirelings', who minister only to themselves, climb 'into' the church, but are never truly in it.

Milton was a man of earnest political convictions, unafraid to risk his life for the English Commonwealth. He was lucky to escape a traitor's death when the monarchy was restored in 1660. Censorship then made it impossible for him to publish any overt criticism of the Stuart kings; but he does include some covert satire in *Paradise Lost*, and self-contradicting puns play a significant part in it. This is how he describes the meeting of naked Adam and the angel Raphael:

> Meanwhile our primitive great sire, to meet
> His godlike guest, walks forth, without more train
> Accompanied than with his own complete

> Perfections, in himself was all his state,
> More solemn than the tedious pomp that waits
> On princes, when their rich retínue long
> Of horses led, and grooms besmeared with gold
> Dazzles the crowd, and sets them all agape.
>
> (V. 350–7)

Nakedness always threatens to explode princely pretensions – which is why satirists delight to bring it and royalty together. Milton takes full advantage of the subversive possibilities offered by Adam's unclad body, but his satire is the sharper for not stripping the emperors of their new clothes. Milton's royal exhibitionists shame themselves by flashing real cloth of gold. It is naked Adam who is truly 'solemn' ('grand, imposing'). Milton drives the point home with a lovely pun on 'state' ('in himself was all his state'). Applied to 'princes', 'state' means 'costly and imposing display' (*OED* 17. a). Kings were said to be in 'state' when they paraded 'with great pomp and solemnity; with a great train; with splendid or honorific trappings' (*OED* 17. c). Charles II had paraded in this way when he made his triumphant entry into London on 29 May 1660. Three hundred cavalry dressed in cloth of silver led the way, followed by the City Marshal with liveried heralds and trumpeters, and the sheriffs, aldermen and Lord Mayor in scarlet robes. Then came the King on a white horse. More regiments stretched behind as far as the eye could see. Even a royalist would have to admit that Charles's retinue was 'tedious' in one narrow sense. It was 'long (in time or extent)' (*OED* 'tedious' 1. b). Stands for spectators had been erected all along the procession route, and people watched from every window. The streets were hung with tapestries. Fountains ran claret. The dazzled crowd was 'all agape'. The roar of cannons and the cries of 'God save the King' were deafening. Milton would have heard the noise in his hiding place in Bartholomew Close. How typical of this poet to mock it all with one naked man. But he does not equate nakedness with shame. Adam humbles the royals because he is more magnificent in his naked majesty than they in their pomp. Adam's 'state' is all the more regal for not having the regal sense. Adam's 'state', the state he carries 'in himself', is his 'bodily form' (*OED* 9. a). Latin *status* means 'way of holding one's body', 'height, stature' (Lewis and Short, *status* A, C). Adam also has 'dignity of demeanour or presence . . . stateliness of bearing' (*OED* 18. a). This is a state that Milton scorns to change with kings.

This play on 'state' might best be described as an 'anti-pun' rather than a 'pun', since the monarchical sense is pointedly excluded rather than admitted. I borrow the term 'anti-pun' from Christopher Ricks, who coined it in an essay on Housman, first published in 1964. Ricks uses Milton to illustrate the term:

[Housman] was fond of that particular kind of pun or anti-pun which creates its double meaning by invoking but excluding. When Milton described something in Paradise as 'wanton', his meaning did not just forget about the fallen sense of the word; it invoked it but excluded it, so that Eve's hair was 'wanton (not *wanton*)'. (1984: 174)

Ricks had described the same kind of effect in *Milton's Grand Style*, where he finds ominous overtones in the rivers that move with 'serpent error' (VII. 302). 'Serpent' and 'error' both mean 'wandering' ('serpent', from Latin *serpere*, is a present participle), but 'rather than the meaning being simply "wandering", it is "wandering (not error)"'. The 'evil meaning', Ricks writes, 'is consciously and ominously excluded' (1963: 110). Ricks gives an ampler definition of the 'anti-pun' in an essay on Lowell first published in *The Force of Poetry*:

> whereas in a pun there are two senses which either get along or quarrel, in an anti-pun there is only one sense admitted but there is another sense denied admission. So the response is not 'this means *x*' (with the possibility even of its meaning *y* being no part of your response), but 'this-means-*x*-and-doesn't-mean-*y*', all hyphenated. (Ricks 1984: 266)

In Ricks's terms, Adam's 'state' means 'bodily form (not pomp)' or 'state (not *state*)'.

One can find 'anti-puns' throughout Milton's poetry. The earliest instance is this from 'On the Morning of Christ's Nativity' (1629). The stars, witnessing Christ's birth,

> Stand fixed in steadfast gaze,
>   Bending one way their precious influence,
> And will not take their flight,
> For all the morning light,
>   Or Lucifer that often warned them thence;
> But in their glimmering orbs did glow,
> Until their Lord himself bespake, and bid them go.
>
>   (lines 70–6)

Lucifer the morning-star is simply doing his duty when he ushers the other stars away from Christ. But 'Lucifer' was also a name for Satan, whose dragon tail 'drew the third part of the stars of heaven' (Revelation 12: 4). As Cleanth Brooks and John Hardy note, the statement that Lucifer often warned them thence 'reminds us of the other Lucifer's desire, sprung from another motive, that stars and men pay as little attention to the great event as possible' (1951b: 98). In Ricks's terms, 'Lucifer' evokes the response 'Lucifer (not *Lucifer*)'.

The Miltonic anti-pun is a variety of prolepsis – the type of anachronism which treats future events as past. Milton's prolepses usually anticipate the Fall. The difficulty comes when we try to describe how they anticipate it. Here critics disagree. For Ricks, Milton's anti-puns evoke the Fall in order to exclude it. For J. Hillis Miller, a tireless advocate of deconstruction, Milton's prolepses collapse the distinction between fallen and unfallen language. Both critics attend to the phrase 'wanton ringlets' (IV. 306), used to describe innocent Eve's hair. For Ricks, 'wanton' evokes the bad sense but shuts it out with a poignant 'not yet'. For Miller, there can be no poignancy, no shutting out, no 'not yet', for the Fall is always already. 'Eve's disheveled wantonness', he writes, 'means that she has in effect already fallen . . . whatever Milton may say' (1991: 294). Miller thinks that Eve lapses into the louche and the lax, but there is a touch of laxity in his own prose – in that flaccid 'in effect' and that rough and ready 'already'. It is evasive to say that Eve is 'in effect' fallen, for 'in effect' might mean nothing more than 'virtually' (*OED* 'effect' 8). Miller's 'already' is both too strong and too weak. It is full of peremptory pre-emption, but it is also weakly acquiescent, surrendering everything on Eve's behalf even as it prevents all reply: 'she has in effect already fallen . . . whatever Milton may say'. It is hard to imagine a criticism more closed and foreclosing than this, and yet deconstruction claims to open eyes and texts. Surprisingly, the claim has found favour with feminists. In their preface to *Re-Membering Milton*, Mary Nyquist and Margaret W. Ferguson praise Miller for 'liberating' Eve from Milton's 'oppressive system of belief' (1987/1988: xiv). But it is Ricks, not Miller, who offers an escape from the stern moral sense of 'wanton'. Ricks allows Eve to be 'wanton' in the innocent sense 'sportive, free, unrestrained' (*OED* 3c). Miller, hearing only the dour sense, dourly rules out any other. Whatever deconstructionists may say, this is not liberating. Miller *claims* to free texts from univocal meanings, but all he really does is turn 'wanton' into a prison – for Eve, for Milton, and for the reader.

The advantage of Ricks's formulation of the anti-pun is that it combines vigilant attention to detail with a truly liberating openness. It is the deconstructionist's 'already' (and its ubiquitous variant 'always already') that shuts things down. The opening lines of Book IX will illustrate the point:

> No more of talk where God or angel guest
> With man, as with his friend, familiar used
> To sit indulgent, and with him partake
> Rural repast, permitting him the while
> Venial discourse unblamed: I now must change
> Those notes to tragic;
>
> (IX. 1–6)

'Venial' is disquieting, even alarming, for it implies that sin (albeit venial sin) has infected Adam even before the Fall. Are we to infer that Adam was always already fallen? Flannagan (Milton 1998b) tries to sweep the problem aside: 'both "venial" ("forgivable") and "unblam'd" emphasize the sinlessness of the encounter between Raphael and Adam and Eve.' But this is vulnerable to an easy rejoinder. If 'venial' means 'forgivable', we still face the difficulty that unfallen Adam needs to be forgiven for something. Fowler (1968 and 1998) tries to get around the problem in another way. He claims that 'venial' has the rare sense 'permissible; blameless' (*OED* 3). This sounds promising, and in a moment I shall argue that it is right. But Orgel and Goldberg (Milton 1991) are unconvinced: '*Venial*. Pardonable (not "permissible" or "blameless", as the *OED* claims [*s.v.* 3], in which case "unblamed" would make no sense): the implication is that Adam is at fault (e.g. for his inquisitiveness about astronomy), but not seriously.'

The problem with this is that it declines to take either the Fall or Milton's words seriously. To say that Adam is 'at fault...but not seriously' merely evades the question of whether one can be a sinless sinner. Like Miller's 'in effect', Orgel and Goldberg's 'but not seriously' is a smudge. It declines the responsibility of choice where Milton requires us to choose. My own view is that 'venial' is an anti-pun, and that the response evoked is 'blameless (not sinful, not even venially so)'. Orgel and Goldberg think that 'unblamed' precludes this reading, and they would be right if 'unblamed' meant 'uncensured for an existing fault'. But 'unblamed' need not mean this. Milton was fond of a Latin idiom in which past participles with a negative prefix signify the strongest possible negation. Latin *invictus* means 'unconquerable, invincible'. When unfallen Eve gazes at Adam with 'eyes / Of conjugal attraction unreproved' (IV. 492–3), 'unreproved' is not a hint that Eve deserves the reproach she does not get. 'Unreproved' means 'irreproachable'. Other instances of this idiom in Milton include 'Teneriff or Atlas unremoved' (IV. 987), 'wise Minerva...unconquered virgin' and 'the uncontrolled worth / Of this pure cause' (*A Masque* 448, 792–3). The past participles respectively mean 'irremovable', 'invincible' and 'indisputable'. Milton was drawn to the idiom when celebrating pure causes, and 'Venial discourse unblamed' is one. 'Venial' and 'unblamed' are both anti-puns, and together they tell us that Adam's discourse is permissible and irreproachable. 'Venial' also plays on Latin *venialis*, 'gracious', to imply that Raphael has been sent by heaven's grace and that the conversation has been conducted on both sides with social graces ('Nor are thy lips ungraceful, sire of men', VIII. 218). I do not deny that 'venial' is ominous. But the ominousness is more, not less, potent for being fended off with a vigilant 'not yet' rather than invited in with a nodding 'always already'. 'Venial discourse unblamed' is what Stanley Fish (the Fish of *Surprised by Sin*, the Fish whose own 'always already' was mercifully not yet) might call 'a trap' for the fallen reader, who finds his or her own sin in it.

I do not mean to imply that Milton's anti-puns always privilege innocence over guilt. Sometimes it is the fallen sense that prevails. This happens with increasing frequency after the Fall. In the last two books of *Paradise Lost* especially, Milton often evokes happy senses only to exclude them:

> To whom thus Michael. Doubt not but that sin
> Will reign among them, as of thee begot;
> And therefore was law given them to evince
> Their natural pravity, by stirring up
> Sin against law to fight;
>
> (XII. 285–9)

Orgel and Goldberg (Milton 1991) think that 'evince' here means 'overcome' (*OED* 1) as well as 'make evident' (*OED* 5). But Michael's whole point is that the Law *cannot* overcome sin. 'Overcome' offers itself as a momentary possibility, but this sense cannot survive line 290, which expressly states that 'Law can discover sin, but not remove.' The scriptural source of the idea is Romans 3: 20: 'by the deeds of the law there shall no flesh be justified in his sight: for by the law is the knowledge of sin.' Michael aggressively limits 'evince' to the stern, reproving sense 'make evident' (*OED* 5). But the optimistic sense is not just absent or irrelevant. In Ricks's terms, 'evince' means 'make evident (not overcome)'.

Milton's finest puns are those that teeter precariously between a fallen and an unfallen sense. Borrowing a phrase that Milton applies to the serpent just before Satan enters it, we might say that such puns are 'Not nocent yet' (IX. 186). The sense of impending doom is too strong to admit the air of untroubled ease evoked by the word 'innocence', but the change from innocence to nocence is pointedly not yet. Not surprisingly, puns evoking a 'not yet' are especially frequent just before the Fall. This is how Milton describes Eve's departure from Adam's side on the morning of the temptation:

> Thus saying, from her husband's hand her hand
> Soft she withdrew, and like a wood nymph light
> Oread or dryad, or of Delia's train,
> Betook her to the groves,
>
> (IX. 385–8)

Eve is 'light' in the innocent senses 'active, nimble, quick' (*OED* 15) and 'free from the weight of care or sorrow' (*OED* 21). But the simile is full of foreboding when we recall that nymphs (even those 'of Delia's [Diana's] train', IX. 387) were often 'light' in the bad sense 'wanton, unchaste' (*OED* 14. b). Eve is not, and never will be, light in that heavy-handed way, but she is 'frivolous' (*OED* 14. a) and she will soon be 'pliant, fickle, ready of belief' (*OED* 16). There is a further prolepsis in 'Betook her to the groves', for 'groves' are often associated with idolatry in the Old Testament, as in 1 Kings 1: 23: 'they also built them high places, and images, and groves, on every high hill, and under every green tree.' Earlier in *Paradise Lost* we have heard of Moloch, who 'made his grove / The pleasant valley of Hinnom' (I. 403–4). 'Groves' still means 'pleasant woods' when Eve 'Betook her to the groves', but the ominous potential is fortified by 'Betook', which here glances at the old sense 'deliver, give up' (*OED* 'betake' 1). Eve will give herself up to grove-worship when she bows before the Tree of Knowledge (IX. 835).

Six lines after 'Betook her to the groves', the proleptic implications of 'light', 'groves' and 'Betook' come to a head in a superb self-contradicting pun: 'To Pales, or Pomona, thus adorned, / Likeliest she seemed' (IX. 393–4). Here I have taken the liberty of citing my own 1998 edition. In his 1998 edition (used elsewhere in this essay and volume), Fowler retains the 1667 version 'Likest she seemed'. 'Likest' became 'Likeliest' in the second edition (1674). Most editors prefer 'Likest', but (as Fowler himself admits) 'Likeliest' is more likely 'as the less common word'. But the real advantage of 'Likeliest' is that it is richer in meaning. Like 'Likest', 'Likeliest' can mean 'most resembling' (*OED* 'likely' A 1), but it also carries the further implication that something is likely to happen. Robert Adams defends 'Likeliest' with this provocative comment: 'Eve is like Pales or Pomona; she is also (like Pales or Pomona) a likely sort of female; the sort who is most likely to get in trouble with Jove, Vertumnus, or Satan' (1955: 84). 'Likeliest' *is* ominous, as is confirmed just twenty lines later when we see Satan searching for Eve 'where likeliest he might find' her (IX. 414). But the phrase 'a likely sort of female' is too jarringly jocular for the tender pathos of Adam and Eve's parting. There is nothing snide about Milton's lines. As I have argued elsewhere (Leonard 2000: 113), Eve is 'likely' in several good senses. She is 'comely' (*OED* 5), and her deportment is 'seemly, becoming, appropriate' (*OED* 6). More than this, Eve in her innocence is 'strong or capable looking' and she 'gives promise of success or excellence' (*OED* 4. a, 4. b). These senses imply that Eve is likely to get *out* of trouble with Satan. 'Likeliest' recapitulates in miniature the whole argument that has just taken place between Eve and Adam. That argument has concerned Eve's *likely* behaviour when left to herself. Thirty lines earlier Adam had said: 'Seek not temptation then, which to avoid / Were better, and most likely if from me / Thou sever not' (IX. 364–6). By 'likely' Adam means 'likely to avoid temptation', but he also implies that Eve is most comely, becoming and capable when she stays by his side. Leaving his side, Eve makes a defiant show of her 'likely' qualities. She wants to prove to Adam that she can be seemly and successful without his help. She fails, but 'Likeliest she seemed' does not gloat over her failure. There is a genuine lightness of step, a tender embracing of possibilities, in the alliterating sequence: '*like* a woodnymph *light*...*Like*li*est* she seemed'. (How heavy, by comparison, is the ponderous tread of 'Likest'.) 'Likeliest' does admit irony, but the word is a triumph because it is true, in some degree, in both the bad and the good senses. The tragedy of Milton's Eve is not that she was 'a likely sort of female', always already 'likely to get in trouble'. Eve's tragedy is that she really was strong and capable, and gave earnest and credible 'promise of success' (*OED* 'likely' 4b), but failed, in the event, to live up to her promise. The pun on 'likeliest' is one of Milton's very best because it captures the delicacy and pathos of the moment, and goes beyond the moment to engage with the central ethical concerns of this great poem. Milton's poetic genius is nowhere more evident than in his wordplay. Deconstructionists often cite, with awful reverence prone, Ferdinand de Saussure's claim that 'man shall learn that he does not speak; he is spoken.' *Paradise Lost* offers a timely and eloquent challenge to this view of language, of free will and of human beings. John Milton is not just spoken. He speaks.

BIBLIOGRAPHY

Writings

Spenser (1978).

References for Further Reading

Adams (1955); Brooks and Hardy (1951b); Corns (1990a); Danielson (1999); Empson (1935, 1951, 1961); Fish (1967); H[ume] (1695); Leonard (1990, 2000); McColley (1983); Miller, J. Hillis (1991); Milton (1957, 1968, 1991, 1998a, b); Nyquist and Ferguson (1987/1988); Ricks (1963, 1984); Stein (1953).

25
Samson Agonistes

Sharon Achinstein

In the early 1640s Milton filled seven pages of a notebook with jottings of outlines for tragedies he thought about writing. Along with a detailed outline for 'Adam unparadized' there were several subjects from British and Scottish history, memos on biblical dramas, including Dinah and 'Christus patiens', and also several ideas about the biblical figure of Samson, with a note of the source in Judges 15 and 16. Milton wrote down possible topics or titles: '*Samson pursophorus or Hybristes*' that is, Samson the Firebrand, or Samson the Violent, was one; another was '*Samson marriing or in Ramath Lechi*'; there was also a note for '*Dagonalia*', the unholy rites at which Samson performed his vindication of God (*CPW* VIII: 556). Perhaps Milton imagined a dramatic trilogy on the life of Samson; or perhaps he was fashioning the multiple characteristics of his title character. The title Milton did choose for his last poetic achievement, *Samson Agonistes*, was taken from the Greek language, and its meaning was Samson as a Combatant in athletic games, Samson in Struggle, Samson the Champion. Classical and Hebraic, Milton's Samson would fuse the two great traditions out of which Milton sought literary power. But of what cause was Samson to be the champion? In the course of the play, as this mystery unfolds, Milton weaves together stories that are intimate, national and divine in a complex drama whose poetry is as haunting as its message is riddling.

Champion of Tragedy

If in *Paradise Lost* Milton sought to 'justify the ways of God to men', in *Samson Agonistes* he defended the cause of classical tragedy. *Samson Agonistes* was titled 'A Dramatic Poem', and it appeared as a work appended to *Paradise Regained* in a slim octavo printed on 29 May 1670, licensed on 2 July, entered in the Stationers' Register on 10 September, and presented for sale in a catalogue of 22 November 1670, offered at a price of 4s bound, a high sum warranted by the fame of *Paradise Lost*. The publisher John Starkey was also publisher of significant books of law and politics, and he subsequently came under severe governmental censure for the private reprinting in 1682 of Nathaniel Bacon's *An Historical and Political Discourse of the Laws and Government of England* (originally published in 1651; see Milton 1943–8: 13–16). Though the volume bore the publication date of 1671, scholars have disagreed over the dates of composition for Milton's drama, debating the political context against which his art may be understood. Is it a work of Milton the political radical, written in the fires of the revolution? Or is it a work written by a Milton in defeat, after the failure of the republican cause and the return to monarchy? The case for composition in the early 1640s is based upon Milton's notes in the Trinity Manuscript, and also the sense that the mid-century was the time for such violent imaginings, similar to the antityrannical message and allusions to classical tragedy prominent in Milton's regicide works. Some critics baulk to think this work, with its return to occasional rhyme, and its violent, disturbing conclusion, could be Milton's 'final word'. And yet there is much to suggest that it is very much a work of the Restoration period. The situation after 1660 offers at least as many parallels to Milton's political thought, and his concerns about failed heroism and his interest in obligations of a religious nature, as well as his debate with Restoration aesthetic theory, could all place the drama squarely within a Restoration context. There are clear references to the fate of the regicides after the Restoration, and the introductory notes on tragedy clearly belong to a Restoration aesthetic debate. As in his polemical charge against the 'bondage' of rhyme in his note added to *Paradise Lost* in 1674, it was characteristic of the late Milton to engage in political conflict by aesthetic means.

With a fresh title page within his 1671 volume, Milton heralded a new beginning which was at once a recovery. Paying homage to Greek tragedy by quoting Aristotle's *Poetics* as an epigraph, Milton in his preface to *Samson Agonistes* proposed 'to vindicate Tragedy from the small esteem, or rather infamy, which in the account of many it undergoes at this day with other common Interludes' (*CPW* VIII: 135). The ruin of tragedy, Milton suggested, was caused by the poor taste and artistic sloppiness of contemporary dramatists, 'the Poets error of intermixing Comic stuff with Tragic sadness and gravity; or introducing trivial and vulgar persons, which by all judicious hath bin counted absurd; and brought in without discretion, corruptly to gratifie the people' (*CPW* VIII: 135). Crowning Aeschylus, Sophocles and Euripedes as 'the three Tragic Poets unequall'd yet by any' (*CPW* VIII: 137), Milton preferred the classical Greek or the modern Italian forms of tragedy to those dramas afflicting the contemporary English stage. He filled three further pages with a brief treatise on tragedy, insisting on its compatibility with Christianity: 'The Apostle *Paul* himself thought it not unworthy to insert a verse of *Euripides* into the Text of Holy Scripture' (*CPW* VIII: 134), he asserted, noting that not only had the German Reformation theologian David Pareus considered the Book of Revelation a tragedy (cf. *Reason of Church-Government* in *CPW* I: 815), but even that the Bishop of Constantinople had been the author of a tragedy entitled *Christ Suffering*. Milton's drama obeyed tradition with its classical components of a Chorus and a tragic hero, and he adhered to the poetic unities of plot, place, decorum (according to which all violence was to be off-stage) and temporality, with the action of the play limited to twenty-four hours. Allusions to classical tragedy are to be found even within the opening lines of his drama, where Milton echoed Sophocles's redemptive tragedy, *Oedipus at Colonus*, as the blind Oedipus was led onstage by his daughter Antigone.

But to write a dramatic poem as a puritan, as Milton did, was to grapple with an aesthetic form condemned by some of that persuasion. During the pre-Civil War years, puritans assaulted theatre in order to reform manners, hoping to direct art towards God (thought to be its proper source and object), to return Sundays to the Lord and, on a more earthly plane, to stave off plague and to control the public by constraining a salient public institution in which dubious morals, sexual licence and political intrigue were thought to lead gullible playgoers into temptation, inebriation, disease or riot. Yet the closure of the theatres by parliamentary edict in 1642 was not entirely due to a puritan campaign; during the decade preceding, the drama was filled with political critique which authorities may have wanted to suppress during a period of political instability (Butler 1987: 136). Milton had successfully authored drama previously in his *Masque*, a work of which he was sufficiently proud to give pride of place as the last English work printed in his *1645 Poems*, and there is nothing in his own writings condemning drama as a genre. The turn to drama in the Restoration was for Milton then no break with a puritan past, but rather a continued development of his experiments with the major literary forms.

After the restoration of the monarchy in 1660, the public theatres sprang back to life. Strongly supported by the crown and court, English dramatic writers created tastes they then satisfied, fashioning drama that traversed foreign vistas (*The Conquest of Granada*), probed the mystique of the Orient (*The Indian Queen*, *The Indian Emperour*, *Mustapha*), unveiled the lives of prostitutes (*The Rover*), exposed plots against tyrannical rulers (*Venice Preserv'd*), pinned characters in heroic conflicts between love and honour (*All for Love*), rewrote Shakespeare (*Romeo and Juliet*, *The Tempest*, Orrery's *Henry V*), satirized politicians and fanatics (*Sir Martin-Mar All*, *The Rehearsal*) and, in their romances, tragicomedies, marriage comedies and twisted political plots, vaunted, mocked and aroused the desires, panting, fears and opportunism of lovers crossed, won and lost. For the first time in English history, women actresses were paid to perform before the public. The Restoration stage became the livelihood for a growing cadre of writers, male as well as female dramatists who sought acclaim from a public and court willing to indulge in the pleasures of leisure, fantasy, travel and sociability. Whether racy, witty, political, heroic or tragicomic, and sometimes all of these, the dramatic arts took a central position among the cultural fora of the Restoration.

Milton's self-styled 'Dramatic Poem', then, was part of a culture war, critical of the dominant modes within the dramatic resurgence in Restoration literary culture. In his dramatic poem, Milton championed a pure tragedy as against a degraded Restoration theatrical culture; called for a purer neoclassicism; and integrated Greek tragedy within a biblical framework. Milton's drama presented Samson, a fallen hero, whose struggle over the course of the drama to recover faith in his Israelite God pitted him against his enemies the Philistines, worshippers of Dagon. The religious themes of the play spoke to a divisive cultural moment in Britain, in which religious controversy had contributed to bloody civil war, and in which backlash against religious dissidents was restricting liberty of conscience for those like Milton who dissented from the Anglican church. In many ways Milton waged a contest within Restoration literary culture, and it is fitting that this, most likely his last poetic work, bears the mark of that contest in its very name.

Champion of Israel

Samson Agonistes fused biblical history with classical tragedy, and nowhere in Milton's works is the alliance between Hebraic poetics and classical form more visible than in that tragedy, though it was never intended to be performed. Tragic action and tragic history combine in a drama that also takes a stand against the contemporary English culture in which Milton the man found himself an outcast. Yet this is also a story of a fallen man brought back to God's care, an intensely personal story of affliction, betrayal and humiliation. It may be the most bitter of Milton's works, as the degraded Samson, once the champion of his people, now maimed, alone, condemned to hard labour in a stinking prison, reflects on his losses and gives voice to his greatest terror, the loss of the special care granted by a God who had favoured him in former times. Samson is the fallen tragic hero, and the drama records the growth of Samson's mind and spirit towards reconciliation with himself and his God. Over the course of the drama, he confronts persons who offer him opportunities to explore his emotional and spiritual state, and also to take decisions about how he will conduct himself. The drama reserves action until the very end, but it is filled with talk, conversations between Samson and his visitors which reveal the changing circumstances of his spiritual condition, and occasions for the combats which give *Samson Agonistes* its title.

Seventeenth-century Protestant poets often aligned the English people with the biblical people Israel; in *Areopagitica*, Milton considered the English to be a chosen nation, pressing his countrymen to deserve God's favour: 'Why else was this Nation chos'n before any other, that out of her as out of *Sion* should be proclam'd and sounded forth the first tidings and trumpet of Reformation to all *Europ*' (*CPW* II: 552). And, on the eve of Restoration, Milton chides the English people for their political failure of nerve, their backsliding towards monarchy after the noble experience of freedom, likening them to the Israelites, who were now 'chusing them a captain back for *Egypt*' (*CPW* VII: 463).

If the people Israel were a common source of historical comparison and religious precedent for Protestant English writers, the figure of Samson was prolific in the polemical literature of the period as a figure admired and discussed by English writers (Wittreich 1986: 215). The story of Samson is found in the Hebrew Bible in the Book of Judges (chs 13–16), and the choice bore political resonance in Milton's day. During the English revolutionary period, the biblical Book of Judges was seen by English radicals as the place to explore a republican form of government, as that book gave the history of a theocracy in which God was the only king and where human leaders were not hereditary monarchs. Judges was also a book in which God's hand in human history was powerfully evident through his workings upon unlikely servants. Figures such as Deborah, Ehud and Samson were all Hebrew heroes, those chosen by God, wise ones who offered spiritual and military leadership to the people of Israel; during the revolutionary decades, these heroes had populated the political tracts, hymns and parliamentary thanksgiving sermons exploring historical precedents for the cause against King Charles. Judges also supplied a list of actions undertaken by the gift of the Spirit, antinomian in implication – that is, where agents were willing to go beyond the law of the land to perform in God's service – and thus the book was highly volatile politically (Burns 1996: 28). When Milton turned to Judges, and to the figure of Samson, he turned to a well-known story, one inviting political readings of an antimonarchical cast. Admiring the heroic Samson in 1651 while defending the tyrannicide, Milton wrote: 'the heroic Samson . . . whether prompted by God or by his own valor, slew at one stroke not one but a host of his country's tyrants, having first made prayer to God for his aid. Samson therefore thought it not impious but pious to kill those masters who were tyrants over his country' (*CPW* IV: 402).

For Milton, Samson held a lifelong interest. He had been a figure for the future glories of the English nation, as Milton prophesied in *Areopagitica*, 'Methinks I see in my mind a noble and puissant Nation rousing herself like a strong man after sleep, and shaking her invincible locks' (*CPW* II: 557–8). But Samson had previously for Milton also been a figure of a degraded, uxorious character, as in *Paradise Lost*, where the fallen Adam awakens in shame from his postlapsarian sexual excesses:

> So rose the Danite Strong
> Hercúlean Samson from the harlot-lap
> Of Philistéan Daliláh, and waked
> Shorn of his strength,
> > (*PL* IX. 1059–62)

If Milton sees in Samson a complex figure, his last poetic work deepens this complexity. In his dramatic rendering, Milton engages directly with the God of the Book of Judges, the God who acted upon and through notorious human figures, but, mysteriously. Milton also adds to the biblical account. The character of Harapha, for instance, is an original invention; so are Dalila's defence and Samson's discussion with the Public Officer. A striking deletion from the biblical account is Samson's prayer to God (Judges 16: 28–30). Milton's drama leaves out the prayer, but includes Samson's words of warning to the Philistine crowd, thus leaving open the question of divine participation in Samson's bloody work. Central to the century of revolution, controversy over prayer had divided English citizens. Was prayer to be the spontaneous expression of the human in search of relation with the divine? Or was prayer to be controlled by set public rituals? Opposition to an imposed prayer book in the pre-Civil War years sparked armed resistance from the Scots and, in the Restoration, the church's imposition of a new prayer book in 1662 divided the orthodox from the nonconforming. By leaving as a textual silence the meaning and the nature of Samson's space for prayer, Milton touches upon this sensitive subject. He consigns inward observance or petition to a private space, subject to no external observation or scrutiny.

In addition to thematic interest, Milton adopted a biblical source as part of his aesthetic programme. *Samson Agonistes* is the most baffling in metrics of all of Milton's poetry. Milton commented that his verse for the Chorus would be *Apolelymenon*, that is, freed from the divisions of the Greek stanzaic forms; but even without stanzaic forms, the verse form in the drama as a whole is irregular, at times adhering to a loose iambic pentameter, occasionally rhyming, but mostly not. Milton's lines are long and short, and the rhythms vary between iambic and trochaic, as the poet experiments with elements of Italian, Hebraic and Greek prosody. As Mary Ann Radzinowicz has shown, Milton incorporated an extraordinary number of allusions to psalms in his work (1978: 368–82). The Hebraic turn in Milton's poetry is signalled by his choice of prosody. Imitating the rhythms and shapes of Hebrew poetry, *Samson Agonistes* does war with contemporary Restoration poetic forms, resisting the conclusiveness of the heroic couplet, with its rigid stanzaic forms reducing all to order through neoclassical balance and antithesis.

Hebrew poetry, unlike that of the English classics, was not based upon accentual-syllabic organization, and instead vaunted parallelism, alliteration and assonance, echoing rhythms within irregular line lengths.

> O dark, dark, dark, amid the blaze of noon,
> Irrecoverably dark, total eclipse
> Without all hope of day!
>
> (lines 80–2)

These lines repeat, and yet the repetitions are not merely parallelisms; they amplify, critique and create paradoxes out of that lamented darkness. Darkness is made all the more dark when cast against the noontime brightness of the sun; and the darkness of an eclipse is indeed all the darker for the instantaneous banishment of light, a light that will in a moment reappear. For the instant, then, this is darkness shadowed only by light. Hebrew poetry abounds in such paradoxes and repetitions, and even though the first two lines above assemble into something like iambic pentameter, the rhythm is disjointed, disrupted, incantatory as well as funereal. In lamenting spasms, Samson wails, 'The sun to me is dark / And silent as the moon' (lines 86–7) as if even the natural hierarchy of sun and moon are reversed. The repeated imagery of darkness presents a world opposed to Samson's nature, his very name, Samson, in Hebrew being connected to *shemesh*, sun. Outcast even to the sun, separated from his namesake, Samson wallows in a darkness that is physical and spiritual, his very meaning obscured. Repetitions of sound and sense heighten the closed world of this drama, Samson's own liability to fatal repetition, marrying twice badly, wielding destruction in a repetitious cycle, but also calling upon God's repeated return.

The language of the Chorus, too, breaks the shapes of accentual-syllabic verse, with lines that are at times voiced as if laughing. They pair rhymes on the 'riddle' of woman's nature:

> *Chor.* It is not virtue, wisdom, valour, wit,
> Strength, comeliness of shape, or amplest merit
> That woman's love can win or long inherit;
> But what it is, hard is to say,
> Harder to hit,
> (Which way soever men refer it)
>   (lines 1010–15)

At other times, the Chorus is striking in its abruptness, the sounds cutting short lines with bluntness of oral expression but the paradox of repetition:

> Which shall I first bewail,
> Thy bondage or lost sight,
> Prison within prison
> Inseparably dark?
>   (lines 151–4)

Shape in Hebrew poetry is given by internal parallelisms which often do not reduce to a single meaning, but which amplify and disperse meaning or sound into con-tradictions (Kugel 1988: 41–5): 'The breath of Heav'n fresh-blowing, pure and sweet, / With day-spring born; here leave me to respire' – note the assonances, the repeated vowel sounds of br*ea*th/h*ea*ven/fr*e*sh and the alliterative sounds of aspiration: *p*ure, *s*weet, *sp*ring, re*sp*ire: these words are linked by sound as well as by sense, and the apposition of 'breath of Heav'n' against 'respire' lays out the contrast between the regenerative graceful air and that of Samson's own breathing.

The Samson of the Bible was also known for his riddling, his dark speech, in which could be enfolded hidden meanings (see lines 1016, 1026). Though his strength is God-given in his body, he also possesses wisdom of the parable; as words constitute his strength, so are they his undoing. Through words, however, Milton achieves a resolution with a Hebraic tradition through which he seeks the strength to recall God's presence in history.

Champion of Christian Violence?

Yet there are deviations from Greek drama. It is unclear whether the Chorus in *Samson Agonistes* is a repository of wisdom or a collection of pat responses; Northrop Frye has described the Chorus 'standing around uttering timid complacencies in teeth-loosen-ing doggerel' (1965: 108). And in matters of dramatic form, Samuel Johnson divided the drama into a classic five-act structure, but complained that the play lacked action, that it 'has a beginning and an end which *Aristotle* himself could not have disap-proved; but it must be allowed to want a middle, since nothing passes between the first act and the last' (1972: 219–20).

Both these deviations from classical drama – the failure of dramatic structure and the unreliability of the Chorus – may, however, be consequences of Milton's Chris-tianizing designs. The Chorus's knowledge, in Milton's apocalyptic world-view, could only be incomplete, since God alone knew God's ways; Samson outgrows their knowledge over the course of the play (Bennett 1989: 124). On the level of dramatic incident, the very absence of observable events is itself the point: the prime dramatic action is that taking place within the heart of Samson, experience occurring on a spiritual level within a Christian salvific framework of repentance and regeneration. That action of inward experience is the great, the heroic action, but one we have difficulty observing from the outside. Many readers are in doubt even at the very end about whether Samson has returned to God; whether his deeds are indeed inspired from above or merely the crazy explosions of a tortured prisoner; suicide, after all, is not sanctioned by Christianity. Though his father and the Chorus construe the ending of the play as a reassurance of God's continued care, none the less these characters are often wrong, as has been evidently seen during the course of the play. This very incomprehensibility of the final action could lead to uncertainty about Milton's political and artistic intentions for his drama (Fish 1989: 569). If, in his reformation of drama, Milton replaces external action with internal, his Christianizing thwarts our dramatic expectations, rendering invisible the moralizing certainties we hunger for. But that cosmic uncertainty about God's ways and means may be the condition of faith.

In addition to reworking the classical models of action, Milton's preface also insisted that this was a drama never intended to be performed on a stage. Conscious of the power of reading in an age of print, Milton makes action internal in another way. This was to be a drama performed in the minds of believers. Resituating the forum for the articulation of great moral themes from the vast public theatres of classical tragedy, and from the public stage of decadent Restoration culture, Milton produces a private drama, a combat within. If Milton gave an account of the therapeutic function of tragedy, citing Aristotle's *Poetics*, suggesting that tragedy could be a champion of healing by giving vent to passions, those were to be endured in the situation of reading, in the private spaces of home and heart. Tragedy could be cathartic, and in quoting Aristotle's theory of tragedy, Milton evoked a spiritual function of drama, an inner location for a struggle which drama could relieve or purge. Tragedy arouses conflict and ambivalence, and it provokes dialogue: Milton's Samson embodies the experience of drama by becoming both the hero and the victim, the purger and that which must be purged, filled with passion yet capable of being sacrificed to relieve passion.

If the turn to Samson was a turn to a Hebraic and republican past, it was also a turn to a Christian one, since Samson was familiar to seventeenth-century readers as a type of Christ, not only for his parabolic speech, but as a heroic saviour of his oppressed people, a godly martyr who achieves liberation for his followers. Samson's three visitors may signify the three temptations of Christ (Krouse 1949: 126). Yet the violent conclusion to Samson's drama – one that results not only in the hero's death, but in his possible suicide – seems to negate an image of Christ who had urged turning the other cheek against oppressors and enemies, a pacifist whose teachings about relations to earthly sovereigns had been a source of discussion for early modern Protestant resistance theory. In Romans 13: 1–2, for instance, Paul had preached: 'Let every soul be subject unto the higher powers. For there is no power but of God: the powers that be are ordained of God. Whosoever therefore resisteth the power, resisteth the ordinance of God: and they that resist shall receive to themselves damnation.' Samson's vehement iconoclasm would not reassure earthly monarchs. If Samson is a glorious leader against oppression, then how is his action to be imitated by other godly persons in the here and now? On a broader plane, the play seems to ask: What are God's ways in history, if violent revenge against enemies is the model of heroism? Would this not be contrary to Christ's teaching?

These questions about the 'Christianity' of the drama raised by the matter of the exemplarity of its hero are thrust into relief by the two-handed nature of the volume in which *Samson Agonistes* appeared. What is the relationship between the two poems within the one volume? Milton's cheeky 'To which is added *Samson Agonistes*' on the octavo's title page offers the drama as an afterthought, giving his readers value for money; but the second title page for the drama suggests it stands on its own merits. Samson may represent the bodily, fleshly, physically tormented and brawny hero, a contrast to that hero of the spirit, the wispy Son in *Paradise Regained*, a contrast which represents a Christian perception of the difference between Old Law and New. The two poems may perhaps offer two perspectives: the one in which Jesus stands fast, passively enduring Satan's temptations but never succumbing to vengeful action, and the other in which vengeance turns bloody from the doings of a human actor. Samson may be seen as a type of Christ, that is, a foreshadowing of the true saviour. Or Samson may be seen as a type of false Christ, a premature form, much as the Hebrew Bible is superseded by the Christian, a derelict image contrasting to the true Christ who will effect salvation through grace (Wittreich 1986: 160). *Paradise Regained* may be less pacifist than it appears at first glance. God's creative energies, and his care for his people Israel, are related to his destructive power, but Milton's drama is unsettling in its assessment of the value of humans within a divine scheme. There is still room to think about the ways in which Milton's two works are interconnected.

Within a Christian typological scheme, the dramatic confrontation between Samson and Manoa also presents a paradigm for thinking about divine and human relations. Samson's father Manoa searches for an earthly solution to his son's problems, busily attempting to secure his release by a ransom reward because he hopes to preserve his son's safety and health at all costs. The Christian irony is heavy here;

another Son will indeed become a ransom for his people, and the machinations of this concerned father seem impious, or at least they would preclude Samson's heroism. But Samson will not accept the cost of such a ransom; he knows his purpose is to serve his God, his nation, and that involves something else. To win freedom through a ransom is an ignoble option, as Samson bitterly imagines what his life would be like after his release:

> To what can I be useful, wherein serve
> My Nation, and the work from heaven imposed,
> But to sit idle on the household hearth,
> A burdenous drone; to visitants a gaze,
> Or pitied object, these redundant locks
> Robustious to no purpose clustering down,
> Vain monument of strength;
>
> (lines 564–70)

Manoa's suggestion is premature, and it is the wrong kind of ransom, a literal liberation which none the less would leave Samson's spirit crushed. Perhaps this is a Christian conception of the Hebrew Bible, in which there is a contrast between the world of the material and that of the spirit. As Jesus's teachings reject the letter of the Hebrew Law for the spirit, so Samson believes that a physical liberation is insufficient to secure his place in God's plan. If Manoa's paternal care seeks to preserve his son at any costs, that is the love of a father who would betray his son's birthright call to nobler deeds. Throughout the drama, Manoa can see only the literal side of things; even at the moment of his son's glorious martyrdom, he is at work acquiring the ransom. The higher-called son must reject his father's plans, and Manoa is the first of the interlocutors whom he confronts, in an exchange perhaps representing the first temptation, the temptation to emancipation through human hands. The son's resistance to Manoa may mirror this Christian hermeneutic rejection of alleged Hebraic literalism. Christian typological reading is a mode of ironic reading, supplanting former truths with reversals, supplements, new testaments.

Samson is a saviour, to be sure, but for what kind of God? Is the extreme violence of the ending consistent with a Christian paradigm? This 'dreadful' God seems a vengeful God. If the Christian is meant to supersede the Hebraic in this drama, there are also parallels between the two religions in the salvation plot where God initiates the destruction of the ungodly. Milton's Christian God, however, is also a violent, judging God, the God of the destruction of all but Noah in flood, a God of apocalypse, of blinding accuracy and punishment, capable of rousing fiery virtue 'From under ashes into sudden flame' (line 1691). As Samson announces, 'I begin to feel / Some rousing motions in me which dispose / To something extraordinary my thoughts' (lines 1381–3); he reassures the Chorus as he is reassured by an experience within him, which he understands as warranting his actions.

Milton's understanding of regeneration, 'the inward perswasive motions of ... spirit' (*CPW* VII: 261), fits into an apocalyptic scheme in which human action is dwarfed by the mighty Spirit of God in battle against the forces of Evil. As he surrenders to God's will, Samson admits, 'all the contest is now / 'Twixt God and Dagon' (lines 461–2). If the poem is to be seen as a celebration of the return to God of a fallen man through the stages of despairing abjection, self-abasement, grief, repentance and then God's approval (Radzinowicz 1978: 363), it is also a recognition that God's mystery, his power, exceeds human comprehension, 'the unsearchable dispose / Of highest wisdom' (lines 1746–7). For Milton's audience, this leaves humans in a condition of agony, a tragic condition of incomplete knowledge about the meaning of their lives. In a commentary upon Psalm 8: 4, 'What is man, that thou art mindful of him?', Milton's Chorus asks:

> God of our fathers, what is man!
> That thou towards him with hand so various,
> Or I might say contrarious,
> Temper'st thy providence through his short course,
> Not evenly;
>
>   (lines 667–71)

Milton pushes the question to ask how God reveals his mindfulness of humans, given the contradictions in his actions towards them.

Champion of Masculinity?

If *Samson Agonistes* dramatizes the agon of a man coming to reconciliation with an overpowering God, it also presents a struggle of a more quotidian sort, that between husband and wife. For Samson to become God's champion, the hero must undergo a process taking place over the course of the play, involving confrontation with several interlocutors: his father, his wife, a warrior, and a public officer. There is no question that the most excitement occurs in his confrontation with a woman. The question of Milton's misogyny is often taken up in relation to the figure of Eve in *Paradise Lost*, but *Samson Agonistes* also considers the nature of woman. The figure of Dalila had since medieval times been a symbol for dangerous femininity – there was the 'lemman Delida' in Chaucer's Monk's Tale – and Renaissance writers drew upon that medieval tradition, likening Dalila to Judas, who betrayed Christ. Milton's admired poetic forebear Edmund Spenser had rebuked Dalila in his *Faerie Queene*, warning against the 'wondrous power' of 'Womens faire aspect. To captive men and make them all the world reject' (*Faerie Queene* V. viii. 2, 8–9).

If in Renaissance literature Dalila was archetypal for the dangerous female who could overpower men, Milton both develops that tradition and criticizes it. Female rulers, warriors and amazons are scattered throughout Renaissance English literature:

strong female figures who appeared during a moment of changing economic and cultural circumstances for women. In Reformation England, moreover, the Roman Catholic Church was often figured as a foreign seductress, the canny Whore of Babylon, and Milton's Dalila draws upon this anti-Catholic tradition. Further still, images of the orientalized, luxurious and totally irresistible character Cleopatra had fascinated English dramatic audiences from Shakespeare's *Antony and Cleopatra* to Dryden's *All for Love* (Nyquist 1994: 85–7). Belonging to all these traditions, Milton's Dalila is a destructive female who illegitimately overturns domestic hierarchy by ruling over her husband, and she is physically overpowering. Bedecked in gorgeous eastern attire, perfumed, wily in her opportunism and skilled in rhetorical duplicity, she is strong, sexy and irresistible. For her able tongue, she is aligned with another of Milton's great adversaries, Satan of *Paradise Lost*, and called 'a manifest serpent' (line 997) by the Chorus. The difference from Satan is that Dalila is a woman, and a wife. If Dalila is a 'type' of Satan, beholden to her false god, Dagon, she is also a woman pitted against a man on the battleground of marriage within seventeenth-century debates over the roles of men and women. Milton's *Doctrine and Discipline of Divorce* set out his stand in these debates, in arguing for marriage as an 'apt and cheerfull conversation' between men and women (*CPW* II: 235), and advocating a spiritual, companionate relation between the sexes. Women possessed the moral and spiritual capabilities to serve as fit companions for their husbands, and Milton's views on marriage may be seen as a 'step forward' for women against the misogynistic background of his day.

In *Samson Agonistes*, Dalila may even have been seen as a heroine in her own right. Like the leading figures of the Euripidean drama Milton revered, Dalila resembles the doubled characters of complex powerful women such as Medea and Hecuba (Revard 1987). Dalila attempts through a series of rhetorical gestures to win back Samson's affection; but in her final speech, when she abandons her love-plotting, she instead boasts of the heroism of her betrayal. Although Samson will accuse her, she responds with a perspective of her own people, for whom her actions will be counted virtuous:

> But in my country where I most desire,
> In Eckron, Gaza, Asdod, and in Gath
> I shall be named among the famousest
> Of women, sung at solemn festivals,
> Living and dead recorded, who to save
> Her country from a fierce destroyer, chose
> Above the faith of wedlock-bands, my tomb
> With odours visited and annual flowers.
> Not less renowned than in Mount Ephraim,
> Jael, who with inhospitable guile
> Smote Sisera sleeping through the temples nailed.
>
> (lines 980–90)

Championing Dalila, William Empson calls this 'one of the noblest speeches in Milton' (1981: 221), and it is a powerful defence of radical, inspired, God-provoked action, raised in the high poetic diction of epic and biblical verse. Milton evokes the biblical story (again from Judges) of the Israelite Jael who had comforted the enemy Canaanite military leader Sisera after a day's battle. Once he fell asleep, she committed an act of brutal murder, turning a scene of maternal nurturance into a scene of destruction. With this proud, self-eulogizing boast, Dalila stands strong as a potential heroine; though capable of treachery, violence and bloodshed, she acts in the service of her country. Calling upon the instance of the woman warrior Jael, a Hebrew heroine from the Book of Judges (4: 17–24), whose story as a woman warrior was sung by the great biblical judge Deborah (5: 2–31), Dalila incorporates herself into Deborah's song of military successes. Dalila, then, makes a reasonable case for her actions, explaining that her deeds were in the service of a higher good, that of her God, her country: these are the very terms upon which rest a defence of Samson's actions. Hers is a call for liberty of conscience. Would not Samson's own heroism be judged the same way?

It is typical of Milton to give his adversaries strong arguments; but in Samson's eyes this bid for heroism is hypocritical and self-serving, and it is instantly repudiated by the Chorus. Within the structure of the play, this confrontation, this agon, produces Samson's own commitment to his God, a commitment not performed through rhetoric or even adjudicated through rational argument, but beyond earthly judgement. To Samson, Dalila's speech is idolatrous – all gods are not equal; there is only one true God. Interestingly, and tellingly, Dalila is condemned not solely for her beliefs; it is for how those beliefs ought to have been superseded by her relation of marriage. This is a complex moment in Milton's drama; liberty of conscience is not entirely liberal.

Milton did intend Dalila to be a liar, a temptress. But her bid for liberty of conscience is compelling. According to Samson, Dalila should have surrendered her claims to her nation and followed her husband in his religion and national identity, especially as his is the true God. *Samson Agonistes* presents marital choice as interconnected to religious choice; each become a figure for the other. Dalila to him is not merely a bad woman, an idolater, of an enemy people; she's a bad wife. Dalila, unlike in the Bible, is Samson's lawful wife, and thus her betrayal of him works at several levels: it is a betrayal against a lawful husband, against the Hebrew people, against the Hebrew God, what Samson calls 'matrimonial treason' (line 959). Samson, echoed by the Chorus and vindicated by the play's vengeful violence, gives an account of marital subordination for women, as he charges Dalila:

> Being once a wife, for me thou wast to leave
> Parents and country; nor was I their subject,
> Nor under their protection but my own,
> Thou mine, not theirs: if aught against my life
> Thy country sought of thee, it sought unjustly,

> Against the law of nature, law of nations,
> No more thy country, but an impious crew
> Of men conspiring to uphold thir state
>
> (lines 885–92)

Dalila has usurped the place of the husband; the logic of a sexual double standard suggests that it is the husband alone who may affiliate political identity. Like Adam, who failed to exert proper authority as a husband, Samson has failed in his marital duties. His loss of sight, his imprisonment, are due to his own failures as a husband. If for the Chorus Dalila stands for all women's perfidy, for Samson the condemnation is more particular: by remaining loyal to her own people, Dalila has disobeyed her husband, and thus transgressed against her bond of marriage.

Samson has been called 'Milton's most notorious woman hater' (Swan 1985: 143), and his negative representation of Dalila has been blamed on the misogyny of the seventeenth-century social milieu, and on Reformation anti-Catholic imagery of the feminized Whore of Babylon; it may even be a cheeky engagement with the problem of the Catholic Queen of England, Catharine of Braganza. Yet if Milton's representation of Dalila speaks the languages of seventeenth-century politics and religion, it also evokes the problematic of fashioning a coherent male identity. *Samson Agonistes* works to reinstate some gender rigidity for a couple who have reversed the proper hierarchy within marriage. In *Samson Agonistes*, Samson, like Adam in *Paradise Lost*, is not only easily seduced by the outside of his mate, he also forsakes his masculine role. Milton figures male incapacity in *Samson Agonistes* through scenarios of bodily mutilation, with the gouging of Samson's eyes figured as castration.

Milton's drama thus represents more than the question of the virtue of women; it also asks about manliness. It represents a marriage gone wrong and reveals Samson's hopes of rectifying his gender instability. As he is constantly reminding himself, it was *Samson* who emasculated himself by succumbing to Dalila's power. As Samson puts it, 'She sought to make me traitor to myself' (line 401); much of Samson's early movement in the play is towards accepting responsibility for his part in his failure:

> of what now I suffer
> She was not the prime cause, but I myself,
> Who vanquished with a peal of words (O weakness!)
> Gave up my fort of silence to a woman.
>
> (lines 233–6)

And again, figuring himself as the victim in a passive position, he describes her conquest:

> mustering all her wiles,
> With blandished parleys, feminine assaults,
> Tongue-batteries, she surceased not day nor night
> To storm me over-watched, and wearied out.

> At times when men seek most repose and rest,
> I yielded, and unlocked her all my heart,
> (lines 402–7)

The language here is suggestive on a psychological register; instead of withholding himself, making himself impenetrable, he has instead been vanquished like a fort, made to blab like a woman, and because of a woman. The usual Renaissance way of figuring female weakness was to levy charges against her as unable to control her tongue, a metaphor for her openness to sexual infidelity. Here Samson reverses these marks of gender; instead, he is the one to be penetrated, it is his tongue which has been loosened. Samson understands that he has turned the gender world upside down, exclaiming, 'foul effeminacy held me yoked / Her bond-slave' (lines 410–11). As he recounts the experience of his temptation to her power, he describes a scene of seduction and erotic abandonment, also the rise and fall of his male member. Samson confesses his surrender to Dalila was a fall, a loss of potency figured through sexual detumescence:

> swoll'n with pride into the snare I fell
> Of fair fallacious looks, venereal trains,
> Softened with pleasure and voluptuous life;
> At length to lay my head and hallowed pledge
> Of all my strength in the lascivious lap
> Of a deceitful concubine
> (lines 532–7)

His sexual surrender was also the opportunity for the waste of his physical gift, the occasion for her cutting his hair, a metaphoric castration:

> who shore me
> Like a tame wether, all my precious fleece,
> Then turned me out ridiculous, despoiled,
> Shaven, and disarmed among my enemies.
> (lines 537–40)

Likening himself to a sheared 'wether', a castrated ram, Samson is now a pitiable object on which others gaze in ridicule: a vulnerable creature who has lost his military prowess, intoxicated and degraded, bereft of his manhood. The play may reflect Milton's own lifelong ambivalence about women, representing what Freud would call castration anxiety, a trauma of separation or differentiation from the mother.

If memory of Dalila serves to highlight Samson's self-abasement, now his combat with her becomes a chance to vent his anger, to expose Dalila for her falseness and to reassert his masculine potency. He returns as champion over his erotic desires, master of his verbal prowess. As he dismisses her, he is overwhelmed with violent impulses, and forgives her with a stormy threat: 'My sudden rage to tear thee joint by joint' (line 953). If he has come to resist her perfidy and to find himself culpable, he has also mustered a strength of words, steadfast now in his hate.

Placing his story of gender roles in a cosmic framework, Milton's drama elevates the theme of Restoration drama to an absolute moral plane, rebuking Restoration libertinism or sensualism by appeal to an ethical paradigm of matrimonial relations and the remedy of the proper sexual self-discipline of the male subject. That construction of masculinity is challenged next in his clash with the giant Harapha, the braggart. Harapha of Gath is a Miltonic invention, a novel addition to the account in Judges. To Samson, Harapha offers combat at the most primitive level, and in facing him, Samson puts into verbal form the savagery, the revenge for his mutilation and the violence denied him in the impotence of his marriage and his slavery. Here is an occasion for the Hebrew to recover his lost potency, his masculinity: it is also an occasion to distinguish earthly fame from heaven-honouring action. In this combat of wills, there is the exposure of false heroism against true. In this case, battle will be conducted by means of words, not arms, as Milton transforms the Renaissance tradition of the duel or single-handed combat of Romance into verbal action. Opposing Harapha's lineage of warfare, the world of ancient biblical narrative, Samson will be the David to his Goliath, a symbol of the potency of God to support the small against the mighty, and Samson's chosen mode of heroic combat, that of verbal warfare, may be aligned with the verbal power sought in Milton's own prose polemics (Lieb 1994: 248).

With Harapha, Samson's *agon* adheres to the tradition of athletic contest; but the winner of that contest seeks not earthly fame but divine favour. Milton rejects *gloria* of earthly praise in favour of those actions taken on behalf of God. By confronting Harapha, who offers a comic relief to true heroism, Samson insists that his own heroism was not self-interested, but in the service of heaven: 'I was to do my part from heaven assigned, / And had performed' (lines 1217–18). Harapha, a boastful, blustery, warrior-courtier, is, in contrast, most interested in reputation, and soon he is exposed as a coward. Through this confrontation, Samson regains possession over his strength, refuting Harapha's vigorous boasts by shooting back with renewed vigour: 'My heels are fettered, but my fist is free' (line 1235). The proud giant escapes 'somewhat crestfall'n, / Stalking with less unconscionable strides, / And lower looks' (lines 1244–6), diminished by the combat.

Milton's Champion

In his prefatory poem to the second edition of *Paradise Lost*, Andrew Marvell had likened Milton to Samson the destroyer. Milton's iconoclastic gestures throughout his political career would have given Marvell warrant to judge that the author was responding to his current dispossession with a similar fervour of prophetic destruction. In a Restoration climate of backlash against Milton and the Good Old Cause,

Marvell wondered if the poet would rise up against his enemies again. Shuddering that the blind poet would 'ruin... / The sacred truths to fable and old song', he likened Milton to the hero of Judges:

> (So Sampson groped the Temple's post in spite)
> The world o'erwhelming to revenge his sight.
>
> (PL: 53)

But as Marvell read on, he came to consider *Paradise Lost* to be not an act of 'spite' but one of true prophecy. In the Restoration, public opinion held that Milton had been stricken blind on account of his activities on behalf of a rebellious, regicidal government. Instead, Milton saw his blindness as a kind of election, a sign that true sight was within (Lieb 1994: 186).

One wonders what Marvell made of *Samson Agonistes*. For there, the sense of public shame, the aggression coupled with the futility of action, the incertitude of God's care, pervade Milton's drama. Milton's violent polemical writings of the Civil War years, his regicidal tracts and particularly his *Eikonoklastes* are given renewed vigour in the representation of his destructive hero Samson (Loewenstein 1990: 73). There are many biographical parallels to Milton's own life. Milton did survive the barbaric backlash against revolutionary heroes, and his horror at their fates blasts *Samson Agonistes* with topical reference. As Samson quakes to remember his compatriots, the public spectacle of their humiliation, the situation reflects the execution and the public desecration of the bodies of the regicides after the Restoration (Knoppers 1994: 56–7):

> to the hostile sword
> Of heathen and profane, their carcases
> To dogs and fowls a prey, or else captived:
> Or to the unjust tribunals, under change of times,
> And condemnation of the ingrateful multitude.
>
> (lines 692–6)

The drama's hopes for a violent saviour match those of Restoration radicals and republicans (Worden 1995: 112; Keeble 1987: 195). Samson, too, has experienced mutilation, 'Betrayed, captived, and both my eyes put out, / Made of my enemies the scorn and gaze' (lines 33–4).

Milton's situation after the restoration of monarchy in 1660 may be likened to Samson's. Milton, too, sat in prison, awaiting his fate while his books burnt in bonfires; that experience of uncertainty and terror is captured in the autobiographical moments in *Paradise Lost*, where the poet suffers 'In darkness, and with dangers compassed round, / And solitude' (*PL* VII. 27–8). The dejected Samson, too, begins in despair, fallen from a height. Nevertheless, the Chorus console that God did return to his fallen son:

Semichor. But he though blind of sight,
Despised and thought extinguished quite,
With inward eyes illuminated
His fiery virtue roused
From under ashes into sudden flame,
                                        (lines 1687–91)

Unpredictable, inscrutable and violent, this ending is troubling: what is its advice for the suffering? Although it is tempting to construct a political allegory for Samson, to ally him with the blind and persecuted Milton, to construe him as a symbol for the Good Old Cause (Hill 1977: 437; DiSalvo 1973: 40), it is unclear where this leaves readers. Are they to rise up in revolution against a persecuting regime? To wait patiently until God sends a saviour? What are the signs by which they know the time is right to act? Samson, it is to be remembered, was a great riddler, offering wisdom mixed up in darkness. The drama leaves us with questions relevant not only to the Restoration condition of persecution for dissenters, but to all persons committed to a political outlook. Along with bitterness, there is hope; and if Milton's drama eulogizes an age, it seeks to emancipate others from the violence, rage and despair there contained.

Milton's cause to be championed is multiple, then, as the blind poet engages with aesthetic, political and religious spheres of understanding. At once intensely topical and universal, representing the particular struggles of a single man at war with his wife, his captors, his father and, most of all, himself, *Samson Agonistes* also reaches across time to call upon a supervailing God to explain actions, to reveal the truth. In glorious imagery and profound bitterness, Milton offers different challenges in his drama, a contest of godliness, of virtue, of that which is essential to regain a name feared lost. When the drama closes, 'all passion spent', the contests are, however, not over. Samson, the riddler, leaves us without betraying his secret.

BIBLIOGRAPHY

Writings

Milton (1943–8).

References for Further Reading

Achinstein (1996); Bennett, Joan S. (1989); Burns (1996); Butler (1987); DiSalvo (1973); Empson (1981); Fish (1989); Frye (1965); Hill (1977); Johnson (1972); Keeble (1987); Knoppers (1994); Krouse (1949); Kugel (1988); Lewalski (1970, 1988); Lieb (1994); Loewenstein (1990); Mueller (1996); Nyquist (1994); Radzinowicz (1978); Revard (1987); Swan (1985); Wittreich (1986); Worden (1995).

26
Paradise Regained

Margaret Kean

Reading *Paradise Regained* requires constant and consistent attention. The caution is perhaps surprising given that, unlike *Paradise Lost*'s inspired revelation of suprahuman events, this later Milton poem takes as its subject matter an episode recounted in three of the four Gospel accounts of the life of Jesus. The baptism at the Jordan and the decisive rejection of Satan by Jesus in the desert mark the entry of the Son to his public office and the first proofs of his inherent authority and merit. Given such stable Gospel testimonies, one might expect the poetic narrative to adhere to established parameters. However, defamiliarization is a necessary strategy in Milton's poem as he strives to re-invest his telling of events with the full impact of a revolutionary moment, restoring a sense both of bafflement and of exhilaration to the reading experience. It is not exactly what we might have expected in terms of style or structure, and that is appropriate precisely because of the extraordinary nature of the subject matter. The lifetime of Jesus, Son of God, spans the boundary between the jurisdiction of the Mosaic law and the Christian covenant of grace; the Messiah promised by the Old Testament has arrived, but he comes to live under the Law and thereby both to fulfil the Law and in that fulfilment to surpass it. Milton's poem on the temptation of Jesus in the desert is an attempt not to revisit an inscribed event but to live out an immediate challenge: namely, what does it mean for the man Jesus to have been divinely identified as the Son of God? This reverberating question means that the wilderness setting can be employed not merely as a geographical or scriptural detail but as a means of constructing an internalized landscape of the mind. It is an indefinite locale that functions as an appropriate stage to chart intellectual and psychological activity on the part of the protagonists and also on the part of the narrator and of the reader.

The sense of transition also affects the literary expression and stylistic composition of the poem. The plain style adopted by Milton for *Paradise Regained* is not a backward-looking refraction of his previous textual attitudes but a radical forward step, prophetic stylistics on the brink of a new age. Fittingly, he gives us a debate poem exploring the impact of new priorities on accepted terminology, weighing up established modes of heroism, public duty and kingship, assessing the relevance of ancient civilizations and of inherited philosophies. Meanwhile, the opening of *Paradise Regained* foregrounds its compositional accession, introducing multiple indicators of a prophetic tradition and a poetic inheritance. From the very first line, it is impossible to read this poem without being aware of other texts, specifically scriptural and Miltonic precursors. The bard of the 'happy garden' (I. 1) reintroduces himself in order now to sing of 'the tempter foiled' (I. 5) with 'Eden raised in the waste wilderness' (I. 7). The narration is identified not only with the established bardic voice but with a heightened renewal of the same epic song. We know from *Paradise Lost* that the 'happy garden' of man's prelapsarian innocence is irrecoverable, but Michael's prophetic admonitions in the final books of the epic closed on the promise of regaining a paradise within, happier far.

This new poem undertakes to fulfil that promise, a task that bears a greater responsibility than anything undertaken in the epic. This is to be a phenomenally direct expression of God's redemptive message, but it also remains very much a Miltonic communication. Yet once more within the study of Milton poetics we are required to retrain in order to read aright, although there remain long-standing difficulties in admitting the stylistic superiority of *Paradise Regained* over *Paradise Lost*. While the moral rectitude of the poem is readily acknowledged, the reformed style of *Paradise Regained* has invoked only limited enthusiasm in its readership: it is hard to give up epic grandeur in favour of terse clarity, even when the rewards are intended to be self-evident. Intriguingly, however, the style of *Paradise Regained* does not just reconsider Miltonic epic. The many echoes of Milton's early poems suggest a further conscious assertion of individual continuity and constancy as well as a deeper re-investment of the Spenserian tradition of Protestant poetics as something in itself worthy not to be left unrecorded. A palpable sense of the Spenserian is achieved in *Paradise Regained* through its archaisms, its romance landscape, and the argument based around illusion and chivalric romance with direct echoes of Spenser's texts at Books I. 1–7, I. 25, II. 27 and III. 95. The extent of Spenserian reference to be found in this late poem by Milton is startling. Such an endorsement of a native inheritance now out of fashion is surely intended to challenge the ascendancy of Restoration court tastes. Steven Zwicker has identified just such an oppositional intent in the counter-stylistics of *Samson Agonistes* and suggests that the politics of style in the 1671 volume as a whole be more thoroughly investigated (see Zwicker 1993, 1995).

Throughout *Paradise Regained*, in terms of both style and argument, the poem endorses the individual's ability to choose rational liberation from the restrictions of conventional norms. The liberty to think for oneself under the guidance of the spirit is articulated in the Son's soliloquy and embedded throughout his trial in the desert. Yet, the attempt to return to the primacy of the Son's reading experience, 'of whom they spake / I am' (I. 262–3) can never be complete. Instead, the poetic narration offers an assimilation of textual materials that mirrors the activity undertaken by the Son in the wilderness but with an expanded reference that includes the entire New

Testament. Such a Christian witness is proleptic, but it is authorized in the life of Jesus. He is the cornerstone to a meditation that encompasses the whole Judeo-Christian tradition up to and including the Miltonic canon. One aim of the poem is certainly to place all authorities past and present under scrutiny, making them the subject of debate, and a modern readership may well find it easier to identify this principle by thinking of poetic precursors and stylistic options before turning to the weighty topic of scriptural citation within the poem. The extent of biblical inter-textuality in the poem has exercised much critical attention in recent years, clarifying for an increasingly secular readership the manifold scriptural references. Particularly informative are Mary Ann Radzinowicz's monograph, *Milton's Epics and the Book of Psalms* (1989), which offers a resonant exploration of the lexical, figural and structural influence of the psalms upon the internal stylistics of Milton's poem, and Barbara K. Lewalski's now classic *Milton's Brief Epic* (1966), which gives an exceptionally nuanced reading of the poem's scriptural structures. However, while such critical exegesis is undoubtedly helpful, no reader should allow overdependence upon critical orthodoxy to threaten the primacy of the reading experience.

The structure of *Paradise Regained* in four books should be an indicator of a radical text, intentionally dislocating the three temptations of the Gospel accounts. Yet many of the most influential critics, including Lewalski (1966), have battled to re-assimilate this dissenting structure back into readings based around conventional triads. Similarly, the strong critical agreement on the importance of John's Gospel to the construction of *Paradise Regained* needs careful consideration given that this is the evangelist who makes no direct mention of the temptation in the desert. Wittreich (1979) and Revard (1984) have both argued persuasively that the Johannine focus on the identity of the Son, his outstanding imagery of Christ as the light of truth and the concept of *kairos*, meaning the appropriate or the right time, are influential for the construction of *Paradise Regained*. Yet other aspects of John's revelation, specific-ally his emphasis on spiritual mystery and the superhuman illumination of the Logos, are not required for an understanding of Milton's presentation of the incarnate Son and may even prove misleading. Ultimately, the fit reader of *Paradise Regained* is not the one with the largest bunch of keys to unlock scriptural obscurities but rather the attentive listener, open to the challenge of new beginnings. Although this is a highly sophisticated and erudite text, the basics of right reading are taught within the poem as a matter of plain style and genuine response, with the Son's example as our immediate and sufficient guide. From his first speech in soliloquy, his voice brings clarity to an overly complicated narration. The reader who places his trust in the Son's word admits the ongoing revolutionary stimulus of the poem. That the experience is both active and educative is proven when late in Book IV Satan's irate recapitulation of the Son's life story (IV. 500–40) is judged by the reader through its contrast with the Son's own soliloquy (I. 196–293). The Son's words have been assimilated as an internal guide in our reading experience, allowing us now to do as the Son has done all along: namely, to identify and reject the Satanic version of events without anxiety or dubiety.

The ongoing debate between Satan and the Son repeatedly places Satan on the side of inherited and pragmatic readings of scripture while the Son appears less obedient to standard interpretations of the texts (see, for example, their contrasting usage of the model of Job). At significant moments, the Son is literal, but his basic verity is always a window on to a new truth, the truth of Christian metaphor. The Son's literalism is then imaginative and stimulating in direct contrast to the Satanic inertia inherent in complacent exegesis and placatory tactics. The conclusive moment in the poem is of course when the Son ousts Satan by standing upright and victorious on the temple's pinnacle. This striking achievement is structured as a revelatory crux, at one and the same time a literal and a metaphoric victory. To examine its full implications it is best to consider first the narrative of debate and then the model it constructs for Christian witness.

The devil employs Psalm 91 in a partial citation that mirrors the self-deluding employment of scripture by Marlowe's Dr Faustus. The Son counters with Deuteronomy 6: 16.

> There stand, if thou wilt stand; to stand upright
> Will ask thee skill; I to thy Father's house
> Have brought thee, and highest placed, highest is best,
> Now show thy progeny; if not to stand,
> Cast thyself down; safely if Son of God:
> For it is written, he will give command
> Concerning thee to his angels, in their hands
> They shall uplift thee, lest at any time
> Thou chance to dash thy foot against a stone.
>   To whom thus Jesus; Also it is written,
> Tempt not the Lord thy God, he said and stood.
> But Satan smitten with amazement fell
>
>   (IV. 551–62)

The Son wins with the Law and verifies its worth by embodying the message in his action: he is not going to tempt God and he says so. Yet the integrity of his statement, embodying not just the letter but the spirit of the Law, opens up his status to further examination. There is an energy in the Son's citation that suggests that his literal embodiment of Law amounts to a new meaning, the Logos speaking directly to the Tempter (i.e. when he says 'Tempt not the Lord thy God' what he means is do not tempt me). However, to foreground this Johannine option of superhuman illumination would be to damage the poem's doctrinal balance. The Son must be seen to undergo temptation in all humility as a man, and it does not follow that the Son must be aware in this moment of his own divine nature for his victory over Satan's machinations to be complete. Rather, the scriptural adjustments within the poetic construction, employing Matthew's wording but Luke's ordering of the temptations, only emphasize the point that a man (albeit a perfect man) by employing God's word is sufficient to stand though free to fall. The trap constructed by Satan is one where human action of any sort should mean victory for the tempter. If the pinnacle is precarious, a place where no man can keep his footing, then the choice is between falling to one's death and forcing divine intervention. But it is not necessary to conceive of the pinnacle as anything other than a flat-roofed tower where the choice to stand or fall is dependent on human will. This is the subtler challenge, because, for the Son to deny Satan, his choice must not be in any way about personal action or safety but rather a completely obedient submission to the Father. Such selflessness is incomprehensible to Satan. To respond in such a way is for the Son to express the Father's will not his own, and thereby to reveal himself as a perfect channel for the Father's authority. That achievement introduces a new dual standard of inter-pretation in religious teaching: the Son's response offers Gospel for the godly that follow after him but Law for the reprobate. This is to argue not only that Jesus the man must stand under the Law but moreover that Satan must be overthrown through the Law, a point endorsed by the otherwise inexcusable internal rhyming of 'written' with 'smitten'.

The Son's achievement on the temple's pinnacle embodies the perfect trust placed by the Son in his Father but the vindication of the Son's stance also allows us to access this as a specifically Miltonic model for continuing Christian witness. The wilderness debates in *Paradise Regained* can be thought of as enacting the struggle against the forcing of conscience or rather, given the invincible nature of the Son, expounding the triumph of liberty of conscience in the face of the oppressor (see Bennett 1989). The final book of Milton's epic focused on just this issue, identifying the period before the coming of the Messiah as a time when wolves would usurp church offices and thwart scripture, turning the spirit of truth into codices. The perverse activity was expressed in true Miltonic fashion as an attempt to 'unbuild / His living temples' (*PL* XII. 526–7) while the perpetrators of this heinous crime could not be overthrown until the coming of the Messiah. Now the attempt to chart 'Eden raised in the waste wilderness' leads us to the temple in Jerusalem. Although the Son will continue to live obedient to the Law until Atonement is achieved on the cross and the veil of the temple is rent, here he stands triumphant momentarily revealed as the apex of Hebraic Law and faith. The act is proleptic of Paul's hermeneutic on the internal nature of the Christian Church (1 Corinthians 6), but in Miltonic terms it is also a reconstruction of the crucial Pauline articulation in *Paradise Lost*, 'Before all temples the upright heart and pure' (*PL* I. 18). This is as shifting a set of timescales and as infolded a set of theological ideas as anything in the poem and it is completely Miltonic: all the more so when one reads the baroque phrasing of the angels for the Incarnate Son, inhabiting a 'fleshly tabernacle' (IV. 599), which takes the reader back to an earlier Miltonic poem on a later event, 'The Passion' (line 17). The angelic song of thanksgiving interlinks *Paradise Regained* with *Paradise Lost* and also with the earlier companion poems, 'On the Morning of Christ's Nativity' (the Nativity Ode) and 'The Passion'. It is a climactic hymn of victory encompassing the Christian story from Genesis to Apocalypse, and Milton's poetic witness is a part of that good news. In his first major English poem, the Nativity Ode, the narrator sought to join his voice unto the angel choir. Now that goal is accomplished, and it turns out that the angels have been voicing Miltonic harmonies all along.

This focus on the victories celebrated by the poem is somewhat pre-emptive. To follow our narrator and the Son more fully, we must go back and start where the debate finds its stimulus, in the Baptism at the Jordan. The crossing of the river Jordan as the entry of the long-wandered Israelites into the Promised Land has intense emotional and doctrinal impact. Marking the end of forty years of exile in the desert, it restores the Hebrews to divine favour as the chosen people. Here, in Milton's poem, the river is re-invested through the Son's immersion as a perfected motif of obedience. Sinners come to John the Baptist not as members of a tribe marching with the Ark of the Covenant but as penitent individuals seeking renewal. The willing involvement of the Son in such public rites of humility will ultimately transform symbolic repentance into a model for internalized conversion, opening the way for a new Christian covenant of grace and an internalized model of deliverance. The sub-mergence of the self is a concept easily grasped through the example of the Son's river baptism; in addition, Jesus's obedience in giving himself up to the Baptist and to the flowing waters of the Jordan also makes of the poem a doctrinal continuum. The flow of texts that mark the start of the Son's public office combine past Old Testament witnesses of God's goodness with a new Christian teleology. The inter-section is best seen in the recollection of the event by the Son himself.

> I as all others to his baptism came,
> Which I believed was from above; but he
> Straight knew me, and with loudest voice proclaimed
> Me him (for it was shown him so from heaven)
> Me him whose harbinger he was; and first
> Refused on me his baptism to confer,
> As much his greater, and was hardly won;
> But as I rose out of the laving stream,
> Heaven opened her eternal doors, from whence
> The Spirit descended on me like a dove,
> And last the sum of all, my Father's voice,
> Audibly heard from heaven, pronounced me his,
> Me his beloved Son, in whom alone
> He was well pleased; by which I knew the time
> Now full, that I no more should live obscure,
> But openly begin, as best becomes
> The authority which I derived from heaven.
>
> (I. 273–89)

The Baptist's call for repentance permeates the opening deliberations in *Paradise Regained*, but in the Son's soliloquy it is John's role as witness to the coming of the Messiah that is crucial. The plain style patterning enacts a profound shift from Old Testament models to the Christian antitype. The Son recounts the Baptist's climactic identification of him on the banks of the Jordan in terms that initially suggest an equivalence, the conferring perhaps of status as a fellow prophet in 'proclaimed / Me him'. The real interpretative crux is held back in the Son's narrative in order to re-affirm divine authorization, and only then can the true impact of John's proclamation be admitted, 'Me him whose harbinger he was'. John's work is done in identifying the Messiah and in conferring the sign of baptism upon him. Now heaven responds in the epiphanic descent of the dove and in the audible voice that both possesses and identifies the Son, 'pronounced me his, / Me his beloved Son'. In the Son's account, it is the Father's voice that is climactic, the 'sum of all', a reference not only to events at the Jordan but to his whole life and sense of vocation as recollected in his soliloquy.

Satan's interpretation of the events at the Jordan emphasizes the titular identification of Jesus as Son of God, but that obsession with paternity means that Satan disregards a more inclusive investigation of the role of the Messiah available through meditation upon the whole of the Father's sovereign sentence. In direct contrast, the Son goes from the Jordan into the desert in order to ponder further on the meaning of his recent experiences, and his opening soliloquy will express a crucial interactive relation between Father and Son through its patterned use of the Old Testament Psalms. The Son maintains a personal affinity with Psalm 1 from his earliest years and his opening lines, while the close of his soliloquy crowns his sense of vocation with the divine authorization that is made in the terms of Psalm 2. Psalm 2, known as the coronation psalm, holds a unique prominence in Miltonic texts. It shapes the primary action of the epic (i.e. the Father's revelation of the Son in heaven as related by Raphael in Book V of *Paradise Lost*), provides the impetus for debate in *Paradise Regained* and is, in addition, one of the psalms translated by Milton in 1653 (see Nyquist 1985). It is also a major proof text for the nature and offices of the Son in *De Doctrina Christiana* I. v, 'Of the Son of God'. Meditating on Psalm 2 is, then, something that Milton has himself spent much time doing, and in his poetic texts he engages not just with the psalm's revelatory import and apocalyptic warning but with the direct political challenge implicit in that text's demotion of secular monarchies. Yet the Father's voice at the Jordan does more than just rehearse Psalm 2. The phrasing is so familiar that its relevance can easily be overlooked, but it will be argued here that the Father's blessing of one man 'in whom alone / He was well pleased' holds the new redemptive promise of *Paradise Regained*.

The Son is the true sovereign whose coming was foretold by the psalmist and his authority comes directly from on high, not from priests or prophets. This is new, a revolutionary shift in the theological and political understanding of kingship, yet even more important in Christian terms is the re-opened channel for direct communication between God and humanity. The Son's desert meditations are described by the narrator as an attempt 'the better to converse / With solitude' (I. 190–1) and the terminology is significant. It suggests an internalization of the prelapsarian state, where the balanced mutuality of Adam and Eve as intellectual and emotional soulmates was described in terms of conversation. The essential negotiations within

Paradise Regained are to be found not in the encounter between the Son and Satan but rather in the private colloquy where the Son actively reviews his vocational choices and revealed experiences. In so doing, he is not to be thought of as self-sufficient in any egotistical sense but rather as living in a real sustaining dialogue with a spiritual soulmate. That spirit will be the Son's guide as he enters a 'pathless desert, dusk with horrid shades' (I. 296). As such romance terminology suggests, this wasteland, far from being empty, is littered with hackneyed rhetoric and familiar arguments. It is not the unknown that proves perilous but rather the temptation to return to old ways.

The spirit within guides the Son. By this means, he knows intuitively not to be distracted by Satan's oratory, and his example stands in the text for all willing to follow in his footsteps. The end of Book I gives one marked example. The Son makes an assured declaration of the end of auguries. God has sent his 'living oracle' (I. 460) into the world and the spirit of truth will henceforth dwell 'In pious hearts, an inward oracle' (I. 463). This rigorous declamation sends Satan into rhetorical overdrive. His reaction to the clarity of the Son's statement is to gloss, a response so exaggerated as to seem staged by Milton as a joke at Satan's expense. When his rhetoric finally peters out, not even Satan's politesse as he bows his 'grey dissimulation' (I. 498) can mask the nebulous nature of his activities. His substance, like his rhetorical subject, proves feigned and slowly fades away, so that at the close of Book I and day one, atrophy is the defining quality of Satanic debate. This lack of relevance is reiterated throughout the poem, but the trump card is played when, with the Son standing upright on the pinnacle, Satan slips out of the grammatical frame of the poem altogether, a lost subject unworthy of further consideration (IV. 581–95; and see Milton 1971b: 425).

The potential for the reader to become distracted by rhetorical display is clearly seen when we look at what happens on the second day in the banquet scene in Book II (285–405). This is very much a literary temptation, and the grandeur of the description is all too familiar from past romances. As readers, we are immediately connoisseurs of the table. Our interest is in luxury, both physical and stylistic, but it is also in the relish of sophisticated disputation. Careful scrutiny reveals to us that the banquet violates Jewish dietary laws. 'Grisamber-steamed' (II. 344) sums up the extravagant indulgence of a scene where the attendant striplings serving wine suggest a heady homo-eroticism and the multiple references to romance amours prove sordid. We may also be alert to the suspicion that these meats have been offered to idols, and this will allow us to interpret the scene with reference to Paul's casuistry in resolving the dispute over the consumption of temple offerings in his Letter to the Romans. Whatever our angle, we have involved ourselves in the details of the scene. In contrast, the response by Jesus is shockingly simple, 'Thy pompous delicacies I contemn' (II. 390). His brevity sweeps aside critical niceties to enforce a wider discipline. The true temptation was to 'deign to sit and eat' (II. 336; cf. 368, 377). This is a dietary ethic where one is defined not just by what one eats but by those from whom one is willing to take subsistence. Tasting the wares in looking for a subtle answer to Satanic argument is foolish. It may be unavoidable to have Satan in our midst, but we should not seek to become involved with his schemes.

We might say, then, that the Son's response to the banquet teaches us to discriminate over the company we keep. His rejection indicates a refusal to be compromised rather than a refusal to act, and this is a lesson with important implications for the immediate publication context of 1671. Both poems in the 1671 volume can be seen to address contemporary debates over religious toleration; both reject collaboration with idolatrous masters, advocating instead models of purifying self-sacrifice. Both Old Testament history and the reality of Restoration England make it an undeniable fact for Milton that God's chosen nation can turn reprobate, and such backsliding is the real threat in both 1671 poems (see Knoppers 1994). When in *Paradise Regained* Satan concludes the temptation of the kingdoms with the sight of the city of Rome, he offers the Son an opportunity to reform the seat of all temporal power, as 'All nations now to Rome obedience pay' (IV. 80). The decadence of Rome suggests of course Catholicism and, more obliquely, the Stuart monarchy; the context also implies a lost republican ideal. Satan encourages the Son to usurp power from the debauched emperor Tiberius in order to implement a much-needed programme of reform. The argument is basically that the ends will justify the means, with the Israelite nation restored to liberty, 'A victor people free from servile yoke!' (IV. 102). The Son's reply, however, is a stark and uncompromising repositioning of the model of slavery. A rhetoric of liberty is mere gloss without freedom of conscience, for who 'could of inward slaves make outward free?' (IV. 145).

The Son's message can hope to reach only those who will choose to listen to him. Reprobates who have enslaved themselves to idolatrous practices are not ultimately his concern, 'As for those captive tribes, themselves were they / Who wrought their own captivity, fell off / From God to worship calves' (III. 414–16). The Son's damning pun on 'wrought', meaning to bring about but also quite literally to fashion, combines with the sarcasm inherent in contemplating the transfer of allegiance from a transcendent God to the bathos of bovine worship. A golden calf is of course the generic Old Testament motif for idolatry from the Book of Exodus on through Kings, Chronicles and Hosea, but what is particularly noteworthy here is the specific inclusion of a reference to Bethel and Dan (III. 431). This extends the potential culpability of idolatry even to heroes of the nation, for it was Jehu, famed as the iconoclast who overthrew Jezebel and named by Milton in *Eikonoklastes* as a positive figuration for parliamentary reform, who still retained the idols at Bethel and Dan (see 2 Kings 10: 29). It is not enough for a public figure to seem praiseworthy if he maintains private idols; God's redemptive plan cannot be enacted under such double standards. Now, however, in contrast to such previous fallibility and compromise, humanity can find its true Saviour in a temperate man who lives in perfect obedience to God's will and the Law.

The difficulty of living such a selfless life is highlighted here, because at this moment in the poem the Son independently speculates on the specific outcome of future events. This means that a desire for some future restoration of the Jewish nation is as close as the Miltonic Son comes to having a weak spot. Although the Son remains certain that it is not his role to act as saviour to the lost tribes, he is willing to entertain the possibility that some other means of redemption may be given to them. Book III closes on the Son positing a miracle based on the model of the river Jordan, when the waters of the Jordan rolled back on themselves to allow the Israelites access to the Promised Land. This future deliverance of the lost tribes is speculation, not insight, and it relies on an inherited understanding of the relevance of the river crossing to the Jewish nation rather than on the new dispensation to be authorized through his own baptism. That the Son should base his response so squarely on an Old Testament model suggests that he has not been given any additional comprehension of his own role as divine Saviour. He reasons well but without realizing the full implications of his argument. This is particularly clear in his remarks upon the inefficacy of a mark of election that is merely physical, 'circumcision vain' (III. 425). He is justly severe on those who remain 'Unhumbled, unrepentant, unreformed' (III. 429) but, within his own lifetime, it is not possible for the Son to see that the transition from idolatrous practices to faith that is identifiable in the Old Testament model of the Jordan crossing is itself to be resigned in favour of Christian baptism, the new internalized mark of election.

Aside from this momentary softening the Son is careful to avoid any such restrictive speculation, particularly where his own kingly role is concerned. He relies instead on rejection of Satanic suggestion and will posit only general apocalyptic imagery, such as his reference to the tree and the stone from the book of Daniel (IV. 146–51), an open-ended projection that closes on the elusive statement, 'Means there shall be to this, but what the means, / Is not for thee to know, nor me to tell' (IV. 152–3). This technique appears defensive at first but it builds to a climax in Book IV where the Son is confident enough to posit himself as a riddle, what we might punningly term a 'think-knot'.

> Think not but that I know these things, or think
> I know them not; not therefore am I short
> Of knowing what I ought: he who receives
> Light from above, from the fountain of light,
> No other doctrine needs, though granted true;
> But these are false, or little else but dreams,
> Conjectures, fancies, built on nothing firm.
> The first and wisest of them all professed
> To know this only, that he nothing knew;
>   (IV. 286–94)

The more Satan or the reader launches a head-on assault on the intellectual conundrum, the more stubbornly it denies access; but give a little metaphoric slack and the knot will unravel before your eyes through the light of the spirit (see Lewalski 1966: 354 on the grammatical and stylistic patternings here). This is a rhetorical model for the primacy of the internalized conversation with the spirit; to enjoy the puzzle is to interact productively with God's message, whereas to compete for control of the linguistic convolutions is to exclude oneself from the redemptive plan.

This riddle opens the Son's longest response in the poem (IV. 286–364), which climaxes in the now famous oration on literary taste. Classical rhetoric, philosophy and poetics are to be rejected in favour of the doctrines and beauties of Hebraic scripture, Zion's songs 'to all true tastes excelling, / Where God is praised aright' (IV. 347–8). Many critics have expressed shock that Milton should have included such a renunciation of the classics, but the Son's spirited declamation summarizes much that has been enacted throughout the poem. Both the Son and Milton are teaching what they practise, a radical form of Protestant poetics that aims to reform the concept of a chosen nation. The 'solid rules of civil government' (IV. 358) is the theme, and significantly the Son's concept of a 'happy' state is not nostalgic for a lost Eden but excited by the prospect of future reform of earthly government. His rule will be based on an interactive understanding of the Psalms and Deuteronomy, for 'In them is plainest taught, and easiest learnt, / What makes a nation happy, and keeps it so, / What ruins kingdoms, and lays cities flat; / These only with our Law best form a king' (IV. 361–4). The reference to Law is not an afterthought. From first to last in *Paradise Regained* the Son turns to Deuteronomy to sweep Satan aside, and here his contrast of the happy nation and the ruined state is itself obliged to the binary opposition of blessed and cursed nations found in Deuteronomy 28. Here, as in the Book of Deuteronomy, we can expect that those who listen to the Lord and obey his commands will prosper while those who fail to observe his commandments shall be cursed and enslaved to their enemies. The message could not be plainer: reform or be proscribed. Freely willed obedience to the Lord and thanksgiving for His many gifts are prerequisites for the Son's soon-to-be constituted chosen people, who will enjoy a covenant that links volitional election with a preference for a native tradition of civil stylistics.

This lengthy speech by the Son amounts to a manifesto, an opportunity for him to sketch out his understanding of a reformed state. It has been occasioned by Satan's wily attempt to validate a fusion of the values of pagan antiquity with those of the Hebraic faith and to introduce a concept of self-sufficiency or self-sovereignty to the Son's sense of vocation. Both options would be idolatrous, and it is no coincidence that in introducing the temptation of classical learning in Book IV, Satan directly proposed the necessity of idolatrous compromise, 'How wilt thou reason with them, how refute / Their idolisms, traditions, paradoxes? / Error by his own arms is best evinced' (IV. 233–5). The Son, of course, brushes the temptation aside and sticks to his own agenda. He knows not to enter the mind-frame of idolators, nor would he admit the grating laxity of their style. Yet, although the Son must not compromise his standards, there is an ironic truth to Satan's argument. The construction of *Paradise Regained* is intended to facilitate the rejection of Satan's works and empty promises by insisting on his constant reliance on imitation and parodic techniques.

So, for example, the tempter is repeatedly seen to manipulate biblical texts and specifically to appropriate the Son's own lexicon, restricting the meaning of such crucial concepts as sonship, kingdom, due time or zeal. Similarly, he wilfully misinterprets the Messianic prophecies because he must presume an earthly kingdom to be implied and therefore simulates military struggle as a form of divine glory. Such tactics have disappointed many readers, making this Satan less grand, less mesmerizing, than his epic counterpart, but the aim is to insist on Satan as an obvious fraud, unworthy of our admiration. The means of achieving this come from his own mouth, error by his own arms best evinced.

One central parodic impulse in particular deserves our attention, namely the recurrent topos of reconstituted Edens and an underlying contest to produce the true Paradise Regained. The narrator promises us 'Eden raised in the waste wilderness', but Satanic imitations abound within the text. In Book II, Jesus wakes to a new day and ascends a hill. From that vantage point, he sees 'a pleasant grove, / With chant of tuneful birds resounding loud' (see II. 285–301). The Spenserian dichotomy of art versus nature is highlighted and there are recognizable similarities to the temptation of the Lady by Comus in Milton's *Masque*, but the strongest echoes are of the descriptions of Eden in *Paradise Lost*: the 'woody scene' (II. 294) and the 'chant of tuneful birds' (II. 290) recall Book IV, while the wood nymphs and setting at noon are closer to the temptation proper in Book IX of the epic. Moreover, the narrator specifically contrasts the luxuries of the banquet to the 'crude apple that diverted Eve' (II. 349), and Satan challenges the Son specifically because the banquet cannot be forbidden fruit. As we have seen, the banquet is a temptation not of carnal appetite but rather of influence, and even its introductory description can be identified as an attempt at literary seduction on the model of Edenic attractions. More problematic as a false Eden to be set aside is Athens, acclaimed as 'mother of arts / And eloquence, native to famous wits / Or hospitable, in her sweet recess, / City or suburban, studious walks and shades' (IV. 240–3). The retreats of Athenian academe are a 'sweet recess', a notable phrase once used to describe Satan's rapacious pleasure in beholding the vulnerability of Edenic innocence, figured in the nakedness of Eve (*PL* IX. 455–7). In the later poem, the violatory eroticism of the Satanic gaze has transferred into a trite complicit knowingness that through the promiscuous connotations of 'hospitable' and 'suburban' and the less than favourable tone of 'wits' makes all human delights seem stale. A little later in this same temptation, the dispersal of Socratic knowledge will be explained as a series of 'Mellifluous streams' (IV. 277) watering the philosophic schools of Greece. This is not so very far from the life-giving streams of Eden in *Paradise Lost*, but it would of course be fallacious to conceive of classical philosophy as the recovery of a garden of knowledge. In contrast stands the Son's adoption of the fountain of light metaphor as a way of expressing true enlightenment through faith (IV. 288–90).

When Satan takes the Son up to the top of the mountain to view the known world in Book III, the error of false Edens is literally mapped out. The setting initially reminds us of the Satanic prospect of Eden from the top of Mount Niphates in Book

IV of *Paradise Lost*, where ambition and malice distorted Satan's clear perspective of creational grace, but there is more to be made of a comparison of the mountain-top spectacles in *Paradise Lost* and *Paradise Regained*. In *Paradise Regained*, the detailed description given by the narrator (III. 253–64) suggests the lands lying between the rivers Tigris and Euphrates, i.e., Mesopotamia. This is the area traditionally thought to be the final location of Eden after the great flood reshaped the face of the earth. It is so identified by Milton in Book XI of *Paradise Lost*, where it is prophesied that Paradise will be forced, 'Down the great river to the opening gulf, / And there take root an island salt and bare' (*PL* XI. 833–4). Satan's temptation of the kingdoms, then, shows not a promised land but a lost Eden where postlapsarian human history with its struggles for imperial dominance is staged. The description of this plain as 'pleasant' (III. 255) is therefore particularly evocative given the well-worn etymo-logical pun found in the epic on Eden as a 'pleasant' place (e.g. *PL* IV. 214–15). The word Eden is Hebrew for delight but, as both *Paradise Lost* and *Paradise Regained* teach, postlapsarian humanity cannot hope to recover the physical geography of such a state of being. Instead, a paradise within is to be sought; just as the fertile construct of Eden built up over the course of the central books of *Paradise Lost* was abruptly destroyed in Book XI of the epic (*PL* XI. 829–35) in an iconoclastic purge that cleared the way for that new internalized concept.

The actual temptation of the Messiah in the wilderness is not given a place in the archangel Michael's summary of the life of Jesus in Book XII of *Paradise Lost*, but it is alluded to in the epic narrator's introduction of Michael's visions in Book XI. There, as here in Book III of *Paradise Regained*, it is structured as a temptation on the threshold of spiritual enlightenment. As Michael takes Adam to the top of the highest mountain in Paradise, the event is directly contrasted with Satan's temptation of Jesus, 'Not higher that hill nor wider looking round, / Whereon for different cause the tempter set / Our second Adam in the wilderness, / To show him all earth's kingdoms and their glory' (*PL* XI. 381–4). Displayed in the subsequent epic simile are the riches of four continents, Asia, Africa, Europe and the New World (*PL* XI. 385–411). Gold is the unifying focus, but wherever one looks barbarity and lucre go hand in hand, climaxing in the reference to the mythic El Dorado, the city of gold that epitomizes self-destructive aspirations. The multiplicity of reference points in this the last epic simile in *Paradise Lost* suggests a textual temptation rather than a visual one. Indeed, from the phrasing, it is impossible to tell whether Adam sees these sights at all. This makes it all the more pertinent a precursor for Satan's temptation of the kingdoms in the central books of *Paradise Regained*, where the description of the panoramic view is so extended as to lose all definition (see also Everett 1980). Fighting on the field of iron may seem standard postlapsarian degenerative behaviour, but the war machine in its 'numbers numberless' (III. 310) verges on the diabolic. Any glory here is utterly transient and, as with the banquet in Book II, the Son is not interested in such fool's gold. His overview of the temptation of the kingdoms states quite categorically, 'I never liked thy talk' (IV. 171), and the literary finesse of an entire book is toppled.

None of Satan's parodic presentations of Edenic states proves successful against the Son because he takes not territorial acquisition or personal aggrandisement but the Law as his delight (I. 206–8). Unable to seduce the Son, Satan shifts tack from rhetoric to force. First, he conjures up a storm at night and then, when that proves ineffective, he transports the Son to the heights of the temple. Satanic bluster has not shaken the Son's reserve and nor will atmospherics. 'Me worse than wet thou find'st not' (IV. 486) is the Son's cool dismissal of the terrors of the night. The rebuff initially seems close to banal but the calm authority behind Christ's irony exposes our critical superciliousness. Plain truth cuts through show, so that the only ridiculous figure is Satan, naïve enough either to anticipate the Son's fall away from an inner peace of mind through mere physical discomfort or to attempt an external baptism with rainwater. Following this defeat and incensed by the Son's stoicism, Satan finally rushes the Son to the pinnacle where, with true dramatic irony, in the last-ditch attempt to force the Son off balance, Satan manages only to overthrow himself.

The Son stands on the pinnacle as axiomatic proof, a direct revelation within the poem of God's redemptive intention. This is a universal test of faith, not just for the Son but for Satan, for the angelic host, for the narrator, and for us as readers. Each individual must respond to the resonant message of Christian redemption actualized in the Son's disciplined achievement. The Son standing on the pinnacle offers real insight into a vertical axis of communication between divine transcendence and human temporality. There is nothing more to be debated, only spontaneous hymns of thanksgiving to be sung. As the angelic choirs voice their praises of the Son, the poem forces its readers to look up and consider not just the epiphanic moment but a graceful stylization of kenosis as the Son returns to man's estate. The slow motion descent is baroque, a revised version of meek-eyed Peace spiralling down to assist mankind in Milton's Nativity Ode (lines 45–52). It is precisely because the Son willingly reassumes his humble role on earth that the angels and the narrator can join in proclaiming the victory both of the Son and of the poem. Eden has been raised in the wilderness,

> For though that seat of earthly bliss be failed,
> A fairer Paradise is founded now
> For Adam and his chosen sons, whom thou
> A Saviour art come down to reinstall.
>   (IV. 612–15)

The poem has charted the regaining of Paradise in the good news of the Son's victory over Satan and in the ongoing commitment shown by the Son in his return to assist humankind. The models of Old Testament prophecy have transformed into New Testament promise within a revolutionary poem that educates us not to set our trust in pleasant places but to meditate upon the vital truth of one man in whom the Father was 'well pleased'.

BIBLIOGRAPHY

Writings	*References for Further Reading*
Milton (1971b).	Bennett, Joan S. (1989); Cullen (1974); Everett (1980); Grose (1988); Haskin (1994); Kirkconnell (1973); Knoppers (1994); Lewalski (1966, 1971); Loewenstein (1994); MacCallum (1986); Martz (1980); Nyquist (1985); Quint (1993); Radzinowicz (1989); Revard (1984); Wittreich (1971, 1979); Zwicker (1993, 1995).

PART IV
Influences and Reputation

27

Reading Milton, 1674–1800

Kay Gilliland Stevenson

The general outlines of the story are simple and well known. Early sales of *Paradise Lost* (1667) were slow. The meagre sum paid to Milton by the printer Samuel Simmons (five pounds down, another five pounds after the first impression of 1,300 copies was sold, with additional payments of five pounds to be made after two further impressions of 1,500 copies each) seems somewhat less shocking a bargain when it is noted how long it took Simmons to clear his stock; the second payment was not made until 1669. Although during his continental tour in 1638–9 Milton had been warmly received in Italian literary circles, and some flattering verses were then written in his honour, his own countrymen were less ready to acknowledge his merit. Before the Commonwealth and Protectorate period, when most of his energy was devoted to prose, he brought out a collection of *Poems* (1645), but while Edmund Waller's collection in the same year was an immediate success, Milton's volume was not reprinted until after *Paradise Lost*, *Paradise Regained* and *Samson Agonistes* had begun to make a mark. In 1692, the popular bi-weekly *Athenian Mercury* printed the question, amusing to a modern eye, 'Whether Milton and Waller were not the best English Poets? and which the better of the two?' The answer is judiciously balanced:

> They were both excellent in their kind, and exceeded each other, and all besides. Milton was the fullest and loftiest, Waller the neatest and most correct Poet we ever had. But yet we think Milton wrote too little in Verse, and too much in Prose, to carry the Name of Best from all others. (16 January 1691/92, p. 1, question 3)

Qualified as it is, this journalistic note indicates that a poetic reputation was well in the making. Each of the three major works is briefly praised, and approving references to 'Lycidas' and to 'L'Allegro' and 'Il Penseroso' among the 'Juvenile Poems' indicate that they too are accumulating an audience.

It grew large. By the end of the eighteenth century, more than a hundred editions of Milton's poetry had appeared, along with translations into Greek, Latin, Italian,

French, Dutch, German, Spanish, Portuguese and Russian. In a single day in 1760 the entire first edition of the libretto to *Paradise Lost: An Oratorio*, a thousand copies, sold out. Straightforward editions, commentaries, translations, adaptations with varying degrees of faithfulness to the original, imitations, casual allusions all provide evidence for various readings of Milton. As early as 1674 a major contemporary announced the first of many creative reworkings of the epic. In April, John Dryden entered in the Stationers' Register *The Fall of Angells and man in innocence: An heroick opera,* eventually retitled *The State of Innocence, and Fall of Man: an Opera* (1677). In July of the same year the second edition of *Paradise Lost,* now in twelve books rather than in ten, appeared, with judicious commendatory verses by Andrew Marvell. Thereafter, major land-marks which are sign or cause of Milton's accelerating reputation are the illustrated folio edition published by Jacob Tonson in 1688, the explanatory notes of Patrick Hume in 1695, Joseph Addison's set of eighteen *Spectator* papers in 1712, and the production by Richard Bentley of *Paradise Lost: A New Edition* in 1732, which by its notorious suggestions for emendation provoked intense attention to every detail of the text.

Students of Milton are, understandably, alert to signs of his impact on English literature, that is, both on subsequent writers and on readers' assumptions about Milton's place in an emergent sense of English literary history. We might also note silences. In an essay 'Of Poetry' published in 1690, the distinguished statesman and prose stylist Sir William Temple vigorously asserts that by 'true poetry' he means epic; he dismisses smaller genres as the choice of those 'wanting either Genius or Application for Nobler or more Laborious Productions, as *Painters* that cannot Succeed in great Pieces, turn to Miniature' (325–6). For Temple, the essential poets are Homer and Virgil (295–8); among the moderns, only Tasso, Ariosto, and Spenser 'have made any Atchievement in *Heroick* Poetry worth Recording' (324–5). Milton's name is never mentioned. When Temple ignores Milton, however, he also ignores Davenant and Cowley, whose reputations were still high.

Although Milton's *Paradise Lost* and *Paradise Regained* are the seventeenth-century epics which still attract an audience, it is useful to remember that these works appeared within a living tradition of English heroic verse, a tradition in which some poets followed Spenser's precedent of planning more than they finished. Sir William Davenant's incomplete *Gondibert* (1651), medieval Italian adventures written in quatrains, was warmly commended by Thomas Hobbes (1651/1673). Abraham Cowley, described by Milton's nephew Edward Phillips as 'the most applauded Poet of our Nation both of the present and past Ages' (1675 pt 1, p. 1), published four books (of a projected Virgilian twelve) of his rhyming biblical epic *Davideis* (1656). Richard Blackmore's *Prince Arthur* (1695) went through three editions in two years, and its sequel *King Arthur* (1697) may have contributed to his knighthood. Although he finished two further epics centred on British monarchs, *Alfred* and *Eliza*, his afterfame shrinks to an episode of *The Dunciad* where Blackmore, 'Who sings so loudly, and who sings so long', wins a contest on the grounds of volume and voluminousness (Pope 1963, 'Dunciad Variorum' II. 256). Despite Milton's own hesitation about whether he lived in 'an age too late' for epic, ambitious and able writers continued to see the genre as an alluring challenge. Dryden followed his adaptation of *Paradise Lost* by announcing in the dedication to *Aureng-Zebe* (1676) his plan to turn from drama to epic: 'Some little hopes I have yet remaining . . . to make the world some amends for many ill plays by an heroic poem.' It is a promise he did not fulfil, except as a translator, but he continues to express admiration for epic as 'certainly the greatest work of human nature' ('A Discourse Concerning Satire' [1693]; 1962, II: 96). Some of his less generous comments on Milton, such as the taunt that he wrote in blank verse because he had little talent for rhyme (1962, II: 84–5), may be coloured by defensiveness and rivalry. While epic remains a viable option for living writers, discussion of Milton's versification, diction and choice of subject has a practical edge. John Dennis, in *The Grounds of Criticism in Poetry* (1704), promises 'to mark his defects with so much the more exactness, because some of them ought to be avoided with the utmost Caution, as being so great, that they would be Insupportable in any one who had not his extraordinary Distinguishing Qualities' (Dennis 1939, I: 334).

Pope, at the end of his life, was planning an epic on Brutus, the legendary founder of Britain. Although only a fragment survives, it demonstrates a significant shift from the couplets Pope used in his translations of Homer to Miltonic blank verse. By placing the direct object first and delaying the appearance of the imperative verb until the start of the fifth line, he recalls Milton's imitation of Virgil in the opening lines of *Paradise Lost*:

> The Patient Chief, who lab'ring long, arriv'd
> On Britains Shore and brought with fav'ring Gods
> Arts Arms and Honour to her Ancient Sons:
> Daughter of Memory! from elder Time
> Recall; and me, with Britains Glory fir'd,
> Me, far from meaner Care or meaner Song,
> Snatch to thy Holy Hill of Spotless Bay,
> My Countrys Poet, to record her Fame.
>
> (Pope 1963: 836)

The patriotic note struck here is one often heard in general accounts of epic, closely associated with a nation's fame, and specifically in comments on Milton's significance. In 1704 Dennis describes Milton as having 'resolved, for his Country's Honour and his own, to present the World with an Original Poem' (1939, I: 333). He repeats and expands the point in 1711:

> He who is familiar with Homer, and intimate with Virgil . . . requires something that is far above the Level of Modern authors, something that is great and wonderful. If I were to recommend a *British* Poet to one who had been habituated to *Homer* and *Virgil*, I would for the Honour of my country, and of my own Judgment, advise him to read *Milton*; who often equals both the *Grecian* and the *Roman* in their extraordinary Qualities, and sometimes surpasses them, is more lofty, more terrible, more vehement, more astonishing, and has more impetuous and more divine Raptures. (I: 408)

Voltaire in 1727 wryly acknowledges the failure of France to produce anything comparable; Milton's achievement is treated as an example of national genius (Shaw-cross 1970: 248).

Invited by the publisher Jacob Tonson to contribute commendatory verses to the handsome folio edition of 1688, Dryden produced an epigram printed under an engraved portrait of Milton:

> *Three* Poets, *in three distant Ages born,*
> Greece, Italy, *and* England *did adorn.*
> *The* First *in loftiness of thought Surpass'd,*
> *The* Next *in Majesty; in both the* Last.
> *The force of* Nature *cou'd no farther goe:*
> *To make a* Third *she joynd the former two.*

At face value, this high praise now seems both generous and just. Milton is acknow-ledged as the ornament of English letters, uniting the strengths of Homer and of Virgil. There are reasons, however, for not taking it at face value in 1688. The fulsomeness of commendatory verses in most seventeenth-century volumes is conventional. When, after circulating in manuscript for some years, the text of Dryden's 'opera' *The State of Innocence* (1677) appeared in print, his fellow dramatist Nathaniel Lee supplied verses politely granting that 'To the dead Bard, your fame a little owes, / For *Milton* did the Wealthy Mine disclose / And rudely cast what you could well dispose' ('To Mr. Dryden, on his Poem of Paradice', lines 11–13; Dryden 1994). Dryden's epigram, almost perfunctory, echoes the easy, graceful, but clearly hyperbolic compliment offered much earlier by an Italian friend, printed with Milton's *Poems* of 1645:

> *Graecia Maeonidem, jactet sibi Roma Maronem,*
> *Anglia Miltonum jactat utrique parem.*
> (Selvaggi 1645: 4)

Or, as the lines were translated by William Cowper:

> *Greece, sound thy Homer's, Rome, thy Virgil's name,*
> *But England's Milton equals both in fame.*
> (Cowper 1808: 3)

What in the mid-seventeenth century was outrageously flattering could later appear as measured homage. By the mid-eighteenth century, Milton's epic was seriously treated as comparable to ancient masterpieces and worthy of the same careful treat-ment. This attitude is explicit in the language Thomas Newton used in 1749: 'My design in the present edition is to publish the *Paradise Lost* as the work of a classic author cum notis variorum' (1749: a2^r).

Among early praise for the epic, Marvell's verses in the edition of 1674 are con-vincing precisely because carefully argued, noting the dangers as well as the achievements of Milton's bold plan. 'Bold' is Marvell's first rhyme-word (linked with 'vast Design unfold') and 'sublime' is set against 'rhyme' in his final couplet. The invigorating energy of Milton is what many of his admirers celebrate, again and again, in the decades which follow. In *The Annual Miscellany for the Year 1694* (the fourth of the anthologies nicknamed 'Dryden's Miscellanies' or 'Tonson's Miscellanies'), the young Addison published a versified history of English literature, 'An Account of the Greatest English Poets'. His account of great poets begins with Chaucer, Spenser and Cowley.

> But *Milton* next, with high and haughty Stalks,
> Unfettered in *Majestic Numbers* Walks;
> No vulgar *Heroe* can his Muse ingage
> Nor Earth's wide Scene confine his hallow'd Rage.
>   . . .
> Whilst ev'ry Verse, array'd in Majesty,
> Bold, and sublime, my whole Attention draws,
> And seems above the Critics nicer Laws.
>   (lines 56–9, 65–7)

Bold, sublime, unfettered, high: these are adjectives which recur in Miltonic criticism. The scenes on which Addison focuses tend to be favourite choices throughout the eighteenth century. His most sustained praise is for the battle scenes, which 'stun the reader with the din of war' (line 73); after Book VI, it is the 'first gay scenes of *Paradise*' (line 77) which he explicitly admires. Given Milton's play with chronology, Addison here may mean either Book IV, where the reader first sees Eden, or Book VIII, where Adam recounts earlier experience, his first moments of consciousness. Almost two decades later, in the series of *Spectator* papers on the epic, Addison says of Adam's speech to Raphael:

> There is no Part of the Poem more apt to raise the attention of the Reader, than this Discourse of our great Ancestor; as nothing can be more surprizing and delightful to us, than to hear the Sentiments that arose in the first Man while he was yet new and fresh from the hands of his Creator. (*Spectator* No. 345; 1965, I: 281)

In comparison, despite a lovely phrase on Milton's 'Exuberance of Imagination' in Book IV, Addison finds the description of Paradise there comparable to still-life paintings: although ornamental and beautiful, suggestive of Adam and Eve's happiness, these passages do not hold his attention long (*Spectator* No. 321; 1965, I: 170).

Concentration on the terrestrial scenes leads to viewing Milton in a rosy or domestic light. Cherishing his pictures of married love, Richard Steele invents, in a *Tatler* essay of 11 October 1709, a wedding feast at which the celebrations include recitation from Book IV of *Paradise Lost* of the passage beginning 'Hail wedded love' (IV. 750). In the final issue of the same year, describing the sorrow of a family gathered around a deathbed, he again thinks of Book IV and of Eve's celebration of companionship and conversation in the lines beginning 'With thee conversing I forget all time' (IV. 639–56). As he savours the quotation, which catalogues the beauties of Paradise, Steele almost abandons the sad scene from which the periodical essay began. Analysing what is pleasing about the description, noting both the variety of imagery and 'the Recapitulation of each particular Image, with a little varying of the Expression', he remarks on genre:

> It may further be observed, That though the Sweetness of these Verses has something in it of a Pastoral, yet it excels the ordinary Kind, as much as the Scene of it is above an ordinary Field or Meadow. (Steele, 30 December 1709: 449–50)

Slightly earlier, in *An Essay upon Pastoral* (1695), Edward Howard, Earl of Suffolk, repeatedly links praise of pastoral life with Eden, and with Adam and Eve in their state of innocence. In 1725 he fills out a slim volume of his own pastoral dialogues, *The Shepherdess's Golden Manual*, with 'Elegancies Taken out of Milton's Paradise Lost'. A more consecutive version of the epic than it sounds, this is a Reader's Digest selection of about a thousand lines, a tenth of the whole. Howard jettisons almost all of Books I–III and V–VIII, and all but the end of Book XII, providing bridging subtitles to identify passages like the scene in which 'our great progenitor conferring with Raphael the Angel, Eve modestly withdraws among the Flowers', but omitting the substance of that conference between Adam and Raphael. Boldness here disappears into picturesque landscape and domesticity. Richard Jago similarly prunes the epic. As he explains in an afterword to *Adam, or the Fatal Disobedience* (1784), his procedure in attempting to turn *Paradise Lost* into an oratorio (never performed) was to collect beautiful passages, 'confining himself to those passages which have a more immediate reference to the principal story, and omitting what was more remote and digressive' (Jago 1784; Stevenson and Seares 1998: 170). Almost all the words are Milton's, but as Jago selects and modifies his material, Eden takes on a curiously languorous atmosphere. Two of the three acts open with the human pair sitting or reclining – not, as Milton first shows them, 'Godlike erect' (IV. 289). A more intelligent though still radically shortened adaptation, the 1760 oratorio *Paradise Lost*, with a libretto by Benjamin Stillingfleet and music by Handel's younger friend John Christopher Smith, also focuses on Adam and Eve. Through a framing chorus of angels, however, Smith and Stillingfleet manage to give at least a hint of the War in heaven, the Creation and, climactically, the restoration of Paradise through the Incarnation. But abridgement of *Paradise Lost* is a perilous undertaking. As Samuel Johnson declares, 'There is perhaps no poem, of the same length, from which so little can be taken without apparent mutilation' (1905, I: 175).

While some readers focus, in selected passages, on a tamed Milton, domestic or pastoral, others emphasize his energy, even strenuousness. The descriptive and meditative Milton of 'Il Penseroso' is close to James Thomson throughout *The Seasons*, but an explicit passage of praise in 'Summer' stresses his exhilarating qualities:

A Genius universal as his Theme;
Astonishing as Chaos, as the bloom
Of blowing Eden fair, as heaven sublime
(lines 1569–71)

The artist Jonathan Richardson varies Addison's verb 'stun' to describe himself as 'dazzled' when, in his teacher's painting-room, he first came across *Paradise Lost* (1734: cxviii). In his preface to copious explanatory notes (546 pages, after a biographical introduction of 132 pages), Richardson comments that 'a Reader of *Milton* must be Always upon Duty; he is Surrounded with Sense, it rises in every Line, every Word is to the Purpose; There are no Lazy Intervals'. Furthermore, he continues: 'His Silence has the Same Effect, not only that he leaves Work for the Imagination when he has Entertain'd it, and Furnish'd it with Noble Materials; but he Expresses himself So Concisely, Employs Words So Sparingly, that whoever will Possess His Ideas must Dig for them' (1734: cxliv). Effort is, however, accompanied by sumptuous pleasure; he learns much of the poem by heart, to 'Store up in my Mind Passages to Regale and Nourish my Mind with at All times' (1734: cxix).

As a mark of popular opinion that reading Milton was exciting but demanding, there are light verses written by the musicologist Charles Burney. In a letter to his wife, written on 19 December 1751, he briskly catalogues the ancient and modern authors they happily read together, and asks:

Among the bards who mount the skies
Whoe'er to such a height could rise
As Milton? he, to whom 'twas given
To plunge to Hell, and mount to heaven.
How few like thee – my soul's delight!
Can follow him in every flight?
(Burney 1991: 5)

His questions seem to be focused on range and sublimity, but whether Milton was 'too hard' for an ordinary reader is a problem to which commentators will return.

The sublimity or boldness of Milton posed a particular problem for neoclassical critics. How were his daring flights to be reconciled with rules based on Homer and enunciated by Aristotle? Was he 'irregular' or could he be measured by established standards and found successful? The contrasting answers to these questions are interesting as one among other instances of contradictory responses to Milton's work. A study of how he was read, during the century or so after his death, often means noting antitheses. Stunning warfare or pastoral bliss, soaring and plunging verse – the contrasts sort out Milton's readers according to their own energies and tastes. He appears pastoral, domestic or sublime from varying points of view. His affinities with painting and with music are explored by readers who most appreciate the visual or aural arts. The eighteenth-century critical habit of analysing Beauties and Faults in some sort of judicious balance is important in keeping enthusiasts for Milton from lapsing into idolatry.

In *The Grounds of Criticism in Poetry* (1704) Dennis puts the case for transgression of the epic rules in strong terms, while at the same time praising the daring genius with which Milton 'made his Country a glorious present of the most lofty, but most irregular Poem, that has been produc'd by the Mind of Man'. On the question of genre, he cautiously calls *Paradise Lost* 'something like an Epick Poem'. That hesitation, however, is not a sign of disapproval, but an acknowledgement that Milton's poem 'by virtue of its extraordinary subject, cannot so properly be said to be against the rules, as it may be affirmed to be above them all'. Dennis asserts that Milton was completely aware of what he was doing, and that he deliberately resolved 'to break thro' the Rules of *Aristotle*' (1939, I: 333). The phrasing implies liberation rather than transgression. Pointing out that Aristotle was a descriptive rather than prescriptive critic, Dennis acknowledges that in the *Iliad* the primary conflict is between man and man, between Achilles and Hector, with the gods secondary. Aristotle's statements about epic rest on observation of what Homer did. In Milton's plot, however, all the characters except Adam and Eve are infernal or divine. It follows that the primary conflict is 'the Devil on one side and Man on the other: and the Devil is properly his Hero, because he gets the better' (I: 334). Perhaps Dennis is picking up from Dryden's dedication to his translation of the *Aeneid* an off-hand comment that Satan is the hero of *Paradise Lost* (1697; Dryden 1962, II: 233). As this long-running question begins to find a place in Miltonic criticism, it is worth pausing to note how thoroughly Aristotelian these neoclassical critics are, resting their assertions on the primacy of plot over character. Dennis spells out the basis for his judgement: Satan wins in the temptation scene; the implicit comparison with Hector and Achilles is useful; Hector is defeated, but is far more admirable than his opponent.

Although in his youthful verses on the greatest English poets, Addison threw off a line asserting that Milton 'seems above the Critics nicer Laws', he set out in his systematic survey of *Paradise Lost* to 'examine it by the Rules of Epic Poetry' (*Spectator* No. 267; 1965, II: 539). The set of eighteen *Spectator* papers, published on a series of Saturdays between January and May 1712, measures Milton's work in comparison with that of Homer and Virgil. Six general essays consider the Fable, Characters, Sentiments and Language, with Addison concluding that 'he excels, in general, under each of these Heads' (*Spectator* No. 291; 1965, III: 35). He next surveys Beauties and Defects, then devotes one essay to each of the twelve books of the epic. The paper on Defects is especially interesting, not simply for the faults Addison admits (primarily those of diction) but for his defence of Milton against faults others have alleged. He takes up Dryden's charges that the plot is imperfect because its outcome is unhappy, and the notion that Satan is the hero, and attacks them together. He notes the mortifying scene in Book X when Satan, not allowed to remain triumphant for long, returns to hell. Furthermore, the final book cheers and comforts Adam and Eve with visions of the enemy's defeat, and promises of Paradise restored. As for the hero, if one must name one, it is the Messiah (*Spectator* No. 297; 1965, III: 59).

The importance of Addison's *Spectator* papers lies not only in his specific comments and full critical examination of *Paradise Lost*, but in the implication that anyone in Britain who is reasonably literate would be interested in the poem. Given its immense circulation, and multiple readers for each copy delivered to a country house or urban coffee-house, the *Spectator* enlarged Milton's audience simply by assuming that it already existed. How much help, apart from Addison's survey of the epic, did such an audience need?

The first major guidebook appeared early. In 1695 Patrick Hume provides a prospectus of his offerings on the title page of a 321-page folio volume, issued separately or bound with Tonson's edition of the epic:

> Annotations on Milton's Paradise Lost. Wherein The Texts of Sacred Writ relating to the Poem, are Quoted; The Parallel Places and Imitations of the most Excellent Homer and Virgil, Cited and Compared; All the Obscure Parts render'd in Phrases more Familiar; The Old and Obsolete Words, with their Originals, Explain'd and made Easie to the English Reader.

These references to 'All the Obscure Parts' and to 'Obsolete Words... made Easie' may be as frightening as reassuring. The second word of Hume's learned notes gives Paradise in Hebrew characters; quotations of parallel passages from Greek and Latin poetry are plentiful. The work pays tribute to Milton as a poet worth explication, well on his way to being treated as a 'classic'. Occasionally, as he promises on the title page, Hume paraphrases passages of Milton's verse in order to make sentence structure and meaning clear.

Difficulties perceived in reading Milton were related to the qualities which were admired. Richardson's life of Milton reports that 'He Acquir'd Betimes an Uncommon Stock of Learning, and all Those Languages in which the Variety and Sublimity of Humane Knowledge is Treasur'd up' (1734: xii). What here is seen as a strength can also be a burden to ordinary readers, producing 'an Unpleasing Mortification from a sense of their Own Deficiency, as well as Regret for what they Lose' (1734: clxvi).

In 1745, 'A Gentleman of Oxford' reduced the entire poem to paraphrase, *The State of Innocence: and Fall of Man. Described in Milton's Paradise Lost*, a version whose popularity is indicated by the number of reprints. The British Library holds at least five different London editions and one issued in Aberdeen. Few editors are so explicit, or as daunting, in defining what one must know before reading *Paradise Lost*. He catalogues what, he alleges, are necessary fields of learning: understanding of rhetoric, mathematics, history, astronomy 'and all the other human arts and sciences'. Nor is that all that the readers of Milton should master: 'Besides which it is necessary they should understand the Hebrew, Chaldee, Arabic, Syriac, Phoenician, and Egyptian, and all the dead languages, with the living and modern ones, in all their different dialects.' Such a prescription sounds like a parody of the superaddressee described in Bakhtin's 'The Problem of the Text', that ideal audience 'whose absolutely just responsive understanding is presumed, either in some metaphysical distance or in

distant historical time' (Bakhtin 1986: 126). Our Gentleman of Oxford soon, however, reveals a double sense of imagined audiences, a magnificent remote one for
Milton's poem and a dependent proximate one for his own publication. Concerned for
those who 'passing by the most instructive passages, or else uncertainly guessing at
their meaning and reading altogether doubtfully, lose the pleasure and benefit', he
offers large quantities of aid:

> It was not thought sufficient to pick out lines here and there, and explain them only, for
> it is impossible to know which part may be difficult to each reader; for which reason, the
> whole is render'd into plain and intelligible prose, the sense preserv'd, and nothing
> omitted that may make it clear to all readers: care being taken not to let any word pass,
> whether proper names of men or places, or technical words, without a note, to make
> them appear plain, and doing the same by all the mythology or fables of the ancients. It
> must certainly be a great ease, to have recourse to such a transcript in prose, and the help
> of such a number of explicit notes. (A2ᵛ)

Although the Preface begins with the words 'The poem', the poetry is what is entirely
omitted from the volume. Prose paraphrase has an honest place in the history of
understanding *Paradise Lost*, or indeed any text. In 'Discourse and the Novel', Bakhtin
considers the standard school exercises of 'reciting by heart' and 'telling in one's own
words' as ways of assimilating and transmitting another person's words (Bakhtin
1981: 341–2). A letter by Benjamin Stillingfleet, when he was planning an edition of
the epic (abandoned when he heard that Thomas Newton's was forthcoming),
describes writing out paraphrases of difficult passages as part of his process of coming
to understand them. There is a great difference, however, between process and
product. From Patrick Hume's commentary onward, in editions by Bentley, Newton
and other scholars, paraphrases are offered from time to time to indicate one way of
reading the passage, but these interpretative rephrasings are meant to be heard against
Milton's own lines. The audience for the Gentleman of Oxford's volume, though
possibly to be imagined with both that and a text of the poem before him, may be too
sensible of the 'great ease' offered by prose alone.

Furthermore, the extensive 'Historical, Philosophical and Explantory Notes',
though ostentatiously educational on their own, lure attention away from the poem
towards matters of fact. Mechanically identifying any proper noun, this editor distract-
ingly emphasizes potential difficulties of the text in the very process of providing
information meant to be helpful, and when the notes interrupt reading, this helpfulness
can be a hindrance, disrupting the rhythm of the lines which pull the understanding
forward with the cumulative force of their sense. Half the first page of text is given to
'Sinai, Heb. from Seneh, a bush, or thorn', and while a reader with no echoes of the Old
Testament ringing in his ears needs to know that 'God appeared theron frequently to
Moses', the information that 'The mountain is round, takes 7,000 steps to the top, has
some olive-trees, date-trees, &c. and several chapels, monasteries, cells, and mosques,
&c.' is closer to a geography classroom or travel brochure than to the poem.

More sensitive to the needs of an unlearned audience, John Wesley edited *An Extract from Milton's Paradise Lost. With Notes* (1763, reprinted 1791). In a preface 'To the Reader', he asserts 'this inimitable work, amidst all its beauties, is unintelligible to abundance of readers: the immense learning which he has everywhere crowded together, making it quite obscure to persons of common education', creating difficulties 'almost insuperable'. The cluster of words he chooses – inimitable, unintelligible, immense, obscure, insuperable – verge on parody of Milton's invocation to Light. Nonetheless, Wesley's editorial procedure shows great confidence, inviting direct and intimate responses to Milton by 'persons of common education'. Despite omitting 'those lines which I despaired of explaining to the unlearned', he preserves a larger proportion of the original poem than other abridgers do, printing over 80 per cent of the lines. Crisp, brief notes provide just enough information to avert frustration in someone uncertain about whether a proper name denotes a place or a mythological figure. Most significant, however, and in contrast to his comments on unintelligibility, Wesley marks with an asterisk about a fifth of all the lines he prints, as particularly suitable for learning by heart. Here he encourages, and shows his faith in, the possibility of real understanding, not as a matter of immediate and intellectual assent but as a process of taking the poem's words into the reader's consciousness, where they continue to reverberate. Such internalizing of Milton's language is a far cry from distrust, distance or distaste; what is encouraged, and assumed to be available, is nourishment, assimilation.

Although Wesley speaks of Milton as 'inimitable', he was often imitated. That Milton was an energizing rather than an inhibiting force on major poets of the eighteenth century is eloquently demonstrated by Dustin Griffin. It would be foolish here to try to summarize the arguments he presents in *Regaining Paradise: Milton and the Eighteenth Century*. The point to be made is not a large one about influence, but a more modest observation that the proliferation of comic poems written in explicit imitation of Milton is a sign of how large a readership he had acquired. Parodies depend for their effect on knowledge of the original. 'The Splendid Shilling' by John Philips (printed twice in 1701, with an authorized edition in 1705), skilfully adapts Milton's blank verse cadences and evocative geographical references in a poem about living in poverty, 'from Pleasure quite debarr'd' (line 115). Other poets too trust that their familiarity with Milton will be matched by that of their readers. 'Fanscombe Barn. In Imitation of Milton' by Anne Finch, Countess of Winchilsea (1713), relies on memory of the prelapsarian conversations of Adam and Eve. John Armstrong's *The Oeconomy of Love* (1736, often reprinted, with an authorized edition of 1768), which focuses on a pair of young lovers before and after their first sexual experience, asks readers to enjoy both his handling of plot, the loss of innocence, and echoes of Milton's language.

Objection to such a parody as sacrilegious shows a tendency to treat the poem, as well as its subject, as sacred. Some began to find reading and memorizing *Paradise Lost* a pious exercise, like reading the Bible. To some serious-minded men, however, it was matter of concern whether the combination of doctrinal matter and poetic imagination verged on the blasphemous. Dennis put the theoretical case that a poet writing Christian truths has an advantage over a poet of similar talent whose material is false (1939, I: 251). Others, including Shaftesbury and Johnson, were more nervous about tampering with biblical stories and awesome religious incidents. Gibbon questions whether the Infinite Being, God himself, in contrast to the fabulous deities of pagan religion, was a proper character for poetic invention (Shawcross 1970: 145; 1972: 251). Handel turned down at least two proposals to make *Paradise Lost* into an oratorio, even though Mrs Delany, one of the aspiring librettists, cited the approval given by her husband, a Doctor of Divinity. Handel's settings of 'Il Penseroso' and 'L'Allegro' (padded out by *Il Moderato*) and of *Samson Agonistes* were a success, but, like most of Handel's other oratorios, *Samson* is an Old Testament story not central to faith and doctrine. What was appropriate in a church was to some minds sharply different from what was appropriate in a theatre (Stevenson and Seares 1998: 66–9).

What Milton called 'my advent'rous Song' (*PL* I. 13) invited translation into literal music. The passage which particularly attracted composers was the morning hymn of Adam and Eve, 'These are thy glorious works, parent of good . . .' (V. 153–208), set at least half a dozen times within the eighteenth century, for performance alone or as part of a larger work, climactically by Haydn. A simple setting by John Ernest Galliard is interesting partly because of its gender distinctions, clear in his division of lines between Adam and Eve. Retaining Milton's words, which are based on Psalm 148, inviting all of creation to join in praise of the Lord, Galliard assigns to Eve the appeals to stars, moon, mists and fountains: he gives to Adam addresses to sun, the air and elements, winds and pines. In the most ambitious of the musical interpretations of *Paradise Lost*, the 1760 oratorio, Benjamin Stillingfleet and John Christopher Smith make Eve's part particularly prominent and attractive. Her songs associate her with the beauty of the natural world, and with the pathos of departure from Paradise. In keeping with an eighteenth-century delight in Milton as the poet of marital love, the duets of Adam and Eve emphasize harmony with God and with one another. Only in the morning hymn and evening hymn do they sing together. Recrimination after the Fall is minimized; there are only two short passages of recitative in which Adam blames Eve, and Eve has only lines of penitence and entreaty.

Interpretation through visual arts offers further insights into how Milton was read during this period. Milton's descriptive passages were often compared with paintings. A special section of Richardson's index to his *Explanatory Notes* lists forty-four 'Pictures' on which he has commented (1734: 544–5). The sense of Milton as pictorial is so strong that in 1776 Richard Graves uses comparison with Milton as part of a compliment to Gainsborough. There were a dozen illustrated editions of the epic before the end of the eighteenth century, inviting comparison and analysis. How imposing, degenerate or attractive Satan is made is, in particular, one of the clearly significant indicators of variant readings. Hume's *Annotations* include reproof for the artist responsible for the final illustration in Tonson's folio, showing the expulsion from Paradise. The artist had been looking at other paintings, rather than at the poem, and therefore misrepresents Milton's description. Hume tartly comments on the inaccuracy of interpretation in the engraved illustrations of 1695. His annotation to XII. 637 'In either hand, &c' reads: 'The Angel led our Parents, loath to depart from their beloved Seat, in each hand, which the Designer of the Copper Plate has not well exprest, representing him, *shoving them out*, as we say, *by Head and Shoulders*' (321).

Questions of taste and accuracy lead us back to the many editions of Milton's poetry published during the century. Richard Bentley's simple title, *Milton's* Paradise Lost: *A New Edition* (1732), scarcely indicates how sweeping, or in Pope's word 'slashing', his proposed revisions of the text are. When the master of Trinity College, Cambridge brought his experience of classical texts to *Paradise Lost*, he was quick to find fault with lines printed in the poet's lifetime and in subsequent editions, asserting that the text was full of 'monstrous faults' (1732: a2^r). Fortified with all the assurance that senior membership in a great university sometimes gives, he barely conceals, under his invention of a careless scribe and printer and an untrustworthy editorial friend who garbled the blind poet's lines, an assumption that the scholar knows better than even Milton himself what he meant to say or should have meant to say, and thus can supply the appropriate wording. Bentley decently prints his proposed emendations as notes rather than as part of the text, and he admits that some changes are bolder than others:

> though the Printer's Faults are corrigible by retrieving the Poet's own Words, not from a Manuscript, (for none exists) but by Sagacity, and happy Conjecture: and though the Editor's Interpolations are detected by their own Silliness and Unfitness; and easily cured by printing them in the *Italic* Letter, and inclosing them between two Hooks; yet *Milton's* own Slips and Inadvertencies cannot be redress'd without a Change both of the Words and Sense. (Bentley 1732: a2^v)

He proceeds therefore to italicize hundreds of lines or phrases as slips, spurious interpolations, or 'flat Nonsense' (1732: a3^v). At the end of the epic, he proposes improving Milton's lines

> *They hand in hand with wand'ring steps and slow,*
> *Through* Eden *took their solitary way.*
> (XII. 648–9)

to

> THEN *hand in hand with* SOCIAL *steps their way*
> *Through* Eden *took*, WITH HEAV'NLY COMFORT CHEER'D.

The tone of his notes on the faults of the lines he wishes to improve is characteristically rational, if inability to recognize complexity is rational: 'how can the Expression be justified, *with wand'ring steps and slow?* Why *wand'ring?* Erratic steps? Very improper: when, in the Line before, they were *guided by Providence*' (1732: 399).

A flurry of responses followed. *A Friendly Letter to Dr. Bentley*, in sixty-four pages, ironically compliments the learned doctor on the paper and font of his edition, but then moves quickly to a far from friendly attack on the bathetic literal-mindedness of his emendations. With some asperity, the writer objects to such changes as 'showers' to 'sow'd' in the phrase 'where the gorgeous East with richest hand / Showers on her kings barbaric pearl and gold' (*PL* II. 3–4). Bentley had pointed out that gold and pearl do not come from clouds but from the sea and underground, an argument his correspondent calls 'unanswerable; unless our Gainsayers, merely for the sake of Contradiction, may say, that *Milton* (like all other Poets) was apt to make use of Metaphors, and other kind of figurative Ways of expressing himself' (1732: 35).

The great service done by Bentley was to motivate scrupulous attention to each word and image in *Paradise Lost*. Ill-judged as his own approach was, it led to greater scrutiny of every detail of the text. Responses to his edition are also interesting in indicating how much readers of Milton are engaging in dialogue with other readers. Sometimes the impression of edgy conversation is explicit in titles, as in Zachery Pearce's three-volume reappraisal, *A Review of the Text of Milton's Paradise Lost: In which the Chief of Dr. Bentley's Emendations are Consider'd; And several other Emendations and Observations are offer'd to the Public* (1732). Sometimes layer upon layer of earlier comments produce a more genial effect, an ongoing symposium. The first variorum edition, Thomas Newton's *John Milton: Paradise Lost, A Poem in Twelve Books, with Notes of various Authors*, appeared in 1749.

Some readers stand outside the conversation through resolute single-mindedness and devotion to their own specialities. The Reverend John Gillies edits *Milton's Paradise Lost Illustrated with Texts of Scripture* (1788). James Buchanan, a grammarian, provides *The first Six Books of Milton's Paradise Lost, Rendered into GRAMMATICAL Construction* (1773), an extraordinary example of professional deformation. He was content to have rearranged only half the epic into what he calls 'natural order' because he is confident that even a young person provided with his volume 'will, by reading three or four books, become tolerable masters of ellipsis and transposition; and, by the time they have read all the six, be able to read not only the whole poem, but every English classic, whether in prose or verse, with taste and judgment' (Buchanan 1773: 15).

Although a bee can be heard buzzing in the bonnet of another editor, Capel Lofft, it is a more musical bee. On the title page of his edition of *Paradise Lost, Books I–II*, the prominence of phrases about 'The Original System of Orthography restored; the punctuation corrected and extended', at first glance suggests kinship with Bentley or Buchanan. Instead of proposing major changes or seeing the poem as a series of grammatical examples, however, Lofft hears its poetic cadences, and thus provides 'Notes, Chiefly Rhythmical'. Details of punctuation, spelling and even capitalization are important to him because of the way the smallest variation 'obscures the sense, reduces the energy, and impairs, or even destroys, the harmony of the period' (Lofft 1793: xvii). His own energetic and rhythmic phrases invite reading aloud.

From Patrick Hume's notes of 1695 onward, most editors and commentators are generous in their notes on 'parallel places and imitations', identifying echoes of classical authors and sacred scripture. Why recognition of parallels matters to a reader is a question taken up in two essays with similar titles but very different points of view. William Lauder launched an aggressive attack on Milton's originality, first in the *Gentleman's Magazine* (1747) and then in a free-standing volume, *An Essay on Milton's Use and Imitation of the Moderns, in His Paradise Lost* (1750). He accumulates some fascinating passages for comparison, such as an image in Du Bartas and in Milton of the Holy Spirit 'brooding' over Creation. Sourest of all Milton's readers, Lauder never shows a flicker of pleasure in parallels which could lead to sharper definition of an author's individual tone and genius. Instead, he indignantly rails at Milton's ingratitude. *Paradise Lost* was, he charges, 'compiled out of all authors, ancient or modern, sacred or profane, who had any thing in their works, suitable to his purpose; not do I blame him for this unlimited freedom, but for his industriously concealing it' (1750: 77). As ready as Bentley to invent biographical material to strengthen an imaginary case, he proposes that Milton's training his daughters to read aloud to him in languages they did not understand was a ploy to avoid 'intrusting them with so important a secret as his unbounded plagiarism'. He knew, after all, how 'loquacious' women are (161).

An altogether more positive sense of intertextuality is found in *An Essay upon Milton's Imitation of the Ancients in His Paradise Lost, with some Observations on the Paradise Regain'd* (1741). This writer sets out to consider how recognition of parallels contributes to a reader's enjoyment. He begins by citing Aristotle on 'the Pleasure Mankind takes in Imitations'. It follows, he affirms, 'That, when one good Poet imitates another, we have a double Pleasure; the first proceeding from comparing the Description with its Object; and the second, from comparing the one Description with the other from which it was imitated' (Anon. 1741: 4). Thus there is a layered, a threefold pleasure in observing how Milton is imitating Virgil who was imitating Homer. Quite contrary to Lauder, for whom borrowing is a mechanical process, the writer emphasizes the creative reshaping involved in imitation, and, like Aristotle, finds the roots of literary responses in deep-seated human tendencies. Because 'we have in our Nature, a Principle to be delighted with what is New', imitation is best when it involves both 'Likeness' and 'a due Variation' (Anon. 1741: 5).

*

More than a hundred editions of Milton's poetry appeared before the end of the eighteenth century. Who were the readers? There are, roughly, four groups who leave traces: editors, who by the nature of their work must be close readers; critics who comment at some length, often, in the standard formula of their time, identifying both Beauties and Faults; fellow poets, demonstrating that imitation is the sincerest form of flattery; and that elusive creature, the common reader.

Adapters and editors with varying cultural backgrounds reveal in their work shifting assumptions about what is central in Milton's epic. Remarks of those engaged in polishing the text, recasting it in shorter forms, or providing embellishments vary in assertiveness or anxiety. The issue here is not that of influence, but of access. Bentley readily entertains 'Conjectures, that attempt a Restoration of the Genuine Milton' (1732: a1ᵛ). Jago, removing what he saw as 'remote and digressive' in order to focus on domestic scenes, mildly proposes that by arranging passages for music he may make the beauties of the poem 'more universally admired, by means of an alliance with that sister-art, whose expressive strains are the only additional ornament of which they were capable' (Jago 1784; Stevenson and Seares 1998: 171). Buchanan expresses the hope that, by providing paraphrases and notes along with the poetic text, he might 'make this first English classic universally read with ease and delight' (1773: 1). Richardson and Wesley, more forthright about the educationalist's problems, clarify the double message of heavily annotated editions, which imply either obscurity in the poem or deficiencies in its audience (Richardson 1734: clxvi). Comments from those engaged in emendation, annotation, selection or more radical rewriting sometimes raise a question: is their intention to improve the poem, the text or the reader?

BIBLIOGRAPHY

Writings

Addison (1965); A Gentleman of Christ-Church College, Oxon. (1732); A Gentleman of Oxford (1745); Anon. (1741); Armstrong (1736); Bakhtin (1981, 1986); Bentley (1732); Blackmore (1695, 1697, 1705, 1723); Buchanan (1773); Burney (1991); Cowley (1656); Cowper (1808); Davenant (1651); Dennis (1939); Dryden (1962, 1994); Dunton et al. (1691–7); Finch (1713); Galliard (1728); Gillies (1788); Graves (1776); Hobbes (1651/1673); Howard (1695, [1725]); H[ume] (1695); Jago (1784); Johnson (1905); Lauder (1750); Lofft (1793); Milton (1688); Newton (1749); Phillips (1675); Pope (1963); Richardson (1734); Selvaggi (1645); Shawcross (1970, 1972); Steele (1710–11); Stevenson and Seares (1998); Stillingfleet (1746, 1760); Temple (1690); Thomson (1726–46, 1981); Waller (1645); Wesley (1763, repr. 1791).

References for Further Reading

Good (1915); Griffin (1986); Labriola and Sichi (1988); Moore (1990); Moyles (1985); Oras (1931); Pointon (1970); Walsh (1997).

28
Milton: The Romantics and After

Peter J. Kitson

For the Romantic writers, Milton was, to a greater extent than Shakespeare, the prime precursor poet. Whether we think in terms of traditional notions of influence, more sophisticated notions of the anxiety of influence, or the poststructuralist orthodoxies of intertextuality, Milton is generally the poet most often invoked and alluded to in the period. Older views stressing the unimportance of Milton's standing in the eighteenth and nineteenth centuries have been vanquished by a number of critics who have demonstrated just how deep and pervading the poet's presence was for poets and critics who followed in his wake (see Shawcross 1972; Griffin 1986; Wittreich 1979). Whether this presence was a pernicious, dictatorial and debilitating one, or liberating and inspirational for his successors, has been a hotly debated issue. Ezra Pound and T. S. Eliot, in the twentieth century, famously arraigned Milton as a literary oppressor who introduced into English literature an ornate and formal style of writing, 'the Chinese wall of Milton's blank verse', which blighted poetic generations to come with a 'dissociation of sensibility' severing common experience from poetic expression (Eliot 1957). More recently, Harold Bloom (1973) argued that all later poets had to struggle creatively against this patriarchal forebear in an oedipal contest to free their own poetic voice, if successful, or to lapse into silence if not. Bloom's argument, which was chiefly applied to the Romantic poets, has not met with general favour. Most critics writing on Milton's influence now seem to regard his presence as enabling and creative, though Bloom's hypothesis of a poetic agon does provide a clue to why the Romantic poets felt compelled to take on their literary predecessor (see Jarvis 1991).

Milton fascinated the Romantic period. As a poet he had written the greatest epic in English literature and was thus someone worthy of emulation. As Dustin Griffin demonstrates, Milton was also the pre-eminent British poet, and in a period in which a 'British' national identity was being formed (see Griffin 1986: 36–9; Colley 1992: 155–208), Milton's example was crucial. In 1799 Josiah Boydell opened his 'Milton Gallery', at which paintings by Fuseli and others were exhibited. Milton could be said to match the achievements of the ancients, and the increasing interest in Britishness in the period, fuelled by colonial and imperial expansion, led many to look to the 'British Homer' who explored a range of heroic 'British' themes. For De Quincey, Milton's work constituted 'one column of our national achievement', Shakespeare being the other (Wittreich 1970: 466). Coleridge, in *Biographia Literaria* (1817), described Milton and Shakespeare as the two ideal poets, 'the two glory-smitten summits of the poetic mountain', not rivals but 'compeers'. Shakespeare is protean, 'passing into all the forms of human character and passion', while Milton is egotistical, 'attracting all forms and things to himself, into the unity of his IDEAL' (Wittreich 1970: 223–4). The Romantics were, in writing about Milton, engaging in their own form of canon formation, championing the poet against the criticisms of Samuel Johnson's disapproving account of Milton's character and politics in his 'Life of Milton' (1779), and using Milton as an example of a kind of art they wished to emulate, as opposed to the tamer verse of the eighteenth century. Both Coleridge and De Quincey claimed that Milton had anticipated the Kantian distinction between the powers of the Reason and the Understanding (Wittreich 1970: 221– 462). In the pages which follow, I will attempt to sketch the magnitude of Milton's influence on the Romantics as Patriot and Poet, discussing the impact of his life, his political persona, his theodicy in *Paradise Lost* and his depiction of Satan, the character most fascinating to the Romantic poets.

Milton as Patriot and Republican Hero

Crucially, Milton was a revolutionary poet for a revolutionary age, a poet who could be variously invoked from a variety of differing political persuasions. For Wordsworth and Coleridge, Milton was a republican hero, an example of virtue and morality who stood out against the corruption of the times in which he lived. In his sonnet 'London', composed in 1802, Wordsworth apostrophized the elder poet: 'Milton! thou shouldst be living at this hour', representing him in an image of republican austerity and virtue:

> Thy soul was like a Star, and dwelt apart:
> Thou hadst a voice whose sound was like the sea:
>   (Wittreich 1970: 111)

In another sonnet he idealized the Commonwealthmen 'the later Sydney, Marvel, Harrington/Young Vane, and others who called Milton Friend'. These were 'Great Men' no longer 'among us' in this world lacking a 'master spirit' and a manifesting 'a want of Books and Men!' (Wittreich 1970: 111).

Coleridge too sought spiritual and revolutionary inspiration from Milton. In his miniature Miltonic epic, 'Religious Musings' (1794–6), it is 'MILTON's trump' that announces the millenarian renovation of earth and the end of earthly tyranny (Wittreich 1970: 155–6). Like Wordsworth, Coleridge was deeply influenced throughout his life by the seventeenth-century republicans, especially Milton and James Harrington. In his radical pamphlet *The Plot Discovered* (1795), Coleridge appealed to those 'Sages and patriots' who 'do yet speak to us, spirits of Milton, Locke, Sidney, Harrington!' (Wittreich 1970: 156). The indebtedness of Wordsworth and Coleridge to Milton and the Commonwealthmen for their early radical views, as well as their later conservative opinions, has now been established beyond doubt (see Fink 1948; Kitson 1991; Leask 1988; Morrow 1990).

Milton was also available as a stick to beat the so-called 'Lake School' of poets, Wordsworth, Coleridge and Robert Southey, who renounced the political radicalism of their youth for the conservatism of their maturity. Byron, in the 'Dedication' to *Don Juan* (1818), contrasted the republican consistency of Milton with what he regarded as the Lakers' apostasy. Though 'fallen on evil days and evil tongues', Milton did not 'loathe the sire to laud the son', despising both Charles I and Charles II, and ending his life 'the tyrant-hater he begun'. His example was poorly imitated by the Poet Laureate of the time, Southey, who in his youth attacked George III but later praised the Prince Regent. Milton was the stern prophet of republicanism who, like Samuel, froze the 'blood of monarchs' (Wittreich 1970: 516–17). Shelley, also an opponent of the establishment of his day, looked to Milton as an example of republican virtue: 'Blind, old, and lonely', 'unterrified' despite the persecutions of the 'priest, slave, and the liberticide', Milton's clear spirit still 'reigns o'er the earth' (*Adonais*, Wittreich 1970: 540). In 'Milton's Spirit' Shelley dreams of Milton's spirit arising and shaking 'all human things built in contempt of man . . . sanguine thrones . . . impious altars . . . Prisons and citadels' (Wittreich 1970: 536). For Keats also, Milton was a part of his 'patriotic lore' (Wittreich 1970: 547), and in 1818 he lamented to his brother George and his wife that there were no longer patriots prepared to 'suffer in obscurity for their Country', that 'We have no Milton, no Algernon Sidney' (Wittreich 1970: 553). Nicholas Roe (1997) has shown how Keats's education at Enfield School brought him into contact with English republican ideas, a sympathy manifested in his early poem 'Lines Written on 29 May, the Anniversary of Charles's Restoration' which decries the remembrance of Charles I's execution, advocating a more seemly act of national contrition for the fates of 'gallant' Sidney, Russell and Vane (Roe 1997: 47–9). Keats, who mixed in the republican and dissenting circles that centred on James Henry Leigh Hunt and his journal the *Examiner*, could write in a marginal note concerning *Paradise Lost* (I. 591–9) that Milton's 'very wishing should have power to pull that feeble animal Charles from his bloody throne' an exertion which 'must have had or is yet to have some sequences' (Wittreich 1970: 556). Ironically, Milton's bodily presence itself interrupted into the living world in 1790 when his grave was opened, prompting William Cowper to thunder:

> Ill fare the hands that heav'd the stones
>   Where Milton's ashes lay
> That trembled not to grasp his bones,
>   And steal his dust away.
>   (Shawcross 1972: 363)

If, in these instances, it seems as if it is Milton's persona as an austere and stern republican exuding virtue which captivates the Romantic poets, so tempted themselves by the egotistical and solipsistic, there is much evidence that both Wordsworth and Coleridge, among many, were as familiar with the writings of his left hand as they were with the works of James Harrington and Algernon Sidney, mediated to them in a number of forms. The early radical thought of both poets, along with their later conservative opinions, were informed by seventeenth-century republican writing, in particular Milton's *Tenure of Kings and Magistrates*, *Of Reformation*, *Areopagitica* and *The Readie and Easie Way to Establish a Free Commonwealth*, Harrington's *Oceana* and Sidney's *Discourses* (see Fink 1948; Kitson 1991; Kitson 1992). Coleridge's *The Plot Discovered*, which laments the expiring of liberty under William Pitt's repressive regime, draws on Milton's jeremiad, *The Readie and Easie Way*, which deplores the prospect of the imminent return of Charles II. In this the two poets were hardly alone. The Commonwealthman tradition maintained throughout the eighteenth century by a small group of republican thinkers, such as John Toland, Walter Moyle and James Burgh, flamed up again in the early years of the French Revolution (see Robbins 1959). Milton's name was frequently invoked in the debate about the French Revolution by Richard Price and others. The prose works were readily available in republican and deist John Toland's three-volume edition of 1698 (Toland also edited an influential edition of Harrington's works) and in versions of Thomas Birch's edition of 1738. These editions were standard until Charles Symmons's new six-volume edition of 1806. The radical publisher Joseph Johnson also produced editions of Milton's and Sidney's political works. In addition, Milton's *Pro Populo Anglicano Defensio* and *Areopagitica* were translated into French in several editions in the early days of the French Revolution (see Shawcross 1974: 292–391; Shawcross 1972: 8; Kitson 1992: 226). Editions of separate works were also available and, as Shawcross points out, Milton's works were accessible in English, or original Latin, for any interested reader in the eighteenth century (Shawcross 1972: 5–6).

Milton was also the subject of several influential biographies in the period. William Hayley, who was to be the patron of William Blake, published an adulatory *Life* in 1794 (revised 1796). Of all the available lives, Hayley's was the most important for the Romantic poets and artists. Hayley emphasized the independence, energy and power of Milton's self: he was 'the man of our country most eminent for energy of mind, for intensity of application, and for frankness and intrepidity' and was 'all of men living, the most perfectly blameless in his sentiments of government, morality, and religion' (Griffin 1986: 32). Charles Symmons's 'Life' of 1806 for his new edition of Milton's prose works similarly affirms the 'virtuous and amiable, the firm and consistent Milton' against the detractions of Johnson and others. Symmons harnessed Milton's republicanism to the 1688 settlement, arguing that Milton 'preferred a republic, (and who can blame him?) to that unascertained and unprotected constitution' (1806: 503). Hayley and Symmons were reacting against the view of Milton, deriving from Samuel Johnson and David Hume, as an austere and dangerous radical. Hume's influential *History of England* (1762) had deplored the 'greatest genius' of the age having engaged with 'fanatics' and 'prostituted his pen in theological controversy' in the cause of 'the most violent measures of party' (Shawcross 1972: 237).

Hayley and Symmons were hardly alone in their defence of Milton; as well as the standard histories of the age there were also histories which attempted to rehabilitate and praise the seventeenth-century republican and dissenting traditions, such as John Banks's *Life of Oliver Cromwell* (1769), Daniel Neal's *The History of the Puritans* (1735, reprinted 1793), Catharine Macaulay's *History of England* (1768–81), and William Godwin's great *History of the Commonwealth* (1824–8). Godwin's *History* sought to re-appraise the English republican tradition in the aftermath of the impact of the French Revolution. Godwin describes how Milton, though preferring a sequestered life, could not refuse public office, determined as he was to devote himself to 'the service of that scheme of a republic, which above all earthly things he loved' (Godwin 1824–8, III: 17). For Godwin, Milton was a sincere republican of the same school as Sir Henry Vane. In an interesting exchange in Sir Walter Scott's undeservedly neglected Civil War novel *Woodstock* (1826), Colonel Everard recites lines from Milton's *Comus* to demonstrate to his royalist uncle, Sir Henry Lee, that the Revolution had created poets as well as saints and prophets. Admiring the lines, Sir Henry is shocked to learn of their authorship: 'What! John Milton, the blasphemous and bloody-minded author of *Defensio Populi Anglicani!* – the advocate of the infernal High Court of Fiends; the creature and parasite of that grand impostor . . . Oliver Cromwell' (Scott 1887: 321).

Sir Henry's view of Milton was not one that was to find general favour as the nineteenth century wore on. The Romantics were the prelude to that great historiographical revolution that would establish Cromwell as one of the heroes of nineteenth-century nonconformity. Thomas Carlyle's seminal edition of *Oliver Cromwell's Letters and Speeches with Elucidations* (1845) was to be the main means of effecting this change, but Godwin's *History* and Thomas Babington Macaulay's essay 'Milton' (1825) to some extent paved the way. Macaulay considered Milton to be a great poet, but he also admired his public conduct in the great conflict between 'liberty and despotism'. Independent of the factions, but sharing in many of their characteristics, Milton's opinions 'were democratic' but his tastes harmonized better with those of 'monarchy and aristocracy'. Looking forward to the concerns of nineteenth-century liberalism, Milton fought for that 'species of freedom which is the most valuable, and which was then the least understood, the freedom of the human mind'. Like the brothers in *Comus*, Milton cherished the 'noble aim' to 'reverse the rod, to spell the charm backward, to break the titles which bound a stupefied people to the seat of enchantment' (Macaulay 1878: 14, 26, 27). Unlike Godwin, Macaulay is keen to disassociate Milton and the Parliamentarians from the republican tradition, claiming them as part of the Whig tradition of liberal politics. Milton, like John Hampden, combined for him the best of both puritan and Cavalier values. It would be nearly twenty years later that Carlyle would provide the first real understanding of the dynamics of puritanism.

Macaulay's championing of Milton as a poet and liberal patriot was written in the wake of the discovery of the manuscript *De Doctrina Christiana* in 1823 and its publication in Latin and English by Bishop Sumner in 1825. Although this discovery might have made a significant difference to the way that Milton was perceived in the 1790s, in the 1820s, when nonconformity tended to be less radical, it occasioned less notice. More or less believing the document to be genuinely Milton's, his admirers were led to accept that the author of *Paradise Lost* was an antitrinitarian and heretical on other opinions. Although many had suspected *Paradise Lost* of Arian beliefs, it was generally held, as Symmons put it in 1806, that Milton's theological opinions were 'orthodox and consistent with the creed of the Church of England' (414). Macaulay, convinced the manuscript was a 'genuine relic of the great poet', accepted that Milton was thus an Arian and a believer in polygamy, adding that no one could have read *Paradise Lost* without 'suspecting him of the former; nor... acquainted with the history of his life, ought we to be much startled at the latter'. More surprising, however, were the opinions expressed concerning 'the nature of the Deity, the eternity of matter, and the observation of the sabbath' (Macaulay 1878: 2). Coleridge, reacting against his own earlier Unitarian beliefs in 1814, claimed that the Satan of *Paradise Regained* is represented by Milton as 'a sceptical Socinian' (Wittreich 1970: 207), although it was not until after the publication of *De Doctrina Christiana* that he realized that Milton was, indeed, 'a high Arian in his mature life' (Wittreich 1970: 278). Published in 1848, at the end of the Romantic period, Thomas De Quincey's 'Life of Milton' could confidently celebrate the achievements of a sublime national poet, defending *Paradise Lost* and the greatness of Milton's character and achievement against the inveterate malice of 'Dr. Sam.' and the punier pedantries of Walter Savage Landor and Robert Southey. In 1859, Dr Johnson, 'the worst enemy that Milton and his great cause have ever been called on to confront' is soundly dismissed by De Quincey as he establishes *Paradise Lost* as 'ideally grand... beyond the region of ordinary human sympathies, as the Elgin marbles and the other sublime works of antiquity' (Wittreich 1970: 500, 507).

Natural Supernaturalism

Milton's presence as a poet, as well as a political prophet, is also substantial in the Romantic period and beyond. Several scholars have attempted to chart and discuss the magnitude of this, variously in terms of influence (anxious or otherwise) or as readerly intertextuality. I would here like to hint at several ways in which Miltonic themes are most present in Romantic period writing.

For the Romantics, Milton was one of the most accomplished writers of the sublime, a mode that they valued highly. De Quincey commented how 'In Milton only, first and last, is the power of the sublime revealed' (Wittreich 1970: 480). It was Edmund Burke, more than any other writer, who established Milton as *the* sublime poet for the Romantic Age. In his *A Philosophical Enquiry into the Origin of Our Ideas of the Sublime and Beautiful* (1757) Burke identifies 'Obscurity' as one of the qualities of the aesthetic experience we describe as sublime, obscurity raising the imaginative powers. Instancing Milton's description of Satan in *Paradise Lost* (I. 589–99), Burke comments that:

> Here is a very noble picture; and in what does this poetical picture consist? In images of a tower, an archangel, the sun rising through mists, or in an eclipse, the ruin of monarchs, and the revolution of kingdoms. The mind is hurried out of itself, by a croud of great and confused images; which affect because they are crouded and confused. (Burke 1958: 620)

Burke was to go on to use the sublime in his political writings dignifying and mystifying the eighteenth-century mechanism of government, most famously in his description of the French monarchy in *Reflections on the Revolution in France* (1791). His hijacking of the Miltonic sublime for the reactionary cause was to be answered by William Blake who, as Morton Paley (1999) argues, constructs a human-centred sublime as an alternative to Burke's apotheosis of power (48–50). The Unitarian Coleridge was also to apply Milton's radical millenarian sublime against Burke in his early work 'Religious Musings'.

Milton's importance to the Romantics as the accomplished epic poet who composed a theodicy made him a target of emulation, or even rivalry. In different ways Blake, Wordsworth and Coleridge all tried to rewrite *Paradise Lost* for their own age. M. H. Abrams in *Natural Supernaturalism* (1971) developed an influential 'Miltonic' paradigm within which to discuss Romantic poetry. Abrams argued that the Romantics typically structured their poems in terms of a circuitous journey from innocence to experience, and from this state to a higher form of innocence. This internalized quest begins with the child's unconscious conviction of a primal unity between itself and the natural world, but subsequently undergoes a fall from that unity into an experience of alienation, division and isolation. In so doing the Romantics internalized the *Paradise Lost* narrative, substituting powers of the mind for its divine and Satanic energies. The Romantic fall, like the fortunate fall, or *felix culpa*, of *Paradise Lost*, is an essential part of the process of the mind's restitution and reintegration with the powers of nature. Like Adam, the Romantic self at the close of the journey has attained a higher state of consciousness, verging on the transcendental, as it comes to an awareness of the workings of nature and the human mind and the affinity between subject and object. For Abrams, Romantic poetry secularizes and humanizes the Milton myth of innocence, sin, fall and redemption. Central to Abrams's point is that Romantic poets, such as Wordsworth and Coleridge, turned away from their early involvement in radical politics and their support of the French Revolution and relocated their political aspirations in the realm of art and imagination, finding, like Milton's Adam and Eve 'A paradise within...happier far' (XII. 587). Herbert Grierson had earlier contrasted Milton's loyalty after the Restoration to the 'Good Old Cause' with Wordsworth's loss of faith in political change, resurgent patriotism and deepening visionary introversion, and this reading of the movement from revolutionary idealism to a concern with individual mental and moral regeneration has remained influential in Wordsworthian criticism to this day (see Jarvis 1991: 77–83). Certainly in later life Wordsworth and Coleridge were to use Milton's disgust, as powerfully expressed in *The Readie and Easie Way*, with the English people who preferred Charles II to the English republic as a way of expressing their own disillusionment with popular politics. In a 'Lecture on Milton and the Paradise Lost' of 1819 Coleridge writes that Milton was:

> As every truly great poet has ever been, a good man; but finding it impossible to realize his own aspirations, either in religion or politics, or society, he gave up his heart to the living spirit and light within him, and avenged himself on the world by enriching it with this record of his own transcendent ideal. (Wittreich 1970: 245)

Coleridge, like Wordsworth, used Milton as a kind of bridge to negotiate his own movement to political conservatism. The radicalism of their youth and the conservatism of their later years could both find precedents in Milton. Coleridge comments in 1815 that 'Milton became more and more a stern republican, or rather an advocate for that religious and moral aristocracy which, in his day, was called republicanism, and which, even more than royalism itself, is the direct antipode of modern jacobinism' (Wittreich 1970: 215) – a sentiment with which Wordsworth concurred when he criticized those who represented the poet as a 'democrat', defining him instead as 'an aristocrat in the truest sense of the word' (Wittreich 1970: 136).

The pattern of 'Natural Supernaturalism' and its origins in Miltonic theodicy are shown in Wordsworth's 'Prospectus' to 'The Recluse', published in 1814 as a preface to *The Excursion* (1814). In this Wordsworth invokes the aid of his great epic predecessor Milton: '"fit audience let me find though few" / So prayed, more gaining than he asked, the Bard – / In holiest mood' (Wordsworth 1936: 590). Wordsworth is attempting, like Milton, to 'weigh / The good and evil of our mortal state'; but his approach is to be psychological. Like the earlier prophetic poet, he must 'sink deep' and ascend aloft to worlds 'to which the heaven of heavens is but a veil'.

> All strength – all terror, single or in bands,
> That ever was put forth in personal form –
> Jehovah – with his thunder, and the choir
> Of shouting Angels, and the empyreal thrones –
> I pass them unalarmed. Not Chaos, not
> The darkest pit of lowest Erebus,
> Nor aught of blinder vacancy, scooped out
> By help of dreams – can breed such fear and awe
> As fall upon us often when we look

> Into our Minds, into the Mind of Man –
> My haunt, and the main region of my song.
>
> (Wordsworth 1936: 590)

Wordsworth thus rewrites *Paradise Lost*, situating its story within the human mind, establishing its status as the founding myth of human psychological development. In Wordsworth's theodicy, Paradise may be regained in this world, but not by political means. It is only when the 'discerning intellect of Man' is 'wedded to this goodly universe / In love and holy passion' that we achieve harmony (1936: 590). The Romantic quest is thus to arouse the victims of eighteenth-century empiricist philosophies, which stress the material and the physical, 'from their sleep of death' (590). Wordsworth's 'high argument' is for a recovery of the innocent vision of childhood in the rational adult. This is the new heaven and earth that are promised in Revelation. Wordsworth's resituating of the Apocalypse in the mind of man is developed at length in *The Prelude*, where the young Wordsworth falls from a childhood in which his sense of self is merged with that of nature, into a period of adulthood division and alienation fuelled by his experiences in the city of London and his disillusionment with the process of the French Revolution, moving from that state to a period of redemption and the healing of the rupture between self and the world achieved through the creative power of imagination, and aided by nature, his sister and his sympathetic friend Coleridge. The re-unification of mind and nature is celebrated by the apocalyptic vision Wordsworth achieves on the summit of Mount Snowdon in Book 13 of the 1805 *Prelude*. From the opening lines of *The Prelude*, where the poet echoes *Paradise Lost* (XII. 646) envisioning that 'the earth is all before me' (*Prelude* 1805, I. 14) and deciding against taking for his epic 'some old / Romantic tale by Milton left unsung' (I. 180–1), the poem is suffused with Miltonic allusions and echoes.

Coleridge also takes on the Miltonic mantle in his own poetry. His *Religious Musings* (1794–6) attempts a Unitarian version of *Paradise Lost* in which humankind is brought to universal redemption by the workings of a divine imagination in a millenarian vision following the French Revolution. Shortly afterwards Coleridge was, like Wordsworth, to locate this process in the human mind itself, as is arguably the case in the retelling of the myth of the Fall in 'The Rime of the Ancient Mariner'. Most obviously Miltonic ideas and images are apparent in 'Kubla Khan', which is a condensation of Miltonic subjects and themes. Kubla's pleasure garden recalls the unfallen paradise of Book IV of *Paradise Lost*:

> And here were gardens bright with sinuous rills,
> Where blossomed many an incense-bearing tree;
> And here were forests ancient as the hills,
> Enfolding sunny spots of greenery.
>
> (lines 8–11)

But Kubla's mighty fountain and river, unlike those of Eden, are not self-renewing; instead, they run down to 'a sunless sea' of death. Coleridge's poem also contains a Satanic woman 'wailing for her demon-lover' (line 16) and 'an Abyssinian maid' who sings a paradisiacal song of 'Mount Abora' (originally Amara), recalling Milton's naming of one of the false Edens in Book IV of *Paradise Lost*. Coleridge's poem finishes with the inspired prophet-poet (Bacchic rather than Miltonic) whose 'flashing eyes' and 'floating hair' inspire awe and dread (line 50).

Wordsworth and Coleridge were not the only poets in the period to be indebted to Milton for the mediation of paradisial themes and the rediscovery of the persona of the prophet-poet. The most rigorous rewriting of Milton's work was, however, that of William Blake. His *Songs of Innocence and of Experience* (1794) arguably demonstrate the pattern of Natural Supernaturalism, placing Eden and Fall in symbolic states of the human mind. For Blake, redemption is available in this world and the divine attributes are found in human forms:

> For mercy, pity, peace and love
> Is God our father dear;
> And mercy, pity, peace and love
> Is man, his child and care.
> ('The Divine Image', lines 5–8)

These ideas are given a more complex form in Blake's poem *Milton*, which adapts his mythological system of division, dispersal and reorganization, as enunciated in the *Four Zoas*, to personal and narrative concerns. While composing the poem, Milton was resident in Felpham, Surrey from 1800 to 1803 under the patronage of Milton's editor and biographer William Hayley. Hayley features prominently in the poem as an unimaginative misinterpreter of Milton's work and also as a version of Satanic self-hood. Blake had known Milton's works since childhood, claiming that 'Milton lovd me in childhood & shewd me his face' (Wittreich 1970: 37). Hayley had written his influential 'Life of Milton' only a few years before Blake's poem was composed and was currently editing Cowper's annotations to Milton's poems, a project in which Blake was supposed to participate (but did not) by engraving illustrations. Between 1801 and 1809 Blake produced watercolour illustrations for three of Milton's major poems, including two sets of illustrations for *Paradise Lost*. Blake saw Milton as the greatest and most inspired artist in English national life, yet one who had gone astray, misled by his classical learning, his puritanical religious beliefs and his commitment to a rational philosophy. Milton thus preached a distorted message and one that Blake wished to recast in his own terms. Subtitling his poem *To Justify the Ways of God to Men*, Blake shows how Milton gave to the nation a false image of God as a tyrannical lawgiver residing apart from humanity and not as a friend among them. Blake presents a narrative of how Milton's soul in heaven was purified and how the malign influence of the old Milton is countered as a new Milton descends to earth, entering Blake's body through his foot and inspiring him with the status of prophet-poet for his own generation. *Milton*, in complex style, retells the story of the fall of Satan along Blakean lines, where Satan's error is to assume activities that are not rightly his and to effect a self-righteousness which shuts him out from heaven. The poem prophesies the apocalyptic transformation of the Giant Albion and the reorganization of a divine humanity through the power of imagination (Jesus). At the close of the poem Milton re-integrates himself with his female emanation Ololon, ushering in the Apocalypse of Imagination, but before doing so he preaches a message purged of his previous errors:

> To cleanse the face of my spirit by self-examination,
> To bathe in the waters of life; to wash off the not-human
> I come in self-annihilation & the grandeur of inspiration
> To cast off rational demonstration by faith in the Saviour;
> To cast off the rotten rags of memory by inspiration;
> To cast off Bacon, Locke & Newton from Albion's covering;
> To take off his filthy garments, & clothe him with imagination;
> To cast aside from poetry all that is not inspiration,
>   . . .
> These are the destroyers of Jerusalem, these are the murderers
> Of Jesus, who deny the faith & mock at eternal life;
> Who pretend to poetry, that they may destroy imagination
> By imitation of nature's images drawn from remembrance.
> These are the sexual garments, the abomination of desolation
> Hiding the human lineaments as with an ark & curtains
> Which Jesus rent & now shall wholly purge away with fire,
> Till generation is swallowed up in regeneration,
>   (pl. 40, line 37; pl. 41, lines 1–7, 21–8)

In different ways Wordsworth, Blake and even Coleridge managed to rewrite Milton's work for their own age. Less successful was John Keats. Keats, whose poetic persona often tended to the passive and the self-effacing, found Milton's work to be less easy to assimilate into his own poetic styles and concerns. Certainly Keats possessed the same admiration for the elder poet's work as his contemporaries. He famously illustrated the workings of the poetic imagination by comparing it to 'Adam's dream' in *Paradise Lost* (VIII. 452–90): 'he awoke and found it truth' (Wittreich 1970: 547). Nevertheless Keats seems to have discerned a certain remoteness from humanity in Milton's work. In 1818–19 he began a close study of *Paradise Lost* as a prelude to composing his own Miltonic epic, *Hyperion*. Keats had chosen the form of the Miltonic epic in an attempt to discipline his poetic style after the critical debacle of *Endymion* (1817). He selected the story of the fall of the Titans and their replacement by the Olympian gods as a suitably Miltonic subject. The work deals with the fall of the sun god Hyperion and the apotheosis of his new rival Apollo. He was, however, unable to complete the third book of the poem and published the work as 'Hyperion. A Fragment' in 1820. Although it is difficult to see how Keats could have filled out the poem to epic proportions, he blamed his inability to continue with the work on the unnaturalness of the Miltonic idiom. In a number of letters he commented on the difficulties of writing Miltonic epic. 'Miltonic verse', he argued 'cannot be written but in an artful or rather artist's humour'; *Paradise Lost* constitutes a corruption of language and a 'beautiful and grand curiosity'. Ultimately Keats found the Miltonic style uncongenial for his own poetic voice; standing on his guard against Milton, he admits that 'Life to him would be death to me' and such verse could only be written 'in the vein of art' (Wittreich 1970: 561–2). When Keats returned to the Hyperion myth, he beautifully recast its form into a Dantean dream vision, 'The Fall of Hyperion. A Dream'. Ironically, the second version of the poem is closer to its Miltonic origins as Keats interrogates his own poetic vocation in a postparadisial world, himself visiting the ruins of Eden and eating 'the refuse of a meal / By angel tasted, or our Mother Eve' (lines 30–1). The goddess Moneta affords the poet a vision of the fall and suffering of the Titans, in the manner of Adam's vision; however, for Keats the progress of history is imaged cyclically and not eschatologically.

Romantic and Miltonic Satanism

If the canonical Romantic writers attempted to rewrite the Miltonic epic for their own time, naturalizing the Miltonic pattern of innocence, fall and redemption, they were also inevitably drawn towards Milton's characterization of Satan. The common notion that the Romantic poets celebrated the Satanic energies of Milton's adversary is not entirely accurate, although certainly, among the second generation of Romantic writers, there was a tendency to glamorize the apostate angel. William Godwin, one of the first writers in the period to defend Satan's conduct, wrote in his *Enquiry Concerning Political Justice* (1793) that Satan's rebellion occurred because:

> he saw no sufficient reason for that extreme inequality of rank and power which the creator assumed. It was because prescription and precedent form no adequate ground for implicit faith. After his fall, why did he still cherish the spirit of opposition? From a persuasion that he was hardly and injuriously treated. He was not discouraged by the apparent inequality of the contest: because a sense of reason and justice was stronger than a sense of brute force; because he had much of the feelings of an Epictetus or a Cato, and little of those of a slave. (Godwin 1978: 309)

Godwin frequented the literary group circulating around the radical publisher Joseph Johnson of which William Blake was a member. Blake's more famous avocation of Romantic Satanism might well have been informed by radical discussions of Milton's work. In his *The Marriage of Heaven and Hell* (1793) he represents Satan as energy, demonized by the orthodox as evil. Blake's Satan is here very different from his later incarnation in *Milton*, serving the function of one-half of the dialectic of humanity, opposed to all repressive codes, philosophical, religious and sexual. He presents a Satanic reading of *Paradise Lost* which, he argues, constitutes the history of the repression of energy by reason:

> But in Milton the Father is destiny, the Son a ratio of the five senses, and the Holy Ghost vacuum!
>
> *Note.* The reason Milton wrote in fetters when he wrote of angels and God, and at liberty when of devils and Hell, is because he was a true poet, and of the Devil's party without knowing it. (Pl. 6, lines 50–5)

Blake's representation of Milton as an artist psychologically imprisoned by outworn creeds and needing a demonic reading of his work to liberate him is one that has been attractive to many twentieth-century critics, such as Denis Saurat and William Empson, but it was a very idiosyncratic view in the Romantic period itself. Shelley comes closest to the Blakean admiration of the Satanic. Shelley, who along with Byron was named as a part of the 'Satanic School' of poets by the contemporary reviews, was generally sympathetic to the strain of Enlightenment rationalism of d'Holbach, Hume and Godwin. In *Queen Mab* (1813) he speculates how, when the absurdities of the 'miserable tale of the Devil, and Eve, and an Intercessor' will perish with the age that gave it sustenance, 'Milton's poem alone will give permanency to the remembrances of its absurdities' and that men will 'laugh as heartily at grace, faith, redemption, and original sin, as they now do at the metamorphoses of Jupiter, the miracles of Romish saints, the efficacy of witchcraft, and the appearance of departed spirits' (Wittreich 1970: 529). Convinced of the importance of *Paradise Lost* as a great epic poem, Shelley believed that Milton's imagination transcended his Christian beliefs. In his 'On the Devil, and Devils' (*c.*1819) and again in his *Defence of Poetry* (1821), Shelley credits Milton with fleshing out the absurdities of the Christian tradition of the Devil, creating a Satan who exudes grandeur and energy:

> Milton's Devil as a moral being is far superior to his God, as one who perseveres in some purpose which he has conceived to be excellent, in spite of adversity and torture, is to one who in the cold security of undoubted triumph inflicts the most horrible revenge upon his enemy, – not from any mistaken notion of bringing him to repent of a perseverance in enmity, but with the open and alleged design of exasperating him to deserve new torments. (Wittreich 1970: 535)

Shelley, anticipating Empson, argues that from the evidence of the poem, Milton might not actually have been a Christian but one merely conforming under the extreme pressures of the time, his poem containing 'within itself a philosophical refutation of that system of which . . . it has been a chief support' (Wittreich 1970: 537). Shelley's view that great poetry at once and same time inhabits and confutes the spirit of the age in which it was composed is close to Blake's notion that Milton must be called upon to purge himself of his errors. Shelley, however, was not completely happy with the heroism of Milton's Satan. Satan's 'benevolent and amiable disposition' is warped into that of a tyrant by the punishments of a cruel and vindictive God, becoming 'like a man compelled by a tyrant to set fire to his own possessions' and to inflict the most 'subtle and protracted torments' upon his 'dearest friends' (Wittreich 1970: 536). Shelley's own preferred tragic hero is instead the resister of oppression who will suffer himself rather than inflict misery upon others, even in revenge. He thus found the character of Prometheus, who combines the power, energy and grandeur of Satan with the benevolence and suffering of Christ. In this 'Preface' to *Prometheus Unbound* (1819) he comments that

> The only imaginary being resembling in any degree Prometheus, is Satan, because, in addition to courage, and majesty, and firm and patient opposition to omnipotent force, he is susceptible of being described as exempt from the taints of ambition, envy, revenge, and a desire for personal aggrandisement, which, in the Hero of Paradise Lost, interfere with the interest ... Prometheus, is, as it were the type of the highest perfection of moral and intellectual nature, impelled by the purest and truest motives to the best and noblest ends. (Wittreich 1970: 531–2)

Of all Satan's qualities, it is his indomitable will that most attracts and frightens the poets of the later age, obsessed as they were with the dangers of solipsism and alienation. Satan became for many an emblem of a powerful mind cut off from human sympathy and finding in its own desires the supreme motive for action. For Coleridge in 1819, Satan could serve as an analogy for the dangers of Romantic Prometheanism and the rise of Napoleon:

> The character of Satan is pride and sensual indulgence, finding in itself the sole motive of action. It is the character so often seen *in little* on the political stage. It exhibits all the restlessness, temerity and cunning which have marked the mighty hunters of mankind from Nimrod to Napoleon ... Milton has carefully marked in his Satan the intense selfishness, the alcohol of egotism, which would rather reign in Hell than serve in Heaven. (Wittreich 1970: 244)

The poet has, however, thrown around Satan 'a singularity of daring, a grandeur of suffering and a ruined splendor, which constitute the very height of poetic sublimity' (Wittreich 1970: 244).

This Satanic abstraction is explored in a great variety of Romantic period writing, often concerned with the alienated individual whose sense of self becomes the only point of moral reference. A substantial number of Romantic and Gothic hero-villains from Wordsworth's Rivers in *The Borderers* (1793) to Ann Radcliffe's Schedoni in *The Italian* (1797) are depicted as Satanic figures who commit great crimes to justify an intense egotism. Most obviously, Byron's cynical romantic heroes are Satans *manqués*. Byron explored this character in a substantial number of poems. His drama *Manfred* (1817) presents us with a Faustian magician, tormented by the death of his love

Astarte, who, it is hinted, was his sister. Rejecting all aid and solace, human or otherwise, Manfred expires declaiming lines highly allusive to the soliloquies of Satan from *Paradise Lost*:

> I bear within
> A torture which could nothing gain from thine.
> The mind which is immortal makes itself
> Requital for its good or evil thoughts,
> Its own origin of ill and end,
> And its own place and time; its innate sense,
> When stripped of this mortality, derives
> No colour from the fleeting things without,
> But is absorbed in sufferance or in joy,
> Born from the knowledge of its own desert.
>
> (III. iv. 127–37)

Like Blake, Byron was keen to retell the myth of the Fall from a Satanic perspective. His play *Cain: A Mystery* (1821) includes a sympathetic Lucifer and a theological perspective that looks towards the Manichaean dualism Byron favoured elsewhere in his work. Byron's Lucifer is a reasonable spirit who refuses to believe that truth is established simply because God says it is so:

> I have a victor – true; but no superior.
> Homage he has from all – but none from me:
> I battle against him, as I battled
> In highest Heaven. Through all eternity,
> And the unfathomable gulf of Hades,
> And the interminable realms of space,
> And the infinity of endless ages,
> All, all, will I dispute! And world by world,
> And star by star, and universe by universe,
> Shall tremble in the balance, till the great
> Conflict shall cease, if it ever shall cease,
> Which it ne'er shall, till he or I be quench'd.
>
> (II. ii. 229–445)

Lucifer delights in pointing out the absurdities of the Christian system and the arbitrariness of a deity who as 'conqueror will call the conquer'd / *Evil*' (II. ii. 443–4). In Adam's family brother and sister love and produce children, but incest will become a sin for their posterity. So, too, Byron returns his play to Genesis, denying, on scriptural grounds, that Lucifer is the serpent who tempted Eve, whatever Milton and the fathers have decided. Satan also appears in more comic mode in Byron's *The Vision of Judgment* (1821), as an urbane and aristocratic gentleman arrived to claim the soul of the recently deceased George III.

Milton and Women Romantic Writers

The writers discussed so far have all been male. Milton's influence, or effect, on women writers generally is a vexed issue. Sandra Gilbert and Susan Gubar have argued that Milton functioned as a colossal bogeyman poet for subsequent female writers. Detailed scholarly work on the women writers of the period is still largely a recent critical activity and it may well be that Gilbert's and Gubar's paradigm will not stand the test of time. Certainly not all women writers in the period were repelled by Milton's work. In 1822 Sarah Siddons published her own abridgement of *Paradise Lost* and Eliza Bradburn composed a prose paraphrase of the poem. Mary Robinson's 'Ode Inscribed to the Infant Son of S. T. Coleridge' alludes to the cosmology of *Paradise Lost* in its apotheosis to the 'Spirit of Light'. While some of these activities may have been of a secondary kind, female responses to *Paradise Lost* were not necessarily any more submissive or obedient than those of their male contemporaries. Joseph Wittreich in his *Feminist Milton* (1987) argues convincingly that women writers, such as Mary Wollstonecraft and Mary Shelley, chose to subvert *Paradise Lost*, turning a 'poem that men would often use against women . . . to their own advantage'. For Wittreich, Milton, despite his reputation for misogyny, was a sponsor of early feminists (Wittreich 1987: 80, 81). Wollstonecraft certainly criticizes Milton's picture of woman as formed 'For softness . . . and sweet attractive grace' (IV. 298), equating this with the 'Mahometan' strain of thinking that deprives women of souls and sees them as designed to minister to the appetites of men. Wollstonecraft does, however, praise Adam's expressed desire for a mate equal in 'fellowship' to 'participate / All rational delight' (VIII. 389–91), a passage in which she says Milton 'seems to coincide' with her (Wollstonecraft 1989: 88–90). Wollstonecraft often quotes Milton on earthly love as being a 'scale to Heavenly', in connection with her conviction that the passions, refined by the reason, would be directed to a republican or democratic universal benevolence characteristic of the beneficent Creator. Jane Austen, though not expressly featuring Milton's work in her novels, refers to him in her letters in a way which makes him stand for political sincerity and uprightness, as opposed to modern insincerity and corruption. When referring to a meeting with Edward Austen's friend Stephen-Rumbold Lushington, an MP, she writes:

> I am sure he is clever & a Man of Taste. He got a vol. of Milton last night & spoke of it with warmth. – He is quite an M.P. – very smiling, with an exceeding good address, & readiness of Language. – I am rather in love with him. – I dare say he is ambitious and Insincere – he puts me in mind of Mr Dundas. (Austen 1995: 240)

Here Austen ironically counterpoints Milton, the principled and sincere patriot, with the modern type of politician. This appraisal of Milton as the touchstone for political integrity is similar to that of the male Romantic writer, though expressed indirectly.

The most thorough engagement with Milton by a female writer in the period, however, is seen in Mary Shelley's *Frankenstein* (1818), which also shares the second-generation Romantic penchant for taking Satan's perspective on things. Shelley's novel is a modern version of the creation myths of classical and Christian history. It is subtitled *The Modern Prometheus* and quotes on its title page Adam's lines from *Paradise Lost*:

> Did I request thee, Maker, from my clay
> To mould me man? Did I solicit thee
> From darkness to promote me,
>   (X. 743–5)

Victor Frankenstein is a Promethean rather than a Satanic figure who succeeds in creating life from an assemblage of human and animal parts, thus implying that the principle of life itself is not derived from an external divine agency but a property of the organization of matter. Abandoned by his creator, the creature feels at first the puzzlement of Adam as to the reason for the Creation and his own moral responsibility, and then the hatred and envy of Satan as he is excluded from the society he craves. Among the books that the Creature is given by the De Lacey family is *Paradise Lost*, in which he reads of an 'omnipotent God warring with his creations'. The Creature sees himself as like Adam 'created apparently by no link to any other being in existence' but without Adam's perfection and God's care. The 'fitter emblem' of his condition is rather Satan as he experiences 'the bitter gall of envy' rising at the happiness of others (Shelley 1993: 178). The Creature marks his life in terms of its difference from that of Adam ('no Eve soothed my sorrows, or shared my thoughts') and its similarity with Satan's ('I, like the arch fiend bore a hell within me'), declaring 'everlasting war' against humanity (Shelley 1993: 180, 186). Frankenstein's materialist creation of his hybrid species is not simply an unholy parody of God's creation of humankind, as Mary's 1831 'Preface' encourages us to believe. Rather, it is used as a vehicle to discuss the problem of evil in a material world, where the processes of creation are natural or unnatural but not supernatural, and crime and murder result not from original sin but from social exclusion and deprivation.

Despite Keats's claim that Milton's literary influence was nearly murderous to him, we can see that general trend of the influence was certainly enabling as poet after poet wrestled with their great forebear. To categorize the 'influence' as a 'line of vision' in which the poets regarded themselves as 'spiritual men who would usher in a new order and a new age' (Wittreich 1975: 141) or as anxious competitors killing off their literary father (Bloom) is to admit the enormous importance of the presence of Milton in the early nineteenth century. Romantic period writing is important in that it established Milton, with Shakespeare, as a pillar of the nation's cultural achievement, as well as beginning the recognition of Milton's status as republican and Commonwealthman. The Romantic reworkings of *Paradise Lost*, the Romantic lives and histories of the period, all contributed to a more sophisticated understanding of the totality of Milton's work. As Lucy Newlyn (1993) has argued in her brilliant study of the ways in which *Paradise Lost* was read in the period, Milton's work was not a monolith, but contained within a hard authoritarian 'supertext' a soft ambiguous 'subtext'. Newlyn's book brings back to us the ambiguous and contested nature of Milton's presence in the period, as the heterodoxies and varieties of Romantic reading (of which this essay has provided only a brief and limited account) respond to a Miltonic text that is also exciting, various and multifaceted. Ironically, it was the Romantic excitement when confronted with Milton's poetry (and not just *Paradise Lost*) which centralized the poet's canonical place in English literature in England and America, a process aided by the later nineteenth-century understanding and appreciation of the puritan mind in the work of Carlyle and Ruskin and in Masson's six-volume biography of the poet.

BIBLIOGRAPHY

Writings

Blake (1989); Burke (1958); Byron (1970); Coleridge (1991); Godwin (1824–8, 1978); Hayley (1970); Keats (1970); Macaulay (1878); Scott (1887); Shawcross (1972); Shelley, Mary W. (1993); Symmons (1806); Wittreich (1970); Wollstonecraft (1989); Wordsworth (1936, 1979).

References for Further Reading

Abrams (1971); Austen (1995); Bloom (1973); Brisman (1973); Colley (1992); DiSalvo (1983); Dunbar (1980); Eliot (1957); Fink (1948); Gilbert (1978); Gilbert and Gubar (1984); Grierson (1937); Griffin (1986); Havens (1961); Jarvis (1991); Kitson (1987, 1991, 1992); Leask (1988); Morrow (1990); Newlyn (1993); Paley (1999); Robbins (1959); Roe (1997); Schulz (1985); Shawcross (1974); Wilkie (1965); Williamson (1962); Wittreich (1968, 1975, 1979, 1987).

PART V
Biography

29
The Life Records

Gordon Campbell

The lives of early twenty-first-century middle-class Englishmen are well documented; we regularly fill in forms, write letters and sign cheques, and others write to and about us. The lives of seventeenth-century middle-class Englishmen are not in this respect markedly different, and it is possible to reconstruct many lives in a degree of detail that at times approaches an account of what someone did every day. The life records of Milton and his immediate family consist of about 2,000 references in some 600 documents housed in more than fifty archives; there are also references to Milton in the printed books of the seventeenth century, most of which testify to his public life as a polemicist rather than his relatively unnoticed career as a poet. These documents enable the scholar to assemble a detailed outline of Milton's life, but in the absence of a diary they can say little about his interior life or even his domestic life: serious scholars hesitate to make inferences about the private Milton who seems at times to be glimpsed through the distorting prism of an incomplete documentary record.

There are inevitably missing pieces in the jigsaw of life records, and the discovery of new documents often requires scholars to realign old pieces of evidence. Vast amounts of unexplored seventeenth-century material survive in public and private archives; the records of the Court of Requests (a minor equity court abolished in 1641) in the Public Record Office, for example, run to millions of pages. The labours of Milton scholars regularly produce new documents in such repositories, so the number of life records is slowly increasing. In the 1930s J. M. French assembled the known records of Milton's life (including many legal documents that he had discovered), which he published in a huge five-volume compendium as *The Life Records of John Milton* (1949–58); W. R. Parker added many more records (particularly from parish registers) in his monumental two-volume *Milton: A Biography* (1968), the second volume of which contains 528 pages of notes that document details of Milton's life and a double-columned 274-page index that enables the scholar to navigate in the cross-currents of Parker's notes. By the time that I produced a revised edition of

Parker's biography (1996) and my own *Milton Chronology* (1997), the number of known life records had increased by about a third since French had published his edition, thanks to scholars such as Leo Miller and John Shawcross. This process of recovery is unending; as I draft this paragraph early in 2000, a document has just been discovered in the archives of the Vice-Chancellor's Court in Cambridge which provides a topical context (and a new date) for a speech known as *Prolusion* 6 that Milton delivered to his fellow students in Christ's College.

In addition to these documentary records, there is a scattering of autobiographical remarks in Milton's poetry and prose (collected by John Diekhoff as *Milton on Himself*, 1939) and a series of early biographies (collected by Helen Darbishire as *The Early Lives of Milton*, 1932). This early biographical material includes a biographical preface to an edition of Milton's *Letters of State* by Edward Phillips (Milton's nephew), an anonymous unpublished biography (Bodleian MS Wood D4) attributed by Darbishire to John Phillips (Edward's younger brother) but now known, on the basis of two recently discovered letters in the City Record Office in Hull (BRL 794 and 795), to be in the hand of Milton's amanuensis Cyriack Skinner, and some scruffy notes taken by John Aubrey early in the 1680s (now Bodleian MS Aubrey 8). Skinner's biography and Aubrey's notes were both plundered by Anthony Wood for his biography of 1694.

In this chapter I propose to survey Milton's life records with a view to demonstrating what they show about Milton's life. I can mention only a tiny proportion of those records, but I have attempted to make my selection representative of the variety of documents available to the scholar. Readers should remain cognisant of the strictures that I have set out above: records are partial, and they delineate only the outward contours of a life that we value chiefly because of the expression of an undocumented inner life that is in some measure articulated in Milton's poetry.

Childhood and Education, 1608–1625

Some details of Milton and his family are known only from the flyleaf of his family Bible (now British Library Add MS 32,310); in the mid-1640s Milton started to record the birth of his children on the flyleaf, beginning with a retrospective entry about his own birth and those of his brother Christopher and his nephews Edward and John Phillips. Of his own birth he says 'John Milton was born the 9th of December 1608 *die Veneris* half an howr after 6 in the morning'; the Latin phrase *die Veneris*, which means 'Friday', enables the scholar to consult a calendar for 1608 in order to confirm that Milton's record of his birth is at least internally consistent. In 1649 Milton supplied the same date and time for his birth to an astrologer who subsequently cast his horoscope (now Bodleian MS Ashmole 436/1, fol. 119); see Harry Rusche (1979), 'A Reading of John Milton's Horoscope'; this document is not an independent witness, because the astrologer's informant was Milton, but it does confirm that Milton was at least consistent. The document that ratifies Milton's stated date of birth is the Parish Register of All Hallows Church, Bread Street (now Guildhall Library MS 5031), which records his baptism on 20 December 1608. One of the documents that enable scholars to chart the business life of Milton's father shows that on the day that his first son was baptized, Milton's father did not take the whole day off work; the evidence is a receipt (now Dulwich College Muniment 503) which he signed on the same day. These business records document in considerable detail the commercial activities of Milton's father, who was a prosperous scrivener; by the seventeenth century the profession of scrivener had extended far beyond the work of a scribe to include the functions of notary, financier and investment broker. The business was conducted in the house on Bread Street, so it seems likely that Milton had observed his father's profession at close quarters.

The family records of Milton's childhood and youth enable scholars to calculate the annual family income and to glimpse the vocation of Milton's father as a composer, but on the key matter of Milton's schooling there is a gap in the records. The sole contemporary evidence that Milton was educated at St Paul's School is the entry in the Admissions Book at Christ's College, Cambridge (now in the archives of the college), which records that Milton had studied under Alexander Gil at St Paul's School. This speck of evidence is the basis for scholarly reconstructions of Milton's schooling, notably Donald Clark's *John Milton at St Paul's School* (1948) and the first volume of H. F. Fletcher's highly speculative *The Intellectual Development of John Milton* (1956). For all their endeavour, the learned authors of these two books fail to answer convincingly the central question of when Milton began to attend St Paul's, which may have been as early as 1615 or as late as 1622. The early records of the school were lost along with the school buildings in the fire of 1666, so there is no definitive evidence from that quarter. Milton's nephew Edward Phillips, who was not born until 1630, wrote in his *Life of Milton* (1694) that his uncle 'was entered into the first rudiments of learning' at 'Paul's School', and Milton's brother Christopher told John Aubrey that Milton 'went to school when he was very young'; these remarks imply an early date, possibly 1615. On the other hand, Edward Phillips says that Milton was sent to school 'together with his brother'; if 'together' means 'at the same time', then it seems unlikely that Milton would have entered much before December 1622, when his brother Christopher had his seventh birthday. Milton's own recollection in *Defensio Secunda* that he had studied till midnight 'from the age of 12' may imply that he had entered school sometime after his twelfth birthday on 9 December 1620. All of these records are suspect, because they are distant recollections or hearsay, and because we know that some of them are inaccurate. Edward Phillips, for example, recorded that Milton had been born in 1606 (instead of 1608) and that he had gone up to Cambridge at fifteen (instead of sixteen); such errors sap confidence in his dating of Milton's schooling. The closest we come to a solid date is Milton's claim in the headnote to *Epitaphium Damonis* that he had known Charles Diodati since childhood (*a puerita*); Diodati matriculated at Oxford on 7 February 1623, aged thirteen, so his friendship with Milton at St Paul's must have been established before that date.

Cambridge, 1625–1632

Milton's student years have been extensively studied, notably in the second volume of H. F. Fletcher's *The Intellectual Development of John Milton* (1971) and in the conference papers collected by Ronald Shafer in *Ringing the Bell Backward* (1982); in both cases, the surviving life records constitute a sandy foundation for such substantial scholarly edifices. The academic literature is filled with muddled accounts of these records composed by scholars who have never seen them and whose grasp of the distinction between college documents and university documents has not been as firm as it might have been.

The Admissions Book of Christ's College records that on 12 February 1625, on payment of ten shillings, Milton was admitted to the college as a minor pensioner under William Chappell. This formal record of admission to his college may not denote Milton's arrival in Cambridge (which may have been in time for the beginning of the Lent Term on 13 January), nor should it be confused with his matriculation at the university, which was entered in the University Matriculation Book on 9 April 1625. In the course of the Lent Term of 1629 (13 January–27 March) Milton supplicated (i.e. formally petitioned) for his BA (University Archives, Supplicats 1629, fol. 331) and in the course of the Lent Term of 1632 (13 January–23 March) he supplicated for his MA (University Archives, Supplicats 1632, fol. 270). These supplications are routinely confused with subscriptions: in 1629 Milton subscribed to the Articles of Religion by signing the University Subscription Book (University Archives, Subs 1, p. 286), because subscription was a requirement for conferment of the BA, and on 3 July 1632 he again signed the Subscription Book (Subs 1, p. 377), this time to qualify for the MA. John Fenwick, the Fellow of Christ's who received the supplications in 1629, seems to have dictated the supplication formula to the graduands and then signed each one himself. This labour-saving device has left scholars with an early example of the hand that Milton used for writing Latin, and so has implications for the Miltonic Latin juvenilia preserved in a leaf now in the Harry Ranson Humanities Research Center in Austin, Texas (Pre-1700 Manuscript 127), which is said to be an autograph. Perhaps it is, but its handwriting does not closely resemble that of the supplicat of 1629.

Most of the other life records of this period document the life of Milton's father rather than the activities of the son, but such records may include blurred reflections of the life of the younger Milton. Documents in the Public Record Office (in Kew) dated 25 May and 11 June 1627 recording that Milton's father purchased property in St Martin in the Fields and subsequently lent £300 to Richard Powell (Milton's future father-in-law) are signed by both Milton and his father; the signatures of the younger Milton may seem to be of merely antiquarian interest until it is realized that both documents were signed in London at a time when Milton was supposed to be in Cambridge, where the Easter Term ran from 4 April to 6 July. The most likely explanation for Milton's absence from Cambridge during termtime is that this was the term during which he fell out with William Chappell and was in consequence rusticated (i.e. suspended). Milton's biographers have traditionally placed the rustication in the previous year, when Milton is assumed (without any evidence) to have composed *'Elegia prima'*. If that poem does indeed refer obliquely to Milton's expulsion from Cambridge, then it should be assigned to 1627. Two apparently insignificant legal documents may hold the key to the true date of Milton's rustication.

Hammersmith and Horton, 1631–1638

The two groups of records which have proved to be significant for our understanding of Milton's life in the early 1630s are a set of Chancery Town Depositions discovered in the Public Record Office in the late 1940s and the poor relief registers of Hammersmith, found in the Hammersmith and Fulham Record Office in 1996. The publication of the Chancery depositions in 1949 showed that from 1631 to 1635 the Milton family lived not in Horton (in present-day Berkshire), as had been believed for 250 years, but in the village of Hammersmith, which was relatively close to London. Such discoveries take an inordinately long time to penetrate the sclerotic body of conventional wisdom, and fifty years after this discovery, chronologies of Milton prefixed to editions of his poems still routinely place Milton in Horton rather than in Hammersmith during this period. The recently discovered poor relief records (Hammersmith and Fulham Record Office PAF/1/21) refine the dates of the Chancery depositions, in that they demonstrate that the elder Milton was assessed for poor relief in Hammersmith as early as 10 April 1631, but, much more importantly, they associate Milton's father with the Laudian chapel-of-ease at Hammersmith: the documents that chronicle the foundation of the chapel are also in the Hammersmith and Fulham Record Office (DD/818/56). Bishop Laud had consecrated the Chapel of St Paul on 7 June 1631, and by May 1633 Milton's father had become a churchwarden; these discoveries dispose of the venerable assumption that Milton grew up in a puritan household. It would seem that during the vacations of his final year at Cambridge and for the three succeeding years, Milton attended services of a Laudian complexion; scholars who want to depict the youthful Milton as a radical-in-waiting have yet to contend with the problems raised by these documents.

On 12 May 1636, according to a document which was in the archive of the Company of Scriveners in the nineteenth century (but can no longer be identified), Milton's father was discharged at his own request from his membership of the Court of Assistants (the Company's governing body) because of his 'removal to inhabit in the country'. This lost entry reflects the retirement of Milton's family from Hammersmith to the village of Horton, which was then in Buckinghamshire, but has since 1974 been in Berkshire, near Heathrow Airport. The identity of the unnamed place in the country is first revealed in a document in the records of the Court of Requests (PRO Req 1/141, fol. 218), which states that on 1 April 1637, the elder Milton was living in Horton.

Milton's two great works of the mid-1630s are *Comus* and 'Lycidas'; in both cases, there are contemporary records that may cast a flickering light on Milton's intentions and on the historical moments at which he composed the masque and the elegy. *Comus* was performed on Monday 29 September 1634 at Ludlow Castle. Sentimental Miltonists with happy recollections of Shakespeare productions in Regent's Park and an anachronistic notion of the importance of the author in the seventeenth century have imagined that *Comus* was acted outdoors, and that Milton himself played the part of Comus in what was essentially a children's party. The record in the Ludlow Bailiffs' Accounts (in the Shropshire Record Office) to the effect that civic officials 'were invited to the maske' is in some measure an antidote to such fantasy, in that it demonstrates that the performance was a civic occasion rather than a domestic one. More problematically, two historical incidents, one national and one local, have been linked to Milton's masque. The national incident was the execution in 1631 of the Earl of Castlehaven, brother-in-law of the Countess of Bridgewater, in whose presence the masque was performed; the execution was for sexual offences, and since 1960, when Miltonists first stumbled across this infamous episode, *Comus* has been interpreted as a ritualistic cleansing of the family; see Barbara Breasted (1971) and John Creaser's riposte (1984). Similarly, the judgement of the Earl of Bridgewater on the case of Margery Evans, a serving maid who had been raped while travelling alone, has been adduced as an historical circumstance relevant to Milton's masque (Marcus 1983).

The occasion of 'Lycidas' was the death of Edward King, a younger contemporary of Milton at Christ's College. Two clusters of life records may be relevant in some measure to an understanding of Milton's poem: first, it is possible to reconstruct Milton's circumstances in Horton in 1637, and second, one can consider the life records of Edward King, which were collected in a special issue of *Milton Quarterly* in December 1994 as *Edward King, Milton's Lycidas: Poems and Documents*. Both groups of documents illustrate the limitations as well as the usefulness of life records. In the first group, one might take into account the evidence of the parish register of Horton, where Milton was living that year. The register (which is now in the Buckinghamshire County Record Office in Aylesbury) lists a dozen deaths from plague in the first half of the year; did these deaths contribute to the complexion of 'Lycidas'? The register also records that Milton's mother Sara died on 3 April. Milton seems not to have written a poem in her memory: does her death colour 'Lycidas'? Or, further afield, did the death of Ben Jonson on 16 August mark Milton's poem? The records of Edward King are similarly problematical, because the relationship of King's life and death to Milton's poem can be understood only through the prism of Milton's own emotions, which are embodied in his poem rather than in the life records of either himself or King. Indeed, these records may prove to be wholly inadequate indicators of Milton's state of mind and creative process; perhaps one should turn to public events that may have touched Milton, such as the public mutilation on 30 June of William Prynne, John Bastwick and Henry Burton, whose crime was to have offended Laud (see Leonard 1991).

Italy, 1638–1639

In May 1638 Milton left England for a tour of the continent that was to last approximately fifteen months. His travels and their effect on his writing have been studied by scholars; the most recent collection of essays on the subject is *Milton in Italy: Contexts, Images, Contradictions* (Di Cesare 1991). The main records of this visit are Milton's own retrospective account in *Defensio Secunda* and the scattered records in Italy, most of which are printed in French's *Life Records*. Scholars have chosen to play down a third source, that of the research of Salmasius, who alleged that while in Italy Milton became a male prostitute, 'selling his buttocks for a few pence' (*paucis nummis nates prostituisse*); this allegation, which was denied by Nicholas Heinsius in a letter of 21/31 January 1653 (French 1949–58, III: 316), may throw light on the enigmatic accusation of John Bramhall in May 1654 that Milton was sent down from Cambridge and banished from the society of men because of actions so shameful that if they were revealed Milton would hang himself, but both records have been set aside because they do not accord with the image of Milton that his champions wish to create. Such records raise a specific problem about the evidential value of hostile reports, in this case uncorroborated slurs by known enemies, but also point to the general problem of tendentiousness in allusions; indeed, all descriptive records embody the perspective of their authors, and to that extent cannot be taken at face value.

The surviving records of Milton's journey to France, Italy and Geneva enable the scholar to construct his itinerary, but precise dates are in short supply, and in Milton's own account the figures that he provides for the length of stay in each city are rounded off and presented with an eye to their symmetry. In the spring of 1638 Milton received his passport, which was really an exit visa that allowed him to leave England. The passport itself, which was a letter from the Earl of Suffolk (written in his capacity as Warden of the Cinque Ports), has disappeared, but Milton kept the covering letter from his friend Henry Lawes, who had secured the passport, and placed it in his Commonplace Book, which is now on permanent display in the British Library (Add MS 36,354). Sir Henry Wotton, who had served as ambassador in Venice, advised Milton to travel 'the whole length of France to Marseilles, and thence by sea to Genoa, whence the passage to Tuscany is as diurnal as a Gravesend Barge' (BL Add MS 28,637, fol. 1, an eighteenth-century transcription of the lost original). Milton adapted this advice to his own purposes, and travelled first to Paris, then south to Nice and along by sea to Genoa; he then sailed to Leghorn (Livorno) and travelled inland, first to Pisa and thence to Florence, possibly arriving in June 1638.

Milton visited at least two of the Florentine academies, one of which was the Svogliati (literally 'the will-less'), the Minute Book of which survives in the Biblioteca Nazionale (MS Magliabecchiana, Cl. IX cod. 60). Milton's name first appears in the minutes of 16 September (6 September in the English calendar, so the date is usually written '6/16'), when he read a poem in Latin hexameters to the assembled academicians, who thought it *molto erudita*; the identity of the poem is not known. This record of Milton's attendance raises the question of whether he had been elected a member. A tantalizing entry in the Minute Book for 28 June/8 July records that an English man of letters (*letterato Inglese*) had attended a meeting of the Academy and expressed his wish to become a member; the following Thursday (5/15 July) two new members were elected: one is named, but there is a blank in the text where the second name should appear. May we infer that the secretary had failed to catch a foreign name, that the foreign name was that of the *letterato Inglese* and that the English man of letters was Milton? The answer is probably, but not certainly, 'yes'. Six years later, in 1644, Milton claimed in *Areopagitica* to have visited Galileo in Florence. There is no independent record of this visit, but it is not improbable: Galileo's illegitimate son Vincenzo was among those whom Milton met at the Svogliati, and Milton could have visited the old man either in his house in Arcetri or in Vincenzo's house on the Costa San Giorgio, where Galileo was staying for medical treatment. We only know of this visit because Milton chose to mention it while making a polemical point in *Areopagitica*; one wonders what other important meetings have been lost to history simply because there is no surviving record.

Does Milton's poetry constitute a life record? The mention of Vallombrosa in *Paradise Lost* (I. 303) was the seed of a tradition that Milton had visited the monastery there, and the descriptions of hell in Milton's epic have been adduced as evidence that he visited the geysers of the Lardello region near Florence and the Phlegraean Fields near Naples, but these are frail foundations for an argument about Milton's itinerary. Milton was not an impressionist painter who took his images directly from the landscape, but rather a seventeenth-century poet whose images are overwhelmingly literary in origin.

Milton travelled to Rome, where he signed the Pilgrim Book of the English College when he dined there on 20/30 October 1638, and near the end of the year he travelled to Naples, where, Milton later recalled, Giovanni Battista Manso presented him to the Spanish vice-regal court. There must be a record of Milton's audience, but the Neapolitan archives in Simancas (in Spain) have not yet been searched for that important life record.

In Naples Milton decided to travel no further south; he turned back, returning first to Rome and Florence, and then via Bologna and Ferrara to Venice, where he shipped home the books that he had collected, which included a case of music books. Thereafter he travelled to Verona and Milan before crossing the Alps to Geneva. He may have arrived in May, but the first solid evidence of his arrival is his entry (dated in another hand) in an *album amicorum* now in the Houghton Library at Harvard University (MS Sumner 84, Lobby XI.3.43):

> ———if virtue feeble were
> Heaven it self would stoop to her.
> Cælum non animu[m] muto du[m] trans mare curro
> Junii 10° 1639   Joannes Miltonius Anglus

The English lines are cited from *Comus* (lines 1021–2) and the Latin is adapted from Horace's *Epistles* (I. xi. 27); the latter may be as close as life records can approach to a disclosure of the state of Milton's mind: Horace's original line (*cælum, non animum, mutant, qui trans mare currunt*) observes that they who cross the sea change their sky but not their mind; Milton transforms the line into a determined boast: 'When I cross the sea I change my sky but not my mind'. Openmindedness was not a virtue in the seventeenth century; Milton and his contemporaries valued conviction.

Schoolmaster and Polemicist, 1639–1648

Milton's life records in the 1640s are relatively thin, and they reflect a comparatively settled period in his life. It was probably the death of Milton's sister Anne that led to her two boys (Edward and John Phillips) moving in with their uncle, who thus stumbled into a teaching career. Some time in 1640 Milton moved with his nephews into a large house in Aldersgate; the tax records document his presence there on 29 April 1641 (Guildhall MS 1503/5). A poll tax levied in July declared Milton and his servant Jane Yates to be liable; on 3 August both Milton and his servant were listed as tax defaulters (PRO E179/252/1) and in September Milton was taxed £6 (Guildhall MS 1503/6).

    The central event in Milton's domestic life in the 1640s was his first marriage, of which no record has been found. Milton's nephew Edward Phillips later described how at the end of 1642 Milton had gone to Forest Hill in Oxfordshire to collect an interest payment from a Justice of the Peace called Richard Powell and had returned a month later married to Powell's seventeen-year-old daughter Mary. Within a few weeks, the marriage had broken down and Mary had returned to her parents. No life record casts any light on this catastrophe, but lack of evidence has not inhibited speculation that there were political differences (the Powells were a royalist family) or that Milton was a tyrannical husband. In 1645 rumours reached the Powell family that Milton planned to remarry. Divorce permitting remarriage was available only to those influential enough to secure a private Act of Parliament. Ecclesiastical courts were empowered to grant only judicial separation (which was also called divorce). Is it possible that Milton planned to seek an annulment? In Milton's England there were only three grounds for annulment: a pre-contract to a third party; consanguinity; and male impotence over a period of three years. Might Milton have hoped that what may have been an unconsummated marriage and his subsequent three years of chastity would gain him an annulment? The life records supply no answers, but it is not surprising that Milton turned his mind to the need for new divorce laws. Whatever the truth of the matter, Milton and his wife were reunited in 1645, and their daughter Anne was born on 29 July 1646. Milton wrote the date and time in his family Bible (BL Add MS 32,310) and Mary wrote the same details into her Bible; Mary's Bible was lost in the late eighteenth century, but her entries were transcribed by Thomas Birch in 1750, and are now in the British Library (Add MS 4244 fol. 52ᵛ).

Public Servant, 1649–1660

On 30 January 1649 King Charles was executed, and six weeks later, at noon on 13 March, the Council of State decided to invite Milton to be Secretary for Foreign Tongues. Two days later, on Thursday 15 March, Milton was appointed to the post at an annual salary of £288 13s 6½ d. The House of Lords was abolished on Saturday and the monarchy on Monday, and on Tuesday Milton took the oath of secrecy. Two days later, on Thursday 22 March 1649, he was given his first assignment, the translation into Latin of letters to be sent to Hamburg. This degree of detail in our knowledge of Milton's first week as a civil servant is characteristic of the documentation of Milton's early years in the post, before he went blind. The documents that he produced, however, are problematical, because it is difficult to ascertain to what extent, if any, Milton contributed to their composition. If he was merely translating the words of other men, these letters are less clearly Miltonic than they would be if he was also responsible for the English originals. The only certain conclusion that can be drawn from these letters, which are known as the *Letters of State* or *State Papers*, is that they show how Milton was discharging the duties required of him by the Council of State.

Our knowledge of Milton's whereabouts is more detailed in this period than in any other, and there is one short spell, from October 1651 to March 1652, when the diary of a German diplomat called Hermann Mylius gives an almost daily account of Milton's professional life (on the diary, see Miller 1985). Mylius had come to London to renew a treaty on behalf of his employer, the city-state of Oldenburg, and his opposite number in the English civil service was Milton; Mylius's diary records their exchanges in detail. On 9 January 1652, for example, Mylius records that Milton had visited him in his lodgings near Whitehall in the morning, and had then ridden into the City (*Ist in die Statt gefahren*), returning that afternoon to collect the draft of a treaty before returning to the Council of State. The question of why Milton was riding into the City of London seems to be resolved by another document, an excise bond that Milton had purchased eight months earlier: an annotation on the bond records that on 9 January Milton had collected £16 in interest, and that collection would seem to account for Milton's journey to the City that day.

The detailed documentation of Milton's professional life in this period contains two puzzling gaps, which together constitute the only protracted period in his life in which he simply disappears. On 14 July 1651 Milton's translation of a Letter of State to the King of Spain was approved, so he was probably in Westminster on that date, in case revisions had been required. On 30 July one Christoph Arnold of Nuremburg met Mylius at the Old Exchange, and told him that Milton was *vier meilen* away. If these four miles were in German measure, then Milton must have been about 18 English miles away from the Old Exchange, perhaps in Horton; if the miles were English, he may have been in Hammersmith. On 16 October Mylius noted in his diary that Milton had returned from the country (*vom Land*) the previous day. Where had he been? The problem is compounded by a similar absence the following year: we know that Milton's daughter Deborah was born on 2 May 1652, that his wife Mary died three days later and that his son John died about six weeks after that, but the parish records are silent about these events, and the burial place of Mary and John is not known. Milton had a flat in Whitehall, but it would seem that his family was living elsewhere. The surviving life records cast no light on Milton's domestic circumstances during this period.

It was about this time that Milton became totally blind; the final stages of the onset of blindness can be traced through various life records. Milton had signed his name in the autograph book of Christoph Arnold (now British Library MS Egerton 1324) on 19 November 1651; he gives the place as London rather than Westminster (the address of Milton's Whitehall flat), so it is likely that he was visiting either Samuel Hartlib or Theodore Haak, both of whom were living in London, and signed the *album amicorum* on the same day. A fortnight later, on 1 December 1651, Johan Oste, the Secretary of the Dutch legation, reported that Milton was almost blind. On 3 January 1652 Mylius visited Milton, and subsequently recorded that Milton was suffering from suffusion of the eyes (*suffusione oculorum*). The recurrence of the medical term 'suffusion' in *Paradise Lost* (III. 26) may imply that Mylius was reporting Milton's term for his loss of sight. On 5 March Mylius met Milton for the last time, and recorded that he was 'wholly deprived of his sight in his forty-second year'; Milton had turned forty-three in December 1651, so the report may contain dated information. Milton's helplessness is recorded in a note (discovered in 1995) dated 11 July 1652 in a copy of his *Eikonoklastes* in Canterbury Cathedral Library: 'the man that wrot this booke is now growne blind and is led up and downe'. This calamity was compounded by the death of Milton's wife Mary on 5 May 1652; Milton had become a widower with four young children, including a three-day-old baby. Parish registers record that he married Katherine Woodcock on 12 November 1656 (Guildhall MS 3572) and that she died on 3 February 1658. The account recording funeral expenses survives in the College of Arms (Painters' Workbook I.B.7, fol. 46b). Milton was a gentleman of some standing, and clearly thought that a funeral overseen by the College of Arms reflected his public status.

For the student of the political Milton, the most frustrating lack in the life records for this period is that of a document which demonstrates that Milton ever met Oliver Cromwell. The Victorian notion of Milton as Cromwell's secretary may have been a fantasy, but no surviving record enables us to replace the fantasy with a fact. It could be argued that both men worked in the Palace of Whitehall and so must have at least passed each other in the corridor, but proof is wanting. In the absence of such proof, any argument about the nature of the relationship between Milton and Cromwell must be regarded as entirely speculative.

With the advent of the Protectorate in December 1653, responsibility for foreign affairs was to pass from the Council of State to Oliver Cromwell and his Secretary of State, John Thurloe. The fact that Milton now worked for an individual rather than a committee means that there are no detailed records of his activities as a servant of the Protectorate. There is no reason to interpret this gap in the historical record as a sign that he had stopped working, though his loss of sight had inevitably limited the speed at which he could work. The best guide to this period is Robert Fallon's *Milton in Government* (1993).

Epic Poet, 1660–1674

On 1 May 1660 the Convention Parliament invited Charles II to return to England as a monarch with limited powers. Four days later Milton prudently transferred the excise bond which he had bought in May 1651 to a young friend, Cyriack Skinner. The restoration of Charles II was proclaimed on 8 May, and Edward Phillips records that when Charles entered London in triumph on 29 May, Milton was in hiding in Bartholomew Close, in West Smithfield. A warrant for his arrest was issued on 16 June, and his regicidal books were condemned to be burnt. Milton was not named in the Act of Oblivion of 29 August, and so escaped the death penalty, but at some point in the autumn he was arrested and imprisoned in the Tower of London. On 15 December he was pardoned, and ordered to be released from custody and to pay a fee of £150 for his imprisonment. Why was he pardoned? Two copies of his pardon were lodged in the State Paper Office and, although neither survives, both were listed in eighteenth-century indices (Warrant Books and Signet Office) that are now in the Public Record Office. Milton's fame has meant that souvenir hunters have stolen such documents, a phenomenon that probably explains the paucity of Milton documents in the Hartlib papers at Sheffield University. The loss of the documents means that we have no solid evidence of the reason for the pardon; a Dutch newsletter published a few months later claimed that Milton was 'freed through good promises' (*nu uytging door goe belaften*), but the life records provide no evidence to corroborate or discredit that claim. As for the imprisonment fee, the *Journal of the House of Commons* records that Andrew Marvell protested on Milton's behalf that the fee was excessive, but we do not know the outcome of the protest: the matter was referred to the Committee of Privileges, whose judgement has not survived.

Milton's notoriety meant that he had to live quietly in Restoration England, and for the next few years the life records are distinctly thin. On 11 November 1663 he declared his intention to marry Elizabeth Minshull (Lambeth Palace MS FM1/3B, fol. 149), and he did so on 24 February (Guildhall MS 8990); Elizabeth was twenty-four, and was destined to outlive her husband by more than fifty years. The autobiography of the Quaker Thomas Ellwood, who had been imprisoned in Newgate for refusing to take the Oath of Allegiance, provides a glimpse of Milton in the summer of 1665, and the publication of *Paradise Lost* in the autumn of 1667 provides another cluster of life records. Milton had written *Paradise Lost* in the years 1658–63, but the political thaw which would permit publication did not arise until 1667. In June 1665 Thomas Ellwood arranged for Milton to rent a cottage in Chalfont St Giles from Anne Fleetwood, daughter of the regicide George Fleetwood; on 1 July Ellwood was incarcerated in Aylesbury Prison, and shortly thereafter Milton arrived in Chalfont to escape from the plague that was 'growing hot in London'. When Ellwood was released the following month, he called on Milton 'to welcome him into the country'. Milton gave Ellwood a manuscript copy of *Paradise Lost*, and asked him to comment on it. In due course Ellwood returned the manuscript to Milton, and commented that 'thou hast said much here of Paradise Lost, but what hast thou to say of Paradise Found?' When Milton returned to London, probably in February 1666, Ellwood visited him again, and Milton showed him a copy of *Paradise Regained*, explaining that 'this is owing to you, for you put it into my head by the question you put to me at Chalfont, which before I had not thought of.' What is the significance of this life record? Professional students of Milton have tended to dismiss Ellwood as a simple Quaker, and to assume that Milton was simply being kind, adducing as evidence the fact that *Paradise Lost* describes the regaining of paradise in the final book. Such superiority seems to me quite unwarranted. Ellwood was a prominent figure in the Quaker movement and the editor of George Fox's Journal (1694), and he was no more foolish than many professional students of Milton: it is not at all unlikely that Milton was thanking Ellwood for giving him the idea of a sequel to *Paradise Lost*.

The title page of the first edition of *Paradise Lost* gives its date as 1667, but its precise date of publication has yet to be discovered. It has long been known that the poem was registered for publication on 20 August, and there is a mildly improbable story that Sir John Denham rushed into Parliament (which had reconvened on 10 October) waving a sheet of *Paradise Lost* 'wet from the press' and proclaiming it to be 'part of the noblest poem that was ever wrote in any language or in any age'. More reliable evidence came to light in 1992 with the discovery in the letters of John Beale to John Aubrey (then in Christ Church, Oxford and now in the British Library) of a series of references to Milton. On 11 November Beale discussed rhyme with what seems to be reference to *Paradise Lost*, and on 18 November he speaks explicitly of *Paradise Lost*.

The greatest chronological puzzle in Milton studies is the date of *Samson Agonistes* (see Sharon Achinstein, ch. 25 in this volume), and no life record offers definitive information. The absence of evidence has not proved to be an effective bulwark against dogmatic belief, and Miltonists argue passionately for a variety of dates. The emergence of a single scrap of paper could quell the argument, but to date no life record has been forthcoming except for the comment of Edward Phillips that the date of composition 'cannot certainly be concluded'.

Posthumous Documents

Milton's will is a posthumous document, because it was not committed to paper until a month after his death. Milton had dictated a nuncupative (i.e. oral) will to his brother Christopher in the summer of 1674, and six months later Christopher was required to give an account of what John had said. 'As near as [he could] now call to mind', Milton had said

Brother, the portion due to me from Mr Powell, my former wife's father, I leave to the unkind children I had by her; but I have received no part of it, and my will and meaning is they shall have no other benefit of my estate than the said portion and what I have besides done for them, they having been very undutiful to me. And all the residue of my estate I leave to the disposal of Elizabeth, my loving wife. (PRO PROB 24/13, fol. 238ᵛ)

Christopher goes on to say that Milton's wife Elizabeth and their maid Elizabeth Fisher were in the room at the time, but that he did not know whether they had heard him declaring his will. This will is a famous document, and is often cited by those who think that Milton mistreated his daughters, especially as one of those daughters, Anne, was declared by Christopher Milton to be 'lame and helpless' (C24/587/46).

What is less well known is that ten days after Christopher testified, the maid Elizabeth Fisher and her sister Mary were examined about Milton's will (PRO PROB 24/13/311–313). Mary, who spoke first, explained that she had been in the kitchen of Milton's house at about noon on a day about two months previous, and that Milton and his wife Elizabeth had been having dinner. Milton 'did then speak to his said wife and utter these words, viz "Make much of me as long as I live, for thou knowest I have given thee all when I die at thy disposal"'; she went on to say that Milton had 'talked and discoursed sensibly and well and was very merry'. Elizabeth Fisher corroborated this testimony, but traced the origins of Milton's remark to the quality of the cooking: Elizabeth Milton had 'provided something for the deceased's dinner which he very well liked', whereupon Milton said 'God have mercy, Betty, I see thou wilt perform according to thy promise in providing me with such dishes as I see fit whilst I live, and when I die thou knowest that I have left thee all.' Elizabeth Fisher went on to say that subsequent to this occasion she had several times heard Milton say 'that he had made provision for his children in his life time and had spent the greatest part of his estate in providing for them and that he was resolved that he would doe no more for them living or dying'. The tone of this remark is markedly different from that recalled by Christopher on an earlier occasion. Under questioning, Elizabeth Fisher went on to tell quite a different story. Milton had told her

that a little before he was married to Elizabeth Milton his now relic, a former maidservant told Mary, one of his daughters..., that she heard the deceased was to be married, to which the said Mary replied to the said maidservant that that was no news to hear of his wedding but if she could hear of his death that was something – and further told this respondent that all his said children did combine together and counsel his maidservant to cheat him the deceased in her marketings, and that his said children had made away some of his books and would have sold the rest of his books to the dunghill woman.

Here is abundant testimony to the effect that cruel children were duping their helpless father and stealing books from his library; as for the disabled daughter,

Elizabeth Fisher explains that 'Anne Milton is lame but hath a trade and can live by the same, which is the making of gold and silver lace and which the deceased bred her up to.' Thus one life record portrays Milton as a spiteful parent and the other depicts him as a responsible parent; the one depicts the children as victims, the other as culprits. The testimony of two maidservants is an antidote to the acidic recollections of Milton's brother. This sharp contrast is a salutary reminder of the partiality of life records.

BIBLIOGRAPHY

Manuscripts (Including Books with Manuscript Annotations)

Austin, Texas, Harry Ranson Humanities Research Center
Pre-1700 Manuscript 127
Aylesbury, Buckinghamshire County Record Office
PR 107/1/1 (Horton Parish Register)
Cambridge, Christ's College
Admissions Book
Cambridge, University Library
University Archives
Matriculation Book (entry for 9 April 1625)
Subscription Book Subs 1, pp. 286 and 377)
Supplicats 1629, fol. 331
Supplicats 1632, fol. 270
Vice-Chancellor's Court.1.52, fols 132–3
Canterbury, Cathedral Library
Milton, *Eikonoklastes* (Elham 732)
Florence, Biblioteca Nazionale
MS Magliabecchiana Cl. IX cod. 60 (Svogliati Academy, Minute Book)
Harvard, Houghton Library
MS Sumner 84, Lobby XI.3.43 (Cardoini Album, signed by Milton)
Hull, City Record Office
BRL 794 and 795 (letters by Cyriack Skinner)
London, British Library
Add MS 4244 (miscellaneous biographical and literary memoranda by Thomas Birch)
Add MS 28,637 (Francis Peck's transcriptions of Milton's poems, etc, which includes Sir Henry Wotton's letter)
Add MS 32,310 (Milton's family Bible)
Add MS 36,354 (Milton's Commonplace Book)
MS Egerton 1324 (Christoph Arnold's *album amicorum*)

MSS Evelyn Letters 63, 64 and 67 (letters from John Beale to John Aubrey
London, College of Arms
Painters' Workbook I.B.7, fol. 46b
London, Dulwich College
Muniment 503 (muniment witnessed by JM's father)
London, Guildhall Library
MS 1503/5 and /6 (Miscellaneous Rate and Subsidy Assessments, St Botolph's Parish, Aldersgate)
MS 3572 (Parish Register, St Mary the Virgin, Aldermanbury)
MS 5031 (Parish Register, All Hallows, Bread Street
MS 8990 (Parish Register, St Mary, Aldermary)
London, Hammersmith and Fulham Record Office
DD/818/56 (Copies of Papers Relating to Hammersmith Chapel)
PAF/1/21, fols. 68, 85, 92^v (Poor Relief Registers)
London, Lambeth Palace Library
MS FM1/3B (Allegations for Marriage Licences)
London, Public Record Office (Kew)
C24/587/46 (Chancery Town Deposition)
C54/2715/20 (indenture recording purchase of property by Milton's father)
C152/61 (staple bond as security for loan by Milton's father to Richard Powell)
E179/252/1 (Exchequer Subsidy Rolls)
IND/1/8/8911 (Index to Warrant Books, 1660–1722, A–P)
PRO PROB 24/13 (PCC Deposition Books, 114 vols)

Req 1/141, fol. 218 (Court of Requests, Mis-
cellaneous Books, 210 vols)
SO4/5 fol. 164 (Index to Signet Office Docket
Books, 1660–1737)
Oxford, Bodleian Library
MS Ashmole 436/1, fol. 119 (Milton's horo-
scope)
MS Aubrey 8 (part of Aubrey's 'Brief Lives')
MS Wood D4 (anonymous life of Milton by
Cyriack Skinner; printed in Darbishire, who
attributes it to John Phillips)
Rome, English College
Pilgrim Book
Shrewsbury, Shropshire Record Office
Ludlow Bailiffs' Accounts for 1634

*Writings and References for Further
Reading*

Breasted (1971); Campbell (1997); Campbell and
Postlethwaite (1994); Clark (1948); Creaser
(1984a); Darbishire (1932); Di Cesare (1991);
Diekhoff (1939); Ellwood (1714); Eyre, Rivington and Plomer (1950); Fallon, Robert T.
(1993); Fletcher, Harris F. (1956/1971); French
(1949–58); Leonard (1991); Marcus (1983);
Miller, Leo (1985); Parker, William R. (1968,
1996); Rusche (1979); Shafer (1982); Whitelocke (1990).

Consolidated Bibliography

Works of John Milton

Milton, John (1638) 'Lycidas', *Obsequies to the memorie of Mr. Edward King* in *Justa Edovardo King naufrago*. Cambridge.

Milton, John (1645) *Poems of Mr John Milton, Both English and Latin, Compos'd at several times*. London.

Milton, John (1673) *Poems, & c, Upon Several Occasions. By John Milton. Both English and Latin, & c, composed at several Times. With a Small Tractate of Education*. London.

Milton, John (1688) *Paradise Lost.* (Tonson's folio edition, with illustrations.) London.

Milton, John (1931–8) *The Works of John Milton*, gen. ed. Frank Allen Patterson, 18 vols in 21. New York: Columbia University Press. Cited in the text as *WJM*.

Milton, John (1937) *Paradise Regained, the Minor Poems, and Samson Agonistes*, ed. Merritt Y. Hughes. New York: Odyssey Press.

Milton, John (1943–8) *John Milton's Complete Poetical Works reproduced in photographic facsimile*, ed. Harris F. Fletcher. Urbana: University of Illinois Press.

Milton, John (1953–82) *Complete Prose Works of John Milton*, gen. ed. Don M. Wolfe, 8 vols. New Haven: Yale University Press. Cited in the text as *CPW*.

Milton, John (1957) *Complete Poems and Major Prose*, ed. Merritt Y. Hughes. New York: Odyssey Press.

Milton, John (1967) *The Prose of John Milton*. ed. J. Max Patrick et al. Garden City, NY: Doubleday.

Milton, John (1968) *The Poems of John Milton*, ed. John Carey and Alastair Fowler. London and Harlow: Longmans, Green and Co.

Milton, John (1970) *John Milton. Poems, Reproduced in Facsimile from the Manuscript in Trinity College, Cambridge, with a Transcript*. Menston: Scolar Press.

Milton, John (1971a) *The Complete Poetry of John Milton*, ed. John T. Shawcross. New York: Anchor Books.

Milton, John (1971b) *Complete Shorter Poems*, ed. John Carey. London: Longman.

Milton, John (1972) *John Milton. Poems, Reproduced in Facsimile from the Manuscript in Trinity College, Cambridge, with a Transcript*. Menston: Scolar Press.

Milton, John (1973) *A Maske: The Earlier Versions*, ed. S. E. Sprott. Toronto: University of Toronto Press.

Milton, John (1974) *Selected Prose*, ed. C. A. Patrides. Harmondsworth: Penguin.

Milton, John (1991) *A Critical Edition of the Major Works*, ed. Stephen Orgel and Jonathan Goldberg. Oxford and New York: Oxford University Press.

Milton, John (1997) *Complete Shorter Poems*, ed. John Carey, 2nd edn. London and New York: Longman. Cited in text as *CSP*.

Milton, John (1998a) *The Complete Poems*, ed. John Leonard. London: Penguin.

Milton, John (1998b) *The Riverside Milton*, ed. Roy Flannagan. Boston and New York: Houghton Mifflin.

Milton, John (1998c) *Paradise Lost*, ed. John Leonard. Harmondsworth: Penguin.

Milton, John (1998d) *Paradise Lost*, ed. Alastair Fowler, 2nd edn. London and New York: Longman. Cited in text as *PL*.

OTHER WORKS

A Gentleman of Christ-Church College, Oxon. (1732) *A Friendly Letter to Dr. Bentley Occasion'd by his New Edition of Paradise Lost*. London.

A Gentleman of Oxford (1745) *The State of Innocence: and Fall of Man. Described in Milton's Paradise Lost*. London.

Abraham, Lyndy (1998) Milton's Paradise Lost and 'the sounding alchymie'. *Renaissance Studies* 12, 261–76.

Abrams, M. H. (1971) *Natural Supernaturalism: Tradition and Revolution in Romantic Literature*. New York: Norton.

Achinstein, Sharon (1994) *Milton and the Revolutionary Reader*. Princeton: Princeton University Press.

Achinstein, Sharon (1996) *Samson Agonistes* and the Drama of Dissent. *Milton Studies* 33, 133–58.

Adams, Robert (1955) *Ikon: John Milton and the Modern Critics*. Ithaca: Cornell University Press.

Addison, Joseph (1965) *Notes Upon the Twelve Books of Paradise Lost* (1719). A reprint of the eighteen papers on *Paradise Lost* published in *The Spectator* between 5 January 1712 and 3 May 1712. *The Spectator*, ed. Donald F. Bond, 5 vols. Oxford: Clarendon Press.

Allen, Don Cameron (1970) *The Harmonious Vision: Studies in Milton's Poetry*, 2nd edn. Baltimore and London: Johns Hopkins University Press.

Alpers, Paul (1996) *What is Pastoral?* Chicago and London: University of Chicago Press.

Anon. (1741) *An Essay upon Milton's Imitation of the Ancients in His Paradise Lost, with some Observations on the Paradise Regain'd*. London.

Aristotle (1973) *Aristotle: The Poetics*, trans. W. Hamilton Fyfe, Loeb, vol. 23. Cambridge, MA: Harvard University Press.

Arminius, James (1956) *The Writings of James Arminius*, trans. James Nichols and W. R. Bagnall, 3 vols. [1853; repr.] Grand Rapids, MI: Baker Book House.

Armitage, David (1995) John Milton: Poet against Empire. In D. Armitage, A. Himy and Q. Skinner (eds), *Milton and Republicanism* (pp. 206–25). Cambridge: Cambridge University Press.

Armstrong, John (1736) *The Oeconomy of Love*. London.

Attridge, Derek (1982) *The Rhythms of English Poetry*. London: Longman.

Auerbach, Erich (1953) *Mimesis*, trans. Willard Trask. Princeton: Princeton University Press.

Austen, Jane (1995) *Jane Austen's Letters*, ed. Deirdre La Faye. Oxford: Oxford University Press.

Austin, Warren B. (1947) Milton's Lycidas and Two Latin Elegies by Giles Fletcher the Elder. *Studies in Philology* 44, 41–55.

Ayers, Robert W. (1974) The Editions of Milton's *Readie & Easie Way*. *Review of English Studies* 25, 280–1.

Bacon, Francis (1857) *Works*, ed. J. Spedding, R. L. Ellis and D. D. Heath. London: Longman & Co. et al. *New Organon* (1620); *Sylva Sylvarum* (1626), vol. 2; *New Atlantis* (1626), vol. 3.

Bacon, Francis (1965) *The Advancement of Learning*, ed. G. W. Kitchin. London and New York: Dent & Dutton, Everyman's Library.

Baillie, Robert (1646) *A Dissuasive from the Errours of the Time*. London.

Bakhtin, M. M. (1981) *The Dialogic Imagination: Four Essays*, trans. Caryl Emerson and Michael Holquist, ed. Michael Holquist. Austin: University of Texas Press.

Bakhtin, M. M. (1986) *Speech Genres and Other Late Essays*, trans. Vern W. McGee, ed. Caryl Emerson and Michael Holquist. Austin: University of Texas Press.

Barker, Arthur E. (1940–1) The Pattern of Milton's *Nativity Ode*. *University of Toronto Quarterly* 10, 167–81.

Barker, Arthur E. (1942) *Milton and the Puritan Dilemma, 1641–1660*. Toronto: University of Toronto Press.

Barker, Francis (1984) *The Tremulous Private Body: Essays on Subjection*. New York and London: Methuen.

Barnaby, Andrew (1990) Machiavellian Hypotheses: Republican Settlement and the Question of Empire in Milton's *Readie and Easie Way*. *Clio* 19, 251–70.

Bauman, Michael (1987) *Milton's Arianism*. Frankfurt: Peter Lang.

Baxter, Richard (1669) *Directions for Weak Distempered Christians*, pt I. London.

Baxter, Richard (1677) *Naked Popery*. London.

Baxter, Richard (1681) *A Third Defence of the Cause of Peace*. London.

Baxter, Richard (1696) *Reliquiae Baxterianae*, ed. Matthew Sylvester. London.

Belsey, Catherine (1988) *John Milton: Language, Gender, Power*. Oxford: Basil Blackwell.

Benet, Diana Treviño (1994) Hell, Satan, and the New Politician. In D. T. Benet and M. Lieb (eds), *Literary Milton: Text, Pretext, Context* (pp. 91–113). Pittsburgh: Duquesne University Press.

Benjamin, Walter (1969) Theses on the Philosophy of History. In *Illuminations*, ed. H. Arendt, trans. Harry Zohn (pp. 253–64). New York: Schocken Books.

Bennett, Joan S. (1987) Virgin Nature in *Comus*. *Milton Studies* 23, 21–32.

Bennett, Joan S. (1989) *Reviving Liberty: Radical Christian Humanism in Milton's Great Poems*. Cambridge, MA: Harvard University Press.

Bennett, Martyn (1997) *The Civil Wars in Britain and Ireland, 1638–1651*. Oxford: Basil Blackwell.

Bentley, Richard, ed. (1732) *Paradise Lost: A New Edition*. London.

Berkeley, David Shelley (1974) *Inwrought with Figures Dim: A Reading of Milton's 'Lycidas'*. The Hague and Paris: Mouton.

Binns, J. W. (1972) William Gager on the Death of Sir Philip Sidney. *Humanistica Lovaniensia* 21, 221–38.

Birch, Thomas (1753) An Account of the Life and Writings of Mr. John Milton. In *A Complete Collection of the Historical, Political, and Miscellaneous Works of John Milton*, 2 vols, 2nd edn. London.

Blackmore, Richard (1695) *Prince Arthur: an Heroick Poem in Ten Books*. London.

Blackmore, Richard (1697) *King Arthur: an Heroick Poem in Twelve Books*. London.

Blackmore, Richard (1705) *Eliza: an Epick Poem in Ten Books*. London.

Blackmore, Richard (1723) *Alfred: an Epick Poem in Twelve Books*. London.

Blake, William (1989) *The Poems of William Blake*, ed. W. H. Stevenson. Harlow: Longman (reissue; first publ. 1971).

Blessington, Francis C. (1979) *Paradise Lost and the Classical Epic*. Boston and London: Routledge & Kegan Paul.

Bloom, Harold (1973) *The Anxiety of Influence*. New York: Oxford University Press.

Blum, Abbé (1987) The Author's Authority: *Areopagitica* and the Labour of Licensing. In M. Nyquist and M. W. Ferguson (eds), *Re-Membering Milton: Essays on the Texts and Traditions* (pp. 74–96). New York and London: Methuen.

Breasted, Barbara (1971) *Comus* and the Castlehaven Scandal. *Milton Studies* 3, 201–24.

Bridges, Robert (1921) *Milton's Prosody*, rev. edn. Oxford: Clarendon Press.

Brisman, Leslie (1973) *Milton's Poetry of Choice and Its Romantic Heirs*. Ithaca and London: Cornell University Press.

Broadbent, J. B. (1960) The Nativity Ode. In F. Kermode (ed.), *The Living Milton* (pp. 12–31). London: Routledge & Kegan Paul.

Brooks, Cleanth and John Edward Hardy (1951a) Essay in Analysis: *Lycidas*. In C. Brooks and J. E. Hardy (eds), *Poems of Mr John Milton: The 1645 Edition with Essays in Analysis* (pp. 169–86). New York: Harcourt, Brace. Repr. in C. A. Patrides (ed.), *Milton's Lycidas: The Tradition and the Poem*.

Brooks, Cleanth and John Edward Hardy (1951b) *Poems of Mr John Milton: The 1645 Edition with Essays in Analysis*. New York: Harcourt, Brace & Co.

Brown, Cedric C. (1985) *John Milton's Aristocratic Entertainments*. Cambridge: Cambridge University Press.

Brown, Cedric C. (2000) A King James Bible, Protestant Nationalism, and Boy Milton. In A. Boesky and M. Crane (eds), *Form and Reform in Renaissance England: Essays in Honor of Barbara Kiefer Lewalski* (pp. 271–87). Newark, DE: University of Delaware Press.

Buchanan, James (1773) *The First Six Books of Milton's Paradise Lost, Rendered into Grammatical Construction*. Edinburgh.

Buhler, Stephen M. (1992) Kingly States: The Politics in *Paradise Lost*. *Milton Studies* 28, 49–68.

Burke, Edmund (1958) *A Philosophical Enquiry into the Origin of Our Ideas of the Sublime and Beautiful*, ed. J. T. Boulton. London: Routledge & Kegan Paul; New York: Columbia University Press.

Burnett, Archie (1981) *Milton's Style: The Shorter Poems, Paradise Regained, and 'Samson Agonistes'*. London and New York: Longman.

Burney, Charles (1991) *The Letters of Dr Charles Burney, Volume I: 1751–1784*, ed. Alvaro Ribeiro. Oxford: Clarendon Press.

Burns, Norman T. (1996) 'Then Stood up Phineas': Milton's Antinomianism and Samson's. *Milton Studies* 33, 27–46.

Bushell, Thomas (1636) *The Severall Speeches and Songs, at the presentment of Mr. Bushells Rock to the Queenes Most Excellent Majesty. Aug. 23. 1636*. Oxford.

Bushell, Thomas (1659) *Mr. Bushell's Abridgment of the Lord Chancellor Bacon's Philosophical Theory in Mineral Prosecutions*. London. (Paginated by section.)

Butler, Martin (1987) *Theatre and Crisis, 1632–42*. Cambridge: Cambridge University Press.

Byron, George G., Baron (1970) *Byron: Poetical Works*, ed. Frederick Page. Oxford: Oxford University Press.

Cable, Lana (1995) *Carnal Rhetoric: Milton's Iconoclasm and the Poetics of Desire*. Durham, NC and London: Duke University Press.

Calvin, Jean (1960) *Institutes of the Christian Religion*, ed. John T. McNeill, trans. Ford Lewis Battles, 2 vols. Library of Christian Classics. Philadelphia: Westminster Press. (Original work publ. 1556.)

Campbell, Gordon (1987) Nathaniel Tovey: Milton's Second Tutor. *Milton Quarterly* 21, 81–90.

Campbell, Gordon (1997) *A Milton Chronology*. London and New York: Macmillan.

Campbell, Gordon and Norman Postlethwaite, eds (1994) *Edward King, Milton's Lycidas: Poems and Documents*. Special issue of *Milton Quarterly* 28, 77–111.

Campbell, Gordon et al. (1997) The Provenance of *De Doctrina Christiana*. *Milton Quarterly* 17, 67–121.

Cartwright, William (1651) *Comedies, Tragicomedies, With other Poems*. London.

Chaney, Edward (1998) *The Evolution of the Grand Tour: Anglo-Italian Cultural Relations since the Renaissance*. London: Frank Cass.

Charles I (1649) *Eikon Basilike: The Pourtraicture of His Sacred Maiestie in His Solitudes and Sufferings*. n.p. Wing E268.

Christopher, Georgia B. (1976) The Virginity of Faith: *Comus* as a Reformation Conceit. *English Literary History* 43, 479–99.

Cirillo, Albert (1962) Noon–Midnight and the Temporal Structure of *Paradise Lost*. *English Literary History* 29, 372–95.

Cirillo, Albert (1969) 'Hail Holy Light' and Divine Time in *Paradise Lost*. *Journal of English and Germanic Philology* 68, 45–56.

Clark, Donald L. (1948) *John Milton at St Paul's School*. New York: Columbia University Press.

Cogswell, Thomas (1989) *The Blessed Revolution: English Politics and the Coming of War, 1621–24*. Cambridge: Cambridge University Press.

Coleridge, Samuel Taylor (1991) *Poems*, ed. John Beer. London: Dent (re-issue; first publ. 1963).

Colie, Rosalie L. (1966) Time and Eternity: Paradise and Structure in *Paradise Lost*. Repr. in *Paradoxica Epidemica*. Princeton: Princeton University Press.

Colie, Rosalie L. (1973) *The Resources of Kind: Genre-Theory in the Renaissance*, ed. Barbara K. Lewalski. Berkeley: University of California Press.

Colley, Linda (1992) *Britons: Forging the Nation, 1707–1837*. New Haven: Yale University Press.

Collinges, John (1669) *Par Nobile*. London.

Collinson, Patrick (1967) *The Elizabethan Puritan Movement*. London: Jonathan Cape.

Collop, John (1656) *Poesis Rediviva: or, Poesie Reviv'd*. London.

Conklin, George (1949) *Biblical Criticism and Heresy in Milton*. New York: King's Crown Press.

Corns, Thomas N. (1982) *The Development of Milton's Prose Style*. Oxford: Clarendon Press.

Corns, Thomas N. (1990a) *Milton's Language*. Oxford and Cambridge, MA: Basil Blackwell.

Corns, Thomas N. (1990b) Milton's *Observations on the Articles of the Peace*: Ireland under English Eyes. In D. Loewenstein and J. G. Turner (eds),

Politics, Poetics and Hermeneutics in Milton's Prose (pp. 123–34). Cambridge: Cambridge University Press.

Corns, Thomas N. (1992a) *Uncloistered Virtue: English Political Literature, 1640–1660.* Oxford: Clarendon Press.

Corns, Thomas N. (1992b) Milton and the Good Old Cause. In T. N. Corns, *Uncloistered Virtue: English Political Literature, 1640–1660* (pp. 269–93). Oxford: Clarendon Press.

Corns, Thomas N. (1994) *Regaining 'Paradise Lost'.* London and New York: Longman.

Corns, Thomas N. (1995) Milton and the Characteristics of a Free Commonwealth. In D. Armitage, A. Himy and Q. Skinner (eds), *Milton and Republicanism* (pp. 25–42). Cambridge: Cambridge University Press.

Corns, Thomas N. (1998a) Milton's Antiprelatical Tracts and the Marginality of Doctrine. In S. Dobranski and J. Rumrich (eds), *Milton and Heresy* (pp. 39–48). Cambridge: Cambridge University Press.

Corns, Thomas N. (1998b) The Poetry of the Caroline Court. The 1997 British Academy Warton Lecture on English Poetry. *Proceedings of the British Academy* 97, 51–73.

Corns, Thomas N. (1999) Duke, Prince and King. In T. N. Corns (ed.), *The Royal Image: Representations of Charles I* (pp. 1–25). Cambridge: Cambridge University Press.

Cowley, Abraham (1656) *Poems.* London.

Cowper, William (1808) *Latin and Italian Poems of Milton Translated into English Verse.* London.

Cox, John D. (1977) Poetry and History in Milton's Country Masque. *English Literary History* 44, 622–40.

Crashaw, Richard (1957) *The Poems, English, Latin, and Greek, of Richard Crashaw,* ed. L. C. Martin, 2nd edn. Oxford: Clarendon Press.

Creaser, John (1984a) Milton's *Comus:* The Irrelevance of the Castlehaven Scandal. *Notes and Queries* 229, n.s. 31, 307–17.

Creaser, John (1984b) 'The present aid of this occasion': The Setting of *Comus.* In D. Lindley (ed.), *The Court Masque* (pp. 111–34). Manchester and Dover, NH: Manchester University Press.

Cressy, David (1980) *Literacy and the Social Order: Reading and Writing in Tudor and Stuart England.* Cambridge: Cambridge University Press.

Crump, C. G., ed. (1900) *The History of the Life of Thomas Ellwood.* London: Methuen.

Cudworth, Ralph (1964) *The True Intellectual System of the Universe.* Facs. repr. Stuttgart-Bad Cannstatt: Friedrich Frommann Verlag. (Original work publ. 1678.)

Cullen, Patrick (1974) *Infernal Triad: The Flesh, the World, and the Devil.* Princeton: Princeton University Press.

Curtius, Ernst R. (1953) *European Literature and the Latin Middle Ages,* trans. W. R. Trask. New York: Harper. (Original work publ. 1948.)

Cust, Richard (1987) *The Forced Loan and English Politics 1626–28.* Oxford: Clarendon Press.

Cust, Richard and Ann Hughes, eds (1989) *Conflict in Early Stuart England.* London: Longman.

Daiches, David (1971) The Opening of *Paradise Lost.* In F. Kermode (ed.), *The Living Milton: Essays by Divers Hands* (pp. 55–69). New York: Macmillan.

Daniells, Roy (1963) *Milton, Mannerism and Baroque.* Toronto: University of Toronto Press.

Danielson, Dennis (1982) *Milton's Good God: A Study in Literary Theodicy.* Cambridge: Cambridge University Press.

Danielson, Dennis (1999) *The Cambridge Companion to Milton,* 2nd edn. Cambridge: Cambridge University Press.

Darbishire, Helen, ed. (1932) *The Early Lives of Milton.* London: Constable.

Davenant, Sir William (1651) *The Works,* 2 vols. London.

Davidson, Robert (1993) Jeremiah, the Book of. In B. Metzer and M. D. Coogan (eds), *The Oxford Companion to the Bible* (pp. 343–7). New York: Oxford University Press.

Davies, Godfrey (1955) *The Restoration of Charles II, 1658–60.* San Marino, CA: The Huntington Library.

Davies, H. Neville (1975) Laid Artfully Together: Stanzaic Design in Milton's 'On the Morning of Christ's Nativity'. In Maren-Sofie Rostvig (ed.), *Fair Forms: Essays in English Literature from Spenser to Jane Austen* (pp. 85–146). Cambridge: D. S. Brewer.

Davies, H. Neville (1985) Milton's Nativity Ode and Drummond's 'An Hymne of the Ascension'. *Scottish Literary Journal* 12, 5–23.

Davies, Stevie (1983) *Images of Kingship in Paradise Lost: Milton's Politics and Christian Liberty.* Columbia, MO: University of Missouri Press.

Demaray, John G. (1968) *Milton and the Masque Tradition: The Early Poems, 'Arcades', and Comus.* Cambridge, MA: Harvard University Press.

Dennis, John (1939) *The Critical Works*, vol. I, ed. Edward Niles Hooker. Baltimore: Johns Hopkins University Press.

Derrida, Jacques (1974) *Of Grammatology*, trans. Gayatri Spivak. Baltimore: Johns Hopkins University Press.

Descartes, René (1984) *The Philosophical Writings of Descartes*, trans. John Cottingham, Robert Stoothoff and Dugald Murdoch. Cambridge: Cambridge University Press.

Di Cesare, Mario A., ed. (1991) *Milton in Italy: Contexts, Images, Contradictions.* Binghamton, NY: Medieval and Renaissance Texts and Studies.

Diekhoff, John S. (1939) *Milton on Himself.* London: Oxford University Press.

Diekhoff, John S., ed. (1968) *A Maske at Ludlow: Essays on Milton's Comus.* Cleveland: Case Western Reserve University Press.

Dietz, Michael (1997) 'Thus sang the Uncouth Swain': Pastoral, Prophecy and Historicism in *Lycidas. Milton Studies* 35, 42–72.

DiSalvo, Jackie (1973) 'The Lord's Battells': *Samson Agonistes* and the Puritan Revolution. *Milton Studies* 4, 39–62.

DiSalvo, Jackie (1983) *War of the Titans: Blake's Critique of Milton and the Politics of Religion.* Pittsburgh: Pittsburgh University Press.

Disraeli, Isaac (1859) *Curiosities of Literature.* London: Routledge.

Dobranski, Stephen B. (1998) Licensing Milton's heresy. In S. Dobranski and J. Rumrich (eds), *Milton and Heresy* (pp. 139–58). Cambridge: Cambridge University Press.

Dobranski, Stephen B. (1999) *Milton, Authorship, and the Book Trade.* Cambridge: Cambridge University Press.

Dobranski, Stephen B. and John P. Rumrich, eds (1998) *Milton and Heresy.* Cambridge: Cambridge University Press.

Dod, John and Robert Cleaver (1612) *A Godly Forme of Housholde Governement: For the Ordering of Private Families according to the directions of Gods word.* London.

Dohrn-van Rossum, Gerhard (1996) *History of the Hour: Clocks and Modern Temporal Orders*, trans. Thomas Dunlap. Chicago: University of Chicago Press.

Donne, John (1967) *The Complete Poems of John Donne*, ed. John T. Shawcross. Garden City, NY: Doubleday.

Donne, John (1968) *Poetical Works*, ed. Sir Herbert Grierson. London: Oxford University Press. (First publ. 1937.)

Donnelly, Phillip J. (1999) 'Matter' versus Body: The Character of Milton's Monism. *Milton Quarterly* 33, 79–85.

Drummond, William (n.d.) *The Poems of William Drummond of Hawthornden*, ed. W. C. Ward. London: Routledge (The Muses Library).

Drummond, William, of Hawthornden (1976) *Poems and Prose*, ed. Robert H. MacDonald. Edinburgh and London: Scottish Academic Press.

Dryden, John (1668) *Of Dramatick Poesie.* London.

Dryden, John (1962) *Of Dramatic Poesy and Other Critical Essays*, ed. George Watson. London: Dent.

Dryden, John (1994) *The State of Innocence. The Works of John Dryden*, vol. XII, ed. Vinton A. Dearing. Berkeley: University of California Press.

Dubrow, Heather (1995) *Echoes of Desire: English Petrarchanism and its Counterdiscourses.* Ithaca: Cornell University Press.

Dunbar, Pamela (1980) *William Blake's Illustrations to the Poetry of Milton.* Oxford: Clarendon Press.

Dunton, John et al., eds (1691–7) *The Athenian Gazette: or Casuistical Mercury Resolving all the most Nice and Curious Questions Proposed by the Ingenious of Either Sex.* London.

DuRocher, Richard J. (1993) The Wounded Earth in *Paradise Lost. Studies in Philology* 93, 93–115.

DuRocher, Richard J. (1994) Careful Plowing: Culture and Agriculture in *Paradise Lost. Milton Studies* 31, 91–107.

Durston, Christopher and Jacqueline Eales, eds (1996) *The Culture of English Puritanism, 1560–1700.* London: Macmillan.

Dzelzainis, Martin (1995a) Milton's Classical Republicanism. In D. Armitage, A. Himy and

Q. Skinner (eds), *Milton and Republicanism* (pp. 3–24). Cambridge: Cambridge University Press.

Dzelzainis, Martin (1995b) Milton and the Protectorate in 1658. In D. Armitage, A. Himy and Q. Skinner (eds), *Milton and Republicanism* (pp. 181–205). Cambridge: Cambridge University Press.

Edwards, Karen (1999) *Milton and the Natural World*. Cambridge: Cambridge University Press.

Edwards, Thomas (1645) *Gangraena*. London.

Egan, James (1976) Milton and the Marprelate Tradition. *Milton Studies* 8, 103–21.

Eliot, T. S. (1936) A Note on the Verse of John Milton. *Essays and Studies* 21, 32–40.

Eliot, T. S. (1947) Milton. *Proceedings of the British Academy* 33, 61–79.

Eliot, T. S. (1957) *On Poetry and Poets*. London: Faber & Faber.

Elledge, Scott (1966) *Milton's 'Lycidas'*. New York: Harper & Row.

Ellwood, Thomas (1714) *The History of the Life of Thomas Ellwood*. London.

Empson, William (1935) *Some Versions of Pastoral*. London: Chatto & Windus.

Empson, William (1951) *The Structure of Complex Words*. London: Chatto & Windus.

Empson, William (1961) *Milton's God*. London: Chatto & Windus.

Empson, William (1967) *Some Versions of Pastoral*. Harmondsworth: Penguin. (First publ. 1935.)

Empson, William (1981) *Milton's God*. Cambridge: Cambridge University Press.

Erbery, William (1648) *The Armies Defence, or, God guarding the Camp of the Saints*. London.

Eriksen, Roy, ed. (1997) *Contexts of Baroque: Theatre, Metamorphosis, and Design*. Oslo: Novus Press.

Evans, J. Martin (1968) Paradise Lost *and the Genesis Tradition*. Oxford: Clarendon Press.

Evans, J. Martin (1978) Lycidas and the Dolphins. *Notes and Queries*, n.s. 25, 15–17.

Evans, J. Martin (1998a) *The Miltonic Moment*. Lexington: University Press of Kentucky.

Evans, J. Martin (1998b) *The Road from Horton: Looking Backwards in 'Lycidas'*. Victoria: University of Victoria Press; rev. in *The Miltonic Moment* (Evans 1998a). Lexington: University Press of Kentucky.

Evelyn, John (1661) *Fumifugium: or, The Inconveniency of the Smoak of London dissipated*. London.

Everett, Barbara (1980) The End of the Big Names: Milton's Epic Catalogues. In J. Carey, (ed.), *English Renaissance Studies: Presented to Dame Helen Gardner in Honour of her Seventieth Birthday* (pp. 254–70). Oxford: Clarendon Press.

Eyre, G. E. B. and C. R. Rivington, eds, and H. R. Plomer, transcriber (1950) *A Transcript of the Registers of the Worshipful Company of Stationers from 1640–1708 AD*, 3 vols. New York: P. Smith.

Fabian, Johannes (1983) *Time and the Other: How Anthropology Makes its Object*. New York: Columbia University Press.

Fallon, Robert T. (1981) Milton in the Anarchy, 1659–60: A Question of Consistency. *Studies in English Literature* 21, 123–46.

Fallon, Robert T. (1993) *Milton in Government*. University Park: Pennsylvania State University Press.

Fallon, Robert T. (1995) *Divided Empire: Milton's Political Imagery*. University Park: Pennsylvania State University Press.

Fallon, Stephen M. (1991) *Milton Among the Philosophers: Poetry and Materialism in Seventeenth-Century England*. Ithaca: Cornell University Press.

Fallon, Stephen M. (1994) Intention and its Limits in *Paradise Lost*: The Case of Bellerophon. In D. T. Benet and M. Lieb (eds), *Literary Milton: Text, Pretext, Context* (pp. 161–79, 246–9). Pittsburgh: Duquesne University Press.

Fallon, Stephen M. (1998) 'Elect Above the Rest': Theology as Self-representation in Milton. In S. Dobranski and J. Rumrich (eds), *Milton and Heresy* (pp. 93–116). Cambridge: Cambridge University Press.

Fell, Margaret (1660) *A Declaration and an Information from us the People of God called Quakers*. London.

Filmer, Sir Robert (1991) *Patriarcha and Other Writings*, ed. Johann P. Sommerville. Cambridge: Cambridge University Press.

Finch, Anne, Countess of Winchilsea (1713) 'Fanscombe Barn. In Imitation of Milton'. *Miscellany Poems*. London. Also in *Selected Poems of Anne Finch, Countess of Winchilsea*, ed. Katharine M. Rogers (1979). New York: Frederick Ungar.

Fincham, Kenneth (1990) *Prelate as Pastor: The Episcopate of James I*. Oxford: Clarendon Press.

Fink, Zera S. (1948) Wordsworth and the English Republican Tradition. *Journal of English and Germanic Philology* 4, 107–26.

Fink, Zera S. (1962) *The Classical Republicans: An Essay in the Recovery of a Pattern of Thought in Seventeenth-Century England*, 2nd edn. Evanston, IL: Northwestern University Press.

Fish, Stanley (1967) *Surprised by Sin: The Reader in 'Paradise Lost'*. New York: St. Martin's Press.

Fish, Stanley (1971) *Surprised By Sin: The Reader in Paradise Lost*, repr. Berkeley: University of California Press.

Fish, Stanley (1972) Reason in *The Reason of Church Government*. In S. Fish, *Self-Consuming Artifacts: The Experience of Seventeenth-Century Literature* (pp. 265–302). Berkeley: University of California Press.

Fish, Stanley (1980) What is Stylistics and Why Are They Saying Such Terrible Things about It? In *Is There a Text in This Class?* (pp. 66–96). Cambridge, MA and London: Harvard University Press.

Fish, Stanley (1987) Driving from the Letter: Truth and Indeterminacy in Milton's *Areopagitica*. In M. Nyquist and M. W. Ferguson (eds), *Re-Membering Milton: Essays on the Texts and Traditions* (pp. 234–54). New York and London: Methuen.

Fish, Stanley (1989) Spectacle and Evidence in *Samson Agonistes*. *Critical Inquiry* 15, 556–86.

Fish, Stanley (1990) Wanting a Supplement: The Question of Interpretation in Milton's Early Prose. In D. Loewenstein and J. G. Turner (eds), *Politics, Poetics, and Hermeneutics in Milton's Prose* (pp. 41–68). Cambridge: Cambridge University Press.

Fish, Stanley (1994) There's No Such Thing as Free Speech, and It's a Good Thing, Too. In S. Fish, *There's No Such Thing as Free Speech* (pp. 102–19). New York: Oxford University Press.

Fish, Stanley (1998) *Surprised by Sin: The Reader in Paradise Lost*, 2nd edn. Cambridge, MA: Harvard University Press.

Fletcher, Angus (1971) *The Transcendental Masque: An Essay on Milton's Comus*. Ithaca: Cornell University Press.

Fletcher, Harris F. (1956, 1971) *The Intellectual Development of John Milton*, 2 vols. Urbana: University of Illinois Press.

Fludd, Robert (1659) *Mosaicall Philosophy: Grounded upon the Essential Truth of Eternal Sapience*. London.

Forrest, James F. (1974) The Significance of Milton's 'Mantle Blue'. *Milton Quarterly* 8, 41–8.

Fowler, Alastair (1982) *Kinds of Literature: An Introduction to the Theory of Genres and Modes*. Cambridge, MA: Harvard University Press.

French, J. Milton (1949–58) *The Life Records of John Milton*, 5 vols. New Brunswick, NJ: Rutgers University Press.

Frere, W. H. and Douglas, C. E. (1907) *Puritan Manifestoes: A Study of the Origin of the Puritan Revolt*. London: SPCK.

Frye, Northrop (1965) *The Return of Eden: Five Essays on Milton's Epics*. Toronto: University of Toronto Press.

Gallagher, Philip (1990) *Milton, the Bible, and Misogyny*. Columbia: University of Missouri Press.

Galliard, John Ernest (1728) *The Hymn of Adam and Eve, Out of the Fifth Book of Milton's Paradise Lost*. London.

Gardiner, Samuel Rawson, ed. (1906) *Constitutional Documents of the Puritan Revolution, 1625–1660*, 3rd edn. Oxford: Clarendon Press.

Gardner, Helen (1965) *A Reading of 'Paradise Lost'*. Oxford: Clarendon Press.

Geneva Bible, The (1560) Facsimile with an introduction by Lloyd E. Berry (1969). Madison, Milwaukee, and London: University of Wisconsin Press.

Giamatti, A. Bartlett (1966) *The Earthly Paradise and the Renaissance Epic*. Princeton: Princeton University Press.

Gilbert, Sandra M. (1978) Patriarchal Poetry and Women Readers: Reflections on Milton's Bogey. *Proceedings of the Modern Language Association* 93, 368–82.

Gilbert, Sandra M. and Susan Gubar (1984) *The Madwoman in the Attic: The Woman Writer and the Nineteenth-Century Literary Imagination*. New Haven: Yale University Press.

Gillies, John, ed. (1788) *Milton's Paradise Lost Illustrated with Texts of Scripture*. London.

Godwin, William (1824–8) *History of the Common-wealth of England. From its Commencement, to the Restoration of Charles the Second*, 4 vols. London.

Godwin, William (1978) *An Enquiry Concerning Political Justice.* Harmondsworth: Penguin.

Goldberg, Jonathan (1983) *James I and the Politics of Literature.* Baltimore: Johns Hopkins University Press.

Good, John Walter (1915) *Studies in the Milton Tradition.* University of Illinois Studies in Language and Literature, vol. 1, nos 3–4.

Graham, James (1870) *Selections from the Prose Works of John Milton.* London: Hurst & Blackett.

Grant, W. Leonard (1965) *Neo-Latin Literature and the Pastoral.* Chapel Hill: University of North Carolina Press.

Graves, Richard (1776) On Mr. Gainsborough; equally excellent in landskip and portraits. *Euphrosyne*, 131–2.

Green, Ian (1996) *The Christian's ABC.* Oxford: Clarendon Press.

Green, Jonathon (1996) *Chasing the Sun: Dictionary-Makers and the Dictionaries They Made.* London: Cape.

Greenblatt, Stephen (1980) *Renaissance Self-Fashioning from More to Shakespeare.* Chicago: University of Chicago Press.

Gregerson, Linda (1995) *The Reformation of the Subject: Spenser, Milton, and the English Protestant Epic.* Cambridge: Cambridge University Press.

Grierson, Herbert J. C. (1937) *Milton and Wordsworth, Poets and Prophets: A Study of Their Reactions to Political Events.* Cambridge: Cambridge University Press.

Griffin, Dustin (1986) *Regaining Paradise: Milton and the Eighteenth Century.* Cambridge: Cambridge University Press.

Grose, Christopher (1988) *Milton and the Sense of Tradition.* New Haven: Yale University Press.

Grossman, Marshall (1987) *Authors to Themselves: Milton and the Revelation of History.* Cambridge: Cambridge University Press.

Guibbory, Achsah (1986) *The Map of Time: Seventeenth-Century English Literature and the Ideas of Pattern in History.* Urbana: University of Illinois Press.

Guibbory, Achsah (1996) Donne, Milton, and Holy Sex. *Milton Studies* 32, 3–21.

Guibbory, Achsah (1998) *Ceremony and Community from Herbert to Milton: Literature, Religion, and Cultural Conflict in Seventeenth-Century England.* Cambridge: Cambridge University Press.

Guillory, John (1983) *Poetic Authority: Spenser, Milton, and Literary History.* New York: Columbia University Press.

H[ume], P[atrick] (1695) *Annotations on Milton's 'Paradise Lost'.* London.

Hadfield, Andrew (1998) *Literature, Travel and Colonial Writing in the English Renaissance, 1545–1625.* Oxford: Clarendon Press.

Hale, John K. (1995) *Paradise Lost*: A Poem in Twelve Books, or Ten? *Philological Quarterly* 74, 131–49.

Hale, John K. (1997) *Milton's Languages: The Impact of Multilingualism on Style.* Cambridge: Cambridge University Press.

Hall, Joseph (1640[/1]) *An Humble Remonstrance to the High Court of Parliament.* London.

Haller, William (1963) *Foxe's Book of Martyrs and the Elect Nation.* London: Cape.

Haller, William and Davies, Godfrey, eds (1944) *The Leveller Tracts, 1647–1653.* New York: Columbia University Press.

Hamers, Josiane and Blanc, Michel H. A. (1989) *Biliguality and Bilingualism*, 2nd edn. Cambridge: Cambridge University Press.

Hammond, William (1655) *Poems.* London.

Hanford, James Holly (1910) The Pastoral Elegy and Milton's *Lycidas. Proceedings of the Modern Language Association* 25, 403–47. Repr. in *John Milton, Poet and Humanist: Essays by James Holly Hanford* (Cleveland: Press of Western Reserve University, 1966).

Harriot, Thomas (1972) *A Briefe and True Report of the New Found Land of Virginia (1590)*, ed. Paul Hulton. New York: Dover.

Harrison, Thomas Perrin, Jr, ed. (1939) *The Pastoral Elegy: An Anthology.* Austin: University of Texas.

Haskin, Dayton (1994) *Milton's Burden of Interpretation.* Philadelphia: University of Pennsylvania Press.

Hassel, R. Chris, Jr (1979) *Renaissance Drama and the English Church Year.* Lincoln: University of Nebraska Press.

Havens, Raymond Dexter (1961) *The Influence of Milton on English Poetry.* New York: Russell & Russell.

Haverstein, Daniela (1999) *Democratizing Sir Thomas Browne: 'Religio Medici' and its Imitations*. Oxford: Clarendon Press.

Hayley, William (1970) *The Life of Milton. Second Edition, 1796*. Facsimile reproduction with an introduction by Joseph Anthony Wittreich. Gainesville, FL: Scholars' Facsimiles and Reprints.

Helgerson, Richard (1983) *Self-Crowned Laureates: Spenser, Jonson, Milton, and the Literary System*. Berkeley: University of California Press.

Helgerson, Richard (1992) *Forms of Nationhood: The Elizabethan Writing of England*. Chicago and London: University of Chicago Press.

Herbert, George (1974) *The English Poems of George Herbert*, ed. C. A. Patrides. London: Dent.

Herbert, George and Vaughan, Henry (1986) *The Oxford Authors: George Herbert and Henry Vaughan*, ed. Louis L. Martz. Oxford and New York: Oxford University Press.

Herrick, Robert (1956) *The Poetical Works of Robert Herrick*. Oxford: Clarendon Press.

Herrup, Cynthia B. (1999) *A House in Gross Disorder: Sex, Law, and the 2nd Earl of Castlehaven*. London and New York: Oxford University Press.

Highet, Gilbert (1949) *The Classical Tradition: Greek and Roman Influences on Western Literature*. Oxford: Clarendon Press.

Highet, Gilbert (1957) *The Classical Tradition: Greek and Roman Influences on Western Literature*, new edn. Oxford and New York: Oxford University Press.

Hill, Christopher (1958) *Puritanism and Revolution: Studies in Interpretation of the Seventeenth Century*. London: Secker & Warburg.

Hill, Christopher (1969a) *Puritanism and Revolution*. London: Panther Books. (First publ. 1958.)

Hill, Christopher (1969b) *Society and Puritanism in Pre-Revolutionary England*. London: Panther (repr.; first publ. London, Secker & Warburg, 1964).

Hill, Christopher (1972) *The World Turned Upside Down: Radical Ideas during the English Revolution*. London: Maurice Temple Smith.

Hill, Christopher (1977) *Milton and the English Revolution*. London: Faber; New York: Viking.

Hill, Christopher (1978) *Milton and the English Revolution*, repr. Harmondsworth, England: Penguin.

Hill, Christopher (1984) *The Experience of Defeat: Milton and Some Contemporaries*. Harmondsworth: Penguin.

Hill, Christopher (1993) *The English Bible and the Seventeenth-Century Revolution*. New York: Penguin.

Hobbes, Thomas (1651, 1673) The Answer to Sir William D'Avenant's Preface before Gondibert. In *The Works of Sir William Davenant*, vol. I (pp. 21–7). London.

Hobbes, Thomas (1986) *Leviathan*, ed. C. B. Macpherson. Harmondsworth: Penguin. (Original work publ. 1651.)

Hobbes, Thomas (1990) *Behemoth or the Long Parliament*, ed. Ferdinand Tönnies, intr. Stephen Holmes. Chicago and London: University of Chicago Press.

Hobbes, Thomas (1996) *Leviathan*, ed. Richard Tuck. Cambridge: Cambridge University Press.

Holstun, James (1987) *A Rational Millennium: Puritan Utopias of Seventeenth-Century England and America*. Oxford: Oxford University Press.

Hoopes, Robert (1962) *Right Reason in the English Renaissance*. Cambridge, MA: Harvard University Press.

Howard, Edward, Earl of Suffolk (1695) *An Essay upon Pastoral*. London.

[Howard, Edward, Earl of Suffolk] (1725) *The Shepherdess's Golden Manual. To which is annex'd Elegancies Taken out of Milton's Paradise Lost*. London.

H[ume], P[atrick] (1695) Annotations on Milton's 'Paradise Lost'. London.

Hunt, Clay (1979) *Lycidas and the Italian Critics*. New Haven: Yale University Press.

Hunter, William B. (1989) The Obedience of Christ in *Paradise Regained*. In *The Descent of Urania: Studies in Milton* (pp. 106–13). Lewisburg, PA: Bucknell University Press.

Hutton, Ronald (1985) *The Restoration: A Political and Religious History of England and Wales, 1658–1667*. Oxford: Clarendon Press.

Ide, Richard S. and Joseph A. Wittreich (1983) *Composite Orders. Milton Studies* 17.

Illo, John (1988) *Areopagiticas* Mythic and Real. *Prose Studies* 11, 3–23.

Jago, Richard (1784) *Poems, Moral and Descriptive*. ('Adam, or The Fatal Disobedience' is also included in the Chadwyck-Healey English Poetry Full-Text Data Base; Jago's 'Advertisement' and instructions 'To the Composer' are reprinted in Stevenson and Seares 1998: 170–2.)

James, William (1902) *Varieties of Religious Experience*. New York: Modern Library.

Jameson, Fredric (1981) *The Political Unconscious: Narrative as a Socially Symbolic Act*. London: Methuen.

Jarvis, Robin (1991) *Wordsworth, Milton and the Theory of Poetic Relations*. Basingstoke: Macmillan.

Jefferson, Thomas (1950–95) *Papers of Thomas Jefferson*, 27 vols, ed. Julian Boyd. Princeton: Princeton University Press.

Jensen, Kristian (1996) The Humanist Reform of Latin and Latin Teaching. In J. Kraye (ed.), *The Cambridge Companion to Renaissance Humanism* (pp. 63–81). Cambridge: Cambridge University Press.

Johnson, Samuel (1905) *Lives of the English Poets*, ed. George Birkbeck Hill, 3 vols. Oxford: Clarendon Press.

Johnson, Samuel (1963) *The Lives of the English Poets*, selected and introduced by S. C. Roberts. London: Fontana.

Johnson, Samuel (1972) *Rambler* 139–140 (1751): *Samson Agonistes*. In J. Shawcross (ed.), *Milton, 1732–1801: The Critical Heritage* (pp. 217–22). London: Routledge.

[Jones, Roger] (1663) *Mene Tekel; Or, The Downfal of Tyranny*. n.p.

Jonson, Ben (1947) *The Oxford Jonson*, ed. C. H. Herford, Percy and Evelyn Simpson, vol. 8. Oxford: Clarendon Press.

Jonson, Ben (1965) *Ben Jonson*, ed. C. H. Herford, Percy and Evelyn Simpson, vol. 8 (of 11). Oxford: Clarendon Press.

Justinian (1975) *The Institutes of Justinian: Text, Translation and Commentary*, ed. and trans. J. A. C. Thomas. Amsterdam and Oxford: North-Holland.

Keats, John (1970) *The Poems of John Keats*, ed. Miriam Allott. Harlow: Longman.

Keeble, N. H. (1987) *The Literary Culture of Nonconformity in Later Seventeenth-Century England*. Leicester: Leicester University Press; Athens, GA: University of Georgia Press.

Keeble, N. H. (1995/6) 'Till one greater man Restore us...': Restoration Images in Milton and Bunyan. *Bunyan Studies* 6, 6–33.

Keeble, N. H. and Geoffrey F. Nuttall (1991) *Calendar of the Correspondence of Richard Baxter*, 2 vols. Oxford: Clarendon Press.

Kelley, Maurice (1941) *This Great Argument: A Study of Milton's* De Doctrina Christiana *as a Gloss upon Paradise Lost*. Princeton: Princeton University Press.

Kelley, Maurice (1973) Introduction to The Englishman John Milton's Two Books of Investigations into Christian Doctrine. In *CPW* VI (pp. 3–116). New Haven: Yale University Press.

Kenyon, J. P. (1976, 1986) *The Stuart Constitution 1603–1668: Documents and Commentary*. Cambridge: Cambridge University Press.

Kermode, Frank (1966) *The Sense of an Ending: Studies in the Theories of Fiction*. Oxford: Oxford University Press.

Kerrigan, William (1974) *The Prophetic Milton*. Charlottesville: University Press of Virginia.

Kerrigan, William (1983) *The Sacred Complex*. Cambridge, MA: Harvard University Press.

Kerrigan, William and Gordon Braden (1986) Milton's Coy Eve: *Paradise Lost* and Renaissance Love Poetry. *English Literary History* 53, 27–51.

Kidd, Colin (1999) *British Identities before Nationalism: Ethnicity and Nationhood in the Atlantic World, 1600–1800*. Cambridge: Cambridge University Press.

King, John N. (1990) *Spenser's Poetry and the Reformation Tradition*. Princeton: Princeton University Press.

Kirkconnell, Watson (1973) *Awake the Courteous Echo: The Themes and Prosody of Comus, Lycidas and Paradise Regained in World Literature with Translations of the Major Analogues*. Toronto: University of Toronto Press.

Kitson, Peter J. (1987) Coleridge, Milton and the Millennium. *The Wordsworth Circle* 17, 61–6.

Kitson, Peter J. (1991) 'The electric fluid of truth': The Ideology of the Commonwealthsman in Coleridge's *The Plot Discovered*. In P. J. Kitson and T. N. Corns (eds), *Coleridge and the Armoury of the Human Mind: Essays on His Prose Writings* (pp. 36–62). London: Frank Cass.

Kitson, Peter J. (1992) 'Sages and patriots that being dead do ye speak to us': Readings of the English Revolution in the Late Eighteenth Century. In J. Holstun (ed.), *Pamphlet Wars: Prose in the English Revolution* (pp. 205–30). London: Frank Cass.

Knoppers, Laura Lunger (1990) Milton's *The Readie and Easie Way* and the English Jeremiad. In D. Loewenstein and J. G. Turner (eds), *Politics, Poetics, and Hermeneutics in Milton's Prose* (pp. 213–25). Cambridge: Cambridge University Press.

Knoppers, Laura Lunger (1994) *Historicizing Milton: Spectacle, Power, and Poetry in Restoration England*. Athens, GA: University of Georgia Press.

Knox, R. Buick (1967) *James Ussher Archbishop of Armagh*. Cardiff: University of Wales Press.

Kolbrener, William (1997) *Milton's Warring Angels: A Study of Critical Engagements*. Cambridge: Cambridge University Press.

Kranidas, Thomas (1982) Words, Words, Words, and the Word: Milton's *Of Prelatical Episcopacy*. *Milton Studies* 16, 153–66.

Kranidas, Thomas (1983) Style and Rectitude in Seventeenth-Century Prose: Hall, Smectymnuus, and Milton. *Huntington Library Quarterly* 46, 237–69.

Krouse, Michael F. (1949) *Milton's Samson and the Christian Tradition*. Princeton: Princeton University Press.

Kugel, James (1988) *The Idea of Biblical Poetry: Parallelism and its History*. Baltimore: Johns Hopkins University Press.

Labriola, Albert C. (1984) Portrait of an Artist: Milton's Changing Self-Image. *Milton Studies* 19, 169–94.

Labriola, Albert C. and Edward Sichi, Jr, eds (1988) *Milton's Legacy in the Arts*. University Park: Pennsylvania State University Press.

Lacy, Norris J., ed. (1986) *The Arthurian Encyclopedia*. Woodbridge: Boydell & Brewer.

Lake, Peter (1989) Anti-Popery: The Structure of a Prejudice. In R. Cust and A. Hughes (eds), *Conflict in Early Stuart England* (pp. 72–106). London: Longman.

Lake, Peter (1993) The Laudian Style: Order, Uniformity and Pursuit of the Beauty of Holiness in the 1630s. In K. Fincham (ed.), *The Early Stuart Church, 1603–1642* (pp. 161–85). Basingstoke: Macmillan.

Lanyer, Aemilia (1993) *The Poems of Aemilia Lanyer: Salve Deus Rex Judaeorum*, ed. Susanne Woods. New York and Oxford: Oxford University Press.

Lauder, William (1750) *An Essay on Milton's Use and Imitation of the Moderns, in His Paradise Lost*. London.

Le Comte, Edward (1978) *Milton and Sex*. London: Macmillan.

Le Goff, Jacques (1980) *Time, Work and Culture in the Middle Ages*, trans. Arthur Goldhammer. Chicago: University of Chicago Press.

Leask, Nigel (1988) *The Politics of Imagination in Coleridge's Critical Thought*. Basingstoke: Macmillan.

Leavis, F. R. (1936) *Revaluation: Tradition and Development in English Poetry*. London: Chatto & Windus.

Leishman, J. B. (1969) *Milton's Minor Poems*. London: Hutchinson.

Leonard, John (1990) *Naming in Paradise: Milton and the Language of Adam and Eve*. Oxford: Clarendon Press.

Leonard, John (1991) 'Trembling Ears': The Historical Moment of 'Lycidas'. *Journal of Medieval and Renaissance Studies* 21, 59–81.

Leonard, John (2000) 'Thus They Relate / Erring': Milton's Inaccurate Allusions. *Milton Studies* 38, 96–121.

Leslie, Michael and Timothy Raylor (1992) *Culture and Cultivation in Early Modern England: Writing and the Land*. Leicester and London: Leicester University Press.

Lewalski, Barbara K. (1959) Milton: Political Beliefs and Polemical Methods, 1659–60. *Proceedings of the Modern Language Association* 74, 191–202.

Lewalski, Barbara K. (1966) *Milton's Brief Epic: The Genre, Meaning, and Art of Paradise Regained*. Providence, RI and London: Brown University Press and Methuen.

Lewalski, Barbara K. (1970) *Samson Agonistes* and the 'Tragedy' of the Apocalypse. *Proceedings of the Modern Language Association* 85, 1050–62.

Lewalski, Barbara K. (1971) Milton: Revaluation of Romance. In H. Baker (ed.), *Four Essays on Romance* (pp. 55–70, 82–7). Cambridge, MA: Harvard University Press.

Lewalski, Barbara K. (1985) *Paradise Lost and the Rhetoric of Literary Forms*. Princeton: Princeton University Press.

Lewalski, Barbara K. (1988) Samson and the 'New Acquist of True [Political] Experience'. *Milton Studies* 24, 233–51.

Lewalski, Barbara K. (1998) Milton's *Comus* and the Politics of Masquing. In D. Bevington and P. Holbrook (eds), *The Politics of the Stuart Court Masque* (pp. 296–320). Cambridge: Cambridge University Press.

Lewis, C. S. (1942) *Preface to Paradise Lost*. Cambridge: Cambridge University Press.

Lewis, C. S. (1967) *A Preface to 'Paradise Lost'*. London, Oxford and New York: Oxford University Press. (First publ. 1942.)

Lieb, Michael (1970) Milton and the Kenotic Christology: Its Literary Bearing. *English Literary History* 37, 342–60.

Lieb, Michael (1981) *Poetics of the Holy: A Reading of* Paradise Lost. Chapel Hill: University of North Carolina Press.

Lieb, Michael (1989) *The Sinews of Ulysses: Form and Convention in Milton's Works*. Pittsburgh: Duquesne University Press.

Lieb, Michael (1994) *Milton and the Culture of Violence*. Ithaca: Cornell University Press.

Lindley, David, ed. (1984) *The Court Masque*. Manchester and Dover, NH: Manchester University Press. (See esp. the essays by Norbrook and Creaser.)

Lipking, Lawrence (1996) The Genius of the Shore: Lycidas, Adamastor, and the Poetics of Nationalism. *Proceedings of the Modern Language Association* 111, 205–22.

Lloyd, Michael (1958) Justa Edouardo King. *Notes and Queries* 203, n.s. 5, 432–4.

Locke, John (1689) *A Letter Concerning Toleration*. London.

Locke, John (1987) *A Paraphrase and Notes on the Epistles of St. Paul to the Galatians, 1 and 2 Corinthians, Romans, Ephesians*, ed. Arthur W. Wainwright, 2 vols. Oxford: Clarendon Press.

Lockyer, Roger (1981) *Buckingham: The Life and Political Career of George Villiers, First Duke of Buckingham, 1592–1628*. London and New York: Longman.

Loewenstein, David (1990) *Milton and the Drama of History: Historical Vision, Iconoclasm, and the Literary Imagination*. Cambridge: Cambridge University Press.

Loewenstein, David (1993) *Milton: Paradise Lost*. Cambridge: Cambridge University Press.

Loewenstein, David (1994) The Kingdom Within: Radical Religious Culture and the Politics of *Paradise Regained. Literature and History* 3, 63–89.

Loewenstein, David (1998) Treason against God and State: Blasphemy in Milton's Culture and *Paradise Lost*. In S. Dobranski and J. Rumrich (eds), *Milton and Heresy* (pp. 176–98). Cambridge: Cambridge University Press.

Loewenstein, David (2001) *Representing Revolution in Milton and His Contemporaries: Religion, Politics, and Polemics in Radical Puritanism*. Cambridge: Cambridge University Press.

Loewenstein, David and James Grantham Turner, eds (1990) *Politics, Poetics, and Hermeneutics in Milton's Prose*. Cambridge: Cambridge University Press.

Lofft, Capel, ed. (1793) *The First and Second Books of Paradise Lost . . . The Original System of Orthography Restored; The Punctuation Corrected and Extended, With the Various Readings: And Notes; Chiefly Rhythmical*. Bury St Edmunds.

Love, Harold (1993) *Scribal Publication in Seventeenth-Century England*. Oxford: Clarendon Press.

Low, Anthony (1985) *The Georgic Revolution*. Princeton: Princeton University Press.

Lucan (1928) *Pharsalia*, trans. J. D. Duff, Loeb, vol. 220. Cambridge, MA: Harvard University Press.

Ludlow, Edmund (1978) *A Voyce from the Watch Tower, Part Five: 1660–1662*, ed. A. B. Worden. London: Royal Historical Society.

Macaulay, Thomas Babington (1878) *Critical and Historical Essays Contributed to the* Edinburgh Review. London: Longmans, Green, Reader, & Dyer.

MacCallum, Hugh (1986) *Milton and the Sons of God: The Divine Image in Milton's Epic Poetry*. Toronto: University of Toronto Press.

Maclean, Hugh, ed. (1974) *Ben Jonson and the Cavalier Poets*. New York: W. W. Norton.

Magnus, Elizabeth (1991) Originality and Plagiarism in *Areopagitica* and *Eikonoklastes*. *English Literary Renaissance* 21, 87–101.

Manning, Samuel (1862) *Selections from the Prose Writings of John Milton*. London.

Marcus, Leah S. (1983) The Milieu of Milton's *Comus*: Judicial Reform at Ludlow and the Problem of Sexual Assault. *Criticism* 25, 293–327.

Marcus, Leah S. (1986) *The Politics of Mirth: Jonson, Herrick, Milton, Marvell, and the Defense of Old Holiday Pastimes*. Chicago: University of Chicago Press.

Marjara, Harinder Singh (1992) *Contemplation of Created Things: Science in 'Paradise Lost'*. Toronto: University of Toronto Press.

Marotti, Arthur F. (1982) 'Love is not love': Elizabethan Sonnet Sequences and the Social Order. *English Literary History* 49, 396–428.

Martindale, Charles (1986) *John Milton and the Transformation of Ancient Epic*. London: Croom Helm.

Martz, Louis L. (1972) Who is Lycidas? *Yale French Studies* 47, 170–88.

Martz, Louis L. (1980, 1986) *Poet of Exile: A Study of Milton's Poetry*, re-issued as *Milton: Poet of Exile*. New Haven and London: Yale University Press.

Marvell, Andrew (1984) *Complete Poetry*, ed. George de F. Lord. London: Dent.

Masson, David (1877–94) *The Life of John Milton: Narrated in connexion with the political, ecclesiastical, and literary history of his time*, 7 vols. London: Macmillan.

Matthews, A. G., ed. (1934) *Calamy Revised*. Oxford: Oxford University Press.

McColley, Diane (1983) *Milton's Eve*. Urbana: University of Illinois Press.

McColley, Diane Kelsey (1997) *Poetry and Music in Seventeenth-Century England*. Cambridge: Cambridge University Press.

McColley, Diane Kelsey (1999a) All in All: The Individuality of Creatures in *Paradise Lost*. In C. W. Durham and K. P. McColgan (eds), *'All in All': Unity, Diversity, and the Miltonic Perspective* (pp. 21–38). Selinsgrove: Susquehanna University Press.

McColley, Diane Kelsey (1999b) Ecology and Empire. In B. Rajan and E. Sauer (eds), *Milton and the Imperial Vision* (pp. 112–29 and 336–8). Pittsburgh: Duquesne University Press.

McEachern, Claire (1996) *The Poetics of English Nationhood, 1590–1612*. Cambridge: Cambridge University Press.

McGee, J. Sears (1976) *The Godly Man in Stuart England: Anglicans, Puritans, and the Two Tables, 1620–1670*. New Haven: Yale University Press.

McGuire, Maryann Cale (1983) *Milton's Puritan Masque*. Athens, GA: University of Georgia Press.

McLachlan, H. J. (1951) *Socinianism in Seventeenth-Century England*. Oxford: Oxford University Press.

Miller, J. Hillis (1991) How Deconstruction Works. *New York Times*, 9 February 1986, sec. 6: 20. Repr. in *Theory Now and Then* (pp. 293–4), Durham, NC: Duke University Press.

Miller, Leo (1980) Milton's Clash with Chappell: A Suggested Reconstruction. *Milton Quarterly* 14, 77–87.

Miller, Leo (1985) *John Milton and the Oldenburg Safeguard*. New York: Loewenthal Press.

Miller, Leo (1989) A German Critique of Milton's Areopagitica in 1647. *Notes and Queries* 234, 29–30.

Miller, Leo (1990) On Some of the Verses by Alexander Gill which Young Milton Read. *Milton Quarterly* 24, 22–5.

Minturno, Antonio Sebastiano (1559) *De Poeta*. Venice.

Monck, George (1659) *Three Letters from the Lord General Monck*. Edinburgh.

Monck, George (1660a) *A Letter of General George Monck's . . . {to} the Gentry of Devon*. London.

Monck, George (1660b) *The Speech of His Excellencie, the Lord General Monck, Deliver'd to the Members of Parliament*. London.

Monck, George (1660c) *A Letter from the Lord General Monck, and the Officers here, to the several and respective Regiments*. London.

Montaigne, Michel de (1893) Of Crueltie. In *The Essays of Montaigne done into English by John Florio, anno 1603, The Second Booke*. London: David Nutt.

Montrose, Louis A. (1991) The Work of Gender in the Discourse of Discovery. *Representations* 33, 1–41.

Moore, Leslie E. (1990) *Beautiful Sublime: The Making of Paradise Lost 1701–1734*. Stanford: Stanford University Press.

Mordaunt, John Viscount (1945) *The Letter-Book of John Viscount Mordaunt, 1658–1660*, ed. Mary Coate. Camden third series, vol. LXIX. London: Royal Historical Society.

More, Henry (1978) *The Immortality of the Soul*, repr. in *A Collection of Several Philosophical Works*, 2 vols. Facsimile. New York: Garland. (Original work publ. 1659, *Collection* in 1662.)

Morrill, John (1993) *The Nature of the English Revolution*. London and New York: Longman.

Morrow, John (1990) *Coleridge's Political Thought: Property, Morality and the Limits of Traditional Discourse*. Basingstoke: Macmillan.

Moseley, C. W. R. D. (1991) *The Poetic Birth: Milton's Poems of 1645*. Aldershot: Scolar Press.

Moyles, R. G. (1985) *The Text of Paradise Lost: A Study in Editorial Procedure*. Toronto: University of Toronto Press.

Mueller, Janel (1996) Just Measures? Versification in *Samson Agonistes*. *Milton Studies* 33, 47–83.

Mueller, Janel (1998) Milton on Heresy. In S. Dobranski and J. Rumrich (eds), *Milton and Heresy* (pp. 21–38). Cambridge: Cambridge University Press.

Mumford, Lewis (1934) The Monastery and the Clock. In L. Mumford, *Technics and Civilization*. New York: Harcourt, Brace and Co.

Mundhenk, Rosemary Karmelich (1975) Dark Scandal and the Sun-Clad Power of Chastity: The Historical Milieu of Milton's *Comus*. *Studies in English Literature, 1500–1900*, 15, 141–52.

Myriell, Thomas (1623) *The Christians Comfort*. London.

Nayler, James (1656) *The Power and Glory of the Lord, Shining out of the North*. London.

Newlyn, Lucy (1993) *'Paradise Lost' and the Romantic Reader*. Oxford: Clarendon Press.

Newton, Thomas, ed. (1749) *Paradise Lost: A Poem in Twelve Books. A New Edition with Notes of Various Authors*, 2 vols. London.

Nichols, Fred J. (1973) 'Lycidas', 'Epitaphium Damonis', the Empty Dream and the Failed Song. In J. Ijsewijn and E. Kessler (eds), *Acta Conventus Neo-Latini Lovaniensis* (pp. 445–52). Leuven: Wilhelm Fink Verlag München.

Norbrook, David (1984a) *Poetry and Politics in the English Renaissance*. London and Boston: Routledge & Kegan Paul.

Norbrook, David (1984b) The Reformation of the Masque. In D. Lindley (ed.), *The Court Masque* (pp. 94–110). Manchester and Dover, NH: Manchester University Press.

Norbrook, David (1999) *Writing the English Republic: Poetry, Rhetoric and Politics, 1627–1660*. Cambridge: Cambridge University Press.

Nuttall, Geoffrey F. (1967) *The Puritan Spirit: Essays and Addresses*. London: Epworth Press.

Nyquist, Mary (1985) The Father's Word/Satan's Wrath. *Proceedings of the Modern Language Association* 100, 187–202.

Nyquist, Mary (1994) 'Profuse, proud Cleopatra': 'Barbarism' and Female Rule in Early Modern English Republicanism. *Women's Studies* 24, 85–130.

Nyquist, Mary and Margaret W. Ferguson, eds (1987, repr. 1988) *Re-Membering Milton: Essays on the Texts and Traditions*. New York and London: Methuen.

Oras, Ants (1931) *Milton's Editors and Commentators from Patrick Hume to Henry John Todd (1695–1801): A Study in Critical Views and Methods*. Oxford: Oxford University Press.

Orgel, Stephen (1975) *The Illusion of Power*. Berkeley: University of California Press.

Orgel, Stephen and Roy Strong, eds (1973) *Inigo Jones: The Theatre of the Stuart Court*, 2 vols. Berkeley and London: University of California Press and Sotheby Parke Bernet.

Orwell, George (1957a) Inside the Whale. In *Inside the Whale, and other Essays*. London: Penguin.

Orwell, George (1957b) The Prevention of Literature. In *Inside the Whale, and other Essays*. London: Penguin.

Otten, Charlotte (1975) Milton's Haemony. *English Literary Renaissance* 5, 81–95.

Pagden, Anthony (1982) *The Fall of Natural Man: The American Indian and the Origins of Comparative Ethnology*. Cambridge: Cambridge University Press.

Pagitt, Ephraim (1662) *Heresiography, Or a Description and History of the Heretickes and Sectaries Sprang up in these Latter Times*. London.

Paley, Morton D. (1999) *Apocalypse and Millennium in English Romantic Poetry*. Oxford: Clarendon Press.

Palmer, Herbert (1644) *The Glasse of Gods Providence Towards his Faithfull Ones*. London.

Parker, Samuel (1673) *A Reproof to the Rehearsal Transprosed*. London.

Parker, William R. (1968) *Milton: A Biography*, 2 vols. Oxford: Clarendon Press.

Parker, William R. (1970) *Milton's Debt to Greek Tragedy in* Samson Agonistes. New York: Barnes & Noble (repr; first publ. Baltimore: Johns Hopkins University Press, 1937).

Parker, William R. (1996) *Milton: A Biography*, 2nd edn, rev. Gordon Campbell, 2 vols. Oxford: Clarendon Press.

Parry, Graham (1981) *The Golden Age Restored*. Manchester: Manchester University Press.

Patrides, C. A., ed. (1983) *Milton's Lycidas: The Tradition and the Poem*, 2nd edn. Columbia: University of Missouri Press.

Patterson, Annabel (1988) 'Forc'd fingers': Milton's Early Poems and Ideological Constraint. In C. Summers and T.-L. Pebworth (eds), *The Muses Common-Weale* (pp. 9–22). Columbia: University of Missouri Press.

Patterson, Annabel (1993) *Reading Between the Lines*. London: Routledge.

Paul, Robert S. (1985) *The Assembly of the Lord: Politics and Religion in the Westminster Assembly and the 'Grand Debate'*. Edinburgh: T. & T. Clarke.

Pecheux, Mother Mary Christopher (1976) The Dread Voice in *Lycidas*. *Milton Studies* 9, 221–41.

Peltonen, Markku (1995) *Classical Humanism and Republicanism in English Political Thought 1570–1640*. Cambridge: Cambridge University Press.

Pepys, Samuel (1970, 1974) *The Diary of Samuel Pepys*, ed. R. Latham and W. Matthews, vols. 1 and 8. Berkeley and Los Angeles: University of California Press.

Philipot, Thomas (1646) *Poems*. London.

Phillips, Edward (1675) *Theatrum Poetarum, or a Compleat Collection of the Poets, Especially the most Eminent, of all Ages*. London.

Plattes, Gabriel (1639) *A Discovery of Subterraneall Treasure*. London.

Pocock, J. G. A. (1975) *The Machiavellian Moment: Florentine Political Thought and the Atlantic Republican Tradition*. Princeton: Princeton University Press.

Pocock, J. G. A. (1987) *The Ancient Constitution and the Feudal Law: A Study of English Historical Thought in the Seventeenth Century*. Cambridge: Cambridge University Press.

Pocock, J. G. A. and Gordon J. Schochet (1993) Interregnum and Restoration. In J. G. A. Pocock (ed. with Gordon J. Schochet and Lois G. Schwoerer), *The Varieties of British Political Thought 1500–1800* (pp. 148–79). Cambridge: Cambridge University Press.

Pointon, Marcia R. (1970) *Milton and English Art*. Manchester: Manchester University Press.

Pope, Alexander (1963) *The Poems*, ed. John Butt. London: Methuen.

Porter, William M. (1993) *Reading the Classics and Paradise Lost*. Lincoln, NE and London: University of Nebraska Press.

Potter, Lois (1989) *Secret Rites and Secret Writing: Royalist Literature, 1641–1660*. Cambridge: Cambridge University Press.

Power, Henry (1664) *Experimental Philosophy*. London.

Prince, F. T. (1954) *The Italian Element in Milton's Verse*. Oxford: Clarendon Press.

Prynne, William (1637) *A Breviate of the Prelates intolerable usurpations*. London.

Prynne, William (1644) *Twelve Considerable Serious Questions touching church government*. London.

Prynne, William (1648) *A Plea for the Lords*. London.

Puttenham, [George] (1589) *The Arte of English Poesie*. London.

Quarles, Francis (1969) *Hosanna or divine poems on the passion of Christ and Threnodes*, ed. John Horden. Liverpool: Liverpool University Press.

Quilligan, Maureen (1983) *Milton's Spenser: The Politics of Reading*. Ithaca: Cornell University Press.

Quinones, Ricardo (1972) *The Renaissance Discovery of Time*. Cambridge, MA: Harvard University Press.

Quint, David (1983) Sannazaro: From Orpheus to Proteus. In *Origin and Originality in Renaissance Literature* (pp. 43–80). New Haven: Yale University Press.

Quint, David (1993) *Epic and Empire: Politics and Generic Form from Virgil to Milton*. Princeton: Princeton University Press.

Radzinowicz, Mary Ann (1978) *Toward* Samson Agonistes*: The Growth of Milton's Mind*. Princeton: Princeton University Press.

Radzinowicz, Mary Ann (1987) The Politics of *Paradise Lost*. In K. Sharpe and S. N. Zwicker (eds), *Politics of Discourse: The Literature and History of Seventeenth-Century England* (pp. 204–29). Berkeley: University of California Press.

Radzinowicz, Mary Ann (1989) *Milton's Epics and the Book of Psalms*. Princeton: Princeton University Press.

Rajan, B. (1978–80) 'Lycidas'. In W. B. Hunter, Jr et al. (eds), *Milton Encyclopedia*. Lewisburg: Bucknell University Press.

Ralegh, Sir Walter (1997) *The Discoverie of the Large, Rich and Bewtiful Empyre of Guiana*, ed. Neil L. Whitehead. Manchester: Manchester University Press.

Raleigh, Sir Walter (1900) *Milton*. London: Edward Arnold.

Raymond, Joad, ed. (1993) *Making the News: An Anthology of the Newsbooks of Revolutionary England, 1641–1660*. Moreton-in-Marsh: Windrush Press.

Raymond, Joad (1996a) *The Invention of the Newspaper: English Newsbooks, 1641–1649*. Oxford: Clarendon Press.

Raymond, Joad (1996b) The Cracking of the Republican Spokes. *Prose Studies* 19, 255–74.

Reid, David (1993) *The Humanism of Milton's 'Paradise Lost'*. Edinburgh: Edinburgh University Press.

Revard, Stella P. (1984) The Gospel of John and *Paradise Regained*: Jesus as 'True Light'. In J. H. Sims and L. Ryken (eds), *Milton and Scriptural Tradition: The Bible into Poetry* (pp. 142–59). Columbia: University of Missouri Press.

Revard, Stella P. (1987) Dalila as Euripidean Heroine. *Papers on Language and Literature* 23, 291–302.

Revard, Stella P. (1997a) *Milton and the Tangles of Neaera's Hair: The Making of the 1645 Poems*. Columbia and London: University of Missouri Press.

Revard, Stella P. (1997b) Sporting with Amaryllis: 'Lycidas' – Classical Ode and Renaissance Pastoral. In Stella P. Revard, *Milton and the Tangles of Neaera's Hair* (pp. 164–204). Columbia and London: University of Missouri Press.

Richardson, J., Father and Son (1734) *Explanatory Notes and Remarks on Milton's Paradise Lost, With the Life of the Author, and a Discourse on the Poem*. London.

Ricks, Christopher (1963) *Milton's Grand Style*. Oxford: Clarendon Press.

Ricks, Christopher (1967) *Milton's Grand Style*, pb. London, Oxford and New York: Oxford University Press.

Ricks, Christopher, ed. (1968) John Milton, *Paradise Lost*. London: Penguin.

Ricks, Christopher (1984) *The Force of Poetry*. Oxford: Clarendon Press.

Rilke, Maria (1984) *Duino 'Elegies'*, II. In *The Selected Poetry of Rainer Maria Rilke*, trans. Stephen Mitchell (p. 161). New York: Vintage.

Robbins, Caroline (1959) *The Eighteenth-Century Commonwealthman*. Cambridge, MA: Harvard University Press.

Roe, Nicholas (1997) *John Keats and the Culture of Dissent*. Oxford: Clarendon Press.

Rogers, John (1996) *The Matter of Revolution: Science, Poetry and Politics in the Age of Milton*. Ithaca: Cornell University Press.

Rosenblatt, Jason (1994) *Torah and the Law in Paradise Lost*. Princeton: Princeton University Press.

Roston, Murray (1980) *Milton and the Baroque*. London: Macmillan.

Røstvig, Maren-Sofie (1975) Elaborate Song: Conceptual Structure in Milton's 'On the Morning of Christ's Nativity'. In Maren-Sofie Røstvig (ed.), *Fair Forms: Essays in English Literature from Spenser to Jane Austen* (pp. 54–84). Cambridge: D. S. Brewer.

Rudrum, Alan (1989) Henry Vaughan, The Liberation of the Creatures, and Seventeenth-Century English Calvinism. *The Seventeenth Century* 4, 33–54.

Rugge, Thomas (1961) *The Diurnal of Thomas Rugg, 1659–1661*, ed. William Sachse. Camden third series, vol. XCI. London: Royal Historical Society.

Rumrich, John (1995) Milton's God and the Matter of Chaos. *Proceedings of the Modern Language Association* 110, 1035–46.

Rumrich, John (1996) *Milton Unbound: Controversy and Reinterpretation*. Cambridge and New York: Cambridge University Press.

Rusche, Harry (1979) A Reading of John Milton's Horoscope. *Milton Quarterly* 13, 6–11.

Ryken, Leland and Sims, James H. (1984) *Milton and Scriptural Tradition: The Bible into Poetry*. Columbia: University of Missouri Press.

Sallust (1995) *Sallust*, ed. J. C. Rolfe. Cambridge, MA and London: Harvard University Press.

Sanchez, Reuben (1997) 'As a burning fire shut up in my bones': From Polemic to Prophecy in *The Reason of Church Government* and *The Readie and Easie Way*. In *Persona and Decorum in Milton's Prose* (pp. 60–76). Cranbury, NJ: Fairleigh Dickinson Press.

Sasek, Lawrence A., ed. (1989) *Images of English Puritanism: A Collection of Contemporary Sources, 1589–1646*. Baton Rouge, LA and London: University of Lousiana Press.

Saurat, Denis (1925) *Milton: Man and Thinker*. New York: Dial Press.

Scanlan, Thomas (1999) *Colonial Writing and the New World, 1583–1671: Allegories of Desire*. Cambridge: Cambridge University Press.

Schneewind, J. B. (1998) *The Invention of Autonomy: A History of Modern Moral Philosophy*. New York: Cambridge University Press.

Schoenfeldt, Michael (1993) Gender and Conduct in *Paradise Lost*. In J. G. Turner (ed.), *Sexuality and Gender in Early Modern Europe: Institutions, Texts, and Images* (pp. 310–39). New York: Cambridge University Press.

Schulz, Max (1985) *Paradise Preserved: Recreations of Eden in Eighteenth Century England*. Cambridge: Cambridge University Press.

Schwartz, Regina M. (1988) From Shadowy Types to Shadowy Types: The Unendings of Paradise Lost. *Milton Studies* 24, 123–39.

Schwartz, Regina M. (1990) Citation, Authority, and *De Doctrina Christiana*. In D. Loewenstein and J. G. Turner (eds), *Politics, Poetics, and Hermeneutics in Milton's Prose* (pp. 227–40). Cambridge: Cambridge University Press.

Schwartz, Regina M. (1993) *Remembering and Repeating: On Milton's Theology and Poetics*. Chicago: Chicago University Press.

Schwartz, Regina M. (1998) *The Curse of Cain: The Violent Legacy of Monotheism*. Chicago: University of Chicago Press.

Schwyzer, Philip (1997) Purity and Danger on the West Bank of the Severn: The Cultural Geography of *A Masque Presented at Ludlow Castle, 1634*. *Representations* 60, 22–48.

Scott, Jonathan (1992) The English Republican Imagination. In John Morrill (ed.), *Revolution and Restoration: England in the 1650s* (pp. 35–54). London: Collins & Brown.

Scott, Walter (1887) *Woodstock or The Cavalier: A Tale of the Year Sixteen Hundred and Fifty-One*. Edinburgh: Adam & Charles Black.

Scoufos, Alice-Lyle (1974) The Mysteries in Milton's Masque. *Milton Studies* 6, 113–42.

Selvaggi (1645) 'Ad Joannem Miltonum'. In *Poems of Mr. John Milton, Both English and Latin, Compos'd at several times*, p. 4. London.

Sennett, Richard (1980) *Authority*. London: Secker & Warburg.

Sensabaugh, George F. (1964) *Milton in Early America*. Princeton: Princeton University Press.

Shafer, Ronald, ed. (1982) *Ringing the Bell Backward*. Indiana: Indiana University of Pennsylvania.

Shakespeare, William (1997) *The Riverside Shakespeare*, ed. G. Blakemore Evans. Boston: Houghton Mifflin.

Shapin, Steven and Shaffer, Simon (1985) *Leviathan and the Air-Pump: Hobbes, Boyle, and the Experimental Life*. Princeton: Princeton University Press.

Sharp, Andrew, ed. (1998) *The English Levellers*. Cambridge: Cambridge University Press.

Sharpe, Kevin (1989) The Foundation of the Chairs of History at Oxford and Cambridge: An Episode in Jacobean Politics. In K. Sharpe, *Politics and Ideas in Early Stuart England: Essays and Studies* (pp. 207–30). London and New York: Pinter.

Sharpe, Kevin (2000) *Reading Revolutions: The Politics of Reading in Early Modern England*. New Haven and London: Yale University Press.

Shawcross, John T., ed. (1970) *Milton: The Critical Heritage*. London: Routledge & Kegan Paul.

Shawcross, John T., ed. (1972) *Milton 1732–1801: The Critical Heritage*. London and Boston: Routledge & Kegan Paul.

Shawcross, John T. (1974) A Survey of Milton's Prose Works. In M. Lieb and J. T. Shawcross (eds), *Achievements of the Left Hand* (pp. 292–391). Amherst: University of Massachusetts Press.

Shawcross, John T. (1991) *John Milton and Influence: Presence in Literature, History, and Culture*. Pittsburgh: Duquesne University Press.

Sheehan, Bernard W. (1979) *Savagism and Civility: Indians and Englishmen in Colonial Virginia*. Cambridge: Cambridge University Press.

Shelley, Mary W. (1993) *The Essential Frankenstein*, ed. Leonard Woolf. Harmondsworth: Penguin.

Shelley, Percy Bysshe (1853) *Queen Mab*. Boston: J. P. Mendum.

Shelley, Percy Bysshe (1948, repr. 1973) *A Defence of Poetry*. London: Porcupine Press.

Sherman, Sandra (1993) Printing the Mind: The Economics of Authorship in *Areopagitica*. *English Literary History* 60, 323–47.

Sherman, Stuart (1996) *Telling Time: Clocks, Diaries, and English Diurnal Form 1660–1785*. Chicago: University of Chicago Press.

Shifflett, Andrew (1998) *Stoicism, Politics and Literature in the Age of Milton: War and Peace Reconciled.* Cambridge: Cambridge University Press.

Shumaker, Wayne (1951) Flowerets and Sounding Seas: A Study in the Affective Structure of *Lycidas*. *Proceedings of the Modern Language Association* 66, 485–94. (Repr. in C. A. Patride, ed., *Milton's Lycidas: The Tradition and the Poem*.)

Sidney, Philip (1595) *The Defence of Poesie.* London.

Sidney, Philip (1989) *Sir Philip Sidney*, ed. Katherine Duncan-Jones. Oxford: Oxford University Press.

Sims, James (1962) *The Bible in Milton's Epics.* Gainesville: University of Florida Press.

Skerpan, Elizabeth (1992) *The Rhetoric of Politics in the English Revolution 1642–1660.* Columbia and London: University of Missouri Press.

Skinner, Quentin (1978) *The Foundations of Modern Political Thought*, 2 vols. Cambridge: Cambridge University Press.

Skinner, Quentin (1998) *Liberty before Liberalism.* Cambridge: Cambridge University Press.

Smith, Nigel, ed. (1983) *A Collection of Ranter Writings from the 17th Century.* London: Junction Books.

Smith, Nigel (1989) *Perfection Proclaimed: Language and English Radical Religion 1640–1660.* Oxford: Clarendon Press.

Smith, Nigel (1990) *Areopagitica*: Voicing Contexts, 1643–5. In D. Loewenstein and J. G. Turner (eds), *Politics, Poetics, and Hermeneutics in Milton's Prose* (pp. 103–22). Cambridge: Cambridge University Press.

Smith, Nigel (1994) *Literature and Revolution in England, 1640–1660.* New Haven and London: Yale University Press.

Sommerville, J. P. (1986) *Politics and Ideology in England, 1603–1640.* London and New York: Longman.

Sowerby, Robin (1994) *The Classical Legacy in Renaissance Poetry.* Harlow: Longman.

Spenser, Edmund (1965) *Spenser, Poetical Works*, ed. J. C. Smith and E. De Selincourt. London: Oxford University Press.

Spenser, Edmund (1978) *The Faerie Queene*, ed. Thomas P. Roche, Jr. Harmondsworth: Penguin.

Sprott, S. Ernest (1953) *Milton's Art of Prosody.* Oxford: Basil Blackwell.

Spurr, John (1998) *English Puritanism, 1603–1689.* Basingstoke: Macmillan.

Steele, Richard, ed. (1710–11) *The Lucubrations of Isaac Bickerstaff, Esq.* [=*The Tatler*]. Also *The Tatler*, ed. Donald F. Bond, 3 vols. (1987), Oxford: Clarendon Press.

Stein, Arnold (1953) *Answerable Style: Essays on 'Paradise Lost'.* Minneapolis: University of Minnesota Press.

Stevens, Paul (1985) *Imagination and the Presence of Shakespeare in 'Paradise Lost'.* Madison: University of Wisconsin Press.

Stevens, Paul (1988) Discontinuities in Milton's Early Public Self-Representation. *Huntington Library Quarterly* 51, 261–80.

Stevens, Paul (2001) Milton's 'Renunciation' of Cromwell: The Problem of Raleigh's *Cabinet-Council. Modern Philology* 98.

Stevenson, Kay Gilliland and Seares, Margaret (1998) *Paradise Lost in Short: Smith, Stillingfleet, and the Transformation of Epic.* London: Associated University Presses. (Includes full libretto of Stillingfleet's 1760 oratorio.)

Stewart, Stanley (1984) Milton Revises *The Readie and Easie Way. Milton Studies* 20, 205–24.

Stillingfleet, Benjamin (1746) Manuscript Letter to Thomas Dampier, bound in Stillingfleet's interleaved copy of Bentley 1732. British Library C.134.h.1.

Stillingfleet, Benjamin (1760) *Paradise Lost: An Oratorio*. Repr. in Stevenson and Seares (1998), 13–46.

Swan, Jim (1985) Difference and Silence: John Milton and the Question of Gender. In S. N. Garner, C. Kahane and M. Sprengnether (eds), *The (M)other Tongue: Essays in Feminist Psychoanalytic Interpretation* (pp. 142–168). Ithaca: Cornell University Press.

Symmons, Charles (1806) *The Prose Works of John Milton with a Life of the Author*, 7 vols. London: J. Johnson. ('Life' is Volume 7.)

Taaffe, James G. (1968–9) Michaelmas, the 'Lawless Hour', and the Occasion of Milton's *Comus. English Language Notes* 6, 257–62.

Tatham, John (1879) The Character of the Rump. In *The Dramatic Works of John Tatham*, ed. J. Maidment and W. H. Logan. Edinburgh: W. Patterson.

Tayler, Edward W. (1978, 1979) *Lycidas* in Christian Time. In E. W. Tayler, *Milton's Poetry: Its*

Development in Time. Pittsburgh: Duquesne University Press, 1979. Repr. from *Huntington Library Quarterly* 41 (1978): 103–17. Condensed and repr. in C. A. Patrides (ed.), *Milton's Lycidas: The Tradition and the Poem*.

Tayler, Edward W. (1979) *Milton's Poetry: Its Development in Time*. Pittsburgh: Duquesne University Press.

Taylor, Jeremy (1870) *The poems and verse-translations of the Right Rev. Jeremy Taylor*, ed. Alexander B. Grosart. Blackburn: printed by G. Tiplady and Son for private circulation.

Temple, Sir William (1690) *Miscellanea, the Second Part*, 2nd edn. London.

Theis, Jeffrey (1996) The Environmental Ethics of *Paradise Lost*: Milton's Exegesis of Genesis i–iii. *Milton Studies* 34, 61–81.

Thomas, Donald (1972) *State Trials: Treason and Libel*, 2 vols. London: Routledge.

Thomas, Roger (1964) The Break-Up of Nonconformity. In G. F. Nuttall et al., *The Beginnings of Nonconformity* (pp. 33–60). London: James Clarke.

Thompson, E. P. (1991) Time, Work-Discipline, and Industrial Capitalism. In E. P. Thompson, *Customs in Common: Studies in Traditional Popular Culture* (pp. 352–403). New York: New Press.

Thomson, James (1726–46; 1981) *The Seasons*, ed. James Sambrook. Oxford: Oxford University Press.

Tillyard, E. M. W. (1930, repr. 1956) *Milton*. London: Chatto & Windus.

Toland, John (1699) *The life of John Milton, containing, besides the history of his works, several extraordinary characters of men and books, sects, parties, and opinions*. London.

Topsell, Edward (1658) *The History of Four-footed Beasts and Serpents: . . . Collected out of the writings of Conradus Gesner and other authors*. London.

Tuck, Richard (1993) *Philosophy and Government 1572–1651*. Cambridge: Cambridge University Press.

Turner, James Grantham (1987) *One Flesh: Paradisal Marriage and Sexual Relations in the Age of Milton*. Oxford: Clarendon Press; New York: Oxford University Press.

Tuve, Rosemond (1957) *Images and Themes in Five Poems by Milton*. Cambridge, MA: Harvard University Press.

Tyacke, Nicholas (1987) *Anti-Calvinists: The Rise of English Arminianism c.1590–1640*. Oxford: Clarendon Press.

Tyacke, Nicholas (1991) The 'Rise of Puritanism' and the Legalizing of Dissent, 1571–1719. In O. P. Grell, J. I. Israel and N. Tyacke (eds), *From Persecution to Toleration* (pp. 17–49). Oxford: Clarendon Press.

Tyacke, Nicholas (1998) Introductory chapter to Nicholas Tyacke (ed.), *England's Long Reformation*. London: UCL Press.

Vane, Henry (1655) *The Retired Mans Meditations*. London.

Vane, Henry (1662a) *The Face of the Times*. London.

Vane, Henry (1662b) *The Tryal of Sir Henry Vane*. London.

Virgil (1960) *Eclogues, Georgics, Aeneid*, trans. H. Rushton Fairclough, 2 vols. Cambridge, MA: Harvard University Press.

von Maltzahn, Nicholas (1991) *Milton's* History of Britain: *Republican Historiography in the English Revolution*. Oxford: Clarendon Press.

von Maltzahn, Nicholas (1993a) Dating the Digression in Milton's *History of Britain*. *Historical Journal* 36, 929–43.

von Maltzahn, Nicholas (1993b) Laureate, Republican, Calvinist: An Early Response to Milton and *Paradise Lost* (1667) *Milton Studies* 29, 181–98.

von Maltzahn, Nicholas (1995) The Whig Milton, 1667–1700. In D. Armitage, A. Himy and Q. Skinner (eds), *Milton and Republicanism* (pp. 229–53). Cambridge: Cambridge University Press.

Walker, Julia M., ed. (1988) *Milton and the Idea of Woman*. Urbana and Chicago: University of Illinois Press.

Wallace, Dewey D. (1982) *Puritans and Predestination: Grace in English Protestant Theology, 1525–1695*. Chapel Hill: University of North Carolina Press.

Waller, Edmund (1645) *The Workes of Edmond Waller, Esquire*. London.

Waller, Edmund (1991) On St James Park, As Lately Improved by His Majesty (1661) In Alistair Fowler (ed.), *The New Oxford Book of Seventeenth-Century Verse*. Oxford: Oxford University Press.

Walsh, Marcus (1997) *Shakespeare, Milton, and Eighteenth-Century Literary Editing*. Cambridge: Cambridge University Press.

Walwyn, William (1989) *The Writings of William Walwyn*, ed. Jack R. McMichael and Barbara Taft. Athens, GA and London: University of Georgia Press.

Walzer, Michael (1965) *The Revolution of the Saints*. Cambridge, MA: Harvard University Press.

Watt, Tessa (1991) *Cheap Print and Popular Piety, 1550–1640*. Cambridge: Cambridge University Press.

Weber, Harold (1996) *Paper Bullets: Print and Kingship under Charles II*. Lexington: University Press of Kentucky.

Wesley, John (1763, repr. 1791) *An Extract from Milton's* Paradise Lost. *With Notes*. London.

White, Peter (1992) *Predestination, Policy and Polemic: Conflict and Consensus in the English Church from the Reformation to the Civil War*. Cambridge: Cambridge University Press.

Whitelocke, Bulstrode (1990) *The Diary of Bulstrode Whitelocke, 1605–1675*, ed. Ruth Spalding. Oxford: Oxford University Press.

Wilding, Michael (1987) *Dragons Teeth: Literature in the English Revolution*. Oxford: Clarendon Press; New York: Oxford University Press.

Wiles, Maurice (1996) *Archetypal Heresy*. Oxford: Oxford University Press.

Wilkie, Brian (1965) *Romantic Poets and Epic Tradition*. Madison and Milwaukee: University of Wisconsin Press.

Wilkins, John (1668) *An Essay towards a Real Character and a Philosophical Language*. London.

Wilkinson, David (1960) The Escape from Pollution: A Comment on 'Comus'. *Essays in Criticism* 10, 32–3.

Willet, Andrew (1620) *Hexapla: That is, A Six-Fold Commentarie vpon the most Diuine Epistle of the holy Apostle S. Paul to the Romanes*. Cambridge.

Williams, R. (1987) *Arius: Heresy and Tradition*. London: Dartman, Longman & Todd.

Williams, Roger (1644) *The Bloody Tenet of Persecution for Cause of Conscience*. London.

Williamson, G. (1962) Milton the Anti-Romantic. *Modern Philology* 60, 13–21.

Winstanley, Gerrard (1941) *The Works of Gerrard Winstanley*, ed. George H. Sabine. Ithaca: Cornell University Press.

Wittkower, Rudolf (1955) *Gian Lorenzo Bernini: The Sculptor of the Roman Baroque*. London: Phaidon.

Wittreich, Joseph A. (1968) The 'Satanism' of Blake and Shelley Reconsidered. *Studies in Philology* 65, 816–33.

Wittreich, Joseph A., ed. (1970) *The Romantics on Milton: Formal Essays and Critical Asides*. Cleveland and London: Case Western Reserve University Press.

Wittreich, Joseph A. (1971) *Milton's Paradise Regained: Two Eighteenth-Century Critiques by Richard Meadowcourt and Charles Dunster*. Gainesville, FL: Scholars' Facsimiles and Reprints.

Wittreich, Joseph A. (1975) *Angel of Apocalypse: Blake's Idea of Milton*. Madison: University of Wisconsin Press.

Wittreich, Joseph A. (1979) *Visionary Poetics: Milton's Tradition and his Legacy*. San Marino, CA: Huntington Library.

Wittreich, Joseph A. (1986) *Interpreting* Samson Agonistes. Princeton: Princeton University Press.

Wittreich, Joseph A. (1987) *Feminist Milton*. Ithaca: Cornell University Press.

Wolfe, Don. M. (1963) *Milton and the Puritan Revolution*. London: Cohen & West; New York: Humanities Press (repr.; first publ. New York: T. Nelson, 1941).

Wollstonecraft, Mary (1989) *A Vindication of the Rights of Woman*. In M. Butler and J. Todd (eds), *The Works of Mary Wollstonecraft*, vol. 5 (pp. 61–266). London: Pickering & Chatto.

Woodhouse, A. S. P. (1952) Milton's Pastoral Monodies. In M. E. White (ed.), *Studies in Honour of Gilbert Norwood* (pp. 263–72). Toronto: University of Toronto Press.

Woodhouse, A. S. P. and Douglas Bush (1972a) *A Variorum Commentary on The Poems of John Milton: The Minor English Poems*, vol. 2, pt 1. London: Routledge & Kegan Paul.

Woodhouse, A. S. P. and Douglas Bush (1972b) *A Variorum Commentary on The Poems of John Milton: The Minor English Poems*, vol. 2, pt 2. New York: Columbia University Press.

Woodhouse, A. S. P. and Douglas Bush (1972c) *A Variorum Commentary on the Poems of John Milton: The Minor English Poems*, vol. 2, pt 3. New York: Columbia University Press.

Woolrych, Austin (1957) The Good Old Cause and the Fall of the Protectorate. *Cambridge Historical Journal* 13, 133–61.

Woolrych, Austin (1974) Milton and Cromwell: 'A short but scandalous night of interruption'? In M. Lieb and J. T. Shawcross (eds), *Achievements of the Left Hand: Essays on the Prose of John Milton* (pp. 185–218). Amherst: University of Massachusetts Press.

Woolrych, Austin (1980) Introduction to vol. VII. In *CPW* VII (Milton 1953–82, pp. 1–218).

Woolrych, Austin (1993) Dating Milton's *History of Britain. Historical Journal* 36, 929–43.

Worden, Blair (1984) Toleration and the Cromwellian Protectorate. In W. J. Sheils (ed.), *Persecution and Toleration* (pp. 199–233). Oxford: Oxford University Press.

Worden, Blair (1990) Milton's Republicanism and the Tyranny of Heaven. In G. Bock, Q. Skinner and M. Viroli (eds), *Machiavelli and Republicanism* (pp. 225–45). Cambridge: Cambridge University Press.

Worden, Blair (1991) English Republicanism. In J. H. Burns with M. Goldie (eds), *The Cambridge History of Political Thought 1450–1700* (pp. 443–75). Cambridge: Cambridge University Press.

Worden, Blair (1994) Marchamont Nedham and the Beginnings of English Republicanism, 1649–1656. In D. Wootton (ed.), *Republicanism, Liberty, and Commercial Society, 1649–1776* (pp. 45–81). Stanford: University of Stanford Press.

Worden, Blair (1995) Milton, *Samson Agonistes*, and the Restoration. In G. MacLean (ed.), *Culture and Society in the Stuart Restoration: Literature, Drama, History* (pp. 111–36). Cambridge: Cambridge University Press.

Worden, Blair (1998) John Milton and Oliver Cromwell. In I. Gentles, J. Morrill and B. Worden (eds), *Soldiers, Writers and Statesmen of the English Revolution* (pp. 243–64). Cambridge: Cambridge University Press.

Wordsworth, William (1936) *Poetical Works*, ed. Ernest de Selincourt. Oxford: Oxford University Press.

Wordsworth, William (1979) *The Prelude 1799, 1805, 1850: Authoritative Texts, Context and Reception, Recent Critical Essays*, ed. M. H. Abrams, Stephen Gill and Jonathan Wordsworth. New York and London: Norton.

Zagorin, Perez (1954) *A History of Political Thought in the English Revolution.* London: Routledge & Kegan Paul.

Zagorin, Perez (1992) *John Milton: Aristocrat and Rebel.* Rochester: D. S. Brewster.

Zwicker, Steven N. (1987) Lines of Authority. In K. Sharpe and S. N. Zwicker (eds), *Politics of Discourse* (pp. 230–70). Berkeley: University of California Press.

Zwicker, Steven N. (1993) *Lines of Authority: Politics and English Literary Culture, 1649–1689.* Ithaca and London: Cornell University Press.

Zwicker, Steven N. (1995) Milton, Dryden, and the Politics of Literary Controversy. In G. MacLean (ed.), *Culture and Society in the Stuart Restoration: Literature, Drama, History* (pp. 137–58). Cambridge: Cambridge University Press.

General Index